Devotional Hours
with the
Bible

Devotional Hours with the Bible

By
J. R. Miller, D.D.

AMG
PUBLISHERS
Chattanooga, TN 37422

Devotional Hours with the Bible
by J. R. Miller, D.D.
©1997 by AMG Publishers
All Rights Reserved.

Originally published by
Hodder and Stoughton, New York, London: 1909, 1912, and Pickering & Inglis
in London.

ISBN 0-89957-219-7

Library of Congress Catalog Card Number: 97-74613

Printed in the United States of America
02 01 00 99 98   –R– 6 5 4 3 2

Contents

Foreword   xi
Preface   xiii

VOLUME I: THE GOSPEL BY MATTHEW

1.	The Wise Men and the Child	1
2.	John, the Forerunner of Jesus	4
3.	The Baptism and Temptation of Jesus	8
4.	The Beginning of the Galilean Ministry	13
5.	True Blessedness	18
6.	Some Laws of the Kingdom	23
7.	Almsgiving and Prayer	28
8.	Worldliness and Trust	33
9.	The Golden Rule	38
10.	False and True Discipleship	42
11.	Jesus, the Healer	46
12.	The Power of Faith	51
13.	The Mission of the Twelve	56
14.	The Question of John the Baptist	60
15.	Warning and Invitation	65
16.	Two Sabbath Incidents	70
17.	Growing Hatred to Jesus	75

18.	The Parable of the Sower	80
19.	The Parable of the Tares	84
20.	Pictures of the Kingdom	88
21.	The Multitudes Fed	92
22.	Jesus Walks on the Sea	96
23.	The Canaanitish Woman	99
24.	Peter's Confession	103
25.	The Transfiguration	108
26.	A Lesson on Forgiveness	112
27.	Jesus on the Way to Jerusalem	116
28.	The Laborers in the Vineyard	121
29.	Jesus Nearing Jerusalem	125
30.	Jesus Entering Jerusalem	129
31.	Two Parables of Judgment	133
32.	The King's Marriage Feast	138
33.	Three Questions	142
34.	The Lesson of Watchfulness	146
35.	The Wise and Foolish Virgins	150
36.	The Parable of the Talents	154
37.	The Last Judgment	158
38.	The Anointing of Jesus	162
39.	The Last Supper	166
40.	Peter's Denial	170
41.	Jesus in Gethsemane	175
42.	The Trial of Jesus	179
43.	The Crucifixion	183
44.	The Resurrection	187

VOLUME II: STUDIES IN THE SYNOPTIC GOSPELS

Preface to This Volume   193

1. The Birth of John the Baptist Foretold   195
2. The Birth of John the Baptist   201
3. The Birth of Jesus   207
4. The Presentation in the Temple   212
5. The Wise Men Led by the Star   217
6. The Boy Jesus in the Temple   222
7. The Ministry of John the Baptist   227
8. The Baptism and Temptation of Jesus   231
9. The Call of the First Disciples   235
10. The Paralytic Forgiven and Healed   240
11. Feasting and Fasting   244
12. The Use of the Sabbath   248
13. The Appointment of the Twelve   253
14. Poverty and Riches   258
15. The Law of Love   262
16. Hearing and Doing   268
17. The Penitent Woman   273
18. Malignant Unbelief   277
19. The Seed in the Four Kinds of Soil   281
20. The Growth of the Kingdom   285
21. A Troubled Sea and a Troubled Soul   290
22. The Ruler's Daughter   296
23. The Visit to Nazareth   300
24. The Death of John the Baptist   305
25. The Feeding of the Five Thousand   309

26. Mission to the Gentiles   314

27. Wanderings in Decapolis   319

28. The Transfiguration   324

29. The Child in the Midst   328

30. The Two Great Commandments   332

31. The Good Samaritan   337

32. Jesus Teaching How to Pray   342

33. Watchfulness   347

34. Jesus Dines with a Pharisee   352

35. False Excuses   356

36. The Parable of the Two Sons   361

37. Bartimaeus and Zacchaeus   366

38. Christ's Trial Before Pilate   371

39. Christ Crucified   375

40. The Resurrection of Jesus   379

41. The Walk to Emmaus   383

42 Jesus Ascends into Heaven   387

Volume III: The Gospel by John

Preface to This Volume   393

1. Christ the Life and Light of Men   395

2. The Witness of John to Jesus   399

3. The First Miracle in Cana   403

4. Jesus Cleansing the Temple   409

5. Jesus and Nicodemus   415

6. Jesus at Jacob's Well   419

7. The Second Miracle in Cana   424

8. Jesus at the Pool of Bethesda 428

9. Christ's Divine Authority 433

10. The Miracle of the Loaves and Fishes 437

11. Jesus, the Bread of Life 441

12. Jesus at the Feast of the Tabernacles 445

13. The Slavery of Sin 449

14. Healing the Man Born Blind 454

15. Jesus the Good Shepherd 459

16. The Abundant Life 464

17. The Raising of Lazarus 469

18. The Supper at Bethany 473

19. Jesus Entering into Jerusalem 478

20. Serving, Following, Sharing 482

21. Washing the Disciples' Feet 489

22. The New Commandment 493

23. How Christ Comforts 500

24. Why Does No One See God? 507

25. The Way, The Truth, and The Life 515

26. The Comforter Promised 520

27. The Vine and the Branches 524

28. The Spirit's Work 529

29. Alone, yet Not Alone 534

30. Jesus Prays for His Friends 542

31. Christ Betrayed 547

32. Jesus Before Pilate 552

33. Pilate Sentencing Jesus 556

34. The Crucifixion of Christ 562

35. It Is Finished!   567

36. The Resurrection   573

37. "Peace Be unto You"   578

38. The Beloved Disciple   584

Foreword

We at AMG Publishers are thrilled to bring you J. R. Miller's *Devotional Hours with the Bible*. We are confident that you will be both uplifted and inspired by this restored collection of Dr. Miller's meditational readings concerning the four Gospels and the life of Jesus Christ. The author's relaxed, conversational writing style will help illuminate passages of scripture in a way you might first think unimaginable. Three of Dr. Miller's works from his original *Devotional Hours with the Bible* series have been combined into a single volume, and they are as follows: *The Gospel by Matthew* (Hodder and Stoughton, London: 1909), *Spiritual Studies in the Synoptic Gospels on the Life of Christ* (Pickering & Inglis, London), and *The Gospel by St. John* (Hodder and Stoughton, London: 1912).

In creating this new edition of *Devotional Hours with the Bible,* we at AMG Publishers have made a few minor changes to the original text to help make its content more clear for modern readers. We have updated spelling in accordance with how our language has changed over the years, and in some cases unusual forms of punctuation have been simplified. Some Scripture references have been inserted into the text in brackets. Readers should also be aware that points of current events mentioned by Miller are from the late nineteenth and early twentieth centuries.

Our desire is that this volume may help readers deepen their knowledge and love of the Gospels and instill a yearning in them to be more like Christ.

Preface

There are two methods of studying the Bible. One is, verse by verse, giving close thought to every word, even looking into etymology and grammatical construction, so that the exact sense of the text may be learned. Such study is important. Many rich shades of meaning are often revealed by intelligent and scholarly exegesis. Commentaries that take us over the Bible in this microscopical way are valuable. We need every particle of light on the Scriptures we can get.

Then another way of studying the Bible is in order to get from it practical lessons for our own daily common life. What does the passage teach us? What Divine instruction have we in it for ourselves? It is the latter purpose that is in mind in this book. It is not a commentary in the usual sense. It is not an exegetical study of the Scriptures that is proposed. No textual criticism is given. There is no discussion of questions of dates, of localities, of authorships, or archaeological researches. Its single aim is to suggest some of the spiritual and practical lessons which may be gathered from great passages.

The book does not attempt to cover every chapter; to do this would make it altogether too long—it deals only with what appear to be leading and representative portions of the Bible.

It is a book for use in the inner chamber where life receives its impulses for conduct, for duty, for service, and for devotion. The Bible is a very ancient book, but it is also a book for today. It brings us face to face with God, and its teachings are meant to guide us in all our ways.

J. R. M.

Volume One

The Gospel by Matthew

1

The Wise Men and the Child

Scripture Reading: Matthew 1 and 2

The Gospel of Matthew begins with a genealogy. Then comes the story of the birth and infancy. Jesus was born at Bethlehem. This was the most wonderful event of human history—the coming of the Son of God in human flesh into this world. Love was born that night. True, there was love in the world before. Mothers loved their children. Friend loved friend. Natural affection was common. But the love which we know as Christian love had its beginning in the birth of Jesus Christ. It is well for us to note, however, that the historical event of Christ's birth is not that which saves us. He must be born again in us.

> Though Christ a thousand times in Bethlehem be born,
> If He's not born in thee, thy soul is all forlorn.

This greatest event in history made little stir in the world. Usually when heirs to a throne are born whole realms ring with joy. But when the Messiah was born, there was no earthly rejoicing. A few humble shepherds came and looked with wonder on the new-born Babe that lay in the young mother's arms—but that was all. The Jews had been looking for their Messiah, but did not recognize Him when He came. His advent was quiet. There was no blare of trumpets. Noise and show are not necessary accompaniments of power. The mightiest energies in this world are often the quietest. The grace of God always comes quietly. Angels minister noiselessly. The most useful Christians are not those who make the most ado at their work, but those who in humility and simplicity, unconscious of any splendor in their faces, go daily about their work for their Master.

We cannot understand just how the wise men were led to Jerusalem. They said they saw the King's star in the East and were led by it. There has been a great deal of speculation as to the character of this star, whether it was a natural or a supernatural appearance. But no matter—whatever it was, it led these men to the feet of Christ. Even the faintest glimmerings of spiritual light should be welcomed by us and their guidance accepted. We should not wait to know all about Christ, and to see Him in all His glory, before we set out to seek Him. We should follow the first faint gleams, and then as we go on the light will brighten, and we shall see more and more of Him, until at length we behold Him in all His blessed beauty, face to face. Certainly there is no one in Christian lands in these days who does not have a great deal more light to guide him to the Christ than these wise men had.

The Herods have an unenviable record in New Testament history. When this Herod, Herod the Great, heard the inquiries of the wise men, he was greatly troubled. Hearing of Christ does not always bring joy. It brought gladness to the humble shepherds and to the wise men, but to Herod it brought great distress. Christ's name makes bad men think of their sins and then of the judgment. It is only when we see Christ and want to have Him for our Friend that the thought of Him is sweet and pleasant. "For you therefore that believe is the preciousness." Those whose faith is fixed upon Him are never terrified by thoughts of Him.

Herod, unable himself to answer the question of the wise men, turned to the scribes and asked them where the Messiah should be born. It did not take them long to give the answer. They could even give chapter and verse, and could tell the very name of the town in which the Messiah was to be born. These facts were all down in their books. Yet we do not see that they made any use of their knowledge. They could tell the wise men where the Christ was to be born, but they did not themselves take one step toward Bethlehem to search for

Him, when they learned of His birth there. Most of us know our Bible well, and can tell others glibly enough where and how to find the Christ. But have we ourselves gone to the place where He is, to search for Him and to worship Him?

The scene when the wise men found the Child-king was very beautiful. They saw only a little baby lying in a young mother's arms. There was no crown on His head. No glory gleamed from His face. His surroundings were most unkingly, without pomp or brilliance. The child did nothing before them to show His royalty—spoke no word, wrought no kingly act of power. Yet the wise men believed and worshiped Him. Think how much more we know about the Christ than they did. It is easy for us to find kingly marks in Him. Shall we be behind the wise men in our adoration?

The wise men did more than adore—they opened their treasures and offered gifts of gold, frankincense and myrrh which they had brought all the way from their own home. The sincerity of their worship was thus attested by the costliness of their gifts. The treasures they had brought were of great value—the most costly things they could find, the best they had to give. It is not enough to give Christ a homage that costs nothing. He asks for our gifts, the offerings of our love, our service, the consecration of our lives. Giving is the test of loving—the measure of our loving is what we are willing to give and sacrifice.

There are many ways of laying our offerings at the feet of Jesus Christ. He Himself does not need our money, but His cause needs it. The extension of His kingdom in this world at home and abroad requires money, and this must be brought by His followers. Those who have no interest in the saving of others, in the sending of the Gospel to those who have it not, have not themselves really tasted of the love of Christ.

2

John, the Forerunner of Jesus

Scripture Reading: Matthew 3:1–12

The time of John's coming was not accidental. It was "in those days,"—that is, when Jesus was still living in Nazareth. Jesus was now about to begin His public ministry and John was ready to go before Him to prepare the way for Him. Every man is made for his own time and work. John would not have fit in at any other date in the world's history.

John is not a very attractive person to our modern Christian eyes. He appears harsh, rugged and stern, and we think of gentleness and kindliness as ideal traits in a beautiful life. But there is need for stern, rugged men in Christ's kingdom as well as for kindly, tender-hearted men. The storm has its ministry as well as the sunshine, winter its mission as well as summer, John the Baptist his work as well as John the beloved disciple.

John came "a man, sent from God," a man with a message. He preached in the wilderness—not in the temple courts, nor in the synagogues, but away from the common haunts of men—and the people flocked to hear him. The burden of John's preaching was in one word—"Repent." This is not the gospel, but it is a call which goes before the gospel. We must repent before we can receive forgiveness. We are in danger of making religion too easy a matter, and of being altogether too patient and tolerant with ourselves. Christ does not come to an un-

4

repentant heart. We must make sure, too, that we do thorough work in our repenting. Repentance is not merely a little twinge of remorse over something wrong. It is not simply a burst of tears at the recollection of some wickedness. Nor is it shame in being found out in some meanness, uncleanness, or dishonesty. Confess and turn from your sins, is the meaning of the call. Repentance is the revolution of the whole life. Sins wept over must be forsaken and given up. Repentance is a change of heart, a turning the face the other way. It is well for us to make diligent quest and be sure that we abandon the wrongdoing we deplore, that we quit the course we regret, that we turn away from the sin we confess. He who bewails a sin and confesses it, secretly intending to return to it again, has no good ground to hope that he is forgiven.

The kingdom of heaven was at hand, John declared. What did he mean? He did not mean heaven, but a life on the earth in which heaven's kingdom ruled. The preacher meant that the King had come and was about to declare Himself. They were to repent to be ready to receive Him. When we pray, "Thy kingdom come," we ask that heaven's rule and heaven's life may come into our hearts, our homes, our lives, our community.

John was not as anxious to have his name blazoned before men as some people are. He was spoken of and speaks of himself as "the voice of one crying in the wilderness." The Bible does not trouble to attach men's names to every little piece of work they do. It matters little whether we are mentioned or not in connection with the things we do for the Master. It is just as well to be an anonymous "voice," speaking well for Christ, as to be known as some famous doctor. The Christian worker who always strives to keep his name before people lacks somewhat at least of the mind that was in Christ.

Part of John's commission was to make straight paths for Christ's feet, paths to reach men's homes and hearts. He will never go in any crooked paths, and if we wish Him to walk with us we must see that the paths are straight. All sin's ways are crooked. That is what iniquity means, inequities, unequal ways. The only straight ways are those which run along the lines of God's commandments. The great railroads are continually getting the curves out of their tracks, to make them straight, that trains may run more rapidly. They spend millions in straightening their tracks. Are there any crooked ways in our lives? If so, they should be made straight, that the feet of Christ may run easily and swiftly in them.

John was a sensationalist. He did not wear the dress of other men. He was like Elijah in his garb. The old prophet was girt with a girdle of leather about his loins; the new prophet, too, had his raiment of camel's hair and wore a leather girdle. His food was that of the very poor—locusts, roasted, boiled or baked, and wild honey. His poverty was not affected but was real, a symbol of his sincere unworldliness. He was sent from God, God's messenger, not man's.

John did not spare the people to whom he preached. Among his hearers were the great men of the nation, but as he looked into their faces he knew that their hearts were full of sin, and he called upon them to bring forth fruits worthy of repentance. They must prove by putting away their sins that their confession was genuine. It will not be enough to tell people we are Christians—they will wait to see the evidence of it in our lives. If a man, hitherto living an evil life, unites with the church on Sunday and goes back Monday morning to his worldly ways, will his neighbors credit his Sunday's profession? The heart is the important member in all spiritual life, but the heart makes the life; and if the life be evil, the heart has not been changed. The way to prove that we have really repented is really to repent, and then the fact will speak for itself.

Throngs flocked to hear the great preacher of the wilderness— "Jerusalem, and all Judea, and all the region round about the Jordan." Confession of sin was the gate of admission to baptism. Baptism meant cleanness—its necessity implied uncleanness, but the afterlife was white.

But John saw some coming for baptism whose sincerity he had reason to doubt. Some of them thought they could get into the kingdom of heaven on their genealogy. They belonged to the family of Abraham, and thought this was sufficient. But John assured them that they must have more than good ancestry to commend them. God, he told them, could not be mocked. The ax was lying at the root of the trees to cut down every one on which fruit was not found. The picture is very striking. An ax leaning against a tree implies warning and also patience— delay to see if the tree will yet prove fruitful. But the delay is not to be forever. The ax at the tree's root suggests, also, thorough work—not pruning, merely, to make the tree more fruitful—the time for that is past—but judgment. We are the trees. If we are fruitless and useless, not living up to our privileges and opportunities, not filling well our place in the world, the ax is lying beside us, warning us that only God's patience spares us, and the time for cutting down will soon be at hand.

The humility of John appears in all the story of his life. He claimed no greatness. The coming of throngs to his preaching did not turn his head. He knew the secondary importance of his part in the work—he baptized only with water, and water could cleanse only the outside. The real work would be done by one who could baptize the heart. Washing the body is a good thing, but it does not make one morally better, does not improve one's character. The change which will make a life like Christ's must take place in the heart, and can be produced only by the Spirit. Water baptism is right as an ordinance and as an emblem of the inner cleansing; but if we depend upon it for salvation, without submitting ourselves to the Divine Spirit, we shall find our trust in vain.

John foretold the work of the Messiah as one of separation. He would gather the wheat into his garner, the chaff he would burn up with unquenchable fire. There is a great difference between wheat and chaff. Wheat has life in it. Wheat grains drop into the earth, grow, and yield a harvest. Wheat is food; it makes bread and satisfies hunger. Wheat is valuable; it is highly prized in the market. But chaff has no life in it; it does not grow, and only rots in the ground. It is not food; it satisfies no hunger. It is of no value; nobody buys chaff, and it is good only to throw away or to burn. What sadder thing is there in this world than a human life made to be golden wheat, to feed men's hunger, yet proving only worthless chaff?

3

The Baptism and Temptation of Jesus

Scripture Reading: Matthew 3:13 to 4:11

The beginning of Christ's ministry was marked by two important events—His baptism and His temptation. There were thirty silent years, without any manifestation of Divine power save the beautiful, sinless life which Jesus lived. We must think of those years, however, as part of the Incarnation. The Divine character was revealed not only in miracles and heavenly teachings, but in sweet, beautiful living.

John said that he was not worthy to unloose the shoes of the Coming One. Now when he recognizes this glorious One waiting before him to be baptized, he shrinks from the performance of the rite. He would have refused. "I have need to be baptized of Thee, and comest Thou to me?" But Jesus insisted on receiving baptism from John. "Suffer it to be so now: for thus it becometh us to fulfill all righteousness." The words are full of meaning. The event was of great importance in the life of Jesus.

For one thing, it was the identifying of Himself with humanity. He stood for us men and our redemption. He had no sin, but His people were sinful and He died for them. It was also the acceptance by Jesus of His Messianic work. The years of preparation were ended, and the time had come for Him to begin His public ministry. The call came, bidding Him turn away from His quiet life and manifest Himself to

His people. We can think of Him shutting up the carpenter's shop and leaving it forever. Then He stood before the Baptist at the Jordan and was baptized. He had a glimpse that hour of all that lay before Him in His Messianic ministry. The shadow of the cross fell upon the green banks and on the flowing water, fell also upon the gentle and lowly soul of Jesus as He stood there. He knew for what He was being baptized—the mission of redemption. We do not know to what we are devoting ourselves, what our consecration may mean, when we stand up and give ourselves to God. In a certain sense we go forth in the dark. Yet we may trust God with the guidance of our lives and should devote ourselves to the will of God without question or condition.

John obeyed the wish of Jesus and baptized Him. The baptism of Jesus became the occasion of a Divine testimony to His Sonship. Luke tells us that as He was being baptized He prayed, and as He prayed the heavens were opened unto Him. Prayer brought down upon Jesus the Holy Spirit. This was Heaven's answer to Christ's consecration. This was the Divine anointing for His public ministry. Instead of a horn of oil poured upon His head, the mere emblem of grace, He received all the fullness of the Spirit. The Spirit came in the form of a dove. It is usual to think of the dove as in its nature in some way a symbol of the character and disposition of the Spirit. Dr. Horton quotes an old commentator: "The bird (the dove) is a lover of men and bears ills patiently; for, robbed of its young, it endures and lets the robbers approach it just the same; it is the purest of creatures and delights in sweet odor." The first mention of the dove in the Bible is as a messenger of good news, bearing an olive leaf. An old legend relates that when Jesus was dying a dove sat on the cross above His head, and the legend has been interpreted to mean that even after the blood of the Lamb of God was given to redeem the world, it is needful that the Spirit shall come to soften men's hearts and incline them to yield to God.

There was another manifestation at the baptism—first, the open heavens, second, the descending of the Spirit, then a voice. The voice was the testimony of the Father to His Son. "This is My beloved Son, in whom I am well pleased." From Matthew's account it would seem that the voice spoke to the people, declaring to them that Jesus was the Messiah. From Luke's Gospel it would appear that the words were spoken to Jesus Himself, assuring Him of His mission and of the Father's pleasure in Him. This was the real, the inner meaning of the baptism of Jesus. From this time His consciousness of Messianic authority was clear.

After this came the temptation. It was necessary that Christ should be tempted before He offered Himself as the Redeemer of the world. The first Adam was tried in Eden and failed. The second Adam must also be put to the test before he could go forth as Lord of men. Several reasons may be suggested why He must be tempted. One was because He was human and must meet every human experience. His temptations were real—He "suffered being tempted." Another reason was that until He had met and overcome the tempter He was not ready to offer Himself to men as a strong and victorious Savior. The Spirit is not the tempter, but it is said expressly that Jesus was led by the Spirit, driven, Mark says, to be tempted. He must be tried, tested, proved, before He went forth to His Messianic work. We know now that Christ is able to deliver us out of the hands of Satan and to defend us against his fiercest assaults. But if He had not Himself been put to the test, in all points tempted like as we are, yet without sin [Heb. 4:15], we could not have had this perfect confidence. Another reason why Jesus was tempted was that He might understand from personal experience the nature and power of His people's temptations and thus be able to sympathize with them in their struggles. In the Epistle to the Hebrews we are told that because of His earthly experience of temptation He can now in heaven be touched with the feeling of our infirmities.

There are very practical lessons we may learn from this narrative of our Lord's temptation. One is that Satan times his temptations to our hours of weakness or our periods of special stress. He does not tempt us with something we do not want, but with something that appeals to our cravings at the time. Jacob could not have bought Esau's birthright for a thousand messes of pottage if Esau had not been hungry that day. Satan watches, and when he finds us exhausted and weary, he takes advantage of our condition. He comes to the boy when he is lonesome and homesick, tempting him to seek companions that will ruin him.

Jesus was hungry after His long praying and fasting, and Satan tempted Him to use His Divine power to turn stones into bread. Many temptations come to people who are hungry. They are tempted to be dishonest, to take employment that is sinful, or in some other way to sell themselves to get bread. We need to be watchful against the tempter always, but especially in the times of our weakness and craving.

Why would it have been wrong for Jesus to exert His Divine power to provide bread for His hunger? Is it wrong to feed one's hunger? Jesus afterwards made bread by miracle to feed the hunger of thousands. Why would it have been a sin for Him to supply bread in this supernatural way for Himself when He was hungry? For one thing, it would have been receiving direction from the Evil One instead of from His Father. Another reason was that He was in this world to live as men live. If He had used His Divine power to help Himself over the hard points of human experience, He would not have understood our life, for we cannot do this. Therefore, He never wrought a miracle for Himself. He met life just as we must meet it, enduring hunger, thirst, weariness, pain, wrong, without having recourse to supernatural power. Still further, it would have been distrusting His Father for Him to make bread of the stones. He was under the Divine care, and God had given Him no command to turn stones into bread. He must wait till His Father provided for His hunger.

The answer of Christ to Satan's temptation is very suggestive. He said that man shall not live by bread alone, but by every word of God. Our physical wants are not our only wants. Sometimes men excuse their sin by saying, "Well, I must live," as if hunger excused theft or fraud. But it is not true that we must continue to live, or that living is in itself the best thing for us. It is true, however, that we must obey God's commandments and do His will. We would better any day starve than commit even the smallest sin to get food. Getting bread should not be our first object in living—indeed, it is not our business at all. Life's first duty is to obey every word of God, and then God will provide for our wants.

The second temptation was to presumption. The tempter asked Christ to throw Himself down from the pinnacle of the temple, quoting words from an old Psalm [Ps. 91] to prove that He would not be hurt, but that God would take care of Him. Thus, the tempter whispered, He would prove to the people that He was their Messiah. What would have been wrong in this? Jesus said it would have been tempting God. If the Father for any reason had commanded Him to leap from the pinnacle into the street, then He could have claimed the promise of protection. But if He had thus accepted the suggestion of the tempter, the promise would have been void. We cannot claim protection in danger which we enter without the Divine bidding. Only when God sends us and guides us do we have the Divine shelter about us.

The third temptation was the boldest of all. Christ had just entered upon His public ministry, and at the end of it He saw the cross. Satan suggested to Him the worldly way of honor and power instead of the lowly way of suffering, sacrifice and shameful death. This temptation Satan uses continually with men. He shows them visions of wealth, of worldly success, and says: "Now all this may be yours—I will give it all to you. True, you must give up some of your old notions. You must get over some of your scruples. But throw these away and this door is open to you, and see where the path leads—to all splendor and brilliance. You will be a millionaire. You will go to Parliament. You will have all the pleasure you want." Too many people yield to this temptation. The old ways of prayer, obedience, simple honesty and faithfulness, seem dull in contrast with the flowery paths which the vision shows. Yes, but we must look on to the end, beyond the glamour of the tempter's vision, before we can conclude that what Satan promises will be a good thing for us.

4

The Beginning of the Galilean Ministry

Scripture Reading: Matthew 4:12–25

In Matthew's gospel the story of the first months of our Lord's public ministry is omitted. Several chapters of John's gospel come in between verses 11 and 12 of Matthew's fourth chapter. The mission of John the Baptist was to go before Christ and prepare His way. When he had done this, introducing Him to the people, John's work was really ended. But he continued to preach for some months until he was arrested by Herod and cast into prison. Then it was that Jesus went into Galilee. Why He did this we are not told. Some suppose it was to avoid John's fate, but this scarcely seems a sufficient reason. Indeed, in Galilee he would be nearer to Herod than in Jerusalem. Is it not more likely that it was just because John was now shut up in prison and his voice silenced that Jesus went to Galilee? John had spoken of Jesus coming after him, and He came at once and began to speak.

He dwelt in Capernaum. At that time Capernaum was an important city on the Sea of Galilee. Now nobody knows certainly what its site was. It was a city of wonderful privilege. For a long time Jesus made His home there. It was exalted to heaven in thus having the Son of God walk on its streets, speak His blessed words to its people, and do His works of mercy and love in its homes of suffering and sorrow.

13

But in spite of all this honor and favor shown to Capernaum, Jesus was rejected there.

Matthew tells us that it was in fulfillment of prophecy that Jesus went to Capernaum. He was needed there. It was a region of moral and spiritual darkness. It is such places that always draw Jesus. Human need in every form appeals to His compassion. When men travel over the world they usually visit regions in which they will see scenes of beauty, of grandeur, of wonder. But Jesus was in this world to do good, to save the lost, to change wildernesses into gardens of roses, and He went where there was the greatest need, the deepest darkness. Churches sometimes move away from sections of cities which have been emptied of prosperous homes and the attractions of fashion. Whatever may be said of the expediency of following the drift of population with our churches, we need to beware of abandoning decaying communities, of taking away from the people who remain the blessings of the gospel. Jesus did not go into Galilee as a sightseer, but as a missionary. He was a teacher come from God to tell the people of the love of God for them. The same words were used of John the Baptist in describing His ministry. Yet there was a great difference in the two men and in their preaching. John spoke sternly and severely. He spoke of the fire, the fan, the ax of the punishment of sin. Jesus came with gentle and winning words.

Yet His first call, like John's, was to repentance. All men need to repent. We never can reach the gates of heaven unless we repent. The prodigal son had to rise and leave the far country, and walk back all the painful way to his father's house, before he could be restored to favor and be at home again. That is what every impenitent man must do. The first step in coming to Christ is repentance.

We must be sure that we know just what this word means. Some persons imagine that if they are sorry for doing wrong they have repented. But sorrow for a wrong way does not take us out of that way. Tears of penitence will not blot out sin; we must turn about and walk in holy paths. Repentance is ceasing to make blots on the record, and beginning to live a fair, clean, white life.

It was a familiar and homely scene which Jesus saw one day as He was walking beside the sea. "He saw two brethren . . . casting a net into the sea; for they were fishers." It is interesting to notice the kind of people Jesus sought for His disciples. He did not look for great and famous men. He did not go up to the temple and gather about Him rabbis and priests. He wanted men who were openhearted, ready to listen to the truth and believe it, men who could be influenced by Him for good, whom He could train in the ways of His kingdom.

Jesus is always looking for men who will become His disciples. He has a great work in hand, and needs and calls for helpers. He wants those who will believe His message. He does not take prejudiced men, men whose opinions are so obstinately held that they will not listen to His words nor accept His teachings; He wants teachable men. He does not choose those who are wise in this world's wisdom, for they might not readily accept the wisdom of God which He teaches. Nor does He seek idlers. He goes among those who are busy in the duty of the day. He found a king for Israel in a boy who was keeping sheep. He found a prophet to succeed Elijah in a young man who was plowing in the field. He found a missionary for India in a humble shoemaker, busy at his bench, ready for the Divine call, unable ever to say "No" to God. If we would be chosen to take a part in Christ's great work we must seek to be ready for it, with heart warm, mind open to receive truth, and ready for any service to which God may call us.

First of all, they must go with Christ. This meant, in their case, leaving their business and attaching themselves to His household. It may not mean that to us—ordinarily we are to continue in the calling in which we are when we give ourselves to Him. But always it means joining ourselves to Him in heart and life. It means the complete surrendering of the mastership of our lives. No longer are we our own; we belong to Him. We are to go where He bids us to go and do what He bids us to do. We are to think of His interests, not of our own. There can be no serving of Christ, no doing of His work, without first being with Him. "Without Me," he said, "ye can do nothing" [John 15:5]. But with Him, we are ready for any service, any duty, any work, and nothing is impossible to us.

First, they were to be with Him, and then He would make them fishers of men. They had been fishers of fish; they were to give up their old calling and take a higher one. The lessons of patience, quiet waiting and persistence which they had learned in their daily and nightly work on the sea would be of use to them in their new duties. They were to fish in the dark waters of sin for perishing men and save them, take them alive. Christ would teach them their new calling—"I will make you fishers of men." It was holy service to which He called them, and calls us. He does not want us to follow Him just for the joy of His salvation and the comfort of His friendship—He wants us to be His that we may win others also to be His.

Instantly these fishermen dropped their tackle and their nets, left everything and went away with their new Master. They were not a moment in deciding. They loved Him, and they were most glad to go with Him. "They straightway left the nets and followed Him." Sometimes the sneer is heard, "They had little to leave!" True, it was not much in money value. Yet these nets and this fishing business were all they had. It was by these that they got their living. Now at the call of their new Master they gave up all, cut themselves off from means of support, burnt their bridges behind them, and in simple obedience and faith went with Him. That is what we should do when we hear the call of Christ. We should obey instantly, without questioning. No matter how great the sacrifice involved, we should make it cheerfully for His sake. Though to obey cuts us off from our ordinary means of livelihood and leaves us without provision even for tomorrow, we should not hesitate. Christ will take care of His servants when they are faithfully doing His will. "Straightway" is also an important word in the sentence. A great many people are forever postponing duties. When Christ calls, they say, "Yes, tomorrow." But every call should be answered instantly. Get this "straightway" into all your obedience.

The charge never could be made against Jesus, that He thought only of men's spiritual needs and neglected their bodily wants. Continually we see Him doing good in common ways and helping people in their common needs. Here He is "teaching," "preaching," "healing." He did not give good advice, exhort people to be true and honest, and then be indifferent to their sufferings. He fed them when they were hungry, opened the eyes of their blind, cured their sick children, healed their diseases. Always this is the law of Christ's ministry. He cares for our whole being. Every trouble of ours whatsoever, whether of body, mind, or soul, moves Him with compassion.

It is a great comfort to us to know that our Lord is not indifferent to our diseases, that He would use them for our spiritual benefit, that He is ready to give us the grace we need if we endure them patiently and submissively, and that He will heal us when His wise purpose in our affliction has been accomplished. Jesus is the great Healer—He is continually healing all manner of sickness and disease among the people. Wherever the Christian missionary goes, the hospital is set up alongside the chapel. In our church work we should think of men's bodies as well as of their souls, if we would wholly fulfill Christ's mission and purpose.

This picture of Jesus ought also to be a great comfort to all those who are suffering. He is going about everywhere healing. Is He any less strong now than He was then? Does He love us less than He loved the sick people in Galilee? Will He not heal us, too, in the way that is best? In the sick-room of every Christian, Jesus sits, to give cheer. The sufferer may know, as he prays for healing, that his prayer will be heard and answered. Sickness has a mission—it sets lessons for us to learn. It is very unfortunate if one who is sick recovers and is not better in heart and life afterward. We should pray that the sickness may fulfill its mission in us and for us, and then that we get well.

"And His fame went throughout all Syria." No wonder. Such blessed news could not be suppressed. When Jesus healed all the sick people in one town, it could not be otherwise than that the report would fly abroad, reaching other towns. It is not to be wondered at that everyone who had a sick friend, hearing about the great Healer, would then want to bring that friend at once to Him. Thousands of people poured out to find Him who had this marvelous power. Whenever Jesus saves a sinner, the news should go out, and others who have unsaved friends should bring them at once to Him. We who know about Christ's power to heal and save should go everywhere telling the news that those who are in their sins may be roused up to seek Him as their Savior.

5

True Blessedness

Scripture Reading: Matthew 5:1–16

Emerson's advice to Lincoln about hitching his wagon to a star is the lesson Jesus sets for us in the Beatitudes. These blesseds shine like stars far above us in their brightness and heavenliness. We may say that we never can reach them and that therefore there is no use in our trying to reach them. But the Master would have us strive after the highest attainments.

It has been noted that if the world would make a set of beatitudes they would be just the reverse of those that Jesus spoke. None of the classes pronounced blessed by Him would be called happy by the world. The poor in spirit, the meek, those who hunger for goodness and holiness, are not the world's favorites. These are not the qualities natural men consider most worthy of quest.

The first beatitude is for the lowly ones. "Blessed are the poor in spirit." This beatitude is not for the poor in an earthly sense, for one may be very poor and yet proud; and one may be rich in worldly goods and yet be lowly in spirit, in disposition. The Bible everywhere praises humility. God dwells with the humble. Christ refers only once in the Gospels to His own heart, and through the window He opens then it is this picture that we see—"I am meek and lowly in heart" [11:29]. To be poor in spirit is to be rich toward God, while pride of heart is spiritual poverty. Humility is the key that opens the gate of prayer,

18

while to the loud knocking of pride there comes no answer. The kingdom of heaven belongs to the lowly. They may wear no earthly crown, but a crown of glory, unseen by men, rests upon their heads even here.

The second beatitude is for those who mourn. We do not usually regard mourners as blessed. We pity them and think their condition unenviable. Christ, however, has a special beatitude for those who are sorrowful. Probably He means particularly penitent mourners, those who are sorrowful on account of their sins. In all this world there is nothing so precious in the sight of God as the tear of contrition. No diamonds or pearls shine with such brilliance in His sight. It was Jesus Himself who said there is joy in the presence of the angels of God over one sinner that repenteth [Luke 15:10]. Truly blessed, therefore, are those who mourn over their sins. They are comforted with the comfort of God's pardon and peace.

But the beatitude refers also to those who are in sorrow. Blessing never is nearer to us than when we are in affliction, if we submit ourselves to God in love and trust. Someday we shall understand that we have received our best things from heaven, not in the days of our joy and gladness, but in the time of trial and affliction. Tears are lenses through which our eyes see more deeply into heaven and look more clearly upon God's face than in any other way. Sorrow cleanses our hearts of earthliness and fertilizes our lives. We grow the best when clouds hang over us, because clouds bear rain and rain refreshes. Then God's comfort is such a rich and blessed experience that it is well worthwhile to endure any sorrow in order to receive it.

The third beatitude is for the meek. Meekness is not a popular quality. The world calls it a craven spirit that leads a man to remain quiet under insult, to endure wrong without resentment, to be treated unkindly and then to give kindness in return. Men of the world say that the disposition of meekness is unmanly, that it shows weakness, cowardice, a lack of spirit. So it might be if we looked to the world for our ideal of manhood. But we have a truer, a diviner example for our model of manliness than any that this world has set up. Jesus Christ is the only perfect man who ever lived in this world, and when we turn to His life we see that meekness was one of the most marked qualities of His character. He was gentle of disposition, never provoked, patient under wrong, silent under reproach. When He was reviled, He reviled not again.

When He suffered, He threatened not. Possessing all power, He never lifted a finger to avenge a personal injury. He answered with tender love all men's wrath, and on His cross, when the blood was flowing from His wounds, He prayed for His murderers. Meekness is then no craven spirit, since in Christ it shone so luminously. Then it is not an impoverishing, but an enriching grace. The meek shall inherit the earth.

The fourth beatitude is for those who hunger and thirst after righteousness. This, strangely, is a beatitude for dissatisfaction. We know that peace is promised to the Christian, and peace is calm repose and satisfied restfulness. The words hunger and thirst appear to suggest experiences incompatible with rest and peace. But when we think more deeply, we see that spiritual hunger must form a part of all true Christian experience. Hunger is a mark of health. It is so in physical life; the loss of appetite indicates disease. So a healthy mind is a hungry one; when one becomes satisfied with one's attainments, one ceases to learn. In spiritual life, too, hunger is health. If we become satisfied with our condition of faith, love, obedience and consecration, we are in an unhappy condition. There is no growth after that. Often invalids die amid plenty, die of starvation, not because they can get no food, but because they have no appetite. There are many professing Christians who are starving their souls in the midst of spiritual provision, because they have no hunger. There is nothing for which we should pray more earnestly than for spiritual longing and desire.

The fifth beatitude is for the merciful. Cruelty is opposed to everything Divine and heavenly. All that is unloving is condemned in the Scriptures. Blessing cannot come to the resentful, the unforgiving, the vindictive, to those who have no sympathy with distress, no hand to help human need. In our Lord's picture of the last judgment, in the twenty-fifth chapter of Matthew, those on the right hand are those who have been kind, gentle, patient, thoughtful, ministering to suffering and want. Jesus Himself set an example of mercifulness. His miracles were for the relief of those who were suffering.

We must note in this beatitude also that we receive in life what we give—the merciful shall obtain mercy. The unmerciful shall find the gates closed upon them when they cry for help. A boy stood before a perpendicular crag, and when he began to shout he heard the echo of his own voice. When he spoke gently, a gentle voice responded. When he spoke angrily, he was answered back in angry tones. It is so in life. Those who show kindness to others receive kindness in return. Those who are bitter, selfish and cruel find this a loveless world to live in.

The sixth beatitude is for the pure in heart. There is no beatitude for anything unclean. There is no room with God for anything that defileth. If we would enter heaven we must prepare for heaven here. To a child who expressed a wonder how he could ever get up to heaven, it was so far away, a wise mother's reply was, "Heaven must first come down to you; heaven must first come into your heart." Heaven must really be in us before we can enter heaven. Just as we become pure in heart are we made ready for the heavenly life.

But what is heart purity? It is not sinlessness, for none are sinless. A pure heart must be a penitent heart, one that has been forgiven by Christ, cleansed by His grace. It is one also that is kept pure by obedient living and close communion with Christ. An essential part of true religion before God is, to keep one's self unspotted from the world. It is an evil world in which we live, but if we carefully follow our Master, doing His will, keeping our hearts ever open to the influences of the Divine Spirit, we shall be kept, Divinely kept, from the corruption about us. As the lily grows up pure and unstained amid the soiled waters of the bog, so does the lowly, loving, patient heart of a Christian remain pure in the midst of all this world's evil.

The seventh beatitude is for the peacemakers. Too many people are not peacemakers. Some people seem to delight in finding differences between neighbors or friends which they try not to heal, but to widen. Christ's beatitude is for those who seek always to make peace. When we find two persons in danger of being estranged by some misunderstanding, we should seek to get them together and prevent their falling apart. If we would be true peacemakers, we must never be quarrelsome or easily offended. Paul says that love is not provoked, that is, it does not take account of little or great hurts, but is patient and forbearing [see 1 Cor. 13]. It is a great thing to be a peacemaker. Of the peacemakers it is said, "They shall be called sons of God."

The eighth beatitude is for those who are "persecuted for righteousness' sake." Some people avoid persecution by conforming to the world, by being very careful never to offend the world. But Christ wants us to be loyal and true to Him whatever the cost may be. Blessing comes upon those who suffer persecution for Christ's sake. Paul spoke of the wounds and scars he had received in persecution as marks of Jesus, honorable decorations. We must notice, however, that it is when we are persecuted for righteousness' sake that we get this beatitude. Sometimes people suffer for doing wrong, but the blessing cannot be claimed in this case. It is when we do the will of God and suffer for it that we can claim the Divine blessing.

We are commanded to rejoice and be exceeding glad when called to suffer reproach and injury for Christ's sake. It is not easy to do this, although many Christians have actually rejoiced in pain and trial, so strong was their faith. Ignatius, on his way to Rome to be thrown to wild beasts, wrote exultantly, "Now I am beginning to be a disciple . . . now am I made the fine flour, ground by the teeth of the wild beasts, to be the bread of God."

In two striking figures Jesus showed His disciples what they were to be in the world, how they were to bless it by the influence of their lives. "Ye are the salt of the earth." You are, by living your new life in the world, to keep it from rotting. This seemed a strange thing to say that day to a little handful of fishermen, but these men and their successors have done just that for the world through the centuries. We know what salt is and what its influence is. We are to be the salt of the earth, not merely in the words we speak, but especially in the influence of our lives. We must take heed therefore that the salt we are does not lose its savor, its power to bless. We must make sure that the world is purified, sweetened and made better in every way by our living in it.

"Ye are the light of the world." We are lamps which Christ lights and which are to shine upon the world's darkness for its enlightening. We must remember that the light of heaven can reach other lives and brighten the world only through us. We must see to it, therefore, that the light in us never fails. We must never allow it to be covered up by any bushel. The object of the shining is not to glorify the lamp, but to honor God. We are not to parade our virtues, but to brighten the world and lead men to love our heavenly Father.

6

Some Laws of the Kingdom

Scripture Reading: Matthew 5:17–26; 38–48

We are not to think of Christianity as a new religion, distinct from that of the Old Testament. Rather, the one is a development from the other. Jesus was careful to say, "I came not to destroy, but to fulfill." Then He added, "Verily I say unto you, Till heaven and earth pass away, one jot or one tittle shall in no wise pass away from the law, till all things be accomplished."

This is the law of all life. No particle of matter is ever destroyed. Its form may be changed, but nothing of it passes out of existence. A log of wood may be burned in the fire, but it is not destroyed. Some of it lies in ashes and some of it escapes into the air in the form of smoke and steam and chemical elements, but not a jot or a tittle of the wood has been destroyed. All the wisdom of the ages still exists in the world. The songs men have sung, the words they have spoken, are living in the hearts and lives of our race. Our age is the inheritor of all past ages. Christianity holds all that was good and true and beautiful in Judaism. Jesus destroyed nothing of the religion of Moses. He was the fulfillment of all the prophecies. What went before Him was blossom; in Him the fruit appeared. The blossom was not destroyed—it only fell off because it had fulfilled its purpose.

The Old Testament is not antiquated and outgrown. It, too, is the Word of God. Wherever we find Divine truth we are to accept it.

23

Of course, there is a difference in the relative importance of Scripture words—there are least and there are greatest commandments, but he who breaks the least has grieved God and sinned against Him. He who obeys every word of God, however small it may seem, has lifted himself up in the rank of God's children.

The Sermon on the Mount teaches the spirituality of all true obedience. The scribes and Pharisees were great sticklers for the letter of the law, but they went little farther. They missed its spirit. They interpreted "Thou shalt not kill" literally as condemning murder, but they did not think of applying it to murderous thoughts. Jesus spoke startlingly, "But I say unto you, that every one who is angry with his brother shall be in danger of the judgment." That is, anger is murder. So serious is this interpretation of the law that Jesus says we cannot truly worship God while we have bitterness dwelling in our heart. Hatred must give place to love when we stand before God. If we have wronged another, and the hour of prayer comes with the wronged yet unrighted, we must stop before the altar, interrupting our worship until we have gone to the one we have wronged and confessed and been forgiven. Perhaps we do not always think how serious an offense to God an unforgiving spirit is. Quarreling is not only ethically unlovely; it is also wickedly and spiritually evil.

Acts are bad, but thoughts are taken note of in the presence of God. There is sin in a lustful look as well as in an unchaste act. Our thoughts have moral quality. Jesus enters into particulars and names certain sins which His disciples should carefully avoid. The Christian life should be without spot or blemish. One lesson He taught was reverence in speech. "I say unto you, Swear not at all." He does not refer to oaths taken in the courts of law, but to profanity in speech. Men were in the habit of swearing by heaven, by the earth, by Jerusalem, or by their own head, by something, always. There is much irreverence in the conversation of many people in our day. Those who indulge in it often do it almost unconsciously. Some people—far too many—are recklessly profane. The profanity one hears in many places, even from the mouths of boys, is shocking. But there are many who think they never use profanity whose speech is full of such forms of oaths as Jesus here refers to. We need to guard against every form of profanity in our speech, however veiled it may be. "Hallowed by Thy name," we say in the Lord's prayer; we should be careful that God's name is always hallowed in our thought and in our conversation also, that it is never used lightly or irreverently.

Jesus made a plea also for simplicity of speech. "Let your speech be, Yea, yea; Nay, nay: and whatsoever is more than these is of the evil one." There is a common tendency to exaggeration and over-emphasis in speech. Many persons always try to say things in a strong and emphatic way. They are not content to say yes or no and stop with that. They rarely tell anything precisely according to the bare facts, but color even the most common happenings. It would be a great deal better if we would learn to use simple words without exaggeration of any kind. Someone says, "The more swearing, the more lying." It would be well if we would remember that in speaking we are always overheard by One to whom the least shade of dishonesty is repulsive, and who is grieved by any profanity.

It was the custom in the old days to return evil for evil, hurt for hurt, injury for injury. "An eye for an eye, and a tooth for a tooth," was the law. It is the common law yet with too many people. Our hearts urge us to seek revenge, and forgiving injuries is not natural with us. It is a law of the kingdom of heaven, which we are slow in learning. Even many who call themselves Christians claim that they have a right to return evil for evil. A person who returns kindness for unkindness, who does an obliging act for one that was disobliging, is not commended as a manly man. The almost universal feeling is that an offense must be punished. But that is not the way Jesus teaches us to do when we have been wronged. "I say unto you, Resist not him that is evil: but whosoever smiteth thee on thy right cheek, turn to him the other also." We are to endure wrong patiently. We are to forgive those who have injured us.

This is one of the hardest lessons we have to learn in becoming Christians and in the cultivation of the Christian graces. It is hard when others treat us unjustly to keep on loving them and to be ready any moment to do them good. Yet that is what Jesus did, and He wants us to be like Him. He suffered wrongfully, and went on loving. He taught that we should forgive those who have injured us. When one of His disciples asked Him how often they should forgive others, and suggested seven times as a fair number, Jesus told him that not seven times, but seventy times seven, they should forgive. That is, they should never cease to forgive.

The word of Jesus which tells us that when one compels us to go a mile with him to show him the way and give him help on his journey, we should go two miles, is suggestive of the spirit of all true Christian life. Some people do the best they possibly can do for others. They try to carry out the teaching of love in a very literal fashion. But they never go an inch farther than they are required to go, they never pay a penny more than the law demands. Jesus said, however, that we should cultivate the two-mile religion, doing more than we are expected to do, going farther in helping others than we are required to go. Love should always abound in us. We are never to measure and calculate our kindness to others, giving just so much and no more. Generosity is to be the law of all our life. Anybody can go one mile with another, but we are to do more than others and go two miles.

The law of love to neighbors was taught in the Old Testament, but, like other Divine teachings which were not easy, the people made their own glosses over the Divine commandment, changing the sense to suit their own natural feelings. They interpreted this ancient law thus, "Thou shalt love thy neighbor, and hate thine enemy." They defined neighbors to include only certain pleasant, congenial people, people who were kind to them, people whom they liked. Jesus taught a higher law. "But I say unto you, Love your enemies, and pray for them that persecute you." According to His teaching our neighbor is anyone who needs our help. The parable of the Good Samaritan was Christ's own illustration and explanation of the meaning of the commandment to love our neighbor. It was a Jew who was hurt, and lay bleeding by the roadside. It was a hated and despised Samaritan who proved neighbor to him, stopping on his way, at much cost to his own interests, caring for the man, nursing him, and providing a place in which he might recover. No matter who it may be that needs any help, ministry or comfort from us—we are not to ask about his nationality, whether he has been a good friend to us in the past, or not, or whether he belongs to our set—we are to help him, because he is one of God's children.

The Divine example is referred to in enforcing the lesson. God is kind to the sinner as well as to the righteous man. "He maketh His sun to rise on the evil and the good, and sendeth rain on the just and the unjust." When He finds anyone in distress He does not ask who he is. He imparts blessing to all alike. Since God is patient with those who wrong Him and neglect Him, if we are God's children we must show the same spirit.

The Master thus sets the highest standard for His followers. It is not enough for them to be as good as other people are—they must be better. "What do ye more than others?" was His question. Anybody can love those that love him. Anybody will salute those who salute him graciously. The Christian is to do more. "Ye therefore shall be perfect, as your heavenly Father is perfect." We should keep before us always the question, "What do ye more than others?" Christian boys among their friends must not be content to live as the world's boys do—they must do more than they do, they must be better than they are. The Christian carpenter must do his work better than the carpenter who does not know Christ and follow Him. The Christian girl must be more gentle, more patient, more thoughtful, more unselfish, more kind, than worldly girls are, because she belongs to Christ. In all life's affairs, we must remember that having given ourselves to Christ there rests upon us an obligation for a more beautiful life, for nobler service, for sweeter living, for larger usefulness, for Christlike helpfulness, because we represent our Master, and are called to be perfect, even as our Father in heaven is perfect.

7

Almsgiving and Prayer

Scripture Reading: Matthew 6:1–15

It was characteristic of the Pharisees in our Lord's time that they sought publicity and display for their religious acts. They made their prayers in as conspicuous a way as possible so that the people would observe them, mark their devoutness and be impressed with their fervor and their earnestness. This was one thing in which the disciples of Jesus were told that their religion must differ from that of the scribes and Pharisees.

They were to take heed not to do their righteousness before men. This does not mean that they were not to be good before people—they were to live righteously everywhere. There are many Divine words bidding us to be careful of our conduct in the presence of others. Jesus Himself in this same Sermon said, "So let your light shine before men; that they may see your good works, and glorify your Father." We are to live all the while so that we shall be blameless, that those watching us, to find fault, shall have no reason for speaking against us. We are to show always to all men an example which shall honor Christ.

What is forbidden is, that we do our righteousness before others in order to be seen of them. We are to live for the eye of God, to get His praise. Some of those who professed great devoutness in Christ's time, making much show of piety in the presence of men, were in their inner life cruel, unmerciful, grasping and unholy. The lesson Jesus taught was lowly humility, devoutness of heart, a goodness which did nothing for display, but was always and everywhere true, faithful, genuine, thinking only of pleasing God.

One special example in illustration of the lesson Jesus gives is regarding the giving of alms. It was the custom of some of the people in those days to give their alms very ostentatiously. If they did not literally sound a trumpet, announcing their gifts, they at least let all people know that they were contributing to the poor and how much they were contributing. They wanted praise for their generosity. The motive was, not to relieve distress, but to "have glory of men." Jesus says they received their reward. That is, they had the name of being charitable. Their deeds were known and talked about. They did not give their alms to please God or because they cared for the poor, and so they had no honor from God, and no love from men as their reward.

Jesus teaches in contrast, in a very emphatic way, the true manner of giving alms. "When thou doest alms, let not thy left hand know what thy right hand doeth: that thine alms may be in secret: and thy Father who seeth in secret shall recompense thee." The lesson would seem to be that our doing good to others should be, as far as possible, absolutely in secret. When others need our help in their distress we are not to withhold it, but we are not to speak to others of what we do. We are even, as it were, not to let ourselves know of it. We are to give out of love to those who need to be helped, not humiliating them by making a spectacle of our kindness. Our giving, too, is to be only for the eye of God. Then He will reward us and recompense us.

The lesson is applied still further to prayer. "When ye pray, ye shall not be as the hypocrites: for they love to stand and pray in the synagogues and in the corners of the streets, that they may be seen of men." They do not pray to God at all, and their real desire is not to receive blessings in answer, but to have men think they are very devout. They have their reward—that is, they get what they seek for; men see them. We all need to guard against the performance of our acts of devotion for men's eyes and not for God's.

Jesus does not mean to teach that we are never to pray in the presence of others. Public prayer is a duty. What He is pressing is that we are not to do any religious act to have men see us and think us religious. We are to pray to God only and our prayer will receive His answer of love and grace. In all our life of love and service the same rule should be observed. We should never seek honor for anything we do. We should shrink from praise and publicity. To show consciousness of our goodness and any worthy service we have done is a blemish. We should hide away rather from praise of men.

Florence Nightingale, having gone like an angel of mercy among the hospitals in the Crimea until her name was enshrined deep in every soldier's heart, asked to be excused from having her picture taken, as thousands begged her to do, that she might drop out and be forgotten and that Christ alone might be remembered as the author of the blessings which her hand had distributed in His name.

"When thou prayest, enter into thine inner chamber, and having shut thy door, pray to thy Father." The Pharisees chose public places as their places of private devotion. They wanted people to see how devout they were. Jesus bids us guard against all such display of our religion. He teaches here also the duty of secret prayer. We are to go away alone—other persons about us disturb our thoughts. Then we are to shut the door to keep out all the world, that we may be entirely alone with God. He only is to hear us when we pray, and in Him alone must our dependence be. No one can afford to leave out of his life the daily secret prayer. Jesus went often apart to meet with God.

The form of prayer which Jesus gave His disciples was not meant as the only prayer they were ever to use, but as showing the spirit in which they should pray and the scope of their requests. "Our Father who art in heaven." This is the golden gate of prayer. If we enter the temple at all we must enter it as God's children. Of what open and loving access the name Father assures us. We know that He to whom we speak has a father's heart, a father's gentleness, a father's yearning for his child. A true earthly parent withholds from his child nothing that is good, so far as his ability goes. God withholds from His children nothing that is really good. We should learn also from a little child how to pray to God. We should come to Him in simplicity, with childlike confidence, with unquestioning trust, with yearning love.

"Hallowed be Thy name." To hallow is to honor, to make holy. If we pray this prayer sincerely we will hallow the Divine name in our own heart, we will pray with reverence and love. Good Christian people sometimes grow very careless in speaking of God. They become so accustomed to using His sacred name in prayer and conversation that they utter it lightly, as if it were the name of some familiar friend. A miner with black, grimy hand plucks a pure flower from the stem. It seems almost a profanation to touch that beautiful flower with the soiled fingers. But what shall we say to our taking on our unclean lips the holy name of God? We should learn to hallow this blessed name in our speech. Then we should hallow it in our life. We are God's children and we bear His name. We must take heed that in every act of ours, in our behavior, in our whole character and influence we should live so that all who see us shall see in us something of the beauty of God.

"Thy kingdom come." God's kingdom is where God is king. In praying this petition we are to think first of our own heart. The one place we can surrender to God is our own life. We cannot surrender our neighbor's heart to God. A mother cannot make God king in the heart of her child. But each one of us is master in his own life and can choose who shall rule in it. In praying "Thy kingdom come," our prayer means nothing at all if it does not first of all invite the Divine King to become our king, to rule in us. Then the prayer widens, and we ask God to set up His kingdom in our home, in our community, then over the whole world.

"Thy will be done in earth, as it is in heaven." Some people always quote this petition as if it meant only submission to some painful providence, as if God's will were always something terrible. They suppose it refers only to losing friends or money, to adversity or calamity, or to being sick or in some trouble. But this is only a little part of its meaning. It is for the doing of God's will, not the suffering of it, that we here pray. Our desire should be always to let God's will be done by us and in us. It is easier, however, to make prayers like this for other people than for ourselves. We all think others ought to do God's will, and we do not find it a difficult prayer to make that they may do so. But if we offer the petition sincerely, it is a prayer that we ourselves may do God's will as it is done in heaven. We can pray it, therefore, only when we are ready for implicit, unquestioning obedience.

Then it may—sometimes it does—mean the giving up of a sweet joy, the losing of a gracious friend, the sacrifice of some dear presence, the going in some way of thorns and tears. We should learn always to make the prayer and then to hold our life close to the Divine will, never rebelling, nor murmuring, but sweetly doing or bearing what God gives us to do or bear.

"Give us this day our daily bread." This seems a small thing to ask. Why are we not taught to pray for bread enough to last a week, a month, or a year? It seems for one thing that Jesus wanted to teach here the lesson of continual dependence. He taught us to come to God each morning with a request simply for the day's food, that we might never feel that we can get along without Him even for one little day. Another lesson He wanted to teach us was that we should live by the day. We are not to be anxious about tomorrow's needs—we are to think only today's. When tomorrow comes it will be right to seek provision for it and to take up its cares and duties.

"Forgive us our debts, as we also have forgiven our debtors." The first part of this petition is not hard to pray. But the second part is not so easy. When someone has done us an injury and we are feeling bitter and resentful over it, it is not easy to ask God to forgive us as we forgive. Perhaps we do not forgive at all, but keep the bitter feeling against our brother in our heart; what is it then that we ask God to do for us when we pray, "Forgive us as we forgive?" God has linked blessing and duty together in this petition in an inseparable way. If we will not forgive those who have wronged us, it is evident that we have not the true spirit of repentance to which God will grant remission of sins.

"Bring us not into temptation." We ought never to seek any way in which we shall have to meet temptation. Temptation is too terrible an experience, fraught with too much peril, ever to be sought by us or encountered save when God leads us in the path in which it lies. So if we make this prayer we must go only where duty clearly calls us. If we meet temptation there, God will keep us from evil.

8

Worldliness and Trust

Scripture Reading: Matthew 6:19–34

The Christian life is very simple if only we understand it. It has only one principle—single-hearted devotion to God. Paul stated this principle when he said, "To me to live is Christ" [Phil. 1:21]. Jesus states it here also when He says, "Seek ye first His kingdom, and His righteousness."

In our present passage we have a whole scheme of life. To begin with, we must find something real and permanent to live for. It concerns the matter of possessions. Earth's banks are not absolutely safe, and if they were, they are not eternal. We are immortal, and we must find a place of deposit secure for immortal years. "Lay not up for yourselves treasures upon earth, where moth and rust doth corrupt, and where thieves break through and steal: but lay up for yourselves treasures in heaven, where neither moth nor rust doth corrupt, and where thieves do not break through nor steal."

How can we lay up treasures in heaven? By living for God, by committing our lives to Jesus Christ, by spending our money for the glory of God. There are men who possess little money or property when they leave this world, but are rich in treasures laid up in heaven. Paul had only the clothes he wore, an old cloak and a few sacred parchments, when his martyrdom came, but he was rich beyond measure in glory. There are millionaires here who will be beggars in the other life, and there are poor men here who will have an inheritance of glory in heaven.

Single-heartedness is the secret of true life. "Ye cannot serve God and mammon." Some people seem to think they can keep on safe terms with God and at the same time maintain close relations with the world. The Master's teaching here shows us that it is impossible to be half God's and half the world's. There is room for only one lord in our life, and we must settle who this will be. If we belong to God, the world is our servant. It seems strange indeed that anyone with an immortal soul should be willing to have mammon—money—for his god. Money may do much good and be a great blessing if it is used for God, but when a man gets down upon his knees to his money, crawls in the dust for its sake, and sells his manhood to get it, it has only curse for him. One who truly serves God cannot give money half his heart. God will share a human heart with no other lord.

A great many people are talking now about the secret of happy living. The Master gives it here. "Therefore I say unto you, take no thought for your life" or "be not anxious." Anxiety is very common. There is a great deal of worrying in the world, even among good people. One does not meet very many whose faces shine always with the light of a perfect peace. The majority of faces show lines of care. Not many people pass undisturbed through all manner of experiences. Is worrying a sin, or is it only an infirmity? There certainly are a great many cautions and warnings in the Bible against worrying.

But how can we help it? Paul tells us how to keep it out of our life. "Be careful for nothing" or "In nothing be anxious." But how can we obey this counsel? What shall we do with the things that we would naturally worry about? Here is the answer: "In everything by prayer and supplication with thanksgiving let your requests be made known unto God." That is, instead of worrying about matters that would naturally fret us, we are to put them out of our own hands into God's hands by prayer. Then we have this assurance: "The peace of God, which passeth all understanding, shall guard your hearts and your thoughts in Christ Jesus" [Phil. 4:6, 7].

It will help us with our lesson if we look carefully at the connection of the words as they stand in the Gospel. "Ye cannot serve God and mammon. Therefore I say unto you, Be not anxious." That is, anxiety comes from serving mammon. We say we are God's children, yet when mammon seems to be failing, then we begin to worry. That is, we trust mammon more than we trust our Father. We feel safer when mammon's abundance fills our hands than when mammon threatens to fail and we have only God. If we truly served God only, we should not be afraid, though we have nothing of mammon, not even bread for tomorrow.

Jesus illustrates His teaching: "Behold the fowls of the heaven, . . . your heavenly Father feedeth them." Elsewhere Jesus says that not even a sparrow is forgotten by our Father. The sparrows are the most useless and the most troublesome of all birds. You can buy two of them for a farthing. Yet God watches over them, and not one of them shall fall to the ground without His permission. If God so cares for quarrelsome sparrows, He will care much more for His own children. We are of more value than many sparrows. Two souls are worth more than a thousand farthings—it took the blood of the Son of God to buy us back from bondage. Birds do not bear the Divine image. They have no spiritual nature. The God who cares for the soulless little bird will surely care much more thoughtfully, more tenderly, for a thinking, immortal being, capable of eternal life. God is our Father—He is not the birds' father; He is their creator and provider, but they are not His children. A woman will give more thought to her baby than to her canary. Our heavenly Father will provide more certainly for His children than for His birds.

Worrying is also most useless. "Which of you by taking thought [being anxious] can add one cubit unto the measure of his life?" A Chinese philosopher illustrated the uselessness of worry in this way: "The legs of the stork are long, the legs of the duck are short; you cannot make the legs of the stork short, neither can you make the legs of the duck long. Why worry?" A short person cannot, by any amount of anxiety, make himself an inch taller. Therefore, why should he waste his energy and fret his life away in wishing he were taller, and in worrying because he is not?

Worrying about a coming trouble does not keep the trouble away. Worrying over a loss does not bring back that which is gone. People find obstacles, difficulties and hindrances in their life. There are hard conditions in their lot. But is there any use in worrying over these things? Will it make them any easier? Will anxiety cure the lame foot, remove the ugly mole, reduce the undesired corpulency, or put flesh on the thin body? Will fretting make the heavy burden lighter, the hard work easier, the rough way smoother? Will anxiety keep the winter away, put coal in the bin, or bread in the pantry, or get clothes for the children?

Even philosophy shows the uselessness of worrying, since it helps nothing and only wastes one's strength, unfitting one for doing his best. But religion goes farther than philosophy, and tells us that even the hard things, the drawbacks, the obstacles, may be changed into blessings if we meet them in the right spirit. So we learn that we should quietly and with faith accept life as it comes to us, fretting at nothing, changing hard conditions to easier if we can, but if not, using them as a means for growth and advancement.

The fact that God cares for us ought to keep us from worry. "Why take ye thought for raiment? Consider the lilies." Does God really care for flowers? Yes, He weaves for them their matchless garments and fills their little cups with fragrance. Yet they live but for a day. If God clothes these frail plants so gloriously for only a few hours' beauty, will He not far more surely clothe His own children? It is told of Mungo Park, the great traveler, that once in the desert he was famishing for drink, and could find no water. In his exhaustion he had sunk down in the hot sands in despair, and had given up to die. He saw a tiny shoot of moss growing in the sand, and the thought came to him, "God tends this little plant. He placed it here and He is watering it. Surely, then, He will not forget me, but will provide for me, too." He roused up from his despair and passed on and was saved.

Here we come upon the great central principle of Christian living. "Seek ye first His kingdom, and His righteousness; and all these things shall be added unto you." That is, we are to put all the energy of our thought and life into one effort—to do God's will. We are not to take thought about our raiment or food—that is God's matter, not ours at all. We are to take thought, however, about our duty, our work, the doing of God's will, the filling of our place in the world. Too many people worry far more about their food and raiment, lest they shall be left to want, than they do about doing well their whole duty. That is, they are more anxious about God's part in their life than about their own. They fear that God may not take care of them, but they do not have any fear that they may fail in faithfulness to Him.

It will be a great point gained if we learn here once for all that providing for our wants is God's matter, not ours; and that our first and only care should be our duty, the doing of our work. This God will never do for us, but if we are true to Him we shall never have any occasion to fret ourselves about our care. Suppose we are nearly starving? Well, we must go on, doing our duty in the circumstances, and not worrying; and in due time, perhaps at the last moment, but somehow or other, and in some way, the Lord will provide. Or if not, He will take us home.

9

The Golden Rule

Scripture Reading: Matthew 7:1–12

When someone asked Raphael how he made his wonderful pictures, he replied, "I dream dreams and I see visions, and then I paint my dreams and visions." The teachings of Christ, if reverently received, fill our mind with dreams and visions of spiritual beauty. But there is something we must do if we would receive from these teachings the good they are intended to impart—we must get them wrought into our own life.

The lesson on judging is not an easy one. We may as well confess that most of us are quite prone to the fault which is here reproved. Of course, the teaching is not that we should never have any opinions concerning the actions of others—we cannot avoid having judgments either of approval or disapproval. It is not understood either that we shall never express condemnation of the acts of others; we are required to censure men's evil courses. A little later in this same Sermon on the Mount Jesus bids His disciples beware of false prophets which come in sheep's clothing, while in reality they are ravenous wolves. It is not an easy-going acceptance of all sorts of people that is taught. What we are forbidden to do is to be censorious. Rather, we are to treat others as we would have them treat us.

There are reasons enough why we should not judge others. One is, that it is not our duty. We are not our neighbor's judge. He does not have to answer to us. God is his Master, and to Him he must give account.

Another reason is that God is patient with men's faults, and we represent God. If He bears with a man's shortcomings, surely we should do so, too. He is patient with people in their indifference to Him, in their disobedience, in their selfishness. Should we be more exacting with others than God is? Should we exercise severity where He shows leniency?

Another reason we should not judge others is because we cannot do it fairly. We see but the surface of people's lives. We do not know what has been the cause of the disagreeable features, the faults, we see in them. Perhaps if we knew all we would praise where we condemn. A young man was blamed by his fellow clerks for what they called his stinginess. He did not spend money as they did. They did not know that an invalid sister in another part of the country, shut away in her room, with none but her brother to care for her, received nearly all of his monthly salary.

Another reason for not judging others is that we have faults of our own which should make us silent about the failings of others. When we glibly condemn our neighbor's shortcomings, we assume that we ourselves are without shortcomings. But quite likely we have a beam in our own eye at the very time we are pointing out to our brother the mote in his eye. A mote is a mere speck; a beam is a great log. The meaning is that we make more of a little speck we see on another's life or in his conduct than we make of a very large fault in ourselves. Our first business certainly is with ourself. We shall not have to answer for our brother's faults, but we must answer for our own. It is not our business to look after his blots and blunders, but we must look after our own. We should be severe in dealing with our own faults and then we will be able to help in curing the faults of others.

Another reason against judging is that the law of love requires us to look charitably at the faults and sins of others. "Love covers a multitude of sins" [see 1 Pet. 4:8]. An artist placed his friend in the chair so that the blemish on one side of his face would not show in the picture. That is the way love prompts us to see our friends and neighbors, and show them to others—exhibiting the noble things in them and throwing a veil over their defects.

Still another reason for not judging others is that when we do, we are setting a standard for the judging of ourselves by others. "Judge not, that ye be not judged. For with what judgment ye judge, ye shall be judged." If you criticize others you must expect them to criticize you, and they will. Those who deal gently with the acts of others may expect gentle treatment by others in return. People will give back to you exactly what you give to them.

The Master has more to say here about prayer. The promise is very large. "Ask, and it shall be given you." Thus our Father throws wide open the doors of all His treasure houses. There seems to be nothing of all His vast possessions which He is not ready to give His children for the asking. "All things are yours, and ye are Christ's" [1 Cor. 3:21–23]. We need not try to trim down the promise, and yet we must read into it other teachings about prayer. Elsewhere we are taught that in all our praying we must say, "Thy will be done" [6:10]. That is, we must submit all our requests to God's love and wisdom. We do not know what things will really be blessings to us. What would not be, our Father will withhold.

We get an important lesson here, too, on the manner of prayer, in the words "ask," "seek," "knock." They teach importunity and growing earnestness. Much that is called praying is not worthy of the name—is not praying at all. We have no burning desire, and there is neither importunity nor intensity in our asking. What did you pray for this morning? Do you remember?

The Father-heart of God is unveiled in the words about bread and a stone, a fish and a serpent. It is far more likely to be the other way, however—what we ask would be a stone to us, would not be a blessing, and God, knowing what we really need, gives us a loaf instead of the stone we cried for. We know certainly that our Father is kinder to His children than earthly parents are to theirs—as much kinder as His love and His ability to give are greater than the largest human love and ability. Yet we must emphasize the words "ask," "every one that asketh," etc. Some people never ask and then wonder why they do not receive. Then, we must ask with the highest motives. "Ye ask, and receive not, because ye ask amiss, that ye may consume it upon your lusts" [James 4:3]. Selfishness in prayer gets no answer.

The Golden Rule, as it is called, is wonderfully comprehensive. It bids us consider the interests of others as well as of ourselves. It bids us set our neighbor alongside of ourself and think of him as having the same rights we have and requiring from us the same fairness of treatment that we give to ourself. It is in effect a practical way of putting the command, "Thou shalt love thy neighbor as thyself" [Lev. 19:18]. It gives us a standard by which to test all our motives and all our conduct bearing on others. We are at once in thought to change places with the person toward whom duty is to be determined, and ask: "If he were where I am and I were where he is, how would I want him to treat me in this case?" The application of this rule would instantly put a stop to all rash, hasty actions, for it commands us to consider our neighbor and question our own heart before doing anything. It would slay all selfishness, for it compels us to regard our neighbor's rights and interests in the matter as precisely equal to our own. It leads us to honor others, for it puts us and them on the same platform, as equal before God, and to be equal, too, before our own eyes. The true application of this rule would put a stop to all injustice and wrong, for none of us would do injustice or wrong to ourselves, and we are to treat our neighbor precisely as if he were ourself. It would lead us to seek the highest good of all other men, even the lowliest and the humblest, for we surely would like all men to seek our good.

The thorough applying of this Golden Rule would end all conflict between labor and management, for it would give the employer a deep, loving interest in the men he employs and lead him to think of their good in all ways. At the same time it would give to every employee a desire for the prosperity of his employer and an interest in his business. It would put an end to all quarreling and strife in families, in communities, among nations. The perfect working of this rule everywhere would make heaven, for the will of God would then be done on earth as it is in heaven.

10

False and True Discipleship

Scripture Reading: Matthew 7:13–29

There are two gates—one narrow and one wide—and two ways corresponding thereto. The easy way is not the good way. This is true in a very wide sense. It is true in the life of a child. There is a broad way of indulgence and indolence, but we know where it leads. There is a way of patient obedience in duty, and the end of this is worthy life and noble character. It is true in young manhood and womanhood. There is a way of pleasure, of ease, which leads to unworthy character. There is a way of self-denial, of discipline, of hard work, and this leads to honor. Then there is a broad way of selfishness and sin which never reaches heaven's gates; and there is a way of penitence, of devotion to Christ, of spending and being spent in His service, whose end is a seat beside the King on His throne.

It is a reason for great thankfulness that there is a gate into the spiritual and heavenly life and into heaven at the end. The glorious things are not beyond our reach. They are high, on dazzling summits, but there is a path that leads to them. We must note, however, that the gate is strait, that is, narrow. Some people have a way of saying that it is very easy to be a Christian. But really it is not easy. It was not easy for the Son of God to prepare the way for us. It was necessary for Him to come from heaven in condescending love and give His own life in opening the way. Jesus said also that any who would reach the glory of His kingdom must

42

go by the same way of the cross by which He had gone. He said that he who will save his life, that is, withhold it from self-denial and sacrifice, shall lose it, and that he only who loses his life—gives it out in devotion to God and to duty—shall really save it [see 16:24, 25]. In one of His parables, too, Jesus speaks of salvation as a treasure hid in a field, and the man who learns of the treasure and its hiding-place has to sell all that he has in order to buy the field [see 13:44]. In another parable the same truth is presented under the figure of a merchant seeking goodly pearls, who had to sell all his stock of pearls that he might buy the one peerless pearl [13:45].

The truth of the difficulty of entrance into the kingdom is put in another way in this Sermon on the Mount. There are two roads through this world and two gates into the other world. One of these ways is broad and easy, with a descending grade, leading to a wide gate. It requires no exertion, no struggle, no sacrifice to go this way. The other road is narrow and difficult and leads to a narrow gate. To go this way one has to leave the crowd and walk almost alone—leave the broad, plain, easy road, and go on a hard, rugged path that often gets difficult and steep, entering by a gate too small to admit any bundles of worldliness or self-righteousness, or any of the trappings of the old life. If we get to heaven we must make up our minds that it can be only by this narrow way of self-denial. There is a gate, but it is small and hard to pass through.

Jesus forewarned His friends against false prophets who should come to them in sheep's clothing, but who inwardly would be ravening wolves. There is something fearful in the eagerness of Satan to destroy men's lives. He resorts to every possible device. He sends his agents and messengers in forms and garbs intended to deceive the simple-minded and unwary. He even steals the dress of God's own servants in order to gain the confidence of believers and then destroy their faith and lead them away to death. There always are such false teachers and guides. They try to pass for sheep, but the sheep's covering is only worn outside, while inside is the heart of a hungry, bloodthirsty wolf.

Many young people in these times fall under the influence of persons who have caught smatterings of skeptical talk which they drop in the form of sneers or mocking queries into the ears of their confiding listeners. They laugh at the simple old cradle faiths which these young Christians hold, calling them "superstitions." Then they go on to cast doubt upon, or at least to start questions about, this or that teaching in the Bible, or to caricature some Christian doctrine and hold it up in such a light as to make it look absurd. Thus these "false prophets" poison the minds of earnest young believers, and often destroy their childhood faith and fill them with doubt and perplexity.

Jesus makes it very plain in His teaching that not profession but obedience is the test of Christian life. "Not every one that saith unto Me, Lord, Lord, shall enter into the kingdom of heaven; but he that doeth the will of My Father . . ." It is not enough to believe in Christ, intellectually, even to be altogether orthodox in one's creed. It is not enough to seem to honor Christ before men, praying to Him and ascribing power to Him. Jesus tells us that some at least who thus seem to be His friends, publicly confessing Him, shall fail to enter the heavenly kingdom.

Why are these confessors of Christ kept out of the heavenly kingdom? What are the conditions of entrance into this kingdom? The answer is given very plainly. Those alone enter the kingdom who do the will of the Father who is in heaven. No confession, therefore, is true which is not attested and verified by a life of obedience and holiness. "Simply to Thy cross I cling" is not all of the gospel—it is only half of it. No one is really clinging to the cross who is not at the same time faithfully following Christ and doing whatsoever He commands. To enter into the kingdom of heaven is to have in one's heart the heavenly spirit. We must do God's will. We cannot have Christ for our Savior until we have Him also as our Master. We pray, "Thy will be done, as in heaven, so on earth." If the prayer is sincere, it must draw our whole life with it in loving obedience and acquiescence to the Divine will.

The illustration at the close of the Sermon on the Mount makes the teaching very plain. "Therefore whosoever heareth these sayings of mine, and doeth them, I will liken him unto a wise man, which built his house upon a rock." Everything turns on the doing or not doing of God's word. Both the men here described hear the words, but only one of them obeys, and thus builds on the impregnable foundation. These two houses were probably very much alike when they were finished. Indeed, the house on the sand may have been more attractive and more showy than the house built farther up on the hillside. The difference, however, lay in the foundations.

There were two kinds of ground. There was a wide valley, which was dry and pleasant in the summer days, when these men were looking for building sites. Then away above this valley were high, rocky bluffs. One man decided to build in the valley. It would cost much less. It was easy digging, and the excavations would be less expensive, for the ground was soft. Then it was more convenient also, for the bluffs were not easy of access. The other man looked farther ahead, however, and decided to build on the high ground. It would cost a great deal more, but it would be safer in the end.

So the two homes went up simultaneously, only the one in the valley was finished long before the other was, because it required much less labor. At last the two families moved into their respective residences, and both seemed very happy. But one night there was a great storm. The rains poured down in torrents until a flood, like a wild river, swept through the valley. The house that was built on the low ground was carried away with its dwellers. The house on the bluff, however, was unharmed.

These two pictures explain themselves. He who built in the valley is the man who has only profession, but who has never really given his life to Christ, nor built on Him as the foundation. The other man who built on the rock is he who has a true faith in Christ, confirmed by loving obedience. The storms that burst are earth's trials which test every life—the tempests of death and of judgment. The mere professor of religion is swept away in these storms, for he has only sand under him. He who builds on Christ is secure, for no storm can reach him in Christ's bosom.

11

Jesus, the Healer

Scripture Reading: Matthew 8:2–17

After the Sermon on the Mount, we have narratives of many healings. The first was that of a leper. The case was remarkable because the disease was loathsome, contagious and incurable. The leper's cry to Jesus was very earnest. He worshiped Him and said, "Lord, if Thou wilt, Thou canst make me clean." He had no doubt of Christ's power to cure him—"Thou canst,"—but he seems uncertain regarding His willingness to do it. Instantly came the answer, "I will." As He said this He reached out His hand and touched him. Straightway the cure was wrought. The man was ready to go back again to his home and to take his place once more in society. Marvelous was the touch of Christ always. It never took defilement; it was so full of health that it cleansed the utmost loathsomeness. The same touch that changed the leper's flesh into cleanness changes the worst lives into whiteness and wholeness.

The next act of healing was wrought on a slave. A Roman centurion had a servant who was very sick and a great sufferer. Somehow the centurion had heard of Jesus and the wonderful works He was doing, and he went to Him beseechingly and told Him of his trouble. We learn more about this soldier from seeing him at Jesus' door. He was greatly distressed, and yet it was not his child that was sick—it was only his slave. This tells us what kind of a man the centurion was—he had a gentle heart. All of us are continually betraying ourselves through the little windows of our common, unconscious acts. By the way a boy treats his dog or his pony, or birds and insects, especially by his treatment of his sisters, and by his manner toward his playmates, and toward the poor and the weak, he is showing what is really in him.

We see here also the immortality of good deeds. It is sweet to be remembered, long after one has passed out of life, by what one has done. It was a great while ago that this centurion went on his errand, but here we find his gentle deed set down among the memorials of Christ's own life. Ages since, a beautiful fern leaf grew in a shaded valley, and as it fell it sighed that it would have no memorial. But the other day a man of science broke off a piece of rock, and there his eye traced

> Leafage, veining, fibers, clear and fine—
> And the fern's life lay in every line.

So it is that good deeds are kept in memory. This one of the centurion's is found imbedded on a gospel page. Every good deed done in Christ's name is recorded in God's books and on human lives. It is worthwhile, therefore, to train our hearts to gentle thoughts and our hands to gentle deeds.

Jesus received the Gentile soldier most graciously and said at once He would accompany him home and heal the servant. Here we have a revelation of the heart of Christ. He was quick to respond to every cry of suffering. It will greatly help us in our thoughts of Christ in heaven, to remember that He is the same now that He was while on the earth. He is still quick to hear our prayers and respond to our requests. His heart is yet tender and full of compassion toward pain. The gospel pages are not records of what Christ was, but glimpses of what He is.

Another lesson here is for ourselves. It is said that Dr. Livingstone rarely ever offered a prayer, even in his early Christian life, in which he did not plead to be made like Christ in all his imitable perfection. This should be the daily prayer of every Christian. We should seek to have Christ's great kindness of heart. The world is full of suffering and we ought to seek in all possible ways to give comfort, relief or help. We have power to scatter happiness, to relieve distress, to give cheer and hope. We may not be able to heal diseases, but we can love people in Christ's name, and give them courage and strength to go on with their troubles and be happy.

But the centurion shrank now in his lowliness from having Jesus enter his home. This was true humility. We cannot truly see Christ and not be humbled. The reason we are so proud and self-conceited is because we do not see Him. If our eyes but beheld Him in the glory and splendor of His Divinity, all our vain pretensions would instantly shrivel. We should look at Christ with a long, loving gaze until a sense of His Divine greatness fills our hearts.

Another thing here to be noted is the centurion's conception of Christ. He thought of Him as a great Commander with all the forces of the universe under Him. The soldier knows only one duty—to obey—and all these forces know only to obey Christ. Christ is the Commander of the army of the universe—"Captain of the Lord's host." The stars and planets are under Him and obey Him, all winds and tempests and all the powers of nature are subject to His sway. All diseases, all events, come and go at His word. This ought to give us great confidence in the midst of dangers of whatsoever kind. Diseases and pestilence are only Christ's soldiers. They are obedient to His will and can never transcend it nor go contrary to it. They can go only where and as far as He sends them. Death is one of His soldiers, too, and can do only His command. Why then should we dread death, since it is the obedient servant of our King? So of all events and occurrences—they are but the messengers of our Master and cannot harm us. It was not necessary for Jesus to go to the centurion's house to heal his slave. He had only to speak the word, and the illness would obey Him and flee away.

The centurion's great faith wrought a great cure. "As thou hast believed, so be it done unto thee." Blessing depends upon faith, the measure of blessing upon the measure of faith. Little faith gets little help. We have all God's fullness from which to draw, and there can be no limit to our receiving save the capacity of our believing. It is because we have such small faith that the answers to our prayers are so meager. If we prayed for our friends as the centurion prayed for the healing of his servant, there would be more conversions.

The next case of healing was wrought in the home of one of the disciples. Jesus blesses homes. It was after a Sabbath service in the synagogue. When Jesus entered the house He found the woman lying sick of a fever. We are not told of any request for healing by any of the family. The thought seems to have been the Master's own. He saw her sick, and

His heart was full of compassion. The record is very beautiful. "He touched her hand, and the fever left her." What strange power has that touch! There are other fevers besides those that burn in people's bodies. There are fevers of the mind, of the soul. There are fevers of discontent, of passion, of ambition, of lust, of jealousy, of envy, fevers of anxiety, of remorse, of despair. All of these, all life's fevers, the touch of Christ has power to heal. Let Him only touch the hot hand and the fever will flee away and quietness and peace will come.

"The fever left her; and she arose, and ministered unto Him." She could not minister until the fever was gone. Nor can we minister while life's fevers are burning within us. But when the fever leaves us we at once arise and begin to serve the Master. It would add immeasurably to our power among men and to the influence of our lives if we would always get the touch of Christ upon our hands at the beginning of each day. Archdeacon Farrar says of his mother: "My mother's habit was, every day, immediately after breakfast, to withdraw for an hour to her own room, and to spend the time in reading the Bible, in meditation, and in prayer. From that hour, as from a pure fountain, she drew the strength and the sweetness which enabled her to fulfill all her duties, and to remain unruffled by all the worries and pettinesses which are so often the intolerable trial of narrow neighborhoods. As I think of her life, and of all it had to bear, I see the absolute triumph of Christian grace in the lovely ideal of a Christian woman. I never saw her temper disturbed; I never heard her speak one word of anger, or of calumny, or of idle gossip. I never observed in her any sign of a single sentiment unbecoming to a soul which had drunk of the river of the water of life, and which had fed upon manna in the barren wilderness. The world is the better for the passage of such souls across its surface." Let other weary mothers wait each morning to get the touch of Christ before they go to the day's tasks and frets. Then the fevers of life will leave them, and they will enter upon a day of quiet peace and gentle ministry.

The closing words of our passage present a most remarkable picture. "When even was come, they brought unto Him many possessed with demons: and He cast out the spirits with a word, and healed all that were sick." It would seem that there were scores and hundreds healed in one hour.

At even, ere the sun was set,
　The sick, O Lord, around Thee lay;
O in what divers pains they met!
　O with what joy they went away!

Once more 'tis eventide, and we,
　Oppressed with various ills, draw near:
What if Thy form we cannot see?
　We know and feel that Thou art here.

Thy touch has still its ancient power;
　No word from Thee can fruitless fall:
Hear in this solemn evening hour,
　And in Thy mercy heal us all.

12

The Power of Faith

Scripture Reading: Matthew 9:18–34

Only comparatively few of our Lord's healings are recorded. He seems never to have refused to heal any who came to Him or were brought to Him. Besides, He healed some for whom no one interceded. Here it was a ruler—an exceptional case, for the rulers were not His friends. Probably this man's great distress led him to seek healing for his child even in spite of his dislike of Jesus. The ruler and his prejudice were lost in the father.

The man came himself, saying, "My daughter is even now dead." Trouble comes just as inevitably and as resistlessly to the mansions of the great and rich as to the homes of the lowly and poor. None are exempt. We can build no walls and set up no doors to exclude sickness and death. This is one lesson. Another is, that when sickness or any other trouble comes to us, we ought to send for Christ. We are to send for physicians, too, in sickness. They are God's ministers of healing. Usually God requires our cooperation in all that He does for us. But we should also send for Christ. He alone has original power to heal. Life is His gift and is under His care. Health is His alone to give. Medicines unblessed by Him give no relief. Only at His bidding can anyone be restored from illness. While we use all the means within our reach, we should use them with prayer for Divine blessing on them and in dependence on Divine power. Whenever anyone is

51

sick in our house we should send for Jesus and put the case in His hands.

Jesus was always eager to help those in trouble. He arose at once at the ruler's request and followed him to his home. It seems strange, when we think who the man was, probably unfriendly to Jesus, that He should so quickly rise and follow this ruler. But it was always thus. He did not wait to make inquiry concerning the man, whether he was worthy or not, before going with him. The man that needed Him was the man He wanted. In this alacrity in doing good Jesus was only showing the alertness of Divine love. In heavenly glory now He is as quick to hear and as prompt to answer our cries as He was that day in His earthly humiliation. He is always at our call. He never has so much to do or so many calls to answer that He cannot attend to our case. Indeed, when we come to Him with any need, He has no other thing to do but attend to us. We should be like our Master in all this. We should be quick to respond to the calls of need and distress about us. We ought to train our hearts to sympathy and thoughtfulness, and our hands to quick, gentle ministry in Christ's name.

Then came an interruption as the Master was hastening with the ruler to his house. "Behold, a woman . . . came behind Him, and touched the hem of His garment." The street was thronged with persons waiting for an opportunity to get near to the Healer. The "hem of His garment" is always within reach of earth's sufferers. He has gone up now on high, out of our sight, but His garment floats everywhere. We never can get beyond the sweep of its folds. We can always come near enough to Christ to reach out a trembling finger and touch His garment and find healing. Of course, we must not make a mistake about this border. It is not a crucifix, nor is it some relic of a dead saint, nor is it a bit of the wood of the true cross. It is not even the Bible, for touching the Bible will do no one good. Nor is it the Church and its ordinances; for we may belong to the Church and observe its ordinances, and get no benefit to ourselves. To touch the border of Christ's garment is to touch Christ Himself. His garment is His life, His love, His Spirit, His grace.

A human physician, if hurrying on such an errand, would probably have refused to listen to any calls for help on the way, as the ruler's child was actually dying. But Jesus stopped quietly and turned to see the woman who had touched Him. Mark says He asked, "Who touched My garments?" How did He know that one touch amid all the jostling of the crowd? The multitudes were close about Him, pressing up against Him. Many of them touched Him. The disciples thought it strange that He should ask such a question. The people could not help touching Him. But there was one touch different from all the rest. There was something in it which sent a thrill through Him. There was a heart's cry in it, a piteous, earnest supplication. It was a touch of faith. It was not like the jostling of the crowd—an accidental or unconscious touch, the mere touch of nearness. It was intentional. There was a soul's cry in it. So, amid all the rude pressure of the multitude, He recognized it and turned about to see her that had done this thing.

Jesus always knows the touch of true faith and prayer among all the touches of this great world. In one sense all men are near to Him, for He is everywhere present. We cannot move without pressing up against Him. But when among all earth's millions one person intentionally reaches out a hand to feel for Him, to touch Him with a purpose, with a longing or a desire, to seek for some blessing, or to crave some help, He instantly knows the pressure of that touch and turns to answer it. He knows when a hungry heart wants Him, no matter how obscure the person, how poor, or how hidden in the crowd.

Notice His graciousness in answering the woman's prayer. "Jesus turning and seeing her said, Daughter, be of good cheer." This was a bit of Christ's wayside work. He was hastening with Jairus to his home, to restore his dying child, and healed this poor woman on the way. We would call it incidental work, unpurposed, unplanned. The things we set out in the morning to do are not by any means all the things that we do in any well spent day. If we have the life of Christ in us, everyone that touches us gets some blessing from us. While busy at our work we speak kindly to those who meet us or who are near us, and an influence of warmth, cheer or encouragement, or an inspiration toward better living, goes from us to them. We meet one in trouble as we hurry by, and stop to give a word of comfort. We hear of a case of distress and we send or carry relief. Thus, if we have the spirit of Christ, our wayside service will be a most valuable and important part of our work in this world.

We do not know how long Jesus was detained in healing and comforting the woman on the way. "Jesus came into the ruler's house, and saw the flute-players." The child was dead and they were preparing for the funeral. So it seemed that He had tarried too long on the way. To us it appears that He ought not to have stopped at all to heal or talk with the woman. She could have waited. The child of Jairus was dying and there was not a moment to lose. But when we read the story through to the end we are glad that He did stop to help the woman. We learn from His delay that Jesus never is in a hurry. He is never so much engrossed in one case of need that He cannot stop to consider another. He is never so pressed for time that we have to wait our turn. No matter what He is doing, He will always hear instantly our cry for need. Another thing we learn from this delay is that Jesus never comes too late; never waits too long. True, the ruler's child died while He lingered, but this only gave Him an opportunity for a greater miracle. He delayed that He might do a more glorious work for this family. There is always some good reason for it when Christ seems to delay to answer our prayers or come to our help. He delays that He may do more for us in the end.

"The maid is not dead, but sleepeth." This was Christ's word always about death. He said His friend Lazarus was asleep. He says the same of all His friends. They are not dead. Indeed, they never lived so really, so richly, so fully, as they live when we call them dead. They are away from all the limitations of earthly life, set free from the hampering prison of the flesh, cleansed of all sin, "spirits of just men made perfect." Christ changed the whole aspect of death for His people. To them it is but the passage to life—rich, blessed, glorious life. Even bodily death is a sleep, and sleep is not a terrible experience. It is restful and refreshing, and then we wake again from sleep and live on beyond it. So the body sleeps, and will rise again renewed and wearing immortal beauty. Christ called this child from her sleep very soon; it will be longer before He will call those whom we lay down in death's sleep, but He will surely wake them in His own time, in the blessed, glorious morning. It is wonderful comfort to us to know that Christ has care of our sleeping dead and has the keys of their graves and can call them when He will.

Another phase of human need is met in the next incident. "Two blind men followed Him." There are a great many people blind in another way. They can see certain things, but certain other things they cannot see at all. They can see mountains and plains and blue skies, and human faces, and money and real estate, and all earthly things; but they cannot see

God, nor heaven, nor the beauty of holiness, nor the inheritance of believers, nor any of the unseen things of blessedness and Divine glory. They can see only material things, which are not enduring nor eternal; but they cannot see spiritual things, which alone are real. Natural blindness is a sore loss. A blind man misses all the glorious beauty of this world. He cannot see where to go and has to be led by the hand. But spiritual blindness is an infinitely more sore loss. Christ alone could give sight to the blind. He opened eyes that had always been closed. He alone can open the eyes of the spiritually blind. If we cannot see spiritual things, we should call upon Christ to have mercy upon us.

Always faith was required. "Believe ye that I am able to do this?" The men must have faith before Jesus could heal them. When we come to Him asking Him to do anything for us, He wants to know if we believe that He is able to do it. Once a father came to Him for his demoniac son, and his prayer was, "If Thou canst do anything, have compassion on us, and help us." But the "if" marred the request—the father was not sure that Jesus could cure his son, and Jesus sent him back to get a better faith. "If thou canst!" He answered. "All things are possible to him that believeth." As soon as the man could say, "Lord, I believe; help Thou my unbelief," Jesus cured the boy [Mark 9:22–24]. May it not be that the reason why many of our prayers are not answered is because we do not believe that Christ is able to do what we ask of Him? If we can believe, He can give what we ask. If we cannot believe, He cannot do anything for us.

13

The Mission of the Twelve

Scripture Reading: Matthew 9:35—10:15, 40–42

Jesus never rested. He went about doing good. His work is summed up here in three words—teaching, preaching, healing. He was in this world to seek and save the lost, and He went everywhere on His holy mission of love. He did not stay in one place, because then other places would have been neglected. He knew that He had blessings for the sad, suffering world, and His soul was burdened until He had borne these blessings to everyone's door. So He went everywhere, from house to house. He was a shepherd seeking the lost, and we can see Him pressing through the dark ravine, up the steep cliffs, out upon the wild crags and over the rugged mountains, through storm and darkness, cold and heat, searching for the lost sheep. That is what He wants us to do now, for we are left in this world in His place, to carry on His work.

"When He saw the multitudes, He was moved with compassion on them." Christ's compassion was wonderful. The sight of suffering humanity filled Him with grief. We have a picture here of the way the world of people looked to Jesus. They were "distressed and scattered, as sheep not having a shepherd." This means that they were neglected by those who ought to have been their friends and helpers. The rulers were intended to be shepherds to their people. Instead of this, they showed them no love, no kindness, no care, but wronged them,

56

robbed them. Jesus was among them as a true shepherd, and His heart was full of compassion toward them.

Out of the deep pity of His heart Jesus begins now to plan for the great work of saving men. "The harvest truly is plenteous, but the laborers are few." He seems to have been almost appalled at the vastness of the work as He looked out over His own people and thought of their condition. But His vision was not limited to His own country. He had come to save the world, the whole world, all nations. No wonder He said to His disciples, "The harvest truly is plenteous." To meet the great need there must be many laborers enlisted. This is the beginning of the great missionary movement which is now reaching out all over the world.

"The laborers are few," said the Master as He looked upon the great fields with their vast human needs, their sorrows, their hungering. Indeed, Jesus himself was the only laborer at that time. The apostles were only a handful and they were still untrained.

Note the first word His heart uttered as He thought of reaching the world with mercy. "Pray ye therefore the Lord of the harvest, that He will send forth laborers into his harvest." The Lord of the harvest is God Himself. At that time the chief duty was prayer that the Lord would send forth laborers. Men were first to be called for the work and then trained for it. There is still need for making the same prayer, for even yet the laborers are few in consideration of the vastness of the field to be harvested. But few young men are entering the Christian ministry, and the ranks are growing thin. The gates of missionary lands are open, and the money is ready to send men into the fields, but the men are not offering themselves.

Already Jesus had chosen the twelve apostles. Luke tells us of this. It is said that He spent all night in prayer to God before choosing these men. He thus sought His Father's guidance in making His choice and His blessing on the men to be chosen. The work of the kingdom was to be committed to their hands, and it was of the greatest importance that they should be in every way the right men. We have a suggestion here also as to the importance of choosing our personal friends. It should be with prayer. Their influence upon our lives will be vital and far-reaching and only God can choose them for us.

Here we have a description of the mission and work of the apostles. "He . . . called unto Him His twelve disciples, and gave them power."

First He called them to Him. No one is ready to go out for Christ until he has come to Him. Discipleship must come before service. There is no place to start but at the Master's feet. We must lie on His bosom and catch His Spirit. It is not enough to attend colleges and theological seminaries and be graduated from these. It is not enough to be commended by committees and mission boards; everyone who would go as a worker for Christ or as a missionary must first come to Christ. Christ must choose and call His own apostles and send them out with His benediction. None are ready to go until Christ has given them power and authority. He is the King, and He only can commission any to represent Him. If we want them to help Christ save the world we must personally surrender ourselves to Him and let Him prepare us and then send us out with authority to represent Him.

The names of the apostles are given. They were not famous men when they were chosen. They were very plain and ordinary men; but afterward they became men of wonderful power, and all the world felt their influence. We see out of what common stuff Christ can make great men, holy saints and heroic missionaries. There is something in His method of preparing His apostles that those who would be preachers and teachers should note. He took these men into His family and kept them there for three years. He lived with them, pouring the light and the love of His holy life upon their dull, sinful lives, until they were literally permeated with His Spirit. Thus He stamped His own impress upon them so that they were ready to go out and repeat His life and teaching among men. Perhaps many of us scatter our work too much. If we would select a few persons and give to them continually our strongest and best influence, month after month, and year after year, carrying them in our prayers, and in our thoughts, and doing all we can to impress them and make them noble, true and Christlike, might we not do more for our Lord in the end than by trying merely to touch a hundred or a thousand lives?

The apostles had their field laid out for them. They were not to go into the way of the Gentiles. This was not the final command; it was only for the first tour of the country. The Gentiles were not always to be left out from the proclamation of the gospel. The great final commission was universal; they were to carry to every creature under the heavens the news of salvation. But as yet the gospel was not ready to be proclaimed everywhere. The blood of the Lamb of God had not yet been shed. The alabaster box of the Savior's precious life had not yet been broken to pour out the ointment. For the present the messengers were not to go beyond the limits of the Jewish nation.

The great law of Christian life is that we receive in order to give, that we are blessed in order that we may be a blessing. "Freely ye have received, freely give." Christ has liberally blessed us, but the blessing is not for ourselves alone. The things He has given us we are to pass on to others. He wants to reach the many through the few. We sin against Christ, and therefore against others, if we keep in our own hands and do not use the good things He has so generously bestowed upon us. We take the bread and are to pass it to those who are hungry. We receive the cup and are to give it to those next to us. We are disloyal, therefore, to Him if we close our hands and hold the blessings He gives us in tight clasp just for ourselves. Let us freely pass on all that Christ has so freely given to us.

14

The Question of John the Baptist

Scripture Reading: Matthew 11:1–19

John was a brave man and a firm believer in Jesus as the Messiah, but in his prison questions arose. "When John heard in the prison the works of the Christ, he sent two of his disciples." There were some things which he could not make out himself, and he sent promptly to Jesus to ask Him about them. That is just what we should learn to do in all our perplexities. There often are times when all seems dark about us. We cannot understand the things that are happening to us. We are apt to get very much worried and disheartened. The true Christian way in all such experiences is to take the matters at once to Christ.

John's faith in the Messiahship of Jesus wavered in his hard circumstances. "Art Thou He that should come?" Some people think that John could not really have been in doubt. It is impossible, they say, that such a brave, grand man should ever have wavered in his confidence. They forget that John lived in the mere dawn of Christianity, before the full day burst upon the world. He had not the thousandth part of the light that we have, yet do we never have our questions? The truth is, there are very few of us who are not sometimes disheartened without a hundredth part of the cause John had. But that is usually the way. We are amazed at every person's blindness or dullness but our own. Other people's failures look very large to us, but we do not see our own at all. We wonder how

60

Moses, once, under sorest provocation, lost his temper and spoke a few hasty and impatient words; while we can scarcely get through a single sunny day ourselves without a far worse outbreak at a far smaller provocation. We wonder how the beloved disciples, with all his sweet humility, could once show an ambition for a place of honor, while we ourselves are forever miserably scrambling for preferments. We say, "Isn't it strange that the people of Christ's time would not believe on Him when they saw all His power and love?" Yet we do not believe on Him any more readily or any more fully than they did, though we have far greater evidence. We think it strange that the Baptist grew despondent when his trials were so great, though many of us are plunged into gloom by the merest trifles.

Somehow Jesus was not realizing John's expectation as the Messiah, and he thought that possibly there was yet another to come after Him. "Look we for another?" It is the same yet with many people. When everything is bright and sunny they think they surely have found Christ, and their hearts are full of joy. But when troubles come and things begin to go against them, they wonder whether after all they really have found the Savior. They begin to question their own experience. Christ does not do just the things they thought He would do for them. Their religion does not support them as they supposed it would do. If they are indeed Christians, why does Christ let them suffer so much and not come to relieve them? So they sink away into the slough of despond, sometimes losing all hope.

But we see from John's case how unnecessary all this worry is. Of course, we must have some earthly trials. Christ does not carry us to heaven on flowery beds of ease. We must expect to bear the cross many a long mile. The true way is never to doubt Him. Suppose there are clouds, the sun still shines behind them, undimmed, and the very clouds have their silver lining. Suppose we have disappointments, Jesus is the same loving Friend as when all our hopes come to ripeness. There is no need to look for another; all we want we find in Him. If we turn away from Him, where shall we go?

When John's messengers came with their question, Jesus did not give a direct answer. He went on with His ministry of love and mercy that they might see what His work was. Then "Jesus answered." Jesus always

answers. Many of our prayers to Him are mixed with doubts. Many of
them are full of complaints, fear and murmuring. Still He never grows
impatient with us. He never shuts His door upon us. We must cause
Him much pain by our distrusts and our unhappy fears. We wonder
whether He loves us or not, whether He really has forgiven us or not,
whether or not He will take care of us all through our life. Half the time
we are worried or perplexed about something and are full of frets and
cares. Does Jesus ever get tired listening to such prayers? No, no; He
listens always, and though His heart must often be pained by the dis-
cordant notes of our murmurings and fears, He never grows impatient,
and never chides but always answers. He remembers how frail we are,
that we are but dust, and gives loving answers.

> There's no place where earthly sorrows
>   Are more felt than up in heaven;
> There's no place where earthly failings
>   Have such kindly judgment given.

Jesus let the messengers get their own conclusions from what they
saw. "Go and tell John the things which ye hear and see." Here we see
how Jesus proved His own Messiahship. The best evidence of Christianity is not a long array of arguments, but the things Christianity has
done. The tree's fruits are the best index to the tree's character. Jesus
pointed to the miracles He had wrought. Yet it was not to the miracles
as miracles, merely as wonderful works, that He pointed; it was the
character of these works that proved His Messiahship. The blind received their sight, the lame were enabled to walk, lepers were cleansed,
the deaf were made to hear. All these were works of Divine mercy and
love. Pulling down mountains, walking on the water, floating in the
air, performing remarkable feats of magic, would not have proved our
Lord's Messiahship; the miracles He wrought were never ostentatious,
never for show, but were acts of love, done to relieve suffering, lift up
fallen men, give joy and help, and thus manifest the Divine character.
Once He walked on the water, yet it was not for show, but in carrying
relief to His imperiled and terrified disciples.

Jesus said nothing about John while the messengers from John were
there, but when they were gone He spoke of him. "As they departed,

Jesus began to say." What a beautiful thing this was for Jesus to do for His friend! The people and the disciples would misunderstand John's perplexity about the Christ, and would be sure to misjudge Him, thinking Him weak and vacillating. Jesus would not rest a moment until He had removed any unfavorable impression about John that might have been left in anyone's mind. He was most careful of the reputation of His friend. The lesson is very important. We should always seek to guard the good name of our friends. We should not allow any wrong impression of them or of their acts to become current. We should hold their name and honor sacred as our own. If we find that anything they have done is likely to leave an unfair or injurious impression on others who do not know all the circumstances, we must try to set the matter right. It is very sad to see persons sometimes even apparently glad to find others unfavorably regarded. Instead of hastening to remove or correct wrong impressions, they seem quite willing to let them remain and even to confirm them by significant silence or by ambiguous words. Surely that is not the Christlike way.

John was not a weak man, blown with every breeze. He was not a "reed shaken with the wind." That is what many people are. A reed grows in soft soil by the water's edge. Then it is so frail and delicate in its fiber that every breeze bends and shakes it. There are people of whom this is a true picture. Instead of being rooted in Christ, their roots go down into the soft mire of this world and are easily torn up. Thus they have no fixed principles to keep them upright and make them true and strong, and they are bent by every wind and moved by every influence. They lack nothing so much as backbone. The boy that cannot say no, when other boys tease him to smoke or drink or go to places he ought not to go, is only a reed shaken with the wind. The girl who is influenced by frivolities and worldly pleasures, and drawn away from Christ, and from a noble, pure, beautiful life, is another reed. They are growing everywhere, these reeds, and the wind shakes them every time it blows. Who wants to be a reed? Who would not rather be more like the oak, growing with roots firm as a rock, which no storm can bend?

It was a splendid commendation that Jesus gave His friend. "There hath not arisen a greater than John the Baptist." So a man may sometimes have doubts and perplexities of faith, and yet be a very great man.

Christ does not cast us off because we sometimes lose faith. Of course, we ought never to have any doubts about Christ, or about His way being the best way, but if ever we do yield to such discouragements, we must not think we have lost our place in Christ's love. He makes a great deal of allowance for our weakness and for the greatness of our trials, and keeps on loving us without interruption. Thousands of good people have their times of despondency, and Jesus is always gentle and tender to all in such experiences. He does not chide. He does not break the bruised reed, nor quench the smoking flax. He restores the sick or wounded soul to health.

15

Warning and Invitation

Scripture Reading: Matthew 11:20–30

It seems strange to hear Jesus upbraiding. His words usually were most gracious and loving. Here, however, we hear Him speaking in tones of sharpness and severity. Yet the phase of His character which is now revealed is not inconsistent with other representations of Him in the Gospels. We must not think of Jesus as having no capacity for anger. He was all love, but love can be severe, even terrible. While He was a friend of sinners and went to His cross to redeem the ungodly, He hated sin. He was just and holy.

We should notice carefully, however, the reason for this upbraiding. It fell upon the cities in which Jesus had done most of His mighty works. These were not His first words to the people of these cities. There had been long months of loving ministry, with miracles of mercy, with words of grace, revelings of the Father-heart of God, and offers of eternal life, before He spoke the words of chiding we now hear Him speak. But the people of these favored cities had been unaffected by all this love. They had gone on in their sins, unrepentant. They had accepted Christ's gifts of love, but had not accepted Him as their Lord. They had taken His help, His kindness, the things He had done for them so lavishly, but they had rejected Him.

The upbraiding of these cities was because after all that He had done for them, after all their spiritual opportunities and privileges, they had rejected Jesus. It was not impatience on His part that made Him severe. He had not grown weary loving even without return. But the fact that the cities had received so much Divine favor made their sin in rejecting Christ far greater.

Tyre and Sidon, great commercial cities which had been denounced by the prophets for their sins, would have repented, Jesus said, if such Divine blessings as had been shown to Chorazin and Bethsaida had been given to them. Sodom was the great historical example of wickedness in the history of the world, and its destruction was a notable instance of judgment. But even Sodom would have repented if it had received such calls and had enjoyed such privileges as had Capernaum. And Sodom's judgment would be more tolerable than that of Capernaum.

There is something startling in what Jesus says here about the doom of these Galilean cities, and the reason for it. They had had high privileges, and had disregarded them. What then about the places in our own day which have had exceptional privileges and have not improved them? What about those who have been brought up in Christian homes, amid the most gracious influences, who have seen Christ continually and have known the beautiful things of His love from infancy, and after all have kept their hearts closed upon Him, refusing His love? The question with which we are really personally concerned is not Chorazin, its site, its doom, or Capernaum, the improbability of its identification, but ourselves, our privileges and what we are doing with them.

"More tolerable." So we would better have been born and brought up in some heathen land, never hearing of Christ, than to have had the highest Christian privileges and then to have turned our back on the Savior of men. In the end we are responsible for our own salvation. Even God cannot save us but by our consent. Even the Son of God, coming to our door, and pressing His mercy upon us, cannot bless us unless we receive Him. We can make the whole work of redemption— the love of God, the cross of Christ, the striving of the Spirit—in vain, so far as we are concerned. We may perish with Christ at our door. Christian privileges will not save us. The question after all is, "What are you doing with Christ?"

The other part of our passage is in a different tone. Here we find mercy again in its most gracious mood. The invitation in the closing verses is better understood when we have studied the great words that precede it. "All things are delivered unto Me of My Father," said Jesus. All things had been put into His hands, all power, all mercy, all gifts, all life. This ought to be a great comfort to us, amid this world's mysteries and perplexities, when there are things which threaten to destroy us. It is Jesus Christ, the Christ of the gospel, in whose nail-marked hands are all our affairs.

There can be no revealing of the Father save as Jesus Christ wills to reveal Him. It is very important then to learn how He dispenses the revelation which is in His hand exclusively. Will He impart it only to a few great saints, to a little company of wise men, to certain rare spirits? The answer is in the gracious invitation which follows, "Come unto Me, all ye that labor and are heavy laden, and I will give you rest." Yet there is a distinct class of persons to whom the gracious invitation is especially given—"all ye that labor and are heavy laden." This does not mean the rich, the noble of birth, the high of rank, the wise, the great among men. It includes the lowly, the oppressed, the overburdened, the weary, those who are in any distress. Need is the only condition. There is no one anywhere who desires the blessings of love, of mercy, of grace, to whom this wonderful invitation is not given and who may not claim it and accept it with all confidence.

Perhaps no other of Christ's words has given comfort to more people than this promise of rest. It meets every heart's deepest longing. What is this rest? It is not cessation from work. Work is part of the constitution of human life. It is necessary to health, to happiness, even to existence. God works. "My Father worketh," said Jesus, "and I work" [see John 5:17]. There is a curse on idleness.

> Rest is not quitting
>   The busy career:
> Rest is the fitting
>   Of self to one's sphere.

It is rest of soul that Jesus promises. The life is at unrest. It is all jangled and can have no rest until it is brought into harmony. Sin is the cause of this universal human unrest, and rest can come only when forgiveness has come. And this is the first rest that is promised. Everyone who comes to Christ is forgiven.

There are two rests promised. "I will give you rest." This rest comes at once. Every weary one who comes to Christ in penitence and with repentance is forgiven, reconciled and restored to Divine favor. Then there is a rest which comes later and only through self-discipline and patient learning. "Take My yoke upon you, and learn of Me . . . and ye shall find rest." To take Christ's yoke on us is to take Him as our Master, to let Him rule our life. The thought of a yoke is suggestive of bondage and humiliation. But the yoke of Christ has nothing galling or dishonoring in it. "My yoke is easy," He says. He is a gentle taskmaster. He requires entire submission to His will. He will not share our subjection with any other master. We must take His yoke upon us willingly, cheerfully, without reserve. But His commandments are not grievous, His burden is light. Then we will find honor and blessing in it.

A yoke implies two united, serving together, walking side by side under the same load. It is Christ's yoke we are to bear, which means that He shares it with us. His shoulder is under every load of ours. If we have a sorrow it is His, too. In all our afflictions He is afflicted. Thus it becomes a joy to take Christ's yoke. When He is our Master, we are free from all other masters. In bearing His yoke we will find rest unto our souls. Our lives under His sway will be at peace.

Another step in finding rest is to enter Christ's school. "Learn of Me," said the Master. We are only beginners when we first become Christians. A good man said, "It takes a long time to learn to be kind— it takes a whole lifetime." He was right—it does take as many years as one lives to learn the one little lesson of kindness. Paul said, and said it when he was well on in life, "I have learned in whatsoever state I am, therewith to be content" [Phil. 4:11]. We would suppose that such a wonderful man as Paul was did not have to learn the lesson of contentment. We can scarcely think of him as ever fretting about his condition and circumstances. But evidently he did, and it was a long, difficult lesson for him to learn to be content anywhere, in any experience. Even Jesus Himself had to learn life's lessons. In the Epistle to the Hebrews it is said that He learned obedience by the things that He suffered [see Heb. 5:7, 8].

All Christian life is a school. We enter it when we first come to Christ. We begin at the lowest grade. We do not have to wait until we know a great deal before we begin to attend school. School is not for finished scholars but for the most ignorant. We may come to Christ when we know almost nothing. He is a teacher and He wants us to become learners. Gentleness is a lesson which we are to learn. One young girl said, "I never can get over being jealous. I cannot bear to have my friends love anybody else. I want them to love only me." But she must learn the lesson of generosity in friendship. She must learn to want her friends to love others. It probably will take her a good while, the lesson will be a long one, but she must learn it because it is in Christ's curriculum for all His students, and no one can get His certificate of graduation without learning it.

Patience is a lesson that has to be learned. An impatient person is not a complete Christian. Thoughtfulness is another necessary lesson. There are a great many thoughtless Christians. The poet tells us that evil is wrought by lack of thought as well as lack of heart. Many people are always blundering in their relationship and fellowship with others. They say the wrong word, they do the wrong thing. They leave undone the things they ought to have done. They are always hurting other people's feelings, giving pain to gentle hearts. Yet it is all from thoughtlessness. "I didn't mean to offend him. I didn't mean to be unkind. I just never thought." There are few lessons in Christian life that more people need to learn than this of thoughtfulness.

We have to learn to trust. Worry is a sin. It is probably as great a sin as dishonesty or profanity or bad temper. Yet a good many Christian people worry at first, and one of the most important lessons in Christ's school is to learn not to worry. Joy is a lesson to be learned. Peace is another. Humility is another. Praise is a great lesson. All life is a school, and it is in learning these lessons that Jesus says we shall find rest. Christ Himself is our teacher, and with Him we should never fail to learn, though it be only slowly. Then as we learn, our lives will grow continually more and more into quietness and peace. All our questions will be in the faith that accepts God's will as holy and good even when it is hardest.

16

Two Sabbath Incidents

Scripture Reading: Matthew 12:1–14

The question of proper sabbath observance arose several times during our Lord's public ministry. The Jewish law made careful provision for the keeping of the seventh day of the week, but the Rabbis had added many rules of their own, making the Sabbath really a burdensome day. Jesus did not recognize these added requirements, and hence often displeased the rulers by what they considered violations of the law.

The criticism at this time was caused by our Lord and His disciples going through the grain fields on the Sabbath. They were probably on their way to the morning synagogue service. The disciples were hungry, and as they walked along by the standing grain, which was then ripe, they plucked off some of the heads and, rubbing them in their hands and then blowing away the chaff, they ate the grains.

The Pharisees were always watching Jesus that they might find something of which to accuse Him. There are two ways of watching good people. One way is to watch them to see how they live that we may learn from their example; the other way is in order to criticize and find fault with them. It was the latter motive which prevailed with the Pharisees. They went along with Jesus, not because they loved to be with Him, but as spies upon His conduct. The conduct of Christians is always watched by unfriendly eyes, eyes keen to observe every fault.

We need to live most carefully, so as to give no occasion for just censure. Yet the example of Jesus shows us that we are not to be slaves of traditional requirements which have no authorization in the word of God.

Good people can find better business than to play the spy upon the lives and conduct of others. The unfriendly espionage of these Pharisees on Jesus and His disciples appears in our eyes very far from beautiful. We are behaving no better, however, than the Pharisees did if we keep our eyes on others for the purpose of discovering flaws. Perhaps they do not live quite as they should live; but are we their judges? Do we have to answer for them? Then, perhaps, our sin of censoriousness and uncharitableness is worse than the sins we find in them. There are some people so intent on trying to make other people good that they altogether forget to make themselves good.

When the Pharisees said to Jesus that His disciples were doing that which was not lawful on the Sabbath, He reminded them of what David did when he and his companions were hungry. "Have ye not read?" It was in their Scriptures. David, fleeing from Saul, went to Ahimelech very hungry, he and his companions, and asked for something to eat. There was no bread about the place save the shewbread. It was not lawful for any but the priests to eat this bread. But the men's need satisfied the custodian of the tabernacle that he might deviate from the letter of the law in this emergency [see 1 Sam. 21:1–6].

The act of the disciples in plucking and rubbing out the heads of grain to satisfy their immediate hunger was a work of necessity and therefore not a sin. Though the letter of the law may have been violated, yet it was not violated in its spirit. What works of necessity are cannot be established by minute rules and regulations. The settling of the question must be left in each particular case to the enlightened consciences of faithful followers of Christ.

Jesus made a startling claim when He said to His critics, "One greater than the temple is here" [see v. 6]. It is usually supposed that He refers to Himself. But a marginal reading suggests "a great thing," meaning the law of love. That is, love is always the highest law. This different rendering seems to be favored by the words which follow. "If ye had known what this meaneth—I will have mercy, and not sacrifice—ye would not have condemned the guiltless." Love would have made you think of the men's need as higher than the observance of the letter of a Sabbath rule. No Divine law means to have men go hungry.

Then Jesus uttered another startling word, "For the Son of man is lord even of the Sabbath day." He thus claimed the right to interpret the laws of the Sabbath. In Mark 2:27 we have also this strong assertion, "The Sabbath was made for man, and not man for the Sabbath." The Sabbath was part of the Divine constitution which God had ordained for His children. Christ came not to destroy, but to fulfill. He took the Sabbath, therefore, and stripped from it the burdensome regulations which men had attached to it, and put into it its true spiritual meaning. He set the Church free from the cumbersomeness of a rabbinical Sabbath, and made it a day of joy and gladness, a type and foretaste of heaven.

Almost immediately afterwards another question of Sabbath observance arose. It was in the synagogue. A man was present who had a withered hand. Again the Pharisees were watching Jesus to see what He would do. They asked Him if it was lawful to heal on the Sabbath day. They were not humble seekers for the truth, but were looking for a ground of accusation against Him. It was a violation of the rules of the Pharisees to attend the sick or even console them on the Sabbath. Jesus knew the intention of the Pharisees in their question and bade the man arise.

Then He asked them, "What man shall there be among you, that shall have one sheep, and if it fall into a pit on the Sabbath day, will he not lay hold on it, and lift it out?" In this He appealed to simple common sense. Whatever their traditions said about the Sabbath day, the practice of the people would be on the merciful line. The Talmud says that if the animal is in no danger in the ditch it should be allowed to remain unrelieved over the Sabbath. But the form of our Lord's question shows that this was not the practice of the people. "What man shall there be among you, that shall have one sheep, and if it fall into a pit on the Sabbath day, will he not lay hold on it, and lift it out?" Then He added, "How much then is a man better [or more valuable] than a sheep!" If it was right to help a sheep out of a pit on the sabbath, it certainly was right to relieve a human sufferer from his sickness on that day.

So we have the lesson, "Wherefore it is lawful to do good on the sabbath." It is right for physicians to attend to their patients on the Lord's day. It is right for those whose duty it naturally is to nurse the sick to care for them on the Sabbath. It is right to visit the sick when they need our sympathy and when we can carry to them blessing or cheer. It is right to visit those who are in affliction when we can carry comfort to them; to visit the poor when we can minister to their needs or relieve their distresses. It is especially right to go out among the unsaved, when we can do anything to bring them to Christ. It is right to gather neglected children from the streets and from Christless homes, and bring them under the influence of Divine grace.

We must be careful not to pervert our Lord's teaching here. Not all kinds of work can be brought into the class indicated in the words, "It is lawful to do good on the Sabbath day." It was the Jewish Sabbath concerning which Jesus was speaking here, and our Christian Lord's day is in every way more beautiful, more joyous. Yet we need to keep most holy guard over it, for there are many influences at work to rob us of it. There was a time when very much of the old rabbinical spirit was exercised in some parts of the world toward the Christian Sunday. Now, however, the tendency is in the other direction, and we are in danger of losing the sacredness of this day. The Lord's day is not well kept when its hours are devoted to mere social purposes. The best preparation that can be made for its proper observance is to prepare for it as far as possible on Saturday. This was the old-time way. Everything was done on Saturday that could be done to lighten the burden of the work on Sunday. Someone tells us the story of a man who was trying to get his negro servant to do some unnecessary work on Sunday. He reminded the servant that Jesus had said it was lawful to pull a donkey or an ox out of a pit on the Sabbath. "Yes, massa," was the ready reply, "but not if it fell in on Saturday."

Jesus never was deterred from His work of mercy by the censorious criticism of His enemies. He bade the man to stretch forth his hand. The arm was withered, dried up, dead. How could the man stretch it forth? But when Jesus gave the command it was implied that He would also give power to obey. The man must make the effort to do what he was bidden to do. That was the way he showed his faith. Then with the effort came new life unto the dead arm.

Whenever Christ gives us a command He is ready to give us strength to obey it. We may say the thing required is impossible, but it is the privilege of the Christian to do impossible things. Anybody can do possible things; but when Christ is working in us and through us we need not ask whether the things He commands are possible or not. "I can do all things through Christ that strengtheneth me" [Phil. 4:13]. People often say that they cannot begin a Christian life because they have not the strength to do what Christ requires of them. True, but if they will begin to obey, they will be enabled to obey, helped by the Master Himself.

17

Growing Hatred to Jesus

Scripture Reading: Matthew 12:22–32, 38–42

The heart of Christ was a great magnet that ever drew to it all human suffering and human need. The description given of Him in a quotation from Isaiah [42:3], in the verses immediately preceding this incident, are wonderfully suggestive. His compassion and His gentleness are depicted in the words,

> A bruised reed shall He not break,
> And smoking flax shall He not quench?

This prophetic picture of the Messiah found its perfect realization in the life of Jesus. He was the friend of the frail, the feeble, and the bruised. In those days men despised the weak. The deformed and the incurable were not considered worth saving, but were thrust out to perish. Jesus, however, had special compassion for that which was crushed or broken. He invited the weary to come to Him. The sick, the lame, the blind, the paralyzed and all sufferers soon learned that He was their friend. Wherever He went throngs followed Him, and these throngs were made up largely of those who were distressed and those who had brought distressed friends to be helped or healed.

Now it was one possessed with a demon, and also blind and dumb, that was brought to Him. Nothing is told of the manner of the cure. All we learn is that "He healed him, insomuch that the blind and dumb

75

spake and saw." No wonder the multitudes were amazed. "Is not this the son of David?" they asked. They thought that possibly a man who did such wonders might be the Messiah, yet it did not seem to them that He was. Or it may be that they feared to give expression to the feeling, knowing how bitter the Pharisees were against Him.

When the Pharisees heard what the people were suggesting, they became greatly excited and set to work to account for Jesus and His power. They felt that they must account for Him in some way, must give the multitude some explanation of Him which would satisfy them and prevent their concluding that He was the Messiah. In Mark's account of this incident we learn that there were scribes and Pharisees present that day who had come down from Jerusalem to watch Jesus and to make a report of what they saw and heard. They set to work to create in the minds of the people the impression that Jesus was working in cooperation with evil spirits and that it was through their power that He did the wonders they had seen Him do. So they answered the people's question, "Is not this the son of David?" by saying, "This fellow doth not cast out devils, but by Beelzebub the prince of devils." Beelzebub seems to have been an infamous name for Satan, probably having its origin in the story of Ahaziah's idolatry in inquiring of Baal-zebub, lord of flies, a Philistine deity [see 2 Kgs. 1].

One thing to notice here is the admission that Jesus had really done wonderful works, had actually wrought miracles. They did not attempt to deny this. They felt that some explanation must be given to the plain, simple-minded people who were following Jesus in such numbers. There was no doubt about the supernatural works. We find the same admission throughout the whole story of Christ's public ministry. Herod believed that Jesus had wrought miracles, and in his remorse imagined that John, whom he had beheaded, had risen from the dead. No opponent of Christ in those days ever even hinted that He did no miracles.

Another thing to notice here is the strange explanation these learned men gave of the miracles of Jesus. They frankly admitted them, but to account for them without confessing that He was the Messiah they said that He was in league with the prince of evil. The giving of such an explanation of the power of Christ shows a prejudice that was not only stubborn but debased. Of course, it was intended also to discredit Jesus by impugning His character. They said He was an agent of the devil.

Jesus claimed to be the Son of God and said He was doing His Father's will and the works of His Father. They sought thus to slander Him and make Him an impostor, an enemy of God.

Wicked men often resort to the same course in our own days when they are seeking to destroy the influence of Christianity. They cannot deny the good that is done, but they seek to account for it by alleging wrong motives in those who do the good. Sometimes they try to blacken the names of those who represent Christ. They start evil stories about them, to defame their character. That is, they accuse the saints of being in league with Satan.

The answer of Jesus to this charge is clear and convincing. "Jesus knew their thoughts." He understood well their motives. He knows all men's thoughts. We can carry on no schemes or conspiracies without His knowing of them. We can keep no secrets from Him. His answer was: "Every kingdom divided against itself is brought to desolation." This proved at once the absurdity and preposterousness of the charge His enemies had made. They said He was an agent of Satan. Yet He was not doing the work of Satan, but the work of God. Satan had a man under his power whom he was destroying. Jesus had taken the man, driven out the demon, opened his eyes and ears and healed him. Who could believe that He was in league with the Devil and was thus undoing the Devil's ruinous work? "If Satan casteth out Satan; he is divided against himself." This shows the folly of their charge. All the works of Christ were good works. He came to bless men, to save them, to heal the sick, to make the lame walk, to raise the dead. Are these the works of the Evil One?

One of the strongest evidences of Christianity is in what it does for the world. In chapter 11 when the disciples of the imprisoned John the Baptist came asking for Christ, inquiring whether Jesus was indeed the Messiah, they were told to tell John what they had seen Jesus doing—"the blind receive their sight, and the lame walk, the lepers are cleansed, and the deaf hear, and the dead are raised up." These were all works of love, and they proved that Jesus was the Messiah, the Son of God. Men are trying to prove today that He is not Divine, denying His miracles, taking away every vestige of the supernatural from His person, His life, His work. But look at Christianity, not as a creed merely, but as a re-generating force. Look at the map of the world and find the white spaces which show the effect of Christianity in the countries where it has gone. Was it an impostor that wrought all this? Was it one in league with Beelzebub who left all these records of blessing, who transformed these countries? Was it an agent of Satan that made the home life of Christian lands, that built the churches, the asylums, the hospitals, the orphanages, the schools, and that has given to the world the sweetness, the beauty, the joy, the comfort, the fruits of love, which are everywhere the results of Christian teaching and culture? Could anything be more absurd than trying to account for the mighty works of Christ by saying the devil did them through Him?

Jesus gives the true explanation of His works in the words: "But if I cast out devils by the Spirit of God, then the kingdom of God is come unto you." Christianity is the kingdom of God in battle with the kingdom of evil. The work of Christ in this world is to destroy the works of the devil. This is a work in which every follower of Christ has a part. "He that is not with Me," said the Master, "is against Me; and he that gathereth not with Me scattereth abroad."

One of the most frequently misunderstood of all the words which Jesus spoke is found in His reply to His defamers: "Wherefore I say unto you, all manner of sin and blasphemy shall be forgiven unto men; but the blasphemy against the Holy Ghost shall not be forgiven." Does not this seem to refer to the act of the Pharisees in imputing to the prince of evil works which Jesus had done through the Spirit? One writes, "The conclusion of the whole is—you are on Satan's side, and knowingly on Satan's side, in this decisive struggle between the two kingdoms, and this is blasphemy against the Holy Ghost—an unpardonable sin."

Thousands of people, however, have stumbled at this word of Christ's and fallen into great darkness, fearing that they themselves had sinned a sin which never could be forgiven. There is not the slightest reason why this saying of Christ should cause anxiety to any who are sincerely striving to follow Christ. It may be said that those who have any anxiety concerning themselves and their spiritual state may be sure that they have not committed such a sin. If they had, they would have no anxiety. Actually, the only unforgivable sin is the sin of final impenitence. All sin that is confessed and repented of will be forgiven. "This sin of blaspheming the Holy Spirit is unforgivable because the soul which can recognize God's revelation of Himself in all His goodness and moral perfection, and be stirred only to hatred thereby, has reached a dreadful climax of hardness, and has ceased to be capable of being influenced by His beseeching. It has passed beyond the possibility of penitence and acceptance of forgiveness. The sin is unforgiven because the sinner is fixed in impenitence, and his stiffened will cannot bow to receive pardon."

"Much torture of heart would have been saved if it had been observed that the Scripture expression is not sin, but blasphemy. Fear that it has been committed is proof that it has not; for if it has been there will be no relenting in enmity nor any wish for deliverance."*

Accustomed as we are to think of the gentleness of Jesus, His lips ever pouring out love, it startles us to read such words as He uses here in speaking to the scribes and Pharisees who were contending with Him. "O generation of vipers, how can ye, being evil, speak good things? for out of the abundance of the heart the mouth speaketh." We are reminded of the manner of the Baptist's speech, when he was calling men to repent. But we must not forget that love is holy, that roses become coals of fire when they fall upon unholiness.

The scribes and Pharisees demanded a sign, something that would assure them that Jesus was what He claimed to be. Sincere and earnest inquirers after truth always find Christ most patient in answering their questions and making their real difficulties plain. When Thomas could not believe on the testimony of the other disciples, and demanded to see for himself the hands with the print of the nails, Jesus dealt with him most patiently [John 20:24–28]. He is always gentle with honest doubt and quick to make the evidence plain to it. But the men who here demanded a sign were not honest seekers after truth. Jesus knew their thoughts and spoke to them in words of judgment. They were an evil and an adulterous generation—estranged from God, false to Him. They had had signs, but they had disregarded them. Nineveh repented at the preaching of Jonah, and before them now was a greater Preacher than Jonah. The queen of the South came from afar to hear the wisdom of Solomon, and a greater Man than Solomon now stood before them. But they believed not, repented not. Impenitence gets no sign.

---

* Dr. Miller gives no source for the quoted material.

18

The Parable of the Sower

Scripture Reading: Matthew 13:1–9; 18–23

Jesus was always teaching. On this particular day His pulpit was a fishing boat, from which He spoke to the multitudes standing on the shore. Perhaps there was a sower somewhere in sight, walking on his field, carrying his bag of grain and slinging his seed broadcast. The sight may have suggested the parable.

Christ Himself is the great Sower, but we all are sowers—sowers of something. Not all who sow scatter good seed; there are sowers of evil as well as of good. We should take heed what we sow, for we shall gather the harvest into our own bosom at the last. "Whatsoever a man soweth, that shall he also reap"—that, and not something else [Gal. 6:7].

In the parable the seed is good—it is the word of God. The soil likewise is good—it is all alike, in the same field. The difference is in the condition of the soil.

The first thing that strikes us in reading the parable is the great amount of waste of good there seems to be in the world. On three parts of the soil nothing came to harvest. We think of the enormous waste there is in the Lord's work, in the precious seed of Divine truth which is scattered in the world. What comes of all the sermons, of all good teaching, of the wholesome words spoken in people's ears in conversation, of wise sayings in books? What waste of effort there is whenever men and women try to do good! Yet we must not be discouraged or hindered in our sowing. We should go on scattering the good seed everywhere, whether it all grows to ripeness or not. Even the seed that seems to fail may do good in some way other than we intended and thus not be altogether lost.

> What though the seed be cast by the wayside
> And the birds take it—yet the birds are fed.

The wayside is too hard to take in the seed that falls upon it. There are many lives that are rendered incapable of fruitfulness in the same way. They are trodden down by passing feet. Too many people let their hearts become like an open common. They have no fence about them. They shut nothing out. They read all sorts of books, have all kinds of companions, and allow all manner of vagrant thoughts to troop over the fields. The result is that the hearts, once tender and sensitive to every good influence, become impervious to impressions. They feel nothing. They sit in church, and the hymns, the Scripture words and exhortations, the appeals and the prayers fall upon their ears, but are not even heard. Or, if they are heard, they are not taken into the mind or heart, but lie on the surface.

"The birds came." The birds always follow the sower, and when a seed lies within sight they pick it up. The wicked one "snatcheth away that which hath been sown." So nothing comes of the seed which falls on the trodden road.

The lesson at this point is very practical. It teaches our responsibility for the receiving of the truth which touches our life, in whatever way it is brought to us. When we read or listen we should let the word into our heart. We should give attention to it. We should see that it is fixed in our memory. "Thy word have I hid in mine heart," said an old psalm writer [Ps. 119:11]. "Give God a chance . . . His seed gets no fair opportunity in a life which is like a trafficking highroad."

The next kind of soil on which the seed fell was stony—only a thin layer over a hard rock. There is none of the fault of the trodden wayside here. The seed is readily received and at once begins to grow. But it never comes to anything. The soil is too shallow. The roots get no chance to strike down. The grain starts finely, but the hot sun burns up the tender growths because they lack depth of rooting.

There are many shallow lives. They are very impressionable. They attend a revival service and straightway they are moved emotionally and begin with great earnestness. But in a few days the effect is all worn off. Life is full of this impulsive zeal or piety which starts off with great glow but soon tires. Many people begin a book, read a few chapters and then drop it and turn to another. They are quick friends, loving at first, but it is soon over.

One of the pictures of the crucifixion represents the scene of Calvary after the body of Jesus had been taken down and laid away in the grave. The crowd is gone. Only the ghastly memorials of the terrible day remain. Off to one side of the picture is a donkey nibbling at some withered palm branches. Thus the artist pictures the fickleness of human applause. Only five days before, palms were waved in wild exultation as Jesus rode into the city.

The goodness of too many people lacks root. The resolves of too many lack purpose. The intentions of too many lack life and energy. There are many shallow lives in which nothing good grows to ripeness. What this soil wants is the breaking up of the rock. What these shallow lives need is a thorough work of penitence, heart-searching and heart-breaking, the deepening of the spiritual life.

The third piece of soil in which the seed fell was preoccupied by thorns whose roots never had been altogether extirpated. The soil was neither hard nor shallow, but it was too full. The seed began to grow, but other things were growing alongside of it, and these, being more rank than the wheat and growing faster, choked it out.

Jesus tells us what these thorns of the parable stand for. They are the cares, riches and pleasures of this world. Cares are worries, frets, distractions. Many people seem almost to enjoy worrying. But worries are among the thorns which crowd out the good. Martha is an illustration of the danger of care [see Luke 10:40, 41]. There are plenty of modern examples, however, and we scarcely need to recall such an ancient case as hers.

Riches, too, are thorns which often choke out the good in people's lives. One may be rich and his heart yet remain tender and full of the sweetest and best things. But when the love of money gets into a heart it crowds out the love of God and the love of man and all beautiful things. Judas is a fearful example. The story of Demas also illustrates the same danger. A good man said to a friend: "If you ever see me beginning to get rich, pray for my soul."

The pleasures of the world are also thorns which crowd out the good. It is well to have amusements, but we must guard lest they come to possess our heart. We are not to live to have pleasures; we are to have pleasures rather only to help us to live.

The fourth piece of soil was altogether good. It was neither trodden down, nor shallow, nor thorny; it was deep plowed and clean. Into it the seed fell and sank and grew without hindrance. By and by a great harvest waved on the field.

This is the ideal for all good farming. The farmer must have his field in condition to receive the seed and to give it a chance to grow. That is all the good seed needs. This is the ideal, too, for all hearing of the word of God. If only we give it a fair chance in our life it will yield rich blessing.

19

The Parable of the Tares

Scripture Reading: Matthew 13:24–30; 36–43

The sower is Christ Himself. He always sows good seed in His field. When He was living here He went up and down the country, dropping the words of life wherever He found a bit of heart-soil that would receive them. It is wonderful to think of the blessings which have come to the world through the words of Christ. They have changed millions of lives from sinfulness to holiness. They have comforted sorrow. They have guided lives through the world's perplexed paths. They have been like lamps for the feet of countless hosts.

In this parable, however, Christians themselves are the seeds. "The good seed, these are the sons of the kingdom." Everyone who has received into his heart the grace of God becomes himself a living seed. Wherever a good seed grows, it springs up into a plant or a tree. Every good life has its unconscious influence, diffusing blessings, making all the life about it sweeter. Then it yields fruit. Paul talks about the fruit of the Spirit in the lives of those who receive the Spirit—love, joy, peace, long-suffering. There are also fruits in the activities of the Christian life, in the words one speaks, in the things one does, in the touches of life upon life.

We here come upon the truth of an Evil One who is in the world, an enemy of Christ, marring or destroying Christ's work. The Bible does not tell us about the origin of evil, but it everywhere takes for granted

84

that there is a kingdom of evil, at the head of which is the great enemy of God and man. Evil is not dropped accidentally into lives or homes or communities. The bad work is done designedly. "While men slept, his enemy came and sowed tares also among the wheat, and went his way."

People sometimes wish that there was no evil in the world. But, unfortunately, the feet of the Adversary go in every path. He is always watching for opportunities to steal in and do mischievous work while no one is watching. He is represented here as coming by night when good people are asleep. Our hours of greatest peril are those in which we are least conscious of peril. What can we do to protect ourselves in these unsheltered, unwatched times? If a man knows that a thief is coming, he will be on the watch. But the thief does not come then—he comes when he knows that no one is watching. How can we keep ourselves safe from the dangers we know not of? All we can do is to keep our lives ever in the hands of the sleepless Christ.

We are in danger of underestimating the enmity of Satan, and the evil wrought by his sowing. His own distinct purpose is to destroy the work of Christ. Whenever any good seed has been sown in a heart, he comes and tries to get some bad seed in among it. He whispers his evil suggestions in our ears, even while we are reading our Bible, praying, or partaking of the Lord's Supper. The devil is far more busy among good people than among the bad. Those who are wholly given over to sin he can afford to let alone—they are safely his already; but those who are trying to be Christians he seeks to destroy. Young people need to guard against the baleful evil which seeks entrance in vile books and papers, in indecent conversation or unchaste pictures. When an officer in General Grant's presence was about to tell an obscene story, he glanced about him and said, "There are no ladies present." The general promptly answered, "But there are gentlemen present." Nothing that should not be said in the presence of a lady should be said in any presence.

In the early stages of growth the tare or darnel is so much like wheat that the two can scarcely be distinguished. Evil in its first beginnings is so much like good that it is often mistaken for it. By and by, however, as they grow, the true character of the tares is revealed. Seeds of evil sown in a heart may not for a while make much show. A child under wrong influences or teachings may for a time seem very innocent and beautiful, but at length the sinful things will show themselves and will shoot up in strength. Many a man falls into ruin at mid-life through bad habits which he began to form when he was a boy. The time for young people to keep their hearts against evil is in the time of their youth.

The farmer's servants wished to clean out the tares before they had come to ripeness. The farmer said, however: "No, you would do more harm than good if you began to do this. Wait until the harvest, and then we will separate the tares and the wheat." Good men must live among the evil in this world. Sometimes they grow together in the same home, or in the same group of friends, or are associated in the same business, dwelling in constant communication and association. Even in the apostle family there was one traitor. Besides the impossibility of making a separation, there is a reason why the evil should remain—the hope that they may be influenced by the good and may yet themselves be changed into holiness. Every Christian should be an evangelist, eager in his desire and effort to bring others into the kingdom of God.

In Old Testament days God tolerated many evils like polygamy, divorce, blood revenge, and did not root them out at once because the people were not then ready for such heroic work. We are not to grow lenient and tolerant toward sin, but we are to be wise in our effort in rooting it out. Especially must we be forbearing and patient toward the sinner. If our neighbor has faults, we are not to rush at him with both hands and begin to claw up the tares by the roots. We must be patient with his faults, meanwhile doing all we can by love and by influence to cure him of them. We are never to lower our own standard of morality nor to make compromise with evil; we must be severe with ourselves; but in trying to make the world better, we need much of the wise patience of Christ.

There will be at last a complete separation between the good and the evil. Hypocrites may remain in the Church in this world and may die in its membership and have a royal burial, but they cannot enter heaven. This solemn word should lead all believers in Christ to honest and earnest self-examination. Are we wheat, or are we tares? The same law applies to the good and the evil in our own lives. In the holiest character there are some things not beautiful. In the worst men there are some things that are fair and to be commended. But in the end the separation will be complete and final.

When the disciples had an opportunity of speaking to the Master alone they asked Him what this parable meant. "Declare unto us the parable of the tares of the field." That is what we should always do with our difficulties concerning the teaching of Christ, and with all perplexities concerning our duty as Christians—we should take them all to the Master himself. Some things may be explained to us at once by careful reading and study of Christ's teaching. Some things that once were obscure and hard to understand become very plain as we go on; experience reveals them to us. Then the office of the Holy Spirit is to guide us into all truth.

Some people talk about this world as if it belonged to the devil. Indeed, Satan himself said that all the kingdoms of the world were his. It looks sometimes, too, as if this were true. But really this is Christ's world. After His resurrection Jesus Christ sent His disciples forth into all the world, claiming it, bidding them go everywhere to make disciples of all the nations.

Jesus taught plainly that there is a personal spirit of evil, called the devil. He says here distinctly, "The enemy that sowed them is the devil." The devil is the enemy of Christ. No sooner had Jesus been baptized than Satan began his assaults upon Him, seeking to overcome Him and destroy Him. Satan is the enemy also of every Christian. He takes the utmost delight in getting his poison into the lives of Christ's followers. Sometimes people think that they can play with evil safely, but it is always perilous play, and everyone who thus ventures will surely be hurt. One great comfort we have in thinking of Satan as the enemy of souls and our enemy is that Christ overcame him at every point. While Satan is our enemy, strong and alert, he is a vanquished enemy. We cannot ourselves stand against him, but with Christ's help we can stand. "In all these things we are more than conquerors through Him that loved us" [Rom. 8:37].

20

Pictures of the Kingdom

Scripture Reading: Matthew 13:31–33; 44–52

The parables of Jesus are unforgettable pictures. They are stories laden with truth. Some preachers tell stories which thrill those who hear them, and yet they are tales with no lesson. The parables of Jesus are homely and interesting, and yet they are vital with spiritual meaning.

The mustard seed is little, so small that one can scarcely see it. Yet it has life in it, and when it is sown in a field it grows and becomes a tree, so large that the birds come and nest in its branches. There would be no reason for our Lord's telling us about this little seed and its plant merely as a bit of natural history. It is beautiful and interesting even in this way, but He had a further purpose in His parable. He uses it as an illustration of His kingdom in the world. "The kingdom of heaven is like to a grain of mustard seed." Christianity began in a very small way. A little baby lay in a manger, sleeping its first sleep—that was the beginning of the kingdom of heaven in this world. A kingdom implies a king. Christ ruled over a very small kingdom that night. His mother loved Him as mothers always love their children, and He reigned in her heart. Some shepherds came in during the night and saw the Child-King and worshiped Him. Their lives were never the same again, for one who has had a vision of Christ can never lose the influence out of his heart. They returned to their lowly duty—keeping watch over their flock—but they were better shepherds afterwards and better men. The kingdom of heaven had entered their hearts.

But the beginning of the kingdom was small indeed—like a mustard seed. For thirty years it seemed to have no appreciable growth. The child grew, but dwelt in a lowly home in a peasant village. His childhood was not unusual. He was not a precocious boy. There was no halo about His brow. Nothing showed that He was kingly. There were no flashings of divinity on His face. He did no brilliant things. He wrought no miracles. He went to school and learned His lessons, but revealed no greatness. According to the rules of His people He entered the carpenter's shop at twelve as an apprentice, and for eighteen years worked at the carpenter's bench. "The kingdom of heaven is like unto a grain of mustard seed . . . which indeed is less than all seeds."

We know what the kingdom of Christ is today. It has touched many lands with its holy influence. It has become a great tree with many widespreading branches. On its boughs the birds sit and sing. In its shadows the people rest. Its fruits feed the hunger of multitudes. The tree is still growing. The great missionary movement of today is extending it, and it is destined to fill all lands. "The kingdom of heaven is like to a grain of mustard seed, which a man took, and sowed in his field: which indeed is the least of all seeds; but when it is grown, it is the greatest among herbs, and becometh a tree, so that the birds of the air come and lodge in the branches thereof."

The next parable tells of the pervasive and permeating influence of the gospel of Christ. "The kingdom of heaven is like unto leaven, which a woman took, and hid in three measures of meal, till it was all leavened." Usually in the Bible leaven stands for something evil. It was a symbol of sin in the Mosaic dispensation. Paul exhorts believers to purge out the old leaven. But here it is used in a good sense. The teaching is very apt. Leaven works secretly and silently. It makes no noise. It works pervasively, creeping out through the dough till every particle of it has been affected. Thus it is that the influence of Christianity permeates society, penetrating everywhere, touching every institution, changing all things.

The illustration may be widely applied. Thus individual lives are changed. The leaven of Divine grace in the heart works out until the whole character is changed. Henry Drummond in one of his books tells of a girl whose life was transformed into great spiritual beauty. Her friends wondered what had wrought the change. At length the secret was discovered in a verse of Scripture which she carried in a locket— "Whom having not seen ye love" [1 Pet. 1:8]. The leaven works also in communities. Neighborhoods are changed, transformed by the gospel. In mission lands there are many notable illustrations.

The truest work of Christianity is quiet. It is a religion less of organization than of personal influence. It is not always the most active person who does the most for the advancement of the kingdom of God; often it is the quiet man or woman whose life is holy and beautiful, that really does the most for the changing of other lives. Many an invalid, who cannot take any active part in the affairs of the Church, yet exerts a sweetening and ennobling influence in a home, in a community, which far surpasses in its value the busy ministry of one who is always going about, talking, doing good.

The lesson from the leaven is that it does its work by being put into the midst of the loaf. It will not do any good if laid on the shelf, in however close proximity to the dough. It must be in the mass. There are some Christian people who seem to feel no responsibility for the touching or influencing of other lives. They incline to keep away from people and to be exclusive. But leaven will never do its work if kept wrapped up in a dainty vessel. A Christian man can do good only by going among people. Thus Jesus did—He was called a friend of publicans and sinners. He ate with them and mingled with them in all social ways, and His pure, loving, gentle life left its impress on their lives. Jesus did not teach His disciples to hide away from people, to keep out of the world, but to live in the world, to be friends of men, to seek to influence others by being with them. He said they were salt, but salt to do its work, to perform its mission, must be rubbed into that which it is to preserve.

We need to take the lesson. Be leaven wherever you are. Let your goodness be felt. Let your kindness touch others. Let your example have in it a contagion of joy, of peace, of unselfishness, of sweetness, of purity, which shall be a benediction everywhere. Be sure that you make one little spot of the world better, cleaner, whiter, brighter, gladder because you live in it.

In another parable Jesus speaks of a "treasure hid in a field; the which when a man hath found, he hideth, and for joy thereof goeth and selleth all that he hath, and buyeth that field." There were no banks in ancient times, especially in unsettled countries. It was common therefore to hide treasure in the ground. Not infrequently did one come upon such concealed treasure. Of course, Jesus had spiritual treasure in His thought, as He is illustrating the kingdom of heaven. We do not dream of the wealth of invisible riches that are always close to us as we go through this world. A man may work for years in a field, digging and plowing over it, not thinking of anything of value in it, and then suddenly someday discover that there are valuable minerals or even gems hidden under his pick and plow.

Dr. Newell Dwight Hillis says:

> Lecturing in Kentucky recently, I saw a cave of diamonds, newly discovered. One day a farmer, plowing, thought the ground sounded hollow. Going to the barn he brought a spade and opened up the aperture. Flinging down a rope, his friends let the explorer down, and when the torches were lighted, behold, a cave of amethysts and sapphires and diamonds. For generations the cave had been undiscovered and the jewels unknown. Wild beasts had fed just above those flashing gems, and still more savage men had lived and fought and died there. And yet just beneath was this cave of flashing jewels.

We do not know what hidden treasures of spiritual good there are all the while so close to us that our hand could take them if we saw them. Sometimes we come suddenly upon them, and then we should instantly seize them and appropriate them, whatever it may cost us. The man in the parable sold all he had and bought the field in which the treasure was concealed. We should be ready to give up all we have to get the spiritual riches that we find.

The parable of the pearl teaches almost the same lesson as that of the hidden treasure. "The kingdom of heaven is like unto a merchant man seeking goodly pearls: who when he had found one pearl of great price, he went and sold all that he had, and bought it." The merchant sought goodly pearls—the best that could be found. Then when he heard of this best of pearls, he was willing to give up all he had that he might possess it. Too often, we do not live for the best things. When we find something even better than the good we should be eager to possess it, no matter if we have to give up all we have to buy it.

21

The Multitudes Fed

Scripture Reading: Matthew 14:13–21; 15:29–39

It was just after the death of John the Baptist. John's disciples went and told Jesus of their great sorrow. Their grief touched the heart of their Master, and He withdrew, seeking a little season of quiet. The best comforter in our times of trouble is God, and when our hearts are sore we can do nothing so wise as to flee into the secret of His presence.

Jesus went out in a boat to cross the lake. But the people saw the boat departing and flocked around the lake to meet Him on the other side. He had not been long in His quiet retreat when the multitude began to gather, eager to see Him. Although He was seeking rest, His compassion drew Him to the people that He might help them.

It was always thus that Jesus carried people's sorrows. When He looked upon the great throng who had flocked after Him and saw among them so many suffering ones—lame, sick, blind, palsied—His compassion was stirred. When we remember that Jesus was the Son of God, these revealings of His compassion are wonderful. It comforts us to know that there is the same compassion yet in the breast of the risen Christ in glory. He did not lose His tenderness of heart when He was exalted to heaven. We are told that as our High Priest He is touched by every sorrow of ours. Every wrong that we suffer reaches Him. Every sorrow of ours thrills through His heart. It was not their hunger, their poverty, their sickness, nor any of their earthly wants, that appeared to

Him their greatest trouble, but their spiritual needs. Our worst misfortunes are not what we call calamities. Many people may seem prosperous in our eyes, and yet when Christ looks upon them He is moved with compassion, because they are like sheep with no heavenly Shepherd.

Yet the first help Christ gave that day was the healing of the sick. He thinks of our bodies as well as our souls. If we would be like Him, we must help people in their physical needs, and then, like Him, also, seek further to do them good in their inner life, their spiritual life. There are times when a loaf of bread is a better evangel than a tract. At least the loaf must be given first, to prepare the way for the tract.

As the day wore away it became evident that the people were very hungry. They had brought no provisions with them, and there were no places in the desert where they could buy food. Combining the stories in the different Gospels, we get the complete narrative of what happened. Jesus asked Philip, "Whence are we to buy bread, that these may eat?" [John 5:5]. Philip thought it was impossible for them to make provision for such a throng. "Two hundred pennyworth of bread is not sufficient for them, that everyone of them may take a little." The apostles could think of no way to meet the need of the hour but by dispersing the people. "Send the multitudes away, that they may go into the villages, and buy themselves victuals." To this suggestion the Master answered, "They need not depart; give ye them to eat."

We are like the disciples. We are conscious of having but little of our own with which to help or bless others, and we conclude hastily that we cannot do anything. If we feel responsibility, we meet it by deciding that it is impossible for us to do anything. Our usual suggestion in such cases is that the people go elsewhere to find the help they need. We suggest this person or that person who has means, or who is known to be generous, thus passing on to others the duty which God has sent first to our door. We are never so consciously powerless and empty in ourselves as when we stand before those who are suffering, those in perplexity, or those who are groping about for peace and spiritual help. Our consciousness of our own lack in this regard leads us often to turn away hungry ones who come to us for bread. Yet we must take care lest we fail to do our own duty to Christ's little ones.

Jesus said to His disciples that day, "They need not depart; give ye them to eat." That is precisely what He says to us when we stand in the presence of human needs and sorrows. He says, "Feed these hungry people." There is no use sending them to the world's villages—there is nothing there that will feed them. Nor need you send them to people who seem to have more than you have—they have no duty in the matter. Whenever Christ sends to us those who are in need, whether it be for physical or spiritual help, we may not lightly turn them away. The help they actually need we can give them. They would not have been sent to us if it had been impossible for us to do anything for them. If we use the little we have in Christ's name, He will bless it so that it shall feed the hunger of many.

We learn how to use our resources of ability by studying the way the disciples fed the multitude that day. The first thing they did was to bring their loaves and fishes to the Master. If they had not done this they could not have fed the people with them. The first thing we must do with our small gifts is to bring them to Christ for His blessing. If we try with unblessed gifts and powers to help others, to comfort the suffering, to satisfy people's spiritual hungers, we shall be disappointed. We must first bring to Christ whatever we have, and when He has blessed it, then we may go forth with it.

The miracle seems to have been wrought in the disciples' hands as the bread was passed to the people. They gave and still their hands were full. In the end all were fed. So with our small gifts, when Christ has blessed them, we may carry comfort and blessing to many people. It was a boy who had these loaves. Here is a good lesson for the boys.

Someone says that this boy was a whole Christian Endeavor Society himself. He and Jesus fed thousands of people with what ordinarily would have been a meal for but one or two. The boys do not know how much they can do to help Christ bless the world through the little they have. The young girl who thinks she cannot teach a class in Sunday-school, and takes it at last tremblingly but in faith, finds her poor barley loaf grow under Christ's touch, until many children are found feeding upon it, learning to love Christ and honor Him. The young man who thinks he has no gifts for Christian work finds, as he begins, that his words are blessed to many.

We must notice, also, that the disciples had more bread after feeding the vast multitude than they had at the beginning. We think that giving empties our hands and hearts. We say we cannot afford to give or we shall have nothing for ourselves. Perhaps the disciples felt so that day. But they gave, and their store was larger than before. So the widow's oil was increased in the emptying [1 Kgs. 17:12–16]. The disciples said that Mary's ointment was wasted when she poured it upon the Master's feet [John 12:3–8]. But instead of being wasted it was increased, so that now its fragrance fills all the earth.

22

Jesus Walks on the Sea

Scripture Reading: Matthew 14:22–36

It was after the feeding of the five thousand. As we learn from John's account the people were so excited by this miracle that they wished to take Jesus by force and make him king. To prevent this act Jesus sent the multitude away and then went up into a mountain for prayer.

Before going into the mountain, however, He sent His disciples out upon the sea in the boat, to go before Him to the other side. The record says He "constrained" them. It ought to have been a comfort to them that night, in the midst of the storm, to remember that their going out upon the lake was not at their own suggestion—then they might have thought it a mistake—but that the Master had bidden them to go. They were in the way of obedience, and when we are doing Christ's will we are under Divine protection, and need fear no storm.

We must not expect that every voyage we take at Christ's bidding shall be without storm. We may be pleasing God and yet meet dangers. When we find obstacles in something we are doing under God's guidance, we may not conclude that we have made a mistake, and that these difficulties are indications that we ought not to have taken such a course. On the other hand, such troubles are not meant to discourage us, but to inspire us to stronger faith and greater endeavor.

"He went up into the mountain apart to pray." No doubt His prayer was partly for Himself. There had come to Him a temptation of earthly honor and power—and He sought relief and strength in prayer. Then He prayed also for His disciples. Mark tells us that from this mountaintop He saw them that night on the sea, distressed in rowing. Jesus always sees us when we are toiling in any tempest, any struggle, and speaks for us to His Father.

"In the fourth watch of the night Jesus went unto them, walking on the sea." He did not come to them immediately—indeed, it was almost morning when He appeared. The boat in the wild storm represents Christ's friends in this world in the storms of life. Sometimes we think we are forgotten, that Christ does not see us, or does not care. Here we have an illustration. From His mountaintop He sees His disciples in their struggles in the wild sea. He does not forget them. He watches that no wave shall engulf them. Then at the right time He comes to them with help. So it is in all our experiences of danger and distress. He is interested in our earthly life. Some people tell us sneeringly that there is no one who cares, no one who thinks of us. But the picture here is the true one. Christ cares, watches, keeps His sleepless eye upon us, keeps His omnipotent hand on all affairs so that no harm can come to us on ocean or on shore.

When He came He came as no other friend could come. "He went unto them, walking on the sea." No human help could have possibly arrived to them that night in the wild sea. Their friends, though standing on the shore, and seeing their peril, could not have done anything for them. So we may stand and look at our friends in their sorrow, and our hearts may break for them, but we can do nothing. We cannot get to them through the wild waves. But there is One who can reach them—Jesus can walk on the roughest billows as if they were a crystal floor.

Sometimes Jesus alarms His friends by the way He comes to them. It was so that night. "When the disciples saw Him walking on the sea, they were troubled." In their terror and superstition they thought it must be an apparition, and they were frightened. Yet it was their best friend, and He was coming to deliver and save them. They were terrified because He came in such a strange way. It is the same with us often. He comes in the black cloud of trial, sickness, loss, bereavement, disappointment, and we think it is some new peril, when really it is our Savior. We should learn to see Christ in every providence, bright or painful. The sternest things of life carry in them, if only we have faith to receive them, Divine blessing and good.

"It is I; be not afraid." As soon as the disciples heard the voice of Jesus they recognized Him, and their fear changed to joy. So it was with Mary at the sepulcher. He whom she took to be the gardener was her own Master; she knew Him as soon as He spoke her name [John 20:15, 16].

Then comes the story of Peter's venture and failure. Peter was always impulsive. As soon as he heard the voice of Jesus, and knew who it was that was walking on the waves, he was seized with a desire to rush to meet Him. "Bid me come unto Thee," he cried. Jesus said, "Come," and for a time Peter walked on the waves and did not sink. His faith was simple, and he was upheld by Divine power. But soon he took his eye off his Lord and looked at the tossing waves and instantly he began to sink. That is the way most of us do. We go a step or two as if we were borne up on wings, while our faith is strong and our eye is fixed upon Jesus. But soon we begin to look at the dangers, and then our faith trembles and we begin to sink. If we could always keep our eye upon Christ, not thinking of the perils, our faith would not fail.

"Jesus stretched forth His hand, and caught him." In his fear and helplessness Peter did the right thing—he turned to Jesus for help, crying, "Lord, save me." Said an old Alpine guide to a tourist who was timid at some point of danger, "This hand never lost a man." Christ never lost a man out of His hand.

As soon as Jesus was in the boat with the disciples, the storm was over, the boat was at the land, and the tired rowers, after their long night of toil, dropped their oars, and all went on shore. So will it be at the end of life, if we have Christ with us. As the morning breaks we will pass out of the storm into the quiet calm and will find ourselves on the shore of eternal blessedness.

23

The Canaanitish Woman

Scripture Reading: Matthew 15:21–28

Jesus seems to have gone out of His own country into the borders of Tyre and Sidon seeking a little quiet. He needed rest. He entered a house and would not have it known that He was there. But He could not be hidden. A Canaanitish woman somehow heard of His being there and came straightway to Him. Her daughter was in a distressing condition.

This woman was a Gentile, and yet she must have known something of the true God. How she had learned about Jesus we are not told. No doubt the fame of His ministry of healing had reached her. So when she heard that He was in the house of a neighbor, she became instantly determined to see Him.

The world is full of sorrow. Few are the homes in which there is not some grief or affliction. Many are the sad mothers who move about through the world, carrying their heavy burden of pain or grief. No wonder this mother was glad when she heard of Jesus coming to her neighborhood. No wonder she was so persistent in her pleading that He would heal her child.

We may notice here that while the trouble was in the child it was the mother's heart that carried the burden. Whenever we see a child sick or in any pain or distress, and the mother watching, the mother suffers more than the child. Children never can understand how the hearts of their parents are bound up in them.

To this woman's intense pleading with Jesus, her appeals to His mercy, her cries of distress, Jesus answered her not a word. This is one of the strangest incidents in the entire story of Jesus. Usually He was quick to hear every request made of Him by any sufferer. Scarcely ever had anyone to ask twice for His help. His heart instantly responded to cries of distress. Often He gave the help unasked. Yet now He stood and listened to this woman's piteous pleading, and answered her not a word. Like a miser with hoards of gold, at whose gates the poor knock, but who, hearing the cries of need and distress, yet keeps his gates locked and is deaf to every entreaty, so Jesus stood unmoved by this woman's heartbroken cries. Why was He thus silent? Was this a weak hour with Him, when He could not give help? The most compassionate man has days when he can do nothing, but there never were such hours in the life of Jesus. Was it because He was so engrossed in His own coming sorrow that He could not think of any other one's trouble? No, for even on the cross He forgot His own anguish, and prayed for His murderers and cared for His mother. Evidently the reason for His silence was to draw out the woman's faith. He was preparing her to receive in the end a far richer, better blessing than she could have received at the beginning.

Our Lord sometimes yet seems to be silent to His people when they cry unto Him. To all their earnest supplications He answers not a word. Is His silence a refusal? Does it indicate that His heart has grown cold, or that He is weary of His people's cries? Not at all. Often, at least, the silence is meant to make the supplicants more earnest, and to prepare their hearts to receive better blessings.

The woman's cries seem to have disturbed the disciples. They grew almost impatient with their Master for keeping her waiting so long. They wanted her daughter healed because they could not endure the mother's crying. Yet Jesus was in no haste to yield to her imploring. He is not so tender-hearted that He cannot see us suffer when suffering is the best experience for us. He does not immediately lift burdens from our shoulders when it is needful for our growth that we bear the burdens longer. There is about some people's ideas of Christ a mushy sentiment, as if He were too gentle to endure the sight of suffering. Here we get a glimpse of a different quality in Him. He does not promise always to save us from suffering—His promise rather is to bless us through the suffering. It is possible to be too tender-hearted toward pain and distress. It is possible for parents to be too emotionally kind to their children. Uncontrolled pity is positive weakness, and often works great injury.

Christ's gentleness is never too tender to be wise and true as well as tender. He never makes the mistake of yielding to anyone's entreaties so long as denial is better than the granting of the favor. He never lets us have what we want because He cannot bear to say "No" to our tearful cries. Nor is He so emotionally kind that He cannot bear to punish sin. He will not let even His truest disciples go unchastened when only by chastening can He save them or best promote their spiritual growth.

But one thing we must not forget—it is love that prompts what seems severity in Christ. He was silent here that in the end He might give the full, rich blessing which He wished to give this woman, but which in the beginning she could not receive. He denies us our requests and is silent to us when we cry, that He may draw out our faith and give us His best blessings in the end.

Jesus told the woman that it was not "meet to take the children's bread and cast it to dogs." This seemed a strange word to fall from the lips of the gentle Christ. If it had been some Pharisee who spoke to this poor woman as a dog, it would not have seemed out of keeping. Even if Christ's own disciples had spoken thus to her, we could have understood it, for they had not yet departed from Jewish prejudices, nor had their hearts grown gentle with love for all humanity. But it certainly seems strange to hear the sympathetic, loving Jesus speak to the lowly sufferer at His feet as a Gentile dog. We can understand it only when we remember that in all His treatment of her He was trying her heart, training her faith, schooling her into truer submission and more earnest believing.

Both the woman's humility and her alert, eager faith appear in her answer, "Truth, Lord: yet the dogs eat of the crumbs which fall from their masters' table." She was not hurt by the offensive words Jesus had used. She was willing to be as a little dog under the Master's table. She was ready to grant to the Jews the children's place at that table. The position Jesus had assigned to her quite satisfied her. For the dogs under the table did not starve. The children were first served, and then the pieces of bread they let fall, rejected, or did not eat, belonged to the dogs at their feet. All she asked was the portion which usually went to the dogs. Even the crumbs from that table were enough for her. Thus her humility and also her faith were shown in her answer, and in both she is an example to us. We should come to Christ with a deep sense of our unworthiness, ready to take the lowest place; and we should believe that even the crumbs of His grace are better than all the feasts of this world.

> Not worthy, Lord, to gather up the crumbs
> > With trembling hand that from Thy table fall,
> A weary, heavy laden sinner comes
> > To plead Thy promise and obey Thy call.

> I am not worthy to be thought Thy child,
> > Nor sit the last and lowest at Thy board;
> Too long a wanderer and too oft beguiled,
> > I only ask one reconciling word.

It is most interesting to trace the growth of this woman's faith. There were many difficulties in her way, but she surmounted them all. She was a Gentile and her Healer was a Jew. When she first came to Jesus she was repulsed and called a dog. But none of these discouragements chilled the ardor of her faith or hindered her in her determination. So at last she got the blessing and won from the lips of Jesus one of the highest commendations ever given by Him to anyone—"O woman, great is thy faith." Large faith gets large blessings; small faith receives but small favors. We should go to God making large requests, believing His promises. We should never be discouraged by delays, by seeming repulses, by obstacles and hindrances. We should fight our way to victory. With infinite fullness in our Father's hand, we should not live in spiritual hunger as so many of God's children do. This is a wonderful saying—"Be it unto thee even as thou wilt." These words simply throw heaven open to our faith. We can get—we do get—what we will. So upon ourselves comes the responsibility of the less or the more blessing which we receive from the bountiful God.

24

Peter's Confession

Scripture Reading: Matthew 16:13–28

Jesus had led the disciples to a quiet place, away from crowds and excitements. The time had come to declare to them His Messiahship. It was a new epoch in His ministry.

He asked two questions. The first referred to the opinion of the people concerning Him. "Whom do men say that I the Son of man am?" The disciples told Him that there were different opinions about Him. Some thought He was John the Baptist risen again; others, that He was Elijah returned to earth; still others that He was Jeremiah, or some other one of the old prophets. There still is a wide diversity of opinion among people concerning Jesus. Some think He was only a man, others, that He was a great teacher, but nothing more. Others then think that He was the only-begotten Son of God, Divine as well as human.

Jesus asked another question, "But whom say ye that I am?" What other people thought about Him was not half so important as the opinions the disciples themselves had of Him. We may be able to state what the creeds say about Jesus Christ, and yet never have brought ourselves to answer the more important question, "Who do you think that I am?" Some people tell us that it makes very little difference what our beliefs are, even about Christ—that conduct is everything in life. But it is of greatest importance what we think of Christ. If we think of Him as only a man, though the best of men, the wisest of teachers, we may learn much from His words and from His life; but can one only a man be to us all that we need to find in Him to whom we look for salvation? We may change the question a little and ask: "What is Jesus Christ to you? Is He only in your creed, or is He also in your life as your personal Savior, Lord, Friend, and Helper?" This is the question that decides our relation to Christ.

Peter was always the first one to answer Christ's questions. Sometimes he answered rashly and unwisely; this time he answered well. "Thou art the Christ, the Son of the living God." It was a noble answer. Jesus was the Messiah promised through the ages, come at length to save His people from their sins. This is the true thought about Christ. God sent Him to earth on an errand of love. He became man, thus drawing close to us. He is also the Son of God, Divine, possessing all power, infinite in His love and grace, able to do for us all that we need, and to lift us up to eternal life and glory. If our belief is like Peter's, and Christ is all to us in our life that we make Him in our creed, we are resting on the Rock.

The true test of every creed, of every system of theology, of every life's hopes, is, "Is Christ in it?" Too many people, however, have Christ only in their creeds, and not in their lives. There is a story of a little deaf boy whom the mother takes with her to church. He loves to have her find the hymns, though the music never thrills his quiet ear nor touches his tender heart. He looks at the words, however, guiding his little finger over every line, to the end. If he finds the name of Jesus there, he is satisfied, and sits absorbed to the close of the singing. But if he cannot find this sacred name in the verses, he closes the book and will have nothing more to do with it. The true test of every creed, every system of theology, and every life's hopes, is Jesus. If Jesus be not there, there is nothing to give rest, nothing to bring life and salvation.

Peter had made a noble confession, and now Jesus said to him, "Thou art Peter, and upon this rock I will build My church." Peter was the new name which Jesus had given to Simon when Andrew brought him and introduced him. Jesus saw in Simon the possibilities of a noble future and so He said to him, "Thou shalt be called Peter." The new name was a prophecy of his future. Jesus sees the best that is in people and tries to inspire them to reach the best. At that time Peter was very far from being a rock, which means stability and strength. But, by and by, he became rocklike, firm and strong, under the training and discipline of his Master. Whatever view we take of the meaning of the Lord's words, it is a great comfort to know that Christ's universal Church is indeed founded upon a rock, an impregnable rock.

As soon as Peter had declared that Jesus was the Messiah, Jesus lifted the veil and gave the disciples a glimpse of what Messiahship meant to Him. They were thinking about a worldly Messiah. Jesus swept all this dream away and told them that, instead of being an earthly conqueror, He was going to a cross. That was the way marked out for Him from the beginning—the will of God for Him, God's plan for His life. They were so overwhelmed by His saying that He must be killed that they had no ear for the bright, joyous word, the note of victory, which came after—that He would rise again the third day. However, Jesus Himself saw through the darkness to the light that shone beyond. He knew that He must suffer and die, but He knew also that the grave could not hold Him and that He would come again. It is always in the story of Divine grace as it was with Jesus Christ—the cross is the way to glory. Beyond every dark valley in the Christian's path is a hilltop bathed in light.

Peter was always making mistakes. Jesus commended his confession. But a little later we again find him speaking rashly and ignorantly. When Jesus had said that His Messiahship meant suffering and death, this impulsive disciple, in his great love for his Master, possibly, too, lifted up by the praise of his confession which the Master had given, sought to interfere. "Be it far from Thee, Lord: this shall not be unto Thee." He would have held his Master back from His cross. But suppose Jesus had listened to love's entreaty that day and had not gone forward; what would the world have lost? We should never meddle with God's plans, whether for ourselves or others. This is one of the dangers of friendship. A loved one of ours is called to some hard service, to some great self-denial or sacrifice. In our warm-hearted affection we try to hold our friend back from the costly calling. We may say almost as Peter said, "This shall never be unto thee."

The answer of Jesus to Peter's rash though loving restraint is full of suggestion. "He turned, and said unto Peter, Get thee behind Me, Satan." What Peter said had proved a temptation to Jesus, suggesting to Him an easier way in place of the way to the cross. The friends of Paul once tried to keep him from going to Jerusalem when a prophet had foretold that he would be seized and bound there. Paul begged his friends not to weep and break his heart by urging him not to go on to peril which had been foretold. They were only making it harder for him to do his duty. It is a constant danger of friendship that we shall try to keep our loved ones from hard tasks to which God is calling them.

Jesus lifted another veil. He told his disciples that not only was the way of the cross God's way for Him, but also that His followers must go by the same way. "If any man will come after Me, let him deny himself, and take up his cross, and follow Me." We never can go after Christ and walk only on flowery paths. There is no way to heaven but the way of self-denial and sacrifice.

We may notice that it is "his" cross, that is, his own cross, that each follower of Christ must take up and bear. Each life has its own burden of duty, of struggle, of self-denial, of responsibility. Each one must take up and carry his own load for himself. Each one must bear his own burden. This is a most solemn truth. No one can choose for us, no one can believe for us, no one can do our duty for us. A thousand people around us may do their own part with beautiful faithfulness, but if we have not done our part, we stand unblessed amid all the multitude of those who have done their part and received their reward.

Our Lord closes with the question no one ever has been able to answer, "What is a man profited, if he shall gain the whole world and lose his own soul?" Even the whole world, with all its wealth and splendor, would give no real benefit to us if our lives should be lost. We could not buy pardon, peace nor heaven, even with the treasures of the whole earth in our possession. Then we could not keep the world and carry it with us into the other life even though we had won it all.

Selfishness is unlovely, but it is worse—it is the way of death. The law of Christ's cross runs through all life. A young girl, beautiful, cultured, honored, with a lovely home and many friends, turned away from ease, refinement, and luxury, and went to teach blacks in the South. She lived among them and gave out her rich young life in efforts to lift them up and save them. "What a waste of beautiful life!" said her friends. But was it really a waste? No; losing her life for Christ, she really saved it. If she had held herself back from the duty to which God was calling her, she might have saved her life in a sense, saved herself from cost and sacrifice, but she would have lost her life in the higher sense.

The losing of one's life is an irreparable loss. Whatever we may seem to get in exchange, we get really nothing. For if we gain the whole world, we can keep it but for a little while, and it will have no power to deliver us from death or give us the blessing of eternal life. The world cannot give peace of conscience or comfort in sorrow. It cannot purchase heaven. All we can do with the world is to keep it until death comes. We cannot carry any smallest portion of it with us into the other world. "How much did he leave?" asked one of his neighbors, referring to a millionaire who had just died. "Every cent," was the reply. So it is easy to see that there is no profit, but rather a fearful and eternal loss in gaining even all the world at the price of one's soul.

Then think for how much smaller price than this, "the whole world," many people sell their souls. Some do it for an hour's guilty pleasure, some for a political office, some for money, some for honor which fades in a day. In a newspaper this advertisement appeared: "Wanted—A nice cottage and grounds, in exchange for a lot of choice liquors." No doubt many people answered the advertisement. Men are continually giving home and property and peace and love and life for strong drink. They are selling their souls also in many other ways for trifles pitiably small.

25

The Transfiguration

Scripture Reading: Matthew 17:1–8, 14–20

Three men, Peter, James and John, were with the Master when He was transfigured. All the disciples belonged to His personal family, but these three were taken into the inner circle and enjoyed closest intimacy with Him. On several occasions we find Him choosing the same three for special companionship. In the Garden of Gethsemane these three were chosen to be nearest to Him, that by their sympathy and tenderness they might strengthen Him and thus help Him to endure His sore agony. We know that the holiest will get nearest to Christ. Faith brings men near, while doubt and unbelief separate from Him. Purity of heart brings us close—the pure in heart shall see God. Likeness to Christ fits for close personal friendship. Jesus said that those who serve most self-forgetfully are first in His kingdom. Selfishness keeps us far off. It is a comfort to find that Peter, though a very faulty disciple, was one of those who were admitted to closest friendship with Christ.

It is interesting to learn from Luke's gospel [9:28–36] that Jesus was praying when this wonderful change in His appearance occurred. While He knelt before His Father, the change began to come on His face. It is recorded of certain saintly men that a like change has come upon them when they prayed. We learn thus that prayer has a transfiguring power. Communing with God brings heaven down into our life. It was after Moses had spent forty days on the mountain alone with God that the people saw the dazzling brightness on his face. So it was when Stephen was looking up into heaven, beholding the glory of God, that even his enemies saw his face as if it had been the face of an angel. Only the upward look can give heavenly beauty. Our communings make our character. If we think only of earthly things we shall grow earthly. If we dote on gold, our lives will harden into sordidness. If we look up toward God we shall grow like God. A life of prayer will transform us into spirituality and bring upon us the beauty of the Lord.

Not only was the face of Jesus transfigured, but His very garments shone. A writer suggests that the garments here may represent the circumstances and experiences of the Christian's life. When one lives near Christ, everything that concerns him is transfigured—for example, care. Every life has its cares, its burdens, its anxieties, its experiences that would naturally fret and vex the spirit. Paul tells us that if we make known all our requests to God, the peace of God shall guard our hearts and our thoughts. The same is true of life's toils and tasks. Many of us find life hard, with its incessant duty and drudgery. But when the secret of the Lord is in the heart, we can sing songs of joy even in the most wearisome way. The same is true of sorrow. Every life has sorrow. But if Christ is ours, we have comfort in sorrow. Thus all the garments of life—all life's experiences and conditions—are brightened by peace in the heart.

While the disciples were awed by the shining on the face and garments of their Master, they became aware of the presence of heavenly visitors beside Him. "There appeared unto them Moses and Elijah talking with Him." How they learned who these men were we are not told. Perhaps the Master told them afterward. This was something very wonderful. For more than nine hundred years Elijah had been in heaven and for more than fourteen hundred years Moses had been away from this world; but both reappear here on the earth, still living, speaking and working. There are many proofs of immortality; here is an illustration— we see two men long centuries after they had lived on earth, still alive and busy in God's service. It will be the same with us and our friends— thousands of years after we have vanished from earth we shall still be alive and active. This is a great thought. If we could only get it into our heart, how much grander it would make all life for us! We should then form our plans to cover thousands of years, not merely the little space which we now call time.

The transfiguration was not a purposeless incident in the story of Jesus. Evidently it was intended to prepare Him for what was before Him. It had just been made known to Him that He was to die at Jerusalem. He may not have been depressed—He may have known long before that He was going to the cross. Yet as He now set out on His last journey and saw the end, He needed encouragement and cheer, and it was for this that the transfiguration was given, with its embassy from heaven and its confirming voice. When we keep this purpose in mind the meaning of the several incidents becomes plain.

It is interesting, with this in mind, to think of the talk which these two men had with Jesus. It was about His decease, His exodus from this world, Luke tells us. They had been sent from heaven to comfort and strengthen Him as He set out on His journey to His cross. He would have bitter sorrows and great sufferings, and they came to speak their word of cheer before He entered the experience. No doubt, all the way unto the end, His heart was braver and stronger because of this visitation.

Peter could not keep quiet. Even heavenly glory did not silence him. When he became aware of the wonderful splendor which he was witnessing, he proposed to keep it on the earth and not allow it to depart. "Lord, it is good for us to be here: if Thou wilt, let us make here three tabernacles; one for Thee, and one for Moses, and one for Elijah." Peter was right—it was good to be there. But at this very moment work was waiting for Jesus at the mountain foot. There was a poor demoniac there whom the disciples could not cure. Then, farther off, were Gethsemane and Calvary for Jesus, and for Peter there was Pentecost, with years of earnest apostolic service, and then martyrdom. It is very sweet to commune with God in the closet, at the Lord's table, but we must not spend all of our time even in these holy exercises. While the raptures fill our soul we must not forget that outside human wants and needs are crying for help and sympathy. We may not build tabernacles and keep our heavenly visions; we must get the vision into our heart and then go out to be a blessing to the world.

Then came the other witnessing. Moses and Elijah had come to talk with Jesus about His death, and the blessed outcome it would have in human redemption. Then from heaven the Father speaks, witnessing to the Messiahship of Jesus. The disciples had been greatly startled by what Jesus had said a week before—that He must suffer and be killed.

Their idea of the Messiah had been the kingly and earthly one. Their faith must have been strengthened by the words, "This is My beloved Son," and by the command that they should listen to His voice and to His voice only. Even if they could not understand, and if the things He said seemed to destroy their hopes, they were content now to hear.

There are times when God's ways with us seem mysterious, when we think disaster is coming to every fair prospect in our life. In all such hours we should remember that He who rules over all is the Son of God, our Friend and Savior, and our trust in Him never should fail. We should listen always quietly and submissively to what He says, and when everything seems strange and dark we should never doubt nor be afraid. What so staggered the disciples then concerning the Messiahship of Jesus we see now to have been the most glorious and loving wisdom. So in our strangest trials there are the truest wisdom and the richest love. This voice came out of the cloud; out of the clouds that hang over us come the voices of most divine love.

When Jesus and the disciples came down next morning from the Mount of Transfiguration, they found the other disciples in trouble. In the Master's absence an epileptic boy had been brought to them for healing. They tried to cure him, but failed. When Jesus appeared, the distressed father knelt before Him, pleading that He might have mercy on his son. He told his story in all its pathos—the boy's grievous suffering and his bitter disappointment when the disciples could not cure him. Jesus listened with compassion and then said, "Bring him hither to Me." A word from Him was enough—"The child was cured from that hour."

26

A Lesson on Forgiveness

Scripture Reading: Matthew 18:21–35

Perhaps no other lesson is harder to learn than to be forgiving. It never gets easy to bear injury or wrong. Yet the lesson is essential. We can ask forgiveness for ourselves only when we are ready to forgive those who trespass against us.

Jesus had been speaking to His disciples about forgiving others. He said if anyone sin against us, we should first go and talk the matter over with him privately. Mutual explanations will likely settle the matter. It will be still better if the two kneel and pray together before they begin to talk about their differences. If the matter cannot be settled between the two, then one or two witnesses are to be taken along. If one man still remains implacable, the other has done his part.

It was always Peter who spoke first, and when he heard the Master's words, he asked Jesus how often his brother should sin against him and he forgive him. This question still troubles many people. In some persons' minds patience quite soon "ceases to be a virtue." If they have forgiven another two or three times, they think they have really acted very generously. Peter supposed he was going to the very extreme of Christian tolerance when he suggested that seven times would be a good limit for Christ's disciples. The rabbis said, "Forgive the first offense, the second, the third; punish the fourth." But the answer of Jesus showed that there should be no limit. That is what seventy times seven means—not any definite number, however great, but infinitely. We are to forgive as God forgives us, and He does not keep account of the number of times. He forgives all the multitude of our transgressions. The time never comes therefore when we may say: "I have exhausted the requirements of Christian love. I cannot forgive you anymore."

Jesus told a little story to illustrate and enforce His teaching. He said the kingdom of heaven is like unto "a certain king, which would take account of his servants." We must never forget that there will be a reckoning with God. We are told that on the last day the books will be opened, the books which record men's acts, words, motives, dispositions, tempers. But we do not have to wait until the judgment day to have these reckonings—God reckons with us also as we go along. He is constantly calling men to give account to Him. Sometimes the call is given by the preaching of the word which convicts them of sin and makes them stand trembling before the bar of conscience. Sometimes it is by an affliction which compels men to stop and think of their relations to God, revealing to them their sinfulness. Sometimes it is by a deep searching of heart, produced by the Holy Spirit. There is no man who some time or other is not called, even in this present life, before God for a reckoning.

The reckoning is individual—each one must stand before the judgment seat and give an account of his own life. Among the king's servants "one was brought unto him, that owed him ten thousand talents." We need not trouble ourselves about the exact money equivalent of these figures. It is enough to know that the figures stand for our debt to God, and that this is immense. It makes it plain to think of sin as a debt. We owe to God perfect obedience in act, word, thought, motive. Duty is what is due to God and the obligation is beyond computation. We may flatter ourselves that we are fairly good people, because we stand well in the community; but when we begin to reckon with God, the best of us will find that our debt to Him is of vast magnitude.

It transpired at once that this servant had nothing to pay. There was no possibility that he ever could make up the amount that he owed to his king. So it is with those who are called to make a reckoning with God. There is no possibility that they can ever make up to Him their enormous debt. Many people imagine that in some way they can get clear of their guilt—they do not try to know how. Some suppose they can do it by tears of repentance; but being sorry that we are in debt does not cancel the debt. Some fancy that because their sins do not trouble them anymore, therefore the debt has been overlooked. But forgetting that we owe a man a thousand dollars will not release us from our debt to him. We are hopelessly in debt to God, and have nothing wherewith to pay.

If the law had been enforced, the servant would have been sold and his wife and family and all that he had. But this servant came to his king and begged for time. "Lord, have patience with me, and I will pay thee all." This appeal to the king touched his generous heart. "The lord of that servant, being moved with compassion, released him, and forgave him the debt." This is a picture of the Divine forgiveness. We never can pay the enormous debt we owe to God, but His mercy is sufficient to wipe it all away. Bankrupt people sometimes pay so many cents on the dollar and are allowed by their creditors to go free. But that is not the way God forgives. He does not require anything on our part, because we have nothing to give. We are justified freely by His grace.

One would think that this servant, after being forgiven such an enormous debt, would have gone out with a heart kindly disposed toward all men. But the reverse was the case. He "found one of his fellowservants, which owed him a hundred pence: and he laid hands on him, and took him by the throat, saying, Pay me what thou owest." He had forgotten the way he had been forgiven. A little while ago he was at his lord's feet, pleading for time and for patience. But the memory of this wonderful forgiveness had failed to soften his heart.

What his servant owed him was a mere trifle in comparison with his great debt to the king, yet he demanded payment and refused to show mercy. How is it with us? This morning we knelt at God's feet, implored His forgiveness, and received from Him the assurance that all our sins were blotted out. Then we went out, and someone said a sharp word to us or did something to irritate us, or injured us in some way. How did we treat our fellow who did these little wrongs to us? Did we extend to him the same patience and mercy that God had shown to us in the morning?

Soon again the servant was before his king. His harsh treatment of his fellow servant had been reported. Very stern was the judgment the unforgiving man now heard: "Thou wicked servant, I forgave thee all that debt . . . shouldest not thou also have had compassion on thy fel-lowservant, even as I had pity on thee?" The king was right in his severe censure. The man who had received such kindness at his hand should certainly have been kind to his neighbor who had wronged him in such a little matter. An old Spanish writer says, "To return evil for good is devilish; to return good for good is human; to return good for evil is godlike."

Jesus makes the application of His parable very plain: "So likewise shall my heavenly Father do also unto you, if ye from your hearts for-give not everyone his brother their trespasses." This does not mean that God actually revokes the forgiveness He has once granted. In fact, the person who acts thus never has been truly forgiven. "If you get pardon from God, you will give it to your brother; if you withhold it from your brother, you thereby make it manifest that you have not received it from God."

Thus we are brought face to face with a most definite practical teach-ing which we dare not ignore. Have we the forgiving spirit? An old proverb says, "Revenge is sweet"; but this is not true. "The unforgiving spirit is a root of bitterness from which there springs a tree whose leaves are poisonous, and whose fruit, carrying in it the seeds of fresh evil, is death to all who taste it." A little poem by Charles Henry Webb is very suggestive:

> Revenge is a naked sword—
>   It has neither hilt nor guard,
> Wouldst thou wield this brand of the Lord?
>   Is thy grasp then firm and hard?
>
> But the closer thy clutch of the blade,
>   The deadlier blow thou wouldst deal,
> Deeper wound in thy hand is made—
>   It is thy blood reddens the steel.
>
> And when thou hast dealt the blow—
>   When the blade from thy hand has flown—
> Instead of the heart of the foe,
>   Thou mayest find it sheathed in thine own.

27

Jesus on the Way to Jerusalem

Scripture Reading: Matthew 19:1, 2, 13–26

The words, "He departed from Galilee," have a significance, when we consider the circumstances, which gives them a peculiar sadness. This was our Lord's final departure. He had been brought up in Galilee. Much of His public ministry had been wrought there. In that part of the country He had met with the kindliest reception. He had multitudes of friends in Galilee. He had performed countless miracles there and had been a comforter of numberless sorrowing and suffering ones. Now He was leaving the dear familiar scenes and the people He loved so well. No wonder the throngs followed Him. The farewell must have been tender.

Some incidents of the journey are given. One was a discussion with the Pharisees concerning divorce. Jesus in His words gave most important teaching on the sacredness of marriage. "They are no more twain [two], but one flesh. What therefore God hath joined together, let not man put asunder."

Another incident was the bringing of little children to Him that He might bless them. It is not said that the mothers brought them, but this is probable. The language in Luke strengthens this inference. "They brought unto Him also infants, that He would touch them" [Luke 18:15]. The disciples probably thought their Master ought not to be troubled with babies and little children, and so they rebuked

116

those who were bringing them. But Jesus was moved with indignation when He saw what His disciples were doing, and said, "Suffer little children, and forbid them not, to come unto Me." This was one of the few times when it is said Jesus was angry. It grieved Him to have His disciples try to keep the children away from Him. He would not have anyone kept from coming to Him, but if any are more welcome than others, they are children.

"Do not keep the little children away. Suffer them to come. For of such is the kingdom of heaven. They are dear to God. To thrust one of them away is to thrust God Himself away. Whoever may be kept away, let it never be a little child."

Very beautiful is the picture we see. He welcomed the children to Him, took them in His arms, laid His hands on them and blessed them. We may be sure always of the love of Christ for children, His interest in them, His watchful care over them and His pleasure in every effort to bring them to Him.

Another incident in this journey to Jerusalem is that of the young ruler who came to Jesus with such earnestness and then went away from Him so sadly. All that is told us about this young man's coming to Jesus shows us His sincerity and earnestness. "There ran one to Him, and kneeled to Him." The running shows how eager he was, and his eagerness tells of an unsatisfied heart. He seems to have attained the best that a young man could reach without taking Christ into his life. He was young, with powers fresh and full. He was rich, with the honor, ease, distinction and influence that riches give. The fact that he was a ruler shows the confidence his fellowmen put in him. His moral character was above reproach, for he said, without boasting, that he had scrupulously kept the commandments. He was a man of winning disposition, for Jesus loved him and was drawn to him in a peculiar manner. It would be hard to conceive of a man with more to satisfy him.

Yet with all his good qualities, his worldly advantages, his good name and his conscience void of offense, he was not satisfied. He needed something more to make his life complete.

The question which this young man asked of Jesus is the most important question ever asked in this world. "What shall I do that I may have eternal life?" We do not know how much he understood about the eternal life concerning which he inquired. The fact, however, that he asked the question shows that he had at least some glimmering of the better life for which he hungered. No matter how much pleasure, or how great success, or how high honor one may gain in this world, if at the end of three score and ten years he passes into eternity unsaved, what comfort will it give him to remember his fine success on the earth?

A rich man failed in business. He gathered up the fragments of his wrecked fortune and had in all a few thousand dollars. He determined to go to the West and start anew. He took his money and built a splendid palace car, furnishing it in the most luxurious style, and stocking it with provisions for his journey. In this sumptuous car he traveled to his destination. At length he stepped from the door of his palace and only then thought for the first time of his great folly. He had used all his money in getting to his new home, and now had nothing with which to begin life there. This incident illustrates the foolishness of those who think only of this life and make no provision for eternity.

Answering the young man's question, Jesus turned his thoughts to the commandments. "If thou wouldest enter into life, keep the commandments." He referred him to the law, that he might show him how he had missed the mark, how far short he had come of gaining life by his own obedience. "Thou knowest the commandments." It is easy enough to imagine one's self quite obedient while one puts easy interpretation upon the Divine law. But when one has seen the law in all its lofty purity, in its wide spiritual application, in its absolute perfection, and then has compared his own life with it, he soon learns that he needs a Savior. A pupil may think his writing fair until he compares it with the copy at the top of the page, and then all its faults appear. The young artist may think his pictures fine until he looks upon the works of some great master, and then he never wants to see his own poor painting again. So long as one has no true conception of the meaning of the commandments, he may think himself fairly good; but when he undertakes what the commandments really require, he is at once convicted of sin.

There must have been pity in the heart of Jesus as He looked upon the young man and heard him say glibly, "All these things have I observed from my youth." He did not know what he was saying when he spoke thus of his own obedience. But Jesus very frankly answers his question, "One thing thou lackest" [Mark 10:21]. He was not far from the kingdom of God, and yet he was not in it. Many men are good, almost Christians, and yet not Christians. It may be only one thing that is lacking, but that one thing is the most important of all, the last link in the chain that would unite the soul to the Savior. It is the final step that takes one over the line, from death to life, out of condemnation into glorious blessedness. One may go to the very edge and not step over, may reach the door and not enter. Almost a Christian is not a Christian. Almost saved is still lost.

Jesus made a very large demand upon this young man. He said to him, "Sell whatsoever thou hast, and give to the poor . . . and come and follow Me." This is not a prescription for being saved by good works—that is not the way Christ saves men. He saw this young man's weakness, that with all his excellent qualities his heart was still wedded to the world, and the test which He gave required him to give up that which stood between him and eternal life. He would not be saved by giving his riches to the poor. Charity is not a way of salvation. But the young man could not be saved until his idol was broken. So the only hope was to get him to give up his money and to take Christ into his heart.

It was a hard battle that was fought those moments in this young man's breast. It grieved him not to be able to enter the circle of Christ's followers, but he could not pay the price. "His countenance fell at the saying, and he went away sorrowful." He wanted to go with Jesus, but he could not accept the conditions. Let us think of him after this day. He kept his money, but every time he looked at it he would be forced to remember that he had given up Christ and eternal life for the sake of it. He would see written over his piles of gold and his deeds and bonds—"These things cost me eternal life." His experience was just the reverse of the man who found the pearl of great price [Matt. 13:46] and then sold all he had and bought it. The young ruler found the pearl, asked the price, and considered the purchase, but did not buy it, because he was not willing to pay so much.

As the young man turned away Jesus was grieved, and said to the disciples, "A rich man shall hardly enter into the kingdom of heaven!" So it is not easy to be rich and to be a Christian. Christ spoke many earnest words concerning money and the danger of loving money. Yet not many people seem to be afraid of getting rich. One morning a pastor found on his pulpit desk a bit of paper with these words on it: "The prayers of this congregation are requested for a man who is growing rich."

It seemed a strange request, but no doubt it was a wise one. No men more need to be prayed for than those who are becoming prosperous, becoming rich. Francis Xavier said that among all the thousands who had come to him with confession of sin, not one had ever confessed the sin of covetousness. Men are not conscious of their danger when they are growing rich.

Jesus did not say that a rich man cannot be saved. He said, "With men this is impossible; but with God all things are possible." This means that every man growing rich needs God in order to be saved. If riches master him, he is lost. Unless God be his Lord he cannot enter the heavenly kingdom.

There is a story of a rich man, one of whose ships was delayed at sea. When one day had passed with no tidings, the man was anxious, and with each added day his anxiety increased. At length, however, he awoke to the fact that his money was having a tremendous hold upon him. He then ceased to worry about the ship and became anxious for his own soul. He was determined to break the perilous mastery, and taking the value of his ship, he gave it at once to a charitable object. We all need to deal thus rigorously with ourselves, whether we have only a little money or much, that money may never be our master, but that Christ may be Master always, and money our servant, to do our bidding and Christ's.

28

The Laborers in the Vineyard

Scripture Reading: Matthew 20:1–16

The key to this parable is found in what goes just before. A young man came to Jesus eager to follow him and asked what he must do. Jesus said he must give up his riches and go with Him. The young man found the cost too great and went away sorrowful. Then Jesus spoke seriously to His disciples about how hard it was for a rich man to enter into the kingdom of God. It cannot have been a high spiritual thought which was in Peter's mind when he said to Jesus, "Behold, we have forsaken all and followed Thee; what shall we have?" Evidently he was thinking that they had done a very worthy thing in leaving all and going with Christ. But his question showed a spirit which was not pleasing to the Master, a mercenary spirit, a disposition to get the best out of duty and service and sacrifice. He expected reward and large reward for faithful service.

In true following of Christ such a question is never asked. Love never thinks of wages in anything it does. If, as a man does for another hard and self-denying things, he is always thinking of the way the other will pay him, expecting large compensation, there is no love whatever in what he does. He is a hireling. A mother never asks, as she cares for her sick child, losing rest, suffering, "What shall I get for this?"

The answer Jesus gave Peter assured him that the disciples who had left all should be amply rewarded. But the parable we are now studying is

121

not always thought of as a part of our Lord's answer to the question. The chapter division in the King James Version obscures this fact. In the Revised Version, however, there is no break in the passage. The words, "For the kingdom of heaven is like," connect this parable directly with the foregoing incident and show that Jesus would warn Peter and His disciples against the disposition to bargain and haggle for pay, or to compare their work with that of others, quibbling about proportionate rewards.

The parable makes it plain, first, that an agreement was made with the laborers. The householder needed men, and when the first came they accepted his offer of a penny a day* and agreed to work for that. Later in the day, at different hours, other men were also engaged and sent into the vineyard. Some were even taken on only an hour before the day closed. Evening came and the workmen gathered to receive their pay. It happened that those who were last engaged and had worked only one hour were paid first. They received the full amount for a day's work. We need not raise the question of fairness. It is evident that the men who had been in the vineyard only one hour had not done as much as those who began in the early morning and had wrought all through the long hours. The parable was spoken for a definite purpose—to condemn the greedy, grasping, bargaining spirit, and to commend the thought of doing duty for its own sake whether there is adequate compensation or not. Those who came at later hours made no bargains as to their wages, leaving to him who employed them how much they should receive.

The parable is not meant to be a lesson in business. No doubt it is better usually to have an understanding as to wages, so that there may be no misunderstanding at the time of settlement. But it is in the Father's business that Jesus is giving instructions, and here we need not trouble ourselves to put our contracts down in black and white, and need not ask, "What shall we get for this?"

"When the first came, they supposed that they would receive more; and they likewise received every man a penny. And when they had received it, they murmured against the goodman of the house, saying, These last have spent but one hour, and thou hast made them equal unto us, who have borne the burden and heat of the day." Peter could

---

*The actual currency used was a denarious, which was the regularly accepted pay for a day's labor. *Ed.*

scarcely help hanging his head when the Master came to this part of the parable. He could have no doubt that He had him in mind in what He said about those who clamored for more pay. Peter's words, "We have left all—what then shall we have?" had shown in Peter a feeling at least of satisfaction with himself. Somehow he felt that he had done a good deal for his Master, had made great sacrifices and that he ought to have a substantial reward for it all. Especially had his words revealed a feeling that he and his fellow-apostles should have a greater reward than those who had done less, come into the service later, made smaller sacrifices. When Jesus spoke of the first-hired laborers and their dissatisfaction with the pay they had received, Peter must have felt rebuked.

If these all-day laborers had the true spirit, they would have rejoiced that they had the opportunity to serve so many hours for their Lord. Instead of counting the hours they had wrought and considering themselves overburdened, overwrought, they should have felt themselves honored in the privilege. The Christian who heard the call of Christ in his youth and began in the early morning hours to serve Him should never cease to be glad for his long service. He should not consider the man who gave eleven hours to the world, and then for one hour followed the Master, as more highly favored than himself who had devoted all his life to the service of the Lord. "It is impossible that a man whose chief desire was to advance his Master's work should envy another laborer who had done much less than himself."

These first men were vexed because they did not receive more for their work than those who had come in at later hours. There are some who are envious of others because they seem to have easier work, lighter burdens, more cheerful circumstances. This is an unhappy mood. They think God is not quite just and fair to them. They fret and chafe when they see others called to more prominent positions. They tell of what they have sacrificed, how hard they have worked, how much they have done, and do not hesitate to fret and complain because they have not the recognition they think they deserve. Other men who have been Christians not half as long as they have, and have not given or worked as they have done, are officers in the Church, are talked about and praised among men for their worth and service.

This is a most unwholesome disposition. It makes one wretched and unhappy. The true Christian spirit is glad for all the years of opportunity to do God's service. It begrudges even one opportunity that has been lost. It does not complain that it has served so long—it grieves always that it has not served longer and more faithfully.

The question of pay or reward for Christian work is one that should never have a place in any heart. All service should be inspired by love. Of course, we have to live, and it costs to live. The minister, for example, who devotes his whole life to the work of Christ, has to live. But when Jesus sent out His disciples to preach He warned them especially against anxiety concerning their food and raiment. They were not to provide luxuries for themselves. They were not to have extra garments—they were going out under their Master's command, and He would see that they should be cared for. The minister ought to be supported, ought to have his needs provided for. But when he haggles about the matter, shows anxiety and frets and complains, he is not pleasing the Master, nor practicing the spirit and the disposition which He commends.

The motive in Christian service should always be like the Master's. We should work for love—never for reward. We should never say to Christ, when called to any hard service, "What shall I get for this task, this self-denial, this sacrifice?" We should be ready to go anywhere, to do anything, that the Master would have us do. We should never bargain for any reward, whatever we may do. We know that we shall have a reward, but we should never let that be our motive. We should devote ourselves with all the earnestness and all the energy we have to the service of Christ, whether we are to receive pay for the work or not.

An ancient legend tells of one who went about carrying in one hand a burning torch and in the other a goblet of water, crying, "With this torch I will burn up heaven, and with this water I will put out hell, that God may be served for Himself alone." This parable teaches that all our service of Christ is to be lowly and self-forgetting. We are to be eager to do God's will whatever it may be, serving unto the uttermost, but never thinking of reward. We shall have reward if we are faithful, but our service is never to be for the reward. The true reward is that which comes in the serving itself.

29

Jesus Nearing Jerusalem

Scripture Reading: Matthew 20:17–34

Jesus was setting out for Jerusalem on His last journey. Did He not know that He was going straight into danger? He was safe in Perea; why did He not stay there? Why did He leave this shelter and go straight into the den of lions at Jerusalem? He knew all that awaited Him, but He did not shrink from it; He resolutely set His face to go, because it was the way marked out for Him. The picture shows Him hastening on, striding away before the disciples, as Mark [10:32] tells us, as if He were eager to reach the city and endure what lay before Him there, and could scarcely wait for the slow steps of the disciples. Why was Jesus so eager to suffer? It was because His time had come, and He was eager to do the Father's will. Besides, it was the receiving up to heaven which He saw, and the cross and darkness were forgotten in the triumph and glory beyond. "Who for the joy that was set before Him endured the cross, despising the shame" [Heb. 12:2]. There ought to be wondrous inspiration in Christ's example here for all who are called to suffer and endure for His sake. We should be eager to do God's will however hard it may be; and we should train ourselves to look beyond the suffering and the trial to the blessing and joy that will come after.

He took the disciples apart and told them what lay before Him. "Behold, we go up to Jerusalem; and the Son of man shall be betrayed unto the chief priests and unto the scribes." The astronomer knows, when others do not, that the dark shadow of the eclipse is traveling toward the sun; and Jesus knew, when no others saw it, that the blackness of the cross was approaching Him and would overwhelm Him, and knew the very moment He would enter it. One of Holman Hunt's pictures represents Jesus as a boy in the carpenter shop. It is evening, and He is weary. Stretching out His arms, the light of the setting sun, shining in from the west, casts His shadow on the floor of the shop, and lo—it is in the form of a cross! The artist's thought is that very early in life the shadow of the cross fell upon Jesus, that from the beginning He was conscious of the fact that He must die by crucifixion. What a pathos it adds to the life of Christ to remember this: that all the time, in the midst of His human joys, while He was scattering blessings among others, while He was working miracles of mercy; in all the holy peace and calm of His soul, that dark shadow hung over Him continually—He was going at last to be crucified. Yet the consciousness never kept Him from speaking one gentle word, nor from doing one kindly deed, nor from being cheerful and loving. Knowing from the beginning all that lay before Him, He went on with His daily duty quietly and joyfully. This reveals something of His love for us and His joy in doing the Father's will.

There is a strange contrast between the words of Christ as He spoke to the disciples of His approaching death and the coming of this mother with her ambitious request: "Grant that these my two sons may sit, the one on Thy right hand, and the one on Thy left hand, in Thy kingdom." Mothers should be ambitious for their boys, and want them to have high places. They should make sure, however, that the places they desire for them are really high places. Earth's pinnacles are not always such. Taking out of Herodias's daughter's request its mistaken worldly thought, no parental ambition for a child can be fitter than hers, that her sons should have places near to Christ. It is to be feared, however, that very many parents think more of getting for their children high positions in this world than places near to Christ and high in holiness.

Jesus spoke to the sons in reply, not to the mother: "Ye know not what ye ask." It was an ignorant prayer which they had offered. They did not know what they were asking for. We know that one dark day two malefactors had the places on the Lord's right and left hand. We all many a time ask for things which we would not dare request if we knew what they would cost us. There is a heathen story, says George Macdonald, which tells that once a man asked for this gift—not to die; and it was granted him by the Fates. He was to live on forever. But he had forgotten to ask that his youth and health and strength might last forever also; and so he lived on till age and its infirmities and weakness were weighing him down, and his life grew to be a weariness and a burden to him. Existence (for it could not be called life) was one long torment for him; and then he wished to die and could not. He had asked for a thing which he was totally unfit to enjoy, but he had to take the consequences of it when it was once given. The better way to pray is to let God choose for us and to give what He sees best for us and in the way He knows is the best.

"To sit on My right hand, and on My left, is not Mine to give; but it shall be given to them for whom it is prepared of My Father." So there are places in heaven higher and nearer Christ than others. Surely, too, the high places are worth striving for. We see how men scramble after earth's positions; heaven's are infinitely better. But how can we gain the seats nearest to Christ now, in glory? We have many hints. A little farther on in this passage we are taught that the path of lowly, self-forgetful service leads upward in spiritual life. In Revelation our Lord says that they who overcome in their struggles with sin and trial shall sit with Him on His throne. In Daniel [12:3] we are told that they who turn many unto righteousness; that is, they who are active and successful in saving souls shall shine as the stars, forever and ever. We know also that the "pure in heart" [Matt. 5:8] shall see God. These and many other hints show that the more like Christ we are in character and work here the nearer we shall get to Him both in this world and hereafter.

Jesus was always having difficulty in getting His disciples to understand the spiritual meaning of things. They thought here that rank and official position were the symbols of greatness. "No," said Jesus; "whosoever would become great among you shall be your minister." This seems a strange way of getting on and getting up in the world. According to this, all men's scrambling for place and power is really scrambling downward rather than upward. The real heights in human life are the heights of self-forgetfulness and service. Of course, this does not mean that a Christian is never to accept nor hold a position of honor and trust. A king, ruling millions of people, can be the very highest of servants by ruling only for the glory of God and the good of his subjects. A rich man has an opportunity to get very near to Christ if he uses his wealth to bless the world. It is not the worldly position that settles this question, but the spirit of the life. A servant in a family may be a great deal farther from it than the mistress whom she serves. The kind of serving that our Lord means is that which forgets self and thinks only and always of the need and interests of others.

"The Son of Man came not to be ministered unto, but to minister." The art of photography is now so perfect that the whole side of a great newspaper can be taken in miniature so small as to be carried on a little pin or button, and yet every letter and point be perfect. So the whole life of Christ is photographed in this one little phrase. He came not to be served—if this had been His aim He would never have left heaven's glory, where He wanted nothing, where angels praised Him and ministered unto Him. He came to serve. He went about doing good. He altogether forgot Himself. He served all He met who would receive His service. At last He gave His life in serving—gave it to save others, to redeem lost souls. He came not to be ministered unto, but to minister.

You say you want to be like Christ. You ask Him to print His own image on your heart. Here then is the image. It is no vague dream of perfection that we are to think of when we ask to be like our Master. The old monks thought that they were in the way to become like Christ when they went into the wilderness, away from men, to live in cold cells or on tall columns. But surely that is not the thought which this picture suggests, such a dream of uselessness. "To minister"—that is the Christlike thing. Instead of fleeing away from men, to live with men, so serve them, to live for them, to seek to bless them, to do good, to give our lives for them—that is the meaning of the prayer for Christlikeness.

30

Jesus Entering Jerusalem

Scripture Reading: Matthew 21:1–17

The triumphal entry was one of the most remarkable incidents in our Lord's life. Usually Jesus made no public demonstration, did nothing to draw attention to Himself in any way. Indeed, He avoided publicity; He did not strive nor cry aloud; neither did anyone hear His voice in the streets. He spoke to His disciples confidentially of His Messiahship, but did not publicly proclaim it. On this occasion, however, He made a public demonstration, riding into the city as a king would ride, thus proclaiming to the multitudes, assembling for the passover feast, the fact of His Messiahship. How shall we explain this? May we not say that it was another way of presenting Himself to the people, offering Himself to them as their Messiah, for the last time? A prophet had foretold that He would thus in this spectacular way ride into the city, but He did not do it merely to fulfill prophecy. The prophecy was part of the will of God for him and there was a reason for it beyond the fulfilling of what had been foretold.

Two disciples were sent from Bethphage (house of figs, the precise site undiscoverable now) into an unnamed village nearby, to prepare for the great occasion. Note their obedience. "The disciples went, and did even as Jesus commanded them." They were glad to have a part in the honoring of their Master. No doubt they themselves shared the expectations of the multitude regarding Jesus, hoping that the time had now come for Him to assume His place as King. It was a lowly errand on which they were sent—to bring to their Master the animal on which He was to ride—but they were proud to be chosen for this service. We should be glad always to run any errand, even the humblest, for our Master. If He were here now and wanted to ride somewhere, who would not be glad to lend Him a beast to ride on? Who would not be eager to bring Him His horse and help Him to mount?

Jesus has told us that we may do just such errands for Him if we will, since what we do for any of His little ones, even the least, in His name, is done for Him. We may so set Jesus before us that our very drudgeries shall be made Divine; we may thus transform them into heavenly ministries by doing them for Him. The angels never think about the degree of honorableness in the tasks they are set to do.

Promptly the disciples returned, bringing with them the animals they had been sent to bring. "And brought the ass, and the colt, and put on them their clothes, and they set Him thereon." The ass was a symbol of peace. If Jesus had ridden on a horse, it would have spoken of war, but He was the Prince of Peace. In those days there was nothing degrading in riding on an ass. It was the royal beast.

The disciples were bidden to say to the owner that the Lord had need of the animal. There is nothing that Christ may not use—nothing of ours, however lowly, which may not have its place in advancing His kingdom and glory. It is said that once Queen Victoria was traveling through the Highlands and stopped a little while at the home of a poor woman to rest and sat in a common chair. When the royal party was leaving, one whispered to the old woman that it was the Queen who had been in her home. She took up the chair on which the Queen had been sitting and carried it away, saying, "No one ever shall sit in this chair again, because my Queen has used it." Our King will use anything we have, and what of ours He uses is lifted to highest honor. He has need for our money, our hands, our feet, our lips, and we do well when we hold all our possessions ready at any call of His to be used as He desires.

It was a strange scene—the enthusiasm of the people that day as Jesus rode toward the city. The "multitude spread their garments in the way; and others cut branches from the trees, and spread them in the way." Xerxes, history tells us, when passing over the bridge of the Hellespont, found the road strewn with branches of myrtle, while burning perfumes filled the air. When Alexander the Great was entering Babylon, flowers were strewn before him. It is no wonder that these Jewish pilgrims honored Jesus that day. For the moment they regarded Him as indeed their Messiah. They were escorting Him into the city, as they thought, to take His place on David's throne. They were not deceived, either, for Jesus was really going to His coronation, though not to such a coronation as they thought. He was to be crowned, but with thorns. The people were indeed escorting the Messiah, but not such a Messiah as they were looking for. The time of His triumph was indeed at hand, though not such a triumph as they expected to see. His kingdom was not of this world. His glory was to be reached through ignominy and shame. He was the king of sorrows, because through sorrow He prepared redemption for the world. The strange pageant of that day was a picture, a Divine foreshadowing, of the coming day, when all nations shall join in honoring Christ as King.

Glad were the songs that rang out on the air that morning: "Hosanna to the son of David: Blessed is He that cometh in the name of the Lord." The people were disappointed in a sense. In a little while all their bright hopes had vanished—Jesus went to a cross instead of a throne. Soon "Hosanna" was changed to "Crucify Him!" Soon the palm branches were withered and trodden underfoot by the throngs. Yet the people sang that morning better than they knew. They thought of the restoring of David's kingdom; the King that was coming was really far more glorious than David. They expected liberty from the Roman yoke; Jesus brought liberty from the yoke of Satan and sin. They expected restoration of homes, riches and honors; Jesus has restored us to our place in our Father's family. They looked for prosperity and peace among the nations; He brought the peace of God and the prosperity that comes by righteousness. They expected the conquest of all nations by their Messiah; He will conquer the whole world by His grace and truth. The earthly blessings they looked for as a result of the Messiah's coming were but the shadows of the heavenly joys which He actually brought.

A remarkable scene occurred in the temple. "Jesus went into the temple of God, and cast out all them that sold and bought." The temple was the house of prayer, but it had been changed into a den of robbers, as Jesus says. Not only did these traders desecrate the sacred house by making it a marketplace, but they robbed the people by usury and overcharging. Jesus cast out the traders and the money changers and cleansed the holy place. Thus it is that He would do when He comes as King into our hearts. Made to be temples of God, houses of prayer, homes of purity and peace, sin has turned them into dens of robbers, desecrating them and filling them with unholy things. Christ's first work is to drive out all that defiles them, all that is unholy, and make them ready to be God's dwelling-places.

The rulers were vexed when they saw all that Jesus had done. They seemed to have been especially annoyed by hearing the children singing their hosannas to Jesus. He reminded them, however, that their own Scriptures had foretold this very scene: "Have ye never read, Out of the mouths of babes and sucklings thou hast perfected praise?" Everywhere in the Bible we learn that children are dear to God. He wants their earliest love. He is pleased to hear their voices in songs of praise. A sweeter music rises to heaven from the children's singing than from trained choirs of insincere, formal, or mere professional worshipers. The children should always be in the church services and should join in the songs. The service is completed, perfected by their voices.

The great triumph of Christ is still going on in this world. The palm branches which were waved that day have long since faded, and the music of the songs has died away on the air; but uncounted millions are following in the procession of those who honor Him. Among these are prophets, apostles, martyrs and saints of all ages. Countless multitudes have been gathered from the darkest abodes of sin, and, wearing white garments washed in the blood of the Lamb, are now among those who honor Christ. Old men and boys, feeble women and maidens, all saved by the power of the cross, are now singing the song, "Hosanna to the Son of David."

31

Two Parables of Judgment

Scripture Reading: Matthew 21:33–46

The parable interprets itself. The people of Israel were familiar with the use of a vineyard as an image or illustration of themselves. The prophets had employed it. It is easy to explain the parable in its historical sense, but it has a reference also to us. God is continually planting vineyards and leaving them in the care of husbandmen. He has placed one in your care—it is your own life. He has placed in it many vines, which, if well tended and cultivated, will produce rich fruits. He has put a hedge about it, the walls and defenses of your own home and of the Church, and the restraints and safeguards of Christian friendships and associations. You were not born in a heathen land, your life open and unfenced like a public common, to be trodden down by every unholy foot. God has made every provision for His vineyard that is necessary for its fruitfulness. It is well watered—the influences of Divine grace flow all through your life. He has done for His vineyard all that could be done. It is yours now to keep and care for, not as owner, but as tenant. You are not your own; you belong to Christ [see 1 Cor. 6:19]; your life is His, and you are to keep it and cultivate it for Him. You are really one of God's tenants. He has "assigned" to you a little vineyard, for whose care and cultivation you are responsible. Yet He does not compel you to obey Him, to keep your heart, to bring forth fruit; you are free, but He holds you accountable for the way you keep your vineyard.

The analogy is followed: "When the time of the fruit drew near, he sent his servants to the husbandmen, that they might receive the fruits of it." This is the way the husbandmen were to pay their rent; they were to give to the owner each year a certain proportion of the fruits of the vineyard. God expects us to return something to Him of the fruits of the vineyard He has assigned to us. It belongs to Him, and He has done all that needs to be done to render it fruitful. He expects a proper "rental." The rental of this vineyard was to be paid, not in money, but in the fruit of the vineyard itself. This is suggestive. God is not satisfied with the mere giving to Him of money or of a portion of the earthly possessions that may belong to us. Of course, our money is part of our vineyard and should pay rent, too; a share of its fruits or earnings should be returned to God, to whom it all actually belongs. But the vineyard proper is our own life and we are to pay our rental to God, the owner, in the fruits of our life, in love, obedience, worship, honor, service. No amount of money will ever satisfy God if we do not also love Him and do His will.

This businesslike illustration of our relation to God is very suggestive. We are His tenants, and all we are and all we have belong to Him. Every tenant must pay a proper rent, or he cannot remain on the property that has been assigned to him. The larger our vineyard and the greater our privileges and blessings, the more rent we must pay. If we do not thus make suitable return, we are robbing God.

The reception given to the servants sent to receive the rental was not merely discourteous, it was cruel and an act of rebellion: "The husbandmen took his servants, and beat one, and killed another, and stoned another." The servants who come to us are those that God sends to us to call us to duty. Of course, none of us ever treat the messengers God sends to us as His ancient people treated the prophets. We do not beat our teachers and preachers. We do not stone them and kill them. We are very kind to them. We show them courtesy. We even love them very much and, as a rule, we listen with great respect to what they have to say to us. We never think of arresting them and putting them in prison or of sawing them asunder. Surely, then, this part of the parable cannot have any application to us.

But, wait a moment. On what errand are the servants sent? What is their request of us? They come to get the rental which we owe to God, to receive the fruits which are His due. We do not beat the messengers, but do we grant what they in God's name ask from us for Him? Do we give up our sins when they ask us to do it? Do we yield our hearts to God and begin to love and obey Him and live for Him, when they ask these things of us? We are very respectful to God's servants, but we go on in our evil ways, and they carry back nothing from us, no fruits, to the God whose we are. We treat the messengers with high honor, but the message we disregard and Him who sends it to us we reject and neglect. Nothing is sadder to the heart of a pastor or teacher than this, that while those to whom he bears God's message treat him with finest courtesy and gentlest love, and are kind to him, they do not learn to honor God and love and serve Him.

"Again, he sent other servants more than the first: and they did unto them likewise." We read the story of God's dealing with His ancient people and wonder at His marvelous patience with them. Though they treated His servants so badly He continued to send others. He seemed never to tire of trying to bless them. But is it not our own history as really as it was theirs? As soon as we are old enough to understand anything, God begins sending messengers to us—loving mothers, faithful fathers, godly pastors, teachers and friends, the voices of conscience, of the Scriptures, of the Spirit, the leading of Providence. But we hear the calls, and then go on as before, unheeding, despising, sinning. But God does not grow weary. He continues to send His messengers. Not only is this true of the impenitent, but to every believer He sends again and again, seeking for fruits and finding none. We never can measure God's patience.

But we must remember that there will be a last call.

"But last of all he sent unto them his son." Mark says, "Having yet therefore one son, his well beloved: he sent him last unto them" [Mark 12:6]. There is a matchless pathos in these words when we think of them as referring to God and defining the acts of His love and mercy. All he had left now was his son. His servants had all been sent, and the last of them had been killed. There was no other messenger that he could send unless he should send his son. If he gave him he gave all, for he had not many sons, but one, his only-begotten son. So "he sent him last unto them." He kept nothing back, spared not even his own son, in his great desire to have men reconciled to him. Thus the sending of Jesus was the climax of a long history of gracious acts of love.

There is another thought here. He sent his son last. Then there is no messenger of mercy after Jesus. He is God's best and final gift. There is nothing more that even God in His infinite power and love can do to induce men to be reconciled. When men reject Christ they throw away their last hope of mercy—they lose their last chance. No other messenger will be sent—no other can be sent.

"This is the heir; come, let us kill him, and let us seize on his inheritance." The rulers killed Jesus that the power might still be theirs. There are many now who reject Christ for very much the same reason. They think that the way to get liberty, pleasure and gain is to thrust Christ altogether away from their lives. To become Christians would interfere too much with their plans, perhaps with their business, or with their pleasure. They think that Christian people make great sacrifices. But the Bible puts it very differently. It tells us that those who receive Christ, instead of losing, gain a glorious inheritance; they become children of God, and if children, then heirs to an inheritance unfading. The rulers killed their best friend when they killed Jesus. Had they accepted Him, they would have received His inheritance, becoming "joint-heirs with Christ" [Rom. 8:17]. Rejecting and killing Him, they lost the very inheritance they thought to seize. Those who now reject Christ reject the only One who could give them eternal life. Since Christ is God's last messenger of mercy to men, the rejection of Him is the thrusting away of the last hope of mercy.

"The stone which the builders rejected, the same is become the head of the corner." They did not think Jesus suitable to be their Messiah, and so they rejected Him; now, however, He is King of glory. The very men who rejected Him and crucified Him, when they awake on judgment morning, shall see Him whom they thus despised sitting as their Judge. But again, we must not apply it to the first rejecters only. A great many people now think Christ unsuitable to be their Lord. They do not consider it an honor to be called a Christian. They blush to own His name or enroll themselves among His followers. They do not care to build their life on Christ. But He has now the highest honor in heaven. No highest angel is ashamed to own His name. Redeemed spirits praise Him day and night. The Father has exalted Him to the throne of power and glory. Why then should sinful men be ashamed to own Him as Lord? They should remember further that God has made Him the cornerstone of the whole building not made with hands. No life that is not built on Him can stand. If men ever are saved it must be by this same Jesus whom they are now rejecting.

32

The King's Marriage Feast

Scripture Reading: Matthew 22:1–14

Christ is soon to be condemned by the rulers and put to death, but as He stands now in the holy city He speaks as the Judge, pronouncing the doom upon the people who are rejecting Him as their Messiah. "The kingdom of heaven is like unto a certain king, who made a marriage for his son." The marriage feast suggests two great thoughts concerning gospel blessings. The figure of a feast pictures abundance of provision, and also gladness and good fellowship. Then the figure of marriage suggests the closeness of the relation into which God invites us. Marriage represents the highest ideal of love and friendship. It expresses mutual affection and delight; on the one hand, protecting care; on the other, perfect trust. The blending of two lives in one, which is the meaning of true marriage, suggests the union of Christ and His people in thought, purpose, feeling and motive. We are Christ's, and Christ is ours. Christ and we become one. He lives in us, and we live in Him.

The forms of Oriental life are preserved in the framework of the parable. The king sent forth his servants "to call them that were bidden." They had already received a preliminary invitation, and now they are formally called by the king's messengers. The refusal to accept such an honor was a distinct and intentional insult and showed that they were in heart rebellious and disloyal. The meaning of the parable is plain. God was the King who made the feast. The invitation shows the Divine earnestness in seeking to bless men. God does not merely invite them once and then if they refuse, give no more thought to them; but He invites them again, and most urgently presses upon them the invitation.

We all have been invited many times to the feast of Divine love. The invitations begin to fall upon our ears in childhood, and are repeated all through our life. Dr. Marcus Dods says:

> If God is in earnest about anything, it is about this; if the whole force of His nature concentrates on any one matter, it is on this; if anywhere the amplitude and intensity of Divine earnestness, to which the most impassioned human earnestness is as the idle, vacant sighing of the summer air— if these are anywhere in action, it is in the tenderness and sincerity with which God invites you to Himself.

After all that God had done for His people and all His efforts to win them to accept His love, they treated His mercy with contempt. "They made light of it." That is, they simply ignored the invitation, paid no heed to it, treated it as a matter of no importance, and hurried on to their own business. It is in this way that a large class of people always treat the gospel invitation. They do not oppose Christ in any active way. They do not rush into great wickedness—they are fairly moral people. They speak patronizingly of the gospel and the Church. But they pay no heed to the calls of Christ. They treat them as if the gospel were only a sort of child's play, something for sick people and the very old, but not important enough for them to give thought to. They treat the gospel as if there were no real importance in the messages of love it brings, which break so urgently upon their ears. They regard their worldly business as of far more importance than personal salvation.

Silent neglect is one of the most offensive ways of treating anyone, and those who "make light" of the gospel insult God even more than those who openly refuse its invitations. Yet these people imagine and often say that they have never rejected Christ because they have shown no open enmity to Him. Countless thousands of souls have been lost by simply making light of the guilt and danger of sin and neglecting the way of mercy.

Those who were first invited and made light of the invitation "went their ways, one to his own farm, another to his merchandise." That is, their business was more important in their estimation than their king's feast. It is easy to see the same spirit today. There are thousands who have more interest in their business affairs than they have in the affairs of God's kingdom.

This is the way some of the king's servants treated his son's marriage and the invitation to it which they received. They made light of it, paid no respect whatever to it and went on with their business as if they had never received an invitation to the royal marriage. Then there was another class of the king's servants who rose up in anger against the messengers, laid hold upon them and treated them shamefully and killed them. There are those who are not content with ignoring Christ and His messengers, but become open enemies and violent rejecters.

The king turned to others when the first invited had refused. "They which were bidden were not worthy." This does not mean that those who had been invited were too wicked to be saved, for the gospel is offered for the worst. Their unworthiness was shown in their refusal to accept. The final responsibility when men are shut out of heaven cannot be laid on God—his part is fully and faithfully done. The feast is ready, even at infinite cost. The invitations are given in all sincerity and pressed with Divine urgency. But if men will not accept the mercy, there the matter must end. They will not be compelled to come to the feast. The weakest sinner can refuse the greatest honor of Divine love. The final responsibility rests upon the rejecters. "They would not come" is the reason that they are shut out. The king then bade his servants to go into the partings of the highways—that is, among the Gentiles, and in a little while the tables were filled.

The king came to see his guests, to know whether they had fulfilled the conditions of their invitation. "The framework of the parable presupposes the Oriental custom of providing garments for the guests who are invited to a royal feast." When the king made his inspection, he "saw there a man who had not on a wedding garment." The man came to the feast, but came in his own way, refusing to accept the conditions and to wear the garment prescribed by the king. The man may represent those who enter the Church but do not accept the garment which is the invariable mark of all Christ's true followers. Church membership is not this garment—one may have this honor and not have on a wedding garment. Nor is it baptism or the Lord's Supper—one may observe these sacraments and yet lack the essential mark of true discipleship. The wedding garment is the righteousness of Christ. We do not become Christians merely by associating ourselves with Christians, by adopting the forms of religion. We must have in us the mind of Christ, conformity to God, an abhorrence of that which is evil, a love for that which is good, a sincere desire to honor God and do His will.

Notice also that this garment is an individual matter. One man in all that great company lacked the required dress, and was excluded. Each one must have the garment for himself. God looks at us as individuals, not in companies. Being in a good family, or among holy persons, or in a Church of saintly members, will not excuse the lack in the one of us who may lack the prescribed garment.

When the king asked the man why he had come to the feast without the wedding garment, he had nothing to answer. "He was speechless." He had no excuse to offer. He knew that he alone was to blame for this lack of preparation, since he had rejected what was freely offered to him. So will it be with any who refuse the grace of God. They are not speechless now; they find many excuses when they are urged to accept Christ. But when they stand at length before the Judge, they will be speechless; they will have nothing to say for themselves.

33

Three Questions

Scripture Reading: Matthew 22:15–22; 34–46

The Pharisees, on those last days in the temple, were in continual and bitter controversy with Jesus. They sought to trouble Him, to ensnare or entangle Him in His talk. We may be glad, however, for the questions they asked, because they drew from Him great utterances which are of priceless value to us.

First, they took counsel together and prepared a question which they thought would entrap Him whichever way He answered it. They began by praising His sincerity and truthfulness, as if to flatter Him. Then they asked, "Is it lawful to give tribute unto Caesar, or not?" They thought He could not possibly avoid being ensnared. If He should answer Yes, He would be denounced as lacking in patriotism. If He should answer No, He would be denounced as disloyal to Rome. But He was not ensnared by their question. He knows men's thoughts. He knew their hypocrisy and falseness, and easily baffled them. His answer lays down a great principle. "Render therefore unto Caesar the things which are Caesar's; and unto God the things that are God's." The use of the coinage of Caesar by the people was an admission of his sovereignty. But there was something higher than that. God was over all, and no duty to Him must be neglected. They must be good citizens of Rome, but there was a higher citizenship, and they must also be good citizens of heaven.

The Sadducees came next with their question about the resurrection. They did not believe in the resurrection nor in the existence of spirits, and they thought their question would completely puzzle Him. "In the resurrection . . . whose wife shall she be of the seven? for they all had her." They thought to make the doctrine of resurrection ridiculous. The answer was wonderfully wise. They were thinking only of the earthly life, but in the immortal life all will be different. In the resurrection there will be no marriage. Christ does not mean that the love which binds husband and wife together and grows into such sacredness and beauty in true marriage shall perish in death and have no existence in the resurrection life. Love never dies—it is immortal. It is only the incidents of birth, death and marriage that have no existence beyond the grave.

Then a lawyer had a question to ask Jesus—"tempting Him," the record says. "Which is the great commandment in the law?" The question was a theological one that was discussed much among Jewish teachers, who were proverbially fond of splitting hairs. However, it is an important question for us, too. It is well for us to know which are the first things in life. Jesus answered promptly, "Thou shalt love the Lord thy God with all thy heart." God comes first. Nothing else in all the universe can be put before Him in true living. The first words of the Bible are, "In the beginning God." God was at the beginning, before anything—a grain of sand, the tiniest flower, the smallest thing—was created. There was nothing before God. There is nothing which God did not create. But He is also at the beginning of everything of good and beauty. The same is true in every true heart. We cannot get a blessing until we have God first. Not God first in order, merely, but God first in love, in the place of confidence and trust. He must have the chief place—we must love Him with all our being. It is idle to think of any other religious act or effort until we have begun to love God. This is the beginning of all true religion. Not to love God is not to have taken the first step in a true and holy life.

Then something else follows. "And the second is like unto it, Thou shalt love thy neighbor as thyself." Love for our neighbor is second, in two ways. It must be second in place and in degree. God must be loved supremely. To love any being or any thing more than God is idolatry. It will not do to preach a religion of humanitarianism and not have first "Thou shalt love the Lord thy God." Love to man is second also in the sense that it must spring out of love for God. There must be a first before there can be a second. There can be no love for our neighbor if there is not first love for God. "We love, because He first loved us" [1 John 4:19], We love our neighbor because God loves us, and we love God and because this love warms our heart toward others. But when we truly love God, we will love our brother also.

There has been altogether too little stress put by the Christian Church in the past on this commandment of love to our neighbor. A careful study of the teachings of Christ will show that He Himself insisted continually on love as the very proof and test of Christian life. We cannot get God's forgiveness until we forgive our fellowmen. We are to love our enemies if we would be the children of our Father. By this shall all men know that we are Christ's disciples, because we love one another [see John 13:35]. The epistles, too, are full of teachings concerning the duty of love. Paul's wonderful thirteenth chapter of First Corinthians shows how essential love is, and then shows us the way we must live if we are indeed Christ's. John also makes it plain to us that if we love God we will love our brother also. The claim that we love God cannot be true if it appears that we do not love our brother. "If a man say, I love God, and hateth his brother, he is a liar: for he that loveth not his brother whom he hath seen, how can he love God whom he hath not seen?"

Jesus asked the Pharisees a question, too. "What think ye of Christ?" It was not an easy question to answer. They had very mistaken ideas about their Messiah. Many stumbled at the Messiahship of Jesus because it was not what they were expecting. Even Christ's own disciples did not understand the matter. The Jews were looking for a king who would reign on David's throne—an earthly monarch, a universal conqueror. The Pharisees said the Messiah was to be David's son. Jesus then asked them another hard question. "How then doth David in Spirit call him Lord?" But they had not thought about the particular Scripture to which Jesus referred. If they had, they would have had different ideas of the character and reign of their Messiah.

Jesus then asked them again, "If David then call Him Lord, how is He his son?" No wonder that no one was able to answer Him a word after hearing this question. The question was simply unanswerable on any theory that made the Messiah only an earthly monarch. It is unanswerable also on any conception of the character of Jesus which considers Him as no more than a man. If David called the Messiah his Lord, the Messiah must be Divine, the Son of God. We may worship Him, therefore, and give Him the supreme place in all our lives.

It is thus, indeed, that Christ offers Himself to us in the Scriptures. He claims the supreme individual love of His followers. He who loves father or mother more than Him is not worthy of Him. He claims the place of absolute Master in the life of every man who would be His. We must obey implicitly, unquestioningly, wholly. We cannot take Christ merely as Savior, trusting in Him as our Redeemer, without at the same time taking Him as Lord, as Master, and obeying Him. What David did in calling the Messiah his Lord is what everyone who accepts Him must do. Paul put his whole creed in a single sentence when he said of Christ, "Whose I am, and whom I serve" [Acts 27:23]. The confession of Thomas should be the confession of everyone who receives Christ and believes in Him, "My Lord and my God" [John 20:28].

34

The Lesson of Watchfulness

Scripture Reading: Matthew 24:32–51

It was Tuesday evening. Jesus had left the temple to return to it no more. His last words to the people had been spoken. On the way His disciples called His attention to the temple, perhaps suggesting its magnificence and its solidity. It was indeed a wonderful building. But Jesus said, "There shall not be left here one stone upon another, that shall not be thrown down."

The little company moved out to the Mount of Olives and sat down. A deep solemnity filled their hearts. The disciples asked Him to tell them when the things He had foretold should come to pass. They had in mind three events—the destruction of the temple, the Lord's final coming and the end of the world. He warned them first against being led astray by impostors. He bade them to be in readiness for whatever might come. The parable of the fig tree taught them to expect tribulations. The precise day and hour "knoweth no man, no, not the angels of heaven, but the Father only." The stupendous events would come unheralded. It would be as in Noah's days. The flood came suddenly. Those who were ready entered the ark and were saved, but the rest perished. "So shall also the coming of the Son of man be."

The great lesson Jesus taught His disciples was in the word "Watch!" which sounds in ever-recurring strokes in His discourse like a great bell. Questions as to when or how are discouraged, but they are always to

146

watch. "Watch therefore: for ye know not what hour your Lord cometh."

We must be always watching—watching ourselves, lest we do wrong; watching our Guide, that we may follow Him closely and carefully; watching our duty, that we may always know it and do it; watching for danger, for on every hand danger lurks. It is not a safe world to live in—that is, it is not safe unless we watch, and unless we are in Divine keeping. Satan is so wary, his approaches are so insidious and stealthy, and sin is so alluring and deceptive, that only sleepless vigilance can insure safety.

In this passage, however, the watching is for the coming of Christ, for which we are commanded to be always in readiness. He will surely come, and His coming will be sudden and unannounced. There will be a great final coming of Christ, but really He is always coming. The only way, therefore, to be prepared for Him at any most sudden moment is to be ready all the time. If there is one hour when we relax our vigilance and cease to watch, that may be the hour when He will come.

There is an old legend of a man who waited a thousand years before the gates of paradise, watching for them to open, that he might enter in. At last, yielding to weariness, he slept for just one hour. And during that hour the gates opened for a few moments and closed again. Thus by being off his guard a little while he missed his opportunity. The coming of Christ will be so sudden that no preparation can be made for it after He appears. We must learn to live so that there will not be a moment, day or night, when we would be afraid or ashamed to have Him come into our house or place of business and find us as we are. There is no day which may not be our last. Therefore, we should keep our work done up to the moment, finishing it every evening as if we were never to come back to it anymore.

Christ illustrates His teaching to make it more emphatic. "If the goodman of the house had known in what watch the thief would come, he would have watched." Thieves do not send a notification of the hour when they will break into the house; they make their coming as stealthy as possible. They come when they will be the least expected and when the master of the house is least likely to be watching. If one would be prepared against them when they come, he must always be prepared. Christ will come as a thief in the night. That means that His coming will be without warning, without any token to indicate

His approach. All efforts of wise men to compute the time and settle upon a year or a day when He will come are useless, for Jesus Himself said, "Of that day and hour knoweth no man, no, not the angels of heaven."

What is it to be ready for the coming of Christ? For one thing, it is to be at peace with God, reconciled to Him, saved. In a sense, death is a coming of Christ to individuals, for it ends their probation and ushers them into the presence of God. What is it to be prepared for death? No one is prepared who has not accepted Christ as Savior and Lord, finding forgiveness of sins and new life and love in Him. Nothing could be more terrible than the sudden coming of death to one whose sins are not forgiven and who is thus unprepared to meet his God.

But forgiveness is not the only thing in preparation for death. One's work should be well done. There is a story of a man who had wasted his life and who at last, near the end, found peace in believing. A friend said to him, "Are you afraid to die?" He answered, "No, I am not afraid to die; but I am ashamed to die." He meant that while his salvation was assured in Christ, he was ashamed to go home, having wasted all his years and having done nothing for the honor of his Master. We should do our best possible work every day, that we should never be ashamed to have Christ come.

Jesus sought to make the meaning of His words very clear. "Who then is a faithful and wise servant," He asked, "whom his lord hath made ruler over his household?" The answer is implied in the form of the words used. He is both faithful and wise. Then comes the assurance of reward—"Blessed is that servant, whom his lord when he cometh shall find so doing." Doing how? Doing his work with fidelity. The watching that Christ wants is not sitting at the window and looking out to see Him approach, but diligence in all duty. If a man went away, leaving a servant in charge of a certain work, fixing no time for his return, what should the servant do? Stand in the door, gazing down the road, watching to get the first glimpse of the master's return? No, that is not the kind of watching that would please his master. The way to be ready for Christ's coming is not to sit down in idleness to wait and watch for His appearance, but to keep at one's work with unceasing diligence, so that when He comes He may not find us in the midst of unfinished tasks, away behind with our work.

There can be no better rule in life than to make every day of life complete, to finish everything each night before retiring, so that if we should never come back to our work again, nothing would suffer. A Christian woman was told by her physician that she could not live a great while, and that she might die any hour. She did not, however, drop her work and shut herself away to prepare for death. She went on with all her usual duties, only with more earnestness and greater diligence, knowing now that the time must be short. Some people would suppose that in a case like this, one should give up all active work and spend the short and uncertain time in praying and reading the Bible; but this Christian woman's way was the better way. Long before she had made her peace with God, and all her life had lived in readiness for eternity. When the warning came that the time was growing short, she was not flustered. Thus far she had done her duty as well as she could, and all she had to do now was the work of the few remaining days and hours. This she did with love and faith, and with diligence, and when the Master came, she quietly went away home with Him.

While there is reward for the servant who is faithful, there is punishment for the evil servant who fails in his duty. Judgment will come upon him suddenly. "The lord of that servant shall come in a day when he looketh not for him." That is, the lord of the unfaithful servant. There are several things said here about this unfaithful servant. He is unbelieving. The delay of his lord leads him to conclude that he is not going to return at all. His unbelief leads him to abuse his position—he becomes tyrannical and despotic in his treatment of those placed under his care. Then his own habits become unworthy; we find him eating and drinking with drunken men. These are characteristics of those who reject Christ through unbelief and become unfaithful.

The punishment of the unfaithful servant is vividly described. It is a fearful thing to live regardless of life's sacred trusts and solemn responsibilities. It is a terrible thing to die after having lived thus. We should compare these two pictures—the faithful and the unfaithful servant—and know positively which one of the two is our own portrait.

35

The Wise and Foolish Virgins

Scripture Reading: Matthew 25:1–13

The three parables in this chapter teach great lessons. They are based on the promise of Christ's return. He is surely coming again, when, no one can know. But we should live always so as to be ready for His most sudden coming any moment.

The ten virgins were alike in some ways. An onlooker in the early evening could not have told which were the wise and which the foolish. Each had her lamp. In any Christian congregation the members may all seem alike true friends of Christ as they sit in their pews in common worship or at the Lord's table. The testing comes in other ways.

All the virgins slept while the bridegroom tarried. There was nothing wrong in this. We all have to sleep some time. We should be sure that we are safe against any surprise while we are asleep, that no duty has been omitted before we slept which is essential to a complete life. The wise virgins were ready for the coming of the wedding party at any hour, however long the delay might be. We are not required to wake and watch every moment for the coming of Christ; we are to be ready for the event so that we cannot be surprised. For example, we are not to think every moment of death, but we are so to live always that whenever death may come, however suddenly, it will not find us unprepared. "Not what death finds us doing, but how death finds us furnished, is the important question."

The lamps of the foolish virgins were filled, but they did not hold much oil and would soon burn out, and these maidens had no oil in reserve to refill their lamps when they became empty. This was their folly. The difference in the other virgins was that besides having their lamps filled, they had oil in reserve with which they could quickly refill them when they had burned out.

This is plain enough as regards these virgins. Applied to human lives, the teaching is also clear. The wise Christian is the one who is not content with a mere profession or with external marks of godliness. These may seem to be satisfactory in the easy days when there is no stress, but in the hour of trial they will not stand the test. The essential thing in Christian life is not good morality—the lamps of the foolish virgins represent that. The essential thing is the grace of God in the heart, or real union with Christ. This is represented in the parable by the supply of oil by which the wise virgins were made ready for the need which the midnight brought. If we have only the little lamp of our own life, we may get along while there is no great stress, but in the hour of trial, we shall fail. But if we have Christ with His Divine fullness we can draw from Him for any sorrow, struggle or hard duty.

Midnight came and brought great commotion. The virgins were all sleeping, waiting until they should be summoned to go out to meet the bridegroom. Life is full of emergencies which come so suddenly that there is not time to prepare for them. If we are not ready at the moment of need we cannot become ready. Now it was that the watchfulness of all the virgins was tested. The delay had been so long that all the lamps were burning low. Now appeared the wisdom of the five who had oil in reserve. Their lamps were quickly filled, and they were ready to go with the bridegroom. Now was brought out also the folly of the other virgins. Their lamps were going out and they had no oil to refill them.

It is such occasions as these that test character. They show what is in us. No one is ready for life's sudden emergencies unless he has made preparation in advance for anything that may happen. One who has missed his lessons and trifled in school days will by and by find the doors of opportunity shut to him, because he is not ready to go in. Many a man fails in life because through early neglect he has not the training for his place or business, the reason being that he wasted the time when it was his duty to make the preparation. Many a woman fails in her

homemaking and wrecks her own happiness and that of her family, because at the right time she did not learn the simple household arts which
fit a girl for being a good wife. The foolish virgins missed the wedding
joy and were shut out in the darkness because earlier in the evening they
had not laid up a reserve of oil. Many people's religion fails them in times
of need, because they have not really the word of God laid up in their
heart. "A man has only as much religion as he can command in trial."

It was a natural request that these distressed virgins made: "Give us
of your oil; for our lamps are gone out." At first thought, too, we would
say that the wise virgins should have granted this pathetic request of
their sisters. If you were very hungry and I had even a crust of bread, it
would not be right for me to eat all of my crust myself. We are taught
that we should bear one another's burdens and that the strong should
help the weak. Yet the refusal of the wise is reasonable and right when
we look at it thoughtfully. If you and your neighbor have each signed a
note for a certain sum, to fall due on a certain date, and you by dint of
economy and perseverance have been able to lay by just enough to meet
your obligation, while your neighbor, wasting his hours on trifles, has
made no provision for the day of settlement; and if on the morning
when the note falls due, he should come beseeching you to give him
some of your money to help him pay his debt, would you give it to
him? Does the law of love require that you should?

There is also an important spiritual lesson which the parable is meant
to teach—that the gifts and blessings of grace are not transferable. No
matter how eagerly one may wish to impart them, he cannot do it. If
one woman has improved her opportunities and grown into refined and
disciplined character, while her sister has missed her chance and has
grown up into weak and uncultured womanhood, the first cannot give
of her strength, self-control, and noble spirit to the other, to help her
through some special emergency. If one man has studied diligently and
learned every lesson, at last reaching a position of eminence and power,
he cannot give of his trained ability to his brother, who has trifled
through years, to help to make his life a success. A brave soldier in the
battle cannot share his discipline and courage with a trembling comrade
by his side. In temptation, one who is victorious cannot give part of his
strength to a friend by his side who is about to fall. We cannot share our
forgiveness of sin with our dearest friend. Each one must live his own

life, bear his own burden, and have the grace of the Holy Spirit for himself. No one can give another these gifts.

It was a tragic moment when the foolish virgins got back to the house and found themselves too late: "The door was shut." It had stood open long enough for all who were ready to enter. Then it was closed and could not be opened again. This teaches us the meaning of opportunity. We may apply it to the matter of personal salvation. There is a time to be saved, and when that time is past, the door is shut. Life is full of opportunities. There is a time when we can enter God's family, finding all blessing. Then there is a time when the door is closed, and all the powers of the universe could not open it again.

To the young people every door stands open. They can get an education and a training to fit them for noble, beautiful and worthy life. They can make good friends, friends whose companionship and help would enrich their whole life. They can form good habits which would build up fine character in them and make them respected and influential in the community. They can read good books which will fill their minds and hearts with noble thoughts and upward inspirations. They can win victory over their own lives and become self-controlled and kingly among men. But the doors stand open only a reasonable time—there is not a moment to lose. By and by they will be shut. Then no imploring cry will open them again.

The lesson for all is, "Watch therefore." We know not the day nor the hour. That is true of our Lord's coming. It is true of death. But it is true also of nearly every other experience of life. We go on, not knowing. The future is closed to our eyes. We know not what awaits us at any turning of a street corner, or what we shall have to meet any moment as we go. The only way to be ready for the unknown events of tomorrow is to improve every opportunity of today.

36

The Parable of the Talents

Scripture Reading: Matthew 25:14–30

The particular teaching of this parable is not the same as that of the parable of the virgins. That was the duty of preparation, this is the duty of working—using one's powers and capacities.

Everyone of us has received a talent or talents, some portion of our Lord's goods. The Master has gone away, leaving us to use what of His He has entrusted to us until He returns. Then we shall have to give account to Him. It is not a voluntary matter with us, nor is it a matter of indifference, whether we will be Christ's servants or not. Christ is the rightful Lord of every man. Declining to accept Him and to enter His service does not exempt anyone from the responsibility.

When the lord of these servants went away, he left his property in the hands of his upper servants as stewards or trustees. He "delivered unto them his goods." Perhaps we do not realize how entirely Christ has entrusted His affairs and His interests in this world to His followers. This puts a serious responsibility on us. If the gospel is to get to men, we must proclaim it. If the work of the Church is to be done, we must do it. The only hands Christ has for work in this world are our hands. If the sorrowing are to receive comfort, we must give it. If the world is to see the beauty—the gentleness, the patience, the compassion, the helpfulness—of God, we must be the interpreters of these Divine affections. Christ has delivered His goods to us.

We notice also that in the distribution of talents the same is not given to all. "Unto one he gave five talents, to another two, to another one; to every man according to his several ability." Each person received what he was able to care for. This principle is observed in all Divine endowments. No one has duties allotted to him which he has not the ability to perform. Nothing impossible is ever asked of any person. Men differ in their ability to manage their Lord's affairs, and the talents given into their hands vary accordingly. The merchant does not take the man with capacity only for lifting heavy bales and put him in the counting-room—he makes him a porter. When a woman wants a fine dress made, she does not give the costly materials to a washer woman, a hairdresser, or to a teacher of German or music, but to a skillful dressmaker. Our Master gives each particular disciple the duties he has ability to do. We need never say, therefore, that we cannot do the things that seem to be required of us. We can do whatever we are given by our Master to do. He makes no mistakes in the allotment of tasks.

The story then tells what the servants did with their share of their master's goods. "He that received five talents went and traded with the same, and made them other five talents." This man used faithfully what had been put into his hands, and the result was that it was doubled—his five talents became ten. He used his gifts—traded with them, and in the trading came the increase.

This is the Divine law in all life. God gives one a gift of music, but it is only in its possibilities as yet. It must be cultivated, developed, disciplined, or it never will become of any practical value. Love must be exercised if it is to grow. It is only a capacity at first. The same is true of all human powers, whether of body, mind or heart. The trouble with too many people is that they are indolent and do nothing with their natural gifts, and then these gifts never increase. Talents that are exercised, put to work, traded with, always multiply. "The hand of the diligent maketh rich" [Prov. 10:4]. The boy who is so shy and diffident that he can scarcely speak a word in public, by using his small abilities becomes a great orator, able to sway a vast multitude. The girl whose voice is sweet but undeveloped, puts her talents to use, and by and by sings so as to thrill countless hearts.

The man with the two talents was faithful, too. "And likewise he that had received two, he also gained other two." Not many of us would claim, or at least our more modest friends and neighbors would not claim for us, that we have five talents. This is the distinction of only a few. Many of us would not be quite willing to say we have only one talent. That would seem to put us low in the scale. Perhaps, however, some of us would admit that we have about two talents. It is the great middle class that does most for the world.

It would not do for all to be great—to be five-talented. If all the soldiers were fit for generals, who would make up the rank and file? If all Church members were eloquent preachers, who would do the countless little, quiet services that need to be done? If all men and women were great poets, who would write the prose? There is need for far more common people than great brilliant ones. One Niagara is enough for a continent, but there is need for thousands of little springs and rivulets. A few great men are enough for a generation, but there is work for millions of common folks. So this diversity of gifts is part of the Divine plan. The world needs more people of average ability than it needs of the extraordinary sort, and so we are sure always of being in good company. Lincoln said God must love the common people, for He made so many of them. People who are very great must feel lonesome, for there are so very few of them.

In the case of this two-talented servant, as with that of the five-talented, it was diligent work that redeemed the mediocre man from the obscurity of the commonplace and gave him distinction. Presently he had four talents. The practical lesson in all the parable is the using of our gifts, that, if we really have only two talents, we should not vex ourselves, but should go to work with what we have, and it will grow by and by into something worthy. Dr. William J. Dawson speaks in one of his sermons of the commonness and pitiableness of "contented insignificance." There is no dishonor in one's being lowly and obscure, but it is dishonorable for a man with fine natural gifts, through indolence and lack of earnestness, to remain contented in his insignificance.

The talents were not given to the servants; they were only committed to them to be used. Then there would be an accounting. "After a long time the lord of those servants cometh, and reckoneth with them." There is an important suggestion in this "long time." We are given plenty of time to make use of our talents. It takes time to learn to work well and to develop and train our faculties to their best. Even if we have buried our talents for a season, there is still time to dig them up and try to put them to better use. We owe far more than we can tell to God's patience in waiting so long for us. But we must never forget that the Lord will come, and we shall have to reckon with Him for whatever of His we have.

The character of the reward should be noticed. The successful man was not given a year's vacation that he might take a long rest. He was not given an easier position where he would have less care and less work. The reward for doing his work well was more work. Because he had done well with the little that had been entrusted to him, more was put into his hands. That is the way of honorable promotion among men—not rest and luxury, but a higher position with harder work, increased burden. "Joy" is promised, too—"the joy of thy Lord," the joy which comes of serving, of doing the Lord's work. The deepest joy experienced in this world is the joy which comes of serving.

But one of the servants had failed to do his best with his talent. "Then he which had received the one talent came." The story of the one-talented man is pathetic, and yet it has its startling lesson. If only he, too, had been faithful, doing his best with his little gift, he also would have multiplied his talent. Many who have done the most for the world had only one talent to begin with. The discovery that we have only one talent never should discourage us. We should accept what we have, however small it may be, and set about making the most of it and doing the most with it. The last thing to do with our gift or ability is to despair about it and then hide it away.

The gifts that are not used are lost. "Take therefore the talent from him." In all life it is the same—faculties unused are lost, become extinct. Natural eyes would lose the power of sight if one lived in darkness continually and never used them. The eye that is never turned toward God by and by loses even the power to look toward God. The capacity for believing, which never believes, at length ceases to be able to believe. "Capacity is extirpated by disuse." The lesson comes with tremendous force to the young. If they will not use the spiritual powers God has bestowed upon them, these powers will be taken away from them.

37

The Last Judgment

Scripture Reading: Matthew 25:31–46

This passage gives us a wonderful picture of the last judgment. It is not a parable, but a prophetic presentation of the great scene. The sheep and goats are used as representing the good and the evil.

Christ will be the Judge. He will appear as the Son of man, that is, in His humanity. It is a comfort to think of this, that it will be our Brother whom we shall see on the throne of glory. Christ came first in lowly form. He was born in a stable and cradled in a manger. No retinue of angels then attended Him except the host that sang their song in the shepherd's ears. In His first coming He was lowly and despised. He was so poor that often He had nowhere to lay His head. He had but few followers and made but little name for Himself on the earth. But He will not come this way the second time. He will appear in glory and will be attended by hosts of angels.

For once the whole human family will be together. "Before Him shall be gathered all the nations." Yet in our thought of the grandeur of this scene we must not lose sight of the individuality of the judgment. We shall be there, but none of us will be lost in the crowd; each one shall have a personal judgment. During a war the telegraphic reports from the field say that in a great battle ten thousand men were slain. Not knowing any of them personally, we think only of the vast aggregate number. But suppose some friend of ours—brother or father—

was among the slain; we think no more then of the ten thousand, but of the one. And every one of the ten thousand is mourned in some home—is somebody's father, husband, brother, son, friend. From that battlefield ten thousand cords stretch to ten thousand homes. The heaps of slain are simply ten thousand individuals. So in that countless throng on judgment day, not one person will be lost in the multitude. "Everyone must bear his own burden."

There will be a division that day—the whole human family will not be as one. "He shall separate them one from another." Our Lord's teachings are full of this thought of final separation. The tares and the wheat will grow together until the harvest; but then there will be an infallible separation—not a tare will be gathered into the barn with the wheat. The net draws good and bad fish to the shore, but there the two classes are separated. The ten virgins were together during the time of waiting, but the midnight cry caused an instant, final and irrevocable separation, as the door opened for those who were ready to enter and shut upon those who were unprepared. Nothing is more plainly taught in the word of God than that the evil and the good, the believing and the rejecting, the righteous and the unrighteous shall be separated at the last day, each going to his own place. These separations will cut very close in many cases. "Then shall two be in the field; one is taken, and one is left: two women shall be grinding at the mill; one is taken, and the other is left." When we are sure of our place on Christ's right hand, we should never rest until we are sure also that all those whom we love shall be in the same company.

The King speaks to the people as if He had personally lived among them, "I was hungry, and ye gave Me to eat." It seems from this picture of the judgment that the eternal destiny of men shall be settled by their works. Feeding the hungry and giving drink to the thirsty are mentioned as reasons for the favor shown to those upon the right hand. But a careful study of the passage shows that in the judgment all will turn upon one question—how men have treated Jesus Christ. If they have believed on Him, loved Him, honored Him, and lived for Him, they will be honored by Him, gathered at His right hand and admitted to His kingdom of glory. But if they have not believed on Him, have not honored Him, have not lived for Him in this world, they will be rejected by Him at the last and shut out of the heavenly kingdom.

In other words, all will depend upon whether men believe or do not believe on the Lord Jesus Christ.

But believing in Christ means more than giving assent to a correct creed—it means also a life of obedience and service. The whole of Christian life is love, not only love for Christ, but love for Christ's own. If we love God, we will love our brother also, says the beloved disciple. If we do not love our brother, it is evident that we do not love God. If we have the love of Christ in our heart, it will show itself to all those who belong to Christ. While there is love for all the world, there should be a special love for those who belong to the Master.

The King speaks as if He had come to the people in the great company in many attitudes and experiences of personal suffering and need. "I was a stranger, and ye took Me in; naked, and ye clothed Me; I was sick, and ye visited Me; I was in prison, and ye came unto Me." There is something very pathetic in this thought of Jesus as a stranger, as hungry, or as sick, coming to our doors in those whose appeals are made to us. If we allowed it to enter our heart and exercise its proper effect upon us, it would inspire in us sympathy and love, and would make us very gentle to all who are in need. Mr. Wesley, one winter day, met a poor girl in one of the schools under his care. She seemed almost frozen. He asked her if she had no clothing but the thin garments she was wearing. She said she had not. His hand was in his pocket in an instant, but there was no money there. He went to his room, but the pictures on the wall seemed to upbraid him. He took them down, saying to himself: "How can the Master say to thee, 'Well done, good and faithful servant'? Thou hast adorned thy walls with the money which might have screened this poor creature from the bitter cold! O justice! O mercy! Are not these pictures the blood of the poor maid?" So he sold the pictures to get money to relieve the girl's distress.

Those to whom the King spoke could not understand what He meant. "When saw we Thee hungry, sick, or in prison, and did not minister unto Thee?" Their surprise need not seem remarkable. The truest greatness is not conscious of itself. Moses knew not that his face shone. The best Christians put the lowest value upon their own good works. No doubt many of the commendations and rewards of the righteous in the judgment will indeed be surprises to them. They keep no record of their good deeds. Their sense of personal unworthiness hinders them from seeing anything worthy in what they do. We do not dream of the real value and helpfulness of the things we do. Besides, we do not indeed see Christ in the lowly and suffering ones who come before us, needing love and help—we see only poor, sick, unfortunate people, with no marks of glory, no hints of nobility, no traces of heavenly beauty. We do not see things as they are. Jesus Himself is ever before us in lowly guise. We are unconsciously serving the Master whenever we do in His name the holy things of love. Every lowly, faithful Christian is preparing for himself many a blessed surprise in glory.

Jesus is still in this world. Once He was here in human form, as the Son of man. Now He is here in His Church. "Ye are the body of Christ" [1 Cor. 12:27], said the apostle. The smallest kindness shown to a Christian, even the least, Christ accepts as done to Himself. Parents understand this. Any honor shown to a child, a father receives as shown to himself. If a son is in a strange land and meets with some misfortune, or is sick, and someone finding him there as a stranger in trouble shows him kindness, no greater act done to the parents at home would be as pleasing to them as is that little ministry to their child in a foreign land. Christ loves His people so much that whatever is done to any of them He accepts as if He Himself had been the recipient of the kindness.

The same is true, on the other hand, of any unkindness or any lack of kindness shown to another. "I was a stranger, and ye took Me not in; naked, and ye clothed Me not. . . . Inasmuch as ye did it not to one of the least of these, ye did it not to Me." We must beware how we treat the lowliest Christian, for if we neglect him in his need, it is as if Christ were in the same need, and we had neglected Him.

> Hush, I pray you!
> What if this friend should happen to be—God!

We must learn that we are judged not only by the things we do, but by the things we fail to do. These persons had not been cruel or unkind to any of Christ's little ones—no such charge is made against them; they had not done the kindnesses which they ought to have done. In the parable of the Good Samaritan neither the priest nor the Levite did any harm to the wounded man, and yet they are severely condemned. They sinned against him grievously by not doing the things of love which he needed to have done for him.

38

The Anointing of Jesus

Scripture Reading: Matthew 26:1–16

We enter now upon the last events of our Lord's life. We are within two days of the passover. We have a glimpse of the plotting of the priests and elders, and their desire to take Jesus by subtlety to kill Him. They wished, however, to wait until after the feast, fearing excitement and tumult, and had so determined. The culmination of the plot was hastened, however, by the unexpected treachery of Judas.

The incident of the anointing is given here apparently out of its proper order, probably because of its influence on the treason of Judas. The incident occurred, according to John's gospel [12:1–8], six days before the passover. Judas was offended by Christ's rebuke of his criticism of Mary's anointing, and under the sting of this went to the priest, offering to betray Christ.

Bethany was a sacred place to Jesus. There He found a home of love where His heart was rested many a time after the conflicts and controversies of the day in the temple. There His greatest miracle was wrought—the raising of Lazarus. We know Martha and Mary well. They differed in their dispositions, but they were alike in their warm and loyal friendship for Jesus.

These two sisters had each her own way of expressing her love for her Friend. The other evangelists tell us that Martha served—Martha

162

always served. There are certain people that we never fail to recognize by some unmistakable feature. We always know Peter by his impulsiveness. We know John by his lying upon the Savior's breast at the last supper. We know Thomas as the man who doubted. We know Felix as the man who trembled, and then sent the preacher away for a more convenient season. We recognize Martha wherever we see her by her serving. She represents those whose love for Christ takes the practical form rather than the form of meditation and devotion.

Some people like to criticize Martha and find fault with her; but after all, her type of piety is important in this world where there is so much need for service and ministry. Beautiful as the Mary spirit is, it would not do if all were Marys, for who then would do the work of serving that needs so much to be done? A wife and mother, for instance, who would spend all her time in Bible reading and prayer, giving no thought to her household duties, would not make a very happy home.

> Yes, Lord! Yet some must serve;
>   Not all with tranquil heart,
> Even at Thy dear feet,
> Wrapped in devotion sweet,
>   May sit apart!

The picture of Mary is also familiar. We see her three times in the Gospels, and each time she is in the same posture—at Jesus' feet. When we have our first glimpse within the Bethany home, we find Martha in her characteristic attitude—serving; and Mary we see sitting at the Master's feet, eagerly listening to His words. Our next view of Mary is when Jesus came back to Bethany after the death of Lazarus, and the sisters came out to meet Him. Again, she is at the feet of Christ, this time in deep sorrow, seeking comfort. And here again we find her at the Master's feet, and now it is in an act of honor and an expression of love and gratitude to Him.

We think of Mary, therefore, as a woman who was always at Christ's feet. In the bright, happy days, she sat there as a learner. When grief was in the house and Jesus came, she went to His feet for comfort. Then when the trouble was over, we find her again in her familiar place, honoring Him with her heart's richest and best gifts. There is no fitter place for the redeemed life than at the Master's feet.

Mary came in during the feast and anointed Jesus. We must distinguish this anointing from another by a woman who was a sinner. That anointing was an expression of penitence; this was an outburst of grateful love. Mary brought the best she had, the richest gift in all her possession. Her ointment was very costly. We should bring our best to Christ. No ointment in the world is half so precious to Him as the love of a human heart; we should bring Him our best love, giving Him the first place in our affection. We should give Him the best of our life, the best of our time, the best of our service.

It seems a sad pity that any occasion so sacred as this should be marred by human littleness and meanness. The disciples had indignation. "To what purpose is this waste?" they asked. John tells us that Judas led in the criticism, and when we know this, we are not surprised. Judas thought it was waste when the ointment was poured out on the feet and head of Jesus. There still are many people who think everything wasted that is not coined into dollars, or that does not show in direct practical usefulness. But the truth is, that much of the richest and sweetest blessing scattered in this world is the odor from the breaking of alabaster boxes. It is well to give food and clothing to the poor, but sometimes love and sympathy are better.

One of the most beautiful ministries of modern Christian love is that of the flower missions in many King's Daughters' circles and Christian Endeavor Societies. The little bouquets of flowers that are sent out carry the fragrance of the love of Christ into many hearts and homes and leave untold benedictions there. Yet these flowers are very much like Mary's alabaster box, and some people would call the money wasted that is spent in this way. But the truth is, the odor of love always carries a blessing wherever it reaches. Besides, Christ looks into the heart and is pleased with love there, whether the expression of the emotion take the form of garments for the poor or flowers for the sick room.

It is beautiful to read how promptly Jesus came to Mary's relief when she was blamed. "Why trouble ye the woman?" He asked. It was a shame for big, strong men like the apostles to pounce with such ill manners and cowardly rudeness on a timid young girl like Mary. They ought to have been gallant enough to encourage and praise her deed of love.

"She hath wrought a good work upon Me," said Jesus. This was what gave her act distinction and honor—it was wrought for the Master. Anything done for Christ is lifted up to honor. It is this that makes all lowly Christian service beautiful—it is something done for Jesus. Judas had said the money ought to have been given to the poor. But Jesus said they could always do good to the poor, but they could not show kindness to Him much longer.

Then Jesus said further that this ointment had been poured on His body to prepare Him for burial. Mary probably did not know He was so near death, but Jesus knew it and accepted the honor as for His funeral. We do not know half the real meaning of our lowliest deeds of love. In Mark's Gospel [14:3–9] we read that Jesus said: "She hath done what she could: she is come aforehand to anoint my body to the burying." Many people would have kept that box sealed up, to anoint His cold body. When a man dies, there is never any lack of kind words about him, nor of flowers for his coffin. This is all well in its place, but Mary's way is better. Let us not wait until our friends are gone before we show our love for them, but rather, let us bring our ointment while they are alive to enjoy its fragrance. Fill the lives of your friends with sweetness; speak approving, cheering words, while their ears can hear them and while their hearts can be blessed by them. The flowers you mean to send for their coffins, send to brighten and sweeten their homes before they leave them. Let us learn the lesson today—to anoint our friends beforehand for their burying.

39

The Last Supper

Scripture Reading: Matthew 26:17–30

Jesus left the temple for the last time on Tuesday evening and spent Wednesday in retirement. He gave instructions to two of His disciples on Thursday morning, concerning preparations for the Passover. They were to go to a certain man and tell him, "The Master saith, My time is at hand; I keep the passover at thy house." The man was to be known by a certain sign—he would be carrying a pitcher of water [see Mark 14:13; Luke 22:10]. As women carried the burdens in those days, the sight of a man carrying water was uncommon. Hence the identification would be easy. Evidently secrecy was intended in the choosing of the place for the passover. It is thought that the reason for this secrecy was to keep from Judas the knowledge of the place, as he was watching for an opportunity to betray Jesus. The Master is always coming to people and saying, "I keep the passover at thy house." He wants to be a guest in every family. Blessed is the home that opens to Him and gives Him its upper room as His guest chamber.

It was a sad announcement that Jesus made to the disciples that night when they had gathered about the table. "Verily I say unto you, that one of you shall betray Me." Judas himself was at the table, and possibly one reason why Jesus made this announcement was to give him an opportunity to repent even at the last moment. It is remarkable that not one of the disciples seems to have suspected anyone as the traitor to whom Jesus had referred. They did not begin to say: "I wonder which of us it is? Do you think it can be Andrew? Do you suppose it can be Peter?" Instead of suspicion, each one shuddered at the possibility that he himself might, after all, be the one. "Is it I, Lord?" they all began to say. "Surely not I!" is the more accurate rendering. We should examine ourselves rather than look at others for sins we find condemned.

It is very much easier to see faults in our neighbors than in ourselves, and to think others capable of doing evil things rather than suppose it possible that we should do them. But our business is with ourselves alone. We do not have to answer for the sins of our neighbors. Then it is not enough to ask merely whether we have done such and such things; we should ask also whether we are in danger of committing them. "Let him that thinketh he standeth take heed lest he fall" [1 Cor. 10:12]. We do not know the dark possibilities of evil which lurk in our hearts. We dare not say, when we learn of someone who has fallen into terrible sin, that it would have been impossible for us to have done the same thing. What man has done, man may do.

The answer of Jesus, "He that dippeth his hand with Me in the dish, the same shall betray Me," was not meant to point out any individual as the traitor. He merely meant to indicate the greatness of the crime—that one of those who had eaten at His table, and enjoyed the familiarity of closest friendship—and they all had—was now to betray Him. In the East, those who ate together, by that very act pledged to each other loyal friendship and protection. This made the crime of Judas all the darker and blacker.

What Jesus said about the traitor is very suggestive. He said, "it had been good for that man if he had not been born." It is a great privilege to live. It is a great thing to be able to stay in this world for a certain number of years and leave our impress upon other lives. It is a great thing to sow seeds which may bring multiplied harvests of blessing in the future. But there are those that live who, perhaps, it may have been better had they never been born. Judas had a magnificent opportunity. He was chosen to be an apostle. He would not have been thus chosen if it had not been possible for him to be a faithful and worthy apostle. He might have gone forth to help bring the world to Christ's feet, and his name might then have been written in heaven. Now, however, the face of Judas is turned to the wall and the place is blank which might have been filled with a story of noble deeds. He wrecked all the possibilities of his life by rejecting the Divine will. He left only a black shadow and then passed to his own place in the other world. It would indeed have been better for him if he had not been born.

The story of the Lord's Supper is told very briefly in Matthew. We may notice, however, that Jesus sets aside the ancient passover and substitutes in its place for Christian observance this memorial supper. "Jesus took bread, and blessed, and broke it; and gave it to the disciples." Bread is a fit emblem of Christ's body. By it our bodies are nourished and strengthened. Christ is food to our spiritual life. Unless we feed upon Him we must perish. The giving of the bread to the disciples signified the offer to each one, by Christ Himself, of all the benefits and blessings of His love and sacrifice. Thus Christ ever stands with outstretched hands holding out to every human soul all the precious things of His salvation.

The use of the words, "This is My body," "This is My blood," ought not to occasion any difficulty. Jesus often spoke in a similar way. When He said, "I am the door," no one supposed that He meant He was literally changed into a door, or when He said, "I am the vine," no one ever thought that He meant to say He had become an actual vine. Here it is just as plain that He spoke figuratively, meaning that the bread was an emblem of His body.

We should notice also that the disciples themselves had a part in this supper. Jesus offered Himself to them as bread, but they must voluntarily accept His gift. "Take, eat; this is My body." It is not enough that God loved the world and gave His Son for its redemption. It is not enough that Christ offered Himself as a sacrifice for men. These stupendous acts of love and grace alone will not save anyone. We have a responsibility in the matter. We must reach out our hands and take what is graciously offered to us. Bread must be eaten before it can become sustenance, so Christ, as the bread of life, must be received into our lives before it can become the food of our souls. Much of the failure of Christian life is at this very point—we do not take what Christ offers and even presses upon us. We pray for blessing, while all the time the blessing is close beside us, waiting only to be received and appropriated.

After giving them bread, Jesus took a cup from the table and gave it to them, too. "He took the cup, and gave thanks, and gave it to them, saying, Drink ye all of it." A little later that same evening Jesus Himself took a cup from the hands of the Father and drank it to its bitter dregs. Into that cup there had been poured, as it were, all the world's sorrow. Yet full as it was of the very gall and bitterness of human guilt, He pressed it to His lips and drank it, saying, "The cup which the Father hath given Me, shall I not drink it?"

This cup, however, which Jesus handed to His disciples was a cup of blessing. Into it He Himself poured, as it were, the concentration of all heaven's joy and glory. Again, however, we must notice the words, "Drink ye all of it." It is not enough that the cup shall be prepared and then offered to us. Unless we accept the blessing of Christ's atonement, we shall not be helped.

Jesus said that this cup represented the covenant. "This is My blood of the new testament [new covenant], which is poured out for many for the remission of sins." In ancient times covenants were sealed by the blood of animals. The covenant of redemption was sealed by Christ's own blood. Christ's dying was not an accident—it was part of the great purpose of His life, that for which, above all else, He came into the world. We are saved, not merely by being helped over the hard places, not merely by being taught how to live, not only by having a perfect example set before us, but by having our sins remitted. No one can be saved until he is forgiven, and no man's sin is put away except through the blood of Christ.

Jesus announced to the disciples that this was the last time He would eat with them at an earthly table. "I will not drink henceforth of this fruit of the vine, until that day when I drink it new with you in My Father's kingdom." In telling them this, He gave them great comfort in the assurance that He would sit down with them again, by and by, in the heavenly kingdom. The earthly supper was only a symbol; the heavenly would be a glorious reality.

Jesus left the upper room with a song on His lips. "When they had sung a hymn, they went out into the mount of Olives." He knew where He was going and to what. Just before Him was Gethsemane, with its agony. Beyond this experience would come His trial, and next day His death. Yet He went to these terrible experiences with a song of praise.

40

Peter's Denial

Scripture Reading: Matthew 26:31–35; 69–75

As Jesus walked with his disciples from the upper room on the way to Gethsemane, He warned them of the peril into which they were about to enter. "All ye shall be offended because of Me this night." Their trial would be very great. He quoted from an Old Testament prophet a word which described the situation as it was about to be: "I will smite the shepherd, and the sheep of the flock shall be scattered abroad" [see Zech. 13:7]. He knew what was coming. He would be smitten. He was the Shepherd and had kept His sheep in safe protection thus far. Now He was to be smitten and they would be exposed to the power of their enemies and His.

Yet even in the shadows of the gathering night He saw the breaking of the morning. "But after I am risen again, I will go before you into Galilee." He was to be killed, but He would be raised again from the dead. He was not to be finally torn away from them. Death would not be defeat to Him. He was to lie in the grave, but He would come again and lead them once more, away beyond the grave. Hope never failed in the heart of Christ. He was never discouraged.

Peter was always the first of the disciples to speak. The most holy occasion could not awe nor quiet him. He had heard the Master's warning, but he resented it. There was no need to fear for him, whatever others might do. "Peter answered and said unto him, Though all men

170

shall be offended because of thee, yet will I never be offended." His self-confidence was very strong. It was not possible, he said, for him to be untrue to his Lord. It was Peter's rash boldness that made him weak. Jesus repeated His warning, making it personal. "Verily I say unto thee, that this night, before the cock crow, thou shalt deny Me thrice." Still Peter resented the warning. "Peter said unto Him, Though I die with Thee, yet will I not deny Thee." We would say that such solemn words spoken by the Master could never be forgotten, and that it would be actually impossible for a disciple so forewarned to commit such a sin against his Master that same night. Yet the fact that Peter actually denied Him with such positiveness, and so repeatedly, shows how terrible the temptation was and how weak the strongest friend of Christ is in such an hour.

Gethsemane came next with its hour of anguish. Then came the arrest, on the edge of the Garden, when Jesus was betrayed by one of His disciples and led away to the palace of the high priest. It was far on in the night. "Now Peter sat without in the palace." There are several steps leading to Peter's present position in the court that we must recall in order to understand his denial. It began farther back. Earlier in the evening he disregarded, even resented, the warning that he would deny his Lord that night. That was a serious mistake. We would better listen when God speaks to us in this way. Peter was not a hypocrite. He was sincere, he loved Christ, but he was too self-confident. He lacked that distrust of self which should lead the best and holiest to know that only in Christ are they safe. Peter was weak that night because he sought no Divine help.

Next we find him sleeping when he ought to have been watching. That hour in the Garden was given in order that the disciples might be prepared for temptation. Peter did not improve it and was found unready. He failed in love's duty to the Master. Next was his rashness in drawing his sword. This act made him liable to arrest and led him to try to hide his identity and his connection with Christ, lest he might be seized by the officers. Again we find him following Jesus "afar off." This showed timidity and failing faith. His courage was going. Following at a distance is always perilous. It shows a weakening love and a trembling loyalty. It is in itself a partial denial. The only really safe place is close up to Christ.

Another fatal step was taken by Peter when he went in and sat down among the servants in the court. He was in bad company. He had seated himself among Christ's enemies. His object was to conceal his discipleship. He wanted to be thought one of their company when he sat down among mockers and revilers. He hoped thus to escape detection. Thus he acted denial before he spoke it. Had he been altogether loyal and faithful he would have kept out of such company and as near his Master as possible. The only true and safe thing to do when among Christ's enemies is to take one's right place quietly and firmly at the beginning. Starting wrong puts one in a false position, in which it is almost impossible to be faithful afterward. Peter was in a bad place for a disciple when "sitting without in the palace." He was ready to fall. We must guard against taking the steps that lead to denial of Christ.

Peter's denial was not premeditated, as was the betrayal by Judas. He was caught in the entanglement of circumstances. His first denial was partly owing to the suddenness of the assault and his previous false steps. He was not false at heart, but loved his Master even when denying Him. We must remember that when all the other disciples forsook Jesus, Peter was the only one, save John, who followed Him when in the hands of His enemies. True, he followed Him afar off, timidly, yet he followed. We must keep in mind his character also—impulsive, impetuous, always doing rash things, yet withal bold and loyal. These considerations palliate though they do not excuse Peter's denial. After all, this is one of the saddest chapters in the Bible. This favored disciple, at the twitting of a slave girl, denies his Lord, and then goes on denying Him, with increasing earnestness and with oaths and curses.

There are several things that made Peter's denial peculiarly sad and sinful. One was that he had received so many marks of special favor from his Master. He was not a disciple only, but an apostle. He was one of the three who had been chosen as the Master's particular friends. He has been honored, too, by the Lord on several occasions, even that very night in the Garden when he was chosen to be with Him. He had made the boldest confession of Christ and had also loudly professed his allegiance.

Another aggravation of Peter's denial was that he had been so earnestly forewarned. Even that night he had been told that he would deny Christ and had utterly disregarded the Lord's words, declaring that he could not possibly do such a thing. No railroad engineer runs past a red light. Forewarning makes sin worse because it leaves it inexcusable.

Another thing that made the sin worse was that it was in the Lord's hour of sorest need that Peter had denied Him. If it had been on the Transfiguration Mount, or during the triumphal entry, it would not have been one-hundredth part so bad. But it was when Jesus was deserted and in the hands of enemies. Was that a time for the bravest disciple, the most highly favored friend, the noblest confessor, to turn his back upon his Lord? When the shadow falls on your friend, when the tide turns against him, when others have forsaken him, is that the time for you, his long-time bosom companion, the recipient of his favors, to turn craven and leave him alone? How much Peter might have comforted Jesus in His trial! Instead, however, the only words the Master heard from His friend's lips, as he stood amid enemies and revilers, were words of denial, which cut like sword-thrusts into His heart.

A simple lie becomes a lie sworn to, and then a lie sworn to with imprecations and curses. Simple denial is bad enough, but this apostle even went so far as to invoke curses upon himself if he were a disciple, if he ever knew the man, and to utter oaths to emphasize his denial. How this aggravated his sin!

But how could an apostle who had been with Jesus so long, hearing and using only pure speech, curse and swear in this way? The answer is, that it must have been an old habit with Simon the fisherman, which now cropped out in the excitement. This is a way old evil habits have. It is impossible to root them out so that they will never give trouble again. They are like weeds; you may dig them out and think there is not a root left in the ground, and for a while none may be seen; but someday they will reappear. Bad habits of any kind formed in early life always leave weak points in the character. It is very easy to fall again in sudden temptation where one has fallen before. It is always easy to take old paths on which the feet were once accustomed to go. One who drank in his youth, though he becomes a total abstainer and is true for years, is never as safe at that point as one who never acquired the habit. It is so with lying, swearing, obscenity, dishonesty and all vices.

At last Peter came to himself. "Peter remembered the word of Jesus, which said unto him. . . . And he went out, and wept bitterly." The cock crew, and then Jesus turned and looked upon Peter [Luke 22:61], who, glancing up at that moment, caught his Lord's eye. The cock-crow and the look aroused him to a sense of what he had done. An incident, a remembering, a look, were the means by which the sinning apostle was brought to repentance. We can think of that look. Jesus was in the hands of mocking enemies, and while they were scoffing and beating Him, there fell on His ear the voice of His favored disciple, denying Him with curses and imprecations. Surely this was the bitterest drop in the bitter cup of that terrible night. What pain and sorrow there were in the look that fell upon Peter! But, thank God, the look broke his heart and saved him. He went out into the night, but not like Judas, to despair. He went out into the night, but the angel of mercy went with him and pointed him to hope. He wept bitterly, but the memory of that look—grieved, chiding, yet full of love—told him that he had not yet lost his place in the Master's heart. He repented of his sin and was saved to become one of the noblest of our Lord's apostles. So we may thank God for this sad story, because it shows us such a door of hope when we have sinned.

41

Jesus in Gethsemane

Scripture Reading: Matthew 26:36–56

There was something strangely significant even in the name of the place where Jesus endured His midnight agony. Gethsemane means oil press. It was the place where oil was crushed out of the olives. Olive oil was very valuable. It was used chiefly for food and for lighting. The sufferings of Christ have yielded the highest blessings to the world—food for men's souls, and light to shine in darkness.

We cannot begin to understand the anguish of Christ that night. He said, "My soul is exceeding sorrowful, even unto death." We should take off our shoes as we stand by the edge of the scene. Some of the elements of His suffering, however, may be suggested. Before Him lay the betrayal, the arrest, the trial, then death on the cross. By His pre-vision He saw all these cruelties and tortures. Another element of His suffering lay in the falseness of the human hearts about Him. There were the traitorous kiss of Judas, the denial of Peter, the desertion by the other disciples, the rejection and crucifixion by the people He had come to save. All this He saw from Gethsemane. But that which made the essence of the anguish that night was that He died for sin. "The Lord hath laid on Him the iniquity of us all" [Is. 53:6]. What that meant we never can know. He was dying, the just for the unjust. He bore our sin in His own body on the tree. We may not try to fathom the mystery, but the fact we should never allow to be forgotten.

The humanness of Jesus also appears in the Garden. He craved the sympathy of His friends in His suffering. While they could not lessen the anguish nor bear any part of it for Him, the consciousness that they were close by and were thinking of Him, feeling with Him, would make Him stronger to endure. There is a picture which shows two women seated side by side. One is in deep sorrow. Some great grief has fallen upon her heart and crushed it. Her face tells of deepest affliction. The other woman has come in from without. She is sitting beside the sufferer, in silence, holding her hand, while her face expresses deep sympathy. The near presence of one we love when we are in any trial makes us stronger to endure. This suggests one way in which we may do good. True sympathy with those in trouble is often the best service we can render them.

No longer does Jesus Himself need that we should watch with Him, but in the persons of his little ones He is ever saying to us, "Tarry ye here, and watch with Me." While Jesus wanted His friends near to Him, yet they could not share the actual experience of that hour. "He went a little further, and fell on His face, and prayed." We, too, must meet all our deepest experiences alone. Even our most tender human friends we must leave back a little way. In sorrow others may hold our hands and we may lean upon their strong arm for support; but that is all—the sorrow itself we must endure without companionship. No one can take our pain and bear it, or our sorrow and endure it.

The prayer which Jesus offered in the Garden was very intense, "My Father, if it be possible, let this cup pass from me." Without attempting to fathom the mystery of His experience as He prayed this prayer, we get some suggestions from it for ourselves. For one thing, in all our troubles we should seek refuge in prayer. There is no other place to go. "Being in agony He prayed" [see Luke 22:44]. He let His heart cries go out in pleadings and supplications. Whatever our trial may be, it is a comfort to know that we may take it to God in prayer.

Another lesson is that however earnest we may be in our pleading, we must always submit our requests to the will of God. "Nevertheless, not as I will, but as Thou wilt." How can we know what is best? Even Jesus in His anguish would not trust His own judgment, but said, "If it be possible—as Thou wilt." Our prayers should always be modeled on our Master's. Anything but God's will would be a mistake. It may be that the sorrow from which we implore God to save us is bringing blessings we could not afford to miss. So we can only safely leave all to Him.

It was a bitter disappointment to our Savior when, after His first great struggle, He returned to the disciples and found them asleep. He had longed for their sympathy. He felt that if they were waking and watching He would be stronger to endure the anguish. He came back seeking refreshment and renewal of strength from their sympathy. Instead of watching, however, the disciples were sleeping. We may not chide them, however. How is it with ourselves? Jesus is ever setting us to watch with Him and for Him. Does He always find us awake when He comes? Is He never disappointed in us? Do we never lose interest in His service?

He showed the pain of His disappointment in the way He spoke to the disciples. "What, could ye not watch with Me one hour?" It was to Peter He said this especially, because Peter was the one who had boasted but a little while before that whatever others might do he would be loyal. The time they were expected to watch was short—only "one hour." It is very sad that the help Jesus craved that night from His own disciples they failed to give Him. He is calling us to watch with Him. Even in His Divine glory He still craves human affection, trust and faithfulness. We still may grieve His heart by lack of fidelity. We have constant opportunity of watching with Christ. There always are those that need our sympathy, our cheer, our encouragement, our help. The disciples that night lost an opportunity of lightening their Master's load in His darkest hour. Let us not fail Christ in loyalty, in affection, in service.

Even in the midst of His own anguish He thought of His disciples in their danger, and sought their safety. "Watch and pray, that ye enter not into temptation." It is not enough to pray without watching. An army in the enemy's country never rests a moment without its encircling line of pickets, keeping watch at every point against danger, and reporting instantly every indication of a hostile movement. We are living in the enemy's country, and we dare not pass an hour without watching. But watching is not enough, for we are not able to guard ourselves in danger. Hence we need also to pray continually, asking God to protect us. God means for us to keep our wits about us as we pray, as well as call to Him for help. "Watch and pray."

When Jesus prayed the second time, the form of His pleading was modified. "My Father, if this may not pass away, except I drink it, Thy will be done." While the prayer was not answered directly, the Suppliant was growing stronger, and His will was coming more and more into acquiescence with the Father's will. This is often the way our prayers are answered. The things we ask for are not given to us, but we are strengthened so as to accept the pain and endure it.

Very sad was the word which Jesus spoke when He returned to His disciples the last time—"Sleep on now, and take your rest." Their opportunity for watching with Him was now gone. He did not need them anymore, because the struggle was over. Waking now would do no good, and they might as well sleep on. There is a time for each duty, and the time soon passes. The time to show sympathy with a suffering friend or neighbor is while the suffering is being endured. There is no use in our coming next day when the need is past. The time to watch against a danger is when the danger is impending; there is no use to wake up when its work is done. Watching then will not undo the evil. We may almost as well then sleep on and take our rest.

The betrayal of Jesus is graphically described in Matthew's gospel. It was "one of the twelve" who did it. This makes it terribly sad. It was a strange place to see a disciple—one who had lived with Jesus in such close relations, eating with Him, enjoying all the confidences of His friendship—acting now as guide to those who came to arrest his Master. The kiss, which was the honored token of affection and the sacred seal of friendship, became in this case the token of disloyalty and the sign of treason. The last word Jesus spoke to Judas shows love, ready even then to accept the traitorous disciple. "Friend, wherefore art thou come?"*

There was a bewildered attempt by the disciples to defend their Lord against those who had laid hands upon Him. But they did not know what they were doing. They were loyal and devoted, but powerless in their fright and confusion. Quickly Jesus bade them put up their swords. He was not dependent on human force. He could by a word have had legions of angels sent to His defense. But that was not God's way. His hour had come.

"Then all the disciples forsook Him, and fled." Shall we call them cowards and chide them with abandoning their Lord? Yes, but their Lord was infinitely patient with them.

---

*Other translations including the NIV and NASB render Christ's address to Judas in v. 50 as "Friend, do what you came for." *Ed.*

42

The Trial of Jesus

Scripture Reading: Matthew 26:57–68

We speak of the trial of Jesus, but really it was not a trial. There was no intention of giving Him a fair and just hearing. The Sanhedrin had firmly made up its mind to condemn Jesus, and they went through the form of a trial, not to discover the truth about Him, but to endeavor to get some pretext for what they had determined to do. When we think who Jesus was, looking at Him in the light of our belief in Him as the Son of God, the scenes of His trial reveal His enemies in strange character indeed. Think of men arresting the Son of God, binding His hands, and putting Him on trial in their courts!

Jesus was arrested in the Garden of Gethsemane, just after the close of His anguish there. The effect of His arrest on the disciples was to cause them to scatter and leave Him. While they all fled, John seems to have returned very soon, and we think of him as following close behind his Master on the way to the palace of the high priest. Peter also followed, but "afar off." This was the beginning of his denial.

The rulers had no difficulty in getting men to testify against Jesus. There always are men who can be bribed to do anything. "The chief priests and elders and the council sought false witness against Jesus," that they might put Him to death. Their intention was not to bring out the truth about Him, but to get such testimony as would seem to justify

179

their determination to kill Him. It was false witness they sought—no other kind of witness against Him could be found, for there was none. In all the land there was not a man, woman or child who could truthfully say a word against Jesus. His was the one life in all the world's history in which there was no flaw, no blemish. No wonder the question was asked by Pilate, when the Jews clamored for the condemnation of Jesus, "Why, what evil hath He done?" The rulers could have found thousands of witnesses to tell of the good things He had done, but they could not find even one to testify of any evil against Him. Hence they deliberately sought false witnesses.

But even this testimony was not of any use, for one witness swept away what another had said. They found it not, "though many false witnesses came." There are many in these days, too, who are willing and eager to witness against the Bible and against Christianity, but there is no agreement among them. One man, for example, goes about with his hammer, breaking off bits of rock and studying ancient fossils, saying that his deductions demolish the statements of the Bible. But another man, also hostile to Christianity, follows, with his little hammer, and reports other deductions which sweep away the theories and conclusions of the first. So it is with all opposition to Christianity. One witness antagonizes another. Amid enmities and assaults, the New Testament stands really unassailable, an impregnable rock, and Christ Himself abides, the same yesterday, and today, yea, and forever.

At length, however, two men were found who seemed to agree in their testimony, saying the same thing. Probably they had been drilled and taught just what to say. "At the last came two false witnesses, and said. . . . This man said, I am able to destroy the temple of God, and to build it in three days." Really Jesus never said this. What He did say was, "Destroy this temple, and in three days I will raise it up," referring to the temple of His body. The Jews taught that any word spoken against the temple was blasphemy. Jesus had not said, however, that He would destroy the temple, but that if they destroyed it—meaning His body— He would restore it, foretelling His own resurrection. The witnesses perverted His words, however, so as to give the impression that Jesus had actually spoken blasphemy against the temple. There always are those who insist upon garbling and misrepresenting what Jesus said in order to bolster up their own peculiar opinions.

Jesus remained silent before all that the false witnesses said. "Jesus held His peace." There was no reason why He should speak, for there were no charges to answer. His calmness angered the high priest, and he stood up and fiercely demanded, "Answerest Thou nothing? what is it which these witness against Thee?" Still He answered nothing. There is a time to keep silence. When others say false or bitter things of us or to us, it is usually better not to answer again. Answering does no good when enemies are in such mood. It only irritates them the more—it does not convince them or soften their hearts.

There is something very majestic in our Lord's silence at this time. There He stood, pale and suffering, yet meek, patient, undisturbed, showing no bitterness, no resentment, no anxiety concerning the outcome of His trial. "Who, when He was reviled, reviled not again; when He suffered, He threatened not; but committed Himself to Him that judgeth righteously" [1 Pet. 2:23]. The lesson is for us, and we should not fail to get it—when we are wronged or hurt, when others say false things of us or bitter things to us, we should keep love in our hearts, and say no unloving word and cherish no unloving thought, committing all the wrong, the injustice into the hands of our Father, who judgeth righteously.

But as there is a time to keep silence, there is also a time to speak. Despairing of getting any real ground of charge from the false witnesses, the high priest determined to make Jesus convict Himself. He demanded of Him whether He were indeed the Christ. "I adjure Thee by the living God, that Thou tell us whether Thou be the Christ, the Son of God." Instantly the silence was broken. Not to have spoken now would have been to deny His own Messiahship. To answer would cost Him His life, but He paused not a moment to think of the cost. There come times in everyone's experience when silence would be disloyalty to Christ. We should have courage then to speak the truth regardless of consequences.

Not only did Jesus answer the high priest's question, but He went farther and gave him and his fellow-judges a glimpse of the glory of His power. "Henceforth ye shall see the Son of man sitting on the right hand of Power, and coming in the clouds of heaven." Recall this scene before the council—the pale, meek One, standing there as a prisoner, bound, mocked, spit upon, smitten. Then go forward and think of the other scene which His own words bring up, when this same Holy One shall sit on the throne of His glory, wearing the crown of universal power, and when the priests, scribes and elders of that ancient court shall stand before Him, and recognize Him as the very prisoner on whom they looked with such contempt that night of His trial. Who can conceive of the shame, the remorse, the anguish, of that moment? The rulers supposed that Jesus was on trial before them; really they were on trial before Him.

There are many who are now, treating Christ with contempt, rejecting His mercy, despising His love, refusing to believe His words. There are those who flippantly deny the deity of Christ and laugh at the claims made by His followers for Him. These, too, will be compelled to see Him when He comes in glory to judge the earth. "Every eye shall see Him, and they also which pierced Him" [Rev. 1:17]. How are we treating Jesus Christ? Are we looking on Him in love, believing on Him as our personal Savior, following Him as our Master, cleaving to Him as our Friend; or are we spurning Him from our doors, insulting Him, mocking Him? We must read ourselves and our own relation to Christ into the scene before us.

The last item in the passage is the formal vote of the Sanhedrin on the question of Christ's guilt. When Jesus had answered, the high priest rent his garments, saying, "He hath spoken blasphemy: what further need have we of witnesses? behold, now ye have heard his blasphemy. What think ye?" Instantly came the answer, "He is guilty [or worthy] of death." Thus the vote of the court condemned Jesus as a blasphemer, condemned Him to death because He claimed to be the Messiah, the Son of God. This was the signal for the beginning of mocking and insult. They spit in His face and buffeted Him. They blindfolded Him and smote Him and bade Him prophesy who it was that struck Him.

43

The Crucifixion

Scripture Reading: Matthew 27:33–50

The story of the crucifixion has the most sacred and tender interest for everyone who loves Jesus Christ. It is not merely an account of the tragic death of a good man—He who was crucified was the world's Redeemer, our Redeemer, suffering for us. Some of the old preachers used to say that our sins drove the nails in the hands and feet of Jesus. He died for us. Paul speaks also of being crucified with Christ [see Gal. 2:20]. He means that Christ's death was instead of his death. No other death in all history means to the world what the dying of Jesus means.

They led Jesus out to Golgotha. There He was met by those who offered Him "vinegar to drink mingled with gall." It is supposed that the act was one of kindness, that the mixture was intended to stupefy Him so as to deaden in some measure the awful suffering of crucifixion. But Jesus refused the drink. He would not have His senses dulled as He entered upon His great work of death for the world, nor would He have His sufferings as Redeemer lessened in any degree.

The garments of men who were crucified were by custom the perquisites of the soldiers in charge of the crucifixion. They "parted His garments, casting lots." We love to think of the garments which Jesus had worn. Perhaps they had been made by His mother's hands or else by the hands of some of the other women who followed Him and ministered unto Him of their substance. They were the garments the sick woman and other sufferers had touched with reverent faith, receiving instant healing. What desecration it seems when these heartless Roman soldiers take these garments and divide them among themselves! Then what sacrilege it is when the soldiers throw dice and gamble for His seamless robe under the very cross where the Savior is dying!

"They sat and watched Him there." Roman soldiers kept guard, but they were not the only watchers. There was the careless, heartless watch of the soldiers. They knew nothing about Jesus. They saw three poor Jews on three crosses, and had no conception of the character of Him who hung on the middle cross. It is possible yet and always to look at Christ on the cross and see nothing more than these soldiers saw. We all need to pray to have our eyes opened when we look at Christ crucified, that we may see in the lowly sufferer the Son of God, bearing the sin of the world.

There were also jealous watchers, the enemies of Jesus, so full of hatred that they even hurled scoffs at Him who hung in silence upon that central cross. Then there were loving watchers—the women and John, Christ's friends, with hearts broken as they looked at their Lord dying in shame and anguish. Then there were wondering watchers— angels, who hovered unseen above the cross and looked in amazement upon the suffering Son of God, eagerly desiring to know what this mystery meant.

All the words that Jesus spoke on the cross were full of meaning. One, the very first, was a prayer for His murderers, "Father, forgive them; for they know not what they do" [Luke 23:34]. The words seem to have come from His lips just as the nails were being driven through His hands and feet. The torture was excruciating, but there was no cry of pain, no execration of those who were causing Him such bitter anguish; only an intercession. Dora Greenwell in one of her poems illustrates the story in a striking way. There was a youth who had blotted from his soul every grace of goodness, who one day, in defiance of God, flung up into the air a dagger meant for God's own heart. Out of the sky came a hand that caught the dagger's hilt, and presently there fell from the wound five drops of Christ's dear blood, freely spilt for human guilt. Then a little leaf came floating through the air and fell at the youth's feet. On the leaf was written a prayer for mercy. Overwhelmed by this Divine answer to his terrible defiance, the youth sank upon his knees, looked up to heaven and cried:

> Have mercy, mercy, Lord, on me
> For His dear sake, who on a tree
>   Shed forth those drops and died.

This legend is a beautiful parable of the meaning of the death of Christ. The answer to the world's daring defiance of God was the hands of Christ stretched out to be pierced with nails for the world's redemption.

It was the custom to fasten on the cross a board bearing the name and the crimes of the sufferer. "They set up over His head his accusation written, THIS IS JESUS THE KING OF THE JEWS." It was only in mockery that Pilate wrote this superscription. He did it to vex the Jews. Yet never were truer words written. Jesus was indeed the King of the Jews. They had looked forward to the coming of their Messiah with expectations of great blessings from Him. "He came unto His own, and His own received Him not" [John 1:11]. This was the way they were treating their King. But He is our King, too. The crown He wore that day was a crown of thorns. Thorns were part of the curse of sin, and the crown of Jesus was woven of sin's curse. We have the promise of crowns of glory in heaven, because on Christ's brow rested that day the crown of shame.

"He saved others; Himself He cannot save." Unwittingly in their mockery they spoke a deep truth. Jesus had saved others, and even now He was saving others in the most wonderful way of all—by dying for them. He could have saved Himself, however, from the cross if He had desired. His offering was voluntary. He said, "I lay down my life. . . . No man taketh it away from Me" [John 10:15–18]. He said He could have summoned twelve legions of angels to deliver Him. He could have saved Himself, but then He would not have saved others. The soldier cannot save himself and save his country. Jesus could not save Himself and redeem the world. So He gave His own life a willing sacrifice to redeem lost men.

It was a strange scene that came on at noonday. "From the sixth hour there was darkness over all the land unto the ninth hour." A yet deeper darkness hung around the Redeemer's soul those hours. It was so dark that He even thought Himself forsaken of God.

We never can understand the mystery of it, and we can know only that He wrapped the gloom of death about Himself that we might be clothed in garments of light. He died in darkness that when we walk in the valley of the shadow of death, the light of glory may shine about us. His head wore a matted crown of thorns, that under our heads may be the pillow of peace. He drank the cup of woe that we may drink the cup of blessing.

Elizabeth Barrett Browning, in one of her poems, has pictured with rare beauty the effect of Christ's death upon two seraphim who lingered a little behind the hosts of heaven who had gathered that day around the cross. One of them, as he thinks of the meaning of the wonderful sacrifice, is troubled by the thought that men will now have more reason to love God than even the angels have. The other remonstrates, saying, "Do we love not?" "Yes, but not as man shall," he answered:

> Oh! not with this blood on us—and this face,
> Still, haply, pale with sorrow that it bore
> In our behalf, and tender evermore
> With nature all our own, upon us gazing—
> Nor yet with these forgiving hands upraising
> Their reproachful wounds, alone to bless!
> Alas, Creator! shall we love Thee less
> Than mortals shall?

"Jesus when he had cried again with a loud voice, yielded up the ghost." His loud cry, "It is finished," which John records [19:30], was a shout of victory. His work was completed. The atonement was made. Then followed the word, given by Luke, "Father, into Thy hands I commend My spirit" [23:46]. The shadows were lifted. There was no longer any feeling of forsakenness. Again we hear the sweet name, "Father," showing that the joy had been restored. We see also in this word that death was to Jesus—only the breathing out of His spirit into His Father's hands. We cannot see into the life beyond, but revelation assures us of the Divine presence close beside us. Dying is but fleeing from the body into the arms of the Father. All this is ours because Jesus tasted death for us. Because He had the darkness, we have the light.

44

The Resurrection

Scripture Reading: Matthew 28:1–20

We think of death ordinarily as the end of a man's life. He can do no more work in this world. Only his influence remains. But it was not the end of the life of Jesus Christ. He came again from the grave after a brief rest and took up once more His work of redemption.

The women watched beside the grave after the burial of the body there until they were compelled to hasten into the city before the gates would be shut upon them. Meanwhile they were in deep grief. The Sabbath was a sad and dark day for them. They were eager to get back to the grave to honor their Lord's dead body. So at the very dawn, after the Sabbath, as soon as the gates would be opened, they left their home and hastened away to His grave, carrying spices and ointments to anoint His dead body.

No one saw the resurrection. We are told something, however, of what took place. "There was a great earthquake; for the angel of the Lord descended from heaven, and came and rolled back the stone, and sat upon it." The rulers thought they had the sepulcher well-secured. The stone had been sealed with Pilate's seal, so that to meddle with it would be a high crime. Besides, they had procured a guard of Roman soldiers to watch by the grave. They seem to have expected thus to keep Jesus from rising. When they asked for the guard, they gave this as the reason—"After three days I rise again" [27:63]. They pretended to suspect that the disciples would try to carry away the body by night, to give the impression that their Master has risen. But we see how useless were all their precautions. There was no power in the universe that could keep the body of Jesus in that rock-prison.

The effect of the resurrection and its attendant circumstances upon the Roman soldiers who kept watch was startling. The angel's "countenance was like lightning, and his raiment white as snow: and for fear of him the keepers did shake, and became as dead men." The soldiers were hardened to all sorts of danger. They never recoiled in the presence of any enemy. But when an angel of God stood before them, with shining face and shining garments, they were in great terror.

But the angel who caused such dread in the Roman soldiers spoke with all gentleness to the women who stood before the grave in great sorrow. "The angel answered and said unto the women, Fear not ye; for I know that ye seek Jesus, which was crucified. He is not here; for He is risen, even as He said." This was the first announcement of the Resurrection. It was made by an angel to the Lord's women friends. They had ample proofs of the fact thereafter.

No event in all history is more incontestably sure than that Jesus rose again from the dead. Nor can the importance of the fact be overestimated. Everything depends upon Christ's Resurrection. All the hopes of redemption waited outside that sealed sepulcher. Jesus had said that He would rise; His Messiahship therefore depended from confirmation on His rising. He had made promises to His disciples that He would come again from death and live forever. Indeed, His kingdom depended altogether upon His rising. If He had remained under the power of death, no soul that trusted in Him could have been saved. For a Savior vanquished and held as a prisoner could not be a deliverer of others. A Savior locked in a grave could not appear before God to intercede for men, could not walk with His people in their trials and sorrows, could not lead the dying safely through the valley which He had not Himself been able to pass through victoriously, could not bring believers from death's prison from which He had not Himself been able to come.

These are hints of what depended upon Christ's rising from the dead. Thus we see something of the tremendous importance of the fact which was announced by the angel to the women that early morning. "He is not here; for He is risen." We have a living Christ, therefore, for our Savior. He was victorious over all enemies then, over death, the last enemy. Therefore, He is able to deliver us from all our enemies and from death's power at the last. He stands before God for us, and also walks with us on the earth in all our experiences, a living Friend, to love, to help, to comfort, to deliver, to keep, all who have committed themselves to Him in trusting faith.

The angel sent the women on an errand to the disciples to bear to them the glorious news. "Go quickly, and tell His disciples." They obeyed promptly and with joy. "They departed quickly." On their way Jesus Himself appeared to them. "Jesus met them, saying, All hail." Notice that it was as they were hastening in the path of obedience that they met their Lord. It is always and only in the way of duty that we ever meet Christ, and find blessing and joy. Had the women loitered by the grave instead of hastening away as they were bidden, Jesus would not have appeared to them. It is only in the way of obedience, in the service of love, that Jesus meets us. There are Christian mourners who never go away from the grave where they have buried their loved ones. They hear the words of hope which the gospel brings, but sit still in their grief, and no comfort reaches their sad hearts. Jesus does not meet them. If they would rise and hasten on errands of love to the living, the Divine comfort would come to them. They would meet Jesus Himself in the way, and receive His "All hail!" Grief is often selfish. It forgets the living in its sorrow for the dead. To such mourners true comfort never comes. Rise up and go on errands of service, and Jesus will meet you.

The women worshiped their Master, rejoicing that they had Him back again from the grave. He then Himself sent them on an errand to the disciples. "Go tell My brethren that they go into Galilee, and there shall they see Me." Whenever Jesus makes an appointment with His friends, He will keep it, He will be present, and will have blessings to bestow upon those who meet Him there. Suppose that some of our Lord's disciples had stayed away from the appointed meeting in Galilee, not quite believing His promise, or having other things to do instead, what would they have missed? Or they might have said, "It is a long distance to the place"; or, "The mountain is steep, and I do not like to climb it"; or, "I fear it will rain or be stormy"; or, "Perhaps He will not be there at all—I cannot understand how He can indeed be risen." For any of these reasons or for any other reason some might have been absent that wonderful day. But they would then have missed the glorious sight of the risen Jesus, and would not have received His commission and promise. To the end of their lives they would have regretted that they had not kept their Lord's appointment that day.

Jesus makes appointments with us to meet us at times of prayer in church services, at the holy communion, at some holy appointed place. Sometimes we do not think these appointments very important and are easily influenced to omit them. We never can know what we lose by these failures or neglects. Jesus always comes where He asks us to meet Him, and gives blessings there to those who have been faithful in gathering to wait for Him. We do not know what we may miss by staying away from any appointment with our Master.

The risen Lord's promise to His disciples when He sent them forth is one of great comfort. "Lo, I am with you always, even unto the end of the world." If Jesus had given His commission without adding His promise, His disciples might well have shrunk from going forth to the work to which He assigned them. But having His promise, they could not hesitate.

This assurance was not for the first disciples only; He says to us also, "I am with you always." In what sense is Christ with us always? It is not merely as our departed human friends are with us—in the sweet memories of their lives. It is a real and personal presence. He is present with us as He was with Mary and Martha when He came to them that day after their brother had died. He is present with each one of us, not only on the bright days but on the dark days. Let us believe in the actual presence of Christ with us, and then let us act as if we believed that He is with us. This is the secret of Christian power and Christian peace.

Volume Two

Studies in the Synoptic Gospels

Preface to This Volume

The readings in this volume are from the Synoptic Gospels, following the story of the Life of Christ. In the space of a single volume only a small number of selections could be given.

1

The Birth of John the Baptist Foretold

Scripture Reading: Luke 1:5–23

There was a wonderful preparation of the world for Christ before He came. There was a Jewish expectation of the Messiah. This hope had been diffused throughout the nations by the wide dispersion of the Jewish people, who carried their religion with them and had synagogues in every city, where also their holy books were read. It is wonderful to think what the world owes to the influence of the Jewish people. Amid the hills of Palestine were written a few little books or tracts whose teachings, like leaven, permeated the great nations of Asia and Europe in the time before Christ was born and prepared the world to receive Him. Rome also had done much to prepare the world for Christianity. It had brought all lands under one government. It had built roads everywhere, which became highways for the messengers of Christ. The Greek language was spoken everywhere, thus giving a medium for the carrying of the gospel to all the nations. These and other conditions were favorable to the dissemination of Christianity. This preparation was not accidental, a mere coincidence of events. There is evidence that the preparation was divine. The hand of God was in it.

We have a picture here of the godly home. Yet the time was not propitious to pity. It is not hard to live a beautiful life amid kindly and favoring circumstances. If a child has a sweet home with only gentle influences about it—an atmosphere of love and prayer—it is not strange that the child's life grows up into beauty. On the other hand, if the home is cold and unkindly, without love and prayer and godliness, it seems to us almost a miracle if a child grows up in it loving God and with a true and beautiful character. The "days of Herod" were not days when it was easy to be godly. The times were ungodly and the prevailing spirit was unrighteous. The holy lives which we find here in this story are like lamps shining in the darkness. Amid the almost universal corruption of the priesthood, and the hypocrisy of the Pharisees, this old priest and his wife lived in piety and godly simplicity. The lesson is that we may be good and may live saintly lives, though all about us is evil. We need not be like those among whom we live. No matter how corrupt the times or how unholy the influences, we ought always to strive to be holy and pure.

It is important to know the name and the character of the woman who helps to make the home. "Her name was Elisabeth." A great many Elisabeths will study this lesson. It is pleasant even by a name to be reminded continually of some other one who has lived a noble and beautiful life in the past. No thoughtful Mary can be altogether forgetful of the Marys of the New Testament, especially the Mary who was the mother of our Lord, "blessed among women," and the other Mary whom Jesus loved so tenderly, who sat at His feet as a learner and then anointed His feet with her ointment. There is ever an aroma of sacredness about this name. So the Elisabeths may catch an inspiration from the Elisabeth of this story. We are not told much about her. We know, however, that she was a good woman, one who walked in God's commandments in times when such godliness was rare.

In these days we are hearing a great deal about the "new woman." Some people think that woman heretofore has been living in a kind of darkness, not making much of herself, not realizing the possibilities of her life and her position. She has not understood herself and her power, and has been content to stay in obscurity when she might have stood forth in splendor. Now, however, she has come to a time when she may make more of her life in many ways. No doubt some phases of the thought of the "new woman" are excellent. The last quarter century has been a wonderful era in woman's history. In all ways women have moved forward with tremendous strides. Our colleges have given women opportunities for acquiring an education they could not get before. In church life and work women have advanced to marvelous power and usefulness. In associated work in benevolence women have shown great energy and wisdom. All this is very beautiful. But the new woman is not in all things so lovely as this. There are some things in her of which the better women do not approve. She discards some of the most gentle refinements of the truest type of womanhood. "She tramples on the traditions of the mother who kissed her in the cradle and made a woman of her," says Mrs. Ballington Booth. "Such a woman could never be Christlike, because she is not tender enough. Her mind is too strong to bow down to God." Let the new woman be as beautiful as she can make herself with the help of Christ, but let her be always a woman. A woman needs God to make her life in the way it should be, to give her the beauty and the glory which is her true heritage. A woman owes everything to Christ, who has redeemed her, and she needs Christ as her Teacher, her Master, her Friend, that she may reach the only worthy possibilities of womanhood.

They were truly mated, this goodly pair. "They were both righteous before God, walking in all the commandments and ordinances of the Lord blameless." It is a beautiful thing when both husband and wife are godly. Then they can bow together in prayer and together read God's Word, and together go to the church and sit together at the Lord's table. Too often only one of the wedded pair is a Christian. Sometimes it is the husband, and the wife does not enter into his religious life. Far more often, however, it is the wife only that loves Christ, while her husband leaves her to walk alone in all her inner spiritual life. In either case the marriage lacks one of its holiest and most sacred bonds. The union of wedded life may yield much joy and very sweet happiness where the two enter together into the holy of holies of prayer. But the union means far more when they are one in trusting God and in communing with Him in all the great hours of life. When both are Christians and walk side by side in all obedience, service, and worship, praying together, heaven's sweetest benediction rests over the home.

It is a beautiful thing, also, that we read of this good old couple, that they were "righteous before God." Some people appear to men to be righteous who before God have no such record. Our real character is what our hearts are. So we ought not to be satisfied with doing well the things that men can see us do; we ought to work and live ever for

God's eye. Sometimes we say it is no matter how we do certain things, because no one will see them; but God will see them, and we should never do careless, faulty work for His eye.

The word "commandments" suggests that the holiness of these people was of a very practical kind. Some people's religion is chiefly emotional and sentimental. They talk about loving God, but they pay little heed to the commandments. They may worship together in formal ways, but they are not careful to do the things that are right, that please God. There are too many whose religion is of this kind—all devout feelings, the observance of forms of worship, but little practical religious living. They go from fervent services to practice selfishness, greed, dishonesties, and in-humanities. God is pleased with ardent devotion, but he wants us to prove our religion by obedience, by doing the things He gives us to do, by fidelity in all duty.

Another beautiful word in the description of these good people is the word "blameless." Of course, this does not mean sinless, absolutely fault-less, but only that their lives were so beautiful, so sincere, and faithful that there was nothing in them to blame or rebuke. It is in this way that God wants all His children to live. He wants them to be unrebukable. "That we should be holy and without blame before Him in love." [Eph. 1:4]. "That ye may be blameless in the day of our Lord" [1 Cor. 1:8]. "That ye may be blameless and harmless, the sons of God, without re-buke" [Phil. 2:15]. "I pray God your whole spirit and soul and body be preserved blameless unto the coming of our Lord Jesus Christ" [1 Thess. 5:23]. These are a few of the words of Holy Scripture which indicate the kind of life we are expected as Christians to live in this world.

There was one thing lacking in this godly home. "They had no child." They were not young. They had been married many years, but no child had come to gladden them. Children are a great blessing in a family. They give much joy to their parents. They brighten the home into which they come. They cost much care and toil; but no true par-ent ever counts such cost, for love rejoices in making sacrifices. And the hearts of parents are made glad by the presence of a little child in their home.

The old priest was in his place in the temple that day, and his par-ticular duty was to burn incense on the golden altar. Incense was a symbol of prayer. While the priest was offering it on the altar the people were standing without, engaged in prayer. The prayers arose to God purified and sweetened by the holy offering. It is a beautiful thought that prayers rise up to God as perfume from earth's altars, that true prayer is fragrance in heaven. Readers of Longfellow will remember his poem founded on the old Talmudic legend of Sandalphon. The legend is that the angel of prayer stands at the gate of heaven listening to the sounds that ascend from earth—

> From the spirits of earth that adore,
> From the souls that entreat and implore
>   In the fervor and passion of prayer;
> From the hearts that are broken with losses,
> And weary from dragging the crosses
>   Too heavy for mortals to bear.
>
> And he gathers the prayers as he stands
> And they change into flowers in his hands—
>   Into garlands of purple and red;
> And beneath the great arch of the portal,
> Through the streets of the City Immortal,
>   Is wafted the fragrance they shed.

This old legend does not overstate the acceptableness of prayer as it goes up to God. This symbol of incense teaches the same thing. There is another thing that we should remember, however, in this connection. The burnt offering was offered at the same time that the incense was burning, and the incense itself was kindled by fire brought from the altar of burnt offering. Prayer needs the efficacy of Christ's atonement to make it acceptable. We can pray only in Christ's name and in dependence on His sacrifice.

The vision of the angel that Zacharias saw awed him. We do not know in what form the angel appeared. He was a messenger from God, however, and had come to announce to the priest that he was to have the high honor of being the father of the forerunner of the Messiah.

Sometimes God seems to wait a long time before He gives us what we ask for. One reason is to teach us faith and patience. Another reason is because He has a time for giving us blessing. John could not be born until the date fixed in God's plan, for he was to be the forerunner of the Messiah. We always see in the end that God's time for blessing us is the right time. We may be sure that when God puts it into our heart to pray for something He means to give us that thing in due time.

> The very prayer to thee was given,
> Itself a messenger from heaven.

The angel told Zacharias that now a son was about to be born to him, and he should have joy and gladness. It makes great joy in any true home when a child is born. In this case the joy was unusual, since the birth of John was the token of the speedy coming of the long-promised Messiah. It was like the rising of the morning star which heralds the approach of the day. Not only would the parents rejoice, but many would mingle in the rejoicing. Every child should seek to be a joy to parents, not only in its infancy, but always. Children hold in their hands the happiness of their parents. It is in their power, too, to give them great grief and sorrow. Many children do indeed break the hearts of their parents. Many do it by their bad conduct, their wrong actions. Then there are many children who make great joy for their parents. They do it by their gratitude and love, and by lives that are full of beauty and honor, of which their parents cannot be anything but proud. All children should seek to live in this way. Then it should be the aim, too, to live so that others shall have occasion to rejoice over their birth, because they are blessings in the world.

The angel said further that John should be great in the sight of the Lord. There are people who are great in their own eyes or in the eyes of their friends, who in God's sight are very small. It is well to have people's approval of us and our work, but it is incalculably better to have God's approval. We should strive always to be and to do what Christ would have us to be and to do. It is well to ask ourselves quite often what God thinks of us. We like to please men; let us seek to please God.

Zacharias asked for a sign to prove to him that this astonishing thing should be fulfilled. His request was granted, and the sign given to him was that he should be dumb until the child was born. God wants us to believe His promises without a shadow of doubt, no matter how strange they may be. We should trust God implicitly. Unquestioning faith is not presumptuous; it honors God and brings fullest blessing.

2

The Birth of John the Baptist

Scripture Reading: Luke 1:57–80

It is a stupendous moment when a great man is born. The birth of
few men through the centuries has meant more to the world than
John the Baptist's. Jesus said of him that of all born of woman there
was none greater [see Luke 7:28]. The beloved disciple thus describes
his coming into the world: "There was a man sent from God, whose
name was John" [John 1:6]. It was a great moment in history when
this man was born.

The neighbors of Elisabeth and her kin folk came and rejoiced with
her. The child was circumcised the eighth day, according to the law of
the Jews. At that time his name was given to him. The friends who were
present would have named him Zacharias, after his father. His mother
objected, however, saying that he should be called John. The friends
insisted that this was not a family name and that he ought to be named
after his father. They appealed to Zacharias to decide the matter. Then
he asked for a writing slate and wrote, "His name is John." Then his
speechless tongue was loosed and he spoke in praise to God.

The people were amazed at what had happened. Surely this was no
ordinary child, they said. He would be a great man. "What manner of
child shall this be!" they asked. They saw that the hand of the Lord was
with him. Zacharias, too, the father, was filled with the Holy Spirit, and
spoke under the Spirit's power the words of the great hymn we are now

to study. In this song he breathed the holy thoughts which had been pent up in his heart during his months of silence. This hymn is called the Benedictus.

The hymn begins with an ascription of praise to God: "Blessed be the Lord, the God of Israel." Then it gives the reason for praise: "He hath visited . . . His people." The thought of God paying visits to people in this world is a very beautiful one. There are pleasant stories or traditions of Queen Victoria's visits to peasants' homes in her summer jaunts. But the Bible tells us of stranger things—visits of God Himself to lowly homes on earth. He visited our first parents in the garden of Eden. He visited Abraham and was entertained by him. He visited Jacob at Bethel and at Penuel. He visited Moses in Horeb and at the burning bush. He visited Joshua by the walls of Jericho. But the most wonderful visit that the Lord ever made to this earth was when Christ came and stayed here more than thirty years.

We must not think, however, that God never comes anymore to visit people. Every time any of His children are in trouble He comes to help them. They do not see Him, and often do not even know that He has come, for He comes softly and invisibly. When we are in danger, He comes to deliver us. He always comes on gracious and loving errands, and always brings blessing with Him. It is said here that He wrought redemption for His people. They had been long in low estate, and now He was about to visit them with deliverance. The birth of John was the harbinger of all the blessings of redemption which Jesus Christ was to bring.

So He visits us with marvelous good, though too often we refuse to receive Him or the gracious things He brings to our doors. A Scotch minister heard one day that a poor woman, one of his parishioners, was in great trouble. She could not pay her rent, and the landlord was about to seize her goods. The good pastor hurried away with money to relieve her wants. He knocked at her door, but there was no answer. He went around the little house and knocked at every door, but there was no response from within. Next day he met the woman and told her of his visit. "Why, was it you that knocked so long?" she asked, with a look of grieved shame on her face; "I thought it was the officer come to take my goods, and I had all the doors and windows barred." So God comes to visit us and bring us relief and blessing, and often we refuse to let Him in. When God visits us, it is always to do us good. We rob ourselves when we shut Him out.

The Bible from first to last is a book of redemption. The Old Testament is a long story of divine calls preparatory to the gospel which came at length through Jesus Christ. No sooner were our first parents driven out of Eden than the promise of redemption was made to them. Then all along the centuries the promise was repeated, each time becoming a little clearer and fuller. In Noah's family it was fixed in Shem's line. Later it fell in Abraham's posterity, and Isaac became the child of promise. Of Isaac's sons Jacob was the one in whom the covenant blessing inhered. In Jacob's family of twelve Judah's descendants were pointed out as the Messianic tribe. Later still in Judah the seed of David was designated as that of which the Christ should come. The twenty-second psalm, the fifty-third chapter of Isaiah, and many other passages, foretell the sufferings of the Messiah. Other prophecies delineate His character and life and foretell the victories. Thus on down to Malachi the prophets all point forward to the coming of the Christ and tell of the blessings He is to bring.

We have the summing up of the work of redemption expressed in a few great phrases. One is, salvation from our enemies. The sweetest child, in the most loving home, has enemies who are secretly plotting its destruction. There are people, too, who are enemies of our souls, though meaning us no bodily harm. There are enemies, also, that hide in our hearts—evil thoughts, feelings, tempers, dispositions, passions, and desires. We all have our enemies who hate us and seek our ruin. We need a deliverer, one who will take care of us, shelter us from the assaults of our foes, and fight our battles for us. In any moment of danger we may flee to Him for refuge. Once, when Gustavus Adolphus was marching at the head of his army, a bird was seen in the air, chased by a hawk. The little thing flew lower and lower, the hawk gaining meanwhile, and at last, as the soldiers watched it, it darted down and took refuge in the commander's bosom. So when we are pursued by any enemy we should always fly into Christ's bosom.

We are set free by Christ's redemption, and are then to serve Him, without fear, in holiness and righteousness. Salvation is not merely deliverance from enemies. That is one side of it. We are to serve Christ. He is our Lord and Master as well as our Savior. True Christian life is obedience, service. The service is to be "without fear." We are not slaves. Our Savior is not a hard, stern master. He loves us with infinite love, and we are to serve Him in love; not driven by fear, but impelled by affection. It is to be "in holiness and righteousness." We must be holy, keeping our hearts pure, our hands clean, our lives unspotted from the world. Then we are to serve Him "all the days of our life." It is not an enlistment for a time merely, but forever, when we enter into covenant with Christ.

The greatest thing we who have been redeemed can do is to tell others, who are not saved, what God has done for us—"to give knowledge of salvation unto His people by the remission of their sins." Forgiveness of sins is the heart of salvation. It is sin that has made all the trouble in this world. It is sin that separates between us and God. Had it not been for sin, there would not have been any need for Christ to die. And we never can be saved until our sins are remitted. Some people talk about salvation as if they needed only to stop their bad habits and become respectable. But there is no use to do this while our sins still remain unforgiven. The dwellers on the slopes of Vesuvius make their gardens and build their cottages, set up their homes and try to be happy, forgetting that the fires are only sleeping in the great mountain's heart, and any hour may awake and sweep away all that they have built and gathered. That is a picture of the false peace and delusive hope of those who talk about salvation while their sins are not forgiven. They are building over slumbering fires that will surely someday burst out. Let us not rest until we get our sins forever out of the way; and there is no way of doing this but by laying them all on Jesus the Lamb of God. If we do this in reality, by simple faith in Him, they will never trouble us again.

Everywhere in the Bible, in every picture of God, mercy shines. Mercy is the divine quality that gives hope to sinful souls. We could never find salvation in the justice of God alone, nor in His holiness, nor in His power. All hope and all grace is "because of the tender mercy of our God." There is a story of a man who dreams that he is out in an open field, in a fierce, driving storm. He is wildly seeking a refuge. He sees one gate, over which "Holiness" is written. There seems to be shelter inside, and he knocks. The door is opened by one in white garments, but none save the holy can be admitted, and he is not holy. He sees another gate, and tries that; but "Truth" is inscribed above it, and he is not fit to enter. He hastens to a third, which is the palace of "Justice"; but armed sentinels keep the door, and only the righteous can be received. At last, when he is almost in despair, he sees a light shining some distance away and hastens toward it. The door stands wide open, and beautiful angels meet him with welcomes of joy. It is the house of "Mercy," and he is taken in and finds refuge from the storm, with all the joys of love and fellowship. Not one of us can ever find a refuge at any door save the door of mercy. But here the vilest can find eternal shelter.

The coming of the knowledge of the love and mercy of God is beautifully represented in the dawning of everyday. "The dayspring from on high hath visited us." Think of a world without sun, moon, or stars, and we have a picture of the moral world without the divine love and mercy. "Darkness and . . . the shadow of death"—no light to guide, to cheer, to produce joy and beauty. Then Christ comes. He comes as the dayspring. There were glimmerings of light on the horizon long before He came. The Old Testament times had their gleams of coming day. Like the day, too, this light came from above, down out of the heavens. Then, like the day, His coming changed everything into beauty. Light blesses the world in many ways. It produces all the life of earth. There would not be a bud, a flower, nor a leaf, but for the sun. Nor would there be any beauty, for every lovely thing in nature the sun paints. Think of Christ as light. His love brooding over us causes us to live, and nourishes in us every spiritual grace. Every beam of hope is a ray of His light. What the coming of light is to a prisoner in a darkened dungeon, is the bursting of mercy over a guilty soul. Light gives cheer; and what cheer the gospel gives to the mourner, to the poor, to the troubled! Is it not strange that any will refuse the light? If any would persist in living in a dark cave, far away from the light of the sun, with only dim candles of his own making to pour a few poor flickering gleams upon the gloom, we should consider him insane. What shall we say of those who persist in living in the darkness of sin, with no light but the candles of earth's false hopes to shine upon their souls? There are many such, too. They turn to every "will-o'-the-wisp" that flashes a little beam, anywhere, rather than to Christ. It is like preferring a tallow candle to the sun.

The ultimate mission of light is to show us the way through the world of darkness and "to guide our feet into the way of peace." This is a most beautiful description of what Christ wants to do for us. He first prepared the way of peace. All this world's paths are full of trouble and lead to despair, but Christ built a highway beautiful and safe, which leads to eternal blessedness. It was a most costly road-making; He Himself dies in preparing the way for our feet. Now He comes to us and wants to be our guide and lead us into this way of peace. We never can find our own way, and if we thrust away this blessed guidance, we must go on in darkness forever. The Christian's way is indeed a "way of peace." It gives peace with God, peace in our own heart because sin is forgiven, and then we have peace amid all this world's trials. Some people think a Christian life is hard and unpleasant. But really it is the way of sweetest peace. The only truly, deeply, and permanently happy people are those whose sins are forgiven and who are going with Christ through this world, home.

3

The Birth of Jesus

Scripture Reading: Luke 2:1–20

Not much is told in profane history about the period in which the event of the birth of Jesus belongs. It is said, however, that there are distinct traces that such a census as Luke describes took place. The great emperor commanded that an enrollment of all the world should be made. The emperor did not know, when he issued this decree, that long before he was born there had gone forth another decree from a more glorious King, which unwittingly he was now helping to execute. It had been written by the prophet under divine inspiration that the Messiah should be born in Bethlehem. But Joseph and Mary were living at Nazareth, a long distance from Bethlehem. How should they be brought to Bethlehem so as to fulfill the prophecy? They had no business there. Now comes the emperor's decree which requires them to appear in the town of David to be enrolled.

The birth of this King did not have about it the glamour which usually marks the birth of earthly royalty. He was born in a stable, wrapped in swaddling clothes, after the fashion of the children of poverty, and slept His first sleep in a manger. It is pleasant for us to think that our Savior knows all the phases of human life by experience. He looks upon the baby in the mother's arms with a peculiar interest, for He Himself was once a baby. Many children are born in poverty, and sometimes they think their lot is hard, that they have not a fair chance in this world. But here is Jesus, the Son of God, beginning His life in poverty, and therefore He can sympathize with them.

The shepherds out in the fields were especially favored that night. While they were keeping watch over their flock, an angel stood by them, and a divine splendor shone about them. Their occupation was lowly, but they were faithful in it, and thus honor came to them. If we would have angels visit us, we must stay at our post of duty, no matter how lowly it is. Angels never come to people who are ashamed of their calling or too indolent to be diligent at their proper tasks. The shepherds did not seem to have an easy way of living. They were poor, and had to stay out of doors all night, guarding their sheep. The people in the fine houses, no doubt, if they thought at all of these poor men, thought they had a hard time of it, and pitied them because of their poverty and hardship. The shepherds themselves, it may be, envied the people who lived in the big houses and did not have to work and stay out nights. At least some people in these days whose lot is in the lowly places are envious of those who are rich. But we may be sure that the Bethlehem shepherds were never sorry afterwards that they had to be out in the field that night. Think what they would have missed if, because of discontent or of self-indulgence, any of them had stayed away from their post. They would not have seen the angels, nor would they have heard the good tidings that came, nor have looked upon the wonderful Child in the manger. We need to watch lest sometimes we miss blessings by being absent from our place of duty. Then sometimes the place of blessing may not be in a prayer meeting, but in a field or in a shop or at home, doing some lowly task work. We do not know where the place of honor and privilege in this world may be. We may be sure, however, that it will always be in the place of duty.

The message the angel brought was a glad one. "I bring you good tidings of great joy." Never before had such tidings come to this world. Wherever the gospel now goes it bears the good news. To the soul struggling with temptation it whispers the assurance of victory. To those crushed in defeat it speaks of hope, saying, "You may rise again, and yet attain a beautiful and noble life." To those who are sitting in sorrow it brings comfort, telling of the compassion of God.

The good tidings was indeed wonderful. "For unto you is born this day in the city of David a Savior, which is Christ the Lord." This was the announcement of the most marvelous fact in all the world's history. It was not an unusual thing for a baby to be born—thousands of infants were born that same night throughout the world. It was not a strange thing that the baby was born in a stable—in the East such an occurrence was not unusual. The wonderful thing was that this child was the Son of God. He was the anointed Messiah—He was divine. That the glorious God should thus enter human life as a little child was the marvelous thing.

The angel told the shepherds how they would know the Child when they found Him. "Ye shall find a babe wrapped in swaddling clothes, lying in a manger." They would not find the Baby robed in purple garments, like the child of a prince, but wrapped in swaddling clothes, a child of poverty. They would not find Him sleeping in a palace, but in a stable. Thus the very authentications of the divine character and mission of this Child were the tokens of poverty and humiliation. We see what empty things are the world's marks of greatness. When Christ came He disregarded all the emblems of rank by which men indicate greatness, and wore the insignia of poverty and humiliation. Yet, was He less great because He bore not the world's stamp of greatness? Greatness is in the character, never in the dress or the circumstances. No matter about wearing a crown—make sure that you are worthy of a crown. This mark of the infant Messiah shows us also how Christ touched the lowliest places of life, began among the poorest and plainest of the people. He went down and started at the foot of the ladder, that He might understand our life and know how to help us in the best way.

Earth paid small heed to the advent of the glorious King, but heaven failed not to honor Him even in His humiliation. His birth made no stir in the world's high places, but heaven's angels came and sang their songs of praise. These holy messengers were intensely interested in the great work of redemption on which the Messiah was then entering. We are told that the angels "desire to look into" [see 1 Pet. 1:12] the strange mystery of redeeming love. We know that there is joy in the presence of the angels when one sinner is saved. We are told further that the angels are as "ministering spirits, sent forth to minister for them who shall be heirs of salvation" [Heb. 1:14]. The glimpses we have in the Bible of angels at their everyday work show them always busy in services on behalf of God's children. This ministry has not ceased. Angels' visits are not "rare," as we sometimes say.

The coming of Christ brought peace—"On earth peace." Peace is one of the great words in the Bible. The coming of Christ to this world to live and suffer and die for our redemption was one of God's thoughts of peace toward us, the most wonderful of them all. It shows how much God loves us, that He is willing to do and to sacrifice in order to make peace for us. Christ made peace for us first by bearing our sins, putting them away, that we might come to God and find forgiveness. Then from the cross went forth the proclamation, offering peace to all who would accept it. Paul says, "Being therefore justified by faith, we have peace with God through our Lord Jesus Christ" [Rom. 5:1].

If we study the conduct of the shepherds, we shall find an illustration of very simple faith. They said one to another, "Let us now go even unto Bethlehem, and see this thing." They did not propose to go to see if what the angel had told them was true, but to see the thing which the angel told them they should see. They were so sure that they would find the Babe in the manger, wrapped in swaddling clothes, that they at once went into the town to begin their search. It would be well for us if we had faith as simple, expecting always to find just what God tells us we shall find.

We might suppose, after seeing all that the shepherds saw that night—the vision of the angels and the infant Messiah—they would be too full of ecstasy to think of returning to their own lowly task work at once, at least. We would have been disposed to excuse them if they had not returned to their sheep. Even Peter was once so enraptured with the splendor of the Transfiguration that he begged to be allowed to stay there, beholding the wondrous vision of the mountain. At that very moment, however, human sorrow was waiting at the mountain's foot for the Master's coming, and the rapture of communion must be exchanged for the commonplace of duty. The highest, holiest place for us is always the place of duty. Where their task waited for them these shepherds must go.

There is a legend of a monk at his devotions, to whom was granted a blessed vision of the Christ. The convent bell rang while he bowed before the vision. It was the hour when the blind, the lame, and all the beggars of the parish came to receive their dole, and this monk on his knees before the vision was to distribute alms that day. Should he go, or should he stay? Then the vision said:

Do thy duty, that is best;
Leave unto thy Lord the rest.

Instantly he arose, hastened away, did his work among the poor, then came again, and found the vision waiting where he had left it. Then a voice said, "Hadst thou stayed, I must have fled." The joy of communion with God must never detain us from life's common task work. We cannot keep the rapture of devotion if we neglect the routine of lowly service. Worship was meant to fit us for better work, not to make us less ready for our lowly tasks.

4

The Presentation in the Temple

Scripture Reading: Luke 2:22–39

The first Jewish rite which was observed in the case of a child was circumcision. Jesus was circumcised. The time was when He was eight days old. At that time, also, He received His name, Jesus, as the angel had directed. The next religious observance was His presentation in the temple. This was forty days after His birth. An offering was required in connection with this ceremony. The usual offering was a lamb; but when the mother was too poor to give this she might bring a pigeon or a dove. This was what Mary gave, showing the poverty of her family.

It was while the child was in the temple that this beautiful incident of Simeon occurred. "The same man was just and devout, waiting for the consolation of Israel: and the Holy Ghost was upon him." Old age is not always beautiful. Sometimes the old seem to outstay their usefulness in this world. Sometimes they lose their sweetness of disposition and grow fretful, sour, and discontented. Christian old age should be beautiful to the very close. It should be useful, peaceful, rich in experience, wise in counsel, patient and loving, the harvest of the life, full of ripe, mellow fruit. Simeon is an illustration of such an old age. There are four things said about him here. First he was a righteous man. This means that he was honest and upright in all his dealings with others. Everybody trusted Simeon, or everybody knew that he was good and faithful. If he was a carpenter, he did honest work and charged only honest prices. If he was a merchant, his customers were sure always of getting the kind of goods he represented them to be, and of getting full measure and full weight at honest prices. The times were corrupt, and many men were dishonest, and there was a great deal of sharp dealing, but Simeon never swerved from the strictest righteousness in his dealings with men.

Second, he was devout. He was not merely a moralist. There are some people who boast of their scrupulous honesty and uprightness, while they never bend a knee to God, never speak a word to Him in prayer, never acknowledge Him as their Lord, never think of pleasing Him. Simeon was not that kind of man. He was a righteous man, because he was a God-fearing man.

Third, he looked for Christ. He believed that the Messiah was to come because God had so promised. He did not neglect his duties, however, in watching for the Messiah, but continued diligent and faithful all the while. We need to learn this lesson. Expectation sometimes draws us away from our duty. When Christ comes, He wants to find us watching, in the sense of being ready to welcome Him, but He does not want to find us idly gazing into heaven, looking for Him.

A fourth thing about Simeon was that the Holy Spirit was on him. That is the secret of all true spiritual life. The truly beautiful character is one that is built up by the Holy Spirit. Tennyson was asked what Jesus Christ was to him. It was in a garden, and, pointing to a lovely rosebush, the poet replied, "What the sun is to that bush, Jesus Christ is to my soul." Such is Christ to every believing life. His Spirit enters into the heart and gives it whatever beauty it acquires.

"It was revealed unto him by the Holy Ghost, that he should not see death, before he had seen the Lord's Christ." So he had a great hope in his heart all along his years. He had had many years to wait—we are not told how many—but he believed in God and was sure he would live till he had seen the Christ. It will be a sad thing for any of us if we die before we have seen Christ. We may have seen many great men in our days, but if we have not seen Christ, we are not ready to die in peace. We may have traveled over the world, looking upon the wonderful things of nature and beholding great works of art; yet, if we have not looked upon Christ, we are not prepared for death. But when we have seen Him we are ready to depart, for condemnation is gone from our souls, our admission to heaven is sure, and we have divine companionship for the valley of shadows.

"The parents brought in the child Jesus." It was a beautiful custom among the Jews, this, of bringing their babies to the temple to give them to God. That is what Christian parents do when they dedicate their children to God. They say their little ones belong to God, and therefore they consecrate them to Him, so that as long as they live they shall belong to Him. When children have been given to God, parents should always remember that they really belong to God and should bring them up as God's own. They should teach them that they are God's and that they ought to live for God and do His will.

When a young woman was about to go as a foreign missionary, someone asked her mother if it was not hard to have her go. The mother replied: "When she was a little child I gave her to God. I did not know till now what God wanted her for, but surely I have no right to complain of any use He may choose to make of her life."

"He received Him into his arms" [see v. 28]. The picture is very beautiful—this old man receiving into his arms from the mother the infant Messiah. Jesus had not yet wrought any miracle to manifest His Deity. He had not yet spoken a single word of wisdom. He was but a helpless infant, six weeks old, held in the mother's arms. Artists, it is true, paint a circle of brightness round the head of the child Jesus in their pictures, or show a soft light streaming from Him; but there was no such brightness about Him in reality. He was not different from other children in His infancy, and there was nothing remarkable about His appearance. Yet the Lord had told this old man that this child was to be the Messiah, and he believed it without any proofs. It was a beautiful faith. We see much more in Jesus than Simeon saw. We see all His beautiful, spotless, gentle, pure life. We see His wonderful works, manifesting Deity. We hear His marvelous words of wisdom. We behold Him on the cross. We come after His resurrection and look into His empty grave. We follow Him with our eyes as He ascends into heaven. We see the evidences of His power in the world since He ascended. If Simeon believed when he saw the Christ as a helpless babe, how much more reason have we to believe! Surely we, too, should receive Christ into our arms, opening our whole heart to Him.

"Now lettest Thou Thy servant depart in peace . . . for mine eyes have seen Thy salvation." No one is ready to depart in peace until he has seen God's salvation. But when we have taken Christ into our heart we are prepared for whatever may come. The penitent thief on the cross had time for only one look at Christ, but one look was enough; he was ready then to enter paradise with his Lord. A young man, who died recently, had not accepted Christ until in his last sickness. There was a picture in his room—some representation of Christian peace. The young man said, "There is something in that picture which I do not understand, of which I have no experience." His friends sought to explain to him the Christian's secret of peace, and before the end came he understood it and could say, "Now lettest Thou Thy servant depart in peace . . . for mine eyes have seen Thy salvation." When our heart has seen Christ, nothing has dread or terror for us.

Simeon's words to Mary suggested the importance of Jesus in the world. "This child is set for the fall and the rising again of many." Everyone to whom Christ is offered is affected by Him in some way, and carries away some mark on his life from having touched Christ. A stone in one's path may serve as a step to lift one's feet upward, or one may stumble over it and be hurt, bruised, broken, by it. If we accept Christ as our Savior and Lord, He will lift us up to noble, blessed, eternal life. He said, "I, if I be lifted up from the earth, will draw all men unto Me." There is in Christ a wondrous lifting power. He took His apostles from their lowly life and exalted them to earthly honor and immortality and to heavenly blessedness and glory. So it is with all who accept Christ. But those who reject Him are like men who stumble over the stone which is meant to lift them upward. To those who believe on Christ He is the savor of life unto life. To those who do not believe on Him He becomes the savor of death unto death. Christ is before each one of us. Whether He is set for our falling or rising depends upon what we do with Him.

"A sword shall pierce through thy own soul." The Bodenhausen "Madonna" shows the mother and Child, and then away in the distance, in very dim outline, the forms of three crosses. The suggestion is that even when the mother of Jesus clasped her child in her arms she had some intimation of the end to which He would come. These words of Simeon to the mother are proof enough that this was the truth. The shadow of the cross fell across the young mother, with the babe in her arms. "A sword shall pierce through thy own soul." We know, too, how soon this word began to come true. It was but a little time till the mother had to flee to Egypt with her child to save Him from the sword of Herod.

There is another picture which represents the same truth, though at a later period. The Boy Jesus is represented at the age of thirteen in the carpenter shop, and as He stretches out His arms at the close of the day, the western sun casts His shadow in the form of a cross, on which the mother looks with pained face as prophetic of His end. Many times also in the years of His public ministry the mother's heart must have been pierced when the sword of human hate struck at Jesus. Then, when she stood below His cross, there came the worst of all the thrustings here foreshadowed. Whenever a child suffers in any way, the mother's heart is pierced.

5

The Wise Men Led by the Star

Scripture Reading: Matthew 2

Matthew does not tell us much of the infancy of Jesus. There is something very beautiful, however, in the little we have in this first Gospel. It gives us a glimpse of the way the world, outside of His own country, received Him. There was no room for Him in the inn, and He was born in a stable; but Matthew shows the far East waiting for Him and honoring Him. A little later, too, it shows Egypt sheltering Him. Jerusalem was the place where naturally the Messiah should have been first and most highly honored, but Jerusalem heard of the great event of His coming from the East.

The coming of the wise men to the cradle of Jesus is an intensely interesting incident. The time was probably soon after the presentation in the temple. Paintings often represent the wise men and the shepherds together in the cave-stable, adoring the Christ-child. As the flight into Egypt came immediately after the visit of the wise men, and the Holy Child was probably kept for many months away from the country, it is evident that their appearance was not at the beginning of the life of Jesus, and that they could not have been present with the shepherds.

Who the wise men were we do not certainly know. The historian speaks of the Magi as a priestly caste of the Medes. They were known as interpreters of dreams. They were also reputed to be observers of the heavens, students of the secret things of nature. Whatever the place of these Magi or wise men was, they were highly honored of God in this reception of Jesus Christ.

The birth of Jesus took place at Bethlehem. This was the most wonderful event of human history—the coming of the Son of God in human flesh into the world. Love was born that night. True, there was love in the world before. Mothers loved their children. Friend loved friend. Natural affection was common. But the love which we know as Christian love had its beginning in the birth of Jesus Christ. It is well for us to note, however, that the historical fact of Christ's birth is not that which saves us. He must be born again in us.

> Though Christ a thousand times in Bethlehem be born,
> If He's not born in thee, thy soul is all forlorn.

The wise men came many hundreds of miles to find the newborn King. The journey was long, difficult, perilous, and very costly. If these men endured so much toil and danger in seeking Jesus, we should count no obstacle too great to overcome in our quest of Him. We should be ready to go thousands of miles, if need be, in seeking for Him. No search for Christ, however costly, will be without avail. He is the pearl of great price [see Matt. 13:46], and we shall be well paid for our search, though it cost us the sacrifice of all other things, and though we even have to lay down our life to find Him.

This greatest event of history made little stir in the world. A few humble shepherds came to look with wonder on the newborn Babe that lay in the young mother's arms—but that was all. The Jews had been looking for their Messiah, but did not recognize Him when He came. Their books foretold His coming; but when He came, it was not known by His people that He had appeared. His advent was quiet. There was no blare of trumpets. Noise and show are not necessary accompaniments of power. The mightiest energies in this world are often the quietest. The grace of God always comes without observation. Angels minister noiselessly. The most useful Christians are not those who make the most ado at their work, but those who in humility and simplicity, unconscious of any splendor, shining in their faces, go daily about their work for their Master. For another thing, we do not always know when Christ actually comes to us. He had been born many months, had been welcomed by angels, had been presented in the temple and received with joy there; but Jerusalem had not known that He was there. He was in the world, and the world was made by Him, but the world knew Him not. We speak severely of the treatment accorded to Him by His own people, who were so indifferent to the coming of their Messiah. Yet, why should we complain so of the Jews? Our King is in our midst these very days—do we recognize Him?

We cannot understand just how the wise men were led to Palestine. They said they saw a star in the east, the star of the newborn King, and were led by it. There has been a great deal of speculation as to the nature of the star, whether it was a natural or supernatural appearance. But no matter—whatever it was, it led these men unmistakably to the feet of the Christ. Even the faintest glimmerings of spiritual light should be welcomed by us and their guidance accepted. We should not wait to know all about Christ, and to see Him in all His glory, before we set out to seek Him. We should follow the first faint gleams, and then, as we go on, the light will become brighter and we shall see more and more of Him, see Him more and more clearly, until at length we behold Him in all His blessed beauty face to face. Certainly there is no one in Christian lands in these days who does not have a great deal more light to guide him to the Christ than these wise men had.

The Herods have an unenviable record in New Testament history. Their hands are stained with crime. When this Herod, Herod the Great, heard the inquiries of the wise men, he was much troubled. He thought that he was king of the Jews, and it terrified him to hear of another King of the Jews, whom these strangers from the East had come so far to see. Hearing of Christ does not always bring joy. It brought gladness to the humble shepherds and to the wise men, but to Herod it brought great distress. His name makes bad men think of their sins and then of the judgment. It is only when we love Christ and want to have Him for our friend that the thought of Him is sweet and pleasant. "Unto you therefore which believe he is precious." Those whose faith is fixed upon Him are never terrified by thoughts of Him. There is nothing to fear, but everything to give joy and confidence to those whose trust is in Him.

Herod, himself unable to answer the question of the wise men, turned to the scribes. The wise men wanted to know where they could find the King who had been born in Judea. "We have seen His star," they said. Whatever it was that led them, we know that there was no illusion, and they were not deceived. They had been led, and they had come to the right place.

Herod could not answer their question, but he could easily learn what the Jewish books said about where the Christ should be born, so he called the priests and scribes and asked them where their Messiah should be born. It did not take them long to give the answer. They knew their Bible well. They could even give chapter and verse, and could tell the name of the town in which the Messiah was to be born. These facts were all down in their books.

Yet we do not see that they had made any use of their knowledge. They could tell the wise men where the Christ was to be born, but they had not themselves taken one step toward Bethlehem to seek for Him, nor did they become eager to see their King, when they were so close to Him. We must be careful not to repeat the mistake of these ancient teachers. Most of us know our Bible fairly well, and can tell others glibly enough where and how to find the Christ. But have we gone to the place where He is, to search for Him and to worship Him?

The scene when the wise men found the Child-king was very beautiful. They were very glad. They saw now the Child-king they had journeyed so far to find. They did not doubt for a moment that this was the object of their quest. When they saw Him they fell down and worshiped Him. They saw only a baby lying in a young mother's arms. There was no crown on His head. No glory gleamed from His face. His surroundings were most unkingly, without pomp or brilliance. The child did nothing before them to show His royalty—spoke no word, wrought no kingly act of power. Yet the wise men believed and worshiped Him. Think how much more we know about the Christ than they did. We see Him in all the glory of His life, death, resurrection, and ascension. We see Him sitting at the right hand of God as King of kings, wearing many crowns. It is easy for us to find kingly marks in Him. Shall we be behind the wise men in our adoration?

The wise men did more than adore—they opened their treasures and offered the gifts of gold, frankincense, and myrrh, which they had brought all the way from their own home. The sincerity of their worship was thus attested by the costliness of their gifts. The treasures they had brought were of great value—the most costly things they could find, the best they had to give. It is not enough for us to sing praise to Christ and give Him an homage that costs nothing. He asks for our gifts the offerings of our love, our service, the consecration of our lives. We need to guard against the worship that is only mere sentiment. Love that will not give and sacrifice is not deep or true. Giving is the test of loving—the measure of our love is what we are willing to give and sacrifice. Some people sing missionary hymns with great zest, and when the collection plate is passed they have nothing for it. The wise men not only gave gifts, but gifts that were rich and costly. Some people give, but with such a pitiful attitude that it must pain the Master to receive their offerings. These Magi gave with gladness.

There are many ways of laying our offerings at the feet of Jesus Christ. He Himself does not need our money, but His cause needs it. The extension of His Kingdom in this world, at home and abroad, requires money, and this must be brought by His followers. Those who have no interest in the saving of others, in the sending of the gospel to those who have it not, have not themselves really tasted of the love of Christ. Then we may give to Christ also in ministering to His needy ones. The latter part of the twenty-fifth chapter of Matthew reveals to us this wonderful truth, that those who serve the needy, the suffering, the troubled, in Christ's name, are serving Him.

6

The Boy Jesus in the Temple

Scripture Reading: Luke 2:40–52

After the presentation in the temple came the incident of the visit of the Magi, recorded only in the Gospel according to Matthew, followed by the massacre of the children and the flight into Egypt. When Mary and Joseph and the Holy Child returned from Egypt they went to Nazareth, where they remained till Jesus was thirty years of age. Of these years we have no record, excepting this single incident of the visit to Jerusalem. The life at Nazareth was quiet and uneventful. Each year Mary and Joseph went to the Passover, but until He was twelve Jesus did not leave His home.

It brings Jesus very near to children to have them remember that once He was a child, and now in heaven has not forgotten the experiences of His earthly infancy and childhood years. His family was poor, and He had not the luxuries which many boys enjoy in these days. He had none of the opportunities that we have. There were no books, magazines, or newspapers. He heard the Scriptures read every Sabbath in the synagogue, and in His home He was taught the words of God. When thirteen years of age, He began to learn the carpenter's trade, and from that time until His baptism we can think of Him as working in the carpenter shop every day. It is a comfort now to those who have to work hard to remember that Jesus worked at a common trade, no doubt with long hours and small pay.

The words that describe the growth of the boy Jesus show us that there was nothing remarkable or unusual in His life at that time, so far as people saw. There was nothing precocious about His childhood. Artists put halos about His face in their pictures, but there was no halo there as He lay in His mother's arms. When the shepherds came to seek for the newborn baby they recognized Him not by any marks of divinity, but by His being wrapped in swaddling clothes and lying in the manger. In His infancy He was as helpless as any other infant. There were months before He could talk, and when He began to speak, it was only with a baby's prattling at first, as His mother taught Him. His lessons did not come to Him without study—He had to work hard to learn them.

The nearer we keep to the way of nature in trying to think of the beautiful infancy of Jesus, the better we shall realize the truth about it. The things that happen to boys in our days, happened to Him. An artist painted a picture of Jesus in the home at Nazareth as a little boy in a carpenter shop. He has cut His finger and comes to His mother to have it tied up. No doubt the picture was true of Him more than once. The chief difference between the boy Jesus and other boys was that he always did what he was told to do, was never rude, insolent, or sullen, but had ever a sweet, smiling, shining face, always keeping love in His heart.

Luke tells us that He grew and waxed strong, filled with wisdom; and that the grace of God was upon Him. Most children grow well enough in body, but Jesus grew correspondingly in wisdom. In this respect every child should be like Him. It is a shame to grow up in ignorance. Boys and girls should study their lessons thoroughly, taking every opportunity to acquire wisdom by observation, by reading, and by thought. An oriental proverb says, "Spread wide thy skirts when heaven is raining gold." Heaven is indeed raining gold in the school days of children who have the opportunities which most children in Christian countries have. It is said further that the grace of God—that is, the divine favor and blessing—was upon Jesus. God loves children and is willing always to give them His grace. "Heaven lies about us in our infancy," says the poet.

The account of the first Passover of Jesus is very beautiful. He was twelve years of age. Mary and Joseph had gone to the feast every year, but until now Jesus had remained at home. His going this year was a great event in His life. The incident has been beautifully described as "the solitary floweret out of the wonderful enclosed garden of the thirty years."

The incident of the losing of Jesus by His mother is very interesting. We can readily understand how she did not miss Him until the evening came, thinking that He was somewhere in the caravan. People often lose Christ. Sometimes, like Mary, they do not know that they have lost Him until they have gone quite a distance on their way. There are homes where Christ was once the guest, but in which He no longer abides. He did not leave the home—He was grieved and driven out of it either by indifference, by unbelief, or by sin. There are persons who once walked in close intimacy and friendship with Christ, but who now have him no more with them. They have lost him on the way—perhaps through business cares or household anxieties, or through worldly pleasures. In whatever way Christ may have been lost out of our lives, we should not rest until we have found Him again.

At last the mother found Jesus in the temple, in the midst of the teachers. He was deeply absorbed in what these men were saying to Him, listening to their words and eagerly asking them questions. There was nothing unnatural in this talking of the child with the rabbis. A room in the temple was set apart as a kind of open free school. There the learned teachers sat and taught those who desired instruction. The older students would sit on low benches, and the younger ones on the ground. The teaching was simple and informal. The pupil would ask questions and the teacher would try to answer them. It was in one of these temple schools that the child Jesus was found that day. A new world was opening to Him. Perhaps He was learning about the Messianic promises and hopes of His people. The lesson for young people is that they, too, should be deeply interested in the Bible, eager to learn all they can in every way of its truths.

The mother of Jesus chided Him with His having wandered away from her. "Son, why hast Thou thus dealt with us? behold, Thy father and I sought Thee sorrowing." His answer was very simple, and yet it showed that He was passing into a new phase of His life. "How is it that ye sought Me? knew ye not that I must be in My Father's house?" Our King James Version puts it the "Father's business," and this is very beautiful, too. He was now beginning to recognize His relation to the heavenly Father and His higher obligation to obey Him. The Revised Version, however, renders it "My Father's house." They need not have wondered where He was. Did they not know that He would certainly be in the Father's house? It is a good thing when a young person's heart draws him to places of instruction or of worship, to where he finds uplifting, helpful companionship. We grow like the things we love. If we love pure things, we will grow pure. If we love heavenly things, we will grow heavenly-minded. If we love the Bible, its words will sink into our hearts and permeate all our life, transforming it. If we love the Father's house in this world, we will be prepared for the Father's house in the other world.

Joseph and Mary did not understand the child that God had given them to train. With all His beauty and simplicity of character, something appeared in Him now which amazed them. Neither could they understand His words. It was so all through His life—His friends did not understand Him. They were bewildered as they saw His life and listened to His words. They thought His dying was defeat and failure, and all their hopes of the Messiahship perished that day at the cross. Not until He rose did they begin to understand the meaning and mystery of His death. Even now Christ's friends often fail to understand Him. They cannot see how the trials, the disappointments, the sorrows of their lives can have divine love in them. Someday they will know.

We have here a beautiful glimpse of the homelife of Jesus from His twelfth year until His thirtieth. He turned quietly away from the temple and went back to Nazareth with Joseph and His mother, and there took and kept the place of a child, obeying His parents and proving in all ways dutiful, reverent, and helpful. He found childhood in a lowly home a place large enough for the exercise of His blessed life. Robert Browning, in one of his poems, represents Gabriel taking the place of a poor boy and working for him at his lowly trade as contentedly as if he had been engaged in the highest service of heaven. But here is something more sublime than even the poet's fancy: the Son of God Himself working for eighteen years as a carpenter, patiently, sweetly, simply, and without discontent.

Should any true-hearted child, however great his gifts, consider the child-place in the home unworthy, or a place too lowly, or too small for use of his gifts? Canon Farrar says: "A life spent in brushing clothes and washing crockery and sweeping floors—a life which the proud of the earth would have treated as dust under their feet—a life spent at the clerk's desk, a life spent in the narrow shop, a life spent in the laborer's hut, may yet be so ennobled by God's loving mercy that for the sake of it a king might gladly yield his crown."

7

The Ministry of John the Baptist

Scripture Reading; Mark 1:1–8; Luke 3:1–20

Mark's gospel opens with the title of the book, "The beginning of the gospel." It was not a very promising beginning from an earthly point of view. As we look at the gospel now, it is a great river, whose streams run through all Christian lands and into many portions of heathendom. For centuries men sought in vain for the source of the Nile, at last finding it in the heart of Africa. If we trace back the streams of the gospel to their source, where will our quest lead us? Back to the heart of God we must go, if we would find the real beginning. It began in the love of God. "God so loved the world, that He gave His only begotten Son." The gospel was, first of all, a thought in the Father's heart, a stirring of the divine compassion. Then it grew into a purpose. All great achievements are first thoughts, then purposes, before they become acts. The gospel was first a feeling of love and pity in the divine breast. This was way back in eternity. Far back in the story of creation, when there was only chaos, we are told that the Spirit of God brooded upon the face of the waters. The words indicate that even then God was thinking of His children yet to be, as He was planning and preparing for their good. His love had no beginning.

John the Baptist was a great character. He had been foretold and his work described by the ancient prophets. Evidently John's life was "a plan of God." He was thought about and his mission mapped out long before he was born. He came as God's messenger to prepare the way for the Messiah. He is spoken of as "a man sent from God." Every man is a man sent from God. Many forget that God has anything to do with their lives, that He thought of them before they came, or that He had any purpose in making them and sending them into the world. But we do not drift into this world in any accidental way. God thought about us before we were born, then made us, and sent us to do what He had planned for us to do. If only we realized this truth, it would give a new meaning to our life and a new glory to our work.

God's plan for everyone is noble and beautiful. He never made anyone to live a marred and stained life. He never sent any man into this world to be a curse, to hurt other lives, to poison the springs from which people drink, or to scatter ruin and devastation. He made everyone for a beautiful character and a worthy career. But it is possible for us to spoil God's plan for our own lives. We can carry out the divine purpose for us only by doing God's will day by day as it comes to us.

John was a very humble man. He shrank from human praise and commendation. When they asked him if he were the Messiah, he said he was only "the voice of one crying in the wilderness." He did not care to have his name blazoned. All he wished to be was a voice proclaiming the divine message. The message was:

> Make ye ready the way of the Lord,
> Make His paths straight.

There is a picture which shows a hand holding up a cross. The person is not seen—only the hand. It is good to be a hand that holds up the cross. It is good to be a voice that proclaims the Christ. We would all do well to keep ourselves out of sight and get people to look upon Christ. Too many of us want people to see us, and so project our own personality that we hide the vision of the Christ that we ought to exalt and honor. We want people to see us, to hear and admire what we say, to love us and honor us. But what can we do for them? What can the teacher do for her scholars in their sinfulness and need? What can the preacher do for those who are in penitence and sorrow? We would better hide ourselves away and get people to see Christ. It is enough for us to seek to be only a voice, speaking out clearly to tell men of Christ, while we ourselves remain unseen and unknown. It is enough for us to speak our word or sing our song and pass out of sight, while the word we speak and the song we sing live to bless the world.

The mission of John is described in the words which "the voice" proclaimed: "Prepare ye the way of the Lord." Christ wants a way to be made for Him. He wants a way into people's hearts, our own hearts, first of all. Is the guest-chamber ready? He wants to walk with us; but He will accompany us only on paths of holiness and righteousness, in the way of obedience. He will never go with us in any crooked way. If we expect His company with us, we must see that the paths are straight. Enoch walked with God, because He walked in the same way in which God walked. Then Christ wants us to make ready the way for Him to other hearts and lives. If we can open a door for Christ into people's lives, we have brought them heaven's best blessing.

One great word summed up the substance of the Baptist's preaching. He preached repentance. John taught that those who repented must be baptized; but he made it very clear that his baptism did not cleanse the heart, and that those who were baptized with water must be baptized also with the Holy Spirit. Water is a fitting emblem. It implies that there are stains which need to be cleansed. Yet we know well that water cannot wash off sin's stains. The spot that sin leaves on the little white hand cannot be removed by any amount of washing. All the water of the ocean would not make it white. Only the Holy Spirit has power to remove sin's stains. If we truly accept Christ as our Savior He will wash us in the water of regeneration. We ought to be baptized with water—the Master instituted this ordinance and sacrament—but we need also to submit to the baptism of the Holy Spirit.

John's tribute to Jesus as he announced His coming was very beautiful. He said that he himself was not worthy to perform this lowest of all ministries for the Messiah. As we read these words and think of John's spirit of humility, we must not forget that one night, at the ending of His life, Jesus Himself took water in a basin, and a towel, and washed and wiped the feet of His own disciples. Thus He himself condescended to the place and the task of the lowliest servant. Surely this should rebuke our pride, when we stop to ask whether we are required to perform this or that lowly service for some little one of His.

John's words to those who came to be baptized were searching. We like to say pleasant things to people, sometimes complimentary things.

John had little time for flowers or compliments. He told the people frankly that they were terribly wrong and must get right if they would be saved. We talk to people about their splendid ancestry and about the advantages of heredity; John told his hearers that their fine ancestry would amount to nothing unless their own lives were right. Personal character was the test, he said.

It was solemn warning he gave in the picture of the ax lying at the root of the tree. An ax meant judgment. The business of an ax is to cut down. The doom of sin was clearly told. But the ax was not active. It was lying quietly beside the tree. There was mercy in the delay. Judgment was waiting that the people might have time to repent. God is patient. He does not wish to destroy. He wishes men to repent and be saved. He is slow to wrath. He waits to be gracious.

It is encouraging to see how the people seem to have been affected by John's stern preaching. "What shall we do then?" they asked. They seem to have confessed their sinfulness and to have desired to turn from their evil ways. This should always be the attitude of those who hear voices of warning and calls to repentance. John's answer to the questions of penitence were plain and simple. The man who had two coats should give one of them to the man beside him who had none. This is the great lesson of love which Jesus taught so often. The publicans who were proverbially unjust, extorting from the people more as taxes than they ought to collect, were touched by the preacher's stern words and asked what they should do. "Just begin to be just," he answered. "Exact no more than that which is appointed to you."

These words of John's impress the truth that God wants nothing unreasonable. "He hath showed thee, O man, what is good; and what doth the Lord require of thee, but to do justly, and to love mercy, and to walk humbly with thy God?" [Mic. 6:8].

8

The Baptism and Temptation of Jesus

Scripture Reading: Mark 1:9–13; Matthew 4:1–11

For thirty years the beautiful life of Jesus had gone on in Nazareth. He differed not from the other children with whom He played and attended school, save in the stainlessness and sinlessness of His life. He grew up among plain people. The village where He lived was small, and everyone knew all His neighbors. Jesus was a carpenter, as Joseph had been. We may be sure that His work in the shop was always well-done. He never did it carelessly. A man's religion is shown in the way he does the tasks of his trade or business or other occupation, quite as unmistakably as in his church attendance, his devotions, and his Sunday duties. Jesus did His carpentering conscientiously, honestly, skillfully. He put in good lumber. He was prompt and did not break His promises nor fail to finish His work at the time He said He would.

But one day He went away from His shop for the last time, closed it up, and left Nazareth. He had a call to higher and larger work. The time had come for Him to take up His mission as the Messiah. We are not told how this call came to Him, or anything of the spirit in which He answered it. But no doubt He knew what the call meant, and went eagerly to take up its tasks. Miss S. Alice Ranlett, in a little poem, "The Carpenter," published in *Forward* in 1897, has put in striking way her conception of the feelings of the Master the morning He left His shop:

231

That evening when the Carpenter swept out
    The fragrant shavings from the workshop floor,
And placed the tools in order and shut to
    And barred for the last time the humble door,
And, going on His way to save the world,
    Turned from the laborer's lot forevermore,
    I wonder, was He glad?

That evening when the Carpenter walked forth
    From Joseph's cottage, in the glimmering light,
And bade His holy mother long farewell;
    And through the skies of dawn, all pearly bright,
Saw glooming the dark shadow of a cross,
    Yet, seeing, set His feet toward Calvary's height,
    I wonder, was he sad?

Ah! when the Carpenter went on His way,
    He thought not for Himself of good or ill.
His path was one through shop or thronging men
    Craving His help, e'en to the cross-crowned hill,
In toiling, healing, loving, suffering—all
    His joy and His life to do the Father's will,
    And earth and heaven are glad!

It seems strange to us that Jesus should need to be baptized. The use of water implied symbolically that the person baptized was sinful and needed cleansing; but Jesus was without sin. John recognized the apparent unfitness of performing the rite upon Him which he was performing upon those who came confessing sin and repenting of it. John would have hindered Him, saying, "I have need to be baptized of Thee, and comest Thou to me?" Yet Jesus bade John to perform the rite on Him: "Suffer it to be so now: for thus it becometh us to fulfill all righteousness" [Matt. 3:13-17]. So John baptized Him.

When we ask the reason for this insisting of Jesus that John should baptize Him, several answers suggest themselves. Jesus' baptism was the consecration of Himself to His Messianic mission. He had come all the way from Nazareth to the Jordan expressly to make this consecration. Shall we then say that there is no necessity for public confession, for declaring ourselves on Christ's side and taking our place among His people?

The baptism of Jesus was His public confession. He accepted the divine call and before all the world declared His acceptance of the mission to be the world's Redeemer. We are called to follow Christ, and we should not hesitate to obey the call.

Another meaning of Christ's baptism was that He was now taking His place as one with us, to be our Redeemer. He had no sin of His own, and yet He stood there that day in the place of sinners. His baptism with water was the shadow of that other baptism into which He entered as our Savior. Then His baptism was His consecration to His public ministry. From the bank of the Jordan He saw through to the end. The shadow of the cross fell on the flowing water, fell also across the gentle and holy soul of Jesus as He stood there. Baptism for us implies also the consecration and devotion of our lives to God, whatever that consecration may include.

The divine manifestations which attended the baptism of Jesus were wonderful. "He saw the heavens opened, and the Spirit as a dove descending upon Him: and a voice came out of the heavens, Thou art My beloved Son, in Whom I am well pleased." The descending of the Spirit upon Him was the anointing of Jesus for His Messiahship. Then the Voice from heaven clearly declared His Messiahship. The Father testified that this was His beloved Son, in whom all the promises of grace were given. Jesus thus entered upon His mission as the Messiah, to be the world's Redeemer.

At once Jesus disappeared from the Jordan. "Immediately the Spirit driveth Him into the wilderness." There seems to have been haste—the word "immediately" indicates this. His going from the Jordan into the wilderness was not merely a pleasant saunter of his own for recreation, or to get away from the crowd. The Spirit of God put the impulse into His heart. Notice, too, the strength and urgency of the impulse—"the Spirit driveth Him," away from the Jordan and into the wilderness. The word "driveth" shows the tremendous divine pressure that was on Jesus as He hastened from His baptism and the Father's declaration of His Messiahship. He must pass now instantly to the first step in His preparation.

"He was there in the wilderness forty days tempted of Satan." Why must He be tempted? The answer seems clear. He had come into the world that He might destroy the works of the devil. He must meet the leader of the works of darkness, first of all, and enter upon His conflict with him. If He could not overcome Satan, He could not be the world's Redeemer. The conflict was fierce and terrible. All the power of evil was marshaled for the great battle. Matthew tells in fuller form the story of the method of the temptation and describes the complete victory which Jesus won. Mark gives details which the other Gospel writers do not give. One is that Jesus was with the wild beasts. It was in the wilderness that He spent the forty days and nights, and the wilderness was the home of wild beasts. This fact added to the terrors of the temptation. No doubt Jesus was kept in perfect safety in the midst of the wild beasts. Not one of them would harm Him.

Mark also makes special note of the ministry of angels to Jesus. His words would seem to indicate that the angels attended Him through all the forty days. Matthew in his account of the temptation puts the ministering of angels at the close, after the period of tempting. But the words imply repeated ministration, as if they had come to strengthen Him at different times, between the several assaults of the tempter. This agrees with Mark's statement, which implies continuous ministry throughout the forty days. Heaven's eye was upon Jesus during all the time of His trial, and help was sent in every time of stress. It is the same with us when we are in any struggle or any need. God watches that we shall never be tempted above what we can bear, and that help shall always come at the right moment. We are never left alone in any need or danger.

9

The Call of the First Disciples

Scripture Reading: Luke 5:1–11

The scene of this lesson is the Lake of Gennesaret. "Although God has created seven seas," said the rabbis, "yet He has chosen this one as His special delight." No body of water on the earth is so sacred to the hearts of Christians as this little inland sea. Along its shores Jesus walked, wrought, and talked. At that time its shore was a garden, without break, covered with pleasant towns and villages. Desolation now reigns about it. In our Lord's time it was covered with fishing boats and vessels of all kinds. A great population then crowded its shores. Now the towns have disappeared, and the boats no longer ply on the beautiful waters. Yet everywhere in the sands are the footprints of Him who came to save us. "It is the gem of Palestine, a sapphire fairly set in its framework of hills, but more fairly set in the golden words and works of the Son of God."

In the story of our passage we have one of the experiences of our Master on this beautiful sea. The people thronged about Him to hear Him speak. The crowd became very great, and that He might speak to the people more satisfactorily, He entered one of the fishing boats that were moored by the shore. The fishermen had left their boats and were washing their nets. Using this fishing boat as a pulpit, Jesus spoke to the people. That little boat had done good service many times before in other ways. It had carried people across the lake, it had been used in fishing, but it never had been put to such a use as it was that day, when the Lord preached from its deck to the throngs on the beach. We can find pulpits every day from which we can preach to the people about us. The boy can speak at school, or from his place of duty, or in the office where he works. The girl can find a pulpit among her friends, at her daily tasks, in the social group of which she is a member. No one ever yet lacked opportunities to speak for the Master. Often the little sermons we speak on the way, as we walk, or as we ride on the street cars or on the railroad train, have more effect, a wider reach of influence, than if we stood up in a church pulpit and made a fine address.

After Jesus had spoken to the people, He asked Simon, the owner of the boat, to push out from the shore into the deep water, and to let down his nets. It seemed to Simon that there could be no use in doing this. He had spent the whole preceding night on the sea, dropping the nets and drawing them up again, each time empty. "We have toiled all night, and have taken nothing," was Simon's discouraged answer. This is true of very much of the work that many of us do. We toil hard, but come home weary and empty-handed. We drag our nets all night, and in the morning we have only weeds and a few bits of rubbish in our nets. This is true of what we do in worldly business. The majority of men die poor, with nothing in their hands to show for their toil. Many do the same in their intellectual life. With countless opportunities for learning, they at last die in ignorance. Many persons have the same experience in spiritual work. Pastors toil for years, and seem to have no souls in their nets. Teachers work with their classes, and seem to have no results. There is often a sad pathos in the Christian's life and work. Many of us are like children trying to carry water in buckets with holes. It runs away as fast as we dip it up.

Peter's obedience at this time was very noble and beautiful. According to the rules of fishing, nothing would come of the Master's command. Yet Peter did not think of that. The word of Jesus had supreme authority with him. It was not his to ask why, or what good could come of casting the net again. No appeal against the Master's word was to be considered for a moment. So Peter answered without hesitation, "At Thy word I will." Many of the things our Master calls us to do or to endure do not seem best to us at the time. Yet we may always say to Christ, whatever His bidding may be, whatever He asks us to do or to suffer, into whatsoever mystery of trial or pain He leads us, "At Thy word I will." There need never be the smallest exception to this obedience. Though to our limited vision it seems that only loss can come out of it, still we should heed the Voice that commands, assured that in spite of all seeming ill there must be good in the end.

The result of the obedience proved the wisdom of the command. "When they had done this, they enclosed a great multitude of fishes." Obeying the Master, though it had seemed nothing could come of it, brought its rich reward. Not always do the results come so soon. But obedience to Christ's word always brings good in the end.

We have here an illustration of two kinds of work—that done without Christ's direction, and that done in obedience to His word. The one came to nothing: the other yielded bountiful results. The disciples had toiled all night in their own effort and taken nothing. They dropped their nets at the Master's bidding and drew them up full. In a wider sense, all that we do without Christ's direction comes to naught, while all that we do in His name yields blessing. Somewhere and in some way everything we do for Christ brings blessing. "Your labor is not in vain in the Lord" [1 Cor. 15:58]. "In due season we shall reap, if we faint not" [Gal. 6:9].

The effect of this miracle on Peter was remarkable. He fell down at the feet of Jesus and said, "Depart from me; for I am a sinful man, O Lord." This is a strange scene—Peter imploring Jesus to leave his boat. Yet it was Peter's very love for Jesus that made him say this. In the miracle he had had a glimpse of Christ's power. A vision of divine glory always humbles a true heart. A room may be filthy; floor, walls, and furniture stained; but in the darkness one does not see the foulness. Let the light flash in, and every speck of stain is revealed. We are not conscious of the evil in our own hearts. But when the divine holiness is revealed and flashes its radiance upon us, we see our condition and loathe ourselves. We should seek to see God, for the vision will show us our unworthiness, and then will lead to the cleansing of our lives, to make them more worthy of Him. We never can enter heaven until heaven has first entered into us and filled our whole being with its holiness and purity.

Peter saw in these wonderful words of Christ the unveiling of divine power. "He was astonished . . . at the draught of the fishes." Every day divine works are wrought before our eyes, and we fail to be impressed. Elizabeth Barrett Browning tells us that while some people see the glory of God in the burning bush and take off their shoes, others only stand by and pick blackberries. We should teach ourselves to behold God in even the commonest events in our commonest days. Daily life is full of goodness and the evidences of our Father's thoughtfulness and care. He made the flowers, the hills, the trees, the fields, the rivers, the stars. Are there no manifestations of divine power in these works of God? Then the life of the individual is full of love and power. No person can fail to see in everyday's providence the evidence of God's presence and thought. He provides for us. He sends us countless blessings, and supplies all our needs. He brings friends to us with love, with sympathy, with comfort. In the life of each one of us there are frequent occurrences just as remarkable as the miracles of the fishes. Yet, how few of us take off our shoes and fall down before Christ in wonder!

It is delightful to notice how the fishermen responded to the call of the Master. The call had reached their hearts, and they were not a moment in deciding. They had known Jesus for some time and were most glad to go with Him. We do not know how much He told them of His plans, of what He wanted them to do. Jesus does not usually give us the details of the life to which He calls us. He only asks us to go with Him; and then, as we go on, He shows us the way, step by step. Each day prepares us for the next. One duty done leads to another.

Jesus is always looking for men. The work of saving the world is still filling His heart and His thought. He wants men who will believe His message. He saw that day in these fishermen just the kind of men He wanted to go with Him and be trained for the great work He had in hand. They had had a training in their old occupation which had done much to prepare them for the new work to which they were now called. They had learned patience, persistence, quiet waiting, and diligence in their daily and nightly work on the sea, and these qualities would be of use in waiting, watching, and fishing for men. The words of Jesus about fishing contain a little parable. The sea is the world, and men are the fish that are to be caught and taken from it. The net is Christ's universal church. The figure is found in one of the old prophets, but in a different sense. A very early Christian hymn dwells on the thought:

Fishers of men, the blest,
Out of the world's unrest,
Out of sin's troubled sea
Taking us, Lord, to Thee;
Out of the waves of strife,
With bait of blissful life,
Drawing thy nets to shore
With choicest fish, good store.

The Master's answer to Simon showed what we should do with our amazement and adoration. Instead of being paralyzed by the revealing of glory, Simon was to find in it a new call to service. "Fear, not; from henceforth thou shalt catch men." Idle wonder is profitless. Divine revealing should drive us to a fuller consecration and service. The one thing after feelings is to put them into acts. We should all want to catch men and to save them from their sin, for eternal life and glory. We should all want to be fishers of men. The boys and girls should seek to draw their companions out of the black sea of sin, that they may be saved for heaven.

The response of Simon and of his friends was instantaneous. "They forsook all, and followed Him." This is just what Jesus asked the rich young ruler to do, and what he would not do. Christ may not ask us to give up all in the sense of leaving all; but He does ask us to give up all to Him. He does ask us to believe, to give up body, soul, and property, to go wherever He may send us, and to do whatever He wants us to do. Nothing will be lost to us, however, for He will return to us, a hundred-fold increase, all that we give up or lose in His cause.

10

The Paralytic Forgiven and Healed

Scripture Reading: Mark 2:1–12

Christ Jesus seems to have entered Capernaum quietly, to escape notice. Perhaps He was weary after His incessant labors, and desired to have rest. So He came quietly, perhaps by night, that His coming might not be known. But it soon became noised about that He was in the house. "He could not be hid" [Mark 7:24]. It was impossible for Him to be long anywhere without His presence becoming known. The people were too eager to get to Him with their needs and their sorrows to allow Him to remain quiet even for a little while. They were even rude and unmannerly in their crowding upon Him. But really it never can be kept quiet when Jesus enters any house or any life. There is a diffusiveness in Him, like a fragrance, which cannot be constrained.

A young woman tells of being on an excursion in the woods, when she picked up a branch of sweetbrier and put it in her bosom. She soon forgot what she had done, but all day long she smelled the spicy fragrance. Every woodland path seemed to her to have the same odor, even if there were no sweetbrier visible. She climbed over rocks and walked through dark caves, and everywhere she detected the perfume. She would stand beside different people, with all kinds of flowers in their hands, but still she smelled only the sweetbrier. As the party went home on the boat, she remarked to a friend, "Someone is carrying home a bunch of sweetbrier." When she came to retire, the bunch of sweetbrier dropped from her dress. All day long she had been carrying it, and it had perfumed everything. She said to herself, "How good it would be if I could have such a spirit in my heart that everyone I meet would seem to be carrying the fragrance!" One in whose heart Christ lives has the secret of a sweet life. The sweetness cannot be hid. A little spot, at least, of the world is made better and brighter.

As soon as His presence became known the crowd gathered about the house where Jesus was. From all over the town they came. It was the kindness of Jesus to the sick, the poor, the troubled, that drew so many to Him. Among those who came that day were four men carrying a friend on a stretcher. The man was a paralytic and could not help himself, but he had friends who were ready to assist him. These four men teach us a lesson. We ought to help one another. The strong should bear the infirmities of the weak. If there is a lame boy in the school, the other boys should lend him their legs. If one girl is sickly and not able to go out, the other girls, her neighbors and friends, should try to brighten her loneliness, calling on her, bringing into her sick room tokens of love and sympathy, and sharing with her their joy and gladness. Christians who have been healed by Christ should try to carry to Him their unsaved friends. It is suggestive, too, that four of this paralytic's friends united in helping to get him to Christ. One man could not have carried the burden, nor could two. But when the four men put their hands to the helpless load, it was easily carried. Four friends may unite in efforts to get a lost one to Christ, at least praying together for him.

The earnestness of these men was shown in what they did. They could not get their friend into the presence of Christ because of the crowd in the house and about the door. But they would not be discouraged. They carried him up on the roof, and, making an opening for him, let him down right into Christ's presence. In seeking the salvation of our friends, we should be very earnest. If we really care for them, we will never be discouraged or balked in our efforts to get them to Christ. Too many of our efforts are feeble and transient. We should be willing to make greatest sacrifices and endure anything to get an unsaved friend to Christ.

It is said that Jesus saw their faith. How could He see faith? Faith is not something material. He saw it in what they did. Nobody said a word, so far as we are told; but the four men showed their earnestness and their strong faith in uniting their strength and carrying their helpless burden up the outside stairs, then in breaking up the roof overhead, and in lowering the poor man into the presence of the Healer. Thus, although there was no spoken prayer, there was a prayer in the men's hearts, which found expression in what they did. It was in their determined overcoming of all obstacles that Jesus saw their faith. There are wordless prayers which our Lord hears and answers. We may notice that part, at least, of the faith which Christ saw was in the hearts of the man's friends. We do not know certainly that there was any faith in the man himself. We may exercise faith in behalf of others. Parents may bring a child to Christ, and He will see their faith. Friends may present a friend unsaved or in trouble, and Christ will see faith and send blessing. There may have been faith also in the sufferer—at least in the end. There was in the man's very helplessness, as he lay there on his mat, that which appealed to the pity of Christ. There were no words of pleading, but there was faith, and it found expression in wordless supplication, which was more eloquent than the most beautiful human liturgies. Jesus looked down upon this helpless man and saw faith. We must show our faith in our acts.

It seemed at first as if Christ had misunderstood the wish of the paralytic and his friends. The man had come to have his palsy cured, and instead of doing this Jesus forgave his sins, leaving him still unhealed. Had the Master made a mistake? As we look more deeply, however, we see that He made no mistake. Indeed, the prayer was only over-answered. We do not always know what our deepest need is. We think it is the curing of our sickness, the lifting away of our burden, or the bettering of our worldly condition, when our deepest, most real need is the saving of our soul, the lifting away of our sin, the changing of our relation to God. This man's dumb prayer was for healing—he wanted to be able to walk about again, to use his hands and feet, to become active. The Master looked at the paralyzed limbs and quivering frame and saw deeper, and answered another prayer first, because that was what the poor man needed most to have done. There are a great many troubles we would like to have removed, but which we can keep and still be noble and useful; but our sin we must get clear of, or we shall perish forever. Therefore Christ often does for us the things we need, though we do not ask to have them done, instead of the things we should like to have done.

He answers our heart's needs before He gratifies our mere wishes. Often when we cry for comfort and ease He looks deeper than we can see and says, "It is your sin, My child, that is your sorest trouble." Then He does not give us what we ask because He wants us to seek for the curing of the deadly heart-trouble first. Nothing else that God can give us would be a blessing while our sins are still unforgiven.

Then, after Jesus had forgiven the man's sins, He performed the other healing also. He made the man rise, take up his bed, and go to his house. He first answered the deepest need, and then, when peace had filled the man's soul and he was willing now to go home even with his palsy, if that were God's will, since heaven had come into his heart, then Christ gave him the other gift—healing. The palsy had a mission—it brought the man to the Healer and Savior. When its mission was accomplished it was dismissed as a servant no longer needed. Jesus never causes pain or suffering without some purpose of love. He is not pleased to see us suffer. Every pang of ours goes to His heart. In all our affliction He is afflicted. But He is far too kind to call away the angel of pain before His beneficent work in us is fully produced. The surgeon would be cruel, not kind, who because of the patient's cries should withdraw the knife when his operation was but half done. God's love is not of that sort. He is not too gentle to cause us pain and to leave us to suffer unrelieved, even for years, when suffering has yet a mission incomplete in us. Yet the moment pain's work is finished God sends the messenger away. When this man's soul was saved, Jesus healed the sickness which had been the messenger of blessing to him and whose ministry was now completed.

Here again the man was called upon for an exercise of faith. Jesus bade him rise, and straightway he took up his bed and walked away before all the people. The command to rise seemed a strange one to give to a paralyzed man. He could not lift his head nor walk home. But as we look at the helpless form, he does rise and obey that impossible command. The lesson is that when Christ gives a command, He always gives strength to do it. We have no power in ourselves to do Christ's will, but as we strive to obey His commands the needed grace flows into our soul. Whatever Christ bids us do, He will by His grace enable us to do it, if we simply go forward in unwavering faith and unquestioning obedience.

11

Feasting and Fasting

Scripture Reading: Mark 2:13–22

The first year of Christ's public ministry was a year of obscurity. He was not yet well-known. Then, as He spoke and served, His fame grew. We are now in His year of popular favor—His second year. One scene of enthusiasm follows another. After the healing of the paralytic the people were amazed, and glorified God, saying, "We never saw it on this fashion." Then the record goes on without a break, telling of the Master's going out from the house where He had been hiding, and that all the multitude resorted unto Him. Then He taught them.

In going along the road, Jesus came to a little office or booth by the wayside and stopped by the door. He had an errand there. He was looking for a man whom He might send forth as an apostle, to carry the blessings of the gospel to others. Jesus is always looking for men He can trust to do His errands. If we would have Him choose for us important and responsible work, we should be faithful in our present service, however lowly it may be. We are being tested continually to show whether we will be faithful. He is looking always for those who are diligent and may be depended on. He never chooses an idle man to entrust with any important duty. He wants men who have capacity and who are eager and busy. Then He wants messengers whom nothing can tempt to be unfaithful.

He saw sitting in this little office the man He was looking for. He was sitting at the place of toll, the place where the people passing by with goods stopped to pay the taxes on the things they were carrying. That seemed a strange place for Jesus to find a man for His work, especially a man who should become an apostle. Those who were engaged in this business of collecting customs were not reputable men. They were hated by their people because their work was to gather taxes for the Romans. Usually they were dishonest, or extortionate, taking all they could get. The publicans were regarded as mean and unpatriotic. However, Jesus can take even a bad and disreputable life and out of it make an apostle.

One day Michaelangelo saw a soiled and cast-away block of marble lying among rubbish in an outhouse. Once it was a magnificent block, with great possibilities. But it had been cut and hacked by an incompetent hand, and seemed to be utterly ruined, so that nothing ever could be done with it, nothing beautiful ever made of it. But to the eye of the artist, as he looked upon the stone, a vision of beauty rose, and from the soiled block he carved the wonderful statue of young David, one of the masterpieces of art which the visitor sees at Florence. Many of those who have finally reached the noblest manhood and have done most for the world have thus been rescued by Christ from what seemed hopeless ruin. Levi or Matthew, whom Jesus found that day in the tax-collector's booth, became in the great Master's hand one of the worthiest and most honored of the apostles.

When Jesus saw the man, His eye discerned the possibilities in him, and He called him to come with Him. The word went at once to the heart of the publican, and he dropped all and promptly followed Christ. Thus he set the example for all who hear the same voice. That was the way Saul did, too, when he saw the glorified form before Him and recognized in it the Messiah. He made a complete surrender and asked for his work. We should learn to follow Christ whenever we hear His call. There should be no tomorrow in our answer—now is the accepted time [see 2 Cor. 6:2].

Matthew made a great feast, Luke tells us, inviting his old companions, that he might honor his new Master, and that they might see Him. He set a good example of confession. He seems to have made this feast to let his friends know what he had done, and to introduce Jesus to them. A noble minister used to say he wanted everybody to fall in love with Jesus Christ, his Friend. Everyone who begins to follow Christ should want to have his companions and friends follow Him, too. The scribes and the Pharisees were always envious of the popularity of Jesus, and took every occasion to say slighting things about Him. When they saw Him that day in Levi's house, and the crowds pressing about Him, they accused Him, saying He had chosen bad company in eating with publicans and sinners. Jesus said He was like a physician, and "they that are whole have no need of a physician, but they that are sick." No one would criticize the taste of a physician because he is always going among sick people. He would be a strange physician who would drive around all day, calling only on well people, chatting and eating with them, and refusing to go among the sick. His mission is to the sick, not to the well. Jesus came as a physician. His mission in this world is to the lost. It should not have been thought a strange thing, therefore, that He went among the lost, the fallen, the outcast. These were the very persons He had come to seek. He would not have been fulfilling His mission if He had devoted Himself altogether to the good, the spiritually refined, the pure, disregarding the unholy and disreputable. The mission of the Church today is to sinners. None are too vile to be sought out with sympathy and love. Christians should not spend all their time in fellowship with other Christians. They must think of those who are not living right, and, like their Master, must try to save them.

Fasting was practiced in those days, not only by the Pharisees, but also by the disciples of John the Baptist. These noticed that the followers of Jesus did not fast, and they came and asked Jesus why His disciples did not. He said that it was not the time to fast when He was with them. The Pharisees fasted by the almanac, without reference to their particular condition at the time. Jesus said that there was a time to fast. Fasting indicates penitence, sorrow for sin, humiliation. It would be thought very strange if a family, without any sorrow in their midst, all of them happy, with the circle unbroken, should go into deep mourning. There is no fitness in wearing the garb of mourning when there is joy on every hand. But when one is dead in the home, then it does not seem strange to see the family showing their sadness and wearing the tokens of grief. Jesus said that there was no reason why His disciples should be fasting and sorrowful at that particular time, for He was with them. There would be no fitness in fasting then.

The Master's words are aimed against all empty professions and meaningless forms. When there is cause for mourning, let there be mourning. But when all things are joyous, let there be gladness. Our religion should be natural and sincere, never affected or hypocritical. Over-expressions of religious emotion or feeling are condemned. Christ wants His disciples true through and through, their forms of worship filled with sincerity of heart and life.

The religion of the Pharisees was chiefly one of forms and ceremonies. The religion Jesus had come to establish was one of the heart. He had not come merely to make some little changes in the Jewish forms and ceremonies; He had come to give the world something altogether new—the gospel of God's love and grace. The Jewish forms and ceremonies in their day had a meaning. They were symbolical and typical of great spiritual truths, a sort of kindergarten teaching of God's will. But all these truths and emblems were fulfilled by Christ Himself, and now the old forms are done away, as the blossom is done away when the fruit comes. Christianity needs no other system of types and forms—it is a religion of the heart; it seeks expression in forms of its own. The danger of forms is that they shall come to be depended on instead of vital religion. Jesus did not merely attach certain new lessons and practices to the old wine skins of Judaism; rather, He put life and love and grace, the new things of the gospel, into the new and simple forms of Christian faith.

12

The Use of the Sabbath

Scripture Reading: Mark 2:23—3:6

One of the most important questions which Christian people have to consider in these days is that of the proper use of the Lord's Day. What is its purpose? What place should it occupy among the days? What should it mean to us? How should it be observed? It would be a great calamity to us if we were to lose our Sabbath altogether. We should then have no churches, no religious services, no Christian institutions, no Sunday schools, no Christian fellowship; for it is the Sabbath that is the inspirer and helper of all these institutions and blessings. Jesus loved the Sabbath. He took from it, as then observed, certain things which had grown up about it and spoiled its beauty; but He did not abolish it. He sanctified it, and then gave it back to us an institution of good and of blessing.

One Sabbath Jesus and His disciples were going through the grain fields. We may infer that they were on their way to the morning synagogue service—were going to church, as we would say. There are many evidences that Jesus was always regular in His attendance upon church ordinances. We would think that He did not require the spiritual help which comes from public worship; yet He seems always to have sought it. If Jesus kept up church-going habits, surely we should not think that we can get along without them. We would do well to emphasize this particular part of Sabbath duty. Young people should feel the obligation and realize their own need of what the church can give them. We ought to come together to worship God, to recognize Him before men as our God, and to render due homage and praise to Him from whom all our blessings come.

Then we need the help that the Lord sends from the sanctuary. We need the instruction, counsel, warning, encouragement, and comfort which come from the faithful preaching of the Word. We need the fellowship of Christians, the strength that comes from human sympathy. In our thought about how to observe the Sabbath, let us not forget to get into it a healthful measure of church-going. We may be sure that Jesus and His disciples were not merely taking a walk for pleasure that morning, and that they were not merely traveling somewhere. We need to be careful how we seek our own pleasure on the Lord's Day. We ought to make the Sabbath different from other days—restful, quiet, a day for receiving the divine blessings of health and renewal, as well as spiritual good and enriching.

The Pharisees were exceedingly punctilious in the observance of the letter of the law and, besides this, of the rabbinical rules which had been added from time to time to the law. They also regarded it as their duty to keep a close watch on others and to note any failure in them to follow the rules. They were especially keen in watching Jesus and His disciples. Their motive was not sincere interest in the teaching and example of Jesus, but to criticize Him, that they might accuse Him. They went along with Him, not because they loved to be with Him, but as spies upon His conduct.

We get two lessons. One is that the conduct of Christians is always watched by unfriendly eyes, eyes keen to detect the slightest apparent fault. We should live at all times most carefully, so as to give no occasion for just censure. Yet the example of our Lord's disciples here shows us that we are not to be slaves to traditional opinions which have no foundation in the Word of God. The other lesson is that we can find better business than playing the spy on the life and conduct of our fellowmen. The unfriendly espionage of these sanctimonious religionists on the actions of our Lord and His disciples, appears in our eyes very mean and contemptible. Let us remember that it is no less mean and contemptible for us to watch our fellow Christians in order to discover flaws. Suppose they do not live quite as they should live; are we their judges?

Then perhaps our sin of uncharitableness in watching them may be as great as theirs of some other inconsistency.

The scribes were always referring people to what was written. With a keen irony Jesus reminds them of an incident in their Scriptures which had a bearing on the matter which was troubling them [see 1 Sam. 21:1–6]. David was a favorite Jewish hero, and what he did ought to be taken at least as a precedent. The teaching is for us, too, and its meaning is that "works of necessity" may be done on the Sabbath. It was in the literal sense a breach of the ceremonial law for the priests to give David the shewbread; but it was not a breach of the spirit of the law, for the necessity of hunger overruled the ceremonial regulation. The work of the priests in the temple was also in a literal way a continual profanation of the Sabbath; yet they were "blameless" because their work was necessary for the maintenance of the ordained worship of God. In like manner our Lord taught that the act of His disciples in plucking and rubbing out the heads of grain to get food to satisfy their immediate hunger was a work of necessity, and therefore was not a sin. Though the letter of the law may have been violated, there was no violation of its spirit.

So we get the principle, that "works of necessity" are excepted in the law of the Sabbath which requires the cessation of secular labor. What these works of necessity are cannot be established by minute rules and regulations. This would be to repeat the error of the Jewish teachers, who added to the plain and simple law of God so many of their own traditions as to obscure and bury away the law itself and make their religion burdensome and oppressive. What these works of necessity are can be left to the enlightened conscience of the faithful followers of Christ.

Jesus went further and made a general statement concerning the purpose of the Sabbath which is very important and which we should always remember in thinking of the observance of the day. "He said unto them, The sabbath was made for man, and not man for the sabbath." The Sabbath is part of God's plan of love for man. It was not made for him merely as an arbitrary law, without a reason. It is as much a law of his nature, or in harmony with his nature, as is the night, which bids him cease from toil and seek rest and sleep. It was made for his physical nature. Then it was made also for his spiritual good, to give him opportunity, not for physical rest alone, but for communion with God when the noise of business and of toil has ceased. It was made for man, to promote his highest welfare in every regard.

Jesus clearly showed, both by His own example and by His teaching, that the Sabbath is never meant to be a burden or to work oppressively. Though work is forbidden on the Sabbath, it is not a violation to prepare food sufficient to meet the hunger of our bodies, to lift a beast out of a pit, or to heal a sick man. Not many people are now disposed, however, to make the Sabbath a heavy burden or a cruel yoke. The tendency is the other way. At the same time it is well to understand just what our Lord taught on this subject. Works of necessity are allowed, even though they may seem to violate the letter of the law. So also are works of mercy, works of benevolence. It will be hard, however, to get out of this great saying of our Lord's any excuse for the hundredth part of the secular go-ings-on that men want to bring in under the shield of Christ's teaching.

Jesus went still further, and asserted His own authority over the day. "The Son of man is lord also of the sabbath." Therefore He had a right to interpret the laws for its observance. He does not intimate any inten-tion of abolishing the Sabbath. He had just said, "The sabbath was made for man, and not man for the sabbath." Because the Sabbath was made for man, it came under the Lordship of the Son of man. As Mediator He had all the interests of humanity committed to His hands. The Sabbath was not to be abolished, for it was part of the very divine constitution which the loving God had ordained for His children. Christ came not to destroy, but to fulfill. He took the Sabbath, therefore, and stripped off the temporary ceremonial regulations, and set aside all the burdensome traditional rules, and then put into it its true spiritual meaning, just as He did to the other commandments in the Sermon on the Mount. Under His touch the Sabbath was made new in a sense. The bondage of the letter gave way to the liberty of the Spirit. He liberated His Church from the oppressive burdens of a rabbinical Sabbath and made the day one of joy and gladness, a type and foretaste of heaven.

"He saith unto them, Is it lawful to do good on the sabbath day, or to do evil? to save life, or to kill?" In the account of this incident in Matthew's Gospel [12:11, 12], we learn that Jesus gave an illustration. "What man shall there be among you, that shall have one sheep, and if it fall into a pit on the sabbath day, will he not lay hold on it, and lift it out? How much then is a man better than a sheep! Wherefore it is lawful to do well on the sabbath day." He appealed to simple common sense. The Jews could not but admit that a man should lift his sheep out of the pit on the Sabbath. Whatever their traditions said about such a case, the practice of the people would be on the merciful line. Now Jesus asked: "Is not a man better than a sheep? If it is right to help a sheep out of a pit on the Sabbath, it surely is right to relieve a sufferer from his malady on that day." So we get the lesson that it is right to do good on the Sabbath. It is right for physicians to attend to their patients on that day. It is right for those whose duty it naturally is, to nurse the sick and care for them on the Sabbath. It is right to visit the sick, when we can carry blessing or cheer to them; to visit the afflicted, when we can carry comfort to them; to visit the poor, when we can minister to their needs or relieve their distress; to go out among the unsaved, when we can do anything to bring them to Christ and save their souls; to gather neglected children from the streets and from Christian homes and bring them to the Sunday school and the Church. Jesus here gives us warrant for many works of mercy on His own Holy Day.

When Jesus entered the synagogue, there was a man there with a withered hand. The scribes watched very intently to see whether Jesus would heal this man on the Sabbath. He asked the man to stand forth, as if He would cure him; but first asked the scribes whether it was lawful to do good on the Sabbath. They were not willing to commit themselves in answering His question, and after a little while Jesus proceeded to heal the man. "He saith unto the man, Stretch forth thine hand. And he stretched it forth; and his hand was restored." Jesus would not let the man suffer because of the criticism of the Jews. We get a lesson here. We must not be hindered in doing good by the opposition and the fault-finding of those about us. We must do our good deeds fearlessly, serving Christ regardless of the world's sneers and hindering.

13

The Appointment of the Twelve

Scripture Reading: Mark 3:7–19

W e can hardly realize how wide the influence of Jesus was at this time. The multitude that followed Him came not only from Galilee, but also from Judea, from beyond the Jordan, and even from the Gentile cities of Tyre and Sidon and the country surrounding them. The throng was so great that Jesus with His disciples withdrew to the sea. He wished to do His work without interruption. Thus we have our Lord's example for sometimes withdrawing from opposition. It was not lack of courage that led Him to do this. He knew that the conspiracy of His enemies would in the end be successful, yet He would not throw His life away. Nothing could be gained by His staying in their midst at this time. There was no testimony to be borne. Besides, His work was not yet finished. When, at last, His work was all done, the plots had all ripened, and He knew that the rulers were about to kill Him, He did not withdraw, nor did He show any fear or lack of bravery.

There are times when duty requires us to flee from danger and thus save our lives for further service. We are certainly never to court danger, nor to be reckless in our courage. On another occasion Jesus said to His disciples, "When they persecute you in this city, flee into the next." Christian prudence is an important element in Christian courage. It often requires a higher courage to avoid danger than to rush into it; to flee away from angry enemies than to answer back and incite them to further wrath.

The great report of our Lord's works of mercy and kindness went out everywhere, and multitudes were drawn to Him. One who does good to others will always have followers. The world is full of sorrow and suffering, and hearts hunger for sympathy. When one who has a gentle spirit and a hand whose touch gives blessing comes among men, people welcome him. Love always finds its mission. We are apt to criticize the motive in such following. "For the loaves and fishes," we say. But people know a friend when he comes among them; and when one suffers and has been helped, it is no wonder that other like sufferers come with their needs. Jesus loved the people—that was the secret; He loved them, and they knew it. People always know when a man truly and sincerely loves them. It was written of one of these lovers of his fellowmen:

> His magic was not far to seek,
> He was so human! Whether strong or weak,
> Far from his kind he neither sank nor soared,
> But sat an equal guest at every board.

> No beggar ever felt him condescend,
> No prince presume; for still himself he bore
> At manhood's simple level, and where'er
> He met a stranger, there he left a friend.

The kindness of Jesus was not discouraged by the ingratitude and enmity of men. Though the plots of His enemies drove Him out of the city, they did not stop His doing good. Though some rejected His love, His heart was not closed. Capernaum lost much when He went out of its gates; but on the throngs which followed Him the gracious blessings fell. Persecution scatters the seed which it means to destroy. When the first Christians were driven from Jerusalem, it was only to carry the word into all the countries round about to which they fled. They "went about, preaching" [Matt. 4:23]. Opposition must never silence the lips that carry the words of life. If one rejects and scorns you, bear your message to another. You will always find some ready to receive the blessing you have to give. Especially are the people who have "plagues," who are in any misfortune or distress, ready to press upon him who comes to them with a heart of love and with power to do them good.

The people pressed up close to Him, that they might touch Him. A touch was enough. All that were touched were made whole. Life flowed from Him to them. Health went from His rich, wholesome life and expelled their sickness. So a touch is always enough. Anyone who really touches Christ is healed. But we must be sure to touch Him. It is not enough to be in the crowd that gathers about Him. Only those are healed who touch Him. It is not enough to be in the congregation that worships. One sitting or bowing next to us may receive a great blessing, while we receive none at all. It is because he reaches out his hand of faith and touches Christ; while we, physically as close to Christ as he is, do not put out our hand to touch Him; and therefore, receive no blessing. We ought, as Christ's disciples, to be so full of life and love that anyone who touches us shall get a blessing from us. Just to have their handshake is a benediction. Their mere presence in a sick room gives comfort. It is worth while to be such a person. Do you want to know the secret? It is love. Love people really, truly, genuinely, and there will flow from you always, to every life that touches yours, an influence of healing.

Jesus stood in the throng and called certain men to come to Him. He singled out the persons and called them individually. That is the way He is doing continually—standing and calling men to come to Him. He does not call a crowd—He calls people by name, calls them one by one. Everyone who hears His voice should answer—leave the world's company, step boldly out, cross over the line, and take his place by the side of Jesus. There are several things to be said about the way these men responded to Christ's call. They did it freely. Although He had chosen them out of a whole nation, and called them, there was no compulsion laid upon them to go with Him. They could have refused if they had chosen; Christ never chooses His disciples by force. Then they responded promptly. There was no hesitation. They said nothing about considering the matter for awhile. They did not talk about being unfit or unworthy; they did not tell Him that they were afraid they could not keep their word if they promised to be Christians. They did not say, "Tomorrow we will go." The moment they heard their names called they answered. Then their answer was given in a way that could be understood. Whenever they heard the call they stepped out with firm tread, and, crossing over the space between the crowd and the Master, they joined themselves to Him. It was not done secretly. They did not wait until they were alone with Him, and then tell Him quietly and timidly that they had made up their minds to accept His invitation. They did not propose to be His disciples and yet stay among their old friends and keep on at the old business. They immediately separated themselves from the people about them, and went over to Him, putting themselves absolutely into His hands, to be His and do His bidding so long as they lived. This is the way these men started in their apostleship, and the way everyone should start whom Jesus calls to be His disciple.

He chose the Twelve that they might be with Him. That is the first thing always, before preaching or teaching or working for Christ. We must be disciples ourselves before He will use us to make disciples of others or to carry His messages and blessings to others. He employs none as His servants who are not His followers. One reason why we must first be with Him is that we may be taught by Him. The apostles learned from their Master the things they themselves afterward taught. We cannot do any good work for Christ until He teaches us how to do it. He teaches us by His Word, by His Spirit, through the impact of His own life, through our experiences. This is one reason we should study the Bible so carefully, that we may be able to teach others by our example and by our words the things Jesus would have us teach them. Another reason why we need to be with Him before we go out to testify for Him is that we may be actual witnesses for Him. We never can impress the world by giving second-hand information about Christ, by repeating things we have heard others say, or have read in books, about Him. We must be able to tell what we have seen and learned for ourselves from personal fellowship with Him.

These men were chosen not merely to official place, but for service—"to preach, and to have authority to heal sicknesses." This authority was given to test their commission. When Moses went to the people and to Pharaoh as God's messenger, and when they demanded evidence that God had sent him, he was to work certain signs in their presence to prove his claim. So the apostles had power given to them to perform works of wonder as their credentials. Besides, those works of mercy which they wrought were examples of what the gospel should do wherever it goes. We say there are no miracles now. Is this true? Are no sick people healed now? Are no evil spirits cast out? Are no blind eyes opened, no deaf ears unstopped, no lame made to walk, no dead raised? If miracles are not produced in the physical realm, they surely are in the spiritual.

Eyes are opened to see God and heavenly things. Ears are opened to hear the voice of the Spirit. Fevers of passion are cured. Sicknesses of soul are healed. The evil spirits of greed, lust, selfishness are cast out. These are the credentials of all teaching and preaching. Power is given yet to Christ's ministers and to all His disciples—power to heal the sick and cast out demons.

One of the men chosen was known as Simon, but Jesus gave him a surname—Peter. These two names are suggestive. "Simon" shows the rude fisherman of Galilee, with all his rashness, his ignorance, his imperfection; "Peter" shows the apostle of the Acts and the Epistles; the rock firm and secure; the man of great power, before whose Spirit-filled eloquence thousands of proud hearts bow, swayed like the trees of the forest before the tempest; the gentle, tender soul whose words fall like a benediction; the noble martyr witnessing to the death for his Lord. Study the two names together to see what grace can do for a man. It is not hard to take roses, lilies, fuchsias, and all the rarest flowers, and with them make forms of exquisite beauty; but to take weeds, dead grasses, dried leaves trampled and torn, and faded flowers and make lovely things out of such materials, is the most severe test of skill. It would not be hard to take an angel and train him into a glorious messenger; but to take such a man as Simon, or as Saul, or as John Newton, or as John Bunyan, and make out of him a holy saint and a mighty apostle—that is the test of power. Yet that is what Christ did, and has been doing ever since. He takes the poorest stuff, despised and worthless, outcast of men oftentimes, and when He has finished His gracious work we behold a saint whiter than snow.

The sculptor saw an angel in the rough, blackened stone, rejected and thrown away; and when men beheld the stone again, behold—there was the angel, cut from the block! In one of the English cathedrals is a window, the admiration of all beholders, made by a workman from the bits of glass thrown away by the master. So heaven is filling with glorified souls gathered from the despised and rejected of earth. We should never be discouraged by our unworthiness or our many faults. Christ can take us as we are, and in His hands our life shall grow into purity and loveliness until He presents us at last before the throne faultless and perfect. There is only one thing that needs to concern us—we must make sure that we are in Christ's school, that we really put ourselves into His hands.

14

Poverty and Riches

Scripture Reading: Luke 6:20–26; 16:19–31

The Beatitudes are glimpses of heaven; that is, the conditions they describe are qualities which belong to the heavenly life. Those who live there are lowly, are meek, are pure in heart, hunger after righteousness, are merciful. We cannot think of any persons in heaven who are proud, resentful, or unmerciful, who thirst after worldly power or fame. To get the Beatitudes of the New Testament into our hearts and lives, even as beginnings, is to enter upon the heavenly life.

"Blessed be ye poor: for yours is the kingdom of God." This beatitude is not pronounced on the poor in worldly circumstances; for one may be very poor and yet very proud, or one may be rich in worldly goods and yet be very lowly in spirit. Nor is it on the poor in mind; for mental poverty is not necessarily a state of blessedness, and ignorance certainly is not desirable. It is the poor in spirit, in disposition, on whom the beatitude is pronounced; that is, the lowly in heart, the humble, those who are conscious of their unworthiness. Humility is a spirit that bows reverently before God and then holds its most divine gifts as not too good or too fine to be used in Christ's name in the service of the lowliest of God's creatures. The Bible everywhere speaks its praises of humility. God dwells with the humble. Christ only once opens a window into His own heart, and through this window it is this picture that

258

we see—"I am meek and lowly in heart" [Matt. 11:29]. To be poor in spirit is to be rich toward God, while pride of heart is spiritual poverty. Humility is the key that opens the gate of prayer, while to the loud knocking of pride there comes no answer. The kingdom of heaven belongs to those who are lowly. They may wear no earthly crown, but a real crown of glory, unseen by men, rests even here upon their head.

We are sure always of Christ's sympathy with the poor. He was Himself brought up in poverty. His mother could bring only the offering of the poor when she brought her child to present Him to the Lord. In His public ministry He said He had not where to lay His head. He rode on a borrowed beast on His triumphal entry. He slept in a borrowed grave when He was dead. He understands poverty's conditions. He is the poor man's friend. Poverty itself is not a beatitude; but the poor who love Christ and follow Him have many blessings.

> Come ye who find contentment's very core
> In the light store
> And daisied path
> Of poverty,
> And know how more
> A small thing that the righteous hath
> Availeth, than the ungodly's riches great.

"Blessed are ye that hunger now: for ye shall be filled." Hunger means dissatisfaction, craving, desire, yearning, longing. It strikes us somewhat strangely at first that there should be a beatitude for dissatisfaction. We know that peace is promised to the Christian, and peace is calm repose and satisfied restfulness. The word "hunger" appears to suggest experiences incompatible with rest and peace. But when we think a little more deeply, we see that spiritual hunger must form a part of all true Christian experience. In all life hunger is a mark of health. It is so in physical life; the loss of appetite indicates disease. So a healthy mind is a hungry one; when one becomes satisfied with one's attainments, one ceases to grow. The same is true in spiritual life; hunger is health. If we become satisfied with our faith, love, obedience, our communion with God, and our consecration to Christ, we are truly in a sad condition. We have ceased to grow. Often invalids die amid plenty, die of starvation, not because they can get no food, but because they have no appetite. There are many professing Christians who are starving their souls in the midst of abundance of spiritual provision because they have no hunger. There is nothing for which we should pray more earnestly than for spiritual longing.

"Blessed are ye that weep now: for ye shall laugh." Weeping is not usually considered a blessed condition. We do not think of those having sorrow as fortunate. We pity them, and think their condition most unenviable. Here, however, is a special beatitude for mourners. Probably Jesus meant particularly those who are sorrowing on account of their sins. In all this world there is nothing so precious before God as tears of contrition; no diamonds or pearls shine with such brilliance in His sight. It was Jesus Himself who said that there is joy in the presence of God over one sinner that repents on the earth. Truly blessed, therefore, are those who grieve over their sins; a holy light shines from heaven upon all such mourners. They are comforted with God's pardon and peace. But the beatitude refers also to those who are in sorrow. Blessing is never nearer to us than when we are in affliction. Someday we shall see that we have received our best things from heaven not in the days of our joy and gladness, but in the time of trial and affliction. Tears are lenses through which our dim eyes see more deeply into heaven and look more fully upon God's face than in any other way. Sorrows cleanse our heart of earthliness and fertilize our life. The days of pain really do far more for us than the days of rejoicing. We grow best when clouds hang over us, because clouds bear rain, and rain refreshes.

"Blessed are ye, when man shall hate you." We do not like to be hated. Nor can everybody who is hated take shelter under this beatitude. Many people deserve to be hated. It is only those who are hated for being good and doing good who can claim this blessing. If any of us are suffering in this way, here is comfort for us. There have been times in the history of the Church and in the history of almost every great reform when those who would be loyal and true could be so only at the cost of losing their friends, often at the cost of property and reputation, even of personal liberty—sometimes of life itself. We must read down to the end of the verse before we begin to congratulate ourselves that the hatred we find in our neighbors toward us is a mark of God's favor. "For the Son of man's sake," the verse reads.

"Woe unto you that are rich! for ye have received your consolation." Evidently it is not very safe to be rich. It is not easy to be rich and to be a good Christian. Jesus said a great many words about the rich and about riches which show that they who have wealth are in a perilous position. People would not think of a prosperous man, a man growing rich, as especially needing the prayers of a congregation. Yet perhaps this is the very man in all the community who most needs to be remembered in prayer. Those who are rich or getting rich would better look well to their spiritual state.

15

The Law of Love

Scripture Reading: Luke 6:27–38

There is a great similarity between the discourse in Luke and that given in Matthew. There are also such marked differences that many writers think they were spoken at different times. It matters not, for our purpose, whether they are the same or a different sermon.

The law of love was taught in the Old Testament. If one met his enemy's ox or ass going astray, he was to bring it back to him. But here the teaching goes much farther. "I say unto you which hear, Love your enemies, do good to them which hate you." This is not an easy lesson. It is never easy to be a Christian. The easy way does not lead toward heaven. It takes a new birth to make us Christians at all. Loving enemies is not a natural affection. People talk about the Sermon on the Mount having in it all the gospel they want; but if they try to live it they will find that they need both an atoning Savior and a sanctifying Spirit. Yet Christ wants us to make these teachings the rule of our life. Of course we cannot love enemies just as we love our friends. It is a different kind of love that is required. We cannot take them into our confidence, nor can we make them our intimate companions; but we can desire and seek their good. We can restrain all feelings of resentment and all wishes to return evil for evil. We may have in our heart kindly thoughts and desires for them, and may even seek opportunities to do them favors

262

and kindnesses. If anyone hates us and seeks to do us harm, instead of repaying him "in his own coin," we may do good for evil, continuing to pour out love and blessing. This and all the other precepts of this lesson find in the life of Christ Himself their perfect illustration.

The following incident will be helpful in illustrating love for enemies: At the close of the first day of the battle of Fredericksburg, in the American Civil War, hundreds of the Union wounded were left lying on the ground. All night and most of the next day the field was swept by artillery, and no one could venture to the sufferers' relief.

Many who heard the poor soldiers' piteous appeals felt the pangs of human compassion, but stifled them under dread necessity. But at length one brave fellow behind the stone ramparts where the Southern forces lay gave way to his sympathy and rose superior to the love of life. He was a sergeant in a South Carolina regiment, and his name was Richard Kirkland. In the afternoon he hurried to General Kershaw's headquarters and, finding the commanding officer, said to him, excitedly:

"General, I can't stand this any longer."

"What's the matter, sergeant?" asked the general.

"Those poor souls out there have been praying and crying all night and all day, and it's more than I can bear. I ask your permission to go and give them water."

The general hesitated for a moment, but finally said, with emotion: "Kirkland, it is sending you to your death; but I can oppose nothing to such a motive as yours. For the sake of it, I hope God will protect you. Go!"

Furnished with a supply of water, the brave sergeant immediately stepped over the wall and applied himself to his work of Christlike mercy. Wondering eyes looked on as he knelt by the nearest sufferer and, tenderly raising his head, held the cooling cup to his parched lips. Before his first ministry of love was finished, everyone in the Union lines understood the mission of the noble soldier in gray, and not a man fired a shot.

He stayed there on that terrible field an hour and a half, giving drink to the thirsty and dying, straightening their cramped and mangled limbs, pillowing their heads on their knapsacks, and spreading their army coats and blankets over them as a mother would cover her own children—and all the while he was so engaged, until his gentle ministry was finished, the fusillade of death was hushed. Hatred forbore its rage in a tribute of honor to a deed of pity.

The lesson of love continues, "Bless them that curse you, pray for them which despitefully use you." These counsels are intensely practical. In answer to men's cursings, revilings, and insults we are to return words of peace, kindness, and love. Those who treat us abusively we are to pray for instead of uttering threats against them and imprecations upon them. We remember how Jesus Himself lived out this law of love. There were many who cursed Him and reviled Him, but He never lost the sweetness of love out of His heart. He never on any occasion returned a word of cursing or anger or even of impatience in answer to the bitterest revilings of His enemies. "When He was reviled, He reviled not again; when He suffered, He threatened not, but committed Himself to Him that judgeth righteously" [1 Pet. 2:23]. That is the example for us. We are to be silent when others speak evil of us or to us; or, if we speak, it is to be the soft answer that turns away wrath. We need not worry ourselves about the deserts of those who treat us unjustly, feeling that we should see to their punishment. We are to leave that to God, who judges righteously and who will take care also that no real harm shall come to us from the wrongs which others inflict on us, provided we keep ourselves in His love and in obedient spirit. The lesson has its ideal exemplification in our Lord's prayer on His cross for His murderers. His only answer to the driving of the nails through His hands and feet was, "Father, forgive them; for they know not what they do" [Luke 23:34]. That is the way He wants us to answer the cruelties and injuries which others may inflict upon us.

"Unto him that smiteth thee on the one cheek offer also the other." Christ gave not so much rules for special cases as principles to govern all conduct. We all think of these words as presenting a very beautiful direction for life, and yet we are apt to feel that they cannot be followed literally. Actually turning the other cheek to one who has smitten you in the face would most likely aggravate the person's anger. We take our Lord's example as the true exposition of His precepts. When He was on His trial, one of the officers standing by struck Him with His hand. Yet Jesus did not literally turn the other cheek to the smiter. Instead He calmly protested against the act, saying, "If I have spoken evil, bear witness of the evil; but if well, why smitest thou Me?" At the same time He fulfilled the spirit of His own precept, for He did not resist the wrong. Paul was one of the noblest of Christ's followers, and we have an example in his life. He was smitten on the mouth by the command of the high priest. He did not literally turn the other cheek, but vehemently rebuked him who had committed the outrage. We must therefore look for the true meaning of this teaching in its spirit, and not in its letter. We must be ready to endure not one but many injuries from others. We must be unresisting like our Lord. No wrongs from others should ever turn our love to hate. Christ's own life was an illustration of this. He was treated wrongfully at every step, but His heart never lost its sweetness, its gentleness, its patience, its desire to bless others and do them good.

"Give to every man that asketh thee; and of him that taketh away thy goods ask them not again." If this rule were to be literally carried, out it would put us at the mercy of every idle, greedy, grasping person. The result of such indiscriminate, unregulated giving would be only evil. It would do untold harm to those to whom we might thus give, fostering idleness, pauperism, and selfishness. It is the result of the observation and practical experience of all thoughtful and wise philanthropists that men should give most sparingly and discriminating to the poor. There are many cases where money or its equivalent is really needed; but ordinarily, giving money only harms the beneficiary. Human sympathy, love, cheer, strength to rise again, encouragement and opportunity to work—such help is far better than that which merely gives temporary aid, while it makes the person no more, but less, able for going on afterward. We are indeed to "give to everyone that asketh" us, but the giving must be that which will be a real benefit or blessing—never that which will do harm to a life. We are to give as God gives, generously, freely, lovingly, but always wisely, withholding that which would only hurt. The second part of the precept—"Of him that taketh away thy goods ask them not again"—must also be read intelligently in the light of other Scriptures. It is not meant to place Christians at the mercy of robbers and thieves, forbidding all property rights. The whole verse teaches gentleness, generosity, unselfishness, meekness, and the reverse of grasping greed.

"As ye would that men should do to you, do ye also to them likewise." This Golden Rule sums up the application of the law of love. We thus carry continually in our own conscience the touchstone by which to decide how we should treat others. We are to ask what we would think they should do to or for us if our circumstances were reversed. Yet even here there must be limitations. We might conceive of ourselves as mean, greedy, selfish, grasping, unjust, and then say that if we were in the place of the other person, or he in ours, we would want a great deal. Clearly it would not be in the spirit of the Lord's teaching to bring ourselves to such an interpretation of this Golden Rule, thus stripping ourselves of our possessions to gratify men's selfish greed. We must apply the rule intelligently, considering what would be right and just and truly good. Thus understood and applied, this rule is a wonderful help in shaping our treatment of others. Things which would appear repulsive in others, we must remember, appear no less so when seen in us by others. Things that look beautiful in our eyes when we see them in others, will look no less beautiful in us to the eyes of others.

"If ye love them which love you, what thank have ye? for sinners also love those that love them." Anybody ought to be able to love his friends, to do good to those that are good to him, and to lend to those of whom he expects to receive as much in return. Even the coldest and most calculating selfishness can go thus far in loving, doing good, and giving. It requires no regeneration, no mind of Christ, no help of the Holy Spirit, to help one to follow that sort of life creed. The most wicked heathen can do it, and the most common infidel, if not utterly devoid of shrewdness, will need no Sermon on the Mount to inspire and teach him that this is the wisest way to live. His kindness to others brings kindness to him in turn. His giving and lending put other men under obligation to show him the same favors when he may need them. But Christians must do more than sinners. They are born again, are children of God, have a new heart in them, and are to be like God Himself, loving enemies, doing and lending, hoping for no return.

"Judge not, and ye shall not be judged: condemn not, and ye shall not be condemned." We have no right to be censorious, to criticize others, to sit in judgment on their actions, to pronounce sentence on their conduct. Who made us judges of others? Under what law are they answerable to us for what they do? Besides, we have no wisdom for such judgment of others. We do not know all the circumstances and conditions that enter into human actions. There are often excellent reasons for doing certain things which to us, who do not know these reasons, seem to be unwise, or even wrong. There are elements of character which to us may appear unlovely because we see them in a certain light, but which, seen from a different point of view, in a different light, are really very lovely. In a certain church there is a stained window which, looked at from one point, gives a blurred and very unsatisfactory representation of a scene in our Lord's life, but which, observed from another point, represents the scene in a very beautiful way. The same difference in aspect is often observable in men's conduct and character, as seen from different points by different onlookers. Evidently, therefore, we are not qualified for judging, because of the fragmentary nature of our knowledge of the circumstances and conditions of people's lives. Let us learn to be charitable and tolerant, seeking for the good things and the beautiful rather than the evil and the repulsive.

16

Hearing and Doing

Scripture Reading: Luke 6:39–49

The Sermon on the Mount tells us the kind of persons Christians should be. The Beatitudes with which it opens show us pictures of the character that is like God. There is a legend which says that when Adam and Eve were driven out of Eden, an angel broke the gates into pieces, and the fragments flew all over the earth. The gems and precious stones which are picked up now in different parts of the world are these fragments of the paradise gates. It is only a fanciful legend, but it is true that in the Beatitudes, the Commandments, and other divine revealings of heavenly character we have fragments of the image of God which was on man's soul at the beginning, but which was shattered when man fell. The Sermon on the Mount is full of these gleaming fragments. We should study them to learn God's thought for our lives. Some of these shining words we have in our present study.

The Master said, "Why beholdest thou the mote that is in thy brother's eye, but perceivest not the beam that is in thine own eye?" It is strange how blind we can be to our own faults and blemishes, and how clearly at the same time we can see those of other people. An old writer says, "Men are more apt to use spectacles to behold other men's faults than looking glasses to behold their own." Our Lord's words in this verse point out this human tendency. A man can see a very small speck of dust in his neighbor's eye, while he is entirely unaware of the beam in his own eye. We would say that a beam in a man's eye would so blind him that he could not see the mote in his brother's eye. As Jesus expresses it, however, the man with the beam is the very one who sees the mote and thinks himself competent to pull it out. So it is in common life. No man is so keen in seeing faults in another as he who has some great fault of his own. A vain man is the first to detect indications of vanity in another. A bad-tempered person is most apt to be censorious toward another who displays irritability. One with a sharp, uncontrolled tongue has the least patience with another whose speech is full of poisoned arrows. A selfish man discovers little motes of selfishness in his neighbor. Rude people are the first to be hurt by rudeness in others. If we are quick to perceive blemishes and faults in others, the probability is that we have similar and perhaps far greater faults in ourselves. This truth ought to make us exceedingly careful in our judgment and modest in our expression of censure.

"How canst thou say to thy brother, Brother, let me cast out the mote that is in thine eye, when thou thyself beholdest not the beam that is in thine own eye?" We do not know through what experiences our brother has passed to receive the hurts and scars on his life which seem so ugly, so disfiguring, in our eyes. It would scarcely be in good taste for a dainty civilian, at the end of a day of battle, to criticize the soiled and torn garments and blood-stained face of the soldier just out of the struggle. We do not know through what fierce battles our brother has fought when we look critically upon his character and note peculiarities which offend us. The marks which we call faults may be but the scars received in life's hard battles, marks of honor, decorations of bravery and loyalty, if we only knew it. If we knew the real cause of all that seems unlovely in those we meet, we would have patience with them. "But is it not a kindness to a friend to take the mote out of his eye?" someone asks. If we meet a neighbor with a cinder in his eye, would it not be a brotherly thing to stop and take it out for him? Even if we have a whole lump of coal in our eye at the same time, would it not be a kindly act for us to desire to relieve our suffering fellowman? Then is it not just as true a kindness to want to cure another's fault, even though we have the same fault in more aggravated form in ourselves? If we did it in the right spirit, it would be. But the trouble is that we are not apt to look at our neighbor's faults in this loving and sympathetic way. It is the self-righteous spirit that our

Lord is here condemning. A man holds up his hands in horror at the speck he has found in his neighbor's character, and his neighbor sees in him an immensely magnified form of the same speck. Will the neighbor be likely to be greatly benefited by the rebuke he receives in these circumstances? Suppose a bad-tempered man lectures you on the sin of giving way to temper, or a dishonest man on some apparent lack of honesty, or a liar on the wickedness of falsehood, or a rude-mannered man on some little discourtesy of yours, or a hypocrite on insincerity, what good will such lectures do you, even admitting that you are conscious of the faults?

"Every tree is known by his own fruit." This is very clear in the matter of trees. Nature never deviates from her fixed laws. No one expects to gather grapes off a bramble bush, nor does one ever find thorns growing on an apple tree. Every tree bears its own fruit. The same is true of life. A bad heart does not make a good character, nor produce acts of beauty and holiness. It is a law of life that "as a man thinketh in his heart, so is he." We have it all here in the following verse. "A good man out of the good treasure of his heart bringeth forth that which is good; and the evil man out of the evil treasure bringeth forth that which is evil: for of the abundance of the heart his mouth speaketh." The thoughts make the life. The temple rose in silence on Mount Moriah; no noise of hammer or ax being heard in the building all the time it was in rising, because down in the quarries under the hill, and in the shops in the valley, every stone and every piece of timber was shaped and fitted perfectly before it was brought to be laid in its place. Our hearts are the quarries and the workshops, and our thoughts are the blocks of stone and the pieces of timber which are prepared and are then brought up and laid in silence upon the temple-wall of our character. Think beautiful thoughts, and your life will be beautiful. Cherish holy impulses, unselfish feelings, gentle desires, and your conduct will show beauty, purity, and gentleness to all who see you. The picture upon the canvas is first a dream, a thought in the artist's mind; so all the lovely things we do have their birth in lovely thoughts within us. On the other hand, think unholy thoughts, and your life will be unholy; think impure thoughts, and your character will be stained and blotched; think bitter, unkind thoughts, and your life will be full of unkindness, resentment, and bitterness. No wonder that we are told in the Bible to keep our heart with all diligence, for out of it are the issues of life. If we would be good and live well, we must have our heart renewed by God's grace. If Christ live in us, then all will be well.

"Why call ye Me Lord, Lord, and do not the things which I say?" Confession of Christ is a good thing, but unless the life correspond, it is only a mockery. It is not enough to honor Christ before men, praying to Him and ascribing power and glory to Him. Jesus tells us that those alone shall enter heaven who on earth do the will of the Father who is in heaven. Every confession of Christ must be confirmed and approved by obedience and holiness. "Simply to Thy cross I cling" is not all of the gospel of salvation; it is only half of it. No one is really clinging to the cross who is not at the same time faithfully following Christ and doing whatsoever He commands. We never can enter heaven unless heaven has first entered our heart. We shall do God's will in heaven when we get there; but we must learn to do it here, or we never shall get there.

"Whosoever cometh to Me, and heareth My sayings, and doeth them . . . is like a man which built a house, and digged deep, and laid the foundation upon a rock." All turns on the doing or not doing of Christ's words. Both the men described in these last verses hear the words of Christ, but one of them obeys, and thus builds upon the rock-foundation. The other hears, but does not obey, and builds upon the sand. The men built houses which were probably very much alike, so far as the appearance was concerned. But there were two kinds of ground in that vicinity. There was a wide valley which was dry and pleasant in the summer, when the men were looking for building sites. Then there were high, rocky bluffs. One man decided to build in the valley. It would cost less. The digging was easy, for the ground was soft. Then it was more convenient, for the bluffs were hard to reach. The other man looked farther ahead, and decided to build on high ground. It would cost far more, but it would be more safe. So the two homes went up at the same time, only the one in the valley was finished long before the other. At last the two families had settled in the two residences and were happy. But one night there was a storm. The rain poured down in torrents, and floods swept down off the mountains. The house that was built in the valley was carried away with its dwellers. The house on the bluff was unharmed. The illustration explains itself. He who has built in the valley is the man who has only professions, but has really never given his life to

Christ, nor built on Him as a foundation. The man who built on the rock is the man who has true faith in Christ, confirmed by living obedience. The storms that burst are earth's trials and the tempest of death and judgment. The mere professor of religion, not a possessor, is swept away in these storms; for he has only sand under him. He who is truly in Christ is secure; for no storm can reach the shelter of Christ's love. It is a terrible thing to cherish a false hope of salvation through life, only to find in the end that one has built upon the sand.

17

The Penitent Woman

Scripture Reading: Luke 7:36–50

Jesus did not turn His back on social pleasures. Herein He differed from the Baptist. We are almost certainly right in saying that John would not have gone to the wedding feast at Cana—Jesus went, and went gladly. John, we are quite sure, would not have gone to dinner at the Pharisee's house—Jesus accepted the invitation without a question and without hesitation. His heart was full of gracious love for men, and He sought every opportunity to do good. He was in the world, but His life remained heavenly in its purity and sweetness. Wherever He went, He carried blessing.

The two characters, besides Jesus, in this story, are the woman and the Pharisee. The woman was spoken of as "a sinner." The Pharisee was a sinner, too, but not of the same kind as the woman. Yet he scarcely seems to have been conscious that he was a sinner.

The woman was known as a bad woman; but something had happened just before we see her coming into Simon's house which had wrought a great change in her. Some of the gracious words of Jesus had fallen into her heart and had started there the vision of a better life.

The woman had followed Jesus into the house, drawn by love for Him who had saved her. She carried in her hand a box of costly ointment. She fell at the Master's feet. She wept, bathing His feet with her tears, then drying off the tears with her untressed hair, kissing them, and then anointing them with the ointment. All this was an expression of deep love which was quite in accordance with Oriental ways. It was the grateful act of a truly penitent sinner.

Jesus seems not to have disturbed the woman, and not to have said anything to her. But His host saw what was going on, and his spirit was vexed within him. He said nothing, either, but into his heart came the thought, "This man, if he were a prophet, would have known who and what manner of woman this is that toucheth him: for she is a sinner." According to Simon's religion a good man should keep himself altogether away from all who are not good. The touch of sinners would defile him.

What was the Pharisee's mistake? Did Jesus not know what kind of woman this was? Yes, He knew all about her, her whole past life, all its shame and guilt. But He knew also that she had repented, had given up her sin, had turned to God, and was now a saved woman.

The Pharisee thought that if Jesus had known who the woman was He would have spurned her. But Jesus had come to the world to be a physician, and a physician does not spurn the sick—they are the very persons it is His mission to receive and to help. The lost are the very ones Jesus came to save, and He will not turn His back on one of them. This woman was welcome at His feet just because she was a sinner, now penitent.

Of all those who come to Christ none are so welcome as those who have in their hearts a deep sense of unworthiness. The banished Peri in "Lalla Rookh," wandered everywhere, searching for earth's most precious thing, having been told that when she brings it, the bar will be lifted. Again and again she brought precious things, but it was only when she bore, last of all, a penitent's tear that the gate of heaven opened to her. The dearest thing on earth to God is a heart broken with sorrow for sin. "The sacrifices of God are a broken spirit: a broken and a contrite heart, O God, Thou wilt not despise" [Ps. 51:17].

In a beautiful parable Jesus explained to Simon the secret of the woman's love and her act of devotion. Two debtors, one of whom owed much, the other little, were both forgiven. Which would be the more grateful? Simon was able to answer the question, although it is doubtful if he understood its application.

Two thoughts may be noted here: one is that, though the debts of the two men were different, both were debtors, and neither could pay what he owed. Sinners differ as to the amount of their debt to God, but he who has sinned least is as unable to pay as he who has sinned most.

The other thought is that both were forgiven. That was the only way either could become free from his debt, for neither could pay. The only hope of sinners is in the divine mercy. One man may look with pity upon his fellow in the depths of some great wickedness, yet he himself is a sinner, too, one who must be forgiven or perish. Wonderful is God's forgiveness. It is great enough for the worst sinner. It wipes out as utterly the blackest sins as the least defiling.

Hartley Coleridge's sonnet beautifully expresses the meaning of the scene:

> She sat and wept beside His feet. The weight
> Of sin oppressed her heart; for all the blame
> And the poor malice, of the worldly shame
> To her were past, extinct, and out of date:
> Only the sin remained—the leprous state.
> She would be melted by the heat of love,
> By fires far fiercer than are blown to prove
> And purge the silver ore adulterate.
> She sat and wept, and with her untressed hair
> Still wiped the feet she was so blest to touch;
> And He wiped off the soiling of despair
> From her sweet soul, because she loved so much.

Jesus showed Simon that this woman loved more than he did by comparing her treatment of him with Simon's. She had a deeper sense of her sin, and consequently a deeper sense of the mercy she had received than Simon had. She had wetted His feet with her tears and anointed them with ointment, while Simon had not even given Him water for His feet. The more we realize our sinfulness, the greater is our love for Christ when we are forgiven. It is often true that the worst sinners make the best Christians. They love more because they owe more to Christ. All through Paul's life of wonderful devotion the memory of his past enmity to Christ appears as a motive for his sublime consecration. He sought to burn out the shame of his past wickedness by more intense devotion and more earnest service. If we understood better how much we owe to God's mercy, we would be more earnest in our Christian consecration.

The words of Jesus to the penitent woman were full of comfort. He told her first that her faith had saved her. How that word "save" must have thrilled her! The poor, shame-soiled, sin-ruined thing that the Pharisee would have spurned from his feet—saved! An heir of heaven now, destined to walk the heavenly streets in white!

There is an old legend that Mohammed once, in passing along the way, touched a plant of mallow, and it became a geranium and ever since has been a geranium, pouring fragrance everywhere. Christ did something far more wonderful that day. He touched this sinful soul, and it was transformed into beauty. That is what He is doing everyday, and can and will do for everyone who creeps to His feet in penitence and faith.

Another of Christ's words of comfort to the woman was, "Go in peace." Peace comes with forgiveness. There never can be any true peace while sins are unforgiven. The dwellers on the slopes of Vesuvius plant their gardens and live in their villas and go on with their work and pleasure, and yet they know that beneath them sleep evermore the awful fires of the volcano, which any day or night may burst out and sweep them away to death. The sinner with his life's sin unforgiven can never have true peace. He is sleeping over a volcano. But when sin is forgiven, there is peace with God.

18

Malignant Unbelief

Scripture Reading: Mark 3:20–35

One of the surest ways to hurt a man's reputation is to give him a bad name. That was the course the scribes took with Jesus. They could not deny that He did very wonderful works, for there were the evidences—the demoniacs in their right mind—but they determined to damage or destroy His influence over the people by starting this atrocious slander about Him. They whispered all around that Jesus and Satan were in league, and that He received His power from Satan. "He hath Beelzebub," they said. The same tactics have since been employed many times. Men who are vigorously engaged in destroying the works of Satan are accused of being themselves Satan's agents.

When there is no way of defeating the earnestness or breaking the power of good men, vile tongues resort to slanderous speech. Base stories are started, or suspicions are breathed, or certain acts are misconstrued or misrepresented, or motives are misjudged. Such slanders fly on the wind, and the usefulness of many a godly Christian has been marred or altogether destroyed by them. Yet we must not be surprised if the world treats us as it treated our Master. We may as well make up our mind to the fact that if we are very earnest either in working for the lost or in fighting vice and wickedness, we shall be both misunderstood and misjudged. Some will say we are crazy, and others that we have a devil. The way to escape all such uncomfortable charges is never to rise above the freezing, or at the highest, the temperate point in Christian fervor, and never to break over the lines of eminent respectability in active Christian service. The devil does not worry over easy-going Christians, for he has little to fear from them. But when he finds a very earnest Christian, bold and uncompromising, he tries relentlessly to strike him down, or to render him harmless.

They said of the wonderful things Jesus did, "By the prince of the devils casteth He out the devils." It will be noticed that even His enemies did not seek to deny that Jesus performed miracles; they only tried to account for His mighty works in a way that would blacken His name. Skeptics in these days who deny the miracles of Christ should take note of this fact, that even His worst enemies when He was in their very midst did not attempt to deny them. They confessed that He produced strange works. The Pharisees and scribes confessed it. Herod confessed it, and in his remorse thought that John the Baptist must have risen from the dead. Not one of His opponents ever hinted a doubt concerning the fact of His miracles. "A blasphemous Life of Jesus, compiled from rabbinical authorities, asserts that He wrought His miracles by possessing Himself secretly of the incommunicable name of God, kept in the Holy of holies and carefully guarded there; and that the cause of His death was His deprivation, through the treachery of Judas, of the manuscript in which He had written this name and other mysteries there acquired." Thus, when the theory of demoniacal possession failed, they invented the theory of magic; but they never denied the miracles themselves. There was no open denial of these until the second century in the works of Celsus.

"How can Satan cast out Satan?" That is the way Jesus swept away their slanderous charge. Satan surely would not join hands with Jesus in His work of tearing down Satan's kingdom. Satan would not be so foolish as to help Jesus cast out his tenants and agents. Satan's aim is to get possession of men, and when he has done this he would not turn about and drive out in disgrace the minor demons he had at so much pains got into men's hearts. We should look with great caution, even with suspicion, on professions of interest in the work of Christ from bad men. They have some other motive than the true one. They mean not good, but evil, for the cause of Christ; hurt, not help, for Christ's Kingdom. Satan will never help Christ destroy the works of darkness.

"No man can enter into the house of the strong man, and spoil his goods, except he first bind the strong man; and then he will spoil his house." Thus Christ declared His power over Satan, and gave a hint of what He will in the end accomplish. If He had not been stronger than Satan, He could never have entered his "house" or kingdom at all. Satan met Him at the door, at the time of His temptation, and resisted His entrance with all his power. But Christ was too strong for him and overcame him and entered. That was the beginning of Satan's downfall. At once our Lord began to "spoil his goods," to expel his emissaries from human lives, to rescue Satan's slaves from his clasp, to undo the terrible work he had done in the world. The work of Christianity in this world all these centuries has been "spoiling the goods" in "the strong man's house"; and this work will go on until Satan's kingdom is entirely destroyed, the last vestige of his power swept away, and the last trace of the ruin wrought by him removed, and till the kingdom of Christ has filled the world. It ought to be a great comfort to us in our struggle with Satan to know that Christ is stronger than he, and that we need but to flee to Him for shelter and help in danger. We ought to know, also, on whose side we are in this world; for there are but two sides, Christ's and Satan's, and the sure doom of Satan and all his is utter defeat and chains and eternal darkness. If we are on Satan's side, we cannot escape the ruin which is sure to overtake him and all his.

"Verily I say unto you, All their sins shall be forgiven unto the sons of men." This is a wonderful saying. Mrs. Stowe, in *Uncle Tom's Cabin,* draws a picture of a slave, weary and worn, toiling in the sultry sun. One quotes to him the words, "Come unto Me, all ye that labor and are heavy laden, and I will give you rest" [Matt. 11:28]. "Them's good words," said the old slave; "but who says 'em?" All their value depended upon who said them. If it was only a man, there was little comfort in them. But it was Jesus Christ, the Son of God, who said them; and therefore, they were of infinite value. The same thought applies to these words: "All sins shall be forgiven unto the sons of men." They are good words, but who said them? It was the same Jesus; and therefore, they are true.

"He that shall blaspheme against the Holy Ghost hath never forgiveness." Learned men do not agree in their idea of what it is to blaspheme against the Holy Spirit. But no matter about the exact meaning of the words; they stand here as a warning against a terrible danger. They are like a red light hung over a most perilous rock. While we may not know just what constitutes the sin here warned against so solemnly, it certainly is our duty to keep as far from its edge as possible. And surely all willful and determined resistance to the influence of the Spirit is a step toward this point of awful peril. This utterance of our Lord should lead us to treat with utmost reverence every appeal, persuasion, or bidding of the Holy Spirit; never to resist, but always to yield and submit to His guidance. We have no other Friend in this world who can guide us home. If we drive Him away from us forever we shall be left in the darkness of eternal night. How long we may continue to reject Him and not go beyond the line that marks the limit of hope, we know not; but the very thought that there is such a line somewhere ought to startle us into instant acceptance of the offered guidance.

"Whosoever shall do the will of God, the same is My brother, and My sister, and mother." This seems too good to be true. To be the brother, or the sister of Jesus—did you ever stop to try to think out what it means? Then, for every Christian to be taken by Christ into as close and tender a relationship as His own mother sustained to Him—did you ever try to think that out, remembering that *you* are the one taken into this loving fellowship? Thousands of women have wished that they could have had Mary's honor in being the mother of Jesus. Well, here it lies close to their hand. They cannot have her distinction in this world, but they can have a place just as near to the heart of Christ as she has. How wonderful is divine grace! How strange it is that sinful creatures can be taken thus into the very family of God, and have all the privileges and joys of children of God! We cannot understand it, but let us believe it and think of it until it fills our hearts with warmth and gladness. But we must not overlook the first part of this verse that tells us who are received into this close relationship. If we would be the brothers and sisters of Christ, we must do the will of God.

19

The Seed in the Four Kinds of Soil

Scripture Reading: Mark 4:1–20

Christ taught many of His great lessons in parables. He gave to the disciples this reason, "Unto you is given the mystery of the kingdom of God: but unto them that are without, all things are done in parables." The truth of Christ looks very different as seen from within and from without. It has been compared to the stained-glass windows of a church. One who stands outside and looks at the windows, sees none of their rich beauty, and cannot understand their meaning. They look only like sheets of dull, patched glass. But let one stand within, and all is transformed. The lines, figures, lettering, and the shades and touches of fine coloring appear in all their rich loveliness. So the truths of the gospel may not be attractive to those who are without. The men of the world see no beauty in them. To human wisdom the gospel is foolishness. Many people sneer at the faith of Christians as they talk about leaning on the unseen God and clinging to the promises and hopes of the Scriptures. But when one enters the family of God, all is changed. What seemed foolishness, appears now as the highest wisdom. Where there was no loveliness, there is now the loftiest beauty. What was laughed at, now seems to be worthy of high admiration and praise. Only those who have accepted Christ as their personal Savior and are faithfully following Him can really understand the wonderful things of His love.

After Jesus had spoken this parable of the seed and the soils, His disciples sought an opportunity to have Him explain it to them. When we do not understand our Lord's teaching, the best thing we can do is to go away to Him alone and ask Him to interpret it to us. None of His words are meant to be inexplicable. He wants us to understand what He says, and He will make it plain to us if we ask Him to do so. He has promised that the Holy Spirit will guide us into all truth. That is what we need—to be guided into the truth. Many providences are really parables, things we cannot understand. They are not only dark and mysterious; but frequently, they are very hard to accept and hard to endure. These perplexing things, too, we may take to Christ, and He will make known to us in His own way and at His own time their hidden meaning.

Christ is the great Sower. Men sometimes bring home from foreign countries seeds of plants or trees which heretofore have not grown in our country. They plant these seeds, and in due time we have the fruits of other climates growing in our orchards. So Christ brings to this world seeds of spiritual things, and plants them on the earth in men's hearts and lives. The words of the Bible are heavenly seeds. They are seeds having in themselves a secret of life which makes them reproductive. They will grow when planted, and will produce trees of righteousness, harvests of holiness.

Christ is the great Sower, but we are all sowers, too. If we are Christ's friends, we should sow good seeds wherever we go. We may do this by speaking kindly words, words of sympathy, comfort, cheer, and hope. We may do it also by writing letters to those to whom we cannot speak the word they need. We may do it by scattering words of God, either in our own speech or in leaflets or books. We may do it by living so that the good influence of our lives shall fall like seeds into the hearts of others.

Four kinds of soil are mentioned in this parable. There are those by the "way side, where the word is sown; and when they have heard, immediately Satan cometh, and taketh away the word which hath been sown in them." The wayside soil is beaten down by passing feet. At first soft, the soil hardens more and more until it becomes almost like rock. So human hearts, at first tender and sensitive to every impression, are trodden over by a thousand influences as life goes on, and often grow like the beaten wayside. One way in which human hearts are thus hardened is by resisting good impressions. Another way is by life's ordinary experiences treading over them like passing feet. Still another way is by sinful habits. There is an old legend of a goblin horseman who galloped at night over men's fields, and wherever his feet touched the soil was blasted, and nothing would ever grow on it again. Thus it is with the heart over which the heavy feet of lust, sensuality, greed, selfishness, and passion are allowed to tread. They beat it down into hardness, and at the same time leave a deadly blight upon it. When the seed falls on hardened soil it lies uncovered, not sinking in, and the watchful, hungry birds soon come and pick it up. So Satan does with good seed that falls upon hardened hearts—he comes and takes it away.

There are others, whose hearts are compared to rocky ground, "who, when they have heard the word, immediately receive it with gladness; and they have no root in themselves." The seed sinks in through the thin soil and soon shoots up, but soon withers. This class represents those whose religion is emotional. There is a superficial softness in their hearts which is easily and quickly touched. They begin the Christian life with a fervor which puts older Christians to the blush. If religion were all ease and comfort, they might get along; but there are temptations, crosses, and persecutions, and these emotional people cannot stand such hard experiences and soon are found giving up the struggle and turning back. They have no root; that is, their religion is emotion, not principle. It lacks faith in Christ and love to Him, and depends upon feeling.

Another class is described as "they that are sown among the thorns." The soil had not been properly cleansed. The old roots had not been dug out. The ground was good enough, and the seed good; but the thorns grew too, as rankly as, even more rankly than, the wheat. What are some of these thorns? Jesus says they are the cares of the world and the deceitfulness of riches. Cares are anxieties, distractions, worries. Martha was in danger of having the good seed in her heart choked out by her distracting thoughts concerning her household affairs. Worry is always a peril. Many people have all the good of God's grace in them choked and destroyed by frets and anxieties which they allow to get into their hearts. Many a businessman loses Christ in anxiety about his business affairs. It is no wonder there are so many warnings in the Bible against worry. Then, as for the deceitfulness of riches, thousands of lives have been starved into ghostly spiritual leanness by desire for wealth. The point to be kept in mind is that the love of Christ in the heart and the Christian graces are in danger of being choked out by other affections springing up in the same soil.

The seed on thorny ground is not altogether killed—the growths are so sapped and dwarfed that they bring no wheat to maturity. The wheat amid the thorns grows, but becomes pale and shriveled, yielding no good ripe wheat. So it is in the Christian life in which the thorns are permitted to grow. There are fruits of the Spirit, but they are shriveled and feeble. Men and women may go on working in the church, teaching, preaching, praying, giving; but the life is not healthy and vigorous. The lesson is the importance of the cultivation of the heart after the good seed has been sown in it. We need to keep our hearts with all diligence and to watch the very beginnings of evil in them. We need to, without remorse, cast out anything that threatens our religion. Sometimes God Himself does the weeding. He takes away the wealth that was choking the spiritual life. He lifts out of the bosom the earthly object that is absorbing all the heart's love. The process is painful, but the results are full of blessing.

The fourth kind of soil is the "good ground"—"such as hear the word, and receive it, and bear fruit." The word is received with attention, thought, faith, and prayer. Thus it is kept in the heart, as rich soft soil receives the wheat seed. No birds can pick it away. It settles down deep into the life, no underlying rock hindering its rooting and growth. The soil is diligently watched, no thorns being allowed to spring up to choke out the golden wheat. Thus the good seed of the word has opportunity to grow and to bring forth fruit. The heavenly teachings that are received into the heart reappear in the character, in the conduct, dispositions, act, spirit, service.

20

The Growth of the Kingdom

Scripture Reading: Mark 4:26–32

Jesus loved nature. He saw in it the tokens and expressions of His Father's love and care. It made Him think of His Father. What could be more exquisite, for example, than the thoughts a tiny little flower started in His mind, as we find them expressed in the Sermon on the Mount? He was urging people not to worry, never to be anxious. He wanted to make them fully understand that they were always in God's thought, in His care. Just then His eye fell on a lily growing in its marvelous beauty by the wayside, and He used it to teach a lesson about the care of God. He cares even for the smallest flower, and His hand weaves for it its exquisite raiment. "And why take ye thought for raiment? Consider the lilies of the field, how they grow; they toil not, neither do they spin: And yet I say unto you, that even Solomon in all his glory was not arrayed like one of these. Wherefore, if God so clothe the grass of the field, which today is, and tomorrow is cast into the oven, shall He not much more clothe you, O ye of little faith?" [Matt. 6:28–30].

Our Lord thus saw in every flower something His Father had made and beautified, something He cared for with all gentleness. And of whatever other use the flowers are, He at least wants us to learn from them this truth of confidence and trust, so that we shall never be anxious. The flowers never are.

285

Many of our Lord's words show us His love for nature, His familiarity with it, and with its laws and processes. Our present passage is one that only Mark records for us. Jesus speaks here of the way a seed grows. We have the familiar picture of a sower going forth to sow. In our modern agriculture, with its wonderful machinery, we are losing much of the picturesqueness of the farmer's life as it was in our Lord's day, and even as it was in the days of our fathers. Men do not go forth now with a seed-bag swung over their shoulder. Now they ride out on the great grain drill and, as they drive over the field, plant the seeds deep in the earth.

Still the lesson of the seed is the same in whatsoever way it may be planted. It is a very little thing, but Jesus sees in it and in its mode of growing a picture of something very great, very wonderful, a picture of the kingdom of God. The same laws prevail in things natural and things spiritual. "So is the kingdom of God, as if a man should cast seed into the ground." We are all sowers, casting seeds all our days. We may not be farmers or gardeners, yet everywhere we go we are sowing seeds. We talk to a friend an hour, and then go our way, perhaps never giving thought again to what we said; but years afterward something will grow up in the friend's life and character from the seeds we dropped so unconsciously or without intention or purpose that day. We lend a friend a book, and he takes it home and reads it. We never think of the book again; perhaps our friend never speaks of it, telling us whether he liked it or not. But many years later there is a life moving about among other lives and leaving upon them its impress which was received from the book we lent—something which influenced the course and career of the life.

We think we have but little influence in the world, that what we are or what we say or what we do, as we go about, matters little, leaves little impression on any other lives. Yet there is not an hour when seeds are not dropping from our hands which will stay in lives and grow. Seeds are wonderful things. There is mystery in the secret of life which they carry in their hearts. Diamonds or pearls have no such secret of life in them. Men do not plant them. They never grow. We do not know what marvelous results will come from some slightest word of ours spoken any day. It may not always be good—it may be evil; all depends upon the seed. The farmer sowed good seed, expecting a rich and beautiful harvest. An enemy came one night, while the farmer was sleeping, and sowed tares. And the tare seeds grew and spoiled the harvest. We need to watch what we are sowing these days, lest a trail of evil and ugliness shall follow us. We need to watch what we say in our little talks with the people we meet through the days, lest we leave stain or hurt behind us. Every time the first king of the ten tribes of Israel is mentioned in the history it is in this terrible way—"the son of Nebat, who made Israel to sin." Surely it would have been better never to have been born than to be born and then have such a biography as that.

But it is of the growth of the seed that our Lord speaks here. "As if a man should cast seed upon the earth; and should sleep and rise night and day, and the seed should spring up and grow, he knoweth not how." He does not stay in the fields and watch his seed growing. He only casts it into the ground and lets it grow as it will. He does not dig it up every-day and see how it is growing. When the seed is once in the soil, it is out of the sower's hand forever. Good or bad, it is gone now beyond his reach. You may write a letter full of bitter words. You were angry when you wrote it. Your conscience told you that you ought not to send it, for it would only cause bitterness. You went out to mail it. All along the way as you went toward the post box the voice within kept saying, "Don't mail it." You came to the box and hesitated, for still there was a clamorous voice beseeching you, "Do not send it." But the anger was yet flaming, and you put the letter in the box. Then you began to wish you had not done it. It was too late now, however, for the cruel letter was forever beyond your reach. No energy in the world could get it back. The evil was irremediable.

So it is when one drops a seed into the ground, whether it be good or evil. The die is cast. The seed is in the ground. There is no use to watch it. So it is when one has dropped an evil influence into a life. Until the word was spoken or the thing was done, it was in your own power, and you could have withheld it. Till then you could have kept the word unspoken or the deed undone. But now it is out of your power. No swiftest messenger can pursue it and take it back. The seed is sown, and you can only let it stay and grow. A man goes on with his work, busy in a thousand ways, and the seed he dropped is growing continually, he knows not how, into what form; the word he spoke, the thing he did, is in people's hearts and lives, and its influence is at work, he knows not how.

There is something startling in this thought of how what we have once done passed then forever out of our hand, beyond recall, and how it goes on in its growth and influence in the silence, while we wake and while we sleep. The time to change evil things, to keep them from forever growing into more and more baleful evil, is before we cast the seed into the ground.

There is a strange and marvelous power, too, in the earth, which, when it receives the seed, begins to deal with it so as to bring out its mystery of life. If the seed is not cast into the ground, it will not grow. Planting it seems to be spoiling it; but really it is saving it, making it grow. Jesus said, "Except a corn of wheat fall into the ground and die, it abideth alone; but if it die, it bringeth forth much fruit" [John 12:24]. This was a little parable. Jesus meant that His life could not accomplish its blessed work but by His dying. The same is true of our lives. We can keep them from suffering and sacrifice; we can choose to live selfishly, keep ourselves from hardship and from self-denial, but that will be keeping a seed out of the ground. Then it will never be anything but a seed. Its life can be brought out, and it can grow only through being cast into the ground.

Here again we see how the planting is all we have to do, all we can do. "The earth bringeth forth fruit of herself." We cannot help the soil take care of the seed. Then, in the spiritual meaning of the Master's words, we do not have to help God take care of the good words we speak to others. The seed is divine, and the influences that act upon it are divine. So all we have to do is to get the truth into the hearts of those we would save and build up; God will do the rest. We are not responsible for the growth of the seed, for the work of grace in a human heart. This does not mean that we do not have God in our lives; it means rather that God and we cooperate in all our good work. God made the seed, and God by His Spirit broods over it in the life where it finds lodgment, and so "the earth bringeth forth fruit of herself."

Great is the mysterious power in the earth which touches the seed and enfolds it, and quickens it, and causes it to grow. But this only illustrates the power that works in human hearts and lives, the power of the Divine Spirit. This holy life receives the heavenly truth that is put into the heart, enfolds and quickens it, and brings out its blessed possibilities till we see a new life like unto God's own life, a Christ-life, blessing the world with its beauty and its love.

The growth is natural and progressive: "First the blade, then the ear, after that the full corn in the ear." The farmer does not expect golden grain to come first; it can come only in its time. We should not expect ripeness of experience in the child Christian.

The parable of the mustard seed needs little explanation. Probably only the smallness of the seed was in the Lord's mind, and the largeness of the tree or bush into which the plant grows. The Church of Christ had a very small beginning, and it has grown till now its branches spread over nearly all lands. It is because the seed has life in it that it produces such wonderful power of growth. It is the secret of heavenly life in the words of God that makes them so marvelous in the results that follow their scattering. Such results do not come from the wisdom or the philosophies of men. The Bible is the Book of God. It was given by inspiration of God. This is the secret of its growth.

The story of the English Bible is a most wonderful illustration of the mustard-seed parable. It is three hundred years since our great King James Version was given to the people, and who can estimate the influence of the Book during these years? Think of what it has done in the building up of the character of the English-speaking people of the world. Think what it has done through the institutions of Christianity which have been nourished by it. Think of all the fruits of the Scriptures in personal lives, in education and culture. The kingdom of God as it has extended in the influence of the English Bible, especially in these three centuries, is like a grain of mustard seed, which, when sown upon the earth, has grown up, becoming greater than all herbs, and putting out great branches, so that the birds of the heavens lodge under the shadow thereof.

21

A Troubled Sea and a Troubled Soul

Scripture Reading: Mark 4:35—5:20

There were marked days in the life of Jesus—days in which He did special things or said special words, days that were made bright and memorable by unusual manifestations of grace and love. "That day"—the day at the ending of which our passage belongs, was one of the great days of our Lord's ministry. It was a day of teaching by parables, a form of His teaching now introduced for the first time. Nothing in nature or in common daily life was left unused by the great Teacher. The light, the darkness, the plays of children, leather bottles, foxes and birds, patched and new garments, and even the homely barnyard hen furnished illustrations for His teachings. Thus He brought the great heavenly lessons down into the everyday lives of the plain, common people.

At the close of this busy day Jesus said to His disciples, "Let us pass over unto the other side." Probably His object was to get quickly and quietly away from the crowd, that He might obtain rest. The people gave Him no opportunity for rest while He was within their reach. They pressed upon Him ever in rude and unmannerly ways, so that He could not get leisure even to eat, and scarcely was permitted to sleep. That He was very weary that evening is evident from what follows in the narrative. It is said that the disciples took Him with them even "as He was in the boat"; that is, they left at once in the same boat in which He had been teaching, not waiting for any preparations. The object, probably, was to get away unobserved, that none of the throng might see Him departing and follow Him.

The storm seems to have come up unexpectedly after they put out to sea. It was one of those sudden storms that so often sweep down from the surrounding hills upon the Sea of Galilee. This storm was very violent. The waves poured into the boat, which seemed as if it would be swallowed up by them.

Notice that the presence of Christ in the boat with His disciples did not prevent the coming of the storm. Sometimes people think when they are in trouble that Jesus has forsaken them, or they would not have such hard experiences. If He were with them, they say, He would not permit them to suffer so. But Christ never has promised to keep us out of trouble. When He was about going away, He prayed the Father to keep His disciples, but only from the evil of the world. He did not say evils, but "the evil." There is only one evil. It is not suffering, nor loss, nor persecution—the only evil in the world is sin. If Christ is with us, we shall be kept from sin, but perhaps not from storms, from sufferings, from bereavements and trials.

The most remarkable thing in the story of this night was the sleeping Master. The tempest howled and the waves swept over the boat; but during all the storm, on the cushion in the stern lay Jesus asleep. This tells us, for one thing, how weary He was after the long day's work, so weary that even the terror and the danger of the storm did not awake Him. He slept through it all. But it tells us also of the peace of His heart, which kept Him in quietness and in confidence in the most trying experiences. This peace the Master would give also to us. He would have such a peace in our hearts that we shall not be disturbed nor alarmed by the greatest of dangers or calamities. If Christ is with us, nothing can harm us. That little boat never could have gone down in the waves with the Master on board. The boat was the emblem of the Church—indeed, the whole Church was in it that wild night. Christ is always with His Church, not only in its days of sunshine and prosperity, but also in its days of trial and in the midst of fiercest storms. Never can the Church be destroyed. "The gates of hell shall not prevail against it" [Matt. 16:18].

The disciples in their terror awoke their Master. They even seemed to chide Him for sleeping when they were in such danger. "Carest Thou not that we perish?" He did care. His heart was awake and watching while He slept so soundly in His weariness. We need never fear in any time of darkness, suffering, or perplexity that Christ has forgotten us or that He will allow us to be harmed. In another storm on the same sea [Matt. 14:25-27], when the disciples were also in great peril, Jesus was absent; He was up on the mountain in the darkness. But while away from them, He kept His eye upon them all the night. He saw them distressed in their rowing. Then, in due time, He came to them, walking on the water, and delivered them. Always we are remembered and thought of in heaven. We never can drift beyond Christ's love and care.

While with peace in His heart Jesus slept in quietness in the fierce storm, undisturbed by its roar and by the sweeping of waters over the boat, He heard the first call of the disciples when in their distress they called to Him. There may come times in our lives when Christ appears to us to be asleep. He comes not with deliverance in our danger. He is not disturbed by the mighty storms which to us seem so fearful. But in the wildest fury of circumstances He hears the faintest prayer of those who cry to Him for help and deliverance.

Christ's power over the forces of nature is illustrated in the way He answered the cry of His disciples that night. He arose from the cushion where He had been sleeping so sweetly, and rebuked the wind, and said to the sea, "Peace, be still." Instantly the wind ceased, and there was a great calm. It ought to be an immeasurable comfort to us to know that our Savior is indeed Master of wind and wave, and of all the forces and powers of nature. We need never be afraid in peril of flood or earthquake or storm, for He who is our Friend is Master of all the elements. No wild tempest ever gets away from His control. A Christian woman who was undisturbed in an earthquake said to a friend who wondered at her composure, "Why, I am glad that I have a God who can shake this old earth."

When Jesus had quieted the storm on the sea, He turned to His trembling disciples, whose spirits were swept by a storm of fear, and asked them, "Why are ye so fearful? How is it that ye have no faith?" It was time they had learned to have faith. They had seen enough of faith in Him to teach them to trust and not be afraid in even the most extreme dangers. But how is it with us? Are we alarmed by life's perils? Have we not yet learned to trust?

As soon as Jesus with His disciples came off the sea, He found sufferers waiting for Him. "Immediately there met Him out of the tombs a man with an unclean spirit." In this demoniac we have a sample of the work of Satan when he gets full control in a man. He destroys every beautiful thing in the life, and leaves only ruin. No chains could bind this demoniac. When sin is on the throne, all other influences and constraints become like spiders' threads in comparison. No cord is strong enough to bind the man who has yielded himself to the sway of the Evil One. The love of a godly mother is a strong bond, but many a child tears off this holy chain and rushes into wayward paths. Home ties are strong, but these too are broken asunder by the victim of Satan's ungodly rule.

One feature of this case was that the demoniac cut and gashed himself with stones. This illustrates what in many ways Satan's captives always do. They may not literally go about cutting their flesh with knives or bruising their bodies with stones; but they do gash and bruise their souls. Sin always wounds the life, and one of its fearful consequences is the self-destruction it works. Every sin one commits leaves an ugly scar. We grieve God by our wrongdoing, we harm others when we sin against them; but we always injure ourselves by every evil word we speak, by every wrong act we commit, even by the evil thoughts we think in our hearts. The self-hurt of sin is one of its saddest consequences.

Demons were afraid of Christ. "I adjure thee by God, torment me not." The torment this demon dreaded was in being deprived of the opportunity of tormenting the man of whom he had possession. Demons find their pleasure in working mischief, in destroying the beautiful work of God's hands, and in ruining lives. Good men count that day lost in which they have done no act of kindness to another. Demons count the day lost in which they have stained no pure soul or led no one into sin. We ought to tear off Satan's mask and show him as he is to our own hearts and to the hearts of others. Evil comes to us pretending to be a friend. It holds flowers in its hands and whispers entrancing words, promising rich rewards. "Only do this, and it will bring you pleasure, honor, wealth, joy"; that is the way sin talks. But this is all false. Sin is never a friend to man. It never does good to anyone, but always harm. However plausibly Satan may present his temptations under the color of pleasure, his secret aim is to destroy the soul he tempts. Nothing gives the Evil One such pleasure as to see a fair and beautiful life stained and debauched.

It is most comforting to us to find that Christ is able to dislodge even the most obdurate and persistent demon. No one could bind this demoniac nor resist his superhuman strength. But when the man met Jesus, he met one who was stronger than "the strong man" in possession. It was in vain that the demon adjured Jesus and made a limited show of resistance. At His word the foul spirit was compelled to leave the man he had possessed for so long. No human hand can break the chains of sinful habits. No mere resolution can free one from Satan's bondage. But when Christ comes, He can set the captive free. Those who have long been trying in vain to reform, to break away from evil practices, see in Christ the Friend who alone can deliver them and save them. No demon-power can resist His command. If the poor slaves of Satan would only put themselves absolutely into the hands of Christ, He would free them, drive out their enemy, and save them from his terrible sway.

In the swine, under demoniacal possession, rushing down the steep cliff and perishing in the sea, we have another illustration of the end of all Satan's ruinous work. It is with men as it was here with the swine. It never yet has been known that Satan impelled anyone upward to a better life or to anything noble and lofty; he always drives down steep ways into choking floods. God's way leads upward—it is always uphill to Christ and to heaven. Every divine impulse is toward something higher and better. Christ never yet sent a man downhill. But the devil always drives downward. These poor swine, demon-possessed, rushed down the steep way into the sea and perished. Human souls, demon-possessed, rush down sin's precipitous course and perish. It would be well to keep this picture in our mind when we are tempted in any way by the devil; for if we follow him, this is the way it will surely end with us.

It is strange how the people were affected by this miracle. Jesus had come among them to bless them. He would have gone on, working other miracles, if they had been willing. But the loss of the swine was too much for them. There always are people who hate Christ's religion because it interferes with their wrong business and cuts off the source of their sinful gain. Saloon-keepers oppose revivals because when the devil is cast out of men they do not patronize the saloons any more. But it is always a perilous thing to ask Jesus to go away. He did now as these people asked Him to do—He would not stay where He was not wanted. He went away, carrying with Him the blessings He had brought and meant to leave. So the sick remained unhealed, the lame still continued lame, demoniacs remained demon-possessed. We must be careful never to ask Christ to go away from us. We see Jesus sailing away from this coast, to come back again no more. May He not do the same if we ask Him to leave us?

Jesus knows where He wants His saved ones to witness for Him. This man wished to go with Him, but there was other work for Him to do. There are different ways of serving Christ. Some of His disciples He asks to leave home and friends to follow Him into distant lands. Others He wants to stay at home and bear witness among those who have known them to the grace and love of God. Each one of us may be sure that if we truly put our life into the hands of Christ, He will give us our work where it will do the greatest good. If He wants one young minister to go to the foreign field as a missionary, he must go. But he must not blame his classmate who does not go to the foreign field, but enters the field at home. The home mission service is just as honorable as the foreign. The only question with anyone should be, "What does Christ want me to do; where does He want me to work for Him?" We serve Christ best when we serve in the place and in the manner in which He directs us.

22

The Ruler's Daughter

Scripture Reading: Mark 5:21–43

Jairus was an important man in Capernaum. He was one of the elders. People looked up to him. He was influential in affairs, perhaps rich. But as we see him, we think of none of these things—what strikes us in him is his anguish of heart. Grief brings all men to the same level. A father, as we see him battling with the world, may seem sometimes to lack the tender emotions. But let his child become dangerously sick, and his heart is revealed—a heart of tender love.

The next interesting thing in Jairus is his going to Jesus with his grief. Perhaps he would never have gone to Jesus if this trouble had not come to his own home. Not many men of his class favored Jesus, would invite Him to their homes, or care to be considered among His friends. But the sore sickness of his child and the fact that Jesus was healing so many who were sick, made him ready to go to Jesus, in the hope that his child might be spared to him. We cannot know in this world how much we owe to painful things. Many another father has been driven to Christ by the sickness of his child. Many a mother has been taught to pray and to cling to God by the anguish of her little one.

What Jairus said when he came to Jesus shows that he had faith in His power to heal the sick child. With trembling speech he told Him that his little daughter lay at the point of death, but if only Jesus would come and lay His hands on her, she would not die. We may pray for our children when they are sick. Not always is it God's will that they should recover. This may not be the best thing for them. We should pray in faith, but should then leave our request in God's hands, knowing that He will do what is best. It is right that we should go to Christ with every case of sickness in our home or among our friends. We should send for the physician, too; for God wants us to use human help so far as this will avail. At the same time we should pray; for whether through or independently of means, it is Christ who is the Healer.

Jesus is always quick to hear the cry of human distress. He went at once with Jairus. He did not have to be urged. But on the way there was an interruption. A poor woman, wasted by long sickness, crept up behind Jesus as He was hastening to the ruler's house, and very shyly and stealthily touched the hem of His garment with her trembling fingers. There was a prayer in that touch, a heart's cry, which Jesus heard, though no word was spoken. There was also faith in the touch. The woman may not have understood the theology of prayer. She knew, however, that the One who was passing so near to her had power to heal, and to heal her; and she did the best she knew, and touched the fringe of His garment, believing that in some way she would be healed. So she touched the garment, and instantly healing flowed from Jesus into her body, and she was made well.

She had meant to slip away and lose herself in the crowd, not letting it be known that she was healed; but Jesus called her. He would not allow her to go away without His speaking to her. He wished her to have a full blessing, not a half blessing only. Her disease had been cured, but He wished to give her also a spiritual blessing. Many people in their sickness have only one desire—to get well again. They send for physicians and faithfully use their medicines and try the remedies they prescribe, but they think of no other blessing to be sought. If they pray, it is only for physical healing. But this is most imperfect faith, most meager, inadequate prayer. When we are sick, there are two blessings we should seek. We should desire to recover, if that is God's will. It is our duty to try to get well, that we may take up again our work and go on with it. But at the same time we should try to get some curing of faults, some enrichment of life, some new vision of God, some fresh strength for service from our sickness before it leaves us. It has some mission to us. It would be a great misfortune to us if we should fail to get from it the good, the benefit, the enriching it was meant to bring to us.

This woman had received her healing, but she was on the point of missing the larger help the Master wanted her to have. She was recalled by the Master, came to His feet and told Him all, and received salvation as well as healing.

This was a bit of our Lord's wayside ministry. He was going with the ruler to heal his child. We would say that in view of the fact that the case was so urgent, the Master would pay no heed to the woman's appeal, but would hasten on to the home of the ruler. The little girl was at the point of death, the father had said. Surely there was no time to lose. The child might die if He lingered even a moment. Yet Jesus was not hurried by the urgency of the ruler's importunity. He did not tell the woman He could not wait to heal her. Nor did He ignore the pressure there was in her touch and leave her unhealed. At once healing came to her. That was all the woman wanted, and He might have hastened on with the ruler. But he stopped and turned to speak to her. "Who touched My clothes?" The work of healing was only half done, and He would complete it. So abundant is His grace that He never has to fail to do one act of love because He is in the midst of another.

No harm came from the interruption and the delay. True, the child had died before Jesus reached the ruler's home. It seemed, indeed, that Jesus had lingered too long on the way. If only He had not stopped to talk with the woman in the crowd! Now it was too late for Him to come. "Trouble not the Master," the servants said; "thy daughter is dead." Jesus heard what the messengers said, and comforted Jairus by saying to him, "Be not afraid, only believe." Jesus had made no mistake. He never makes a mistake—He never comes too late.

Jesus went on with Jairus and soon gave back the child to her parents alive. Some whose little ones are dead, as they read this part of the story, may say: "If only Jesus had restored our child after it had died! But He did not." He did not literally restore your dead, yet He comforted you in a way which wonderfully sustained you. Since Christ has died and risen again, dying in Christ means only passing into fuller, richer life. Your child is not dead. You see her not, but she never lived in this world so really as she does now. You have the comfort of knowing also that in the hands of Christ all is well. Then you have the assurance of meeting her again by and by.

Christ has a heart of sympathy and love which will lead Him to take a tender interest in every need or sorrow of ours, and to help us in the best way. Our need is our strongest claim on Him. When the freed slave Sojourner Truth was in great distress over her child, which had been stolen from her and sold, she offered this prayer: "O Lord, if I was rich as You be, and You was as poor as I be, I'd help You—You know I would. And O, do help me. And I felt sure that He would, and He did," continued the poor woman.

23

The Visit to Nazareth

Scripture Reading: Luke 4:16–30

Christ never forgot the place where He had spent His childhood years. We are not given many facts of His life there. Nothing indicates that there was anything unusual in the story of the thirty years He spent there. The more we think of His life at Nazareth as simply natural, without anything unusual, the nearer shall we come to the true conception of the boy and young man who grew up in the lowly village of Nazareth. Our passage today tells of His visit to His old home after He had been away for many months.

"He came to Nazareth, where He had been brought up." It was not an easy place for Jesus to visit. Everybody knew Him. He had lived there for thirty years. He had been playmate and schoolmate with the people of His own age. He had been a carpenter, doing work for many years in the shop and about the town. The young men of Nazareth thought themselves as good as He was, and were not in mood to receive instruction from Him. It is easy for us to understand the prejudice and envy with which people listened to Jesus as He spoke to them that day in their synagogue.

There are some lessons to be taken, however, from our Lord's example in thus going back to Nazareth. One is, that we ought to seek the good of our own neighbors and friends. Many young men go away from plain country or village homes and in other and wider spheres rise to prominence and influence. Such ought not in their eminence to forget their old home. They owe much to it. It is pleasant to hear of rich men giving libraries or establishing hospitals or doing other noble things for the town in which they were born. Among our first obligations is that which we owe to our old neighbors.

Another lesson is, that as young people we ought to live so carefully that when we grow up we may be able to go back to our old home and, in the midst of those who have known us all our life, witness for God. There are some men, good and great now, whose preaching would have but small effect where they were brought up because of the way they lived during their youth. Sins of youth break the power of life's testimonies in later years. A blameless youth makes one's words strong in mature days.

"And he came to Nazareth, where he had been brought up: and, as his custom was, he went into the synagogue on the sabbath day, and stood up for to read" [Luke 4:16]. Here we have a glimpse of our Lord's religious habits. From childhood His custom had been to attend the synagogue service on the Sabbath. Here are good shoe prints for young people to set their feet in. The time to begin to attend church is in youth. Habits formed then stay by us all our life. If our custom is to stay away then from church services, we will be very apt to keep up that custom when we get older. On the other hand, if we go to church regularly from childhood, the custom will become so wrought into our life that in after years we shall not incline to stay away. And the value of such a habit is very great.

"He . . . opened the book, [and] found the place where it was written." The book was part of the Old Testament. Some people have the feeling that the Old Testament is dry and uninteresting. But we see here what precious things Jesus found in it that day in the synagogue. The passage which He quoted drips with the sweetness and tenderness of divine love. It is a great honeycomb of gospel grace. Some men were about to tear down an old frame house, long unoccupied. When they began to remove the weather boarding they found a mass of honey. As they removed the boards at different points they discovered that the whole side of the house, between the weather boarding and the plastering, was filled with honey. People regard the Old Testament as an old, worn-out book, a mere relic of old ceremonial days. But when they begin to open it they find honey, and as they look into it at other points they find that all the passages, in among the histories, the chronicles of war, and the descriptions of ceremonial rites, are full of sweetest honey. Here is a bit of dripping comb, and there are hundreds more just as rich. We do not know what we lose when we do not study the Old Testament.

"The poor . . . the captives . . . the blind . . . them that are bruised." These are the special classes of people to whom Jesus was sent. What a picture this is of humanity! Some people ridicule what the Bible says about a fall. They tell us there never was a fall, and that the world is all right. They talk eloquently about the grandeur of human life. But this eighteenth verse certainly looks very much like the picture of a very bad ruin. Read the description—poor, captives, blind, bruised. There is not much grandeur in that. Anyone who goes about and looks honestly at life knows that the picture is not overdrawn. On every hand we see the wreck and ruin caused by sin. Then suffering and sorrow follow, and hearts and lives are crushed and bruised.

But there is something here a great deal brighter than this sad picture. Light breaks on the ruin as we read that it was to repair just such moral desolation as we see here that Jesus came. He came to preach good tidings to the poor, to proclaim release to captives, and recovering of sight to the blind, and to set at liberty them that are bruised. He saw in all these ruins of humanity something that by His grace He could make beautiful enough for heaven and glory. Christ is a restorer. There are men who take old, dimmed, effaced, almost destroyed pictures and restore them until they appear nearly as beautiful as when they first came from the artist's hand. So Christ comes to ruined souls, and by the power of His love and grace He restores them until they wear His own beauty in the presence of God.

"To preach the acceptable year of the Lord." For the Jews this "acceptable year" closed with the condemnation of the Messiah. Jesus stood on Olivet and looked down upon the city and wept over it and said, "If thou hadst known, even thou, the things which belong unto thy peace! but now they are hid from thine eyes" [Luke 19:42]. When He spoke these words, amid the rush of tears and with loud outcry of grief, "the acceptable year" closed. After that the doom hung over the beautiful city, which in forty years burst upon it in all its woe and terribleness. This is history. But there is another way to look at this matter. There is an "acceptable year" for each soul. It begins when Christ first comes to us and offers salvation. It continues while He stands at our door and knocks. It closes when we drive Him away from our door by utter and final rejection, or when death comes upon us unsaved and hurries us away forever from the world of mercy. Since the past is gone and there is no certain future to anyone, the "acceptable year" to us all is now. Shall we allow it to pass and close while we remain unsaved?

"This day is this scripture fulfilled in your ears." Seven hundred years before had the words been written. Now Jesus reads them and says to the people: "I am the One to whom the description refers. I am the One the prophet meant." The whole Old Testament was full of Christ, and the New is full of correspondences and fulfillments. It is pleasant, too, to take this particular passage and show how Christ indeed fulfilled in His life and ministry the mission which the prophet marked out for Him. He preached to the poor, He healed the broken-hearted. Wherever He went, the sorrowing and the troubled flocked about Him. As a magnet draws steel filings to itself out of a heap of rubbish, so did the heart of Christ draw to Him the needy, the sad, the suffering, the oppressed. He was the friend of sinners. He brought deliverance to sin's captives, setting them free and breaking their chains. He opened blind eyes; not only blind natural eyes to see the beautiful things of this world, but also blind spiritual eyes to see spiritual things. Then He lifted the yoke off the crushed and oppressed, inviting all the weary to Himself to find rest. His whole life was simply a filling out of this outline sketch.

They "rose up, and thrust Him out of the city, and led Him unto the brow of the hill . . . that they might cast Him down." Their envy grew into murderous rage. We see first the danger of allowing envious feelings to stay in our hearts; they are sure to grow into greater bitterness, and may lead us into open and terrible sin. We should instantly check every thought or motion of anger or hatred and cast it out of our heart. This act shows also the natural hatred of God which is in human hearts. We talk severely of the Jews' rejection of their Messiah, but this opposition to God is not exclusively a Jewish quality. Is it not the same with all of us? So long as the divine teaching runs along in lines that are pleasing to us, we assent, and applaud the beauty of God's truth. But when the teaching falls against our own tendencies and dispositions and opinions, we wince, and too often declare our disbelief. They tried to kill Him; is not the rejection of many people now just as violent? They would kill Him if they could.

His word was with authority. His words are always with authority. We remember how all things hearkened to His words and obeyed them. Diseases fled at His command. The winds and waves were quieted and hushed at His word. The water changed to wine at His bidding. The dead in their graves heard His call and answered. Evil spirits owned His lordship. Nothing for a moment resisted His authority—nothing but man. Shall we not take Christ's word as the rule of our faith and of our conduct? Shall we not yield to His authority?

24

The Death of John the Baptist

Scripture Reading: Mark 6:14–29

We have here at the very beginning a serious case of conscience. One would say that Herod was past having such fits of remorse, as his life was so wholly bad. But in even the worst men conscience is not apt to be entirely dead. At least Herod's conscience was only asleep, and when He heard of Jesus going about the country, working miracles, it seemed to him that it must be John the Baptist, whom he had so tragically beheaded, and who had been raised from the dead. Herod's friends tried to quiet him, assuring him that it was not John returned, but a new prophet, who was doing these wonderful things. However, Herod's fear could not be quieted, his remorse was so great. "No, it is John, whom I beheaded; he is risen." Conscience is our best friend so long as we live right. But if we sin, it becomes a torturing fire. We may think we can easily forget our sin, but conscience refuses to forget. Lady Macbeth, in Shakespeare's play, said that all the perfumes of Arabia could not sweeten her murderous little hand. Visitors traveling in Scotland are shown a stone with a spot of blood on it which, it is said, will not wash off. If we would be surely saved from the terrors of the accusing conscience, we must live so as to have the approval of conscience on all our acts.

John the Baptist was a wonderful man. The story of his death is most tragic. It seems utterly inappropriate that a man so noble, so worthy, who had done such a good work, should be brutally killed to gratify the resentment of a wicked woman. For it was Herodias who really caused the death of the Baptist. Wicked as Herod was, he would not have killed John if it had not been for the woman, who never could forgive the preacher for reproving her sin. The part that Herodias played in this crime shows her in a most pitiful light. She was a disgrace to her sex. From the time John spoke so plainly against her sin she was determined that he should die for it. Herod protected him from her plots, but she bided her time.

A "convenient day" came, by and by, and Herodias set herself to accomplish her purpose. It was Herod's birthday. A great banquet was in progress—Herod and the principal men of his kingdom were feasting together. Wine flowed freely, and when the king and his guests were well under its influence, Herodias sent her daughter into the banqueting room to take the part of a common dancing girl in the presence of a party of drunken men. A true mother shields her child from all that would dishonor her. Now, in order to bring about John's death, this mother was ready to degrade her own daughter.

The record says that Herod was pleased by what he saw. He called the girl to him, and in his drunken mood gave her a promise, "Ask of me whatsoever thou wilt, and I will give it thee." She was shrewd enough to demand an oath of him, lest when he was out of his wine he might refuse to do what he had promised. "And he swear unto her, Whatsoever thou shalt ask of me, I will give it thee, unto the half of my kingdom." A man under the influence of strong drink will pledge anything. Many men in such moments have made promises which it has cost them dearly to keep.

The child did not know how to answer Herod, what request to make of him; so she ran to her mother in a dutiful fashion and asked her, "What shall I ask?" Perhaps the child was thinking of a palace that the king might give her, or of some wonderful gems that she would like to wear. But she could not herself decide what to ask. The words in which the mother answered her child's question showed the terrible wickedness of the heart of Herodias. "The head of John the Baptist," she said. At last the moment had come for the full revenge of Herodias. But think of a mother asking her own child to do such a terrible thing!

The story moves on swiftly, and at length the closing scene in the tragedy is enacted. The girl herself must have had a cruel heart to go so gleefully to Herod with the request which Herodias had put into her mouth. "What have you decided to ask of me?" inquired Herod. "The head of John the Baptist," was the girl's answer. The king was shocked and grieved at receiving such a request. How could he grant the girl's request? He shrank from the crime, but in his cowardice he dared not show his hesitation. His courtiers would laugh at him if he did. He must be brave, whatever the cost might be. Anything that belonged to him he was under obligation to give to the child—he had said he would; he had sworn it. But John's head was certainly not Herod's to give to anybody.

The king trembled at the request. He was about to say to the girl that he could not give her what she asked; but there was his oath—he could not break that, so he said to himself. His princes and courtiers would laugh at him if he showed tenderness of heart in such a matter of sentiment as this. So he sent for an executioner and had the great preacher killed in his dungeon, and his head brought on a dish and given to the girl. Herod had kept his promise; but there was murder on his soul.

"How could Herod have refused," asks one, "when he had taken such an oath?" It was a sin to make such a rash promise, and a still greater sin to seal it by an oath. We should never pledge ourselves to do anything which another may ask of us until we know what it is. To keep a promise made thus may require us to sin grievously. But if in a moment of foolish rashness we pledge ourselves to do something wrong, we are still not required to do it. We should break our promise rather than do a wicked thing. In this case Herod ought to have broken his oath. He knew this, but he was afraid of the laughter of his guests, and committed a horrible crime rather than be a man and refuse to do the thing which he knew to be wrong.

Amid all the dark crime and shame of this story one figure stands out noble and heroic, splendid in character, unspotted in whiteness, strong in faithfulness. We are inclined to pity John, as the victim of such a crime. But our pity should be rather for those who robbed John of his life, while for him we have only admiration. John seemed to die prematurely. He was only about thirty-three years of age. He had preached but a year or so, and was then cast into prison, where he lay a long time. It seemed that he was but only beginning his life work. We can think of his disciples and friends lamenting over his early death, and saying, "If only he had lived to a ripe old age, preaching his wonderful sermons, touching people's lives, advancing the kingdom of God, giving blessing and comfort to people—what a benediction he would have been to this world!" But here we see his splendid life quenched probably before he turned thirty-three. Was it not a mistake? No; God makes no mistakes. "Every man is immortal till his work is done." One thing we know at least—John's mission was accomplished. He was sent from God to introduce the Messiah to the people. He did this, and did it grandly. The best life need not be the longest—it must be one that fulfills God's purpose for it. If we do God's will for us, we have lived well, whether it be for eighty years or for only a few months.

John died in a very sad and tragic way, died in a prison, at the hands of a common executioner; yet there was no stain upon his name. He had kept his manhood unspotted through all the years. Men would call his work a failure; it certainly was not a worldly success. Yet it was a fine moral success. Jesus said that among all men born of woman, none was greater than John. Earth's failures may be heaven's truest successes.

The life of John the Baptist is rich in its lessons. For example, he hid himself away and pointed the people always to Christ. He was willing to decrease, that Christ might increase. When his popularity waned and he was left almost alone, with scarcely any friends or followers, he kept as sweet and worked as faithfully as when he was everybody's favorite. He was heroic in reproving sin, even in a king. His whole life was noble. Forgetting himself, he lived for God in the truest and most complete way unto the end.

25

The Feeding of the Five Thousand

Scripture Reading: Mark 6:30–44

After the tragic death of John the Baptist his disciples paid loving honor to his body. Their sorrow must have been very great, for they loved their master. We do not know whether or not John had those lovable qualities which drew men to him and made them his friends, or whether, by reason of his natural sternness and his ascetic severity he failed to be a friend of men, as Jesus was. It is not likely that he drew men to him as the other John did, or as Paul did, or that men loved him as our Lord's disciples loved their Master. Yet it is certain that there must have grown up between the Baptist and his disciples a strong affection, and that they were sorely grieved at his death.

Jesus had sent His apostles on a brief missionary tour. When they returned they made report to Him. "They told Him all things, both what they had done, and what they had taught." No doubt they told Him all they had tried to do, even if they had seemed to fail—how the people had received them, and how sometimes they had rejected them. They would tell Him, too, of their mistakes and blunders. This is what we should do at the close of any work we are doing for our Master—go to Him and make report of it all. It is well, indeed, that every evening we carry to Christ such a report of our life for the day. There could be no better evening prayer than the reporting to Christ the story of the day—simply, humbly, truthfully, fully, confidingly. There will be many confessions in this recital; for we should tell Him all, hiding nothing. If we form the habit of doing this, it will be a restraint upon us many times when tempted to do the things that are not right. We will not want to report anything of which we are ashamed, and we will not do them just because we would not wish to tell Him.

Note also the consideration of Jesus for His disciples. They were very weary after their tour through the country, and needed rest. The throngs that kept coming to them all the time prevented them from obtaining the rest they needed. Jesus now invited them to a quiet place, where they might renew their strength. The form of the invitation should be noted. He did not say, "Go ye yourselves apart," but, "Come ye yourselves apart." We are not to go away from Christ when we seek a vacation, but are to rest with Him. No vacation away from Christ is complete. Too many people drop their religious work when they leave home for a few weeks, and some even forsake the altar of prayer and the Bible. But Christ wants us to take our vacations with Him.

Jesus and the disciples did not get a vacation after all. The people saw them crossing the sea, and, flocking around the shore, awaited the Master when He reached the other side. He was not impatient with the people, however, even though they had robbed Him of the rest He needed. He had compassion upon them. It is always thus. Christ carried the people's sorrows. His heart was touched by their needs and distresses. When He looked upon the great throng, and saw among them many suffering ones—lame, sick, blind, palsied—His heart's compassion was deeply stirred. In heaven He is touched today with the feeling of our infirmities. Some men's sympathy is only in sentiment and fails to show itself in act. The compassion of Christ filled His heart, and then flowed out in all forms of kindness and helpfulness. Then it was not their hunger, their poverty, their sickness, that seemed to Him their worst trouble, but their spiritual need. They were wandering like lost sheep away from the fold, and had no shepherd.

When the question of the people's hunger and what should be done for them came up, the best that the disciples could suggest was that they should be sent away to find food for themselves. That is about all that human wisdom or even human love can do. Perhaps we cannot feed their bodily hungers. Nor is it always best that we should try to do it. Every man must bear his own burden. Doing too much in temporal ways for those who are in stress or need is not true or wise kindness. The best we can do for those who are in need is usually to put them in the way of relieving their own needs. It is better to show a poor man how to earn his own bread than it is to feed him in idleness. But we can always be courteous to any who come to us for help. We may at least in every case show kindness, even when we cannot give the help that is asked. We must take care that we do not coldly turn away those who appeal to us for help. The parable of the Judgment in the twenty-fifth chapter of Matthew teaches us that in the poor, the needy, the sick, and the troubled who appeal to us for help, or whom we see or hear of in any distress, Jesus Himself stands before us. We must be careful lest we someday send Him away hungry.

It was a startling word that Jesus spoke to His disciples, however, when they suggested that the people be sent away to buy bread for themselves. He said, "Give ye them to eat." That is what He is saying all the while to His disciples. He wants them to feed the hungry. There is no use in sending them to the villages—there is nothing there to feed them. Besides, there is no need that we should send them away, for we have food for them. We have but to read the story through to find that the disciples were able to feed even this great multitude, and did feed them. Their scant supply, blessed, by the Master, satisfied every hungry one of all the five thousand. Whenever Christ sends needy ones to us He wants us to give them help, and it will not do for us to say that we cannot do it, that we have no bread. When Jesus gives a command He means to make it possible for us to obey it. It may seem to us that we cannot do it, that we have not the resources necessary; but if we use our little in trying to help, our little will grow into all that is needed for the supply of the want which has been entrusted to us.

When the disciples had made inquiry they found that they had only five loaves and two small fishes, and they never dreamed that so little could be made enough to feed five thousand hungry men. We are always saying that we cannot do anything to bless the world because we have so little with which to work. A young Christian is asked to teach a Sunday school class, and says: "I have no gift for teaching. I have nothing to give to these scholars." A young man is asked to take part in a meeting, but thinks he cannot say anything to help anybody. Christ says to us, "Feed the hungry ones about you," and we look at our stock of bread and say, "I have only five barley loaves—what can I do with these?" We do not think we can do any good in the world, while really we can bless hundreds and thousands if we rightly use our little store.

It is interesting to note the manner in which Jesus enabled His disciples to feed the people. First they brought their loaves to Him. That is what we should always do with our little—we should bring it to Christ, that He may bless it. If the disciples had tried themselves to feed that hungry crowd with their five loaves, they would not have been able to do it. If we try in our own name to bless others, to comfort the sorrowing, to lift up the fallen, to satisfy the cravings of men's souls, we shall be disappointed.

The method of distributing the provision is suggestive. Jesus did not Himself pass the bread directly to the multitude—he gave it through His disciples. Study this picture. Jesus stands here; close about Him stand His disciples; beyond them is the great multitude. Jesus is going to feed the hungry people with the disciples' loaves, but the bread must pass through the disciples' hands. It is in this way that Christ usually blesses men—not directly, but through others. When He would train a child for great usefulness, He puts love and gentleness into a mother's heart and skill into her hands, and she nurses the child for Him. When He would give His word to the world, He inspired holy men, and they wrote as they were moved by the Holy Spirit. When He would save a soul, He sends not an angel, but a man or a woman redeemed already by His grace, to carry the message. This suggests the responsibility of those to whom Christ passes the bread of life. It is not for themselves only, but for themselves and those who are beyond them. Suppose the disciples had fed themselves only from the loaves, and had not passed on the food; the people would still have hungered, while provision enough for them was close at hand.

Notice the careful economy of Christ. He bade them gather up the fragments that were left, that nothing might be lost. Though He had so easily made a little into a great supply of bread that day, yet He would have the fragments saved. We are all apt to be careless about fragments, especially when we have plenty. We should be careful of the fragments of our time. Most of us waste plenty enough minutes every day to make hours. Every moment of time is valuable; in it we may do something to honor our Master and help one of His little ones. Let us take care of the golden moments—the fragments will soon make a basketful. We should let nothing whatsoever be lost of all that God gives us.

26

Mission to the Gentiles

Scripture Reading: Mark 7:24–30

Much of the public life of Jesus was devoted to caring for sufferers. The doctor's little girl told the messenger where she thought her father could be found, as he was wanted immediately, "I don't know, sir; but you'll find him somewhere, helping somebody." When people sought for Jesus and could not find Him, He was usually away with someone in need, doing good, helping somebody. At this time, however, He was trying to get away from the crowd. He certainly was not trying to hide from His enemies, for He never had any fear of men. Probably He needed rest for Himself and His disciples. At least we are told He entered into a house and would have no man know He was there. We are sure Jesus never hides away from those who need Him in their distress. It is never true that He cannot be found. He never shuts the door upon those who pray to Him or those who come to Him in trouble and want to find Him, refusing to see them. We will never find Him absent nor in hiding when we go to Him with any question or any need.

Try as He would, Jesus was not able to get away from the people. His attempts to have a little rest were always thwarted. We are told here, that though He wished to remain in seclusion, He could not be hidden. We cannot hide flowers—their fragrance will tell where they are. Jesus could not be hid from human need—there was something about

His love which revealed Him to all who had any need. In this case it was a mother with a great sorrow who sought Him. Her little daughter had an unclean spirit. We cannot understand how a child could be possessed by a demon, but in this case it was a child. Very great was the mother's distress. This woman had heard in some way of Jesus and of His casting out evil spirits over in His own country. She had never expected that He would come into her neighborhood, as she was a Gentile, living outside the limits of His country. But when she learned from some of her neighbors that the Great Healer had come to the town, and was in a certain house, she lost no time in finding her way to Him. She came with strong faith. She was sure that Jesus could free her little girl from the terrible trouble. She fell at His feet, in the attitude of deepest humility.

Mothers may get a lesson from this Gentile woman. If their children are sick, they should hasten to Christ with them. If they are in the power of any form of evil, they should especially seek the help of Him who alone can give help in such cases. There are unclean spirits besides the demons who possessed people in our Lord's day. Every child is exposed to constant temptations and may receive hurt. In every child there are natural evil tempers and dispositions which, if not cast out, will greatly imperil the life.

The first difficulty in this woman's way was the fact that she was a Gentile. Christ was not sent to her, but the gospel now is for all the world. No nation has any exclusive claim to it. It is for the world. But Jesus devoted Himself only to His own people. Not till after He had died and risen again were His disciples sent to all the nations. The woman's nationality was a barrier. Jesus was not sent to any but the lost sheep of the house of Israel.

Matthew tells us that when the woman began to plead with Jesus, "He answered her not a word" [15:23]. This is one of the strangest incidents in our Lord's whole life. Usually He was quick to answer every call for help. His heart responded instantly and lovingly to everyone who came to Him. A Christ silent to the cry of a mother, pleading for her child, seems so contrary to what we know of the sympathizing and helping Christ that the record seems almost incredible. He was never unsympathetic, unloving, indifferent, or cold. We may be sure, however, that His silence in this case did not show lack of interest in the woman. His heart was not cold to her. All we can say is that the time had not yet come for Him to speak. The woman's faith needed still further development and discipline to bring it to its best. People sometimes think now that Christ is silent to them when they call upon Him in their trouble. No answer comes to their cries. He seems not to come for their distress. But they may always know that the silence is no indication of indifference. Christ's delays are not refusals. When He does not speak to answer our pleadings it is because He is waiting for the right time to speak.

Matthew tells us also that the disciples interfered, begging Him to send the woman away. They seem to have been annoyed by her following after them and her continual pleading. The fact that she was a Gentile may account for this. The Jews had no sympathy for the Gentiles. It took the disciples a long time, even after the day of Pentecost, to be willing to carry the gospel to a Gentile home. Here they wanted Jesus to send the woman away and to stop her annoying cries. This is the way some people try to get clear of the calls of human need even in these Christian days. They cannot stand the cries of those who are suffering. They cannot bear to see those who come with pleas of distress. They turn away from their doors those who come asking for help. They do not know that they are turning away Christ Himself, for He says that in the needy who stand before us, asking for aid, He Himself stands, hungry, thirsty, sick, a stranger. "Inasmuch as ye did it not unto one of the least of these, ye did it not to Me" [Matt. 25:45].

When Jesus did speak to this woman, at length, it was a very discouraging word that He said. "Let the children first be filled: for it is not meet to take the children's bread and cast it unto the dogs." The children were the Jewish people. They were in a peculiar sense God's family. It seems very strange to hear the word "dogs" falling from the lips of Jesus Christ, applied to Gentiles. It does not seem like Him. It would not have been surprising to have heard the disciples use this offensive designation, for they still were full of the Jewish spirit. It was common for the Jews to call the Gentiles by this name. However, Jesus was different. There was never in His heart even a shade of contempt for any human being. No doubt there was something in the tone of voice which Jesus used, or in the look of His eye as He spoke to the woman, that took away from His words the offensiveness. Certainly she was not insulted by what He said. Perhaps she was encouraged by the word "first"—"Let the children first be filled." A first implied a second. Or she may have detected in His language a play upon words which gave her hope. There were little dogs in the home as well as children. She was only a dog, but the dogs had a portion. They lay under the table and got what the children left. The woman with her quick wit seized upon the picture which the words of the Master suggested. She was content to be a dog and to have the dog's share. Even the crumbs off that table would be enough for her.

There is strong faith in her reply. At last she had won her victory. Jesus said to her, "For this saying go thy way; the devil is gone out of thy daughter." In all the New Testament there is no other such striking illustration of the persistence of faith. Obstacle after obstacle was met and overcome. The woman believed from the beginning that Jesus had power to heal her poor child, and she determined that she would not go away without winning from Him the help which she so very much needed.

The lesson for us is that we should never be discouraged by delays in the answering of our prayers. Even God's silence to us should not dishearten us. He before whom we stand can do for us whatever we need to have done. Nothing is impossible to Him. He waits to draw out our faith until it reaches its fullness of power and wins its victory.

If this woman had turned away at any time, discouraged by Christ's seeming repulse of her, by His silence, or by His seemingly scornful words, she would have missed the blessing which at last came to her in such richness. No doubt many people fail to get answers to their prayers because they are not importunate. A man spent thousands of dollars drilling for oil. At last he became weary and gave up the quest, selling his well for a mere trifle. The purchaser, in two hours after he began work, came upon one of the richest oil wells in the country. The first man had lost heart just two hours too soon. The same lack of persistence causes failure, no doubt, often, in praying. Jesus says we should always pray, and not faint; that is, not give up.

We can picture the joy of this mother as she at last went to her house and found her child well. Her home was no longer darkened by this old-time sadness. The child was no longer under the power of the demon, but was happy and well and beautiful. Whatever the trouble with their children may be, mothers should always find the way to Christ and should plead with Him in patience, persistence, and faith, until their children are blessed and happy.

27

Wanderings in Decapolis

Scripture Reading: Mark 7:31—8:10

The activity of Jesus was intense. He was never in a hurry; for hurry is wasteful of time and strength. It spoils one's work. It hinders speed. The man who hurries is nervous and fusses and does not begin to accomplish what the man accomplishes who never hurries. Jesus never hurried. He moved quietly, calmly, as if he had days and days for His work, and yet He never lost a moment. We have all this in the three or four words at the beginning of our passage. "And again, departing from the coasts of Tyre and Sidon, he came unto the sea of Galilee, through the midst of the coasts of Decapolis." Some men lose time between duties—Jesus never lost a moment. If we would get this lesson for ourselves it would add years to our lives. It is in the gaps between tasks that we waste time.

The world is full of broken and imperfect lives, of people who lack or have lost certain powers or faculties. One has lost an arm, another a leg, another lacks an ear, another has only one eye. My doctor told me the other day of a certain man that has had only one lung for twenty years. Here it was his ears the man had lost. "They bring unto Him one that was deaf, and had an impediment in his speech." He could not hear. The loss of the sense of hearing is a most serious one. It is easy to think of what a man loses who cannot hear. We who know what pleasure comes to us through the words of others, through words of friendship

319

reaching our hearts through our ears and giving us thrills of gladness, inspirations of love, feelings of trust and confidence, can imagine in some measure what it would mean never to hear such words anymore. We who receive the exquisite sensations which come to us through voices of sweet song, through the notes of birds, the music of nature which we hear as we walk through the forest or stand beside the sea or listen to the soft breezes and the wild roar of the storm, can understand a little what we should miss if this were a silent world to us. Blindness is the sorest of all losses of the senses, but the loss by deafness is also very great.

This man who was brought to Jesus was deaf. He seems to have been totally deaf. Then, besides, he had an impediment in his speech. What has been called dumbness results usually from deafness. The organs of speech are perfect, but those who cannot hear cannot be taught nor trained to speak. The words here, however, seem to imply that there was some disturbance or some impairment of the organs of speech, so that the man could not make articulate or intelligible sounds.

We should always bring to Jesus our friends who have any defect, or problem. This man's friends brought him to Jesus. That was beautiful. To pray for our sick or our suffering, from whatever cause, and not to use the means that science and medical or surgical skill have brought without our reach, would be to mock Jesus, declining the help He has offered and asking Him to heal in some other way. We are not authorized to pray God to do anything for us that we can do for ourselves. God never works unnecessary miracles, nor can we ask that divine grace will do for us what we can do without special grace. This does not mean that we are not to bring our sick friends to physicians, nor to use any means that are known for their cure or recovery. Men are accomplishing wonders in these days in the way of healing. This does not show that Christ is any less the healer now than He was when He was here in the flesh. It means that He is giving His power to men who, with their science and their skill, are now doing the wonderful things.

The friends of this poor man brought Him to Jesus and besought Him to heal the man. We see at once our Lord's sympathy and interest in the way He received the deaf man. "They beseech Him to put His hand upon him." His response was instant and most gracious. "He took him aside from the multitude." His gentleness and considerateness for the man's infirmities appear in all His treatment of him. The deaf man could not hear the words of Jesus and would miss the tenderness and cheer which those who could hear received from His words and tones. Hence Jesus took other ways of giving him encouragement and confidence. He "put His fingers into his ears, and He spit, and touched his tongue." There was something in each of these acts which would help the man to understand the purpose of Jesus. He was deaf—the touching of his ears would suggest to him that Jesus intended to cure his deafness, and started in him expectation and faith. His speech was disturbed—the touching of his tongue by Jesus with the moisture of His spittle would indicate to the man that He was about to cure the defect. Jesus' looking up to heaven was a prayer, and would turn the man's thought to God as the only Healer. The sigh or groaning of the Master showed the sufferer His sympathy with him in his trouble.

After Jesus had spoken to the man in signs instead of words, on account of the man's deafness, He spoke the one word, "Ephphatha." This word is Aramaic. The writer of the Gospel gives the very word which Jesus used. It means, "Be opened." He spoke to the deaf ears and the disordered speech, and instantly these organs recognized their Master. "And his ears were opened, and the string of his tongue was loosed, and he spake plain."

Thus the cure was complete, and the man made altogether well. This is another illustration of the power of Jesus over all the functions and conditions of the body. It may not be His ordinary way of working to cure such physical defects; yet we need not question His power to do so. There have been instances when, although the deafness remained, the use of the other senses has been so quickened that the deafness has been practically overcome. The case of Helen Keller is perhaps the most remarkable of these in all history. She was blind and deaf. She was taught altogether through her sense of touch, through finger-spelling into her hand. She also learned to speak:

> the method being that of making the pupil feel the vocal organs of the teacher. She learned to speak well, and to tell, with some assistance from finger-spelling, what some people say by feeling the mouth. Her literary style became excellent; her studies included French, German, Latin, Greek, arithmetic, algebra, geometry, history (ancient and modern), and poetry and literature of every description. She had male tutors, but Miss Sullivan was 'eyes and ears'

at all times, by acting as interpreter, and this patient teacher had the satisfaction of seeing her pupil pass the entrance examination of Harvard University. To all time the success attained in educating Helen Keller will be a monument of what can be accomplished in the most unfavorable conditions.[*]

We do not call what was achieved by Helen Keller a miracle. It shows, however, what, no doubt, may be accomplished in other cases through wise and unwearying diligence and through love, helped by the divine blessing. We must note also that the advances of science have put marvelous power into the hands of men who treat diseases and defects of the ear, who now can do what in earlier days it was impossible to do. We hear it said sometimes that certain physicians have produced miracles of cure. They have not produced miracles, however, but secrets of nature have been discovered, so that help once impossible is now possible. It is all the work of Christ, whether done by supernatural power or through the imparting of knowledge by which the once impossible results are now within reach.

Jesus charged the man's friends not to tell any man of what He had done. He often did this. Probably His purpose was to avoid the notoriety which would follow such remarkable works if they were talked about. Such publicity was distasteful to Jesus. Some men like to have people talk about the great things they do and enjoy the excitement that is created by the spreading abroad of the news of their achievements. Jesus, however, shrank from having His good deeds talked about. He sought to do His good works quietly, secretly, and continually asked people not to tell anybody what He had done. He encouraged His friends to do their good deeds in the same spirit. We are not to sound a trumpet before us when we do our almsdeeds. Our life is to be like the dew that falls silently, making no noise, sinking away and disappearing, leaving no record except in the freshening of every blade of grass and the sweetening of all the flowers. So Jesus Himself sought to live and love and serve and slip away unnoticed, only remembered by what He had done. In this case His request was unheeded. So grateful were the friends of the dumb man for what Jesus had done that they could not be quiet about it, but the more He charged them not to tell it, the more they published it.

---

[*] Dr. Miller gives no source for this quotation. *Ed.*

"And they were beyond measure astonished, saying, He hath done all things well; He maketh both the deaf to hear, and the dumb to speak."

The feeding of the four thousand is not the same miracle as the feeding of the five thousand told in all four Gospels. The place of this miracle was in Decapolis. The many cures Jesus had performed had drawn throngs to Him. There was again a great multitude. The country was wilderness and desolate, and "they had nothing to eat." Jesus could not look upon human distress with indifference. "I have compassion on the multitude," He says, "because they have now been with Me three days, and have nothing to eat." He might send them away; but if they started homeward unfed, they would faint by the way. We know that the heart of Jesus has not changed, and that He still has the same compassion on those who are suffering. "Does God care?" people sometimes ask. Does He care when people are hungry? Here the question is answered.

It seems strange that His disciples had forgotten the other occasion, when their Master had provided for five thousand hungry men. "From whence can a man satisfy these men with bread here in the wilderness?" Why they did not remember what Jesus had done only a little while since in similar circumstances seems strange to us. But that is just what most of us do. We do not learn from experience. We forget yesterday's goodness in today's recurrence of need.

28

The Transfiguration

Scripture Reading: Mark 9:2–13

The Transfiguration was one of the most remarkable events in our Lord's life. The object, so far as the disciples were concerned, probably was to restore their confidence in Christ's Messiahship after the staggering blow to their faith which had come to them in the announcement by Himself that He must suffer and be killed. So far as Jesus Himself was concerned, the object of the Transfiguration would seem to have been to strengthen and encourage Him as He set out on His last journey to the cross.

For companions and witnesses on this occasion Jesus had Peter, James, and John. These were His special friends, admitted by Him to His closest friendship. On several occasions we find Him choosing the same three for special companionship. There must have been something in these three men which fitted them for the place of honor to which they were admitted. We know that the holiest will get nearest to Christ. We know, too, that faith always brings us near, while doubt and unbelief separate us from Him. Purity of heart brings us close— the pure in heart see God. Likeness to Christ fits us for personal friendship. Jesus said that those who serve most self-forgetfully are first in His kingdom. Selfishness keeps us far off. No doubt the eye of Christ saw in the three favored disciples reasons why they were best fitted to be witnesses of His glory that night. It was not an accident that these, and not three other men, were with their Lord on that occasion. It is a special comfort to find that Peter, though such a faulty disciple, was one of those who were admitted to closest fellowship with his Master that night.

Luke tells us that Jesus was engaged in prayer when the wonderful change in His appearance took place. From this we learn that prayer has a transforming power. Communion with God brings heaven down into our life. Tennyson said, "Prayer is to me the lifting up of the sluice-gate between me and the Infinite." Prayer lets God's own life into our souls. While we pray we are in the very presence of God. When Moses had spent forty days on the mountain alone with God, and then returned again to the plain, the people saw the dazzling brightness of heaven on his countenance. When Stephen was looking up into heaven at the glory of God as revealed now in holy vision, even his enemies saw his face as it had been the face of an angel. Only the upward look can give heavenly beauty. Our communing makes our character. If we think of earthly things, we will grow earthly. If we dote on gold, our lives will harden into sordidness. If we look up toward God, we shall grow like God. A life of prayer will transform us into spirituality and bring down upon us the beauty of the Lord.

Another strange thing happened that night. There appeared unto Jesus and His disciples two men from heaven, not mere apparitions, but actual men, not men either from the earth, but from heaven—Moses and Elijah. There was something very wonderful in this. For more than nine hundred years Elijah had been in heaven, and for more than fourteen hundred years Moses had been away from this world; and now both reappear, still living, speaking, and working. There are many proofs of immortality, but here is an illustration of the truth. Here we see two men long centuries after they have left the earth, still living and active in God's service. It will be the same with us and our friends. Thousands of years after we have vanished from earth we shall still be alive and active somewhere. If only we can get this great truth into our heart, how much more grand it will make all life for us!

We are told that these men had a talk with Jesus. One of the Gospels gives us the subject of the talk—it was about Christ's decease, His exodus from this world. These men were sent from heaven to comfort and strengthen Jesus for the journey to His cross. He would have bitter sorrows and great sufferings, and they came to cheer Him. We are not told that He was afraid or that He was in danger of growing faint-hearted before He reached His cross, but the bravest and strongest are better for encouragement and cheer. So the heavenly messengers were sent to earth to talk with Jesus about His death, to show Him what it would mean to the world, that He might be strengthened for it. No doubt all the way unto the end of life Jesus was braver and stronger because of this heavenly visitation. No doubt He had such a vision of redemption as He went to His cross that He rejoiced to suffer, that He saw of the travail of His soul and was satisfied.

May there not be a hint in this of the kind of employment that shall occupy the redeemed in the other life? Possibly we may be sent to dis-tant worlds on errands of love to carry help to weary ones. At least we are sure that heaven is not merely a place of inactive rest. Praise will not be the only employment of the glorified ones. They will have op-portunity to serve.

The hearts of the disciples were filled with strange ecstasy that night. So absorbed were they in the blessedness of the vision that Peter pro-posed that they should stay there, offering to build three tabernacles, one for Jesus and one for each of the heavenly visitors. Peter was right—it was good to be there. But at that very moment human need was wait-ing at the foot of the mountain for the Master's coming. Then, farther on, were Gethsemane and Calvary for Jesus, and for Peter there was Pentecost, with years of earnest service, and then martyrdom. It is very sweet to commune with Christ in the closet, at the Lord's table; but we must not spend all our time in these holy exercises. While raptures fill our hearts human wants are crying to us for help and for sympathy, and we must hasten away from our peaceful enjoyment to carry blessing and comfort to those who need.

Another element of the Transfiguration was the witness from heaven. It was the Father who spoke and said, "This is My beloved Son: hear Him." The disciples had been greatly shocked by what Jesus had told them six days before—that He must suffer and be killed. Now from heaven the Father speaks, assuring them that Jesus is indeed the Mes-siah, and that they should listen to His voice, and to His voice only. Even if they could not understand, and the things He said seemed to destroy all their hopes, they must be content to hear. There are times when God's ways with us seem very hard, when we think disaster is coming to every fair prospect in our lives. In all such hours we should remember that He who rules over all is the Son of God, our Friend and Savior, and our trust in Him should never fail. We should listen always quietly and submissively to what He says, and when everything seems strange and dark, we should never doubt or be afraid. What so staggered the disciples then we now see to have been the most glorious and loving wisdom. Through the cross there came to the world the most wonderful blessing the world ever has received. So in our strangest trials there are the truest wisdom and the highest love.

As Jesus and the disciples came down from the mountain the next morning, He charged them that they should tell no man what they had seen until after He had risen from the dead. There are many things that it is hard or even impossible for us to understand at the time, but which become clear enough when other events follow and cast their light upon them. One riding along a road, approaches a building which has no beauty and which seems to be only a confused pile. But when he has passed by and looks back at it, he sees a structure graceful, impressive, and beautiful. He saw it first from the wrong side. One looks at an artist at work on his canvas and sees only rude daubs. The picture has not yet been completed. By and by it is finished and is a rare work of art. We must wait for finished work before we judge. A boy enters the academy, and a page of Greek is put before him, but it has no meaning for him. He cannot read it. He spends a few years in the study of the language, and again the same page is presented to him. Now he reads it off with ease, and every word glows with some high thought. We are in Christ's school now, and there are many things we cannot understand until we get farther on and learn other things, and then the former will be made plain and clear.

29

The Child in the Midst

Scripture Reading: Matthew 18:1–14

Apleasing incident is recorded of Francis Xavier, the Jesuit missionary. Hundreds were coming to him with their needs, their questions, and their heart-hungers, and he was weary almost to utter exhaustion in days and nights of serving. At last he said to his attendant: "I must sleep! I must sleep! If I do not, I shall die. If anyone comes—whoever comes—waken me not, for I must sleep." He then retired into his tent, and his faithful servant began his watch. It was not long, however, till a pale face appeared at the tent-door. Xavier beckoned eagerly to the watcher and said, in a solemn tone: "I made a mistake; I made a mistake. If a little child comes, waken me."

There is something in this wondrously like the Master. He never was so weary but the coming of a little child awoke all His love. His interest in children appears throughout all the Gospels.

It was a strange question which the disciples brought to Jesus, "Who is the greatest in the kingdom of heaven?" These men, although occupying so sacred a place in their Lord's family, were still very human, and had their natural human ambitions. They even seem not to have been free from the passion for official or political positions which afflicts so many people, sometimes even very good people. They had only the earthly idea of the kingdom Christ was to set up. They probably had been discussing the question as to which of them would occupy the

328

highest place in this kingdom. One remarkable feature of biography-writing in the Bible is that it takes no pains to hide the faults of the saints. There is encouragement in this for us; it shows that even the holiest people have their faults and often do foolish things. Of course, this makes no excuse for us, however, for we ought to be very much better than even the apostles were, since we have more light, greater privileges, and better opportunities than they had, and should understand better the teachings of Christ.

There is one proper way, however, of wishing to be great in Christ's kingdom. It is right that we should long to be great Christians. It was said of a certain Christian man that his daily prayer was, "Lord, make me an uncommon Christian." That was a good prayer. There are plenty of common Christians. It is right to pray always, and to strive to meet the level of our praying, "Nearer, my God, to Thee."

The answer of Jesus to the disciples' question was beautiful and very suggestive. "He called a little child unto Him, and set him in the midst of them." He answered their question by an example. "This is greatness," His act said to them. A little child in the midst is used often to teach great lessons to older people. When a new baby comes into a home, God sets it in the midst of a family as a teacher. Parents suppose they are training their child, and so they are, if they are faithful; but the child also teaches and trains them. Thoughtful and reverent parents learn more of the meaning of the fatherhood of God, and the way God feels toward His children, in one week after their first baby comes than they had learned from teachers and books, even from the Bible, in all the preceding years of their lives. Every child's life is a book, a new page of which is turned everyday. Children are not angels, and yet they bring from heaven to earth many fragments of loveliness. Their influence in a home is a constant benediction. They change the center of life in their parents—it is no more self; they begin now to live for their child. They train their parents in patience, in gentleness, in thoughtfulness, in love. While a young child is in a home, a school of heaven is set up there.

After Jesus had set the child in the midst He spoke to the disciples, putting His lesson into words, rebuking their ambition and startling them with most serious words. He said to them, "Except ye be converted, and become as little children, ye shall not enter into the kingdom of heaven." His words implied that they were not now as little children, that their grasping after high places was anything but beautiful. They must be changed in spirit before they could even enter into the kingdom of heaven; that is, before they could have the spirit that belonged to the kingdom.

But the lesson was not for the first disciples only—it is for us also. What do these words say to us? What is it to become as a little child? There is a legend of a man whom the angels loved and wished to have honored. They asked God that some remarkable gift might be bestowed upon him. But he would make no choice. Urged to name something which should be given to him, he said he would like to do a great deal of good in the world without even knowing it. So it came about that whenever his shadow fell behind him, where he could not see it, it had healing power; but when it fell before his face it had not this power.

That is childlikeness—goodness, humility, power to do good, helpfulness, without being conscious of the possession of these qualities. Ambition to win distinction, craving for human praise, consciousness of being good or smart or useful or great—all are marks of a worldly spirit which is neither childlike nor Christlike. Moses knew not that his face shone.

Jesus went on to speak other words about the children, while the little child still stood in the midst. He said, "Whoso shall receive one such little child in My name receiveth Me." Every little child that comes to earth, comes in Christ's name. To receive it is to receive Him. What sacredness this thought gives to every little child that comes to us or makes its appeal to us! We should look with reverence upon it—it comes in Christ's name.

Many wrongs are done to children. Very grave, therefore, is our Lord's word to those who hurt a little one. "Whoso shall cause one of these little ones which believe on Me to stumble, it is profitable for him that . . . he should be sunk in the depth of the sea." There are many ways of causing little ones to stumble. He does it who sets a child a wrong example, thus influencing him to go in the wrong way. He does it who tempts a child to do anything that is not right. It is a fearful thing to offer a boy the first glass of strong drink, or to whisper in a child's ear a doubt, or a sneer at sacred things, or to put a bad book or paper in the hands of a young person.

Jesus also gives us a glimpse of the way children are regarded and cared for in heaven. He said, "Take heed that ye despise not one of these little ones; . . . in heaven their angels do always behold the face of My Father." Children and those of childlike character are the objects of heaven's bravest, strongest care. The angels sent to guard them are those who are most honored of God, and therefore are most powerful in their defense of the little ones entrusted to their care. It would seem, too, that the angels who serve the children are never refused admittance into the presence of God, are not kept waiting at the door, come when they will. There is no little child, therefore, who has not ever with him unseen heavenly guardians who can complain to God of any injury done to their charge, and bring instantly to earth all the power of heaven for his defense. The least sheltered ones, as they appear to us, are the most perfectly sheltered.

Another mark of Christ's love for children and the childlike is shown in the word about the lost sheep. If one of the shepherd's flock strays away, the shepherd leaves the ninety-nine and goes into the mountains and seeks the straying one. If a little child is lost from a home, we know how the whole community is aroused to try to find it. But these words tell us that heaven is aroused to search for the child that strays away from God. Whether human hearts on earth break in anxiety or not, the heart of Christ is full of loving solicitude when a child strays from His fold.

The last words of the passage are precious. "It is not the will of your Father . . . that one of these little ones should perish." It is not the will of God for anyone that he should be lost. He never made a soul to perish; He would have all to be saved. We are sure, therefore, that in all efforts to bring children to Christ and keep near Him, we have the sympathy, the cooperation, and the help of our Father who is in heaven.

30

The Two Great Commandments

Scripture Reading: Mark 12:28–34, 38–44

This scribe admired the way Jesus had answered the questions that were put to Him by His enemies. Jesus always answered well. He never got confused in His replies as often human teachers do. He never erred in His answers to men's questions, for He knew all truth. We know only fragments of the great body of truth, and therefore frequently find ourselves entangled when we attempt to explain difficult matters or to answer questions that are put to us. But Jesus knew truth in all its relations, and those who sought to catch Him in His words could never lead Him into any inconsistency of statement.

The practical lessons from this are important. One is that Christianity has nothing to fear from enemies who try to make its teachings appear self-contradictory. Amid all the assaults of skepticism, Christianity stands ever unharmed and secure. The hammers are shattered and worn out, but the anvil is unbroken. The other lesson is that we may take to Christ all our own questions, our fears, our doubts, our ignorance, our perplexity, and He will always have for us a wise and satisfactory answer.

It is the fashion in these days, in some quarters, to decry creeds. "Little matter what we believe," says one, "if only we live right." But if we do not believe right we will not be likely to live right. The duty of loving God is based upon the truth that there is only one God to be loved. If there were more gods than one, there would be little use in

332

teaching us to love God with all our heart. "Which God?" we might ask. So the doctrine of one God is a most practical one. There is only one God, and this one God is our Lord. What a comfort it is for us to know that the God in whom we trust is the great God of the universe!

He is our God. The little word "our" links Him to us and us to Him in closest relations. If He is our God, we are under obligations to obey Him, to do His will. We belong to Him. Then, if He is our God, He belongs to us, and we have a claim on Him. "The Lord is the portion of mine inheritance" [Ps. 16:5]. Every child of a good father knows with what pride he points to his parent and says, "That is my father." Still greater comfort to a believer is that he is able to point to God and say, "He is my God." All He is is ours—His love, His grace, His goodness, His truth, His mercy.

If God is our God we should love Him. He is the God to whom we owe everything, from whom we came, to whom we go, who cares for us, watches over us, provides for us, keeps us. He is our Father, with all a father's love. We ought to love God for Himself, for what He is in His character—merciful, gracious, holy, loving, good. We ought to love Him, too, for what He has done for us. Surely the commandment is reasonable.

Notice that it is love God asks. Obedience is not enough. One might obey every divine command and not have love for Him whom he obeys. Homage is not enough. We might pay homage to God, and yet have no affection for Him. God must have our love. Nor will a little love do. "Thou shalt love the Lord thy God with all thy heart." Our love for God must be greater than our love for father, mother, sister, brother, husband, wife, child, or friend. It must fill not our heart only, but our soul, our mind, and our strength. That is, it must draw all the powers of our life with it. It must lead us to obedience, to service, to complete consecration. If we love God supremely, He must be the Master of our life. We must be ever ready for whatever duty or service He asks of us.

Some people's religion seems compulsory; they do right because they must, not because they want to do so. All their work has the character of unwilling service. God says, "I want you to love Me," and if we truly love Him, we will fly at His bidding to duty or to sacrifice with eager alacrity. "But how can I learn to love God?" asks someone. "I want to love Him, but I cannot compel myself to do it. I love my father, my mother, my sister; but I cannot see God, and He seems great and terrible when I think about Him. He does not appeal to my heart as my mother does. I feel awe toward Him, but not affection."

It is important to know how we can learn to love God. The incarnation was God coming down near to us, that we might love Him. The glory of Sinai did not make its appeal to men's hearts. But when Jesus went among the people, touching them with His compassion, being their friend, comforting their sorrows, it was not hard for them to love Him. We must get to know God if we would learn to love Him. We should read about Him in the Bible until we know His character, His feelings toward us, what He has done for us, especially in redeeming us. Another way to learn to love God is to begin to trust Him. "How shall I learn to love God?" asked one. "Trust Him," was the answer. "I thought I must love Him before I could trust Him." "No; begin to trust Him, and you will soon learn to love Him."

No other duty comes before this duty of love to God. "This is the first commandment." Until we begin to love God no other obedience is pleasing to Him. We may do a great many things we ought to do, and yet if we do not love Him our doing amounts to nothing. A child may obey all a father's biddings, but if there is no love in his heart, what does the father care for the obedience? A man may be very good so far as his acts are concerned, but if he does not love God his goodness counts for nothing. When Jesus tested the young ruler's love by asking him to give up all he had for His sake, the young man went away sad. He had kept all the commandments from his youth, but he did not love God; at least he loved his possessions more, and gave God up while he clung to his property.

Love to our fellowmen is a very important duty, but it avails nothing unless love to God is behind it and in it. Two comes after one. The second commandment can come only after the first. A good many people boast of their love for men, their humanitarianism. They take the good Samaritan as their model. They are humane, charitable, philanthropic. But this is the whole of their religion. They do not love God, nor worship Him, nor recognize Him in any way. They put the second commandment high up, but they have no first. They do not know God, do not recognize Him, do not love Him. The things they do are very beautiful, and if they first loved God and lived all their life inspired by love for Him, their charities and humanities would be pleasing to Him, and not the smallest of them would go unrewarded. But since they do not love God there can be nothing pleasing to Him in their love for their neighbors.

The second comes after the first. After we have begun to obey the first commandment, the second presents itself and must also be obeyed. He that loves God will also love his neighbor. The two loves are linked together and are inseparable. John says distinctly that he who claims to love God while he hates his brother is a liar [1 John 4:20]. The love of God that does not overflow in love for our brother is not true love.

Jesus was pleased with the scribe's intelligence. He said to him, "Thou art not far from the kingdom of God." If he would only do the truth he knew he would enter into the kingdom; he was yet outside, although so near. There are a great many people who are almost, but not quite, Christians. There are those who know the way of salvation, but do not with their hearts accept Christ. There are those whose character is good and beautiful. They do many of Christ's sayings. They try to keep the second commandment, and seek to be gentle, kind, loving in temper, disposition, and act. They lack only one thing, but that one thing is vital. They are not far from the kingdom of God. Then there are those who are under conviction of sin and have a deep sense of need. They become honest inquirers, like the scribe, asking what they must do. They hear the answer of Christ and still stand hesitating, indecisive, on the point of yielding, yet not yielding to Him. They are not far from the kingdom of God, and yet they are not in it. At the door, with the hand on the latch, is still outside, and outside is lost. There are thousands in perdition who have been almost Christians, and yet have perished forever.

Jesus then turned to the people and said some plain things to them about the scribes. "Beware of the scribes." The scribes were the official interpreters of the Scriptures. It was their duty to make plain to the people the word and will of God. But Jesus said they were not trustworthy leaders. They professed to be guides to the people, but they were not safe guides. They were fond of wearing the garb and having the honor of saintly men. They liked to have people salute them as holy men; they took the chief seats in the synagogue and at feasts; but in their private lives they were bad men. Instead of being the defenders of widows, they used on themselves the widows' money entrusted to them. Then, to balance their embezzlement, they would make longer prayers than ever in the streets. They were the most despicable hypocrites.

The beautiful story of one of these widows and her suffering shows who were the really good people in those days—not the scribes and Pharisees, who put on the saintly airs that covered lives of shameful meanness, hardness, and wrong, but the poor, who were despised and robbed. This widow had higher honor before God than any of the rulers. Her gifts, though too small to be counted, weighed far more in God's sight than all the great shining coins they cast into the treasury.

31

The Good Samaritan

Scripture Reading: Luke 10:25–37

This is one of the great parables which only Luke has preserved for us. If Luke's gospel had not been written, we never would have had this beautiful story. This suggests one reason why we have four Gospels instead of one. No one of the four tells us all about Christ or records all of His sayings. Each one gives facts and incidents and teachings which the others do not give. It takes all four to tell us all that we need to know of our Lord.

The question which this lawyer asked was a very important one, yet it was not asked by one who really wanted to know. He was only a quibbler. Jesus referred this lawyer to the law. "What is written in the law?" The lawyer answered Him, quoting the first and great commandment. The man was glad to show his intelligence and, no doubt, was well-pleased with himself. Then came the quiet word, "Thou hast answered right: this do, and thou shalt live." There are a great many people who can answer right and do no more. They can repeat with glib and fluent tongue text after text of Scripture. They can recite catechism, creed, and confession, without missing a word. But that is not enough. They know the law, but do not obey it. If doing were as easy as knowing, how good we should all be!

Evidently the lawyer was confused by the home-thrust which Jesus gave. He wished desperately to justify himself, and so he asked, "Who is

337

my neighbor?" Under the eye of Jesus he became conscious that he had not been fulfilling this law of love. No doubt he had made the commandment rather easy for himself by convenient trimming. For example, he defined the word "neighbor" to mean only such good, pleasant people as belonged to his own set, those who were congenial, thoroughly respectable, those who could be loved without any distasteful association. No doubt also he had been defining love to mean an easy-going sort of sentiment which did not require any sacrifice.

Jesus told a beautiful story to make plain the meaning of the commandment. The "certain man" who was going down to Jericho was a Jew. This road was proverbially dangerous. It has kept its bad reputation through the centuries. Robbers frequently lie in wait for passers-by, hoping to get plunder. That old road is a type of many paths in this world. That poor man, stripped, wounded, almost dead, is a picture of thousands of people who every day are left hurt, bruised, robbed, ruined, and dying along life's wayside. Last night a body was found in the river and it proved to be that of a woman, young, with rich hair, beautiful face, and graceful form. While the city was quiet she had stolen to the edge and plunged into the cold water, which closed over her with a gurgle and then rolled on quietly as before. A few people dropped a tear of pity as they read of the tragedy in the papers. In one home there was bitter sorrow when the form was recognized. The woman had fallen among robbers, who had destroyed her and left her to die.

God had to send three men along that dangerous road before He got the poor man help. First, a certain priest went down that way. "When he saw him, he passed by on the other side." One would think that a priest would have a compassionate heart, as his work was all about the temple. People who belong to God in this special way, we would think, would be gentle and compassionate. We are surprised, therefore, to see this priest paying no heed to the sufferer he found by the wayside. He seems to have kept away as far as possible from the poor man. Perhaps he was nervous and afraid lest he might be set upon by a robber and hurt or killed. This feature of the story, however, has its meaning for us. We are the "certain priest." We are journeying along life's highways. We are continually coming up to people who are hurt in some way—wronged, sick, in trouble, in peril. Love is the Christian law of life, and we are told distinctly that love works no ill to its neighbor. Yet there are people going about who are continually doing ill to others, working injury to neighbors. We are always coming upon people who have been hurt—not wounded in body, perhaps, but harmed in life, in soul. What do we do when we come upon these unfortunate ones? Do we do anything better than this priest did?

Another man was sent that way when the first one had not helped the hurt man. This time it was a Levite. He also was one of God's ministers, engaged in the service of the Church. The men who naturally would be inclined to help were chosen. The Levite seems to have gone a little farther than the priest, to have shown a little more sympathy. He paused and looked at the sufferer, then went on. He may have uttered a sigh, saying, "Poor fellow, how I pity you!" But that was all. He really did not do anything for him. There are plenty of people of this sort in the world all the while. Pity is cheap. There is no end of comforters of the kind who say, "I am sorry for you." But this only mocks men's grief or suffering. It is practical help men need, not empty words of compassion.

Then came "a certain Samaritan." The Jews hated the Samaritans. Nothing good was ever expected of them. Therefore the sufferer would have little hope of help from this traveler. He would not have even spoken to the man in ordinary conditions. But a strange thing happened. This Samaritan proved to be his friend. He was moved with compassion. Jesus is now answering the lawyer's question, telling him who a neighbor is. It is a beautiful picture that He draws.

A good man in a prayer meeting made this prayer, "O Lord, advertise Thy love through us." A young Christian, when asked if she loved Jesus, was moved to tears, saying in her heart, "What a dim light mine must be if others are not sure, without asking me, that I love Jesus!" A Christian writer has recently said that the deadliest heresy is to be unloving. God certainly advertised His love through the Good Samaritan. The man's love was not so dim that others needed to ask him if he loved God. Certainly he was not guilty of the deadly heresy of unlovingness. He had true compassion. He was not content merely to say a few pitying words—his sympathy took the practical form of doing something, something, too, which cost him seriously. He risked danger, not asking if the robbers might still be lurking in the neighborhood to set upon him. He bound up the man's wounds—that was practical help of the right kind. He stopped the bleeding away of the sufferer's life. He then "set him on his own beast"—he would not leave him there by the roadside. He rested not until he had him safe in a warm shelter, away from danger. He gave up his own comfort in making the unfortunate man comfortable. He loved his neighbor as himself.

He was not even content to get the man into an inn, and then throw off further responsibility. He might have said, "I have done my share in helping this poor man—let some other one look after him now." But he was in no hurry to get the case off his hands. He took care of the man for a time, and then, when he had to go on his way, he provided for a continuance of the care so long as it should be needed.

The Good Samaritan is our Lord's own picture of what Christian love should be in every one of His disciples. We ought to study it with loving interest, getting its spirit into our own hearts. It adds force also to the teaching to remember that it was an enemy whom the Samaritan helped. Christian love is to exercise itself not only in being kind to friends, to those who are gracious and good, but its distinguishing characteristic is kindness to enemies.

In a sense this Good Samaritan is a picture of Christ Himself. The wounded man represents humanity, robbed and beaten by sin, ready to die. The priest and the Levites represent human religions which, at the best, give only a glance of pity and then pass on. But Jesus comes full of compassion, serving and nursing back into life, healing, and wholeness, dying souls. A Chinese Christian thus described the relative merits of Confucianism, Buddhism, and Christianity. A man had fallen into a deep, dark pit, and lay in its miry bottom, groaning and unable to move. Confucius came by, approached the edge of the pit, and said: "Poor fellow, I am very sorry for you. Why were you such a fool as to get in there? Let me give you a piece of advice—if you ever get out, don't get in again." "I cannot get out," groaned the man.

Then the Buddhist priest next came by, and said: "Poor fellow, I am very much pained to see you here. I think if you could scramble up two-thirds of the way, or even half, I could reach you and lift you up the rest." But the man in the pit was entirely helpless, unable to climb up even the smallest part of the way. He could do nothing to help himself. Then Jesus Christ came by, and, hearing the man's cries, he went to the very brink of the pit, stretched down, and laid hold of the poor fellow, and said, "Go, sin no more." That is what Christianity does.

"Which of these three, thinkest thou, was neighbor unto him that fell among the thieves?" That was the Master's question. The lawyer could not help answering, "He that showed mercy on him." Then came the application, "Go, and do thou likewise." It is not enough to hear good lessons or look on good examples; when we have heard and seen, we must go out and do the good things which are so beautiful, which our judgment commends. It is not enough for the artist to have lovely visions—he must get his visions on the canvas, where they will be blessings to the world. It is a precious privilege to look at noble lives and to read heavenly counsels. But we must reproduce in disposition, in act, in character, in our own lives, the excellent things we read. Now we have read the story of the Good Samaritan. Is that all we need to do? No; we must go and do likewise.

32

Jesus Teaching How to Pray

Scripture Reading: Luke 11:1–13

Our passage opens with an illustration of unconscious influence. The disciples saw their Master praying apart from them and yet within their sight, and were so impressed by something in His manner, perhaps His earnestness and fervor, that they wished to learn how to pray as He did. We never can know what the silent influence of our acts may be upon those who see us. One gentle person in a home unconsciously impresses and influences the whole household. One quiet, restful person makes others calmer and more quiet. One faithful, consistent life in a workshop, an office, or a school is a perpetual gospel, touching all the other lives. By simply being good we may start in many others desires to be good also. A young man, lodging once with a stranger at a country inn, where the two were put to sleep in the same room, by kneeling at his bedside before retiring, touched the other's heart and became the means of his salvation and consecration to useful life and service. We never know how far the influence of our example may reach.

We all need to make the same request the disciples made, "Lord, teach us to pray." We do not know how to pray, and there is no one who can teach us so well as Jesus can. We will find many words of Christ on the subject of prayer, all of which it will be profitable for us to study. We do not know what things we are to ask for. We are shortsighted and are apt to plead for comfort and help in the present moment, not thinking of the years before us. We all need to pray and need to be taught how to pray. The passage we are now studying is our Lord's answer to the request of His disciples to be taught how to pray.

The opening word of the Lord's Prayer, "Father," is really a Golden Gate through which we must enter into the temple of prayer. "When ye pray, say, Our Father." We must seek to say it as a child would say it to a father. When we actually do this we are ready to pray. God wants us always to come to Him as little children. If we think of Him in this way as a Father, it puts us into right relations with Him. Ideal human fatherhood means a great deal, and yet in its imperfection and its sinfulness it is only a dim reflection of the Divine Fatherhood. We can get many precious thoughts of God, however, through what we know of human fatherhood on the earth—his love, his faithfulness, his thoughtfulness, his patience, his care. The name also suggests what our feeling and conduct toward God should be. If He is our Father, we are His children, and we should never fail in the duty of children.

The honoring of God's name comes first among the true objects of prayer. "Hallowed be Thy name," we are taught to say, as we enter God's presence. He is holy, He is glorious. The name of God stands for God's character, for all that He is. We should give Him the first place in our hearts. We should be careful that in all our life we honor Him, doing nothing that will misinterpret God to others, or dishonor Him. No lesson more sorely needs to be learned in these days than the lesson of reverence. The profanity of men and boys is something appalling. In many of our churches and Sunday schools there is a painful lack of reverence in worship. To hallow is to make holy. We cannot add to the essential holiness of God, but we can make people see more of His holiness and have higher thoughts of Him. We can talk about His greatness and goodness and love. Then we can show a reflection of His glory in our own lives, so that all who see us shall learn of God from us. It was said of a noble minister that everyone who knew him fell in love with Jesus Christ.

The second petition is a prayer for the coming of God's kingdom. We can help to answer this prayer, first, by letting Christ be our King indeed, ruling in our hearts and lives, over all our feelings, dispositions, thoughts, tempers, words, and acts. We can also help to set up Christ's kingdom in this world by influencing others to accept Him as their King. We are advancing His kingdom when we get even one person to accept Christ as Lord and Master. We can do much also by seeking to overthrow evil and establish that which is good. The kingdom of heaven is heaven begun on earth. Jesus said, "The kingdom of God is within you" [Luke 17:21]. It must begin in our own hearts, and then extend its influence through us wherever we go.

The next petition is a prayer for the doing of God's will by us on earth as it is done in heaven. The kingdom of heaven is really the making of one place on earth like heaven. If God is our Father, His children should live the heavenly life, wherever they are. A thoughtful boy wanted to know how we can get to heaven, since it is so far away. His mother said, "Heaven must come down to you; heaven must begin in your heart." Then it will not be hard to get to heaven. We must have heaven in us before we can be ready to enter heaven.

Many people think of this petition of the Lord's Prayer as always meaning something very hard, something painful. They change their tone as they say the words and speak, "Thy will be done," in a strained, sad voice, as if a friend were dying, or as if they were passing through some great trouble. But the will of God is to be done not merely in the acceptance of crushing sorrow, but also in the acts and duties of our common days. We are to do God's will on the playground, in our schools, in our homes, in our shops, and on our farms—wherever we are. God's will is the law of heaven, and if we would help to make this earth like heaven we must learn to do His will while we stay here. It should be a glad and joyous prayer.

We are apt in prayer to think of our own earthy needs first. Many people never go to God until they have some request to make, some help to ask. But in the Lord's Prayer the petition for daily bread does not come until the prayer is more than half finished. We are to pray first for the honoring of God's name, the coming of God's kingdom, the doing of God's will, and then we are to ask God to give us provision for our bodies. We have the same lesson taught in the Sermon on the Mount:

> Therefore take no thought, saying, What shall we eat? or, What shall we drink? or Wherewithal shall we be clothed? For after all these things do the Gentiles seek; for your heavenly Father knoweth that ye have need of all these things. But seek ye first the kingdom of God, and His righteousness; and all these things shall be added unto you [Matt. 6:31–33].

The prayer teaches us to ask for our bread only day by day, and then only enough for the day. Thus God fed Elijah for many months at the brook Cherith, but only day by day, and the Israelites also for forty years in the wilderness morning by morning. We ask for "our" daily bread, thinking of others as well as ourselves. We are never to be selfish in our praying.

The next petition is for the forgiveness of our sins. God is always glad to forgive us, but in His prayer there is linked a duty also. We are asking God to forgive us as we forgive others. In an album Guizot wrote: "I have learned in my long life two rules of prudence. The first is to forgive much; the second is, never to forget." Under this one day Thiers wrote, "A little forgetting would not detract from the sincerity of the forgiveness." Then Prince Bismarck added these words, "As for me, I have learned to forget much and to ask to be forgiven much."

The latest petition of the Lord's Prayer refers to temptation. God does not promise to lead us in ways in which we shall have no temptations. The prayer we are taught to make is that we may not be allowed to rush needlessly into any danger. We need never fear temptation if it comes in the way of God's leading, for then we shall always have God's protection. But we should never dare to put ourselves into any place of temptation unless we are sent of God. God's design in temptations that come to us is never to lead us to sin, but to have us overcome and grow strong in resistance and victory. The divine thought in temptation is that we may be proved and may grow stronger.

The lesson of earnestness in prayer is taught in the little parable of the friend at midnight. The good man within did not give his neighbor food because the neighbor was his friend, but because the man would not go away from the door until he got the bread he wanted. The lesson is, importunity in prayer. God wants us to be earnest, not rebellious and willful, but always earnest and persistent in our praying. He is pleased when we want things very much and when we believe in His willingness to give them to us. The Syrophoenician woman is an illustration of our Lord's teaching. She knew that Jesus could heal her daughter, and she simply would not be driven away without the blessed gift. Many prayers fail to be answered because the person praying gives up too soon. A little longer patience and continuance in prayer would have brought the answer.

The love of human fatherhood is used in the last verses of our lesson in assuring us that God is willing to give us blessings, even the best that He has to give. We certainly would not say that human fathers are kinder than the Heavenly Father. No true earthly father would mock his son by giving him a stone when he asked for bread. We may turn the words about a little and say also that our Heavenly Father will withhold from us the stone which we unwittingly asked for, supposing it to be bread. God will not give us anything that will harm us, however persistently we may plead.

The best of all gifts is the Holy Spirit. Not only is God willing to give us things we need in this world, things for our bodies, supply for our passing needs; He is willing also to give us the best things of His own love, even Himself, the Holy Spirit. All we have to do is to ask, but the asking must be sincere. It must be earnest and importunate. If we get the richest of God's gifts, and yet do not get God Himself, we have missed the best.

33

Watchfulness

Scripture Reading: Luke 12:35–48

Our Lord often taught the lesson of watchfulness. The duty is one which cannot too frequently be impressed. We are all apt to grow negligent concerning things which we do over and over, day after day, through many years. We need to have our thoughts often called to the duty of unceasing watchfulness in service, instant readiness for anything that may come.

The lesson opens with a counsel concerning girt loins and burning lamps. These figures suggest readiness for instant and intense action. The loose garments must be kept drawn up and girded about the loins, so that without a moment's delay we may be ready for the march, and may not be impeded in our journey. The lamps must be kept always burning, so that whenever the Master may come, we shall be ready to rise and go with Him. A characteristic phrase more than once reappearing in Paul's epistles is, "I am ready." Every Christian should hold himself ready at a moment's notice to do anything or go anywhere at the bidding of his Master.

Men looking for their absent lord, waiting for his return, is the figure used to illustrate the waiting of the Christian for his Lord. No promise of Christ's was given more often or repeated more impressively than that He will come again. The time of the return is indefinite and unknown; but of the fact that He will come there is not the slightest doubt. His coming is always imminent—any hour He may come. These truths are presented in the parable we are now studying. The master is away, and his servants are left in charge of his house. When he will come back, tonight or a month hence, they do not know. But they are so to conduct themselves that, at whatever moment he may return, they will not be confused, and he will not be disappointed.

> If the Lord should come in the morning
>   As I go about my work,
> The little things and the quiet things
>   That a servant cannot shirk,
> Though nobody ever sees them,
>   And only the dear Lord cares
> That they always are done in the light of the sun,
>   Would He take me unawares?
>
> Why do I ask and question?
>   He is ever coming to me,
> Morning and noon and evening,
>   If I have but eyes to see.
> And the daily load grows lighter,
>   The daily cares grow sweet,
> For the Master is near, the Master is here,
>   I have only to sit at His feet.

It is high honor which the Master shows to the servants whom He finds faithful. "He shall gird himself, and make them sit down to meat, and shall come forth and serve them." No honor could ever be higher than this—that the master should bid his servants sit at the table, while he himself takes the servant's place and waits on them. Yet this is just what Jesus will do for His faithful ones at the heavenly feast. He did it, indeed, at the Last Supper, when He washed His disciples' feet. He said also to them, "I am among you as he that serveth" [Luke 22:27]. We cannot understand this, but we know that heaven holds for us surprises of blessedness far beyond our highest dreams. The picture suggests to us also the dignity and nobleness of service. We are taught to think it menial and degrading to serve, but in Christ's kingdom they who serve are the highest. Love always serves, and love is divine.

Christ sought to make it very plain to His people that the time of His coming to them cannot be known. He may come in the second watch, or in the third watch, or in the dawning of the morning. The value of this uncertainty as a factor in life is to press the duty of incessant watchfulness. "If the goodman of the house had known in what hour the thief would come, he would have watched, and not have left his house to be broken through." Of course. But that is just what men cannot know—when the thief will come. Thieves do not send, beforehand, a notice of the hour when they intend to break into a man's house. They come when the master of the house is least likely to be watching. So Christ will come as a thief in the night. This means that His coming in the last days will be entirely unexpected and will be a surprise.

> It may be when the midnight
>   Is heavy upon the land,
> And the black waves are lying dumbly
>   Along the sand;
>
> When the moonless night draws close,
> And the lights are out in the house;
> When the fire burns low and red,
> And the watch is ticking loudly
>   Beside the bed.
>
> It may be at the cockcrow,
> When the night is dying slowly
>   In the sky,
> And the sea looks calm and holy,
> Waiting for the dawn
> Of the golden sun,
>   Which draweth nigh.
>
> Behold, I say unto you, watch;
> Let the door be on the latch
>   In your home:
> In the chill before the dawning,
> Between the night and morning,
>   I may come.

The great lesson impressed in this passage is the duty of readiness for the coming of Christ. While the words had special reference to the great event of the return of Christ to the world, the lesson applies to every coming of Christ. We never can foretell any future, even the nearest to us. We never know what may happen in the next hour. We should so live that any moment of our days and nights we may be ready for any coming of Christ, ready for any duty that may be most suddenly given to us, or ready to die if the call to go home should come to us.

What does this mean? For one thing, it means that we must be at peace with God, reconciled to Him. It means that we must be faithfully following Christ, doing our work day by day, hour by hour, as it is given to us. One who is not saved is not ready for Christ's coming. Death is a coming of Christ to men, for it ends their probation and ushers them into the presence of God. No one is prepared for death who has not accepted Christ as Savior, and is not living in Him.

There is a beatitude in our lesson which we should take into our lives. "Blessed is that servant, whom his lord when he cometh shall find so doing." "So doing"—how doing? Doing his work with fidelity. If a man went away and left a servant in charge of a certain piece of work, fixing no time for his returning, what should the servant do in the master's absence? Sit in the doorway and watch to see his return? That is not the kind of watching that will please his master. He wants his servant to attend to the duties assigned him, and desires to find him, on his return, not idly gazing out at the window, but busy at his work. The way to be ready for Christ's coming, whenever and in whatever way He may come, is not to sit down in idleness and watch for His appearance, but to keep at one's tasks with unceasing diligence, so that when He comes He may find our work all finished.

Again and again is repeated the warning to those who are unfaithful. "The lord of that servant shall come in a day when he looketh not for him." There are several things said about this servant. For one thing, he is unbelieving. "My lord delayeth his coming." As a result of his unbelief he is unfaithful to his duties and to the trust reposed in him. Then, besides unfaithfulness in duty, he is unjust to his fellow servants. He becomes selfish, grasping, domineering, cruel. Then in his own moral habits he becomes debased. He is found eating, drinking, drunken. The punishment of the unfaithful and evil servant is stated clearly in the last verse. It is a fearful thing to disregard life's solemn responsibilities. We should compare these two pictures—the faithful and the unfaithful servant—and know positively which one of the two is our own portrait.

34

Jesus Dines with a Pharisee

Scripture Reading: Luke 14:1–14

Our Savior did not refuse any invitation to a proper social function. In this His example is important for us. He wants His people to be in the world, though not of the world. He does not desire us to withdraw from men, but to live with them in life's common relations, only being careful all the while that we live the true life as citizens of heaven. We are to be the salt of the earth, our influence tending to purify and sweeten the life about us. We are to be the light of the world, shedding brightness upon earth's darkness, helping weakness, comforting sorrow.

John the Baptist would not have accepted the invitation of this Pharisee. He was an ascetic. His theory of life required him to keep out of the world, witnessing against its evil by withdrawing from it. But Jesus did not follow John in this. He gave men a new type of religion. His first public act, after returning from His temptation, was to accept an invitation to a wedding feast. His theory of life was that the truest and most effective protest against the world's evil may be made from within, by living a holy, godly, and beautiful life in the midst of the world's evil.

Jesus had a reason for accepting social courtesies. He wished to show the divine sympathy with all human life. We used to be told that He often wept, but never smiled. But we cannot think of Jesus never smiling.

His whole life was one of gladness. He went among men that they might know He was interested in their lives. Life was not easy for most people in our Lord's day. Their work was hard, and they were not kindly treated by those who employed them. Their burdens were heavy. They were poorly paid. Jesus wanted them to know that He was their friend, that He cared for them, sympathized with them. He was ready for every opportunity to get near to them, that He might do them good. When He attended dinners, feasts, or weddings, He was not satisfied merely to eat and talk over the empty trivialities which are usually discussed around the table on such occasions. He found time always to say some serious, thoughtful words among the lighter things, which those who heard Him would not forget. Some of His most important teachings were given at feasts. Coventry Patmore says:

> Yea, find thou always time to say some earnest word
> Between the idle talk, lest with thee henceforth,
> Night and day, regret should walk.

We scarcely know why this Pharisee invited Jesus to dine with him. We cannot suppose that it was really a cordial, friendly invitation; that he wished either to honor Jesus or to have the pleasure and privilege of entertaining Him and hearing His profitable conversation. Possibly it was a sinister motive which led him to give the invitation—a plot to get Jesus near to him, that he might catch Him in His words or lead Him to do something or say something which could be used against Him. It may be that the presence of the man with the dropsy that day was part of the same evil intention. It was on the Sabbath, and if Jesus would heal this man on that day, there would then be cause for criticism, such healing being considered by the Pharisees a desecration of the Sabbath. Of course, the sick man may have come in of his own accord, drawn perhaps by the hope that Jesus would hear him. But there is room for the suspicion that his being present that day was part of a scheme to get Jesus to violate the Sabbath rules as they were interpreted by the scribes.

Jesus was not afraid of any such plots. He never thought about expediency or diplomacy when an opportunity for doing good came His way. We are told that He "answering spake." What did He answer? No question was asked Him, so far as we are told. Evidently He answered the thoughts of the lawyers and Pharisees who were watching to see if

He would heal the sick man. Jesus is always aware of what is going on within us. Our thoughts are as open to Him as our acts are to our neighbors. We should not forget this when our thoughts and feelings are not what they should be.

The question Jesus asked brought up the subject of Sabbath healing. The Jews considered it wrong. But they did not care to answer Him just now—so "they held their peace." They wanted Him to heal the man, that they might bring their charge against Him. Jesus healed the man. Thus He teaches us to think for ourselves in matters of duty, and not to be influenced by what we suppose other people will say. Too many people take their moralities largely from the opinions of others, doing this and not doing that, to meet the approval of somebody. But that was not the way Jesus did. His rule of life was God's opinion. "I do always the things that are pleasing to Him." That should be our rule of life.

Jesus asked another question. "Which of you shall have an ass or an ox fallen into a pit, and will not straightway pull him out on the sabbath day?" This question His critics would not answer. They admitted that it was right to relieve a dumb animal in such a plight. But if it was right on the Sabbath to help an ox out of a pit, how could it be wrong to help a suffering man out of his trouble on the same holy day? Surely a man is worth more than an ox, dearer in God's sight, and we should be more willing to relieve a man than a beast. Thus Jesus stripped the Sabbath of the disfigurement which human hands had put upon it, and set it forth in its beauty, what God meant it to be when He first gave it to man.

There was another lesson which Jesus wanted to teach that day. So He "put forth a parable." He had noticed that as they took their places at the dinner the guests scrambled for the best places at the table, the seats of honor. There is much of this same spirit yet in the world. One sees it on railway trains, on steamers, in hotels and boarding houses, almost everywhere. Nearly everybody wants the best, and scrambles to get it. Sometimes it is seen, too, where members of families try to get the choicest things on the table, the most comfortable seat, or the brightest, airiest room. Often unseemly strife occurs and bitter wrangles take place between brothers and sisters, each demanding the best. It will be well to study this lesson very carefully and to apply it to ourselves—the kind of application we should always make first in studying Christ's words.

Jesus said, "Sit not down in the highest room." We would say that common politeness would prevent any guest at a dinner from rushing for the seat of honor. It is understood in all refined society that these favored places are for the guests who are specially honored that day. Even these guests, though they know they are to have the distinction, do not take their places unbidden, but wait to be invited to them. "Sit down in the lowest place," said the Master further.

Thus the religion of Christ teaches the most beautiful humility and courtesy. We are not to seek to be ministered unto, but to minister [see Matt. 20:28; Mark 10:45]; not to get distinction and praise, but to live humbly and quietly. Kossuth said that of all natural emblems, he would choose as the emblem for his life the dew. It makes no noise, seeks no praise, writes no record, but is content to sink away and be lost in the flowers and grass blades, and to be remembered only in the fresh beauty and sweetness it imparts to all nature. Those who always demand that they shall be recognized and that their names shall be attached to everything they do, have not learned the mind of Christ. Our aim should be to seek to have Christ honored, then to do good to others, and to be remembered only in the blessing and good which we leave in other lives. Jesus tells us, further, that those who look after their own honor shall fail to be honored, while those who live humbly, modestly, without seeking distinction or praise, shall receive the best promotions.

The last teaching of the passage is also very important. "Call the poor, the maimed, the lame." Mary Lyon used to say to her Mount Holyoke graduates, "Go where nobody else wants to go, and do what nobody else wants to do." That is another version of the teaching of Jesus here. The rich have plenty of invitations—Christian love should seek to give pleasure to those who do not have much of it. If you are at a party, and there is one person present who seems to get no attention, that is the one whom, according to our Lord's teaching here, you should be most interested in and should take particular pains to make happy. Among your neighbors are some who have many things to make up their enjoyment—friends, money, health, books, social opportunities. But there are others who lack in these regards. While you are to love all your neighbors, your love should show itself especially toward the latter class—those who have less and who need you more.

35

False Excuses

Scripture Reading: Luke 14:15–24

"**A**certain man made a great supper." This supper is a picture of the blessings of redemption. The redemption of Christ is said to be great—he who prepares it, its blessings, the numbers who enjoy it, its eternal duration, and the sweetness of its joys—all are great. At a feast men provide the best provisions they can obtain; in the gospel we have the best that heaven has to give. At a feast there is plenty; in the gospel there is infinite abundance. There is pleasant fellowship at a feast, and the gospel brings us into intimate communion with God and into sweet fellowship with other Christians. There is one marked contrast, however—earth's feasts are soon over, while the gospel feast is unending.

Next comes the invitation. "Come; for all things are now ready." One of the things included is forgiveness of sins. Deep in every soul is the consciousness of sin and of separation from God because of sin. There is therefore a craving for the taking away of sin, and peace never can come until this craving is satisfied. Another hunger of the heart is for fellowship with God. The human soul was made for God and never can find rest until it finds it in reconciliation to God and restored communion with Him. Human friendship is very sweet and brings deep joy, but we need also the love of God in our hearts to make the satisfaction complete.

One who did not know the facts would say that this invitation would find universal acceptance. We can scarcely think of anybody declining an invitation to such a festival as this. But instead of universal acceptance, "they all with one consent began to make excuse." Most people are eager to accept social honors. But this is a spiritual feast. It is not this world's dainties that load the table, but the things of God's love. The joy to which men are here invited is not earth's festivity, but the joy of forgiveness and communion with God. To accept this invitation men must leave their sins and enter upon a new life of holiness. The natural heart does not take kindly to this. The begging off of those invited is true to nature.

The excuses given are only excuses—they are not real reasons. The truth is that those invited do not want to come to the supper, and therefore make up pretexts having the appearance of reasons for not accepting the invitation. Men do not like to say bluntly that they will not come to Christ, nor accept His mercy and love. That would seem discourteous. Hence they resort to insincerity and hypocrisy, revealing under all manner of flimsy and empty pretexts their unwillingness to accept Christ as their Savior and Friend.

The excuses which are given are typical. One man said, "I have bought a piece of ground, and I must needs go and see it; I pray thee have me excused." This may be called the property excuse. That was a very costly piece of ground to its new owner when we consider that it kept him away altogether from Christ and deprived him of eternal possessions. Yet there are many fields which have done this very thing. They have cost men their souls. The parable is not overdrawn. There are a great many people who lose their lives for things worth even less than a ten-acre field. Esau got only a plain meal as the price of his birthright. Judas got about twelve or thirteen dollars for his act of treason to his Master which has blackened his name for all generations, and which sent his soul into eternal darkness. Caring for property is always an insidious danger. It is not meant to be a snare to men—business ought to be a help heavenward. It is, when it is followed as our Master means that it shall be followed. Many men, however, are led to give more thought to planning how to make the most of their farms and their money than to the saving of their souls and making the most of their spiritual lives.

The second man offers the business excuse. "I have bought five yoke of oxen, and I go to prove them." He already had engagements for the day on which the feast came, business engagements which he thought he could not set aside—rather, which he would not set aside. He had no thought of postponing the breaking in of his oxen in order that he might attend the great supper. That is, he was not willing to make a little readjustment of his business arrangements even to honor his God and to get a new blessing for himself. The business of trying the oxen certainly could have waited another day, but the man missed the supper altogether while he spent the day out in the dusty field.

Many people are kept away from the church, from religious duties, and from Christ Himself by business occupations. They say they have no time to pray or read the Bible because their work is so pressing. They have no time to go to church, or to take an interest in spiritual affairs, because their worldly duties press them so. One man said the other day that he always played golf on Sunday. His business during the week required every moment of his days. His mind was under a constant strain. In order to be able to begin again this life of stress on Monday, he must have absolute rest on Sunday. He found this relaxation nowhere, he said, as he did in golf.

This is the way many men talk about the matter of religion. They have no time for it. They need Sunday for rest. Yet some of these days they will have to take time to be sick, and then, someday, time to die. What comfort will they get in these hours from all their life of engrossing business cares?

The third man gave pleasure as his excuse. "I have married a wife, and therefore I cannot come." He was so much taken up with the joys of wedded life that he could not turn aside. There is no doubt that home pleasures and delights do often so absorb people as to keep them away from religious duties and even from Christ. Sometimes the very blessings of home life interfere with faithful following of Christ. A loving wife may unintentionally hold her husband back from Christian service by the exactions of her affection. She is unwilling to spare him from her side that he may do the work which the Master would have him do. Peter in his love for his Master would have kept Him from going to His cross. Too often a happy home by its very happiness so satisfies men's hearts that they do not feel the necessity for anything more. We all need to watch that we never allow our home or our love for dear ones to keep us in any sense from our full duty to Christ. If we love father or mother, wife or friend, more than Christ, we are not worthy of Him.

When the master received the "regrets" of his invited guests, he bade his servant go out quickly into the streets and lanes, and bring in the poor, the maimed, the blind, and the lame. The servant did this and reported, "Yet there is room." There is always room. The heart of God is never full. The church is never full—its doors ever stand open and its welcome is ever extended to everyone who will come. Heaven is never full—there are places remaining still unfilled in its many mansions. In the description of heaven in the Book of Revelation we are told that the city has twelve gates, three entering from each point of the compass [Rev. 21:10–13]. These gates forever voice heaven's welcome to all those who will come. They are never shut, by day or by night, and no matter when one may come, he will find ready admission and glorious welcome.

Heaven must be filled. If those who are first invited will not come, the invitation is extended to others and pressed upon them. "Go out into the highways and hedges, and compel them to come in," was the bidding. These words show us the importance of earnestness in those whose duty it is to invite men to the Lord Jesus Christ. We are not merely to find Christ ourselves, and then be satisfied. The first impulse of the true Christian is to seek other lost ones. The words of the parable suggest, first, that we are to go into all the world, wherever there is a lost soul, and invite all men to come. We are to invite them earnestly, to constrain them, to press the invitation upon them. The morning papers the other day told of a policeman rushing into a burning building, climbing the stairways, through flame and smoke, to save a mother and her children. We should have similar earnestness in rescuing perishing souls.

A visitor at the hospice of St. Bernard, in the Alps, tells of one of the noble dogs coming in one morning, holding his head and tail to the ground, and slinking away to a dark corner of his kennel, as if ashamed to look anyone in the face. The monks explained to the visitor that the dog had not been able to find anybody to rescue that morning in the snow, and therefore was ashamed to come in from his search. How will it be with us when we reach the end of our life, if we have not rescued anyone from the storms and the dangers? On the other hand, much of the

joy of heaven will come from meeting those whom we have been allowed
to bring to Christ. Someone writes:

> Perchance in heaven one day to me
>   Some blessed saint will come, and say,
> 'All hail, beloved, but for thee
>   My soul to death had fallen a prey:'
> And oh, what rapture in the thought—
> One soul to glory to have brought!

36

The Parable of the Two Sons

Scripture Reading: Luke 15:11–32

The world would be very much poorer if the fifteenth chapter of Luke's gospel had not been written. The whole chapter should be studied. It is rich in spiritual instruction. It is all about seeking and finding lost things. Publicans and sinners flocked to Jesus, and He received them graciously and kindly. His enemies, however, found fault with Him for being so friendly to these outcast classes. They sought to put social obloquy upon Him by saying that He was the friend of publicans and sinners. The parables of this chapter are Christ's answer to this criticism. He did not deny the charge. He did not apologize for what He had done. He said that was the purpose of His life. His mission was to the lost—it was to save such that He came into the world.

The picture of the shepherd—seeking, finding, then bearing back on his shoulder his lost one, gives us a glimpse of the wonderful depths of love in the heart of Christ. The second parable tells of a lost coin for which the owner searches with lighted candle and broom until she finds it. A coin bears the image of the king and represents the human soul on which God's likeness is imprinted. The third parable tells of a lost boy.

The trouble began in the boy's discontent. His home was happy, but into this paradise sin crept. He became restless, discontented. His father's authority irked him. He began to have dreams of freedom. He

361

would like to be out in the world, away from all restraint. So he demanded his portion.

That is where sin begins. A man wants to have his own way without regard to the divine will. The father "divided unto them his living." He yielded to the son's demand for his portion. This may seem strange. Why did not the father refuse the son's unreasonable request? God does not refuse the demands we make upon Him. The other day one telling of a life of departure from God was disposed to put the blame on God. "Why did God let me leave Him and go away from the life of obedience I was living?" But God holds no one by force in the bonds of a good life. We belong to Him, we owe Him love, obedience, honor, service; but He will never compel us to stay with Him, or to love and obey Him. The stars are held in their courses by laws which they cannot break. Our little planet cannot get its liberty, cannot fly away from the sun's control, however it may weary of the restraints of gravitation. But stars are things. We are moral beings, under moral law, and God never compels us to stay with Him. We can break away if we will.

The story moves swiftly. "Not many days after, the younger son gathered all together and took his journey." From many a home door young men have gone forth to begin a noble career—brave knights to redress wrong; heroic soldiers to fight for country; missionaries to carry the gospel to darkened lands. Then the departure was honorable. But this prodigal's going forth was to shame, dishonor, wretchedness.

Mark the haste. It was not many days after he had demanded his portion when we see him on his way to the far country. Sin's course is swift. When a man has broken away from God's control, he is eager to leave God's presence. Our first parents, after they had sinned, hid themselves from God among the trees. When you have done wrong to a friend you dread to meet him. Sin makes us ashamed to look into God's face. The prodigal could not now endure his father's loving presence, and quickly went away.

The story of sin is always the same—a story of want and ruin. In the far country the prodigal wasted his substance with riotous living. His money was soon gone. But money is not all of a man's "substance." Indeed, money is really not substance at all. It is the most uncertain, unsubstantial thing a man has. Life is substance. Character is substance. Manhood is substance. An artist bought a piece of canvas for a few cents. He then put a picture upon it—an immortal creation—and it was sold for more than a hundred thousand dollars. God put His own image on the soul of man, and now a human life is priceless. Man is God's child, but a little lower than God.

Thus we have hints of the meaning of the "substance" which the prodigal wasted. If money were all a man wasted when he plunges into a sinful life, it were a small matter. Men often lose money, and are still rich as ever, because manhood is left, character is left. But when one goes into sin, though his money remain, though he still is a millionaire, he has wasted that which is worth infinitely more than money—God's blessed, infinite gift of life.

After waste came want. "When he had spent all, there arose a mighty famine in that country." In the famine the boy found himself without friends. It is a pathetic record which says that in his dire need he went and "joined himself to a citizen of that country." He hired himself out. He had made no friends in the far country. He had spent his money there, in banquets and revels and social dissipations, in which evil companions had shared. But now, when he had no money, and was in need, he had no friends. Sin does not bind bonds of affection between human lives. Sinning together does not make people friends. A man spends all he has at a saloon, but when he has no more to spend the saloon-keeper does not become his friend and take him into his house as a brother to shelter him and make a home for him.

So we see this young man, erstwhile a carefree and popular spendthrift, feeding swine for the citizen to whom he had attached himself. This pictures the degradation to which sin drags down a man who leaves God and chooses the evil way.

At last hope dawned. "He came to himself." He had been beside himself in the sad days of his sinning. When a man stops in his evil course, repents, and becomes a Christian, his old companions say, "The man is crazy." But the truth is he was crazy before, and now he is in his right mind—come to himself. Sin is insanity; religion is saneness.

Wonderful is the influence of home. It was a vision of home that first flashed its divine light upon the prodigal's soul. He said, "How many hired servants of my father's have bread enough and to spare!" As he sat there watching the swine and famishing, there came back to him a memory of the days of innocence and plenty in his father's house. Many a man has been saved far on in his years by such a memory. The old home tugs at our hearts, no matter where we wander. The child of sin who has wasted all her beauty in evil, when the hectic flush comes on her cheeks, and the ominous cough racks her body, creeps back home to die in her mother's bosom. The soul's true home is in God. That is where we all belong. In our childhood life heaven lies about us. This is a world of sin, and we are fallen creatures, but there are in us fragments of the defaced image of God—gleams of tenderness, flashes of nobleness, pulsings of good feeling, longings for better things, visions of purity—which tell of an origin above this world. It is a blessed moment when to one living in sin there comes a vision of the love of God and of holiness. Home is the one place in this world whose door is never shut in a man's face, howsoever evil he has made himself.

Quickly the young man made up his mind. "I will arise and go to my father." The glimpse which memory had given him of the home, bright with love and joy, while he was wasting his life in wretchedness, was enough. He saw in a vision his father's house, and beaming there in the doorway he saw the face which had looked into his the morning he came away, with love and yearning. Even the servants in that home had enough and to spare. Relentlessly, the old home drew on his heart.

Many people resolve to do right, and then take no steps toward the doing of it. This young man, however, carried out his good resolve at once. It was not easy to go home. He had come away rich, well-dressed, happy, and proud; he must go back stripped of all, a poor beggar, with penitence and confession. But he did not hesitate. He was too much in earnest to think of the cost of his repentance.

One of the most beautiful pictures of this story is in the picture it gives of the father. "When he was yet a great way off, his father saw him." Evidently he had been watching for his boy. That is a way fathers have—mothers, too. No matter where the child may wander, the loved ones at home never forget him. I knew a home from which a boy had been gone for twenty-seven years. Not a word ever had come from him during that time. Yet not a night passed but the widowed mother sat at the window, hour after hour, watching the street that went by the door, hoping that she might see her lost son returning.

And at last one night he came.

So God watches for the beginnings of repentance. We have not to trudge all the way back and knock at the door to get God's attention when we desire to return to Him. He sees the penitent afar off. And that was not all. This father "ran, and fell on his neck, and kissed him." Every word here has a volume of meaning in it. Let your heart interpret it. The father saw his son in rags, in ruin, and his heart broke. Then he "ran." How glad he was to see his boy returning home! How glad God is to see His child returning!

The son began his confession—a confession he had studied out carefully before he left the far country. He did not ask to be received back as a son, but only as one of the hired servants. Did his father take him at his word and give him a place among the servants? No, he took him back into a son's position. The ring, the robe, the shoes, were all tokens of honor. Then a feast was made. All this is an expression of the love of God for His children who come back to Him in penitence even from their farthest wanderings.

There is one thing we must not overlook in studying this story. It must not be forgotten that, though God forgives and restores, the prodigal never can be as he would have been if he had not gone to the far country. Sin is a terrible thing.

"Are you afraid to die?" asked a visitor of a man who lay on his deathbed, one who had lived a prodigal's life, returning to Christ only in time to die. The man was now grieving, and his friend said to him, "Why, you are not afraid to die, are you?" "No," said the dying man, "I am not afraid to die; but I am ashamed to die. God has done so much for me, and I have done nothing at all for Him."

37

Bartimaeus and Zacchaeus

Scripture Reading: Luke 18:35—19:10

It is said that when a certain French queen was journeying through her country, orders were given that no persons in sadness or in trouble—blind, lame, or suffering—should be allowed anywhere along the way. The purpose was to keep from the sight of the gentlewoman everything that might cause her pain. When Jesus was journeying, however, no such commands were given. On the other hand, all manner of sufferers thronged the waysides, and He never resented them as impertinent intrusions.

Bartimaeus was blind and a beggar. He was sitting by the wayside, holding out his hand to receive alms from those who passed along. He heard a strange noise, the noise of trampling feet, and he asked what it meant. They told him that Jesus of Nazareth was passing by. He knew who Jesus of Nazareth was. He had never passed that way before, and now was the blind man's one opportunity. Bartimaeus knew what that name meant. He knew that Jesus was a great healer, that He could cure the sick, and that He could give blind men their sight. Instantly, as soon as the people repeated the name, his cry broke upon the air, "Jesus, Thou son of David, have mercy on me." The people rebuked the blind man, bidding him keep quiet. But this only increased his earnestness. When the cries reached the ear of the Master He stopped and commanded that the blind man be brought to Him.

The story of Zacchaeus is different from that of blind Bartimaeus. This was also his day of opportunity. Jesus is ever passing by. He does not linger. He may come again—He does continually come again. But He is ever moving on, and the blessing we would get from Him at any time we must get as He passes by. All the days seem alike as they come to us; but each one is really individual and peculiar, coming with its own opportunities, privileges, and blessings. If we do not take just then the gifts it offers, we never shall have another chance to get them, and always shall be poorer for what we have missed.

Zacchaeus was a publican. He was also rich. Usually wealth gives men influence and power. But Zacchaeus was hated and despised, not because he was rich, but because of the way he had received his riches. His occupation was reason enough with his countrymen for hating him. Rightly or wrongly, Zacchaeus was supposed to have grown rich by exactions from his own people. Money, to be even in a worldly sense an honor to a man, must be received in an honorable as well as in an honest way. The luxurious and worldly comforts which money brings are a paltry compensation for the hatred and contempt of one's neighbors and a lack of respect in one's community.

The place of Zacchaeus in Jericho was no enviable one. For greed of gain he had been willing to sacrifice the sweet joy of human approval and commendation, the joy of having friends; but it would have been better far for him to have remained a poor man, approved and honored by his people, having men speak well of him, than to grow rich at the cost of all that made life a gladness and a blessing—the respect and love of his fellows. There are many, too, in towns and cities, whom men hate just as Zacchaeus was hated in his town for having grown rich in dishonorable ways. The exposure of getting rich dishonestly has left many names dishonored in our own days.

When Zacchaeus learned that Jesus was coming that way, he was greatly excited. "He sought to see Jesus who He was; and could not for the crowd, because he was little of stature." It is a golden moment in anyone's life when he begins to want to see Jesus. It is the starting of a new life. The interest of all heaven centers upon a man in this world who begins to pray, to look to God for mercy, to long to become a Christian.

There were difficulties in the way of Zacchaeus. There always are difficulties in the way of a man who wants to find God. The crowd was in the way of Zacchaeus—the crowd is always in the way of those who want to get to Christ. Zacchaeus was little, too little to see over the heads of the people; we are all in some sense too little of ourselves to see Christ. People hide Him from our eyes. We must expect that there will be obstacles in the way of our desire to find Him.

Zacchaeus was eager and determined to see Jesus, and therefore set about the surmounting of the difficulties. "He ran before, and climbed up into a sycamore tree to see Him." The people must have laughed at the rich little man running ahead to climb up into a tree. But Zacchaeus was too earnest to mind the laughter and the sneers. Nothing should ever be allowed to hinder us in a great purpose, especially in getting to see Jesus. Often one has to brave the ridicule of others, but we should never let ridicule hinder us from doing our duty and getting a blessing from Christ. We should not allow ourselves to be laughed out of heaven. Zacchaeus overcame his littleness by getting up into a tree. Men must often overcome disadvantages by expedients. Personal disadvantages often become one's best blessings. The very effort to overcome them makes one a stronger, nobler man.

Zacchaeus was trying to see Jesus that day, but Jesus was also looking for him. "When Jesus came to the place, He looked up." Zacchaeus did a good thing when he climbed up into a tree under which Jesus was about to pass. We should put ourselves in the way of Christ, going where He is to be. He has promised to meet with His people where two or three are gathered together.

It was a strange word that broke upon the ear of the little man in the tree that day. Jesus said to him, "Zacchaeus, make haste, and come down; for today I must abide at thy house." That was far more than Zacchaeus was looking for. He hoped only to get a good view of Jesus as He passed, but his earnestness brought him much more than that. It brought him a divine friendship. Jesus called him. He knew his name. Wherever you are, Jesus knows you are there and knows your name. He knows also what is in your heart, sees the desire there. He called Zacchaeus by name. Bible invitations rain down on the earth for everybody; yet when one touches your ear and heart you hear your own name spoken with it and know that you are personally called. Jesus asked Zacchaeus to come down from the tree. He wanted to meet him. He is always calling people to come down, to get nearer to Him. It is a lowly place where Jesus stands to receive sinners, a place of self-abasement, of penitence. Zacchaeus was bidden to come down in haste. There is always haste in Christ's calls.

Zacchaeus was quick to respond. "He made haste, and came down, and received Him joyfully." He did not hesitate an instant. If he had done so he would have lost his opportunity, for Jesus was only passing through, and soon would have been out of sight. A moment's lingering and indecision, and he would have been gone, and Zacchaeus would have been left unblessed. That is the way thousands of people do who hear Christ's call. They defer obeying, and then the opportunity is soon passed.

The conversion of Zacchaeus seems to have been sudden and very thorough. It was in his own house that he said, "Behold, Lord, the half of my goods I give to the poor; and if I have taken any thing from any man by false accusation, I restore him fourfold." Grace began at once to work in this little man's heart. His acceptance of Christ took hold of his life. It went down into his pocketbook. He is an example for the rich who come to Christ and are saved by Him. All they have belongs to Christ, and everything is truly given to Him if the conversion is genuine. How they shall use their wealth for Christ is a very serious question, which they should answer with great care. Jesus asked one seeker to lay down the whole of his wealth, and then give himself to Him, besides, for ministry. We have easy theories of consecration by which we make out that we may keep our money and then use it for Christ. Yes, but the problem is vital. Do we use it for Him?

Another evidence of the genuineness of the repentance of Zacchaeus was shown in his resolve to make restitution to those whom he had wronged. "If I have taken any thing from any man by false accusation, I restore him fourfold." Here we come upon another too much neglected part of consecration. We say: "Let the past go. We cannot change it. We cannot undo the wrongs we have done. Let us make the future beautiful, pure, and true." This is right in a sense. It is idle to waste time in unavailing tears and regrets. Yet there may be wrongs we have done which we can undo, or at least in a way can set right. If one has spoken false or injurious words against another before his conversion, he should seek instantly to undo the harm so far as it is in his power. Sorrow for sin is not enough if we can in any way make right that which we have marred.

The law of restitution applies to influence; but how impossible it is to recall or undo or gather up that which has gone before.

Jesus saw the sincerity of the man's heart and the reality of his conversion, and said to him, "This day is salvation come to this house." That the man's repentance was genuine was evidenced by such moral changes in his character as always accompany true repenting. Zacchaeus was saved. The publican was now a child of God. It is always so. There is no vain seeking of Christ in this world.

The people murmured at Jesus because He went among the outcasts. He assured them, however, that these were the very people He had come to save. "The Son of man is come to seek and to save that which was lost." Sinners were the very ones He had come from heaven to continue to seek. In another place He illustrated the same truth by the case of a physician, whose mission is to the sick, not to the well. Who would sneer at the physician for choosing sick people to associate with and call upon? Who then should murmur at Jesus for going among sinners, when He came to this world expressly to save sinners?

38

Christ's Trial before Pilate

Scripture Reading: Mark 15:1–15

We speak of Christ's trial before Pilate. Really it is Pilate's trial before Christ that is described in our Scripture. The narrative holds up the Roman governor in such a blaze of light that all the world can see him. The story of this trial begins in the early morning, when Jesus was led to Pilate. During the night the rulers had informally condemned Him to death, but they could not carry out their own sentence without bringing their prisoner to the Roman governor. This was one of the humiliating conditions of their subjection to the Romans. Meanwhile Jesus had been kept under guard during the morning hours, and had been cruelly mocked by the soldiers. It was during this time that Peter's denial occurred, and the pain of the disciple's words as they fell upon Christ's ears was more severe than all the mockeries of the heathen soldiers. As the first streaks of dawn appeared in the east, the members of the Sanhedrin were together again to hasten the formalities, so as to get Jesus on the cross at the earliest possible moment.

When Jesus was taken to Pilate, He was bound. The rulers supposed that their cords would hold Him. Knowing as we do who this Prisoner was, we are sure that no chains of earth could have held Him if He had put forth His power, and therefore that their bonds were useless. We understand also that this quiet submitting to be seized and led away was entirely voluntary. He was led as a lamb to the slaughter, not resisting, exerting no power in His own defense, though omnipotence was His, because He was laying down His life for us.

But what a strange picture this is—the Son of God bound, manacled as a common prisoner, and led away under arrest! What humiliation! But did they shackle the arms of His power with their chains? Did they stain the radiance of His glory with the shame they put upon His name that day? We know that while He Himself wore chains, submitting to them, He is able to break our bonds and set us free.

The rulers had told Pilate that Jesus claimed to be a king. They thus sought to secure Pilate's consent to His execution as one who was disloyal to Rome. "Art Thou the King of the Jews?" asked the governor, referring to what His accusers had charged. Jesus did not look much like a king as He stood there, His hands tied and a cord about His neck. Pilate's question sounds like ridicule. Yet Jesus answered calmly, "Thou sayest it." Where was His kingly power? Where was His throne? Where did His kingdom lie? These questions are not hard to answer today. Millions now bow to Him and worship Him as King of their souls. In heaven He is honored and adored as King of kings. On earth, too, His sway is felt even where He is not acknowledged. His influence has permeated all lands. Righteousness, truth, love, and grace are the characteristics of his reign, and these qualities are entering more and more into the life of all the world.

When the chief priests accused Jesus before Pilate, Jesus answered nothing. Pilate could not understand His silence, and so endeavored to induce Him to speak. "Behold how many things they witness against Thee." But still He was silent. "Jesus yet answered nothing," the record says. We cannot too often remind ourselves of the wisdom of silence under false accusation. It is told of a certain bishop in the olden times, that when most grievously and falsely accused by enemies, he refused to give even one word of denial or to offer any proof whatever of innocence, saying that God knew all about it, and that if it was God's will that he should live under the shadow, he would do it in silence, like his Master on his trial. This is what a Christian should usually do when falsely accused, perhaps not even offering explanation. Jesus at least answered nothing, but "committed Himself to Him that judgeth righteously" [1 Pet. 2:23]. That is, He left His name, His life, and the whole matter of His vindication to His Heavenly Father. There is no spot now on His name, though He died as a malefactor. So may we trust ourselves in God's hands when we are wrongly accused, answering nothing, but committing the whole matter to Him who will judge us righteously.

Pilate was aware from the beginning that the rulers really had no case against Jesus. If he had been courageous and just, he would have delivered Him out of the hands of His enemies. But he could not forget his own interests, and tried in various ways to parry the question of decision. He saw clearly the motive of the rulers. "For he knew that the chief priests had delivered him for envy." The rulers were envious of the influence of Jesus with the people. Envy has led many to a crime. It was envy that led Cain to slay his brother Abel. It was envy that caused Joseph's brothers to hate him and to sell him as a slave, to get him out of their way. In many a school a bright scholar is disliked and even persecuted in many ways because of the envy of his schoolmates. In business the successful man is followed by the envy and the enmity of rivals. In society a popular young person is often assailed by those who are outshone. Many a good name is blackened by envy. We should be on our guard continually against this sinful tendency in our hearts.

One of the expedients to which Pilate resorted in his effort to release Jesus indirectly, without exerting his own authority, was to get the people to choose Him as the one prisoner to be set free at that Passover. But the rulers, determined on the death of Jesus, insisted upon the release of Barabbas, a noted criminal. "Jesus or Barabbas?" was now the question. Barabbas was a robber and murderer. He had been engaged in an insurrection against the Romans, probably was chief in the band. His condemnation was just. Jesus never had done anything but bless men and do them good. No enemy could say a word against Him. No witness had testified that ever He had done the least unkindness to any human being. Yet the people did not hesitate in their choice. They chose the guilty, blood-stained criminal for friendly recognition and freedom, and sent the pure, holy, and gentle Jesus to dishonor and death. Everyone of us have to make a similar choice between Jesus, the holy, blessed, living glorious One, and sin. Which are we choosing?

This determined choice of Barabbas for freedom still left Jesus on Pilate's hands. He was disappointed. He had hoped to get clear of deciding in His case. He was compelled now to do something, either to assert his power and set Him free, or yield to the people's clamor and send

Him to the cross. "What will ye then that I shall do unto him whom ye call the King of the Jews?" Pilate's question is a question which everyone of us must answer—we must do something with Jesus. We take Him to our hearts, to the highest place of love and honor, or we must reject Him. What shall we do with Him? Before everyone of us He stands waiting at our door, and we must ask and answer this very question, "What shall I do with Jesus?" He comes to us in every gentle and gracious way—to be our Savior, our Friend, our Lord, our Guide, and we must either accept Him or reject Him. We may postpone our answer, but delay does not rid us of the question—it only pushes it forward, and when we go on a little we shall meet it again. The question must be answered either by our acceptance or by our rejection of Christ. Not accepting is really rejecting, and, therefore, while we think we have not answered the question, we really have answered it. We should think seriously what the rejection of Christ involves. We know what it involved for Pilate. What will it involve for us? Would we crucify Him afresh?

At length Pilate yielded to the pressure of the rulers and gave sentence that Jesus should be crucified. He did it, we are told, wishing to calm the multitude. That was Pilate's opportunity. He was the one man in all the world who could send Jesus to the cross. No other one could do it. It was a fatal and terrible distinction that was his among men. Whether Jesus should have justice and be set free or should die innocently, he had to settle. The Jews could not touch Jesus without Pilate's consent.

We know what he did with his opportunity. He had not the courage to be true, to be just, to protect the innocent, to maintain right. He knew well that Jesus had done nothing worthy of punishment. He struggled feebly for a time with his conscience, and then gave way, sentencing to death as a malefactor a man he knew to be without sin or fault. Thus he lost his opportunity to do justice and to win for himself an immortality of honor. He went through the farce of washing his hands before the rulers, saying that he was not responsible. But the stain upon his soul no water could wash off; the brand of dishonor marks his name with an immortality of shame. The lesson is for us. We all have our opportunity to stand for truth and right. What shall we do with Jesus who is called the Christ?

39

Christ Crucified

Scripture Reading: Mark 15:22–39

After Pilate had sentenced Jesus, the soldiers crowned Him with thorns, robed Him in purple, and saluted Him in mockery as King of the Jews. Later the purple robe was replaced by His own garments, and Jesus, bearing His cross, was led away to be crucified. Faint from suffering and loss of rest, the burden of the cross was too heavy for Him, and the soldiers seized Simon, the Cyrenian, who was passing by, and compelled him to bear the cross after Jesus.

Simon was an unwilling cross-bearer. There may have been no tenderness toward Jesus in the hearts of the soldiers when they pressed this young man into the service to help Him when He staggered under His heavy load. Perhaps they wanted only to have Him get along faster. Yet it was a compassionate act, whatever its motive. This was one of the kindnesses shown to Jesus on the way. If Simon afterward became a disciple of Jesus, he never ceased to remember with gratitude what even unwillingly he did that day to give comfort to his Master.

Even amidst the terrible scenes of Calvary there were gleams of human pity. One we have seen already—the help Simon gave Him in carrying His cross. Here is another: "They gave Him to drink wine mingled with myrrh." The object was to dull His senses somewhat, as is now mercifully done by the use of anesthetics when surgical operations are to be performed, so that He would not be fully conscious in the

375

terrible agonies of crucifixion. We cannot but be grateful, loving Jesus as we do, that there were women with tender hearts who sought thus to mitigate His sufferings. His refusal of the offered kindness meant no disrespect to them. He tasted the wine, showing His appreciation of their kindness. But He declined it, we may suppose, for two reasons. He would not seek to lessen in any way the bitterness of the cup which His Father had given Him to drink. Then He would not cloud His mind in the least degree as He entered the experiences of the last hour. He would not dim the clearness of His communion with the Father by any potion that would dull His senses and thus impair His full consciousness.

In the fewest words we are told of the crucifixion of Jesus. "They crucified Him." Crucifixion was a terrible mode of punishment. It was reserved for the lowest criminals, and, therefore, set the mark of ignominy on those who were sentenced to endure it. The shame of the cross was the deepest shame that could be put upon anyone man. But there was a yet darker meaning for Jesus in the crucifixion than that which the world saw. This is a mystery, however, which we cannot fathom. We know only this, that He was the Lamb of God bearing the sin of the world. What this great work of atonement meant to Jesus in those hours when He hung on the cross, we can never understand. It is enough for us to know that from His anguish comes our joy; from His stripes, our healing; from His crowning with thorns, our crowning with glory; from His forsakenness, our peace.

The custom was for the soldiers in charge of the crucifixion to divide the sufferer's garments among themselves. In many a home there are garments which we sacredly cherish because some beloved one, now gone, once wore them. We love to think of the garments Jesus had worn. They may have been made by His mother's hands or by the hands of some of the other women who followed Him and ministered unto Him. They were the garments the sick had touched with reverent faith, receiving healing. A peculiar sacredness clings to everything that Jesus ever touched. What desecration it seems to us, then, to see these scoffing Roman soldiers take the garments He had worn in His holy ministry and divide them among themselves as booty! What terrible sacrilege it seems to see them throwing dice there under the very cross, while the Savior of the world hangs upon it in agony! Gambling for that seamless robe which trembling hands had touched in faith to find healing! There is a suggestion in this stripping off of Christ's garments. He hung naked on the cross that we may stand in the final judgment arrayed in robes of beauty. Those soldiers went about after that day wearing Christ's clothes; if we are saved we are wearing the robes of righteousness made by His obedience and suffering.

The cross of Jesus was marked that day so that all the world might know it. Over the Sufferer a wide board was nailed, bearing the title, "King of the Jews." It was the custom thus to indicate the name and the crime of the person suffering. There was no crime to write over the head of Jesus, for not even His enemies had been able to find anything against Him. So Pilate wrote the only charge the rulers had made. He was the King of the Jews—the Messiah who had been promised through all the centuries, longed for, prayed for, waited for. He was the King of whom David was the type. He had fulfilled all the Messianic predictions of the Old Testament. He had brought infinite blessing to the nation. Yet this was the way His own people treated Him. Instead of receiving Him with love and honor whom they had been expecting so long, they had rejected Him, and now had nailed Him on the cross. But He is our King, too. How are we honoring Him?

It was strange company in which Jesus died. "With Him they crucify two robbers; one on His right hand, the other on His left." There were three crosses that day, and each has its own special suggestion for us. On the center cross hung the Savior, dying for the sin of the world. We should study long and reverently this death scene. He died, the Just for the unjust, to bring us to God. He bore our sins in His own body on the tree.

Even during those terrible hours there were manifestations of grace and power on that middle cross. There was a prayer for His murderers which showed His spirit of forgiveness. There was His word to John and His mother which showed His thoughtfulness for her. There was His word to the penitent robber, showing His power to save even in His death hour. There was the cry of forsakenness which gives us a hint of the awful blackness which surrounded the Redeemer as He bore our sins.

On one of the other crosses we see dying penitence. Few are the words we hear, but they are enough to show us the proofs of true regeneration in this man who not until the last hour repented and sought mercy. On the other cross we see dying impenitence. This man saw Jesus, heard His prayer, listened to the words of his companion, and yet was lost. So one may be close to the Savior and yet perish. Men sometimes say, "I will take the chance of the thief on the cross." Yes, but which—for there were two?

A great multitude was gathered that day about the cross, but most of the people were there to mock. Even the chief priests mocked Him. We must remember that it was while He was dying in love for the world that the world was thus pouring bitterness into His cup. Strange return indeed to get for such infinite love! Yet it shows more and more the depth and wondrousness of that love, that even the treatment He received from men while giving His life for men did not chill His love. They said, "He saved others; Himself He cannot save." That is just what love must always do—sacrifice itself, that it may save others. Jesus did not save Himself because He would save the world He loved.

We have a glimpse of the most intense moment of Christ's agony in His cry, "My God, My God, why hast Thou forsaken Me?" We never can understand this cry. We learn here a little more of the infinite cost of our redemption. Then let us never forget that it is because death was so terrible to Him that we can look upon dying as simply passing through a valley of shadows with divine companionship. He "tasted death for every man." He endured death's awful bitterness, that we may die in sweet peace.

The rending of the veil in the temple as Jesus died tells of the completion of His work of redemption. The way of access to God was now opened to all the world. Heretofore none but the priest could enter the Holy of holies; now all could enter.

40

The Resurrection of Jesus

Scripture Reading: Luke 24:1–12

The important question in all that refers to Christianity is, "Did Jesus truly rise again?" Paul says that if He did not rise, our faith is vain, we are yet in our sins, we have no Redeemer [see 1 Cor. 15:14]. Until that morning Death had been an unchallenged conqueror. All the generations of men had been taken captive by him, and not one person had ever returned. True, a few persons had been recalled from his power, but only for a little time, to be reclaimed again after a brief respite. Death never had been really overcome.

Someone has said, "No philosophy will ever satisfy men which cannot throw a plank across a grave." To our natural eyes the grave is a dark chasm over which we cannot pass. Has Christ bridged this chasm for us?

He came to be the world's Redeemer and Deliverer. He conquered every form of evil—sickness, human infirmities, demons. Now He had met the last enemy and apparently had been defeated by him. Death had carried Him down into the prison of darkness and had shut the door upon Him. If He had not risen, that would have been the end. If He were not able to overcome death, He could not be the world's Redeemer. All our hopes, all the hopes of the world, waited outside that sealed door to see if Jesus would come again. Did He rise?

It was the first day of the week, very early. A little company of women were hurrying toward the tomb where their Master had been buried three days before. Worthy of notice is the beautiful and loyal devotion of the women friends of Jesus. Woman's ministry gave Jesus much comfort during His sorrowing years, and now, when He is dead, women are the first to come to His grave. The women friends of Jesus are as brave and tender in their loyalty to Him today as they were when He was on the earth.

What brought these women friends to the tomb that morning? They had no thought that Jesus had risen or would rise again. They supposed that His body still lay in the grave, and they wished to honor it. It was a beautiful sentiment which sought thus to show love's tender regard for the departed. It was fitting to pile fragrant spices in the sepulcher, filling the place with sweet odors. In like manner friends lay flowers on the coffins of their beloved dead in our own time. It is one of love's tender ways of expressing itself. It is fitting and beautiful. But let us not forget to put flowers also upon the pathways of our friends while they live. That is better. It is a poor compensation to allow hearts to starve for acts of kindness along all the years, and then to send elaborate floral designs to be laid on their coffins or graves. Let us be kind to our friends while they are living, and then honor them in death.

As the women hurried on through the dim dawn they were perplexed about the stone which had been rolled to the door. It was too heavy for their feeble strength to roll back, and they asked each other, "Who shall roll us away the stone?" Apparently they did not know that the stone had been sealed with the Roman seal, and that, also, a guard of soldiers had been set to watch the grave. If they had known this, their anxiety would have been still greater. But when they came near enough to see the grave, they found that the stone was already rolled back. An angel had been there before them.

We may get a lesson here about the needlessness of anxiety over difficulties in our way. Wherever God wants us to go He will open the way for us. It is ours only to go straight on, in confidence and faithfulness, doing our simple duty, and leaving to divine love and wisdom the opening of the path, the rolling away of the stones. Impossibilities become easy possibilities when God is leading.

Fearlessly the women entered in and found that the body was not there. This greatly perplexed them. But suppose they had found the body in the grave—what then would have been the conclusion? That would have meant no resurrection, Jesus still held in the clasp of death. The women were disappointed in not finding the body, but in this disappointment lay the glorious hope out of which all our Christian joy comes today.

We should get here a lesson of comfort for our own hearts when we stand by the graves of our Christian dead. The body of our loved one may be in the grave, but the friend we knew and loved is not there—he is with his Lord. Speaking of believers who are departed, Paul says they are "absent from the body," "at home with the Lord" [see 2 Cor. 5:8]. You go to an old house where your friend used to live. You knock, but get no answer. The house is empty. Then you find that your friend has moved to a new house, a larger and better one, on the hill. You stand by the form of your dead and speak, but get no answer. The house of clay is empty. Your friend is not there—he is absent, he has gone away. Where is he? He has moved out of the old house and is now "at home with the Lord." That is the story of Christian death. It is life, not death.

In their disappointment the women had a vision which brought great comfort to them. They saw two forms in dazzling apparel keeping watch over Christ's tomb. One of the evangelists speaks of them as young men. All heavenly life is young. It is a pleasant fancy of Swedenborg's that in heaven the oldest angels are the youngest. The longer they dwell in the glory of that happy home, the younger they become. In heaven all life is toward youth. In this world we grow ever toward feebleness and decay. But in the immortal life all this is reversed. The angels were young men, although they were created before the human race began.

As we look into this empty tomb there are several lessons we should learn. We are assured by it, first, that Jesus actually died. Certainly He was buried there. His head lay there, and His feet lay here. He was surely dead, for Pilate had official inquiry made, and received assurance of the fact before he would give leave for the removal of the body. If any doubt had existed concerning His death, there certainly could be none after the soldier had thrust the spear into His side. Here are the grave cloths, the pieces of fine linen which gentle hands had wound about His limbs. Here is the napkin that covered His face, lying neatly folded by itself. Look closely at the place, for He was here—He was actually dead.

But He is not now in the grave. There is no dead form lying there where He lay yesterday. The grave is empty. But are we sure that He is risen? May not His body have been stolen away? No; for a great stone was rolled to the door and by Pilate's order sealed, so that it could not be removed without breaking the seal. Further, at the request of the rulers a guard of Roman soldiers was stationed by the tomb to watch it. These precautions of Christ's enemies, taken in order that His body might not be disturbed and a story of resurrection started, form important links in the evidence of His resurrection.

Carelessness about sealing or watching the grave would have left room for uncertainty as to the fact of resurrection. But now we can say, without a shadow of doubt, "He is risen." His enemies helped to make the testimony infallible and invincible. Thus the empty tomb declares the resurrection of Christ. Death could not hold Him.

The empty tomb proclaims another precious truth to the Christians. Jesus rose, and so shall all who sleep in Him rise. "For if we believe that Jesus died and rose again, even so them also which sleep in Jesus will God bring with Him" [1 Thess. 4:14].

The angel called the attention of the women to words which Jesus had spoken during His lifetime. They reminded them that He had said He would rise again. The women remembered the words now. It seems strange to us that the disciples should have forgotten the promises of Jesus about His resurrection. If only they had remembered these words they would have been spared their sorrow when they saw Him led to His cross. All the uncomforted sorrow of the disciples during those dark days and nights came from not remembering what Jesus had said to them.

Often it is because we forget what Christ has said to us in His Word that we are in sorrow and in darkness. He has revealed to us the infinite love of His Father; if only we remembered this love we should not be overwhelmed by the strange things of providence which appear to us to be evil and destructive. He has told us that death for a believer is only going to his Father's house; if only we remembered this word, we should not dread to die, nor should we grieve immoderately when our loved ones go from us.

41

The Walk to Emmaus

Scripture Reading: Luke 24:13–35

Sometime in the afternoon of the day on which Jesus rose, two of His disciples, not apostles, but friends, took a long walk into the country. We are not told why they went to Emmaus. Perhaps they had given up hope. Thus it is too often with Christ's friends in these days, when trouble comes upon them. The bright dreams fade, they grow disheartened and turn away as if the sacred beliefs they had cherished so long were only delusions. We see here, however, how needless was the discouragement. No hope really had faded. What they thought was cause for sorrow was the secret of the most blessed hope the world ever has known.

As these men walked along the way they talked together of the strange things which had happened. This was natural. Their hearts were full of these things, and they could not but talk about them. If the conversation of Christian people is sometimes vapid and trivial, it must be because their hearts are not filled with the holy themes which ought to occupy them. Is there much truly religious conversation? What did you talk about yesterday, or last evening, in the long walk you took with your friend? This example suggests to us at least the value of good, earnest, wayside conversation. Most of us walk more or less with our friends. Why should two intelligent Christians talk together for an hour or longer and neither of them say one word better than the idlest chit-chat about the merest nothings?

Now a most interesting thing occurred. As they went on talking together, Jesus Himself drew near and walked with them. That is always the way. Jesus said, "Where two or three are gathered together in My name, there am I in the midst of them." We are met in His name when love for Him draws us together. Then He will always join us. If only idle words are on our lips, if we are gossiping about our neighbors, saying mean and disagreeable things about them; if we are talking of things which are not beautiful and good, we have no reason to expect Christ to draw near and join us. He would not be interested in our conversation, nor would we care to have Him listening to what we are saying. In order to have Christ go with us in our walk, our talk must be of things which will be congenial to Him. This, therefore, is the test—Would Jesus want to enter into this conversation with us? Would He be pleased to hear the words we are saying drop from our lips?

Sometimes we join a group of busy talkers, and suddenly the conversation ceases. They do not want to go on with it in our presence. Would we keep on with this talk of ours without embarrassment or sense of unfitness if Jesus were to come in and sit down visibly in our circle?

He walked with these friends unrecognized. They did not know him. This is often the way with us—Jesus draws near to us and we fail to know that it is He. He comes to us in our sorrow, and we do not see Him by our side. We go on weeping and breaking our hearts, while if we saw the glorious form that is close to us, and knew of the love that is throbbing against our breasts, we would put away our tears and rejoice. Many people fail to recognize the divine love and comfort in their grief and go on as if there were no stars shining in the sky. How many of us are conscious of the presence of Christ with us, or get from it the full comfort, inspiration, and help which we might get?

Sir Launfal, in Lowell's poem, wandered over all the earth in search of the Holy Grail. When at last, after long years had passed, he returned, aged and bent, to his old home—there under his own castle walls did he find the object of his search! So, often would we find close beside us, in the Scriptures we already possess, in the circumstances in which we are placed, in the human tenderness that is about us, the help we are seeking and the truth we need, if only we had eyes to see.

The Stranger showed a deep interest in the two men. The sorrow in their faces and tones touched His heart. Jesus always has a quick ear and sensitive heart for human grief or need. He knows when we are sad, when our burden is greater than we can bear. Then He is quick to express sympathy. He wants to give help.

This conversation shows that Jesus desires His friends to confide in Him. It does good for a burdened heart to tell out its trouble to Him. So when these men spoke to Him of the things that filled their hearts that day, He asked, "What things?" He knew, of course; but He wanted them to speak out their fears and doubts and ask their questions. So, when we are in sorrow, Christ wants us to tell Him of all that troubles or perplexes us. The telling will do us good. Then, by bringing them to Him, we shall have the tangles unsnarled.

Jesus spoke to these disciples out of a loving heart, telling them how slow they were in believing in what the prophets had spoken. He then told them that it behooved the Messiah to suffer the very things which this Jesus they were grieving over had suffered. He told them that if they had only understood the Scriptures their hearts never would have been cast down by the things which had befallen Him. God's way is always the true one. Our way would not bring us to the glory we desire any more than the disciples' idea of the Messiah would have brought salvation to the world. When God sets aside our plans for our lives we may know that His plan, however different from ours it may be, and however it may seem to thwart our plans, is the right one.

> If we could push ajar the gates of life,
>   And stand within and all God's workings see,
>   We could interpret all this doubt and strife,
>   And for each mystery could find a key.

These two men enjoyed a rare privilege that day in having Jesus as an interpreter of the Scriptures concerning Himself—"He expounded unto them in all the scriptures the things concerning Himself." It would be interesting if we could read the interpretations he gave. What a wonderful talk that was! We may be quite sure that He quoted the passages which depicted the sufferings of the Messiah, showing that the cross was part of the divine plan of redemption. Doubtless He quoted the fifty-third chapter of Isaiah. Thus He went over the Old Testament, interpreting it and showing how he had fulfilled these ancient predictions. No wonder their hearts burned within them as He opened to them the Scriptures.

At length they came to the place where their journey ended. He was disposed to go on farther, but they urged Him to abide with them. If they had not thus constrained Him, He would have passed on. Think what they would have missed if He had not gone in with them. We do not know how much of the revealing of divine love and grace we miss continually because of the tameness of our praying. We ought to get a lesson from the example of these disciples, who constrained the Stranger to go in with them and were rewarded by finding in Him the Friend for whom they were so hungering.

When they sat down together at the table for their evening meal, the Stranger took bread and blessed it, and brake, and gave to them. Perhaps it was these familiar acts which revealed Him to them. Or they may have seen the nail mark in the hand that broke the bread. We are not told how, but in some way they came to understand that the Guest at their table was Jesus Himself whom they were mourning as dead, but who was now risen and living. What if our eyes should be opened to see Jesus every time He is beside us, eating with us, walking with us? How radiant would all life then become!

Another suggestion from this Emmaus story is that often it is only as they leave us that we learn the value of our blessings. "Their eyes were opened, and they knew Him; and He vanished out of their sight." How often is it true that only in their vanishing do our friends reveal themselves to us:

> In this dim world of clouding cares
> We rarely know, till 'wildered eyes
> See white wings lessening up the skies,
> The angels with us unawares.

Somehow our eyes are holden and we do not see the loveliness. Faults seem larger and blemishes greater while our friends are close to us. But as they leave us the faults appear faults no longer, "just odd ways," and blemishes are transfigured into shining marks. Why wait for the hour of departing to see the beauty and the good?

42

Jesus Ascends into Heaven

Scripture Reading: Luke 24:36–53

It was in the upper room on the evening of the day on which Jesus arose. The disciples had gathered there, drawn together by their common sorrow and also by the strange things which had occurred that day. The doors were closed and fastened. Suddenly, with no opening of the doors, Jesus Himself appeared among the disciples. They were terrified, but He spoke to them these quieting words: "Peace be unto you." Still further to alleviate their terror He said, "Why are ye troubled? . . . Behold My hands and My feet, that it is I Myself." Doubts always cause perplexity. Doubting cost Thomas a whole week of grief and sadness. Even those who have given up their Christian faith confess that in doing so they lost the sweetest joy out of their lives. Jesus showed the disciples His hands and His feet, that they might see in them the prints of the nails and thus be convinced that He was indeed risen. The prints of the nails is the indubitable mark of Christ where He appears. We see Him always as the suffering One, or as the one who has suffered, for He bore our sins.

Slowly the doubt and fear of the disciples vanished, as they beheld their Master right before them, as they looked at the wounds in His hands and feet, and the marks of the thorns upon His brow, and heard His voice in words of love. He sought then in other ways to make them familiar with the fact that He was risen. He asked them for something to eat, and when they had given Him a piece of a broiled fish, He ate it before them. We see how gentle Jesus is in dealing with the doubts and fears of His disciples. He does not want them to disbelieve. Yet He does not chide and condemn them because they are slow in believing. He is most gentle with those who are seeking to believe. Some Christian teachers are stern and severe with those who even ask questions which seem to indicate doubt or uncertainty as to great teachings. But Jesus deals most lovingly with everyone who has difficulty in believing.

Somehow the disciples had been very slow in understanding the words which Jesus had spoken to them before His death about the manner of His Messiahship. They had been so full of their earthly idea of Him that they could not accept or even understand any suggestion which permitted a completely different view. He reminded them of what He had said. "These are the words which I spake unto you." The cross was no surprise to Jesus. All along His years He saw it standing at the end of His course. The events in His life which had seemed so terrible to the disciples, for a time blotting out all their hopes, were the very things which He had foretold, over and over again, during His ministry. If they had only understood His words, they would have been saved all their perplexity when they saw Him going to a cross. Many of the perplexities of our lives come from the same forgetting of the words of Christ. There are many promises in the Bible, but we forget them just when we most need to remember them. We throw away our life preservers just when we ought to be buckling them about us.

Now Jesus sought to make all things plain to His disciples. "Then opened He their understanding, that they might understand the scriptures." There is a promise which says that the Holy Spirit will guide us into all truth. We sometimes forget that we need to pray God to open our minds, to help us to understand the deep things of His Word. The lessons of the Bible are shy, and hide themselves away from ordinary search; only prayer and reverent love will find them.

The commission of the disciples contained the gospel "that repentance and remission of sins should be preached in His name among all nations, beginning at Jerusalem." They were to begin right where the cross had been set up. We should begin at home, just where we live, to tell the story of Christ. The lighthouse throws its beams far out to sea—a hundred miles from the shore, it is said. Some of the lights are seen—but it pours no light around its own base. The lighthouse, therefore, is not the best picture of an individual Christian life. We should shine, first, close about ourselves. "He does the best in God's great world who does the best in his own little world." We should begin at Jerusalem, touching the lives nearest to us. But that is not to be the end. Every Christian has something to do with getting the gospel even to the remotest ends of the earth.

The first disciples were to be not only messengers, but also witnesses. "Ye are witnesses of these things." How shall people know of things they have not seen, unless others testify of these things to them? The disciples knew personally the story of Christ's life, death, and resurrection. No other persons knew these facts. If the story was to reach the world it must be told by those who knew it. It is our business, after we have seen Christ, to become witnesses of Him to those who have not seen Him. It is not said, "Go and bear witness," but, "Go and be witnesses." The testimony is not to be merely in words—it must also be in the life.

The disciples may well have shrunk from such a tremendous task as their Master put upon them in giving them their commission. But He hastened to assure them that they would not be left unhelped. "Behold, I send forth the promise of My Father upon you." They were to receive the Holy Spirit, and thus would be enabled to deliver their message, live their new lives, and carry the gospel to the ends of the earth. The promise is put in a little different way in the last words of Matthew's gospel: "Lo, I am with you always, even unto the end of the world." Jesus went to heaven when He ascended, but He returned as to His real life, in the Holy Spirit, on the day of Pentecost. Since then the presence of Christ has been as actual among His people in all this world as it was during the days of His incarnation in the little company of friends who knew Him personally.

The story of the Ascension is told briefly. "It came to pass, while He blessed them, He was parted from them, and carried up into heaven." In the last glimpse the world had of Jesus in human form, He was holding out His hands over His friends, blessing them. Ever since that time the hands of the risen Christ have really been spread out over this world, raining benedictions down upon it. Jesus is at the right hand of God, but He has not lost any of His interest in this world, nor has He withdrawn His hands from the work of redemption. He ever lives in heaven to make intercession for us. Then He is always with us in the world, in real, personal presence, so that any one of us may say, "Christ and I are friends."

When the disciples had seen their Master ascending out of their sight they were not overwhelmed with grief, as they had been when He died on the cross. They understood now the meaning of His departure, and their hearts were full of joy and gladness. "They worshiped Him, and returned to Jerusalem with great joy." While they would not see Him anymore, they knew where He had gone, and why. They knew also that He had not left them, that they had not lost Him, but that He had gone out of their sight, that He might become all the more to them, in their spiritual lives and in their power for service.

There was something yet to do before the blessing of Christ's redemption could come upon His disciples. They were to wait for the promise of the Father. So they came down from the Mount of Olives and entered the city, to begin the waiting and prayer, at the end of which the Holy Spirit would come. "And were continually in the temple, praising and blessing God." We cannot always be engaged in prayer and formal acts of worship, but we can have in our lives continually the spirit of devotion. We can always be expecting to find blessing, looking up to God and pleading for it. If we live thus, a life of prayer, of faith, and hope, our weekdays, even when engaged most busily in the work of the world, will be full of song and cheer. If we cannot write hymns which people may sing, we can at least make our lives songs, so that all who see us shall hear the music of love and peace in our life.

Volume Three

The Gospel by John

Preface to This Volume

The spiritual volume of the Gospel according to John is supreme. It would have been easy to extend these readings indefinitely, but it seems best to limit this volume to the size of the preceding ones. The aim has been to make the chapters simple, practical and devotional.

1

Christ the Life and Light of Men

Scripture Reading: John 1:1–18

The first three Gospels begin on the earth; the fourth Gospel begins back in eternity. There are no sublimer words in all language that the first words in John's prologue. They give us a glimpse of the eternal past and show us the Word existing then. In the beginning, before anything else was, He was. Genesis is the book of earthly beginnings, but this first verse of John's gospel carries us back far beyond Genesis. We find precious comfort in human friends when we can rest in their love and know that they are indeed ours, true to us and faithful. Yet all the while, as we lean upon them, we know, too, that they are only creatures of a day. They have not lived long, and their wisdom is only inexperience, their strength only weakness. Their love is liable to change and decay, their very life is only a breath, a mere comma in the great sentence of eternity. But in the friendship of Christ we know that we are in the clasp of One who is eternal—the same yesterday and today, yea, and forever.

We are told also plainly who this divine Friend is. "The Word was God." A word reveals thoughts. We cannot know what is in our friend's heart until he speaks. We never could have known what God's thoughts about us are if He had not spoken to us. Jesus Christ is the Word, that is, the revealer to us of the mind and heart of God. The Incarnation of Christ brings Him very close to us. In His human life He is one of ourselves, our brother, with feelings, affections and sympathies like ours. But when we can add to our thought and experience of Christ's humanity the wonderful truth that He is divine, it puts a marvelous element of strength and security into our trust. The Incarnation is God coming to us with a great heart of love, offering Himself to us. A great preacher says, "In the last analysis Christianity is nothing more or less than a great dear Figure, standing with outstretched arms." God is love, and it is Love, yearning, searching Love, that comes to us in the Word.

All divine revelation has been made to the world through the Word. "All things were made by him." One was showing an old watercolor picture which hung in his room. It was beautiful, but the good man said that nothing among his possessions was so precious to him as this faded bit of painting, because his mother had made it. Everything in nature is made sacred and beautiful to one who loves Christ, when he remembers that his Savior made it. The sweet flowers by the wayside would be sweeter to us if we remembered, as we looked upon them, that the hand of Christ painted them. This is Christ's world. His touch is on everything in it. Everything speaks of Him and of His love.

Christ is also the source of all life. "In Him was life." He is the one fountain of life. No one in the world, save God, can produce life. With all his skill man cannot make the smallest living seed, or create the most infinitesimal particle of matter. Science, with all its wondrous achievements, has never been able to produce life in even the lowest form. No man can make a blade of grass, or the tiniest flower, or the lowest insect. All life comes from Christ.

Our lesson turns now to the revealing of the divine life. First, preparation. "There was a man sent from God." He came as God's messenger, to prepare the way for the divine revealing. Each one of us is likewise "sent from God." We know what John's mission was. We may not know yet what our own mission is, but God will show it to us as we go on, if we are faithful. We may be sure, however, that we are here on no haphazard errand, that we are really sent on some errand, some definite mission. There is some word that we were born to speak, and if we do not speak it, the world will be poorer, some life will not know God's message and will not know what God wants it to do.

John came to tell men of the Messiah. "The same came for a witness, to bear witness of the Light, that all men through him might believe."

Our highest duty in this world is to give honor to Christ, to show some phase of His glory. Some men in their self-conceit think only of making a show of themselves, getting people to see them and praise them. The mission of every Christian is to bear witness of the Light, to point others to Christ, that men may believe. It was said of a great preacher that wherever he went, people, when they saw his life, fell in love with Jesus Christ. They forgot the preacher and thought only of the Master whom the preacher proclaimed, both in his words and in his life. John hid himself out of sight and wanted people to see only Christ. We cannot save any soul, but we can point lost ones to Him who can save. We may bear witness of Christ in many ways. We may do it by our words, telling what He was and what He did for us, and by our life and character, showing ourselves what Christ can do for all who come to Him.

It is strange that when the Son of God came to this world, He was not received. We would say that such a glorious being would have been hailed with highest honor. But there was not welcome for Him. "He came unto his own, and his own received him not." This was one of the saddest things about Christ's mission to the world. For ages He had been waited for and watched for, but when He came He was not recognized—He was even rejected and crucified. We say, "If He came now, He would find a warm welcome." But would He? He does come now as really as He came then. He comes to save us, to be our Friend, to help us in our need, and many of us turn our backs upon Him. He stands yet knocking before many a door which does not open to Him.

There were some, however, who received Christ when He came, and to these He brought wondrous blessings. "As many as received him, to them gave he power to become the sons of God." Here we have the way of salvation made plain. We have only to accept Christ as He comes to us, and we are led into the household of God, among God's own children. We need not understand all about Christ, about His person or His work—there may be a great deal of unexplained mystery about Him. There cannot but be, for the Incarnation is the strangest mystery of all ages. But we do not need to understand everything—all we need to do is to accept Christ as our Savior, our Master, our Friend, and we are led by Him into the full light. Then some day we shall understand. In the experience of divine love our joy will be so full that there shall be no question unanswered, no desire unsatisfied.

The beginning of our passage tells us of the Word existing in the eternity past, the Word with God, the Word as God Himself; now we come to the revealing of the Word: "The Word was made flesh, and dwelt among us." It is not said that the Word was changed into flesh—He continued to be divine. He became flesh. It does not mean, either, that He took up His abode in a human body merely—He took upon Him the whole of human nature, body, soul and spirit. We cannot divide the activity of Christ into two sections and say, "This the divine nature did, and this His human nature did"; the human and the divine were inextricably blended into one. When we see Christ's compassion, His thoughtfulness, His mercy, His kindness, His gentleness, these are divine qualities, revealed in human ways, through human life. It was all divine, all glory.

Christ is the only revelation of God. "No man hath seen God at any time; the only begotten Son, which is in the bosom of the Father, he hath declared him." We never can know God except through His Son. There is no other possible revelation of Him. Christ came in lowly form, and appeared to His friends as a man; but when they learned to know Him, when their hearts had fixed their tendrils about Him, they found that He was divine, the Son of God. If we ever see God and know Him, and enter His family as His own, we must accept Christ. There is no other way. To reject Him is to shut ourselves away from God, in darkness unillumined by a beam of love from His face.

2

The Witness of John to Jesus

Scripture Reading: John 1:19–34

S t. John was a good witness. He had a strange training. He was brought up, not in any school with human teachers, but in God's school, in the wilderness, away from men. At last he came out ready to begin his work. His preaching had tremendous power. From near and far the people came in throngs to hear him, and they were deeply impressed by his words.

The effect produced by the Baptist's work was so great that the authorities at Jerusalem felt it necessary to send a delegation to inquire into it. They claimed to have direction of the religious affairs of the nation, and wished to know the meaning of John's work. These men asked John, "Who art thou?" There was a general unrest at the time, with much feverish excitement concerning the coming of the Messiah. There was a widespread feeling that this event was nigh at hand. The impression that John made upon the people was so great that many thought he might be the Messiah. If John had been so disposed, he might have claimed to be the One who was to come, and would have had a great following. But his loyalty to truth and to his Master forbade this, and he eagerly and with grief at the suggestion replied, "No, no; I am not the Christ." They thought then that he must be some other great personage—Elijah, who was expected by the Jews as the forerunner of the Messiah, or "the prophet"—that is, the prophet "like unto Moses," promised and vaguely looked for. It was felt at least that this preacher by the Jordan was no ordinary man. He was a very great man, and his power as a preacher was startling.

The way John met these questions showed the kind of man he was. If he had been weak and ambitious, he would have been tempted to encourage the people's thoughts about him and to accept the homage they wanted to pay him and to which he knew that he was not entitled. He shrank with pain from all such offers of honor not rightly his, and instead eagerly turned all the expectation and enthusiasm of the people to Jesus. This showed a nobleness in John worthy of his mission. He sought only to honor Christ. He hid himself way out of sight, that nothing in him might win any eye from his Master. This is a lesson we all need to learn.

When asked again to tell who he really was, if not the Messiah nor one of the great men prophesied of, he said that he was only a voice. No matter about his name. He sought no honor for himself. He had been sent with a message which it was essential that the people should hear, while the personality of the messenger was unimportant. "I am the voice of one crying in the wilderness."

Thus he identified himself with a well-known Messianic prophecy, but in his lowliness he had no care to have his own name known. He was only a voice, speaking a word for God, delivering a divine message to men. It is honor enough for anyone to be a voice, a voice uttering heavenly words, words of divine comfort or cheer or hope to those who are weary, discouraged, lonely or in disrepair. Titles and degrees and earthly honors, which some men strive so hard to win, are pitiably empty in comparison with the distinction of being a clear, true voice speaking God's messages to men.

In this part of the story of John we learn two beautiful lessons. One is, the splendor of humility. Humility is the lowliest of the virtues, and yet it is the most divine. Nothing so shows the greatness of the Baptist as his lowliness in declining human honor and praise. The other lesson is that we should be sure we are really a voice, with a message from God, in this world, speaking out distinctly for God. Too many lives mean nothing, stand for nothing, declare nothing to others, make no impression of beauty, of cheer, of holiness. The voice of John's life is heard yet throughout the world, and the world is better, truer, holier, because of it.

We should be a voice with unmistakable note, a voice that shall be heard wherever we go, whose sound will make men happier, stronger, braver, kinder, more like God, and that shall prepare the way for Christ into men's hearts.

John's message was important. It called men to prepare the way for the great Coming One. "Make straight the way of the Lord." "There standeth one among you, whom ye know not; he it is, who coming after me is preferred before me, whose shoe's latchet I am not worthy to unloose." So John turned all thoughts and all eyes away from himself as not worthy even to do this lowest service for Him whose way he had come to prepare. Thus he honored Christ and set Him high above all men, One worthy to receive the deepest worship and the highest praise. John's humility was not feigned. He was so conscious of the real glory of Christ that he felt himself as truly unworthy to perform even the lowliest service for Him. No matter how lofty the place one occupies, Christ is infinitely higher, and it should be our joy to serve Him in the lowliest ways.

John's witness to Jesus continued next day. He was standing among the crowds when a young man was approaching him. Pointing to Him, John said to the people, "Behold the Lamb of God, which taketh away the sin of the world." This was a distinct declaration that Jesus was the Messiah who had been foretold as a lamb led to the slaughter, as the Paschal Lamb, as the atoning sacrifice. This part of the witness of John concerning Jesus must not be overlooked. He saw Him as the Lamb of God. It is not enough to think of the name "lamb" as referring to His gentleness, His meekness, His steadfastness in enduring wrong. The chief thought in the name is that of sacrifice. The paschal lamb prefigured Christ, who was thus foretold as the world's sin-bearer. We must see Christ first as our Savior. In heaven the song of the redeemed is, "Worthy is the Lamb that was slain." Until we see Him as Savior He can be nothing else to us.

John witnesses also to the divine anointing of Jesus as the Messiah. "I saw the Spirit descending from heaven like a dove, and it abode upon him." This was infallible testimony. John had not the slightest doubt of the Messiahship of Jesus. "I saw, and bare record that this is the Son of God." In these days, when so many people are doubting and trying to put doubts into the minds of others, it is well that we have such a testimony as this which tells us positively that He in whom we trust as our Savior and Lord is indeed the Son of God. It gives us an impregnable rock on which to build, in which to find our refuge.

Every Christian should, first, be a witness of Christ in his own life, and secondly, should bear witness to Christ in his confession of the blessed Name, wherever he goes.

3

The First Miracle in Cana

Scripture Reading: John 2:1–11

There were thirty years of silence before Jesus began to speak. The only miracles in those days were miracles of love, of obedience, of duty, of sinless life. At length He began His manifested life, and the first sign He wrought was at Cana.

It is pleasant to remember that Jesus attended a wedding feast at the very beginning of His public ministry. Indeed, this was His first appearance among the people, and the beginning of His signs, as John puts it, was produced at this marriage festivity, where the simple country folk met in all the freedom of their gladness. Christ is a friend not merely for our sorrow hours, but also for our times of joy. Then His presence and His miracle at this time indicate His approval of marriage and give it a holy sanction. We should notice also that He was invited to this wedding. If He had not been invited He would not have gone, for He never goes where He is not desired. If we would have Him attend our weddings and give His blessing, we must be careful that He receives an invitation. No matter who performs the ceremony, Christ's hands should bestow the benediction.

The failing of the wine at this marriage feast is an illustration of the way all earth's pleasure falls short. It comes in cups, not in fountains, and the supply is limited and is soon exhausted. Even amid the gladness at the marriage altar there is the knell of the end in the words, "till death do us part." Human love is very sweet, and it seems to answer every craving of the heart. But if there is nothing but the human, it will not last long enough. One of every two friends must hold the other's hand in farewell at the edge of the valley, must stand by the other's grave, and then walk on alone the rest of the way. The best wine of life and of love will fail. Very striking, however, is the picture here, and true also—the failing wine, and then the Master supplying the want. When human joy fails, if we have Christ with us, He gives us new joy, better than the world's, and in unfailing abundance.

The mother of Jesus came and told Him of the failing of the wine. She had become accustomed to take all her perplexities to Him. That is what we also may do. His answer to His mother was, "Mine hour is not yet come." He seems to have referred to His time for supplying the need. We may notice here, however, our Lord's perfect devotion to His Father's will. We find the same all through His life. He did nothing of Himself; He took His work moment by moment from the Father's hand. He always waited for His "hour." He had no plans of His own, but followed the divine purpose in all His acts. Though appealed to now by His mother, whom He loved so deeply, He would not do anything a moment before His hour had come. We cannot learn this lesson too well. Sometimes we find it hard to wait for God, but in no way is our obedience more beautifully shown than in our self-restraints under the direction of God's will. Too many of us run before we are sent. It requires great patience at times not to put forth the power we have, but to wait for God's time.

The word of the mother to the servants is suggestive: "Whatsoever he saith unto you, do it." She was not hurt by the reply Jesus had given to her, which to some seems harsh. It shows, too, that she did not understand His answer as a refusal to relieve the perplexity of the family in due time. She bade the servants to stand ready now for His bidding, not knowing what He would do, but sure it would be the right thing. "Whatsoever he saith unto you, do it," is always the word for the Master's servants, and we are to take our commands from Him alone. We are not to follow our own impulses in doing things for others, not even the impulses of kindness and affection; we are to wait for the Master's word.

His "hour" was not long in coming. Apparently but a little while after the mother's words to the servants Jesus said to them, 'Fill the waterpots with water"; then at once, "Draw out now, and bear unto the governor." Thus the servants became coworkers with the Master in this miracle. So He calls His people always to be His helpers in blessing the world. We cannot do much ourselves. The best we can bring is a little of the common water of earth. But if we bring that, He can change it into the rich wine of heaven, which will bless weary and fainting ones. The servants helped Jesus in this miracle. The divine gifts of mercy can only get to the lost through the saved. Then, how striking is the other side of the truth—the servants carried only common water from the spring, but with Christ's blessing it became good wine. So it always is when we do what Christ bids us to do; our most prosaic work leaves heavenly results. Our most common work amid life's trivialities, in business, in the household, among our friends, which seems like the carrying of water, only to be emptied out again, is transformed into radiant service, like angel ministry, and leaves glorious blessings behind. We do not know the real splendor of the things we are doing when we do the commonest things of our daily task-work. What seems only giving a cup of cold water to a lowly man is blessed service to one of God's children, and is noted and rewarded by the Father.

We have an impartial witness to this miracle in the ruler of the feast. He knew not whence the wine was. No one had told him that it was only water in the vessel whence it had been drawn. This suggests how quietly Jesus produced this divine sign. He did not announce it, nor advertise it. He said nothing to call attention to what He was going to do. The people about Him did not know of the wonderful work He had done. So He works always quietly. His kingdom comes into men's hearts, not with observation, but silently. An evil life by His words is changed into moral purity. Miracles of grace are performed continually, and no one sees the Hand that works the marvelous transformation. Silently help comes in the hours of need, silently answers to prayer glide down, silently the angels come and go.

It is significant also that "the servants who drew the water knew." They had put the water into the vessels, and knew it was only water. They had drawn out the water, and knew that it was now wine. Those who work with Christ are admitted into the inner chamber, where Omnipotence is unveiled, where the mysteries of His grace are performed. Christ takes into His confidence those who serve Him; calls them no longer servants, but friends. Those who do Christ's will know of His doctrine and see His ways of working. If we would witness Christ's power and glory, we must enter heartily and obediently into His service. Often it is in the lowliest ways and in the paths of the most humble, self-denying service that the most of Christ's glory appears.

We have the testimony of the ruler of the feast as to the quality of the wine. "Thou hast kept the good wine until now." That is what Christ always does—He keeps the best until the last. The world gives its best first, and the worst comes afterwards. It is so in sin—first exhilaration, then remorse. It is so in the chase for wealth, power, fame—first gratification, then disappointment. But in spiritual life it is the reverse of this. Christ Himself had His humiliation, darkness, the shame of the cross, and then came exaltation, power, glory. In Christian life the same rule holds—first the cross, then the crown; first the self-denial, the loss, the suffering, afterwards the blessing, the peace, the joy. We never get to the end of the good things of divine love—we never get to the best even in this world. There is always something better yet to come. Then Christ keeps the good wine, the best wine, to the very last—in heaven. Sweet as is earth's peace to the Christian, he will never know the best of peace until he gets home.

This was Christ's first miracle, but it was not the beginning of His grace and love. The record says that in "this beginning of miracles" Jesus "manifested forth his glory." The word "Manifested" suggests that the glory was there before; it had been slumbering in His lowly human life all along the quiet years of toil and service at Nazareth. Then the glory manifested itself in ways which no one thought of as supernatural—in the beautiful Life that grew up in the Nazareth home, with its attention to daily tasks and duties. The story of the eighteen years from twelve to thirty is told in one short verse, "Jesus increased in wisdom and stature, and in favor with God and man" [Luke 2:52]. The glory was in Him those days, but no one saw it shining out. The neighbors did not think of His gentleness of spirit, His graciousness of disposition, His purity and simplicity of life, as revealings of the divine glory.

Now the glory was manifested for the first time. We say there are no miracles now, but there may be less difference than we think between what we call natural and supernatural. Luther said one day: "I saw a miracle this morning. The sky stretched overhead and arched itself like a vast dome above the earth. There were no columns supporting this dome—it hung there with nothing to hold it up. Yet the sky did not fall." You see the same every day, yet you do not think of calling it a miracle—you say it is only natural. In the life of Christ there were a thousand simple and beautiful deeds. During the days of the feast at Cana, He no doubt was the life of the company. If there was a shy and bashful person among the guests, He was specially kind to that one. If there was one that the others neglected, Jesus sought him out. If there was one in sorrow, Jesus tried to comfort him. But nobody thought of these common kindnesses as miracles. Next hour, He changed water into wine to relieve the embarrassment of the host, and that was manifesting His glory.

It is pleasant to notice, too, that it was in a simple act of thoughtful kindness to a perplexed household that this divine glory was thus manifested. Really it was just a beautiful deed of common kindness. Someone calls this the housekeeper's miracle. It was a most embarrassing occasion. In the midst of a marriage feast the wine failed. There were more guests than were expected, and there was not enough wine to serve them all. The host would have been disgraced if there had been no way of adding to the too meager supply. Jesus, by His timely manifesting of power, relieved the awkwardness of the occasion. He performed the miracle, we may be sure, primarily for the sake of the host, to save him from mortification. When the writer, referred to, calls this the housekeeper's miracle, it is because it shows Christ's sympathy with those who attend to domestic affairs, His thought for them, and His readiness to serve them, relieving them of embarrassment or perplexity. There is no annoyance too small to take to our Savior. He manifested His glory in just this—His great kindness. When we think of the matter carefully, we know that the most divine thing in the world is love. That in God which is greatest is not power, glory, not the shining splendor of deity, as it was shown at Sinai, but love, which shows itself in plain, lowly ways. When the disciples besought the Master to show them the Father, they thought of some brilliant display, some revealing of God which would startle men. Jesus replied: "Have I been with you so long and have you not yet known Me? He that hath seen Me hath seen the Father." He had been showing them the Father in all His days—not alone in His miracles of goodness and mercy, but in the thousand little kindnesses of the common days. It was to His daily life as the disciples had seen it that He referred. He meant that the truest revealing of God to men is not in great theophanies and transfigurations, but in a ministry of gentleness, helpfulness and kindness, such as Jesus Himself had performed.

4

Jesus Cleansing the Temple

Scripture Reading: John 2:13–25

Over and over again in the Gospels we read of Jesus going to the feasts of the Jews and to their synagogue services. In this He set an example for us. We are to follow Him, putting our feet into the prints of His shoes. One of the things we may learn from Him is the church-going habit. He was always faithful in attending religious meetings. He began at the age of twelve to go to the Passover, and went every year as long as He lived. We ought in youth to form habits of faithful attendance upon the ordinances of religion. If young people do not learn in childhood to attend church, it is not likely they will ever form the habit. Children learn readily, and childhood habits do not easily forsake one. There is a great protection for moral and spiritual life in church attendance. It keeps one continually under the influences of holy things. It brings one into the presence of God, where all the impulses are toward the better things. It aids in brotherhood life and Christian fellowship, by which great good comes to every Christian. It helps us to be more useful, tying us up with other good people in work for Christ. Every Sunday-school pupil ought to attend the church services. The example of Jesus should be followed in this as in all other things.

When Jesus entered the temple precincts He was grieved by what He saw—"And found in the temple those that sold oxen and sheep and doves, and the changers of money sitting." No doubt the evil had grown by degrees. Jews coming from foreign countries needed animals to offer as sacrifices. They would have to buy them at the market in the city and bring them to the temple. Men with an eye to business would establish themselves near the temple, so as to get custom. By and by they would begin to herd their animals at the gate, and then soon within, in the court of the Gentiles. So gradual was the encroachment of the business that no one felt shocked when at last the traffic was firmly established in the temple court. It was such a convenience, too, to have the animals and the moneybrokers just at hand, that the people were slow to want things the old way.

It is thus that most wrong customs come in. First only the camel's nose is admitted, then he gets one great foot in, and then another, and by and by his whole immense body is in the tent, and the man has to get out. Thus the world creeps into the church and into the Christian's life. Thus perfectly legitimate business encroaches on the heart's sacred places until all that is tender and holy is driven out. We need to watch lest the world's traffic sets up its stands in the very temple of our lives and desecrates the place where only God would be admitted. It is against the beginnings of the encroachments that we should guard. When the first approaches have been permitted, it is hard to check the advance.

Our Lord's act was not a mere outburst of temper but an expression of His righteousness indignation. It was His Father's house in which He was standing, and He was also Lord of the temple and had a right to cleanse it. He was the Messiah and had authority. The singular manifestation has a meaning also for us who are studying the story. Our hearts are now temples of the Holy Spirit. Christ comes to them to see if they are kept clean for the divine indwelling. What does He find when He comes? Does He hear the clatter of the world's noisy traffic, where only holy voices should be heard? Does He come upon herds of cattle driven up into the sacred precincts, where only God and God's messengers should tread? Does He see the broker's table where the altar of incense should stand? If our heart is the temple of God, we should see to it that nothing undivine, nothing that is unworthy of God, shall ever invade its courts.

How is it, just now, in your heart? Is there any need for Christ to come with His whip of cords to drive out the traders, the sellers of cattle and doves, and the moneychangers?

Very picturesque is the scene. "When he had made a scourge of small cords, he drove them all out of the temple." He did not use the scourge save as a symbol of authority. It was not the men He drove out, but the cattle. He poured out the money. The incident furnishes a remarkable illustration of the power there was in our Lord's presence and voice and manner. It required no violence on His part to awe and impress the men who were so defiling His Father's house. We may notice, too, that He did not touch the birds, did not hurt them, nor open the cages, but bade the merchants remove them.

His next word set forth the character of the offense of the men He was reproving. "Make not my Father's house an house of merchandise." Merchandise is legitimate business in the proper place. It is not sinful. There was nothing wrong in selling animals and doves for sacrifice, or in changing people's money for them, from foreign to Jewish coin. If these sellers and moneychangers had been somewhere else, on some of the city streets, Jesus would not have disturbed them. It was because they were where they ought not to be that His anger was so kindled against them. This is an important distinction. "If I regard iniquity in my heart, the Lord will not hear me" [Ps. 66:18].

Two or three years later Jesus repeated this act in substance. This was at the beginning of His ministry, and the other was at its close. Whatever impression was made in His first cleansing had been forgotten. Things seem to have grown worse. Jesus said they had made the temple court a "den of thieves." His charge implied that the dealers and brokers were dishonest, overcharging, cheating and defrauding. Too often the same may be said of hearts made for God. Into them has come all manner of wickedness. But here we learn that things which in themselves are right enough may become very offensive to Christ because they are where they ought not to be. It is right to have business and worldly work—indeed, not many are doing their whole duty in the world unless they are carrying some share of what are called secular duties. However, there is a place for these things. Meanwhile, no matter how full our hands are of the common tasks, there ought to be a sacred place in our heart into which nothing of this world ever shall come. We are to be in the world to do our share of the world's work, but we are not to be of the world. The world is not to be in us. The problem in sailing a ship is not to keep the ship out of the water, but the water out of the ship. We are commanded, "Love not the world." Christ is to have our love while we are busy doing the things in the world that come to our hands. So we get our lesson—that Christ did not condemn merchandising as something sinful, but found fault with it because it was in the place which ought to have been kept altogether for God.

As His disciples saw their Master's intense earnestness and heard His words, they were impressed with His holiness and His zeal in behalf of God's house. "His disciples remembered that it was written, The zeal of thine house hath eaten me up" [see Ps. 69:9]. These words well describe not this one experience alone, but the whole of the human life of Jesus. The zeal of His Father's house consumed Him, wore Him out. It burned in Him a flame, like the flame of a lamp, until it burned out His whole life. He lived intensely. Love for God and for man possessed Him and ever constrained Him. He did His Father's will until that will led Him to the cross. He loved men so that His life was utterly consumed, poured out, in service for men. One of His words was: "Whosoever will save his life shall lose it: and whosoever will lose his life for my sake shall find it." He never saved His life. He kept back absolutely nothing He had that anyone needed. He never withheld Himself from the sick, the leprous, the demon possessed; He went everywhere, at every call. He never took rest. Virtue went out of Him continually, as He healed and comforted and helped others. His own life was poured out to become life to those who lacked. His own joy was given to be joy to those who were in sorrow, His own love was given to fill the hearts of those that were loveless. So He lived—giving, giving, giving, loving, doing, serving—until at last He died on Calvary to save the lost. So this sentence really tells the story of all His years. It becomes also a fitting motto for every follower of Christ. Zeal for Christ should consume us. "I have only one passion," said Zinzendorf, "and that is Christ."

The Jews demanded of Him His authority for assuming such authority over the temple. He answered in words which we are to hear again as they were used with perverted meaning by the false witnesses on the trial of our Lord: "Destroy this temple, and in three days I will raise it up." The Jews quibbled over His words, and the Evangelist gives us the Lord's meaning: "He spake of the temple of his body." Then he went on to tell us how in the light of the Resurrection the mystery became clear. "When therefore he was risen from the dead, his disciples remembered that he had said this unto them; and they believed the scriptures and the word which Jesus had said." This is an illustration of the need of the "afterwards" to make many things plain. At the time, the disciples probably understood their Master's allusion to "this temple" no better than His enemies did. But by and by events occurred which threw light upon the language, and then its meaning flashed out plainly and clearly. When the temple of His body had been destroyed by the Jews, and He had indeed raised it up in three days, then they understood.

Many other of Christ's words were in like manner enigmas to the disciples when they were spoken. All His references to the cross were such. They never realized that He must die, although many times during His later months He spoke of His coming death. However, when the cross had been set up and taken down, and when the grave had been sealed and then opened, the mystery vanished. To all of us, even yet, there are many truths and teachings which cannot be made plain until we have passed through certain experiences. We could never know that there were stars in the skies if night never came. We cannot know the beauty of the divine promises until we enter the needs the promises were given to meet. The same is true continually of events of our lives; their meaning is wrapped in mystery for us until afterwards. The early story of Joseph of the Old Testament was dark and sad. It could not be understood. It seemed all strange and wrong. It was hard to see divine love and goodness in it. But when the story was finished, the wisdom, the love and the goodness are apparent. There are things in every life which, at the time, seem tangles and puzzles, but which afterwards reveal divine love and grace in every line. The lesson is: When you cannot see, trust and wait.

Evidently Jesus made a deep impression at this Passover. He performed many miracles or signs. What these were we are not told, but many believed on Him. Their faith, however, seems to have been impulsive, and not based on strong conviction. It was not such believing as in the case of the disciples. Jesus saw into the hearts of the people who were ready to believe, and did not accept Him as true followers. "Jesus did not commit himself unto them." Nothing came of His work at this time.

Our Lord's knowledge of men is very clearly stated here. He "needed not that any should testify of man: for he knew what was in man." We should not forget this. There is immeasurable comfort in this truth if we are living truly. He knows our love for Him, though it is so feeble that the world can scarcely know that we love Him at all. This was Peter's refuge when, after his threefold denial, Jesus plied him with the three-fold question: "Lovest thou me?" "Lord, thou knowest all things; thou knowest that I love thee." It is a comfort for us to know that Jesus understands all our struggles, all our temptations, how hard it is for us to be good; and that He has infinite patience with us. It is a comfort, too, for us to know that He is acquainted with the innermost things of other lives as well. He knows the plots, the schemes to do us harm, and is able to shield and protect us from them. What folly is hypocrisy, when we remember that Jesus knows all that is in man! How silly it is to talk about "secret sins," when the deepest thoughts of all hearts are known to Him with whom we all have to do!

5

Jesus and Nicodemus

Scripture Reading: John 3:1–15

Nicodemus is well-known. His story has often been told. We study here the beginning of his Christian life. It is the fashion to speak slightingly of his coming to Jesus by night. It is sometimes said that it was cowardly. But this may not be a fair criticism. Night may have been the best time for him to make his visit. It may have been the only time when he could hope to find Jesus free for an undisturbed hour's talk with him. We must read the story through to the close and see if the subsequent mentions of Nicodemus confirm the charge of timidity or cowardice in him. We shall find that just the reverse is true. It is said that he desired to be a secret disciple. If that was his thought, we know that he did not persist in this kind of discipleship, but that the time came when his secret friendship for his Master grew into majestic strength. We may be glad, therefore, that he came to Christ, even though he came first under cover of darkness. The end of the story justifies its beginning.

The heart of the lesson which our Lord taught Nicodemus is the necessity for the new birth. "Except a man be born again, he cannot see the kingdom of God." The natural human birth is not sufficient. We must begin again at the beginning, and build up our life as if we never had been born. We must be born of the Spirit, or we cannot even see the kingdom of God, much less enter into it. That is, we are not fitted for heaven or the heavenly life while we have our old nature unchanged. We would not enjoy heaven even if we could be taken up and set down in the midst of it, unless our hearts have been changed. A wicked man would not enjoy a prayer meeting in one of our churches where the exercises consist of prayer, hymns, singing and conversation on spiritual subjects. He finds no pleasure in reading the Bible. Think of this man, his heart full of worldliness, without love for God, without the spirit of prayer, finding joy in heaven. To one who was speaking of heaven being so far away and asking how one could ever find the way there, the answer was given: "Heaven must come down to you. Heaven must begin in your heart." Nothing could be truer than this. Heaven must come into our heart before we can enter into the heavenly life. Our nature must be so changed that we shall love holiness, purity, the things that God loves. This change can be made only by the Holy Spirit.

A second natural birth, even if it were possible, would not effect the change. We would be the same being still, with the same desires, the same evil nature, the same hatred of God and of holiness. "Except a man be born of water and of the Spirit, he cannot enter into the kingdom of God." The new birth is more than education—the drawing out of the powers that are in the nature. There would be no improvement in this process. The new birth is more than the refinement produced by good society, by familiarity with beautiful things, by association with gentle and refined people. It is a new life that must come down from heaven into the heart of him who believes. Without this we cannot be made into the likeness of God.

The new life is like its Author. "That which is born of the Spirit is spirit." Like produces like. Everyone who is born of God will bear the features of God's likeness. He will begin to love the things that God loves, and hate the things that God hates. He will be like God in holiness, in forgiveness, in love. If we would know what God is like, we need only to look at Jesus Christ, for He is the image of God; and if we are born again, we will have the same features in us. At first they may be very dim, but they will come out clearer and clearer as we grow in spiritual life. We can tell whether or not we are born again by looking closely at our lives, to see if they bear the marks of the Holy Spirit. Do we put away sin and strive to live holy lives? Do we love the Bible and prayer? Do we love the services of the church and the Lord's Supper? Do we love to be with Christ in Christian fellowship and in personal communion? Is it our deepest desire to have the divine features stamped on our lives?

It would put strong confidence into our hearts if we would learn to think of Christ's words as eternal verities. They are not like any other words. A dying woman cried to the minister who entered her room, to try to comfort her, "Oh, give me a word I can lay hold of!" She felt herself drifting out upon the sea with nothing to which she could hold. We will all need words of this kind as we come into life's crisis places. Nothing but the words of Christ will then meet our needs. Jesus said to Nicodemus, "We speak that we do know, and testify that we have seen; and ye receive not our witness." Very much of human science is only guessing and speculation—we cannot be sure of it. Every now and then some new discovery is made which overturns and sweeps away whole volumes of boasted theories. We have to be all the time buying new books to keep up with the times, and we are afraid to quote from any but the newest editions, lest there may have been some recent discovery which contradicts the older. But Christ's teachings are eternal certainties. He came down from heaven, where from all eternity He had dwelt, and He knew what He taught. We may accept His words without the slightest doubt, and may build our soul's hopes upon them. We need never fear that there will be a revision of these teachings or that anything yet to be made known to us will contradict or set aside what we have already been taught. What Jesus said about God, about God's love, about the way of salvation, about duty, about the judgment, about the future life, is all eternal certainty. We may infallibly believe and unfalteringly trust every word of Christ, and be sure of eternal security.

There is no other infallible teacher but Christ. "No man hath ascended up to heaven." There are some people these days who take it upon themselves to question what Christ revealed about the heavenly life. They talk as if they knew more about these matters than did He who lived from all eternity in heaven, and then coming to earth, told men of the invisible things of God. Christ's words to Nicodemus mean that there is no other one, that there never has been any other one so qualified to speak of heavenly things as was God's own Son, who came to reveal Him. He was an infallible teacher and a true witness. There is no guesswork about the statements which He makes concerning God and God's love for men, God's will and the provision made in the heavenly kingdom for God's children. All manner of books have been written, telling us of "gates ajar" and "gates wide open," and we find whole volumes of guesses and fancies about the other world. But these are of no value whatever when they go beyond what the Son of God has made known to us. We must turn to Christ's words for any real knowledge of the land beyond.

The shadow of the cross lays upon the heart of Christ from the beginning. He knew in what way He was to make salvation for men. He says here, "As Moses lifted up the serpent in the wilderness, even so must the Son of man be lifted up." The reference to the incident of the brazen serpent is instructive—so must Christ be lifted up. He referred to the cross—He knew He must die on it. It was at the beginning of His ministry that Jesus spent the evening with Nicodemus. Even then He knew what was before Him. Why the "must"? Not merely because it had been foretold by the prophets. The prophets foretold it because of the necessity that He must suffer. Only by dying for the world could He save the world.

The way in which bitten ones in the Hebrew camp could be saved by the uplifted serpent illustrates the way lost men can be saved by Christ on His cross. Those who looked, lived; those who behold the Lamb of God shall live. Anyone who looked, whatever his condition, was healed; "whosoever" believes on Christ, no matter who he may be, of what nation or color or condition, shall have everlasting life.

6

Jesus at Jacob's Well

Scripture Reading: John 4:5–15

The record tells us that Jesus in His journey "must needs" pass through Samaria. There was no other way unless He had gone far about. But we may believe that there was another "must needs" for His passing that way—there was this woman at Samaria who needed Him. It was worthwhile to go a long distance out of His way to carry the water of life to a thirsty soul. If He had not gone through Samaria, this wonderful chapter in John's gospel would never have been written, and the New Testament would have been less rich. It is worth our while to think of the way God is always directing our movements so as to bring us to the places at which He wants us to be and to the people He wants us to touch and to help. There are no chance meetings in this world. Jesus met the woman at the well at the right moment. When we are doing God's will He guides our movements, orders our steps, and there is a sacred meaning in our crossing of others' paths.

A well of water in the East was of great importance, and this well, no doubt, was especially valuable. People came from far and near to draw water from it, and weary passers-by were refreshed as they drank of the pure, wholesome spring. It is interesting to think of how many persons along the centuries were helped by the water they drew from its cold depths. It is no longer of value, however—it is now only a useless excavation, a mere relic of the past, choked by rubbish. There are some

419

people like this old well. Once they were full of life, with kindness flowing from them wherever they went, a blessing to all who came near to them. Now the well of love in them flows no more, or only intermittently; it has been choked up by worldliness or by care. We should keep our heart-wells ever open and the water flowing fresh and pure in them as long as we live. Christian love never should cease to pour forth its streams of kindness.

The picture of Jesus being wearied with His journey, sitting down by the well-curb, is very suggestive. He had come a long distance and was tired after His hot journey. Such incidents as this help us to realize the humanness and the human-heartedness of Christ. He has not forgotten, now in heaven, the experiences of earth. He remembers in His glory this day at the old well, how tired He was after His long journey, and how the rest and the water refreshed Him. We need not be ashamed to grow weary, since our Master Himself was weary. We are sure of His sympathy with us, for He understands, too, when we are exhausted by our toils or struggles, and is glad to comfort and strengthen us.

When the woman of Samaria left her home that morning, to go to the well, she did not know what strange thing would happen to her before she returned. She did not know that she would meet a Stranger who would bring to her a new meaning of life and set her feet in new paths. We never know when we set out, any day, what the hours may bring to us, whom we shall meet, what new friend, whose influence that day shall change all our future course. We do not know what may happen any common day that will make all our life different ever after. We should go forth every morning with our hand in Christ's, that He may guide us in the best way, so that we may not reject the good that is offered to us.

Jesus began His conversation with the woman by asking a little favor of her. He said, "Give me to drink." This was better in the beginning of the conversation than if He had offered to do something for her. This was the way to gain the woman's attention. Though so weary that He could not journey farther with His disciples, He was not too weary to be interested in this woman's life. This was a bit of Christ's wayside ministry. He was always ready to do a kindness, even in His resting hours. Much of life's best work is produced in wayside ministries; things we did not plan to do when we set out in the morning, little helpfulnesses which we render as we pass on the way, words of cheer which we speak as we move along the common paths. Often these bits of wayside service mean more than the things in our lives which seem greater, which we plan for with care.

Jesus asked this woman for a little kindness—a drink of water. Who of us would not be glad any day to give our Master a cup of cold water? We say we cannot do anything like this for Him now, for He comes no more to our gate or along our way, a weary man needing our kindness. But He has told us how we may always have this privilege. In the least of His little ones who need our help He Himself comes, appealing to love's ministry [see Matt. 25:40]. We must be careful always lest in our neglecting to show a kindness to some human being we thrust Christ Himself away.

The woman was surprised to have this Stranger speak to her. It was not considered proper in those days, in that country, for a man to speak to a woman in public. Especially was it not customary for a Jew to speak to a Samaritan. The Jews and Samaritans were not in cordial relations. So she answered Him with a question—why He had requested a drink of water from her. The answer which Jesus gave to her flippant question hints at His own character and mission. "If thou knewest the gift of God, and who it is that saith to thee, Give me to drink; thou wouldest have asked of him, and he would have given thee living water." She saw only a weary, dust-covered Jew sitting there by the well, asking for a drink of water. She saw nothing unusual in Him. She did not know that this footsore Man was the Messiah, the Son of God, who had all life and all good in Him, and all things to bestow. He had asked only for a drink of common water, but He would give to her the water of life. Really she was the famishing one—not He; and if only she would ask, He would give her infinite blessing. It is always the same. We go about with our great needs, our hungering hearts, our unrest, our consciousness of guilt, not knowing that close beside us stands the Christ, with all we need in His hands, ready and eager to supply our every want. We go on, meanwhile, chattering about the trivialities of life and the unsatisfactory vanities of earth, not knowing what infinitely greater blessings are within our reach, to be had simply for the asking.

The woman was impressed by what the Stranger said, but she did not yet comprehend His meaning. So she talked to Him about the difficulty of getting water out of that deep well, and asked Him if He were greater than Jacob. Jesus replied again, using the water of the well as a symbol of earthly blessing. "Whosoever drinketh of this water shall thirst again." These words tell the whole story of the thirsts of human life. Men turn everywhere to satisfy them, but at best they find only temporary satisfaction, followed by still deeper thirst.

There is said to be a strange plant in South America which finds a moist place and rests there for a while, sending its roots down and becoming green. When this bit of earth dries up, the plant draws itself together and is blown along by the wind until it finds another moist spot, where it repeats the same story. On and on it rolls, stopping wherever it finds a little water and staying until the water is exhausted. But after all its journeyings it is nothing but a bundle of dead roots and leaves. The life of this plant tells the story of those who drink only at this world's springs. They go on from spring to spring, and at the last, at the end of the longest life, they are nothing but bundles of unsatisfied desires and burning thirsts.

In contrast, Jesus here tells also of the heavenly water which He gives to those who believe on Him. "Whosoever drinketh of the water which I shall give him shall never thirst." In Christ all the soul's cravings are met. There is no want or desire in our nature which cannot in Him find perfect satisfaction. One of the Beatitudes reads, "Blessed are they which do hunger and thirst after righteousness: for they shall be filled." Noah's dove flew from the ark and went on weary wing everywhere, but found only a waste of desolate waters, with no place to alight. Then she flew back to the ark and was gently drawn within, where she found warmth, safety and rest. This story of the dove illustrates the history of every soul that, having wandered everywhere in search of rest, at last returns to God and finds rest in Him.

The saying of Jesus about the well of water in the heart is very suggestive. "The water that I shall give him . . . shall be in him a well of water." Thus every Christian becomes a fountain of blessing in this world. As from the great Fountain, Christ, all the streams of life flow, so from the little fountain in the heart of each believer flows a stream of the water of life to give drink to those who are thirsty. Blessed ourselves, our thirst quenched, our life satisfied, we become in turn centers or sources of blessing to others. Are we indeed wells of water at which others quench their thirst? Does our life make us a blessing to all who come near to us? Do we give forth kindness, patience, thoughtfulness, gentleness and all helpful influences? Or do we pour out bitterness, impatience, angry words, ill temper, selfishness, thoughtlessness?

The answer which Jesus made deeply impressed the woman, and she cried, "Give me this water, that I thirst not, neither come hither to draw." She did not understand the meaning of Christ's words, and yet her pathetic appeal is full of meaning. The first desire of our hearts should be to receive the grace of Christ, that we may no longer be dependent upon this world's pleasures and comforts. It is a weary life which those live who have no source of good save the little springs of earth which soon dry up.

7

The Second Miracle at Cana

Scripture Reading: John 4:43–54

After leaving Sychar, Jesus seems to have gone at once to Cana. He never rested. When His work was done in one place He hastened to another. He was never in a hurry, never flustered, never feverish in His haste, but He never loitered nor lost a moment's time. If we keep our heart at peace, and live according to God's laws, there is little danger of our injuring our health by too much work. Then, even if duty demands serious toil and self-denying labor, it is Christlike not to withhold ourselves from it. "For whosoever will save his life shall lose it." Taking too good care of oneself is the way to make the least of one's life.

Jesus was no exception to the well-known rule that "A prophet hath no honor in his own country." It is a common saying that no man is a hero to his own servant. Those who live in familiar relations with the great or the good are the least likely to recognize the elements of greatness or goodness in them. Many of the men whose names shine in the galaxy of fame, and whose work lives in the world with undying influence, had little honor from those among whom they walked, and perhaps would have little honor today if they were to return and live in the old relations. We often fail to recognize the true excellence of our best friends while they stay with us. It is not until she is gone out of a home that a mother's real value is appreciated. The same is true of each

424

member of the household and of each friend upon whom we lean much and whose life is a great deal to us. Jesus walked among the people in Judea, taught, produced His miracles, and lived out His sweet, beautiful life of love in their midst, but they failed to recognize the Messiah in Him. "He was in the world, and the world was made by Him, and the world knew Him not. He came unto His own, and His own received Him not" [1:10, 11]. We are in danger in these very days of failing to appreciate the blessings of Christianity because they are so familiar to us.

Sickness and suffering are everywhere. No one is exempt from them. Even the mansions of the noble are not sheltered from the invasions of disease. There is no charm in wealth or rank or power to keep fever away. Into the home of this nobleman suffering came. It was only a child, too, who was sick. Even to the youngest, illness comes as well as to the old.

Trouble often sends to Christ those who would not have gone if the trouble had not touched them. It was the sickness of the nobleman's child that sent him to Jesus. He had heard of the great Healer, but probably had never sought Him, nor even thought of seeking Him. But when his child was stricken down and seemed about to die, he remembered what he had heard about Jesus, that He was able to heal the sick and even bring back to life those who were near death. So this great man hastened away all the long distance to Cana to find this Healer. We all owe far more than we know to our troubles. We do not recognize our need of divine help until we are in some sore distress when human help can do nothing for us. Then we turn to God. If we never had a sense of sinfulness we would never seek Christ as our Savior. If we never realized our powerlessness in the midst of temptation, we would never turn to Christ as our helper. Indeed, the Bible becomes a new book to us in times of trouble. Many of the best things in it we never would have found had it not been for some great need which made their meaning real to us. We do not turn with our heart's cravings to God until we realize the insufficiency of this world's friendships and blessings.

The child seemed about to die. The record says "he was at the point of death." The point of death is a point to which all of us must come sometime in our life. We must pass through this world along many different ways, but every one of us comes at last to the point of death. All earthly roads pass that way. No matter how bright the path is on which our feet are now walking, somewhere on it, perhaps far away yet, perhaps closer than we think, awaits this point of death. We should learn to live so that if at any sudden hour we find ourselves facing death, we should not be troubled nor disturbed.

In this nobleman's earnest pleading we have a revelation of a father's heart. He pleaded, "Come down ere my child die." We do not realize the value of father-love as an impulse in this world. The secret which sends thousands of men every day to their tasks, their struggles, their heroisms, is back in the homes from which they come, where children stay. We idealize mother-love, not overmuch, but perhaps sometimes to the exclusion or at least to the forgetting of father-love, which has scarcely a less powerful motive in the inspiring of the noble things of human life. The sickness of a child sent this nobleman miles away to plead with Christ. There was a great faith also in the father's heart—he believed that Jesus could save his child's life. He seems not to have thought, however, that even the Master, with all His power, could do anything without journeying all the way to his home. He thought the Healer's presence necessary to the putting forth of His power. So he insisted on having Jesus go with him to his home, where his child lay dying.

Jesus recognized the father's faith and assured him at once that his child would recover. "Go thy way; thy son liveth." More than twenty miles off the sick boy lay, but the power of Jesus healed him there just as easily as if He had been at the bedside. The word of power flew through the air all that long distance like an electric flash, and on his couch of pain the suffering child suddenly felt a thrill of health. A moment later, and the fever was entirely gone and the child was altogether well. This miracle should have much comfort for us. We cannot now bring Christ in bodily presence to the room where our loved one is lying, but we can pray to Him, and He can heal our friend just as easily from His heavenly home as if He were present where he lies. We can also ask God to bless our friend twenty miles away from us, a thousand miles away, and He can do it just as easily as if the friend were close by our side when we pray.

The father hastened home, and on the way learned that his request had been granted. "As he was now going down, his servants met him, and told him, saying, Thy son liveth." Ever after that day, when he looked upon this child, the father would remember that his boy's spared life was an answer to a prayer. The child would always know, too, that he was living in the world because his father had thought about him one day when he was very sick, and had gone all the way to Cana to speak to Jesus on his behalf. Children do not know how many blessings they are enjoying because their parents, teachers, pastors, and other friends have gone on errands to Christ for them in the days of their need.

The manner of the answer to this nobleman's prayer made a deep impression on the father. He compared the time and learned that the beginning of the child's recovery was at the very moment when Jesus had said that the boy would live. He believed before—now his faith was confirmed. He found it just as the Master had said it would be. There were many other cases in which the words of Jesus were put to the test at once and proved to be exactly true. He told the woman of Samaria all about her past life. He told Peter that the coin would be in the fish's mouth with which to pay the temple tax. He told the disciples they would find a colt tied, and rehearsed the conversation that would take place with the owner, and it all came out just as He said it would. He told the disciples, again, that they would meet a man bearing a pitcher of water, who would conduct them to the guest room; and the words came true. From these illustrations in common life we learn that every word of Christ will be found to be true. He promised salvation and eternal life to those who will believe on Him, and everyone who believes and commits his life to Him will find this promise fulfilled. He said that in the Father's house are many mansions, and that He will come again, to receive to Himself each believer; we shall find this word true. When we pass into the valley of the shadows, we shall find ourselves in the personal care of Christ, and shall be led by Him home, to enter the mansion which He has been preparing for us.

8

Jesus at the Pool of Bethesda

Scripture Reading: John 5:1–15

The pool or spring, called Bethesda, probably was some sort of medicinal spring. There are many such springs both in America and Europe, to which people flock from all parts of the world with their ailments, hoping to have them cured. Supernatural properties were attributed to such springs in ancient days. This spring at Bethesda was probably an intermittent spring which possessed healing virtue for certain kinds of ailments. It was well-known, and its porches were always thronged with patients waiting for the moving of the waters. The curative power of the spring seems to have been confined to the times of its periodic flow. We should note that the fourth verse of our King James Version is omitted from the Revised Version, as it is not found in the most ancient manuscripts.

The man whose case is described in our passage for today had been a sufferer for thirty-eight years. It is not easy to be sick year after year. Prolonged invalidism very seriously tests the quality of life. Some people fret and chafe in such experiences. Pain is hard to bear. Then their illness seems a sad interruption to their activities, breaking into their plans for lifework. It is much easier to go to one's tasks every day, toiling for long hours, than it is to lie quietly in bed, doing nothing, yet keeping sweet. Yet invalidism, when accepted in faith and trust, and endured with patience, often produces very beautiful life. There are shut-ins whose rooms are almost like heaven in their brightness and joy. Some of the most wonderful revelations of divine grace have been made in cases of long and painful illness, when the sufferers have accepted their condition as God's will for them and have found it a condition of blessing. Richard Baxter, who himself had been an invalid for long years, has a note on this passage which is worth repeating: "How great a mercy was it to live thirty-eight years under God's wholesome discipline! Oh, my God, I thank Thee for the like discipline of fifty-eight years; how safe a life is this, in comparison with full prosperity and pleasure!" The furnace fires of sickness burn off many a bond of sin and worldliness. Many now in heaven, no doubt, will thank God forever for the invalidism which kept them from sin when on the earth.

Jesus came down to the Bethesda spring that Sabbath and, as His eye looked over those who were waiting there, He noticed one man to whom His sympathy went out at once. He saw all the sufferers who were sitting in the porches that day, and He was moved with compassion as He looked upon them. He saw them, however, not merely as a company of sad people, but as individuals. He knew the story of each one—how long he had been suffering, how hard his life had been. Among all who were there that day, He singled out one for special thought and help. Probably he had been a sufferer longest. At least this man's case made its appeal to the heart of Jesus. He knows about each patient in a hospital, or each shut-in in a town. This personal interest of our Master in those who are sick or broken in their lives is wonderfully comforting. He knows all about us—our pain that is so hard to bear, our disappointments year after year, growing at last to hopelessness. It is very sweet to be able to say always, "He knows!"

Coming up to this man, Jesus asked him, "Wilt thou be made whole?" He wished to rouse him from his lethargy. He asks the same question now of each one who is in any trouble. He comes especially to those who are spiritually sick, and asks them if they will be made whole. The question implies His willingness and readiness to heal. He can take these deformed, crippled, and helpless lives of ours and restore them to strength and beauty. It seems strange that anyone should refuse to be made whole when Christ comes and offers to do it. If we were sick in body, and He wished to make us well, we would not say, "No." If we were crippled and deformed, and He wanted to make us lithe and straight, we would be glad to accept His offer. Why is it that when He comes to us and asks us if we would have Him make our maimed and crippled souls whole, so many of us say, "Oh, no! "or, "Not yet"?

The man did not answer the question directly, but uttered a complaint. He had been so long used to hopelessness that the song had altogether died out of his heart. He had always been pushed aside when there had seemed a possible chance for him. "I have no man, when the water is troubled, to put me into the pool." Other people always got ahead of him. He had no one to help him, and he could not go himself. There are some persons who really seem to have no friend. Nobody ever gives a thought to them. There are many unsaved people who might almost say the same, "I have no man to help me to Christ." No one cares for their souls. True, there is none who could not come to Christ if he would. Yet Christian people must not forget that the unsaved need the help of those who are saved, that the forgiven must carry the news of mercy to the unforgiven. Part of our mission in the world is to help others to Christ. This man waiting at the fountain's edge is a type of many persons about us—close to the healing waters, with hungry, unsatisfied hearts, needing only the help of a human hand or the sympathy of a loving heart to lead them to Christ, yet never getting that help or that sympathy, and sitting close to the waters year after year, unhealed, unsaved.

It was an important moment for this man when Jesus spoke to him. There was a shorter way of help for him than by waiting for someone to put him into the water. "Wilt thou be made whole? . . . Rise, take up thy bed, and walk." The man might have said: "Why, I cannot rise. That is the very thing I have not been able to do for thirty-eight years. Take up my bed! Why, I could not lift a feather; and as for walking, I could as soon fly. I cannot obey His command until I get strength to do it." There are people who talk just in this way about beginning the Christian life. They plead their helplessness as a reason for their delay. There is a fine lesson for such people in this man's prompt obedience. The moment he heard the command he made the effort to rise, and as he made the effort strength was given to him.

New life came to this lame man with the obeying. Christ never commands an impossibility. When He bids us rise out of our helplessness and begin the Christian walk, He means to give us the grace and strength to do it. The command to take up his bed was a sign that he would not have any more need for it. He had been lying upon it for many years. Now it should be rolled up as no longer required. Some people enter upon the Christian life experimentally. They will try it and see if they can hold out, yet they still keep the way open for return to the old life if they should not succeed in the new. But this is not the way Christian faith is meant to act. We should burn the bridges behind us, that we may not possibly retreat to the country out of which we have come. We should put away the implements of our wickedness, our crutches, our staves and our beds, with no thought of ever returning again to them.

"Take up thy bed, and walk." The word "walk" suggests that the man was not simply to rise up and stand where he was—he was to move out in the paths of duty and service. The invalid is restored that he may take his place and let his hand become busied among the activities of life. We are saved to serve.

Before the man could get far with his bed, he was challenged for breaking the Sabbath. There are people who spoil everything. They find fault with every beautiful thing anyone does. These men knew what had happened to this poor man. We would think they would have rejoiced in him in His restoration. But the fact that he seemed to them to be violating one of their Sabbath rules bulked more largely in their eyes than all the blessings that had come to him. When they told the happy man that it was not lawful for him to be carrying his bed on the Sabbath, he answered that He who had cured him told him to take up his bed and walk. When they asked him who the man was, he said he did not know. He had been made so glad by his healing that he gave no thought to the Healer. Jesus had slipped away in the crowd. Too often, however, men receive benefits without showing gratitude to the person through whom the benefits are received. Many of those who are helped by Christ have but little interest in Christ, and never think of Him, though they owe so much to Him.

But, although the man had shown no regard for his Healer, Christ was deeply interested in him, and followed him up. Finding him in the temple, He said to him, "Behold, thou art made whole: sin no more, lest a worse thing come unto thee." Evidently the man's thirty-eight years of illness had been brought about by some sin in his early life. There are many men who in a lifelong feebleness or infirmity pay the penalty of sins of youth. Very pathetic is the cry of the Psalmist, "Remember not the sins of my youth" [Ps. 25:7]. The man had been healed, but his continued health depended now upon his right living being continued. If he turned back again to the sins which had brought upon him his diseased condition through so many unhappy years, the evil would return in worse form than ever. There is something worse even than thirty-eight years of helplessness. These words have serious warning for everyone who has been forgiven. The condition of forgiveness is repentance, and repentance, if it would prove true, must be final, unconditional and unchanging.

9

Christ's Divine Authority

Scripture Reading: John 5:17–27

The people were angry at Jesus because He had healed the helpless man on the Sabbath. They claimed that He had done wrong by working on the seventh day. The answer of Jesus was, "My Father worketh hitherto, and I work." In the History of the creation we read that God set the example of Sabbath-keeping. After six days of creating, He rested the seventh day. We are living now in God's Sabbath. But the words of Jesus here show us that there is a sense in which God keeps no Sabbath. He never ceases to be active. The worlds do not stop in their orbits to rest when the Holy Day begins. The sun does not veil His face and cease His shining that day. The grass does not stop growing, the flowers do not cease to bloom, the wheat does not pause in its ripening, when the day of rest comes. There is no Sabbath-keeping in God's providence. Nor does His care for His children intermit when the Sabbath dawns. It would be very sad for the world if it did.

The people had found fault with Jesus for healing a man on the Sabbath. They said He had been working, and working was forbidden by the law. This was His answer, "My Father worketh hitherto"—has never ceased to work, is evermore blessing and helping His creatures. Then He added, "and I work." This was in answer to the charge that He had broken the Sabbath in healing the man. For one thing, He put Himself alongside the Father in power and authority. It was an assertion that He was divine. We get here a suggestion of the kind of works that are right for us to do on the Lord's Day. There is not in these words a shadow of defense for ordinary secular work on the Lord's Day, but works of mercy, of religion, of obedience, we may do on the day of rest.

Jesus had claimed equality with His Father in the words, "My Father worketh hitherto, and I work." For Him as well as for His Father there was no need of a Sabbath of rest. Rest is necessary for man. His strength has its limitations. He cannot go on forever, but must stop to renew His strength. Human energy flags and is exhausted, its source is finite and it must be continually renewed. But Christ was not like other men in this. He fainted not, neither was weary. Then He had coupled Himself with the Father in the words, "My Father worketh hitherto," through all the ages, "and I work." He and His Father work together. All divine power was in Him and had always been in Him. He could not grow weary.

Then He added, "The Son can do nothing of himself, but what he seeth the Father do: for what things soever he doeth, these also doeth the Son likewise." From the beginning to the end of Christ's life we find the same oneness with the Father asserted. He did the Father's will, never deviating from it in the smallest particular. We hear Him say continually such words as these: "I seek not mine own will, but the will of the Father which hath sent me"; "My meat is to do the will of him that sent me, and finish His work" [4:37]; "I do always those things that please him" [8:29]. For one thing, these words show us the perfect oneness of the Father and Son. He took all His directions from His Father's lips. He waited at every step for His Father's bidding. The question with Him never was: "What would be pleasant for Me to do? What would further My own interests? How can I do the most good in the world? How can I win the greatest number of friends?" The one question always was, "What is My Father's will for Me today?"

Jesus asserts the Father's love for Him and His complete trust in Him. "For the Father loveth the Son, and sheweth him all things that himself doeth: and he will show him greater works than these, that ye may marvel." Here we have a glimpse of true fatherhood. Love hides nothing. The Father's love for the Son is so perfect that He withholds nothing from Him, has no secrets which He does not reveal to Him. The words tell of the most perfect oneness and unity, life flowing into life, heart opening into heart. It is a oneness of love. There are none of the "sons of God" who are so glorious in their privileges as the "only begotten Son." Yet there is a verse in one of the Psalms [25:14] which says, "The secret of the Lord is with them that fear him; and he will show them His covenant." This would seem to mean that in proportion to our love for God and our trust in Him, He reveals His inner thoughts, the secrets of His love and favor to us. Then Jesus said to His disciples, "I call you not servants; for the servant knoweth not what His lord doeth: but I have called you friends; for all things that I heard of my Father I have made known unto you" [15:15]. Thus Jesus reveals the secret things of His love to those who trust Him.

The works which only the Father can do, Jesus says He also does. "As the Father raiseth up the dead, and quickeneth them; even so the Son quickeneth whom he will." To Nicodemus, Jesus spoke of becoming a Christian as being born again—beginning life as if one had never lived before. Here Jesus represents the natural world as a great cemetery in which all men sleep in graves of death. The beginning of Christian life is spiritual resurrection—those who believe on Christ burst their graves and come into life. The picture is very striking. The natural man is really dead to God and to the things of God. He hears not the voice of the Spirit. He knows nothing of what is going on about him in the spiritual realm. It is just as when Jesus stood before the grave of Lazarus and called the young man's name. The dead heard His voice and came out and began to live. So the spiritually dead who hear the voice of Christ and believe on Him are quickened into a new life.

There is another strong assertion of divinity here, showing that Christ was conscious of being equal with the Father. To God alone belongs the prerogative of judgment. "For the Father judgeth no man, but hath committed all judgment unto the Son." If this power of judging is given to Christ, He must be divine. It is a precious comfort to us, as we think of the judgment day, to know that the Judge on the throne will be Jesus—the same Jesus who died for us, who wears still and shall then wear our nature, and who therefore will understand us. We need not fear Him who once died for love of us. If we are His friends now and here, confessing Him before all men, He will be our friend then, and will confess us before His Father and the angels. But we must not forget the other side of this truth. If we are ashamed of Him and do not confess Him here by love and obedience, we are assured that He will be ashamed of us and will deny us before His Father and the angels.

We must remember, too, that He who is to be our Judge makes common cause with the lowliest of His people, and will say to them, "I was hungry, and ye gave me meat: I was thirsty, and ye gave me drink . . . I was sick, and ye visited me"; or "I was hungry, and ye gave me no meat . . . I was sick . . . and ye visited me not" [Matt. 25:35-40]. We are continually on trial, and the Judge Himself is continually before us. We need to watch how we treat the lowliest of our fellowmen.

> Hush, I pray you!
> What if this friend should happen to be—God?

Jesus tells us here how to be saved. "He that heareth my word, and believeth on him that sent me, hath everlasting life." There are but two steps from the darkness of eternal death into the brightness and blessedness of eternal life. The first thing is to hear Christ's word. The Bible says a great deal about hearing. "Hear, and your soul shall live" [Is. 55:3]. But mere hearing is not enough. One may hear the gospel over and over, and yet be lost. Therefore Jesus said, "Take heed how ye hear." We must hear with a willing spirit, a spirit of obedience. The second step is believing—"he that heareth my word, and believeth on him that sent me." Hearing must be followed by believing. What is it to believe? It is not merely the assent of the mind to the truth. It is believing with the heart, trusting, committing oneself to God. The Revised Version takes out the "on" between "believeth" and "him"—there is not to be even a little preposition between the soul and God.

These are the two steps from death's darkness into life's brightness—hearing, believing. Then comes the blessing—"hath eternal life." Each word burns with light. "Life"—not merely physical life, but life in its largest, fullest, richest, truest sense—the life of Christ in the soul. We are made partakers of the divine nature, and the new life which enters into us makes us children of God, changes us into the image of Christ. "Everlasting life"—not this world's life only, but life in heaven and forever. "Hath everlasting life." I like the present tenses of the Bible. The good things of God's love and grace are not pushed off into the future, but are present possessions. Eternal life begins the moment one hears and believes.

10

The Miracle of the Loaves and Fishes

Scripture Reading: John 6:1–14

The importance of the miracle of the loaves and fishes is shown in the fact that it is the only one of the miracles which all the four evangelists record. Jesus sought rest for His disciples, who were very weary, thus showing His thoughtfulness for them, and took them away. But the looked-for rest was not realized, for the people flocked after Him and a great multitude thronged about Him in a little while, interrupting His rest and calling Him to minister again to the people.

A picture in the Doré gallery represents a great throng of people, rich and poor, young and old, kings and peasants, all turning beseeching looks toward a far-away Figure. It is the Christ, clothed in robes of dazzling whiteness, bearing a cross, beckoning with uplifted hand to these broken-hearted ones and sorrow-laden ones to come to Him for rest. This is always a true picture of Jesus. He invites all the weary and the needy to Him. Wherever He is, those who are hungry-hearted or in distress are drawn to Him. It was so in the old Galilean days. He could scarcely get a moment's rest or quiet. The people would follow Him to His retreats when He sought to be alone. They would break in upon Him even when He was at His prayers. It still remains true that there is something in Christ which draws all men to Him. He had something to give to men which they needed and which no other could give to them.

437

Jesus cares for our physical wants as well as our spiritual needs. When He saw the multitude about Him in the wilderness, His heart was moved with compassion for them. We sometimes forget this part of Christ's thought for us. We know that He cares for our spiritual wants, and has grace ready for every need; but we too often fail to remember that our bodily needs are also in His thought. Many persons do not even pray to God about their secular affairs, they do not ask Him for help in their business or in their household matters. But really nothing which concerns us is a matter of indifference to Him. He who feeds the hungry birds will care for His children.

Jesus spoke of the matter of the feeding of these people to Philip, asking him what they should do, The record says that He did this to prove Philip. Jesus is continually proving His disciples, putting them to the test, to bring out their faith, and to train them in serving. He is constantly sending to us cases of need to see if we will help them, and that we may learn how to help them. He wishes to draw out our interest, our love, our sympathy, our tenderness, our thoughtfulness, and to teach us to do the works of mercy which He leaves us in this world to do. The disciples could not see any possible way of feeding the multitude in the wilderness, and yet the Master meant that they should feed them. Their little blessed and used proved enough. We think we cannot meet the needs and the hungers which appeal to us, but we can if we will. We do not seem able to do much, but even our few words spoken kindly, our tears of sympathy, our expression of love, He can use to do great good to the faint and weary before us.

In answer to our Lord's question, "How many loaves have ye? go and see," Andrew found a boy in the company who had five barley loaves and two little fishes. Happy boy this was to be in that crowd that day with His basket of provisions. Just why he had the provisions with him, we are not told. His small supply was accepted and used by Christ in the working of a great work of kindness. This little incident shows what good even a child with Christ can do. It was a young girl who carried to Syria the news of the prophet's power which led to the healing of the proud general's leprosy [see 2 Kgs. 5]. They laughed at St. Theresa when she wanted to build an orphanage and had only three shillings with which to begin it. But she answered, "With her three shillings Theresa can do nothing; but with God and her three shillings there is nothing which Theresa cannot do." Every child who studies the story of this work should be impressed by the fact that even with His small possessions he can do great things when Christ works with him and uses him.

We should carefully study the method of this miracle. There were several steps. To begin with, the disciples brought the loaves to Jesus. If they had not done this, if they had begun feeding the people with what they had, without first bringing it to the Master for His blessing, it would not have gone far. We must bring our small resources to Christ and put them into His hands, that He may use them. When we have done this no one can tell the measure of good that may be wrought even by the smallest abilities. Whatsoever it is you have in your hand, you can use for God, and He will put His power into it. Then it will accomplish God's will. We need never say we can do nothing with our small ability or resources. God is not dependent on human power.

Notice what Jesus did in working this sign. First, He made the people sit down, that they might be quiet. They could not have been fed while moving about in a crowd. We must do our work in an orderly way. We must get quiet and still if we would have Christ feed us. Then, when the multitude were still, Jesus gave thanks and blessed the loaves before He gave them to the disciples. The blessing of God maketh rich. We ought to pray continually that Christ's touch may be upon us and upon the things we are doing. The letter you write to a discouraged friend lay first before Christ for His benediction, and then it will carry comfort and cheer. The flowers you will carry to a sick room—make a little prayer first that Christ's benediction may be upon them, that they may go laden with the fragrance of His love. Then their power to do good will be increased.

We are told in the other records that Jesus broke the bread before giving food to the disciples. Bread must be broken before it can be eaten. The body of Jesus must be broken before it could become bread for the world. Often Jesus must break us and our gifts before He can make us food for others. We should think also of the responsibility of the disciples that day. Jesus passed the bread through their hands to the hungry multitude beyond them. If they had merely fed themselves with what Jesus gave them, not passing it on, there would have been no miracle and the hungry thousands sitting on the hillside would not have been fed. We are now the disciples, standing between the Master and the hungry people.

Into our hands come the blessings of the gospel, and we must pass them to those about us and beyond us. If we feed only ourselves, take the comfort and the grace for our own lives, and do not pass on the broken bread, we have disappointed our Master and have failed in our duty as His helpers and coworkers, also leaving the waiting people unfed.

After the miracle we have a lesson on frugality and carefulness. The disciples were bidden to gather up the broken pieces that were left over, that nothing might be lost. "Waste not; want not," says the proverb. It seems remarkable that He who could so easily multiply the few loaves into a meal for thousands should be so particular about saving the fragments that remained. But He would teach us economy by His own example. No matter how great our abundance may be, we never should waste anything. After we have fed at our tables there always are hungry people who would be glad of the pieces that are left.

One day Thomas Carlyle stopped suddenly at a street crossing and, stooping, picked up something out of the mud, even at the risk of being knocked down and run over by passing vehicles. With His bare hands he gently rubbed the mud from it. He then almost reverently carried it to the pavement and laid it down on a clean spot on the curbstone. "That," said the old man in a tone of tenderness he rarely used, "is only a crust of bread. Yet I was taught by my mother never to waste anything; above all, bread, more precious than gold. I am sure the little sparrows or a hungry dog will get nourishment from this bit of bread."

The lesson on the sin of waste applies to other things besides bread—to fragments of time, of energy, of influence, of affection. Many people waste whole years in the course of their lives in the little fragments which they lose every day—one minute here, five minutes there, ten minutes later. If, at the end of a year, they could gather up all these fragments which they have wasted, they would have many basketfuls of golden time in which they might do much good. In the mint, where gold and silver coins are made, the sweepings of the floors, the settlings of the water in which the men wash their hands, the very smoke from the furnaces are all carefully searched through for fine particles of precious metals; and it is said that during a year large sums are recovered in this way. If only we would learn to pass through our hands, we should be far richer at the end of our life, and the world would be richer for our living. We should gather up the fragments, the finest golden dust, that nothing may be lost.

11

Jesus, the Bread of Life

Scripture Reading: John 6:22–40

I t was the day after the multitude had been fed so marvelously on the five loaves and the two fishes. So great was the impression made by the miracle that the people were about to take Jesus by force and make Him king. He first sent the disciples away, constraining them to enter the boat and go before Him, alone, unto the other side. Then He sent the multitudes away, and when they were gone He went quietly, unobserved, unto the mountain to pray.

The people had been foiled of their purpose to make Jesus king, and were disappointed. They sought Him, but could not find Him. It is a sad thing to lose Jesus. There is an incident in the days of our Lord's boyhood which tells of His mother losing Him. The family had been to Jerusalem, on the occasion of the Boy's first Passover, and when they started homeward Jesus was unawares left behind, and they had gone a whole day's journey before they missed Him. Great was the anxiety and the distress. Not till they had retraced their steps and sought painfully did they find Him. Many people lost Jesus, some in play, some in pleasure, some in business, some in sorrow, some in sin.

These men who had lost Jesus in the desert, after vainly searching for Him far and near, crossed the sea and found Him on the other side. Then, when they had found Him, they seemed almost to blame Him for disappearing, asking Him, "When camest thou hither?" Jesus

441

answered, revealing to them their real motive in seeking Him, "Ye seek me, not because ye saw the miracles, but because ye did eat of the loaves, and were filled." That is, they sought Jesus, not to honor Him, but only for what they thought He would do for them. We are in danger of thinking of religion only or chiefly from the side of its earthly benefits, for it has the promise of the life that now is as well as of that which is to come. But the higher blessings should be dearer to us than the lower. We should seek Christ for His own sake and for the sake of the honor we may do to Him.

The lesson which Jesus taught the people that day, we should consider well for ourselves. He said, "Labor not for the meat which perisheth, but for that meat which endureth unto everlasting life, which the Son of man shall give unto you: for him hath God the Father sealed." We live in a materialistic age, when the quest of the world is for money, for power, for things of the earth, and not for the things that are spiritual and enduring. Men are toiling and wearing out their life in gathering rubbish out of the dust, not thinking of the heavenly treasures, the spiritual things that are in Christ, and which they might have with half the toil and care. We ought not to spend our life in picking up things which we cannot carry through the grave. If we are wise, we will seek rather to gather treasures which we can take with us into eternity. Really, all we can carry out of this world is whatever we may have of character when we are through with living. The Beatitudes tell us what are the things that will abide. The fruits of the Spirit, of which Paul tells us, are the only qualities which will endure to eternal life.

The people seem to have caught at last from the words of Jesus a glimmering of the truth that there were better things to live for than they were yet striving after, and they asked Him, "What shall we do, that we might work the works of God?" Jesus had said He would "give" them eternal life, but they wanted to "work" for it. People are always making this mistake—instead of accepting life as God's gift they want to earn it. Jesus corrected their mistaken notion in His answer, "This is the work of God, that ye believe on him whom he hath sent." There is abundant opportunity for working for Christ, but working does not come first. Having received eternal life through Christ as a gift, we are to work, presenting our body as a living sacrifice unto God. The first thing in the true life is to believe on Christ, to accept Him as the revealing of God to us, to commit ourselves to Him, and to let Him live in us. Then Christ becomes the inspiration of our life. He lives in us, and our life is just the working out of His life in us.

The people had another question. Jesus had claimed to be the Messiah. What proof could He give? "What sign showest thou then?" They remembered that Moses had given their fathers manna, which proved that he was God's prophet, and they wanted Jesus to do something great which would prove that He was one sent of God. They were thinking all the time of common food, daily bread, for they were poor and life was hard for them. It is not uncommon in our own times to hear practically the same demand for a sign. People want prosperity as a mark of divine favor. They want to find some reward for following Christ. If their religion does not bring them bread and earthly comforts, they think it is not measuring up to its promises. Yet it is not in this way that Christ is to reward those who follow Him. He gives life, with inward joy and peace, and not ease and luxury and wealth.

Jesus answered their demand by telling them that He was doing for them a far greater work than Moses had done. Moses gave only bread for the body. It was not the true, the real bread—bread which answered life's deepest needs. Now God was giving them through Him true bread from heaven. It was not manna, but a person, a life—"the bread of God is he which cometh down from heaven, and giveth life unto the world." Nothing that grows out of the soil of earth will feed a human soul. We were made for God and for heaven, and must feed our immortal nature upon heavenly bread. Nothing but bread will satisfy hunger; nothing but Christ will meet the cravings of a life.

The people begin now to have a true thought of Christ's meaning, although it is still only a glimmering. Instead of asking further questions, however, they make a prayer, "Lord, evermore give us this bread." It was a good prayer, but when they made it they did not know what they were asking. They wanted the bread that had in it the power to bless, and yet they did not know what that bread was. It is often so in our praying—we have a dim vision of something very beautiful, very good, but it is only a shadowy vision to us. It is well that we have an Intercessor to take our poor, ignorant, mistaken prayers and interpret them aright for us, securing for us not what we thought we would get, nor what we would like to receive, but something better, richer, more divine.

Jesus then told them what the bread is that gives life and how they could get it. "I am the bread of life: he that cometh to me shall never hunger." Christ will satisfy all our desires. Some people imagine that the desires of the heart are sinful things, which must be torn out and destroyed. But that is not what Christ purposes to do. He says that our thirsts shall all be satisfied. He does not mean our sinful and selfish desires, the things of our lusts which we think would satisfy us, but our desires purified, such as Christ meant when He said, "Blessed are they which do hunger and thirst after righteousness: for they shall be filled."

Jesus reminded the people that they had not received Him as the one sent from God. "Ye also have seen Me, and believe not." That is, they had not eaten the bread of God of which He had been speaking to them. The assurance that follows is one of the most precious words of all the Bible, "Him that cometh to me I will in no wise cast out." No penitent who ever really comes to Christ shall be turned away.

The closing words of the passage are rich in their revealing of the purpose of Christ's coming into the world. He came to do His Father's will. His will was that of all that the Father had given the Son, the Son should lose nothing. Our part in His great purpose is also made very clear, "This is the will of him that sent me, that every one which seeth the Son, and believeth on him, may have everlasting life: and I will raise him up at the last day."

12

Jesus at the Feast of Tabernacles

Scripture Reading: John 7:37–46

In the chapter from which our passage is taken we find much about how different people regarded Jesus. His brothers did not believe on Him, and yet they urged Him to put on a bold face and go up to the feast. Just what their motive was we are not told. They seem to have wanted Him to make a display of His power at Jerusalem, to show the people there what He was and what He could do. Or perhaps they only taunted Him, professing to believe in His power. Jesus knew that the Jews at Jerusalem were plotting to kill Him, and as His "hour" was not yet come, He declined to go to the feast, but said to His brothers that they should go up. The world did not hate them—no one was plotting for their lives. They would not be molested if they went.

Later, however, Jesus did go up to the feast and taught in the temple. There was a great deal of discussion about Him then, and all sorts of opinions were expressed. The Jews wondered at the wisdom of His teaching, since He had not been trained in their schools, had not sat at the feet of their great rabbis, nor learned wisdom from them. Jesus gave the honor to His Father, saying, "My doctrine is not mine, but His that sent me" [v. 16]. The people wondered who He could be. They sought to take Him, to arrest Him, but no one laid His hand upon Him. There was a divine protection about Him, "because His hour was not yet come" [v. 30]. God watches over the lives of His servants who trust

Him, who are doing His work in the world, and lets no evil touch them. "Every man is immortal till His work is done."

On the last day of the feast Jesus uttered one of His most wonderful words. The temple was thronged, and He spoke, no doubt, in a loud voice that all might hear what He said. He made a great proclamation of His mission, as it were, offering life to all who would accept it. This is one of the great invitations of the gospel. Every word is full of meaning. "If any man thirst, let him come unto me, and drink." "If" marks the one and only condition to which the invitation is addressed. Of course, if we do not thirst we will not care to come to the well to drink. Souls are dying all around us, not because there is no water near, but because they are not thirsty. The words "any man" show us how universal the invitation is. It was not for "any Jew," nor "any intelligent man," nor "any man of good character," but for "any man." No one is left out or overlooked. All the invitations of the gospel are universal in their offer and in their adaptation. "All ye that are weary" receive the invitation to rest which Christ gives. All that are thirsty are invited to come and drink. All who hunger are bidden to eat the bread of life. There is not a person in the world who can say he is not invited to receive the salvation of Christ.

The word "thirst" describes the need which Christ is ready to supply. It is not bodily thirst, but thirst of the soul which He offers to quench. For the soul has its thirsts as well as the body, and there is no spring of water on earth at which these thirsts can be satisfied. The words "Let him come" show us the gate to the fountain flung wide open. There is no barrier or hindrance in the way. No person is shut out. The words remind us, however, that if we would have our thirst quenched by Christ we must come to Him. We must leave our dry, burning wastes where no water is found, and come away to Christ. We cannot find Christ in our sins. Our thirsts will never be satisfied unless we bring them to the fountain. The fact that we are dying of thirst is not alone sufficient to insure us of the quenching of the thirst. There must be a movement made by us, a movement toward Christ, a believing on Him, and acceptance of Him. The word "drink" tells us we must receive Christ Himself into our own hearts if we would have our thirst satisfied in Him. Merely going to the spring and looking at its sparkling waters will never quench anyone's thirst; he who would be satisfied must drink. This implies a voluntary act on the part of each individual. So, looking at Christ in all His beauty and power to help is not enough to bless us—we must take Him into our life by an act of our own, as one takes water in drinking from the fountain, or from a cup, and let His spirit fill our hearts.

Jesus next proceeded to tell of the result of coming to him. "He that believeth on me, as the scripture hath said, out of his belly shall flow rivers of living water." Believing is coming to Christ. To come is to believe, and then to trust oneself to Him. Believing is putting oneself into such personal relations with Christ that His life becomes ours. Every thirsty one who drinks of Christ has thenceforward in himself a fountain of life, a well of water, at which other thirsty ones may drink. This is a beautiful picture of a Christian life. We in turn become little wells of the water of life, filled by Christ Himself, from which the water flows that others may drink. Christ wants every one of us to repeat in our own little measure His great life of love. A spring of water, especially in a hot, oriental country, is invaluable. It is a center of great blessing. Weary ones come to it, and go on their way refreshed.

Someone describes an old homestead, deserted now, with its empty dwelling and unused porches and grass-grown walks. But there is one path on which no grass grows, which is trodden daily by many feet. It is the path to the spring. Nearly every passer-by turns aside to drink of the clear, sweet water of the spring. If we can be like such a spring of water by life's wayside, we shall be an untold blessing in the world. People who are weary, those who have troubled hearts, those who are in sorrow, those who are weak and faint in their journey—all may come and drink of the water of life in us and go on their way stronger and happier. It is a great thing to be a well of water by the wayside, but if we cannot be a well, we can at least be a little spring, giving out its little stream to quench the thirst of some who are weary.

The writer of this Gospel explains further His words about the fountain within the heart. He says that Jesus referred to the Spirit which they that believed on Him would receive. In talking with the woman at the well, Jesus told her that the water He would give those who should drink, would become a well of water in them, springing up into eternal life. The Spirit is God Himself. Hence those who receive the Spirit receive God Himself into their hearts. The new life in a believer is the divine life. It is Christ Himself. We may notice here, too, the two words that are used in the two passages, showing the growth of life in those who receive Christ. Jesus said to the woman that the water should become a well in the heart of the believer. Here He says that from within him who receives the divine Spirit shall flow rivers of living water. The word "rivers" suggests the possibilities of Christian life and influence. When the apostles first came to Christ, the beginning of life in them was very small. But when they went forth, after the day of Pentecost, full of the Holy Spirit, rivers of influence and blessing flowed from them. Our lives should increase in power as we become filled with Christ, and our reach of blessing should grow wider and wider.

A question of origin hindered the faith of some of those to whom Christ spoke that day. They thought that nothing good could come out of the despised province of Galilee. We are familiar already with this argument against the Messiahship of Jesus. Nathanael could not believe that any good thing could come out of Nazareth [see 1:46]. In His case, however, a personal knowledge of Christ instantly swept away His prejudices. A like prejudice applies in many other cases. Lowly circumstances bury much that is good and hinder its recognition among men. Yet we know that the Christ who slept His first sleep in a manger was the Son of God, and His power and glory have filled all earth and heaven. The unconscious testimony of the officers to the power of Jesus is very remarkable. Sent by the rulers to arrest Him, they came under the influence of His words as He spoke to the people. The spell was so strong that the officers returned without arresting Jesus, awed and unable to do anything, and when asked why they had not brought Him as a prisoner they replied, "Never man so spake." Those who come under the influence of Jesus are always impressed by the power of His presence. It is indeed true that "never man so spake." His words are the words of God. If we let them into our hearts they search us and find us. They are convincing words, showing us our sins and faults. They are upbuilding words, kindling and stimulating in us holy desires and aspirations, holding before us divine ideals of life and inspiring us to all heavenly attainments. They are transforming words, imprinting upon our lives the beauty of Christ and sending us to ministry of love. They are words of hope, revealing the true honor and blessedness of those who faithfully follow Christ. The most wonderful things in all this world are the words of Christ. "Never man so spake."

13

The Slavery of Sin

Scripture Reading: John 8:31–40

The title of this day's passage is suggestive. People who live in sin do not confess that they are slaves—they often think they are the only free men, and that Christians are the slaves. But in all this world there is no bondage so terrible as the bondage of sin. The salvation of Christ is not merely the taking away of sin's penalty—if this were all, it would be very incomplete. This would leave us unchanged in heart and life, loving still the old things and the old ways, not disposed to live the beautiful life of holiness, not having the love of Christ in our hearts. The salvation of Christ not only changes our relation to sin's penalty, setting us free, but brings us into God's family, making us God's children. It includes also the breaking of the power of sin over the life and the exaltation of the believer into the full liberty of Christ.

The passage begins by telling how we may be Christ's disciples. "If ye continue in my word, then are ye my disciples indeed." It is not enough to begin—abiding, continuing, is the test. A disciple is a learner, a pupil. It is not enough for one to enter a school. Mere enrollment will not make anyone a pupil. The pupil must continue in the school all through the long course, studying subject after subject, until he has mastered the whole curriculum. The same is true in business and in all callings. Life is a school. The course is a long one. It is not finished in a day, but fills all the days of one's life, The lessons, too, are long ones—

These lessons Thou dost give
To teach me how to live,
To do, to bear,
To get, to share,
To work and play,
And trust away.

The man who is faithful, who persists and perseveres unto the end is the one who succeeds. Missing lessons anywhere in the course leaves a blank. Many begin well, with diligence and earnestness, but lose interest in a little while, let their courage falter, and fail in their course. They grow weary and give up. This is true of many in all lines of work. A writer, speaking of the failure of some ministers to succeed, says that they enter the ministry with great enthusiasm and promise, but after a little while settle down into a dead level, lose their enthusiasm, and soon are heard of no more. It is true also in Christian life. There are thousands who begin to follow Christ, but who, when discouragement comes, give up and sink back again into the world. Jesus told His enthusiastic followers that an ardent beginning was not enough—they must continue unto the end.

Abiding in the word of Christ is given as the essential thing in discipleship. To abide in Christ's word is to obey Him, to do His commandments, not for a day or two only, but faithfully, all through life. It is not enough to know the will of Christ—we must do it. He said that if we are His friends we will do whatsoever He commands us. Obedience, therefore, is a test of discipleship, and obedience must be patient and continuous. It must be without break. It must look to the little things of duty. Dropped stitches in the web make breaks, and then the garment unravels.

There is another way in which we may abide in the word of Christ. Many of His words are promises. The forests in summer days are full of birds' nests. They are hidden in the trees, in among the leaves. The little birds know where they are, and when danger comes, when a storm arises, or when night draws on, they fly at once each to its own nest and hide away there in safety. So the promises of Christ are hidden in the Bible like nests in the trees, and thither we may fly in any danger or alarm, hiding there until the storm is past. There are no castles in this world so strong, so impregnable, so safe, as the words of Christ. "Heaven and earth shall pass away," said the Master, "but My words shall not pass away" [Matt. 24:35 {cf. Mark 13:31; Luke 21:33}].

Jesus then told His disciples how they could be made free from sin's bondage. "Ye shall know the truth, and the truth shall make you free." Christ is a deliverer. He came to open prisons and lead captives out to liberty. There is a story of a stranger who entered an oriental city, and as he walked through the marketplace he saw many birds in cages. His face grew sad, and by and by he asked the price of one of the birds, and paying for it, opened the cage door. The bird flew out and, rising a little way in the air, caught a glimpse of its native mountains far away, and then flew swiftly toward them. The traveler then bought the other cages, one by one, and set the birds free, until all of them had been liberated. That is what Christ, our Liberator, would do for every one of us in our captivity. He would set us free, breaking our chains, opening our prison doors, that we may fly away toward home and safety.

It is the truth, Jesus says, that makes men free. So long as they are ignorant of Christ and of His power to liberate them, they remain in bondage. But when His emancipating word comes to them, they are free. From old Crusading days comes this story: A certain king, on his way back from the Holy Land, was captured by his enemies and cast into prison—where, none of his friends knew. The king had a favorite minstrel who determined to find his master. He went throughout the country, pausing before the door of every prison, singing the songs he had been known to sing in the palace of his king. He hoped to find the captive monarch with his songs. Long he wandered in vain, but at last, as he stood one day before a prison window and sang, he heard a voice within, the voice of him he sought, responding. The old songs sung at the prison windows were heard by the captive, who was thus discovered and soon released. So when the messengers of Christ sing the songs of Christ's love before prison doors, those within hear, and the truth makes them free.

The Jews resented the suggestion that they were in any sense slaves. "They answered him, We be Abraham's seed, and were never in bondage to any man." By what species of deception they imagined themselves free, when at that very hour Roman soldiers stood guard about their city, we cannot understand. But it is the same with spiritual slaves. It is a great privilege to have good ancestry; it is good capital with which to start in life; but beyond a certain point it does not count for anything. The first question may be, "Who was your father?" But the next will surely be, "Who are you?" Every man must bear His own burden. In the end, everyone must stand for himself. These people were depending upon blood, upon their fine ancestry. Sin plays strange tricks with men. Insane people sometimes deck themselves out with tinsel, and imagine that they are some great personages. The devil puts similar notions into the heads of His deluded followers, making them think they are free, when in reality they are pitiful slaves.

Jesus very promptly assured the rulers of the people that they were not free men. He said to them, "Whosoever committeth sin is the servant of sin." Sin makes slaves of those who follow it. Everyone is the servant of some master, the only question being who the master is. Christ asks His disciples to take His yoke and to come under bondage to Him. His is not the bondage of compulsion, but of love and joy. Christ is a blessed Master. His yoke is easy; serving Him lifts one up to eternal glory. What sort of master is sin? What does sin do for its slaves? What life did it ever ennoble, lift up, or bless?

There is a story of a man to whom the devil came, ordering a chain of a certain length. Coming for the chain at the appointed time, he ordered it made longer, and went away. When at last it was finished, he came again, and with it bound the poor man who had fashioned its links at his bidding. So sinners are everywhere building their own prison walls and with their own hands fashioning chains to bind them forever. There is only One in all the world who can set men free from the bondage of sin—Christ Himself. "If the Son therefore shall make you free, ye shall be free indeed." There is no other one who can do this for us. He breaks the chains of personal enslavement on all who follow Him, putting His grace into their hearts and enabling them to overcome evil habits and conquer their evil nature. Sin begins with threads, and weaves ropes and cables about its slaves until they are bound hand and foot in bonds they have no power to break. But even those who are thus bound, Christ can set free. We all need Christ as liberator, emancipator, for we all have chains of some kind forming about us, chains of habit, of desire, of passion, of disposition, which will bind us and drag us down as slaves, unless we come to Christ and have Him free us from our bondage and make us free indeed.

Jesus told the people further that day that, while they were genealogically Abraham's seed, yet they were continually doing inappropriate things, things which the children of Abraham should not do. They were seeking to kill Him, because His word was not allowed to have free course in them. This was not the work of free men. Love is the law of freedom, and love was not in their hearts while they were so bitter against Him. He told them that if they were really Abraham's children they would do the works of Abraham. Their doing the works of the devil proved that they were the devil's children, and not God's. It was not complimentary to these rulers, church dignitaries, to be called children of the devil, but Jesus read their hearts and saw murder and falsehood there under all their fair-seeming and back of their boasted godly ancestry. Wherever these feelings and intentions are found they indicate the devil's work. As the fruit of the Spirit in the heart is love, joy, peace, long-suffering, meekness, gentleness and kindness, so the fruits of the devil's indwelling are hatred, malice, envy, jealousy, and bitterness. If our lives have only the devil's characteristics, we cannot make claim to being God's children.

14

Healing the Man Born Blind

Scripture Reading: John 9:1–11

The narrative of the opening of this blind man's eyes is given only in John's gospel. It is recorded with much minuteness, not merely because of the greatness of the miracle, but also because it was a sign of the spiritual enlightening which Jesus came to give to men. The cure seems to have been performed without request, either from the blind man himself or from any of his friends. The thought of it arose in the compassionate heart of Jesus. The case was pitiable enough. No other physical calamity is sorer than blindness. It shuts a man away in the darkness so that he cannot see anything of the beauty of God's world about him. Besides, blindness made this man helpless. He had to depend on others for everything. Another's hand must lead him wherever he went, another's eyes must see for him, and he must get through another's mind his only dim ideas of form, color and beauty.

The case was still sadder because the man never had seen. Those who have their eyes for a time and then lose them may cherish the memories of the beautiful things they once looked upon. But this man never had seen. He could form no conception of colors, nor could he understand anything about the appearance of objects. The world was a great dark blank to him. Then the blindness of this man was incurable. He was absolutely hopeless in the darkness. His poverty was an added element of distress in his condition. He sat and begged for alms,

454

receiving only such pittances as passers-by grudgingly gave him. No wonder that when Jesus saw him sitting there, saw his blank, sad face, knowing all that lay behind it, and beheld his hand outstretched, He pitied him.

There is another blindness, which is still worse than natural blindness. It is the blindness of the soul's eyes. There are those who see well the beautiful things of nature, but who see nothing of the still more beautiful things of God's love and grace. They have no eyes for the loveliness of righteousness and truth. They see not the divine Hand that moves everywhere in providence. They never behold the face of Jesus Christ, in which shines all the glory of God. There is a whole world of spiritual beauty lying about them, of which they see nothing—the love of God, the divine promises, the hopes of heaven, all the joys of salvation. Men of the world hear devout Christians speak with rapture of the joys of Christian faith and of Christian experience, and say, "I cannot see any such joys as these in religion." It is because they are blind.

In those days the belief was almost universal that every trouble was due to special sin in the person. The friends of Job insisted that the patriarch must have been a great sinner, to bring upon himself so much of the disfavor of God. There is much of the same feeling found yet in the world, even among Christian people. Misfortune is associated in many men's minds with guilt. We often hear it said by those who have had some trouble, "I wonder what sins God is punishing me for now." The disciples, when they saw this poor man sitting in his blindness, imagined that sin either in him or in some ancestor was the cause of his calamity.

It was a very instructive word that Jesus spoke in reply to the question, "Master, who did sin?" He said, "Neither hath this man sinned, nor his parents." He did not mean that the man was sinless, but that his trouble had not been produced by sin. Of course, suffering may sometimes be traced to sin. Sometimes the connection is so obvious that no one can doubt it; sometimes it is so obscure that no one may certainly seek to trace it. But in the case of this man's blindness there was no such cause, and our Lord meant to warn the man's neighbors against the tendency in their minds to look into his life suspiciously and uncharitably seeking some cause in himself or his ancestors for his misfortune. We never should ask, in any case of suffering, "Who is to blame?" Rather, we should set about giving what help it may be in our power to give. Jesus said that the blindness came upon this man "that the works of God should be made manifest in him." His misfortune now became an occasion for the display of mercy. Whatever the cause of the man's blindness, it called now for human sympathy and every possible effort to relieve the trouble and do good to the sufferer. It is interesting also to notice that the man's blindness became a blessing to him in the end, in that it brought him to Christ and resulted in his spiritual awakening as well as in giving of sight. A case of trouble of any kind should not set us to gossiping about who is to blame, but rather should call us to prompt efforts to give help or relief.

Before curing the man, Jesus spoke of the necessity of promptness in doing God's work. He said, "I must work the works of Him that sent me, while it is day." There is no time to lose. Even Jesus felt the pressure of the shortness of the opportunity and the need for doing promptly what had been given Him to do. There are two suggestions in the words: The first is that every one of us has a task to do, and it must be done in our brief day, or it never can be done at all. The other thought is that there is a time during which our deeds must be done, or they never can be done at all. We must sow in the seedtime—when this is past there will be no use in our scattering the grain upon the fields. We must put the wheat into the mill while the water is in the race, for when the water is gone we cannot grind. We must teach the child while he is young, for when he is grown up there will be no opportunity to put the lessons into its heart. It will then be too late. We must visit our sick friend while he is sick—there will be no use in coming with our kindness when he is well, or when he is dead. We must show sympathy to those who are in trouble while the trouble is upon them—it will not be worthwhile to try to help when they lie defeated in the dust. The disciples slept in the Garden during the hour when they should have been watching, and then Jesus said to them, with infinite pathos, "Sleep on now, and take your rest." There was no use in waiting and watching now, for the traitor was already at the gate.

A strange thing in this miracle was the use of the means to which Jesus resorted. "He spat on the ground, and made clay of the spittle, and he anointed the eyes of the blind man with the clay." Jesus did not need the help of any means in working His healings, as human physicians do, for He had all power. Evidently the means were used for the effect their use would produce upon the man's own mind. The blind man had not thought of the possibility of receiving his sight. He seems never to have heard of Jesus as one who could open his eyes. There was in him, therefore, no expectation that he might be cured. Hence the first thing to be done was to arouse his hope and start faith in him. This Jesus did by beginning the processes of healing, spitting on the ground, making paste, and putting it on the sightless eyes. This must have started expectation of cure and faith. Then the man was bidden to go and wash in the Pool of Siloam.

This seems strange, too. He could by a word have healed him, not requiring of him the long walk across the city. Why did He require him to go away and wash? The answer is that the act still further encouraged faith and obedience in the man. We have a similar instance in the case of Naaman. Elisha bade him go and wash seven times in the Jordan [see 2 Kgs. 5:10]. There was no specific virtue in Jordan water—it never had been known to be a cure for leprosy. But the man must obey, thus showing his faith and his submission to the will of God. If he had not washed in Jordan, he would not have been cleansed. A similar test of faith was required in the ten lepers whom Jesus sent to the priests [Luke 17:12–19]. The journey itself would not cleanse them. Yet, if they had not gone they would not have been cured. "As they went, they were cleansed." This blind man would not have been cured of his blindness that day if he had not obeyed and taken the journey to the Pool of Siloam. He must cooperate with Christ in his healing. Some people wait for the evidences of salvation before they will fully accept Christ. But the salvation will not come until they take the step which proves their faith.

The blind man obeyed promptly and eagerly. It was not easy for him to take this long walk through the town. On his eyes were the unsightly patches of clay, and people would laugh at him as they saw him groping along the street. But he did not mind this—he would not be laughed out of the cure which was now so near at hand. Perhaps his friends told him it was all foolishness—that mud never yet had been known to cure anyone's blindness, and that Siloam water had no power to open sightless eyes. Still the man pressed on, amid the laughing people, until he came to the pool. There he washed, and lo—his eyes, which never had seen before, were instantly opened.

When the man's old neighbors saw him going about with his eyes opened, they asked him how the wonderful transformation had come to him. They could scarcely believe that it was the same man they used to know. When a man's life is changed from evil ways to good, people are amazed. In every life conversion works a change. If a man is not in some way better, sweeter in spirit, kindlier, truer, with a more radiant face, and a new light in his eyes, his conversion has not made much impression.

The man's prompt and simple confession of Christ as his Healer shows his sincerity and earnestness. When the people asked the man how his eyes were opened, he answered, "A man that is called Jesus made clay, and anointed mine eyes." He was not afraid to tell how he had been cured. When Jesus has saved us we should never hesitate to confess Him before the world.

15

Jesus the Good Shepherd

Scripture Reading: John 10:1–18

Shepherd is a very homely name for Christ, and yet as used in the Scriptures it is wonderfully rich in its suggestiveness. In the Old Testament there are many allusions to God under this figure of a shepherd. The twenty-third psalm is a Bible classic. Perhaps no other portion of the Scriptures is so widely known or has had such a ministry of blessing in the world as this homely little Psalm. The ancient Christians found in the name "shepherd" a beautiful interpretation of the character and work of Christ. In the catacombs at Rome no other picture is so common as that of the Good Shepherd.

The tenth chapter of John's gospel is so full of great teachings that only a few leading suggestions can be pointed out. At the beginning of the chapter attention is called to the sheepfold. Applied in a spiritual sense, the fold is the shelter which our Good Shepherd provides for His sheep. The sheepfold is an enclosure surrounded by a wall into which in the evening the shepherds lead their flocks, committing them for the night to the care of the undershepherd, who guards the door. In the morning the several shepherds come and knock, and the porter opens the door, and each shepherd calls His own sheep, which know His voice and come out to him. He then leads them out to the pasture for the day. The fold is enclosed by a wall. A wall means defense and shelter. The Bible says much about God's keeping of His people. We are not told, however, that the Lord builds a refuge for them, but that He Himself is the refuge—the divine love and power being a wall of protection between His people and all danger. The safest place in all the world for the sheep of Christ is in the place of confidence and obedience. We have but to obey our Shepherd, staying within the fold, to have His protection. We have only to do God's will, to go where the Good Shepherd leads, to abide where He puts us, in order to be sure of divine defense.

The shepherd's love and care are individual and personal. "He calleth His own sheep by name." It is easy enough for us to understand how a Syrian shepherd may know each of His sheep by name. His flock is small, and he can readily know each one. But when we think of the millions who are in Christ's flock, it seems strange to us that He should know and call each one of all His by name. Yet the truth is made very clear in the Scriptures. It is as easy for our Good Shepherd to know each of His millions personally as for any human mother to know the name of each one of her little group of children. There is great comfort in this teaching. We are not lost in the crowd. Love always individualizes its object. We cannot love a crowd—we may pity a city in distress, as after the horrors of an earthquake, and yet not know one person in it. But if we have a brother, a child, or a friend among the sufferers, we know the one. Our Good Shepherd loves each one of His own.

A little child of poverty, who had been adopted by a kind man, said he was glad to belong to somebody. It is pleasant for us to know that we belong to Christ. He speaks of His sheep as "His own." They are His own because the Father gave them to Him. "Thine they were, and thou gavest them me" [17:6]. They are His own also because He gave Himself for them. "Ye are not your own; for ye were bought with a price" [1 Cor. 6:19, 20]. They are His own, further, because they have voluntarily given themselves to Him. It is very sweet to think of ourselves in this way as belonging to Christ. The words suggest love, closeness of relation, tenderness of affection.

The Good Shepherd presents Himself also as the Guide of His flock. He "leadeth them out." "He goeth before them, and the sheep follow him." He does not drive them—He leads them, and they follow Him. They love Him and also trust His guidance. They know that they are safe wherever He takes them. Sheep need to be led; they have no such instinct for finding their own way as most other animals have. Set certain kinds of dogs down anywhere, miles from where they have been staying before, and they will find the way home by instinct. You cannot lose a dog. But a sheep cannot find its way anywhere. The same is true of human souls. They get lost very easily, and are willful and wayward. They need to be led, and without the divine guidance never could get home. But if Christ leads, we who are His sheep must obediently and cheerfully follow Him. The reason we have so many troubles in life and get so often into difficulty and danger is because we do not follow Him as we should.

Not only are we to follow Christ, but we are to follow Him only. "A stranger will they not follow, but will flee from him: for they know not the voice of strangers." This is always true of sheep. A stranger's voice frightens them, and even when he calls them by their right names, in imitation of their shepherd's voice, they will yet flee from him rather than come to him. They know His voice to be strange and will not answer His calls. It ought to be so with Christ's sheep, too. They should know when the voice they hear is not really their Shepherd's, and should not give heed to it. Voices of strangers continually fall upon the ears of young Christians, especially of inexperienced Christians. There are many temptations which would lure them away from the fold into paths of wandering, ending in ruin. There are false teachings which seek to dishonor Christ and make His believing ones love Him less and trust Him less confidently. There are solicitations of pleasure which lack the note of purity and truth—voices of the stranger. There are invitations to things that appear to offer gain, to promise reward, but which, in reality, have only loss and hurt and ruin to give. Everywhere the voices of strangers are heard, and, unfortunately, too many are willing to listen to these voices. Those who do are lured away, often into peril and destruction. We need to be sure that the voices we hear are of the Shepherd, calling us only and always to things that are beautiful and true and good.

Not only is Jesus the Good Shepherd, but He is also the Door. "I am the door of the sheep." A door is a way of entrance—those who come through Christ are admitted into the blessedness of God. As many as receive Him become children of God [see 1:12]. This is a Door that is always open. We need never fear coming to it and finding it shut. In the representation of heaven as a city, in Revelation, there are twelve gates, three on each of the four sides. No matter from which way we approach, we shall always find a door of entrance.

When we enter the fold through Christ as the Door, we find provision with Him. "By me if any man enter in, he shall be saved, and shall go in and out, and find pasture." The shepherd looks well to the feeding of his flock. He leads the sheep into green pastures. He searches everywhere to find food for them. When one spot is burnt up with the summer heat and has no more provision for his flock, the shepherd takes them elsewhere. So does Christ. Wherever He leads us, we may always be sure that He is taking us to some good, some provision, some blessing. The Bible is Christ's pastureland, and the pasture there is always good. Wherever we open it we find something to feed our hunger. Other books may have poisonous teachings, but every word in the Bible is wholesome food for our lives. The fields of providence are also Christ's fields. In all the common ways of life we find food waiting for us. We may trust Christ absolutely, because we know that wherever He leads us, He is always taking care of us in the right way. When the shepherd led his flock through the dark valley, it was not to terrify them, but to get them to a place where they would find pasture. Sometimes Christ leads His people through dark ways, struggle, trial, loss, but it is always because these are the ways to some good which He has in waiting for them.

The Good Shepherd loves His sheep, loves them so much that He stops at no sacrifice in protecting them and saving them. "The good shepherd giveth his life for the sheep." The Eastern shepherd often has to fight battles for His flock. David tells of killing a lion and a bear in defense of his sheep. Sometimes the shepherd in defending his flock against wild animals is himself, wounded—sometimes he even loses his life in protecting them. Our Good Shepherd has wounds upon Him, and if we ask when He received them, His answer is, "In defending My own."

At present Christ's sheep are widely dispersed. They are scattered over all the world. But at last there will be a great home-gathering, when all the flocks shall be brought together. "Other sheep I have, which are not of this fold: them also I must bring . . . and there shall be one fold and one Shepherd." One of the saddest things about the church as it is in the world today is the separation of believers into different denominations. In heaven all shall be brought together, from the north, the south, the east and the west, and all shall be found at last in the one flock with the one Shepherd.

16

The Abundant Life

Scripture Reading: John 10:10

Christ always wants abundant life. He is infinitely patient with the weak, but He wishes that we be strong. He accepts the feeblest service, but He desires us to serve Him with the whole heart. The smallest faith, even like a grain of mustardseed, has power with God and can remove mountains, but God is best pleased when we have a faith that quails at no difficulties, and accomplishes impossibilities. A believer may have but the smallest flame of life, and yet Christ will not despise it. "Smoking flax shall He not quench." There is a picture of one bending over a handful of cold embers on the hearth, as if he would get them to glow again. Underneath the picture are the words, "It may be there is a spark left yet." This is a picture of the infinite patience of Christ with those who are almost dead spiritually. So long as there is even a spark left He will seek in every way to make the dead live. But with all His gentleness toward the barely living, He wants abundance of life in all His followers. "I am come that they might have life, and that they might have it more abundantly."

Every picture of Christian life which our Lord uses suggests fullness and richness of life. Fruit is the test and measure of it. The fruitless branch is taken away, and the fruitful branch is pruned that it may bring forth more fruit. "Herein is my Father glorified, that ye bear much fruit; so shall ye be my disciples" [15:8]. To the woman at the well Jesus spoke of spiritual life beginning in the heart as a well or spring of water. When we receive Christ, a fountain of divine life is opened in our hearts. At first, however, it is only a little spring, a mere beginning of the life of God and heaven in us. Then, later, Jesus said, "He that believeth on me . . . out of his belly shall flow rivers of living water" [7:38]. The little spring by and by becomes rivers. Christ came to give life and to give it abundantly.

There have been those in all ages whose lives became like rivers in the fullness and richness of their flow. This was true of John and Peter and Paul. Streams of blessing and good poured out from them which reached many lands and thousands of people, and which are flowing today, wherever the gospel is known. There are those whose influence for good touches countless lives.

What is an abundant life? It does not need to be a conspicuous life, one which makes itself heard on the streets. There are some good people who seem to suppose that they are living for a purpose only when they are making themselves seen and heard. Yet there are those who are rich in outward incident but poor in inward experience. One may have abundant life and yet move among men so quietly as almost to be unheard and unknown. Of our Lord Himself it was written, "He shall not strive, nor cry; neither shall any man hear His voice in the streets" [Matt. 12:19]. No other ever had such fullness and abundance of life as He had, and yet no other ever lived and worked so quietly as He did. Noise is not force. The real power in life is in its influence, in its character and personality.

Our Lord puts first in the Beatitudes—humility. "Blessed are the poor in spirit" [Matt. 5:3]. It is the lowly ones who live nearest to the heart of Christ and have most of His life in them. Not those who fill the largest places in the eyes of men, even in the church, nor those whose works attract the most attention, have most of God in them, but those who live humbly, with no thought of human recognition or praise.

The abundant life need not be known by its large money gifts. The tendency in these days is to measure every man's value to the world by charities. Money has its value. Those who contribute to charity, to education, to religion, if their gifts are wisely bestowed, are blessing the world. It is the bounden duty of all who possess wealth to use it in doing good. But money is never the best gift we can bestow on others, and those who cannot give money may yet be really generous givers.

A man's money is not the only thing a man has to give. He can give love, sympathy, encouragement, hope, cheer, and these gifts will help where money would be only a mockery. There are great needs which money has no power to satisfy. There are sorrows money cannot alleviate. It was one of the conceits of ancient poetry that the oarsman Charon was permitted once to visit this world and from the mountaintop to look down upon the cities and palaces and works of men. As he went away he said: "Why, all these people are spending their time building birds' nests. No wonder they fail and are ashamed." Building birds' nests to be swept away in the floods, when they might be building palaces of beauty to abide forever. If all Christians would put the same earnestness into their Christian life and work which they put into their bird-nest building, what would they not accomplish for the kingdom of Christ!

Jesus never gave money. Yet the world has never known such a lavish giver as He was. Imagine Jesus going about with His hands full of coins and dispensing them wherever He went among the poor, the lame, the blind, the beggars, the lepers, the sick—money, and nothing else. What a poor, paltry service His would have been, in comparison with the wonderful ministry of kindness and love He performed in His journeyings through the land! Suppose He had given a coin to the woman who lay at His feet crying for her poor daughter's deliverance. Would that have comforted her? Suppose He had put a handful of money in the hands of the blind beggar at Jericho, instead of opening His eyes—would the generous gift have meant as much to the poor man?

"Silver and gold have I none; but such as I have give I thee" [Acts 3:6], said Peter at the Beautiful Gate to the lame man. Then the man was lame no more. Was not the healing a better gift to the poor man than if he had filled His hands with coins? Was it not better that the man should be made strong, so that he would not need to beg anymore, than that he should have been supported a day or two longer in poverty and mendicancy?

The abundant life may not have money to give, and yet it may fill a whole community with blessings through its gifts. It may go out with its sympathy, its words of comfort, its inspirations of cheer and hope, and may make countless hearts braver and stronger. Let the well of love

in your heart spring up and pour out rivers. That is what it means to
have life abundantly. One writes of another:

> I never crossed your threshold with a grief
>   But that I went away without it; never came
>   Heart-hungry but you fed me, eased the blame,
> And gave the sorrow solace and relief.
>
> I never left you but I took away
>   The love that drew me to your side again
>   Through that wide door that never could remain
> Quite closed between for a little day.

That is what should be said of the ministry of every one of us to
others who turn to us with their needs, their heart-hungers, and their
sorrows—we should be their comfort, strength and help. They should
go away helped. We should always have bread in our hands to give to
those who are hungry. We should always have cheer for those who come
to us disheartened and discouraged. "Can I help thee?" should be our
heart's question, whoever it is that stands before us. The life Christ came
to give is only love—God's love poured into veins, and through us to
those who lack. It is more love we need when we cry out for more life
and more power to do good. It is love that the world needs. Nothing
else will make people happier or better. Ethics will not heal broken
hearts, nor comfort those who are in sorrow, nor quiet a guilty conscience. The only abundant life is the life that is abundant in love.

How can we get this abundant life? Most of us are conscious of the
poverty and thinness of our spiritual life. We faint easily under our
burdens or in our struggles. We are not living victoriously. We are not
filled with the spirit of Christ. We may have other things—we may
have plenty of money; we may have pleasure, power, honor; our hands
may be full of tasks. But there is only a little of God in us, only a little
of heaven. Our brains may be teeming with plans, projects and dreams
of success, but of spiritual life our veins are scant.

Christ came to give us just what we need—life. We can get it only
from Him, and we can take it only as His gift. We have no conception, we who are merely living, with no great, strong, victorious life,
what it is possible for us to become as Christians in this world, if only
we would let the life of Christ possess us fully, wholly.

Henry van Dyke tells of two streams that emptied into the sea.

One was a sluggish rivulet, in a wide, fat, muddy bed; and every day the tide came in and drowned out the poor little stream, and filled it with bitter brine. The other was a vigorous, joyful, brimming mountain river, fed from the unfailing spring among the hills; and all the time it swept the salt water back before it, and kept itself pure and sweet; and when the tide came, it only made the fresh water rise higher and gather new strength by the delay; and ever the living stream poured forth into the ocean its tribute of living water—the symbol of that influence which keeps the ocean of life from turning into a Dead Sea of wickedness.

But there is no way to save our lives from being swallowed up in the bitter floods of sin in this world but by having them full of divine life. A feeble stream of spiritual life has no power to resist the evil of the world. Only the abundant life can keep itself pure and sweet.

A wild gypsy girl was sitting for her picture in an artist's studio in Germany. Opposite to her as she sat hung an unfinished picture of the crucifixion. One day the girl asked, "Master, who is that?"

"That is Jesus Christ, Son of Mary," replied the painter.

"Was He a very bad man, that they treated Him so cruelly?"

"Oh, no! He was the best Man that ever lived," said the artist, carelessly.

"Tell me more about Him," pleaded the girl, who had never heard of Jesus before.

Day after day as the girl came to the studio her eyes remained fixed upon the picture of the Christ on His cross. When her sittings were ended and she was going away, she whispered: "Master, how can you help loving Him who, you say, died for you? If anybody had loved me like that, oh, I'd like to die for him."

Has not the love of Christ for you power to win you to love Him?

Great little story

17

The Raising of Lazarus

Scripture Reading: John 11:32–45

The eleventh chapter of John's gospel introduces us to an experience of our Lord's life which will ever be unspeakably precious to His friends. Here we enter a home which was in a very real way our Lord's own home. Here He found love which was unspeakably rich and dear to His heart in its comforts and blessings. The house in which Martha and Mary and Lazarus lived was one place in which Jesus was always sure of welcome when He came to their door weary, and always sure of refuge when He came from the strifes and enmities of the world.

Into this home there came sore and fatal sickness. Jesus was absent. When Lazarus was stricken, a messenger was sent to Jesus bearing the simple message from the burdened hearts, "He whom thou lovest is sick" [11:3]. We would say that such a message would have brought the Master at once. We think at least that if we had been in His place, we would have made all haste, traveling by night and day, to get to our dying friend. But, strange to say, Jesus, after receiving the message, lingered two days longer where He was. Evidently He was not alarmed, although He knew all the circumstances. Explaining His delay in starting to the home of His friends, we have this remarkable statement: "Jesus loved Martha, and her sister, and Lazarus. When therefore he heard that he was sick, he abode at that time two days in the place where he was."

469

That is, it was just because He loved the sisters and Lazarus that He abode two days longer before He sent out to minister to them. When He reached Bethany at length, Lazarus had been dead four days. In the narrative we have our Lord's conversation with the sisters. Then we have the exquisite picture of the weary and wayworn Christ, standing beside His friends in their grief, weeping with them. But we have more than tears—the same One who weeps calls the dead from the grave, and gives back to the darkened home its light and joy.

Martha was the first to meet Jesus when He reached the village. It was outside the home, in some quiet place. Presently He sent her to call Mary. The message was, "The Master is come, and calleth thee." Mary was sitting in the house in deep grief. Evidently the sisters and brother were bound together in very warm ties of affection. Probably they were orphans, keeping up the old home after father and mother were gone. A good brother is a great comfort and blessing to His sisters, especially when they have neither parent to lean on. Great, therefore, was the grief when Lazarus died. Jesus had been a friend to them all, and when Mary had learned that He had come and that He wished to see her, she rose up quickly and hastened to Him. Jesus sends the same message to everyone who is in sorrow, "The Master is come, and calleth thee." He wants to comfort His friends who are in sorrow. He bids them come to Him with their trouble. No matter how deep the grief is, we should always do as Mary did—hasten to Jesus. He is the only true Comforter.

When Mary came to Jesus she fell down at His feet. A true picture of Mary should always show her there. Mary seems to be grieving, almost complaining, at the Master's long delay in coming to the sad home. She told Jesus that if He had been there, her brother had not died. Perhaps that was true. So far as we are told no one died ever in the presence of Jesus. But the saving of Lazarus from dying was not the best thing for even divine power and love to do that day. When the word came that Lazarus was sick, Jesus said to His disciples that the sickness was "for the glory of God, that the Son of God may be glorified thereby." Curing His friend's fever would have glorified God and His Son, but raising him from the dead was a greater glory. When a friend of ours is sick, it is right for us to pray for His restoration to health, but we do not know that that is the best thing. Perhaps the death of our loved one may be a better thing and more for God's glory than His living longer would be.

We do not know where God wants us to serve Him, nor how He would have us honor Him. It is better that we leave it all with our great Intercessor. The "if" was not a word of faith, but it is a word we are all too apt to use in like cases. "If we had sent for another physician," we say, or, "If we had tried some other remedies, our friend would not have died." But such words are not the language of the quietest trust in God. We are to do what seems to be wisest at the moment, with all the light we have, and then have no regrets or doubts afterwards.

The shortest verse in the Bible is that which contains only the two words, "Jesus wept." This was His first way of comforting Mary. He entered into full and deep sympathy with her. This little verse is a great window in Christ's breast, showing us the depths of His very heart. It tells us that our blessed Lord, though so glorious, has a tender love for us and is touched by all our griefs. This alone is a wonderful comfort to those who are in trouble. A little child visited a neighbor who had lost her baby, and came home and told her mother that she had been comforting the sorrowing one. Her mother asked her how, and she said, "I cried with her." It does us good when we are in trouble to know that some other one cares, feels with us. It brings a sense of companionship into our loneliness. It puts another shoulder under our load. Sympathy halves our sorrows. But when it is Jesus who cares and is touched, weeps with us, and comes up close beside us in gentle companionship, it is wondrous comfort indeed.

When Jesus came to the grave, He gave command that the stone should be taken away. Could He not have taken it away Himself by a word, without any human help? Certainly He could. The power that called the dead back to life could easily have lifted back the piece of rock from the door of the tomb to let the risen man out of His prison. But there is always something left for human hands to do. Christ honors us by making us coworkers with Himself, both in providence and in grace. He makes His work dependent, too, upon our fidelity in doing our little part. He still wants us to take away the stones that shut our friends in their prison.

The manner of the raising of Lazarus is suggestive. We may place together all Christ's calls to the dead He raised. To the daughter of Jairus, His words were, "Maiden, arise." To the young man of Nain, He said, "Young man, I say unto thee, Arise." He calls neither of these by name. Neither of them had been personally known to Him. But Lazarus was His own familiar friend; and therefore, He called him by His dear household name. Death does not destroy personality. Lazarus, in the region of the dead, knew His name, heard it called, and answered to it. In the coming of Lazarus from the grave at the call of Christ we have a glimpse of what will take place at the final resurrection, when the same voice will be heard by all the dead.

When Lazarus came forth at Christ's call, his friends had something to do in assisting him. Jesus bade them, "Loose him, and let him go." His limbs were bound about so that he could not walk freely. It was necessary that these wrappings should be removed in order that he might be free in his movements. Note Christ's economy in miracle. He did not by supernatural power take off these bandages, though He could have done so. Nor did He with His own hands unwrap the clothes and remove them. He bade His friends to do this, thus making them coworkers with Himself. There is here a parable of spiritual things. When a soul hears Christ's voice and comes from its grave of death, there are still many old wrappings of sin, the graveclothes of an old life, chains of bad habits, the bonds of evil companionships and friendships. Lazarus walking forth from his grave with his limbs bound about and his freedom hindered, is a picture of every saved life at the first. The removing of these bonds and hindrances is work which Christ gives us to do for our friends who are beginning their new life. We are to set our friends free. We are to help them overcome their old habits and break off their sinful associations, and in all ways to seek to set them free for loving service.

18

The Supper at Bethany

Scripture Reading: John 12:1–11

The feast given to Jesus was in recognition of the great blessing He had brought to the home in Bethany in the calling back of Lazarus from death. The record says, "They made him a supper." He had turned their sorrow into joy, and the sisters' hearts were full of gratitude. No wonder they were grateful. There are many homes in which this story is read where there is even greater reason for gratitude than there was in this Bethany household. The dead have been brought back from the graves of spiritual death, and live in joy and beauty. Should not Christ be honored in all such households? There, too, should feasts be made for Him, feasts of love and thanksgiving. In every home, also, in which sorrow has been a guest and where Christ has come bringing comfort, there is reason for gratitude.

There are some persons who are well-known in the Gospels by certain features which always appear in them. Wherever she is seen, Martha is known by her serving. Some people criticize her for this feature of life and speak as if she were to blame for the way she took of honoring her Master. It was too material. But Jesus did not say so. He did not reprove Martha for her careful housekeeping, nor for her hearty hospitality, nor for the pains she took to provide well for Him and His disciples. What He reproved in her was not the serving, but her fretfulness, her worry, and her nervous impatience with her sister Mary because she did not choose to honor the Master in the same way. While Martha was busy serving, eagerly preparing a meal for her guests who had come in from their journey, Mary slipped away and sat down at her Guest's feet, to listen to His wonderful words. When Martha saw her there, she was vexed, and giving way to her feeling, chided her, almost petulantly, and spoke almost bitterly to Jesus, as if He ought to send Mary back to her tasks in the household.

It was this that Jesus did not like in Martha—not her serving, but her hurt feeling toward her sister, and her impatient complaint of her to the Master. There is great need for Marthas in the world. Beautiful as is the Mary-spirit, it would not do if all women were Marys, for who then would do the work which needs so much to be done in countless households? For instance, a wife and mother who would spend all her time in Bible-reading, giving no thought to the domestic duties, would not make a very happy home for her family, and certainly would not bless the Master. There is need for service.

> Yea, Lord! Yet some must do
> Life's daily taskwork; some
> Who fain would sing, must toil
> Amid earth's dust and moil
> While lips are dumb!

While we recognize Martha by her serving, we recognize Mary also by her place at the Master's feet. We see her always there, and she is always beautiful there. First, she sat there as a learner, drinking in the Teacher's words. Then she came to Him by and by in her great grief, and found comfort. We see her here again in this incident in the same posture. Now, however, it is at the feast made in Christ's honor. "Then took Mary a pound of ointment of spikenard, very costly, and anointed the feet of Jesus." Another Gospel tells us that she first poured the ointment on His head. Her act was an expression of the tenderest, most humble, most reverent love. We should bring Christ the best we have to bring. The fragrant ointment was a beautiful symbol of the love of a gentle heart. We should bring Christ our deepest gratitude and purest affection. No words could express the love Mary bore to her Master, so she put it into an act.

The record says that the house was filled with the odor of the ointment. Indeed, the whole world has been filled ever since that day with the fragrance of Mary's deed of love. We all should seek to fill our homes with the odors of love. A writer says, "I believe I should be homesick in a mansion filled with angels if my own precious friends whom I love were not within call." While we have our own loved ones about us, we should seek every opportunity to give them the comfort and the joy of love. A home is not made beautiful alone by costly pictures on the walls, by rich carpets on the floors, by costly furniture in the apartments, or by beautiful flowers in every room, but by love which sheds itself abroad in all gentleness, kindness, patience, thoughtfulness, and tenderness.

There always are some to criticize even the beautiful and sacred things that love does. It is said here that even one of the Lord's disciples found fault with Mary's deed. "Why was not this ointment sold for three hundred pence, and given to the poor?" We are not surprised to read in the record that it was Judas Iscariot who began the criticism of Mary's act. He spoke of the pouring out of the oil as waste. It has been noted that the word "waste" here used by Judas means literally perdition, and we remember that Jesus called Judas the son of perdition; that is, a man who utterly wasted His life. There still are people who think everything wasted that cannot be coined into dollars, or that does not result in immediate or direct practical usefulness. But the truth is that much of the sweetest blessing scattered in this world is the odor from the breaking of love's alabaster boxes. It does not coin into money. It is well to give food and clothing to the poor, but sometimes love and sympathy are better.

In some places circles or bands of Christian young people are in the habit of carrying flowers to sick rooms or to homes of pain and sorrow. These flowers are much like Mary's ointment. They do not feed anyone's hunger, nor put clothing on the backs of children, nor put coals into the grate. But the odor of love often carries more real comfort and cheer into homes than would the largest gifts of charity. Besides, Christ looks into the heart, and He is pleased with love there, whether the expression of the emotion take the form of garments for the poor or flowers for the sick room. The life that is given to Christ and spent in the service of love is not lost, not wasted. Love is never lost, even though nothing practical or utilitarian should seem to come of its outpouring. That life only is wasted which is emptied out in sin or spent in idleness, selfishness, or self-indulgence.

The keen criticism of the disciples must have pained the heart of Mary beyond measure. But the gracious commendation of her deed which Jesus promptly gave proved a comfort and brought back the joy. He said she had begun a good work on Him. We cannot know how her loving thought of Him and her sweet honoring of Him strengthened Jesus for His sorrowful way, how He was helped in His struggle in Gethsemane and in the darkness of His cross by the love that Mary lavished upon Him in her anointing. He said also, "Let her alone: against the day of my burying hath she kept this." We do not know that Mary understood that Christ must die and that she planned her anointing of Him with distinct reference to that event. But even if she did not, her anointing was most timely. It fitted into the need of that hour. It brought great joy to the Master, and the joy came to Him at the time when He craved sympathy and love, and when His burdened heart could appreciate the experience.

In Mark's gospel we have the words, "She is come aforehand to anoint my body to the burying." Many people would have kept that vase sealed up until Jesus was dead, and then have brought it out and emptied it on His body. When a man dies, there is never any lack of kind words about him, or of flowers for His coffin. But Mary's way was better. Let us bring our alabaster boxes and break them while our friends are alive to enjoy and be refreshed by the perfume. Let us fill the lives of those who are dear to us with sweetness, speaking approving, cheering, heartening words while their hearts can be warmed and blessed by them. The flowers you mean to send for your friends' coffins, send to brighten and sweeten their homes before they go away. Do not keep the alabaster boxes of your love and tenderness sealed up until they are gone. Speak approving, encouraging words while their ears can hear them.

> What use for the rope if it be not flung
> Till the swimmer's grasp to the rock has clung?
> What help in a comrade's bugle-blast
> When the peril of Alpine heights is past?
> What need that the spurring paean roll
> When the runner is safe beyond the goal?

What worth is eulogy's blandest breath
When whispered in ears that are hushed in death?
No, no! If you have but a word of cheer,
Speak it while I am alive to hear.

19

Jesus Entering into Jerusalem

Scripture Reading: John 12:12–26

The time of the triumphal entry was five days before the crucifixion. There was an immense contrast between the two events. Here we see Him riding as a King into the holy city, followed by a great multitude of wildly enthusiastic people. It is a glimpse in earthly expression of the Messianic glory of Jesus. His reign was to be spiritual, but here once, it took on a form which made its appeal to the senses of mankind.

The other evangelists tell us that disciples had a part in preparing for the great pageant. We learn also that it was Jesus Himself who gave the command for this display. Once before when the enthusiastic multitude would have taken Him by force to make Him a king, He resisted and rejected the honor, sent His disciples away, dispersed the crowd, and fled to the mountain, taking refuge in prayer. Now, however, it is at His own command that this procession is undertaken. He would proclaim His Messiahship in a way that would make appeal to the rejectors. Or we may say that this really was the ride of the King to His coronation, for was not the cross the stairway to the Messiah's throne? The events of this day fulfilled an ancient prophecy. The song that was sung, "Hosanna: Blessed is he that cometh in the name of the Lord," was a joyous outburst from the hearts of the people. Yet we know how soon that "Hosanna" was changed to "Crucify him!" A picture of the cross by Tintoretto represents the scene of the Crucifixion after it was over. It is late in the evening. The cross is empty. The multitude has scattered, and all is quiet. The crown of thorns is lying on a rock near by. Then, in the background, an ass is seen feeding on withered palm leaves. This suggests how short-lived was the enthusiasm of which the palm branches were the emblem, and marks the contrast between the shouts on this Palm Sunday and the angry cries on the following Friday.

The effect of this day's events on different persons is indicated in the passage. The disciples did not then understand what it all meant. Afterwards, however, they remembered that the things which happened that day had been foretold of Jesus in prophecy. We need the "afterwards" to explain many perplexities in our lives. In the light of future events present mysteries become clear. The effect on the multitude was probably transient, and yet we are told that they remembered the raising of Lazarus when they beheld the scenes of the triumphal entry. The effect of the strange events of that day on the Pharisees was still further to embitter them. They said, "Perceive ye how ye prevail nothing? behold, the world is gone after him."

The incident of the coming of the Greeks occurred two days after the triumphal entry. These Greeks were Gentiles. They had learned the Jewish religion and were worshipers in the temple. They had come up from their own country to attend the feast of the Passover. They wished to see Jesus. Why they wished to see Him we are not told. Whatever their definite desire may have been, their prayer is one which should be on the lips of every one of us, "We would see Jesus." This should be the deepest wish and prayer of every heart. The great business of life should be to know Jesus Christ, to get intimately acquainted with Him. It was not enough to know about Him—we should be content with nothing less than personal knowledge of Him as a friend. We cannot see Jesus now in the flesh, but we can see Him by faith as our Savior and take Him into our lives in the most real sense as our intimate companion.

These Greeks came to two of Christ's disciples and asked them to introduce them to their Master. A little child was dying, and she said she was not afraid to die, for she was going to be with Jesus. But she wished so much that her mother would come with her to introduce her. "For you know, mother," said the little one, "that I was always afraid of strangers." But no one will find Jesus a stranger. He loves to be sought and to have people want to see Him. Yet it is always a precious privilege to be permitted to introduce another person to Him.

The reply of Jesus to the request of these Greek visitors was, "The hour is come, that the Son of man should be glorified." By the "hour" He referred to the time of His death, the hour toward which He had been moving through all the years of His life. Every one of us is moving toward our "hour." It is not marked on any earthly calendar; we do not know in what year, or in what month, or day, it lies, but it is fixed in the plan of God, and we shall come to it at the appointed time. It seems strange to us to have Jesus speak of His death as His being glorified. He died on a cross of shame. It seemed to the world as the extinction of all glory for Him. He Himself, however, explained the meaning in the words, "Except a corn of wheat fall into the ground and die, it abideth alone: but if it die, it bringeth forth much fruit." A grain of wheat laid away carefully in a dry place, remains simply a grain of wheat, with no increase. It cannot thus reach its best. It is only when it is cast away, as it seems, and falls into the ground and perishes as to its form, that it is really glorified, springing up into a harvest of golden wheat.

Jesus might have saved Himself from sacrifice and death if He had sought to do so. He might have turned away from His enemies and have found an asylum among the Gentiles. He might have lived to old age, teaching, healing, and blessing the world. Yet, He would not in His years of comfort and quiet usefulness have done the work He had been sent into the world to do. Life is not measured by the number and length of its years, but by the completeness of its devotion to the will of God. Jesus never would have glorified God by fleeing from the sacrifice of the cross to an asylum which would have given Him continued years of comfort and ease. By giving Himself up to death on the cross He became the Redeemer of the world. Christianity, with all its marvelous fruits and blessings, is the real glorifying of Christ. If He had not gone to His cross, this glorifying would never have been attained.

Jesus taught His disciples further that not only must He Himself reach His glory by way of His cross, but that those who would follow Him must also walk in the same way. "He that loveth His life shall lose it; and he that hateth His life in this world shall keep it unto life eternal." There are two ways of living, and we have our choice. We may live for self, taking good care of our lives, not exposing them to danger, not making any sacrifices, caring only for our own interests. We may then prosper in this world, and people will commend our prudence. We may reach old age robust and well-preserved, and may greatly enjoy our accumulated honors and possessions. That is one way of living—loving our life and saving it from the costly service to which we were called, but in the end it is only the wheat kept from falling into the ground to die. There will be no harvest. That is the outcome of selfishness. Its end is death. "He that loveth his life loseth it."

The other way of living is to forget self—not to care for one's own life or to try to preserve it, but to give it out at God's call, to throw it away in unselfish service. People will say you are foolish thus to waste your golden life, thus to sacrifice yourself for the sake of others, or in the cause of Christ. But was Christ foolish when He chose to go to His cross? The redeemed Church is the answer. Ignatius said, when facing the fierce lions in the arena: "I am grain of God. Let me be ground between the teeth of lions, if thus I may become bread to feed God's people." Was the martyr foolish? Did he really waste His witnessing for His Lord? The way to make nothing of one's life is to take too good care of it. The way to make one's life an eternal success is to do with it as Jesus did with His.

20

Serving, Following, Sharing

Scripture Reading: John 12:26

"If any man serve me"; if he would be My servant; if he would belong to Me—"let him follow me"—live as I live, come close after Me in spirit, in manner of life, walk in My steps. "Where I am, there shall also my servant be." To follow Christ here, in this world, in the way He marks out, is to follow Him also in His exaltation, to reward, to heavenly honor. To share His cross is also to share His glory.

If Jesus had taken care of His life, if, for instance, He had gone with these Greeks to their country, He might have been welcomed and have received homage, honor, and love, and have lived many years to teach and heal and do good; but there would have been no Gethsemane, with its tears, no Calvary, with its cross of redemption, no grave of Arimathea, with its resurrection. "Except a corn of wheat fall into the ground and die, it abideth alone: but if it die, it bringeth forth much fruit."

We admit the truth of this in Christ's own life. We understand that He accomplished infinitely more by giving His life in service and sacrifice at an early age than He would have done if He had saved it from suffering and death and devoted it for long years to good deeds. But the same is true of all lives. Christ by His example taught all of us the true way to live. "If any man serve me." That was what Christ's disciples wished to do. They had listened to His call and had joined His company. They meant to serve Him. They believed in Him. They were sure that no one like Him had ever come among men as teacher, helper and leader. They wanted to serve Him.

What is it to serve Christ? Ruskin calls attention to a common form of religious speech which, he thinks, is misleading. We call church worship "divine service." We say our morning service is at ten forty-five, our evening service at seven forty-five. Service in this use of the word means singing hymns, reading the Scriptures, praying, and meditating on some devotional theme. But Mr. Ruskin reminds us that this is not service at all, in the higher sense. "If a child finds itself in want of anything, it runs and asks the father for it. Does it call that doing its father a service? When a child loves its father very much, and is very happy, it may sing little songs about him; but it doesn't call that serving its father. Neither is singing hymns to God, serving God." Of course, in a sense we are serving Christ when we worship Him in a meeting. But this is not all that such service means.

What is it to serve Christ? How are we to serve Him? The answer is here. "If any man serve me, let him follow me." Follow Me? What does that mean? It was sometimes literal following with the first disciples. Andrew and Simon and John and James were fishermen. Jesus bade them follow Him, and they left their boats and nets and fishing tackle, gave up their business, and went with Jesus. Matthew was sitting in a little booth, collecting customs from people who went by, and Jesus said, "Follow me." Matthew left His business and went with the Master. Following Christ may mean the same in our day. If you are in a sinful business and hear the call of Christ, you are to leave the bad business. There are men and women whom Christ wants to follow Him away from home and country, to be missionaries in foreign lands. But the literal following is not always the meaning of the call.

We are to follow Christ in the way of sacrifice. That was the way Jesus lived. He hated His life. This does not mean that He despised life, that He regarded His life as of no account. Sometimes you hear a discouraged man say: "My life is of no value. I cannot be of any use. I can never do anything worthwhile. I may as well die." Jesus did not mean that we are to hate our life in that way. God never made a life to be useless. Jesus said no one shall accept even the whole world in exchange for His life. Think what Jesus must have thought of the value of human lives when He laid down His own life to redeem men. It is a sin to hate your life, to despise it, to regard it as of no value, to throw it away. Love your life, prize it, for it is worth more than worlds. Keep it, cherish it, guard it. Never say you are of no account.

What, then, does Jesus mean when He says, "He that loveth His life shall lose it?" He means loving life more than duty, more than obedience. To hate one's life *in this world* is to give it up gladly in service of others, to lose it in saving others. Recently an English medical journal reported that Dr. Waddell was attending a poor man's child with diphtheria, when the operation of tracheotomy became necessary. The instant clearing of the tube became a matter of life and death, and at the risk of his life, the doctor sucked the tube free of the diptheritic membrane. The child recovered, but the doctor contracted the disease. He hated his life; that is, he thought it not too valuable to sacrifice in the doing of his duty as a physician. The records of every day are full of instances when in hospitals, in private sick rooms, on railway trains, in mines, and in all kinds of service, men and women are illustrating the lesson. The highest example the world ever saw was in Christ's own case, when He gave His life to save the world.

It is easy enough to think of this law of life as a theory. Now and then there comes an opportunity also to illustrate it in some grand way, as some nurse does it, as some true doctor does it, as a mother does it. But how are we going to live this way in the common experiences of everyday life? "If any man serve me, let him follow me." "He that hateth His life . . . shall keep it unto life eternal." We may interpret this law of the cross so as to make it apply to the experiences of the home, the neighborhood, the school, the business office. Victor Hugo attempts it in speaking of the philosophy of life. He says:

> Men hate, are brutes, fight, lie, leave their dream unto the shadows. But share you your bread with little children; see that no one goes about you with naked feet; look kindly unto mothers nursing their children on the doorsteps of humble cottages; do not knowingly crush the humblest flower; respect the needs of birds. . . . Be like him who has a watering pot in His hand, only let your watering pot be filled with good deeds and good words. . . . If you have enemies, bless them—and live with that sweet, unobtrusive authority that comes to the soul in patient expectation of the eternal dawn.

The keynote of the lesson we are trying to learn is self-denial, which is not merely doing without meat during Lent, giving up some customary indulgences for a few weeks, sacrificing a few things you do not care much for. There are few farces enacted in the world equal in emptiness to the farce of pious self-denial, as it is played by a good many people, for example, in the Lenten days, meanwhile living selfishly in all the relations of the common days. Self-denial as Christ practiced it and teaches it is denying yourself—hating your own life, laying it on the altar that some other one may be helped.

Hating your life means stooping down and considering the needs of little children, the loneliness and weariness of old people; it means thinking of persons no one else is likely to think of or care for; being patient with disagreeable people, cranky people, and kind to them; going far out of your way to be obliging to one who would not go out of His way an inch to do a good turn to you; not noticing slights and inattentions, or even slurs and offensive things, save to be all the more Christlike to those who so ungraciously treat you; saying especially kind things of anyone who had been saying unusually unkind things of you. That is what Christ did.

The papers recently told the story of the way a young man gave himself. He was poor, but had a great desire to be a gentleman, then to become a lawyer. He saved enough money from his earnings and his economy to carry him through college. His first year he made a friend, a young man, brilliant, and noble as well. The two were roommates and became devoted to each other, in spite of their differences. During the first summer vacation the father of the well-to-do boy died, and he then had no money to continue his course. He wrote to his friend and told him he could not return to college, that he must abandon his dream of education and go to work.

The friend after a short time wrote to him in this way:

> You have fine capacity and will make a useful man if you have education. I have found out that I would be only a fourth-rate lawyer at best. It will be far better for you to be educated than for me. I have money enough saved to carry me through college. You must take my money and complete your course. I enclose a draft for the amount. I will drop out of sight altogether and lose myself. Do not try to find

me—it will be of no use. Do not refuse the money—you never can return it to me."

This is what Christ spoke of when he advocated the "hating" of one's life. This is self-denial of the noblest kind.

You do not begin to know how many chances you have every day of hating your life in this world, giving yourself to help some other one upward. In the home life the chance comes continually, the chance of giving up your own way to make another happier; to put another upward; of keeping gentle and sweet, instead of becoming irritated and provoked; of speaking a soft answer instead of a cutting one; of taking the heavy end of some burden, that a more frail one may not be crushed; of giving cheer to one who is discouraged. There are a hundred opportunities every day of dropping yourself out and putting another in the way of receiving the favor, of laying selfishness on the cross and nailing it there, and showing love instead. How do the boys treat their sisters? How do people in comfortable homes, with plenty, regard and treat the neighbor who is having pinching times, or has a sick child? Do you hate your life, your comfort, your luxury, in the sense of doing without some of it to show kindness and give help? There is an almost infinite field of opportunities for denying self, sacrificing one's own feelings, desires, preferences, to make life easier, happier, more joyous to others.

There is another sphere of opportunities for living out the doctrine of the cross in everyday life. "Do justice and judgment" [Gen. 18:19; Prov. 21:3], runs the Bible teaching. Have you ever thought how grievously many of us fail in being just to others? We are unreasonable; we are exacting; we are unfair; we are partial. We criticize others unmercifully. We commend very few people; we condemn almost everybody for something. Oh, what ungodly judges of the acts of others we are! Then, do you ever think how little of real forgiveness there is among us, even among Christian people? We talk a great deal about forgiveness, and we pray it every time we say the Lord's Prayer; but how much Christian forgiveness do we practice? "How often must I forgive?" asked Peter. He thought seven times would be enough. "Seventy times seven," said Jesus—that is, without counting. It is hard to forgive an enemy—it is not a natural disposition or act—it is divine—it is Christ in us. But do not forget it is Christian, and you cannot be a Christian yourself in anything: you need Christ living in you. You need Christ in you to forgive as He forgives.

But this is part of our lesson—the cross in daily life. Not to forgive is to love your own life, and that is to lose it in the end. To forgive is to hate your own life, not to insist on having your own way, in demanding your rights, but to bear the wrong, the insult, the injustice, to return good for evil, kindness for unkindness, to turn the other cheek when one cheek is already smarting with the smiting. Oh, what a new world we Christians would soon make if this old earth would only get the law of the cross into our conduct and spirit for a time! What heart-burnings we should cure! What hurts of love we should heal! One of the fine sayings of Lincoln quoted before the recent centenary of His birth was this, "Die when I may, I want it said of me by those who know me best, that I always plucked a thistle and planted a flower where I thought a flower would grow." That is one of the ways of hating one's own life *in this world* as Christ spoke about. It is so easy to plant thistles instead of plucking them up! It is so easy to pluck up roses instead of planting them! It is so easy not to deny ourselves, just to let the old unregenerate self rule our spirit and go on with its bitter jealousies, envyings, resentments, injustices, believing evil of others, judging others. Do you know what such life will come to in the end? "He that loveth his life"—that is, cherishes all these evil things, thinks only of his own wishes, demands always his own way, no matter who is crushed or hurt—"He that loveth his life shall lose it."

"If any man serve me, let him follow me." That is our lesson. It is not easy—it is very hard. Nature never can learn it. When we no longer love our own life, and instead instantly give it up to do a kindness to another, to give help, whatsoever the cost; when we forget our own interest and put another forward instead of ourself—then we are following Christ. "He that hateth his life in this world shall keep it unto life eternal."

There is still another thing to learn—sharing. "If any man serve me, let him follow me; and where I am, there shall also my servant be." Perhaps in this age of materialism we do not look on enough to think what will come after this life is over. "He that loveth his life shall lose it." Look ahead and think what that means—loving self, loving life, losing it, having nothing out of it but death. That is the end of selfishness, living for self, having one's own way. "He that hateth his life in this world shall keep it unto life eternal." That is what came out of Christ's life of self-denial here, His hating His own life. You will reach the same glory. "Where I am, there shall also my servant be." Where is Christ today? Think of being with Him when you have finished your life of serving and following Him here.

Did you ever sit down quietly and think over what you will be, and where you will be, after you are dead? These lines appeared in a religious paper—the author's name not given:

> Think that the grass upon thy grave is green;
>   Think that thou seest thine own empty chair,
>   The empty garments thou wast wont to wear,
> The empty room where long thy haunt hath been;
>
> Think that the lane, the meadow, and the wood,
>   And mountain summit, know thy feet no more,
>   Nor the loud thoroughfare, nor sounding shore—
> All mere blank space where thou thyself hast stood.
>
> Amid this thought-created silence, say
>   To thy stripped soul: 'What am I now, and where?'
>   Then turn and face the petty, narrowing care
> Which has been gnawing thee for many a day,
>   And it will die, as dies a wailing breeze,
>   Lost in the solemn roar of bounding seas.

Think what it will be to be where Christ is. "Where I am, there shall also my servant be." Think of the reward. People sometimes call it sacrifice now, talking dolefully of how much they have given up in their life of self-denial. Call it not sacrifice to give up your own way to give others joy and to do them good, even to give up your life that others may be saved. Sacrifice! "Where I am, there shall also my servant be." Oh, no, not sacrifice, but glory.

> 'Life's weary lessons are all learned,' she said,
> 'And school is out.' We bent, and she was dead.

"Where I am, there shall also my servant be."

21

Washing the Disciples' Feet

Scripture Reading: John 13:1–14

It is supposed that the strife among the disciples as to which was
the greatest led to the incident of the washing of the feet. None of
the disciples was willing to perform the lowly duty of washing the
feet of the others. The service belonged to the youngest or the one of
lowest rank. Then Jesus quietly did it Himself. It was not in a moment
of depression that He performed this deed of lowly humility. He was
fully conscious of His divine character while He knelt before His disciples washing their feet. It was this consciousness of His glory that
made the condescension so stupendous. It would have been no condescension for John or Peter to have washed the feet of the others.

The story of Christ's act of humility is told in very beautiful words.
Jesus did not consider His holy hands too fine for the washing of the
feet of the twelve men who sat around the table. Some of us think we
are too great or too high in rank among men to stoop to any lowly service like this. Our thought of our greatness and our dignity oppresses us
and prevents us from doing the beautiful things of love. That was the
way the disciples thought of themselves. Christ's act of humility is an
answer to all such pride and pretension. Never was there any other
being of such glorious personality as Jesus; yet He did not hesitate to
perform this lowliest of all service. Some of us like to do all our serving
by proxy. We will pay a deaconess or a city missionary for relieving the

489

poor or ministering to the sick, but will not do the work with our own hands. We do not know what blessing we miss in declining to accept such blessed service, nor how much more the service means when we do it with our own hands. "The gift without the giver is bare."

Peter shrank from having his Master perform such menial service for him. It was natural for him to feel thus. It was his deep sense of personal unworthiness that led him to exclaim as he saw his master about to perform the lowly service, "Lord, dost thou wash my feet?" The answer Jesus gave bade him submit, though he could not understand what was being done. Someday it would all be clear to him.

"What I do thou knowest not now; but thou shalt know hereafter." There are many things which Christ does which at the time we cannot understand. They seem mysterious to us. Yet afterwards we shall see the reason for them and find beauty in them. This is true of many of the providences of our lives. At one time Jacob said, "All these things are against me" [Gen. 42:36]. But he lived to see that the very things which he thought were against him were really working for His good. So it always is in the dealings of God with His people. We cannot understand now, but someday we shall know. "The tapestry weavers do their work on the reverse side, looking at the ends and threads, a mystery of tangle and confusion, but not seeing the beautiful picture they are making on the other side. So we are weaving our lives largely on the reverse side." Someday we shall look on the beauty we are unconsciously making in our life today.

There was something generous in Peter's outspoken feeling that he could not allow the holy hands of Christ to wash his feet. It showed his thought of the glory of Christ and his sense of his own unworthiness. But the answer of Jesus was startling. "If I wash thee not, thou hast no part with me." It was not merely the washing of the feet to which Jesus referred. Cleanliness is a virtue, no doubt, and a duty as well; but discipleship could not be made to turn on anything so incidental. This word of Christ implies among other things that no one can be a disciple who insists upon having his own way. Utter self-surrender is the essential condition. We must put ourselves wholly in Christ's hands, and must do just as He bids us, or we can have no part with Him. It is not ours to reason why, or to make any reply—it is ours only to obey. Especially must this word of Christ be considered in its reference to spiritual cleansing. Unless

Christ wash us, we can have no part with Him. No one can be a disciple until he has been cleansed, and only Christ can cleanse us. Some people profess to take Christ as a teacher who yet feel no need of being washed by Him. We must understand that this word is final—that Jesus will receive no disciples who do not submit to Him first to be cleansed by Him. The picture of Jesus with the basin is one of wonderful suggestiveness. He must come to all of us first in this way—that He may wash us.

Peter went then to the other extreme, as his impulsive nature always did. He was willing to submit not only his feet, but his hands and his head. Then Jesus told him that "he that is washed needeth not save to wash his feet, but is clean every whit." Bathing is the cleansing of the whole body, and washing is the rinsing off of the dust that gathers on the feet in walking from the bath to the table. There was no necessity for washing Peter's hands and head—he had just come from the bath, and was clean except that his feet had become soiled with the dust as he walked. But there is a spiritual meaning, too. Peter was a justified and regenerated man—he was "clean." All he needed, therefore, now was that the stains of his daily sinning and from his contacts with the world should be removed. The lesson here is important. Bathing must come before washing. That is, the mere cleansing of daily sins amounts to nothing unless we have first been received by Christ and justified and saved by Him. The acceptance of Christ as our Savior lifts the guilt from our souls and leaves us free from condemnation. Yet after that, even the holiest need daily forgiveness for daily sins.

Jesus taught the disciples the meaning of what He had done. "If I then, your Lord and Master, have washed your feet; ye also ought to wash one another's feet." We must do all lowly service for each other. We should have in our hearts that love which will lead us into the lowliest service for even the lowliest people.

Then Christ's act was more than one of service—it meant the cleansing of faults, the removing of blemishes of character, the washing of stains got in passing through the world. We should seek to rend this service also to each other. We are to help each other to become clean Christians. We are to seek the sanctification, purification, and upbuilding in character of our fellow disciples. Of course, we cannot wash away sins—Christ alone can do that. But we can do something toward making others purer, better and holier. This part of Christian friendship requires great wisdom. It is not easy to reprove the faults of others. We must be careful, first of all, that our own hands are clean before we attempt to cleanse the stains on the lives of others. We must cast out the beam from our own eye before we can attempt to remove the mote from our brother's eye.

22

The New Commandment

Scripture Reading: John 13:34

Jesus was about to leave His disciples. "Yet a little while I am with you." He wanted them to stand together when He was gone. He knew, too, how great a danger there was that they would fall apart. His church which He had come to establish depended on these men. If they were not true and loyal to each other, His work would fail. So, with all earnestness, He pleaded with them to love one another. This would be their safeguard and the secret of their power after He had left them. Nothing but love would hold them together.

Jesus spoke of this last exhortation to them as a new commandment. Why new? Really it was new. There was an old commandment which ran, "Love thy neighbor as thyself." The new commandment is, "Love one another; as I have loved you." Love is the distinct mark of discipleship. "By this shall all men know that ye are my disciples, if ye have love one to another." Christians are to be known in the world, not by the creed they profess, nor by their church membership, but by their love for each other. Love puts a brand on them. Sometimes we hear of a church with strifes and quarrels among its members. What kind of witness is such a church giving to the world for its Master? "By this shall all men know that ye are my disciples, if ye have love one to another." The church which has a right to call itself a church of Christ is one in which the members love one another as Christ loves them.

This puts upon us a serious responsibility as churches and as individual Christians. We dare not be contentious, quarrelsome, biting and devouring one another. The world would then laugh at our profession that we are a company of the friends of Christ. When a man joins a church he assumes the obligation of love. He says, "I will love my fellow Christians as Christ loves me." What does he mean? Does he mean that he will love the gentle, agreeable, congenial, refined members; those who show him a great deal of honor, those who are kind to him, sympathetic, eager to favor and help him? He must love these. But suppose there are among the members some who are not congenial, not obliging, who do not show him deference, whose lives are not lovely—does he have to love these? "By this shall all men know that ye are my disciples, if ye have love one to another." There do not seem to be any exceptions. How was it with the first disciples? Were they all of the lovable kind? John was. He must have been sweet-spirited, good-tempered, affectionate. But how about Peter, Matthew, Andrew, Thomas? Were they all lovable? One of them had treason in His heart. Another denied Jesus. All of them forsook Him in the hour of His great need and sorrow. Yet, how did Jesus love these? He loved on, He loved to the end. How are we to love our fellow Christians? As Christ loves us.

What would be the effect if all Christian people, all who belong to Christian churches, would begin to love one another as Christ loved His first disciples, as He loves every one of us? Paul tells us how true Christian love acts, how it shows itself. It is in personal contacts and associations. "Love suffereth long, and is kind" [see 1 Cor. 13:4]. That is, it bears patiently with others' faults, unkindnesses, ill-treatment, ingratitude, and is kind. It keeps on being kind in spite of all the unkindness it receives. It is kindness that we need always to show—just the art of being kind is all this old world needs—and it must always be kept in our lives. The trouble is, however, that with too many of us our kindness is spasmodic, is shown only when we feel like it and checked continually by things that happen. Nothing ever stopped Christ's kindness—nothing ever should stop a Christian's kindness. Love in the heart should flow out in the life as an unintermittent stream.

Take another line from the picture. "Love . . . doth not behave itself unseemly." That is, it never forgets itself, is never rude, is not supercilious. Bad temper is unseemly. Did you ever notice in the story of the life of Jesus how He always respected people? He seemed to have reverence for almost every person who came before Him, even the worst? The reasons were that He loved everyone, that He saw in each the glorious possibilities of heavenly sonship. If we had our Master's regard for and His deep interest in the lives of men, we would never act unseemly toward even the unworthiest.

A newspaper gives an account of a new society which has been organized by a company of people. It is called "The Take Heed Society." It seems that a member of the company boarded once in a rather sleepy New England town with a prim spinster who was a wonderfully charitable woman. She was never heard to say an unkind word to anybody. Further acquaintance showed that charity and brotherly feeling were almost universally practiced by the people of the village. The good woman made inquiry and learned that they all belonged to a society, and that they had all pledged themselves to speak no unkind words, to think no unkind thoughts, and do no unkind deeds. The people of the little town, who belonged to this organization, never met in a body as other societies do. They had no officers, paid no dues, assessed no fines except individually upon themselves. There was a fine mentioned in the pledge, but this was to be imposed by the offending person upon himself if he ever violated the fundamental rules of the organization. He was to fix His own fine, making it as large as he was able to pay, and it was to be paid, not to the treasurer, but to the first poor and needy person he met. It is said that every member of the company had eagerly joined this Take Heed Society when it was proposed to organize it. It may be worthwhile to start such societies in families, in boarding houses, in Sunday-school classes, in circles of friends. It might help much in getting this law of love—not to behave ourselves unseemly—into every day of life.

"Love is not easily provoked" [see 1 Cor. 13:5]. That is, it does not become vexed or irritated at what another may say or do. It may be noticed, too, that some people even get provoked at inanimate things. A man awkwardly stumbled against a chair, flew into a violent passion, and kicked the chair with great energy. Bad temper is said to be one of the most common of the vices. No other infirmity is so often confessed. A great many people will tell you that they find no other fault so hard to overcome as that of bad temper. They do not seem, either, ashamed to make the confession, and apparently do not consider the fault a serious one. Sometimes it is spoken of apologetically as an infirmity of nature, a family failing, a matter of temperament, certainly not a fault to be taken very seriously, or anything more than a matter of regret. It has been said that ill temper is the vice of the virtuous. Men and women whose characters are noble, whose lives are beautiful in every other way, have this one blot. They are sensitive, touchy, easily ruffled, easily hurt.

But we make a grave mistake when we let ourselves think that bad temper is a mere trifling weakness. It is a most disfiguring blemish. We know that Jesus set for us a perfect model of living. He came to show us in a simple human life how we ought to live, and then how, through His grace and help, we may live; and He was never provoked. You cannot point to a single instance of His becoming even ruffled in temper. He never lost His calmness, His repose of mind, His peace. He was reviled, but reviled not again. He was insulted, but showed no sign. In all His quiet, restrained, and loving life He never once was provoked. When He bids us to love one another as He has loved us, this is certainly part of what He means.

Another part of our lesson concerns life with others in personal contact and association. Paul, in a letter, named several persons who, he said, had been a comfort to him. It is a fine thing to have one say of us that we have been a comfort to him. There are people who have been a comfort to you. You are glad they live. Then there are other people who have not been a comfort to you, who have not made life happier and easier for you. Sometimes you hear one say that a certain person has been a thorn in his side. In a conversation on a railway train, one reports catching this bit of a sentence: "Yes, I suppose she's good—I know she is. But she isn't pleasant to live with." A goodness that isn't pleasant to live with is not the kind Jesus had in mind when He said we should love one another as He loves us. Indeed, being "pleasant to live with" is one of the final tests of Christlikeness in life. Christ, Himself, was pleasant to live with. He never made anybody uncomfortable by His lack of lovingness, by selfishness, by censoriousness, by unsympathetic moods or words or looks. Whatever else you may fail to strive to be at home, among your friends, in your church life and fellowship, do not fail to seek and pray to be pleasant to live with. You are careful never to fail to do the little things of duty. Your friends cannot say that you are inattentive to them, that you leave undone any of the kindly deeds of neighborliness or even of brotherliness, which you ought to have done. But if, meanwhile, you are not pleasant to live with, is there not something lacking? The ideal religious life is one that gives comfort to others as well as help. It is gracious and winning in spirit, and also in manner. It is a blessing to everyone it touches.

Loving one another as Christ loves us must make it easier for others to work with us. A minister was telling me of one or two persons in His church who are excellent workers, full of zeal and energy, always doing things, but he said they had always to draw in shafts—they would not draw double. There are horses that will not pull in a team—they are to be driven single. There are people who have the same weakness. They want to do good, but they must do it by themselves. They will not work with another person. Then, soon it is true the other way—nobody else will work with them. There is a kind of buggy with only two wheels and a seat for one. It is called a sulky, because it obliges the rider to be alone. Some people are happiest when they ride alone, when they work alone. But the love of Christ teaches us a better way. We need to learn to think of others, those with whom we are associated in Christian life and work. It is so in all associated life. It is so in marriage when two lives are brought together in close relations. It is evident that both cannot have their own way in everything. There is not room for any two people to have their own way in the marriage relation. They are one now, occupying only the place of one, and they must live as one. There must either be the displacement of the one by the other, the losing of the one individuality in the other, the giving up of all by the one to the other, or else there must be the blending of the two lives in one. The latter is the true marriage. Each dies, the one for the other. Love unites them, and they are no longer two, but now one—two souls with but a common thought, two hearts that beat as one.

The same process should prevail in Christian life and work. Headstrong individualism should be softened and modified by love. Jesus sent forth His disciples in pairs. Two working together are better than two working separately. One is strong in one point and weak in another. The second is strong where the first is weak, and thus the two supplement each other. Paul speaks of certain persons as yokefellows [see Phil. 4:3]. Yokefellows draw together patiently and steadily, two necks under the same yoke, two hearts pouring their love into one holy fellowship of service. It is very important that Christian people should love one another as Christ loves them when they are called to work together for their Master. None of us should insist on always having his own way. In community of counsel there is wisdom. Jesus says distinctly that when two agree in prayer there is more power in the pleading, and the prayer will be surer of answer.

In our Master's service we should work together in love. It never should have to be said of us that other people cannot work with us. The secret of being agreeable workfellows is love. The Christian who is always wanting to be an officer, to have positions of prominence, to be chairman or president, first in something, has not caught the spirit of the love of Christ, who came not to be ministered unto, but to minister. Love never demands the first place. It works just as enthusiastically and faithfully at the foot of a committee as at the head of it. It works humbly, seeking counsel of the other members, and not asserting its own opinion as the only wise one. It seeks in honor to prefer the other rather than self. It is content to be overlooked, set aside, if only Christ is held up. It is patient with the faults of fellow workers. It strives in all ways to have the Master the real leader in all work. "Love one another; as I have loved you," is the command of Christ. Hold together, stand together. Be as one in love for others which will sacrifice anything, everything, that the Master's name may never suffer any dishonor.

This counsel of Christ calls us to a love like His in building up His kingdom. "As I have loved you." How was that? He loved and gave Himself. We must love and give ourselves. Some people are leaving out the cross these days in their thought of Christ. They preach about His wonderful teaching, His marvelous character, His sublime works, but say nothing about His death. But we need the cross. We can be saved only by a sacrificial love. Then the service of ours which will really bless others must also be a sacrificial service. "As I have loved you" means loving unto the end. We must give our lives for the brethren as He gave His life for us.

It is not easy, but it was not easy for Christ to love us as He did. To love as He did is to let our lives be consumed as in a flame, to let them be burned as on an altar. The trouble with too much of what we call love is that it costs nothing, is only a sort of gilded selfishness, is not ready to give up anything, to suffer, to endure. Oh, profane not the holy name of love by calling such life as that love! To love as Christ loves is to repeat Christ's sacrifice continually in serving, bearing, enduring, that others may be helped, blessed, saved. Christ's love laid itself across the chasm of eternal death to make a bridge for us to pass over, from death to life. "Love one another, as I have loved you." Let us try to know what the words mean, and then let the love of Christ itself into our heart. Then it will not be we that love, but Christ loving in us.

23

How Christ Comforts

Scripture Reading: John 14:1, 2

The words of the fourteenth chapter of John were spoken by the Master to His friends in a time of deep grief which seemed inconsolable. Yet He said, "Let not your heart be troubled." This seemed a strange thing to say to those men that night. How could they keep their hearts from being troubled in such circumstances? To think of all that Jesus had grown to be to them! For three years they had been members of His personal family, enjoying the most intimate relations with Him. How much a friend can be to us depends on the friend. If he has a rich nature, a noble personality, power to love deeply, capacity for friendship, the spirit of pure unselfishness, if he is able to inspire us to heroism and to worthy living, what he can be to us is immeasurable. Think what Jesus Christ, with His marvelous manhood, must have been as a friend to His disciples, and you can understand something of what His going from them meant to them.

Then He was more than a friend to them. They had believed in Him as the Messiah, who was to redeem their nation and lead them to honor and distinction. Great hope rested in Him. His death was, as it seemed to them, the defeat and failure of all their hopes. The announcement that He was to leave them swept away—as they thought—all that made life worthwhile. There are human friends whose death seems to leave only desolation in the hearts and lives of those who have loved them and leaned on them. But the death of Christ was to His personal friends and followers the blotting out of every star of hope and promise. Their sorrow was overwhelming.

Yet Jesus looked into their faces and said, "Let not your heart be troubled." It is worth our while to think of the grounds on which Jesus could reasonably say this to His disciples when they were entering into such great and real sorrow. The first thing He bade them do was to believe. "Let not your heart be troubled: ye believe in God, believe also in me." Thus far they had believed in God. Jesus had taught them a new name for God. They were to call Him Father. He had not been known by this name before, but Jesus used no other name for Him. The word Father is a great treasure-house of love-thoughts. It told the disciples of personal thought, love and care, extending to all the events of their lives. The very hairs of their heads were all numbered. It told them of goodness that never failed. It was a great lesson they had been learning as they came to think of God as their Father. In the shock of the last terrible days; however, the danger was that they would lose their faith in God. But Jesus said to them: "Believe in God. Let nothing take this faith out of your heart. Let nothing take from you what you have been learning from me about God."

"Believe also in me." They had accepted Jesus as the Messiah. You remember the splendid confession made by Peter, "Thou art the Christ, the Son of the living God." In this confession all the disciples had joined. They believed that He had come to be the world's Savior. Now, in the announcement that Jesus was to die at the hands of wicked men, there was danger that they should lose their faith in Him. But to save them from their loss of faith He exhorted them to continue to believe. Not one of their hopes had perished. "Ye believe in God, believe also in me."

We are always in danger of losing faith in time of sorrow or any sore trouble. Many times people are heard asking such questions as, "How can God be a God of love, and allow me to be so bereft, so stripped of good things? Where are now the promises of blessing which are made in the Scriptures over and over again? Has God forgotten to be gracious?" To these questions of doubt and fear the answer is, "Let not your heart be troubled: ye believe in God, believe also in me." Let nothing disturb your faith. Though it seem that God's love has failed, that God has forgotten you, that Christ is no longer your friend, still continue to believe; believe in God, believe also in Christ.

Sorrow is full of mystery. We go everywhere asking, "Why?" "This is not love," we say. "This is not goodness. This is not salvation." We cannot answer the Why. Why should we expect to know why God does this or that? How could we, with our narrow vision and our small knowledge, understand all the plans and purpose of God? God does not want to give us an easy time in this world—He wants to make something of us, and often the way to do this is to give us pain, loss, suffering. A German writer speaks of the "hardness of God's love." Love must be hard sometimes. A writer tells of keeping the cocoon of an emperor moth for nearly a year, to watch the process of development. A narrow opening is left in the neck of the flask, through which the perfect insect forces its way. The opening is so small that it seems impossible for the moth to pass through it. This writer watched the efforts of the imprisoned moth to escape. It did not appear to make any progress. At last he grew impatient. He pitied the little creature and, in a weak kindness to it, decided to help it. Taking his scissors, he snipped the confining threads to make the struggle easier. In a moment the moth was free, dragging out a great swollen body and little shriveled wings. He watched to see the beauty unfold, but he watched in vain. "It never was anything but a stunted abortion, crawling painfully about instead of flying through the air on rainbow wings." Nature's way—that is, God's way—with moths is the only true way, although it is a way of pain, struggle, suffering. Human pity may make an easier way, but the end will be destructive.

God's love never makes this mistake, either in nature or in dealing with human lives. God lets us suffer, if by suffering we will best grow into perfect beauty. When the mystery of pain or hardness comes into our life, let us not doubt. Let us suffer and wait. The disciples thought all their hopes were gone, but in the end they learned that no hope had perished or failed. Blessing and good came out of what seemed irretrievable disaster. "Ye believe in God, believe also in me," is always the word of faith and of comfort. Trust God. Nothing is going wrong. You cannot understand, but He understands.

The disciples were in great distress because their Master was going away from them. They were dismayed as they thought of their loss.

They thought they could not live without Him. But He explained that He was going for their sake. They thought they would not have His help anymore, and He explained that He would still be active in their behalf. "In my Father's house are many mansions. . . . I go to prepare a place for you."

He told them where He was going—to His Father's house. These are precious words. They tell us that heaven is home. On this earth there is no place so sweet, so sacred, so heart-satisfying as the true home. It is a place of love, purest, gentlest, most unselfish love. It is a place of confidence. We are always sure of home's loved ones. We do not have to be on our guard when we enter our home doors. We do not have to wear veils there, hiding or disguising our real selves. Home is a refuge into which we flee from the danger, the enmity, the suspicion, the unkindness, the injustice of the world. Home is the place where hungry hearts feed on love's bread. Mrs. Craik in one of her books has this fine picture:

> Oh, conceive the happiness to know that some one person dearer to you than your own self, some one breast into which you can pour every thought, every grief, every joy; one person who, if all the rest of the world were to calumniate or forsake you, would never wrong you by a harsh thought or an unjust word; who would cling to you the closer in sickness, in poverty, in care; who would sacrifice all things to you, and for whom you would sacrifice all; from whom, except by death, night or day, you never can be divided; whose smile is ever at your hearth; who has no tears while you are well and happy, and your love the same. Such is marriage, if they who marry have hearts and souls to feel that there is no bond on earth so tender and so sublime.

This is a glimpse of what a true home is. The picture is sometimes realized on the earth. There are homes which are well-nigh perfect. But the home sought will be realized fully in heaven. The Bible paints heaven in colors of dazzling splendor, its gates and streets and gardens and streams and fruits, all of the utmost brilliance; but no other description means so much to our hearts as that which the Master gives in these three words, "My Father's house"—home. One writes:

> Life changes all our thoughts of heaven;
> At first, we think of streets of gold,

Of gates of pearl and dazzling light,
Of shining wings and robes of white,
And things all strange to mortal sight.
But in the afterward of years
It is a more familiar place;
A home unhurt by sighs and tears,
Where waiteth many a well-known face.
With passing months it comes more near;
It grows more real day by day—
Not strange or cold, but very dear—
The glad homeland, not far away,
Where none are sick, or poor, or lone,
The place where we shall find our own.
And as we think of all we knew
Who there have met to part no more,
Our longing hearts desire home, too,
With all the strife and trouble o'er.

"My Father's house." That is the place to which we are going. That is the place where those we have lost awhile from our earthly homes, falling asleep in Jesus, are gathering. That is the place to which the angels have carried the babies and the old people, our mothers, our fathers, our friends who have passed out of our sight. What a vision will burst upon our eyes when, some quiet day or night, we shall fall asleep to awake no more on earth, but to awake in heaven, in our Father's house! You have read of men coming over the sea as immigrants, and landing in a strange city as utter strangers—throngs all about them, but not one familiar face, no welcome in any eye, no greeting. But it will not be this way with you when you leave this world and enter heaven. Loved ones will meet you and receive you with joy.

Jesus said also to His disciples, "I go to prepare a place for you." They thought His dying was an interruption of His work. The Messiah they had conceived of was to live and be a glorious earthly King, conquering the world. Suddenly they were told that soon they should not see Him—He would be gone. They were bitterly disappointed. All their hopes were now to perish. Jesus comforts them by telling them that the reason He was going away was to prepare a place for them. Nothing was going wrong with His Messiahship. They had misunderstood it—that was all. He could easily have escaped from the plots of the rulers, the betrayal of Judas, the arrest by the temple officers. But that would have been to fail in part of His work.

The reason He was going away was that He might continue and complete His work in heaven. "I go to prepare a place for you." The thought is very beautiful. How does Christ prepare places for us? We need not understand, but it is a sweet thought to know that He thinks of us as you think of a dear guest who is coming to visit you—lovingly, and prepares for your coming. You good women, when you are expecting a friend you love very much, make the guest room just as tidy and beautiful as you can. You think of the friend's tastes, and prepare the room with this in mind. You put up a picture you think will please him. You lay on the table the books you know he will like. You gather his favorite flowers and place them on the dressing bureau. You do everything you can to make the room beautiful so that he will feel at home in it the moment he enters it. Christ is preparing a room for you.

There is something else here. "If I go and prepare a place for you, I will come again, and receive you unto myself; that where I am, there ye may be also." This is more of the work Jesus went away to do for His friends. First, He would make ready for them, build a home for them, prepare a place. Then, when all things were ready, He would come for them and take them home. That is what He does when we leave this world. Men call it dying, but dying is a gloomy, forbidding word. Jesus said, "Whosoever liveth and believeth on me shall never die." What we call dying is really only Jesus coming to receive us unto Himself. Why, then, should anyone dread to leave this world? It is the Master coming to tell you that your place in the Father's house is ready for you and that He has come to take you to it. When Stephen was being stoned he had a beautiful vision. He saw the heavens opened, and the Son of man standing on the right hand of God. As the mob stoned him, Stephen was calling upon Jesus Christ and praying, "Lord Jesus, receive my spirit" [see Acts 7:58–60]. It was the Savior coming for His servant. The place was ready for him. His work here had been short, but it was all that had been allotted to him. His departure was tragic—he died at the hands of a religious mob; but it mattered not how he was taken away—really it was Jesus who took him away—receiving His spirit into strong, gentle and secure hands.

The comfort to us in our sorrows and bereavements is that nothing has gone wrong, that God's purpose is going on in all the wrecks of human hopes. Your friend passed away the other night. You thought he would have been with you for many years. You had plans covering a long future of happiness. You were appalled when the doctor said your friend could not live. Life to you would be dreary, lonely and empty without this one who had become so dear to you. You say: "My friend stayed so brief a time! I could almost wish that I had not let my heart fasten its tendrils about this dear life, since so soon it was torn away from me." Say it not. It is worthwhile to love and to let your heart pour out all its sweetness in loving, though it be but for a day, and then to have the bliss give way to grief. Richard Watson Gilder writes:

> Because the rose must fade,
>   Shall I not love the rose?
> Because the summer shade
>   Passes when winter blows,
> Shall I not rest me there
> In the cool air?
>
> Ah, yes, because the rose
>   Doth fade like sunset skies;
> Because rude winter blows
>   All bare, and music dies—
> Therefore, now is to me
> Eternity.

24

Why Does No One See God?

Scripture Reading: John 14:8, 9

Christ had just told His disciples that they had seen the Father. Philip was bewildered. What did the Master mean? That was just what the disciples were longing for—to see the Father. "Lord, show us the Father," said Philip, "and it sufficeth us."

There are many sincere Christians today who are longing for fuller, clearer revealings of God. They wish they might see Him. God seems unreal to them. An earnest young Christian wrote: "For some time I have been drifting away from God and have not been able to drop anchor. The more I read and study the life of Jesus, the farther I drift. I find myself ever asking, 'Are these things true? They certainly are very beautiful to read about; but are they true? How do we know they are true?'"

Human hearts are alike in their feelings, their longings, their perplexities of faith; and, no doubt, there are many who sometimes ask the same questions as they read the wonderful story of Christ. "Are these things true? How do we know they are true?"

There is nothing wrong in such questionings. Philip had the same longing. Spiritual things seemed unreal to him. Many of the best people who ever lived have had similar difficulty. There come times in the life of almost every Christian when such questions as these arise.

507

Two girls were overheard one evening by a gentleman, talking with unusual earnestness, as if in perplexity, and one of them said, "Yes, but why has no one ever seen God?" This was all the gentleman heard of the conversation, as he stood near them, waiting for his car; but this single sentence showed their state of mind. Evidently they had been talking about the apparent unreality of spiritual things. Why had nobody ever seen God? They had heard a great deal about God, about His love, His care, His interest in human lives, His kindness. But they had never had a glimpse of Him. How could they know that all they had heard about Him was true? How could they be sure that there is a God? How could they know that the things of Christian faith and hope are real?

Questions will arise with all who think. Does God indeed love me? If He does, why must I suffer so? If He does, how can I explain all the accidents, calamities, and troubles of life? There is nothing wrong in such questions. God is not grieved with us if we ask them, desiring light. Christ is always patient with the questions of honest doubt.

It is not surprising if sometimes we cannot understand the mysteries of Christian faith. All life is full of things we cannot comprehend. Can you explain how on the bushes in your garden, which in March were bare and briery, there were in June masses of glorious roses? In the most common things there is mystery. Linnaeus, the great botanist, said there was enough mystery in a handful of moss to give one a lifetime's study. There really are few things you actually understand and can explain. How do your eyes see? How do your ears hear? Shall we refuse to believe these things because we cannot explain them?

We have read how the cry of the wireless went out from the wrecked ship and was heard far and wide over the sea—a prayer of distress—and how help came swiftly. No one doubts this pathetic experience of the sea. Why, then, should we doubt or question that when a mother sat by her sick child the other night, while the little one hovered between life and death, and pleaded with God, her prayer reached the ears of her heavenly Father? Why shall we doubt or question that God loves us when we believe that our human friends love us? You cannot see the love in the friend's heart any more than you can see the love for you in God's heart. You tell me that your friend is true, is patient, is kind; that he is a refuge, a tower of strength, to you. But you cannot see these qualities in him. Your friend is much away, out of your sight, and you cannot set spies on him to know that he is always faithful. Yet you never doubt him. Evil tongues whisper false things about him, but you refuse to believe them. How do you know that your beliefs in him are true? Why can you not, then, in like manner believe in the love of God, whom you cannot see?

A sorrow breaks in upon the joy of your home. You cannot understand it. But why must you understand? We would be far happier sometimes if we did not try to understand things. Dr. Robertson Nicoll says: "There are some very devout people who know far too much. They can explain the whole secret and purpose of pain, evil, and death in the world. They prate about the mystery of things as if they were God's spies. It is far humbler and more Christian to admit that we do not fully discern a reason and method in this long, slow tragedy of human existence." You remember that Jesus Himself said, "I have yet many things to say unto you, but ye cannot bear them now" [16:12]. Why should we expect to understand God and God's ways?

God does show Himself to us, and we do see Him more often than we think. There is a picture of Augustine and his mother which represents them looking up to heaven with deep earnestness, great eagerness, and longing. One is saying, "If God would only speak to us!" The other replies, "Perhaps He is speaking to us, and we do not hear His voice!" Philip said to Jesus, "Lord, show us the Father." And did you notice what Jesus said to him? "Have I been so long time with you, and yet hast thou not known me, Philip? he that hath seen me hath seen the Father." Philip thought that he never had seen the Father, but Jesus told him that he had been seeing Him all the time He had been with the disciples. What Philip had in mind when he said, "Show us the Father," was some revealing of glory, some outshining of majesty and splendor, a theophany, a transfiguration. That was the way he thought God must appear. When Jesus said, "He that hath seen me hath seen the Father," He referred to His common daily life with His disciples, not to His miracles. Only a small proportion of the things Jesus did were unusual, supernatural. Ninety-nine percent of His acts were simple, common things that did not need Deity to perform. He performed only one miracle in the Bethany home, but in His frequent visits—sitting with the family by the open hearth or at the table, talking with them in the quiet evening, walking with them in the garden, sharing with them the gentle things of friendship—there were a thousand kindnesses which made His name sacred to them.

It was so in all Christ's life. There were a few miracles, showing divine power; there were countless revealings of gentleness, sympathy, thoughtfulness, cheer, encouragement, which were as full of God as the miracles. It was to this part of His life that Jesus referred when He said to Philip, "He that hath seen me hath seen the Father." It was in Christ's most human ways that the disciples saw most of God. His miracles dazzled their eyes and awed them. Many could not have sat at His feet and listened calmly if He had appeared transfigured. John could not have leaned on His breast at supper restfully and quietly if glory had been shining in His face. God is love. Wherever there is love, God is revealing Himself.

> They bade me lift my eyes to Thee
> Who art great Lord and King,
> Enthroned above the cherubim
> Who praise eternal sing;
> And eagerly I gazed above
> As other mortals dare:—
> Such radiant light was all too bright—
> I could not find Thee there;
> And, blinded, and with downcast eyes
> I scarcely saw the Man
> Who walked beside me on my way,
> Though close our pathways ran.
> No pomp, no kingly pride, was there;
> His footsteps pressed the road;
> A staff like mine was in His hand;
> His shoulders bore their load.
> One day I turned and saw His face—
> The pitying human brow—
> 'Brother!' He said, with outstretched hand;
> And I, 'Why, this is Thou!'

Jesus showed the disciples the Father in all the love and sweetness and compassion they saw in Him continually. Do we not see God in similar ways? Does not God reveal Himself to us in a thousand familiar things that we do not think of at all as divine revealings? A writer says that most men are religious when they look upon the faces of their dead babies. The materialism which at other times infects them with doubts of God and immortality drops away from them in this hushed hour.

> There's a narrow ridge in the graveyard
>> Would scarce stay a child in its race;
> But to me and my thought it is wider
>> Than the star-sown vagues of space.

People see God only in the unusual, the supernatural. "If we could see miracles," they say, "we would believe." But the common things are full of God. Moses saw God in one bush that burned and was not consumed. Yet God is as real in every bush in the woods, for those who have eyes to see, as He was in that little tree in Horeb.

Have you never seen God? If you think of God as only burning majesty, shining glory, you will answer, "No—I never saw God." But splendor, Sinai clouds, and flaming fires are not God. God is love. You remember Elijah's vision. A great wind swept through the mountains, but God was not in the wind. An earthquake made the hills tremble, but God was not in the earthquake. A fire swept down over the crags, but God was not in the fire. Then came a still small voice, a sound of gentle stillness—and that was God [see 1 Kgs. 19:11–13].

You have seen God a thousand times in love, in peace, in goodness, in comfort. You see Him daily in providential care, in the sweet things of your home, in friendships, in the beauty of little children. Do not forget that you have been receiving blessings all your life in manifold ways. Do not call it chance, or luck, or good fortune. The heart-hungry girl asked, "Why has no one ever seen God?" Yet she had seen God herself every day, every hour of her life, in the goodness and mercy which had followed her from her infancy.

You were in danger, and there came a mysterious protection which sheltered you from all harm. You called it chance. It was God. You had a great sorrow which you thought you could not possibly endure, and you felt strange, sweet comfort which filled your heart with peace. You thought it came through a friend's gentle kindness. Yes, but it was the loving-kindness of God that brought it. There was a tangle in your affairs which seemed about to wreck everything, and in an inexplicable way it was all straightened out as by invisible hands. You had a crushing loss which threatened to overwhelm you, and suddenly—the loss proved a gain! You were wronged by a professed friend, and the stars in your sky all seemed to go out. That was some while ago, and today you are quietly praising God for the event which was a deliverance from a real misfortune, for there came instead a blessed friendship which fills all your life. Your years have been full of great providences, strange guidances, gentle comforts, answered prayers, sweet friendships, happy surprises of goodness, divine love and help and care. Yet you say you never have seen God, and ask, "How may I know that the beautiful things the New Testament tells me about Christ are true?"

Think of some definite ways in which we may learn that the things of Christian faith and hope are true, and how we have them become more real to us.

First, by experience. In one of the Psalms we read, "They that know thy name will put their trust in thee" [9:10]. It is sometimes said of a man that none know him but to love him. They who truly know God love Him and trust Him. We have to learn by experience to love our human friends. One was telling how he found a particular friend. He had heard much about him. His neighbors spoke well of him, praised him— his unselfishness, his kindness, his sincerity, his helpfulness, his readiness to give time and thought and money in assisting others. But this man never had met him. Some months since circumstances led him to seek his kindly interest. Then he found that all the good he had heard about him was true, and that the half had not been told. Now he believes in him.

In the same way we can only learn to know God. We read in the Bible of His goodness, His justice, His truth, His kindness, His faithfulness. But we must come into personal relations with Him before we can surely know that these qualities are really in Him. When Philip said to Nathanael, "I have found the Messiah, Jesus of Nazareth" [see 1:45, 46], Nathanael sneered at the suggestion that the Messiah could come from so lowly a place as Nazareth. Philip did not argue. He said only, "Come and see." He knew that if His friend would only meet Jesus he would believe. If we can only get people to come to see Jesus, to get to know Him, to experience His love, they will soon believe in Him and follow Him.

The story of the conversion of Lady Aberdeen is well known. She had been long in doubt, wavering, indecisive. In her time of perplexity she sat one day under a tree in her garden, in deep thought. Out of the silence she heard a mystic voice speaking as clearly to her consciousness as if a friend had uttered the words, "Act as if I were, and you will find that I am." She had been asking the very question of my friend's letter, "How can I learn that these things are true?" Was Christ real? She could not be sure. Would He be her friend? Would He bless her as the New Testament says He would? "Act as if I were," said the voice, "and you will learn that I am, and that all these things are true." There is no other way to find out that Christ is, and that the things the Scriptures tell us about Him are true.

Again, if we begin to do the will of God, we shall learn the reality of the spiritual life. Jesus said, "If any man will do His will, he shall know of the doctrine" [7:17]. You are to will to do God's will. This means the most earnest determination, the most unfaltering obedience. As we do the things of God's will as they are made known to us, we shall learn the reality of God and the beauty and blessedness of His love. One who tried to believe there is no God confessed that it was never in His best moments that he felt himself an atheist. Jesus said the pure in heart shall see God. He did not mean only that we shall see God when we get to heaven, and look upon God in His glory. He meant also that those whose hearts are pure shall see God on the earth. They will not be troubled about the reality of the things of faith. They will not ask, "Why has no one ever seen God?" They will see Him themselves. No cloud will ever dim for them the radiance of His face.

Then it is only in Christ that we can see God. Notice the precise words in which Jesus answered Philip's request, "Show us the Father." "He that hath seen me hath seen the Father." In Jesus Christ, therefore, and only in Jesus Christ, can we see God. The Incarnation was God coming to the earth in human life, that men could understand Him. Those who saw Him looked upon the face of God. Those who knew Him knew God. Those who became His friends became God's friends. This privilege is ours. Friendship is the holiest and most sacred of all human relations. Think of all that is possible in ideal human friendship. Then think of all that is possible in friendship with Jesus Christ. There never was another friend like Jesus. Think what His friendship may be to you if you will let it into your life in all its sweetness, its divineness, its power to transform and bless.

But the Christian girl asks: "Are these things true? How do we know they are? They are very beautiful. They were true of the people who knew Jesus personally; but may I have a share in them?" The friendship of Christ is the most real and the most wonderful thing in this world. To very many people there does seem to be an unreality in the things of spiritual life. God seems far away. We cannot see Him. We cannot feel His touch. But this need not be so. Christ wants to reveal the Father to us. He wants His friendship with you to be as real and as close as your friendship with your closest earthly friend. Get acquainted with Christ. Act as if He were what He says He is. Trust His promises—not one of them shall fail. Let His love into your heart—it will fill you with joy and peace; it will transform your life into love and beauty and radiance.

25

The Way, The Truth, and The Life

Scripture Reading: John 14:1–14

The fourteenth chapter of John's gospel is the most familiar chapter of the New Testament. Its words are sweet music. As spoken first, it was the little company of the disciples sitting at the Last supper who heard them. They were in great sorrow. They were about to lose their Master, their best friend. They had hoped that He was the Messiah and were expecting some special manifestation of His power. Now all their hopes seemed to be swept away. Jesus speaks to them as they sit around the table. He seeks to comfort them. He says to them, "Let not your heart be troubled." This seems a strange word to say to them at this particular hour. How was it possible that they should not be troubled when He, their Master, was about to leave them? We may be sure, however, that the words He spoke were not empty or formal. Many things that earthly comforters say to their friends in their times of trouble mean but little. They say, "Weep not. Dry your tears. All will come right," but they have no real comfort to offer. They can give no reason why their friends should not weep, or why all will come right. Their optimism is without foundation. But when Christ said, "Let not your heart be troubled," He knew what He was saying, and there were in His mind clear reasons why He spoke in this strong, confident way. The same is true of the comfort Christ speaks now to us. No matter what the sorrow, how great the loss, how

515

deep the darkness, if we are Christians, the same voice always speaks to us in the same words.

Christ tells the disciples what they should do, how they might cease to be troubled. "Ye believe in God." This was the way their trouble should be comforted. There was no need to ask questions, for their questions could not be answered, or at least they could not understand the answers. But they were to keep their faith in God and in Jesus Christ unshaken, undisturbed, in the midst of all the sorrow. They thought everything was gone, that they did not have God anymore, that all their hopes about Jesus Christ had failed, were only dreams. He tells them that nothing they had believed about God or about Jesus was gone. Their faith in God was to abide. What they had hoped about Jesus Christ was true. They had lost nothing.

This is the foundation of all true comfort. We cannot understand the mystery of sorrow, but if we believe in God and in Jesus Christ, we need not lose our confidence or our peace, whatever the distress may be. A word of an old prophet [Is. 26:4] says, "Trust ye in the Lord forever, for in the LORD JEHOVAH is the everlasting strength." If we are hidden in the cleft of the Rock of Ages* we need not fear any seeming disaster. Another word says, "Thou wilt keep him in perfect peace, whose mind is stayed on Thee, because he trusteth in Thee" [Is. 26:3]. We may always be sure of God's eternal faithfulness and of Christ's unchanging love, and believing these great truths, we may be quiet and confident in the worst calamities.

The first thought Jesus gave His disciples was that all the world is the Father's house. They were greatly distressed by what was transpiring in a little corner of the world. He assures them that the stage of action reached out far beyond the city and the country in which they lived. There are many mansions in the Father's house. They were distressed that He was leaving them, but He was leaving only one of the mansions and going to another. They would not lose Him by His departure, for He would continue to be their friend, and would still be interested in their welfare. "I go to prepare a place for you." Dr. David Smith thus explains the words of Jesus:

---

*The words "the everlasting strength" in Isaiah 26:4 are more accurately rendered in the NIV and the NASB texts "the Rock of Ages." *Ed.*

The disciples were like travelers, and His companionship had hitherto cheered them on their journey. And now He must leave them. But He was not forsaking them. He was only hasting on in advance to make ready for them. And when they arrived He would be waiting for them and would bid them welcome.

His going away was not a desertion of His friends. He was going on their account, to prepare a place for them. The thought of mansions prepared for us beforehand is a very beautiful one. We need not fear that when our time comes to go home there will be no place ready for us. We shall not go to the gate as strangers or aliens, but as those who are expected, those who indeed have been sent for. Jesus assured His disciples not only that He was going on to prepare a lodging place for them, but that when the place was ready He would come again, to receive them unto Himself, that where He would be they might be too. The separation was only apparent, not real, and certainly not final. The relation between them would not be broken by His going away. The ministry of His love which had come to mean so much to them, would not be interrupted by His departure. He was going to leave them in their present lodging place, but it would be only to prepare another lodging place for them in another part of His Father's house.

"I am the way." Christ is the way from earth to heaven, and from heaven to earth. Through Him God comes to us with love and blessing, and through Him we go to God. He is the Mediator between God and man. He is the one ladder down which angels come on their ministries and up which they can ascend to the gates of glory. Christ is the way, and the only way. If we reject Him we can never get home. But if we believe on Him, and love Him, and abide in Him, there never can be any confusion, any mystery, any want unmet, any yearning unfulfilled.

Even now, with all our knowledge of spiritual things, the other life is still full of mystery. When our loved ones leave us we cannot understand where they have gone; and when we think of going ourselves, we cannot realize anything of the way. So it was with the first disciples. Thomas was perplexed about the way of their going where Jesus was going. "We know not whither thou goest; and how can we know the way?" Jesus sought to relieve the mystery. "I am the way," He said. This is the answer to all our longings. Philip thought he knew Christ well. He had been in His family for more than three years. It is possible for us to be with Christ a long time, in His Church, among His people, familiar with the story in the Gospels, and yet not really know Him. There is a great difference between knowing about Christ and knowing Him.

Jesus went on to explain to Philip the meaning of the blessed, beautiful life He had been living with them. "He that hath seen me hath seen the Father." If John had said this about himself we would have called it blasphemy. When Christ said it about Himself, He very clearly claimed to be divine. He was the revealer of God. What men saw in His life was an interpretation of God's own life. When we see Him taking little children in His arms, laying His hands on their heads and blessing them, we see how God feels toward children. When we see the compassion of Jesus stirred by human suffering and sorrow, we learn how our Father is touched by the sight of earthly suffering. When we see Jesus receiving sinners and eating with them, speaking forgiveness to penitents who crept to His feet, and making stained lives white and clean, we learn the mercy of God. When we follow Christ to His cross and see Him giving His life a willing sacrifice in redemption for lost men, we see how God loves this world. So the holiness of Christ was the Father's holiness; His meekness, patience, gentleness and compassion were mirrorings of the same qualities in the Father. If we would see what God is like, we have but to turn to the gospel story. To know Christ is to know the Father.

Now we have another phase of the marvelous teaching. Christ and the Father were one. He who saw the life of Christ saw God. Still more, Christ and His followers were one. His life was in them. "He that believeth on me, the works that I do shall he do also." Christ Himself was going away, and would be missed from the earth. Those He had comforted and helped would long for His visits when He would come no more. There are some good men and women who leave a great emptiness in the world when they go away. The departure of Christ left a great blank in the homes He had been used to visiting. But it was the plan of Christ that His disciples should take His place and go on with the ministry which He had begun. His life was to be taken away, but He would live on in His disciples. If we take off slips from a geranium and put them into the ground anywhere, they will grow and have the same beauty and fragrance as the original plant. All true Christians are parts of Christ, branches of Christ, so to speak; and wherever they may be they will have His likeness and His spirit, His love and gentleness, and will do the same works that He produced. Are we fulfilling our mission as Christians? If not, why not?

There was another link in the chain. Christ was going away, but He would not be out of reach. "Whatsoever ye shall ask in my name, that will I do." They could not see Him face to face in human life and get the things they needed, but they could speak to Him and ask Him for blessings and get them. While Jesus was going away and would be out of sight, He would not be beyond call. His people on earth could speak to Him and, although they saw Him not, He would hear them. The way of communication with Christ has never been broken. We are to pray always in the name of Christ—that is, we are to ask things for His sake, because He is our Savior.

26

The Comforter Promised

Scripture Reading: John 14:15–27

Everything in Christian life is love. "The fruit of the Spirit is love." There are other things that are mentioned as fruit, but love is named first, and all the others are only parts or qualities of love. The one white ray of light is resolved into the seven colors of the rainbow. So love, the white ray that shines from the face of God, separates itself into all the heavenly graces. "The fruit of the Spirit is love, joy, peace, longsuffering, gentleness, goodness, faith, meekness, temperance" [Gal. 5:22, 23].

Love is the one essential in the life which the Holy Spirit produces. Paul tells us we may have great eloquence, tongues of angels, the gift of prophecy, faith that can move mountains, generosity that will give all we possess, the martyr's spirit; and yet, if we have not love we are nothing. Men have been champions of orthodoxy, and yet, lacking love, given to anger, evil temper, resentment. There are those who are devoted to the institutions of religion and who yet fail to show love at home. These do not meet the highest requirement of the gospel. Nothing but love can satisfy the demands of the Holy Spirit.

We must prove our love by our life. "If ye love me, keep my commandments." We cannot live truly except by loving, but we cannot love and not live worthily. It is very easy to say we love a person, but our conduct is the only true index. In one of his epistles John, the disciple

520

of love writes: "Hereby perceive we the love of God, because he laid down His life for us: and we ought to lay down our lives for the brethren. But whoso hath this world's good, and seeth his brother have need, and shutteth up his bowels of compassion from him, how dwelleth the love of God in him? My little children, let us not love in word, neither in tongue; but in deed and in truth" [1 John 3:16–18]. John is speaking of the proof of love to our fellowmen, but the same principle applies to our profession of love to Christ. It is not enough that we sing it in our hymns and say it in our prayers and recite it in our creeds; we must show it in our life by obedience to His commandments. A fruit tree proves its usefulness by bearing fruit. If there is "nothing but leaves," the tree's profession is empty. The rosebush must prove its right to the distinction by putting forth beautiful roses in the season for roses. When we claim to be Christ's friends, we must show it by doing what Christ bids us do.

Promise follows requirement. If we truly love Christ, we will keep His commandments. Then He says, "And I will pray the Father, and he shall give you another Comforter." The "and" is important. It links the promise back to the previous verse. There are four links in the chain. If we love Christ, we will keep His commandments; then He will pray the Father, and the Father will give us another Comforter. The disciples thought they would be sore losers by Christ's leaving them, and so they were, in a sense. It broke their hearts to part from Him. But He assures them that instead of His personal presence another heavenly Friend would be sent to them. The name "Comforter" is a very precious one. Even in the common usage of the English word it is sacred. One who is a comforter to us ministers to us in our sorrows, consoles us when we are in grief. Then the word "another" shows what kind of comforter the Spirit would be—Jesus had been a comforter, and the Spirit would be one like Him. We sometimes wish we had lived when Jesus was on earth, and feel that those who knew Him in the flesh had a privilege no other believers ever again can have. But this word tells us that the Holy Spirit, who came in Christ's place, is all to us that Jesus was to His friends. He may not take away our sorrows, from us, but if not, He gives us strength so that we can bear them. That is part of what the Holy Spirit does for us. He is not, however, merely a comforter in the sense that the word is now used. The word is "Paraclete," which has no precise equivalent in

English. The same word is translated "Advocate" in one of John's epistles, which means one who stands by or stands for one. We may put all our affairs into the hands of this Advocate. He will defend us, intercede for us, be our comrade and friend.

The world does not want to receive the Holy Spirit—"Whom the world cannot receive." It has no love for Him, no eyes to behold His beauty, no ears to hear His words. The world does not want the Spirit as guest. Only those who desire to be holy have any yearning for Him. It is one of the most wonderful proofs of the love of God that the Holy Spirit is willing to live in a corrupt, defiled, loathsome human heart, amid all its sin and uncleanness, for the purpose of cleansing it and making it holy and fit for heaven. It was one of the qualities of the love of Christ that it went out in compassion and longing to the most unworthy. Someone defined the love of God as "loving people He did not like." The Spirit of God takes up His abode in the worst heart, that He may make it clean and holy.

It is wonderful how gently Christ dealt with His disciples that night. He talked with them as a mother about to leave her children would talk to them, mingled counsel with words of love. He knew how lonely they would be when He was gone away from them. They would indeed be desolate in their sorrow and bereavement. We remember how it was with them those days that He lay in the grave. Then for forty days they saw Him occasionally, receiving sweet consolation from Him. After this He went away, but soon He came again in the Holy Spirit, and after that the disciples were never lonely anymore, for they had their Master's presence with them in close and loving tenderness all the while. We ought never to feel desolate if we have Christ. Everything else may be stripped off, and we may be driven out into the world, orphans, homeless; but if we have Christ, we are rich in love and in all heavenly blessing.

The proof of love for God is obedience to His commandments. Then, when love for God is in our lives, God Himself is with us. "If a man love me, he will keep my words: and my Father will love him, and we will come unto him, and make our abode with him." It is a wonderful truth that is declared to us here, that God actually desires to have our love and longs to make His home in our hearts.

One of the great words of the Bible is peace. Our heart hungers for it. Everywhere men search for it, in paths of pleasure, in the avenues of fame. But peace does not come by finding a quiet place to hide in, away from the world's storms. It must begin in the heart. Indeed, the peace a Christian has must be a peace that will hold the heart quiet in spite of the world's storms. Two artists went out to paint each a picture of peace. One painted a silvery lake embosomed deep amid the hills, where no storm ever could touch it. The other painted a wild sea, swept by tempests, strewn with wrecks, but rising up out of it a great rock, and in the rock, high up, a cleft with herbage and flowers, amid which, on her nest, a dove was sitting. The latter is the true picture of Christian peace. "In the world ye shall have tribulation," but "in me ye shall have peace" [see 16:33]. The peace of Christ is a peace that holds the heart quiet in the very heart of the world's trials. This peace is offered to us here as a gift, as Christ's legacy to us. We can get it only by taking Christ Himself into our heart.

27

The Vine and the Branches

Scripture Reading: John 15:1–12

When Jesus says, "I am the true vine," He means that He is the source of the spiritual life of His people, who are compared to branches. What the vine is to its branches, Christ is to all who believe on Him. The branches, down to the smallest twigs, are dependent on the vine. So every believer is dependent on Christ. He is the source of the spiritual life of every Christian. A traveler in Kamchatka who spent many nights in the poor huts of the people tells of His experience. The hut in which he was entertained was dirty, and the people were in every way repulsive. But their kindness was beautiful. They were most attentive to the traveler's wants. The best morsels were put upon His plate. The best bed was given to him. When bedtime came there was family prayer, closing with these words, "Lord, bless our home and bless and prosper our guest." There was something almost heavenly in the spirit of the home, which deeply impressed the visitor. He had found a branch of the true Vine. The life of Christ was flowing in it. There was a vital connection between these kind hearts in Kamchatka and Christ. Wherever a real Christian life is found, there is a little branch of the great Vine. There is no other vine to which any soul can be joined and from which it can be nourished. Other religions may present their legends, their ceremonies, their rules of conduct; but there is no life in any of them. The religion of Christ is more than a creed or a cult, more than a set of moral precepts. It has a great stream of heavenly life flowing from it. All the fullness of God is in it, and of this fullness we all receive.

Another truth suggested in this figure is the dependence of the vine upon the branches. It is easy to see how the branches depend upon the vine, but the only way a vine can bear fruit is on its branches. So the only way Christ can feed the world's hunger is through His disciples. We ought to think of the responsibility of being a branch. The only way to be a good branch is to be full of fruit, the same kind of fruit that Christ bore on His life.

The culture of the vine is also important. Jesus says that the Father is the Husbandman. The care of the branches is in His hands. It ought to be a great comfort to us to know that our life's training and discipline are under the Father's care. If an ignorant, inexperienced, unskillful man were to enter a beautiful vineyard and begin cutting at the vines, he would soon destroy them. He does not know what he ought to cut off. But if the man who comes to prune knows about vines, and has had experience and is skilled, though he may sometimes seem to be destroying a vine, yet we know that he is not making any mistakes and that His most severe and painful prunings are for the good of the vine. We have similar confidence when God seems to be dealing sorely or even harshly with us. The Husbandman is our Father; He has all wisdom and love, and never gives us pain nor cuts away any of our joys except when such pruning is for our good.

The Husbandman does not trouble to prune the fruitless branches, but only cuts them off and casts them away. "Every branch in me that beareth not fruit he taketh away." All through the Bible uselessness meets God's disfavor and condemnation. The wicked are compared to the chaff which the wind drives away. Chaff is of no use; it feeds no hunger; it has no value and no beauty; it is fit only to be burned. The fruitless branch stands for the formal profession of religion. Merely nominal church members without spiritual life are not of any benefit to the church. For a time the Husbandman may be patient with them, waiting while He tried in all ways to bring them into real union with Himself, and to make them fruitful; but when due efforts have been made and there is still no fruitfulness, they are cut away.

It is the fruitful branches which the Husbandman prunes and tends. The motive of His care is that in this way these branches may become more fruitful. "Every branch that beareth fruit, he purgeth it, that it may bring forth more fruit." The pruning process is a very important one. Dead twigs must be cut away. Sometimes there is too much foliage. There is not life enough to nourish all the branches. Some of them, therefore, must be cut off, that what remains may receive full nourishment. There may then be less fruit for the present, but it will be better, richer fruit. The Husbandman does not prune the unfruitful branches—pruning would do them no good, It is the Christian that the Father chastens and causes sometimes to suffer under sore discipline. Mere formal professors of religion are left alone, and often they grow very luxuriant, like unpruned vines. But in their luxuriance there is no spiritual fruit.

Notice also that the object of the Father's pruning is that the branch may be made to bear more fruit. It sometimes seems that the pruning is destructive. Great branches are cut off, and it seems as if the very life of the vine is endangered. But He who holds the knife knows that what He is doing will make the vine in time more luxuriant and its fruit sweeter and more luscious. If only we would bear this in mind when we find ourselves under God's chastening, it would help us to bear the pain in patience and also to cooperate with God in His design to make us more fruitful. Earthly prosperity is often to a Christian like the excessive luxuriance of a vine, which the vinedresser must cut away with his merciless hand in order to save the vine's life.

Jesus reminded His disciples that He had been acting as their Husbandman and Caretaker. "Now ye are clean through the word which I have spoken unto you." For three years He had been teaching them, speaking to them words of correction, of counsel, of exhortation, and these words had trimmed off the faults, the evil habits, and the sinful things from their lives, leaving them now clean. The word of God is the knife which is used in pruning the branches. This word, Paul says, is profitable for reproof, for correction, for instruction in righteousness, that the man of God may be perfect, thoroughly furnished unto all good works. Every time we read the Bible as we should, thoughtfully, yielding our life to its sway, the knife cuts off some twig or branch which is marring our life or hindering its usefulness. We never should shrink from the impact of the words of God, but should let them cut deep as they will into our life, exposing hidden faults, secret sins, and unlovely dispositions.

Since the branches draw their life from the vine, it is essential that their attachment shall always be complete. "Abide in me, and I in you. As the branch cannot bear fruit of itself, except it abide in the vine; no more can ye, except ye abide in me." We might as well try to grow plants without roots as to have a Christian life without attachment to Christ. The kind of fruits Christian lives should bear are indicated by Paul as love, joy, peace, longsuffering, gentleness, goodness, faithfulness, meekness, and temperance. These fruits can grow only when the life of Christ is in the heart. A branch torn from a vine at once withers and dies. Two trees grew in the same yard. One spring, when the time for leaves came, it was noticed that while one of the trees put forth its foliage as usual, the other stood dark and bare, with neither bud nor leaf nor any life. The same warm sunshine fell upon both, and the same spring rains watered the roots of both, but in one there was life, while in the other there was no life. There are men and women, too, who have spiritual privileges in home and church and Christian friendship, but who bear no fruit. It is because they are not really attached to Christ, not rooted in Him, and therefore they have no life in them.

Many are the blessings of abiding in Christ. One is answer to prayer, "If ye abide in me, and my words abide in you, ye shall ask what ye will, and it shall be done unto you." This promise is a great key with which we may open the door of the divine treasury and take from it whatever we need. But we must not overlook the condition—the twofold condition on which the promise depends. First, we must abide in Christ, in close, intimate union and communion with Him. Secondly, Christ's words must abide in us. This means that His words must be received by us into our hearts, that we must love them, meditate upon them, allow them to rule our actions and words, to color our thoughts and feelings, and to inspire our dispositions. When these conditions are fulfilled we can claim the promise.

It is very important that we should understand well how we may abide in Christ. Jesus tells us plainly. "If ye keep my commandments, ye shall abide in my love." Jesus Himself, in His incarnation, was under the same law of obedience. He says, "Even as I have kept my Father's commandments, and abide in His love." Nothing can take the place of obedience in Christian life. In absolutely no other way can we abide in Jesus Christ's love.

One of the great privileges of Christian life is friendship with Christ. Those who abide in Him and do His will shall become His friends. "Ye are my friends, if ye do whatsoever I command you." That is the way we are to show our love for Christ. It is not enough to say we love Him. That is well so far as it goes, and if we prove it by our deeds it is all right. Shortly before His death, Dean Stanley closed a sermon with some quaint lines, the authorship of which he said he did not certainly know.

> Say well is good, but do well is better.
> Do well seems spirit, say well the letter.
> Say well is godly, and helpeth to please;
> But do well lives godly, and gives the world ease.
> Say well to silence sometimes is bound,
> But do well is free on every ground.
> Say well has friends some here, some there,
> But do well is welcome everywhere.
> But say well to many God's word cleaves,
> But for lack of do well it often leaves.
> If say well and do well were bound in one frame,
> Then all were done, all were won, and gotten
>   were gain.

28

The Spirit's Work

Scripture Reading: John 16:1–15

The disciples were in great sorrow. Jesus had told them that He was going to leave them, and they were so absorbed in thoughts of their loss and so overwhelmed that they had not even thought to ask Him where He was going or why He was going away. He seems here to complain of them for this. Their conduct showed selfishness; they were not interested in His glory, but were absorbed in their own grief and loss. It showed also lack of faith, for they were in danger of losing their hope in Him as the Messiah.

We may get a lesson here for ourselves when called to endure bereavement. We are in danger of making the same mistake. When God takes away from us our beloved friends, we are apt to think only of ourselves and our own earthly loss, and not of the joy and glory into which our friends have gone. Is there not in this an element of selfishness? Is it right that we should think only of what we have lost in their departure, and not of what they have gained? Is it not unbelief that sees only the sorrow and the gloom, and not the light that is back of the gloom? Should we not be willing to suffer loss to ourselves when what is loss to us is eternal gain to those we love? We train ourselves in the fellowships and experiences of life to endure cost and hardship that our friends may be helped, benefited, or made happier. Shall we not exercise the same spirit of unselfish affection toward our loved ones who have gone from

529

us into glory when we suffer loneliness and must bear the double burdens which are ours because they are not with us?

The disciples thought that Christ's going away would be an irretrievable loss for them. It seemed the crushing of all their hopes. They saw no silver lining whatever in the dark cloud that was gathering. But now Jesus says to them, "It is expedient for you that I go away." There was silver after all in that black cloud. What seemed an irreparable loss would prove in the end a gain. They did not understand it now, but here were the Master's words assuring them of it. The same is true in the case of Christ's disciples now when He calls away their human friends. We can readily see how it is well for our believing friends when Christ takes them home. They exchange earth for heaven, sin for holiness, and pain for eternal joy. But how about the friends who are left with bleeding hearts to walk on lonely and sad over earth's ways? This word of Christ replies, "It is expedient for you that I go away." The young wife whose husband is called from her may believe that it is better for him to be with Christ. He is doing more exalted service. He sees His Lord's face. His wife, who stays behind, has to meet life's tasks and responsibilities alone, and misses the joy of companionship. But she, too, has her gain. She learns lessons in the hardness of her loneliness she never would have learned in the sheltered and pampered ease of love. The finer possibilities of life are brought out in her. Burden-bearing develops her womanly strength. She grows into a strength and a beauty of character she never would have attained if she had not lost the companionship which made life so restful and quiet. We cannot understand now, and neither could the disciples understand how Christ's departure could be better for them than His staying with them would have been. Afterwards they knew; and afterwards we shall know, too, how even for us the going away of our friends will become a blessing if we in faith submit ourselves to God.

The disciples had no thought that when Jesus was gone from them, He would be more to them than He ever had been in His bodily presence. "If I go not away, the comforter will not come unto you; but if I depart, I will send him unto you." Many people wish they could have known Christ as His personal disciples and other friends knew Him. They think it would have been so much easier to have loved and trusted Him if they could have seen His face and heard His words and felt His touch, if they could have gone to Him with all their questions and perplexities and could have had His help in every experience of need. But Christ Himself says that His staying with His disciples would have been a loss to them, and that His going away would be a gain. Christ has not left the world; He was never so really present with His own disciples when they could see Him as He afterward was, when they could not see Him. The presence of the Holy Spirit in the world is a greater blessing than Christ's continued bodily presence would have been. It is the same presence in a form that can do infinitely more for us. There are limitations to physical presence, but there are no limitations to the divine Spirit. We have lost none of the blessing which those who knew Christ in the flesh enjoyed; on the other hand, He is far more to us now than He was to the first disciples. In the body He could not be present in even two places at the same time; in the Spirit He can be with millions of people in different lands at the same moment.

Jesus tells His disciples of the work the Spirit will do when He comes. "When he is come, he will reprove the world of sin, and of righteousness, and of judgment." The first work of the Spirit is not pleasant work, but painful. He crushes before He heals. He brings terror before He brings joy. He comes first of all to show us our sins. As His light shines upon us we see the stains in our hearts. As His holiness is revealed it shows us how unholy we are. Then, as He lifts the veil, we have a glimpse of the judgment when we must stand before God's bar. Yet this is not unkind work; He shows us our guilt and peril, not to trouble us, but to save us, and then, when we have seen our need and danger, He points us to Jesus Christ the Savior. Some tourists once lost their way in the Alps as night came on. They groped about for a time, not knowing where they were, and at length a terribly violent storm burst upon them, and a lightning flash showed them that they were standing on the very edge of a fearful precipice; a few steps more, and they would have been hurled to death. It was a kind storm that by its lurid flash revealed to them their peril, because thereby it saved them. Terrible are the convicting flashes of the Spirit, sometimes striking terror into the soul; but they are merciful flashes, for they are meant to save.

The sin of which the Holy Spirit convicts is the sin of not believing on Christ. So the worst of sins is the rejection of Christ. He is the Son of God who came to the world to prepare and bring salvation. People think murder is the worst sin, and they think that stealing and lying are terrible sins, and so they are. But do we ever think that no other sin we can possibly commit is so base and so soul-destroying as unbelief in Christ? We should think of this. Unbelievers are very ready to pick flaws in the conduct of professing Christians, and they congratulate themselves that, while they do not believe in Christ, they are better than those who do. Do they remember that, evil as their other sins are, their unbelief is the blackest of them all in God's sight? No moral goodness, however beautiful it may be, makes one acceptable in God's sight while Jesus Christ is rejected in the heart and shut away from the life. It is a terrible thing to reject the Son of God, who comes to us to be our Savior.

Part of the work of the Spirit is to lead us into ever fuller and deeper knowledge. We never can know the truth if the Spirit be not our teacher. We cannot understand the Bible unless the Spirit makes it plain. Men of great intellectual powers have listened to sermons of which they could understand scarcely a word, while some plain, unlettered woman, with threadbare garments, sitting in some back gallery seat, understood every word, her heart being enlightened and thrilled by the blessed truths. She was taught of the Spirit. There are devout men who never open the Bible without a prayer that God would show them its meaning. We must remember also that it is as a guide that the Spirit comes to us. He does not promise to teach us Himself; He will not make any new revelation to us; He teaches through the truth. He comes to guide us to the understanding of the truths already revealed. He honors God's Word, and comes not as a teacher of new truth, but as an interpreter. There is no doubt about the Spirit's readiness to help us into the deepest things of the Scriptures if we are truly ready to follow His guidance. But we must be willing to receive the truth without question, though it sweep away all our own opinions; and to accept it as a rule of our life, though it revolutionize all our conduct.

The great work of the Spirit is to make Christ known. "He shall glorify me: for he shall receive of mine, and shall show it unto you." Even the divine Spirit does not preach Himself, but, remaining unseen, points men to Christ. The Spirit glorifies Christ; that is, makes Him glorious in the eyes of men. As the world saw Jesus, He was far from lovely. His visage was marred; He was despised; He died on a cross of shame; His name was hated and covered with obloquy. But the Spirit came and poured such light upon Him that He appears all glorious in His beauty. In all the world there is no other face so lovely, so radiant, as the face of Jesus Christ. Men who have hated Him, seeing Him only dimly, when the Spirit reveals Him to them as He really is, see Him as the chief among ten thousand, and one altogether lovely.

29

Alone, yet Not Alone

Scripture Reading: John 16:32

The loneliness of Jesus while in this world was one of the most pathetic elements of His experience. There are two kinds of loneliness. One is, when a person is away from all human presences. A man who had been shipwrecked and had drifted for many hours on a piece of wreckage, spoke of the terrible feeling of desolation he experienced when on all the waste of waters he could see no sign of human life, hear no voice, get no ear to listen to His calls of distress. But there is another loneliness. One may be in the midst of people and yet be utterly without companionship. Were you never oppressed with a sense of loneliness in a crowd that surged all about you and pressed close to you on every side? Think of the loneliness of one who lands from a foreign country and enters the throngs on the streets of a strange city, but sees no face he ever has seen before, catches no glance of recognition from any eye. In a surging multitude of human beings he is utterly alone. It takes more than human presence to make companionships; hearts must touch; there must be love and sympathy.

In a sense, Christ was always alone in this world. His very greatness of character made it impossible for Him to find real, deep, and full companionship. All great men are in a sense solitary men. Their exalted life lifts them above the plane in which other people live. They are like the few tall mountain peaks of the earth that lift their heads far above the

534

clouds, and wear their crowns of unmelting snows. The little hills are not lonesome, for there are so many of them, but the giant mountains are lonely in their solitariness because there are so few of them. The world's few great men are solitary because common people cannot rise into companionship with them in thought, in feeling, in purpose. Christ found no fellow, no equal, no real companion, among men.

Then in His work as Redeemer, Christ was alone. He had few friends. There is infinite pathos in such words as these, which describe His personal loneliness: "He was in the world, and the world was made by Him, and the world knew Him not. He came unto His own, and His own received him not" [1:10, 11]. He revealed His feeling of aloneness and sense of homelessness when He said, "Foxes have holes, and the birds of the air have nests; but the Son of man hath not where to lay His head." [Matt. 8:20; Luke 9:58]. Thus in the midst of multitudes, His own people, too, not foreigners, those also He had come to deliver and save, He was alone because hearts and homes were shut against Him.

Then, too, Jesus had a gentle heart, which craved affection and companionship. There are some men with cold, stern natures, who are indifferent to the coldness they meet in the world. They desire no sympathy. They are not pained by men's rejection. Opposition acts as stimulus to them. They almost court unpopularity. But Jesus craved affection and sympathy. We remember how He welcomed love whenever it came to Him; what a strength the beloved disciple was to Him; what a shelter and comfort the Bethany home, with its love, was to Him; how even the slightest tokens of kindness comforted and cheered His heart. We see also His deep craving for companionship in the Garden, when He wanted His closest friends near Him in His bitter agony and so deeply felt the disappointment when they slept and did not watch with Him. Jesus was not, then, a cold, iron man, who was unaffected by the indifferences and rejection of the people. He suffered keenly from every unloving act and touch. This intensified His loneliness.

Here we have another phase of Christ's loneliness. "Ye shall be scattered, every man to His own, and shall leave me alone." The only human relief to His loneliness, along the years of His public ministry, was in the love of His friends; and this love, we know, was very imperfect. These friends, though loyal and devoted, never fully understood their Master. They had an earthly conception of His Messiahship, yet they were very unspiritual. They hurt Him continually by their lack of gentleness, thoughtfulness, and perfect trust. They grieved Him—unintentionally, of course, ignorantly, loving Him still, but giving Him pain every day by the rudeness and harshness of their contacts with His sensitive heart. Very poor and imperfect, indeed, was the companionship which He found even with the gentlest and truest of His human friends.

But now He looks forward to the losing of even this solace and support. "Ye shall be scattered, every man to His own, and shall leave me alone." Even the little company of friends, who had walked with Him along the way, would desert Him in the hour of His supreme trial. We remember how it was. One of those who had eaten bread with Him, dipping His hand in the same dish, betrayed Him. Another, till then His bravest confessor, denied even knowing Him. They all forsook Him and fled. Alone, He was led away to His trial. Alone, He was left to stand before the court and before the governor. Loving and craving love as no other ever loved and craved love, He was left alone, with no pitying eye, with not one friendly voice raised in His behalf. At the close of a life given to love of men and to efforts to save men, He was left with no one confessing to have been helped or saved by Him, no friend, no follower; abandoned to the cruelty of brutal men. Even Barabbas, a notorious criminal, found friends that day, while Jesus, who had given His life to gentle deeds and kind ministries, was dragged away by His enemies through the streets, as if He had been a murderer, with no one to speak a word for Him.

But read what He says of this hour of abandonment: "Ye shall be scattered, every man to His own, and shall leave me alone: and yet I am not alone, because the Father is with me." There was One whose companionship never failed Him for a moment. Through the years when His infinite divine nature found such meager, imperfect fellowship even in the best love of human friends, He had but to turn His face toward His Father to have His hungry heart filled. When His affectionate nature met only misunderstanding, coldness, rejection, antagonism among the people for whose love and trust He so hungered, He would go away at nightfall, apart from men, and on some mountaintop or in some deep garden shade He would commune with One who was all love, who never misunderstood Him, and in whose blessed companionship all of the hungers of His heart were satisfied, and all the hurts of love were healed.

One of the most touching incidents in the Gospels described what occurred at the close of one day in the temple. "Every man went unto His own house: but Jesus went unto the Mount of Olives" [see John 7:53—8:1]. It was evening—night was gathering. It was time for all to go away. But nobody asked Jesus home with him. They went to their own fine houses on the great streets, leaving Him there. Then He, homeless, with no place to go, no place to lay His head that night, climbed the Mount of Olives, and there stayed alone—alone, but not alone, because the Father was with Him.

We may apply the words to experiences in our own lives. We, too, have our times of loneliness. In a certain sense, all life is lonely. Even with sympathetic friends all about us, there is an inner life which one of us lives, in which we are solitary. We must make our own decisions and choices. We must meet our own questions and answer them ourselves. We must fight our own battles, endure our own sorrows, carry our own burdens. Friendship may be very close, so close that it seems to us there is no part of our deepest life which our friend does not share with us; yet there is an inner sanctuary of each human life, into which even the most perfect friendship may not enter.

> "Still in each heart of hearts a hidden deep
> Lies, never fathomed by its dearest, best."

Blessed are they who in this aloneness can say, "Yet I am not alone, because my Father is with me." God is the only friend who can really enter into the inner sanctuary of our life. God's is the only companionship we can really have in the inner experiences of our hearts. God's is the only friendship that can really meet all our soul's deep needs and cravings. Human love is only a little trickling stream; God's is a great river, broadening into a shoreless ocean. Human companionship helps us at a few points; the divine fellowship flows all about us and enters into every experience of ours. We never can be left alone if we still have Christ. When other helpers and comforts flee, He will abide with us. When other faces fade out of view, His face will appear, shining out with perfect love, pouring its holy light upon us. "I am not alone, because the Father is with me."

There are special times when we are alone. Pain sets us apart. We have to endure it alone. In any pain or grief of yours, you may have truest friends about you, but none of them can bear one pang for you. Sometimes we almost blame our friends because they do not come near to us in our trouble, because they do not appear to feel for us or sympathize with us. We say they do not understand us. We think they ought to help us more. But the truth is, we have to live all our inner lives alone. Our friends love us and want to help us, but they cannot. None can fully understand us. None can really help us in any deep and efficient way. Those about us, even those who are our truest friends, who sympathize with us most fully, leave us alone because they cannot share our suffering. But we can always say, "I am not alone, because the Father is with me."

There is a loneliness which is made by the breaking up of homes. A true home is an incalculable blessing to the young lives that nestle in it. It is a shelter where they find protection. It is a school where they are educated, where they learn life's lessons. There is guidance also in a true home. Many of life's hardest questions are answered by wise parents. Blessed is that young man or young woman who takes every perplexity, every mystery, every fear and doubt, every heart-hunger, to the sacredness of love's sanctuary at home and gets wise counsel and guidance.

Home has also its blessed companionships. It is one place where we are absolutely sure of each other, where we need never suspect anyone, where we do not need to be on our guard. Youth has its unexpected longings, its deep cravings, its hunger for affection, its inexperience needing direction. A true home is the very shadow of God's wings, the very cleft of the Rock of Ages, to those who abide in its love. But sometimes the home is torn down and its shelter broken up. Sore indeed is the loss when a young person, used to all that is gentle and satisfying in home tenderness, is driven out to homelessness. Other human friendships are very sweet, but they never can give back home with its rest and comfort. But blessed is he who in earthly homelessness can say, " 'Yet I am not alone': who can look into the face of Christ and breathe out the psalm of peace, 'Lord, thou art my dwelling place; thou art home to my heart.'"

Another time of special loneliness is that of old age. Old people often grow very lonely. Once they were the center of large groups of friends and companions. One by one the loved associates slipped away. Now the old man or the old woman stands almost entirely alone. The streets are full, the church is full; but where are the faces of forty or fifty years ago? There is a memory of empty cribs, of vacant chairs, of little graves, of marriage altars, and then the starting of new homes, perhaps far away. But the old faces are gone. It is young life that now fills the home, the street, the church. Only here and there a companion of forty, fifty years ago remains. The old people are lonely.

Yet Christian old age can say, "I am not alone." No changes take Christ away. Other companions scatter, leaving them humanly alone, but He never departs. Indeed, Christ becomes more and more real to the old, who believe in Him, as other friends drop off and become fewer and fewer. While human friendships filled the life, Christ was not turned to very often, though He was believed in and loved. The joys that were needed were found so easily in the human loves that were always at hand that Christ did not seem so indispensable, so necessary. But as one by one the earthly loved ones dropped off and slipped away, and could not be turned to in the time of need, then Christ began to be more necessary and was turned to more frequently. As the years went on, and more and more of the old friends were missing, Christ grew every day more precious, till now He is almost the only one left. Blessed be the old Christian; he is now drawing near to glory. A little while longer, and he will enter heaven. Soon the old people will pass over, and find again, waiting for them, those who were once their friends here—companions once more, inseparable now, in heaven.

> So long Thy power hath blest me, sure it still
> Will lead me on
> O'er moor and fen, o'er crag and torrent,
> Till the night is gone;
> And with the morn those angel faces smile,
> Which I have loved long since, and lost a while.

But it is not old people only who are left lonely by life's changes. Sorrow touches all ages. There is a continual breaking of human companionships. Blessed are they who can say with every bereavement, "Alone, yet not alone, because Christ is mine, and He never leaves me." Then in Christ also our human ties are made inseparable. We never really can lose each other if we are united in Christ.

> Our own are our own forever; God taketh not
> back His gift;

They may pass beyond our vision, but our
    souls shall find them out
When the waiting is all accomplished and the
    earthly shadows lift,
And glory is given for grieving, and the
    surety of God for doubt.

We may find the waiting bitter, and count the
    silence long;
God knoweth we are dust, and He pitieth
    our pain;
And when faith has grown to fullness, and the
    silence changed to song,
We shall eat the fruit of patience, and shall
    hunger not again."

In Christ we never lose a friend. But this is not all, nor the best. Human loneliness here is filled with the divine presence of Christ. "I am not alone, because the Father is with me."

There is no other loneliness in all human experience like that of dying. We cannot die in companies, or in groups, nor even two and two. We must die alone. Two may walk together for long years, never divided in joy or sorrow. But they cannot die together. Human hands, however long they have held each other, must unclasp as the friends enter the valley of shadows—one taken, the other left. Human faces that have looked into ours through the years, must fade from our vision as we pass into the mists. "I cannot see you," said a dying friend the other night, as the loved ones stood about His bed. "I cannot see you." So will it be with each of us some night. Human friends cannot go beyond the edge of the valley. "Ye shall leave me alone." Yes, that will be true of each of us in our turn. But we need not be alone even in that supreme moment. When the hand of human love unclasps, the hand of Christ will take your hand and lead you through. When human faces fade out, Christ's face will be revealed, with its welcome of infinite love. When you must creep out of the bosom of human affection, and pass into the mystery of death, it will be into the clasp of the Everlasting Arms. So death's loneliness will be filled with divine companionship. "I am not alone, because the Father is with me"

Thus the one great need of life is Christ. If we do not have Christ, what will we do in life's crises? When human joy fades, what will be left? When human companionships are stripped off, who will walk with us the rest of the lonely way? When death comes, and we must drift out from all we ever have known, from earth's refuges and trusts and from earth's familiar places and friends, where shall we go? In whom shall we trust? Who will receive us and lead us home? If we have not Christ, life is hopeless and the universe is homeless for us. But if we have Christ, then, no matter what is taken, He will remain and He will suffice.

30

Jesus Prays for His Friends

Scripture Reading: John 17:15–26

A writer tells of suddenly opening the door of his mother's room one day in his boyhood, seeing her on her knees, and hearing her speak his own name in prayer. He quickly and quietly withdrew from the sacred place, but he never forgot that one glimpse of his mother at prayer, nor the one word—his own name—which he heard her speak to God. Well did he know that what he had seen that moment was but a glimpse of what went on every day in that place of prayer. The consciousness of this fact, he says, strengthened him countless times in duty, in danger, in struggle. In this seventeenth chapter of John's gospel we hear Christ praying just once, a few sentences, but we know that this is only a sample of what is going on forever in heaven, for the Scriptures tell us that He ever liveth to make intercession for us.

Jesus knew that the end had come, the time for Him to make His great sacrifice, to offer Himself for the redemption of the world. He knew how much depended upon this hour. So He prayed that the Father would glorify Him in His sufferings that in turn He might glorify His Father. When we are about entering any sore trial, or taking up any great duty on which much depends, it should be our prayer that God would so sustain us that we may honor Him in the experience and in the way we pass through it. We should dread nothing so much as the dishonoring of God in sorrow, in trial, or in pain, by losing faith, by complaining, by murmuring. The deepest wish and prayer of our hearts always should be that we may be enabled to glorify God in every experience of our lives. "Love's secret," says Faber, "is to be always doing things for God, and not to mind because they are such very little things."

This means that we do nothing, say no word, let no feeling enter our heart that would in any way dishonor God. A great preacher who was subject at times to seasons of excruciating suffering would ask when the paroxysms were over, "Did I complain? I did not want to complain." He wished to endure His anguish without yielding to any expression of pain, and he feared that he had not honored God as he had wished to do. Too many fail in glorifying God in suffering. Allowing themselves to cry out, to fret, to chafe and repine, giving way to feelings of pain, to impatience, to envy or jealousy, to anger and bitterness, to discouragement or despair, is to fail in glorifying God.

Jesus looks back over His past, too, with comfort and satisfaction. He can say to the Father, "I have glorified Thee on the earth: I have finished the work which Thou gavest Me to do" [17:4]. He is the only person that ever lived who could say this. The most faithful of us have done but a little of what God meant for us to do when He made us. The best and most complete human lives are but little fragments in which are left undone many things which ought to have been done. We may take a lesson, too, from Christ's way of accomplishing His work. He did it by simply doing each day the will of His Father. He was only a young man—thirty-three years old—when He died. We think of those dying early as dying too soon, before their work is accomplished. Yet we learn from Jesus that even a young man may leave a finished work. Years enough are given to each one in which to do the work allotted. Even a baby that lives but a day, just looking into the mother's eyes and then going back to God, does its work, all the work that was given it to do. And the young man who dies at thirty-three, with his hands full of tasks, whom his friends mourn as having died prematurely, if only he has lived faithfully while he lived, has accomplished the work that God gave him to do. Not many years, but diligence and faithfulness count with God.

Jesus makes an earnest prayer for His disciples before He leaves them. He knows what lies before them—the persecutions, the struggles, the temptations, and then their weakness, their ignorance, their inability in themselves to meet these perils and difficulties; so He commends them to

His Father, "Holy Father, keep through thine own name those whom thou hast given me." While He was in this world, Jesus had kept them in the Father's name, guarding them so that not one of them had perished but the son of perdition. Now, however, He was about to leave them in the world. He was going back to God, and they would not have His protection, the shelter of His love, His divine strength, to keep them. He knows that the world will hate them and persecute them, even as it had hated and persecuted Him. But He will not leave them alone. He will so keep them that they shall not be overwhelmed in the world's enmity. In great tenderness He commends them to His Father's keeping.

Jesus does not pray that His disciples should be taken out of the world to escape the danger. This would have been the easier way for them, for with Him in heaven they would have been safe from all persecution. But they had a work to do in this world, and therefore they must stay to do it. They were to represent their Master, carrying on His work among men. Hence, He must leave them behind Him. It was for this very work that He had called them and made them His followers. It would be a great deal easier in one sense for Christian people if they were taken to heaven as soon as they had become Christ's followers. Then they would have no cross-bearing, no giving of their lives for others, no struggles, self-denials and sacrifices. But who then would do Christ's work in the world? Who would look after the wandering ones, or rescue those who are tempted? Thus followers of Christ are left to the world after they become Christ's friends, both for their own sakes and for the sake of others. It seems hard to have to fight battles and endure trials, but these battles and trials are means of strengthening and growth. Not those who have the easiest life are really the most favored ones, but those who endure. They are not the most majestic trees that grow in the sheltered valley, but those that are found on hilltops and mountains, where they must encounter fierce storms. When armies return from victorious war, the loudest cheers are not for those who have fought the fewest battles and wear the fewest scars, nor for the flags that are cleanest, but for the regiments that are cut down to the fewest men, and for the colors that have been shot to tatters. So when the redeemed are welcomed home, those who have fought the hardest battles and who wear the most scars will be received with the highest honor.

The prayer that Jesus did make for His disciples was that they should be kept from the evil of the world. There is but one evil in the world.

It is not trouble, not persecution, not suffering nor sorrow. The one and only evil is sin. No matter what comes to us, so long as we do not sin, we have not been harmed. The Revised Version makes the evil personal—"the evil one." We know who this "evil one" is. It is a great comfort also for us to know that Christ our Master is stronger than Satan, and if we are faithful to Him, Satan will have no power to harm us.

Jesus prayed also for His disciples that they might be sanctified in the truth. A man is sanctified when he is given up to God to live for Him only, to think, to feel, to act, to do all things for the glory of God and in God's service of love for men. It means also the cleansing and purifying of the life and character.

Then the prayer of Christ reached out beyond the little group of men who stood about Him that night in the upper room and took in all who ever should believe on Him. "Neither pray I for these alone, but for them also which shall believe on me through their word." We can think of ourselves as remembered that night by the Master before He set out for His cross. The special prayer that He made for all His disciples was that they might be one. Anything that separated them in heart and life, the one from the other, would destroy their unity as believers. The great passion of the Redeemer's heart was that His disciples might be one. The reason He so longed for their unity was that the world might be impressed by their oneness and might be led to believe in Christ. It was a unity of heart and spirit which Christ had in mind, not a mere formal unity. He would have His people bound together in bonds of love. Denominationalism need not be wrong nor harmful if the different churches live together in the spirit of love and unity. But controversy and strifes not only dishonor Christ, but greatly mar the influence of Christianity in the world.

An old legend says that when Adam and Eve were turned out of Eden, an angel broke the gates to pieces, and the fragments flying over the earth are the precious stones which men now gather. A writer makes an application of the legend—he says that the precious stones were picked up by the various religions and philosophies, each claiming that His own fragment alone reflects the light of heaven and is the material of which the gates of paradise were made. But as all these fragments had the same origin, it is the work of Christianity to gather them all back again into one unity, thus reconstructing the gates of paradise. Every Christian represents Christ, and all Christians combined together should represent the spirit of Christ, the love of Christ, the compassion, the patience, the mercy of Christ. We all should seek to be one in spirit, to whatever particular branch of the Church we may chance to belong.

31

Christ Betrayed

Scripture Reading: John 18:1–13

It was after the great intercessory prayer. Jesus now set out on His
journey to the cross. The Garden of Gethsemane was on the way.
This was one of His familiar sacred resorts for prayer, and here He
lingered for an hour. Leaving eight of His disciples at the outer edge
of the Garden to watch, He took three, His closest friends, with Him
a little farther. "Sit ye here," he said to them, "while I go and pray yon-
der" [Matt. 26:36]. He was drawing near to the terrible experience of
the cross and sought help. Before He passed into the darkness He wanted
the lamps of comfort lighted. Though He was the Son of God, He
sought strength and help in prayer and communion with His Father.
We know that the praying in Gethsemane made the darkness of Calvary less dark and the woe less bitter. Indeed, the battle was really fought
under the olive trees, and when the next day came with its darkness and
anguish, He was ready for it and met it all calmly.

The great lesson for us is that the way to prepare for coming perils
and sorrows is by prayer. A season spent with God will make us strong
for any experiences of struggle or duty. It is said that a young officer
under Wellington, when ordered to perform some perilous duty, lingered a moment and then said to his commander, "Let me first have
a grasp of your all-conquering hand, and then I can do it." We need to
feel the grasp of the mighty hand of Christ, and then we can perform

547

any duty, meet any peril, and endure any trouble. A mother whose life was very hard used often to go away upstairs to her room for a little while, when the burdens became unbearable, and she always would come back with a song and a shining face and a brave heart. We should seek the Garden always before we have to take up the cross.

This Garden meant a great deal to Jesus. Often He had come here with His disciples in the troublous times when His enemies were plotting His death. Here we have a glimpse of our Lord's devotional habits. All through His life He had His times for prayer. There were mountaintops where He spent whole nights communing with His Father. We are apt to wonder why He, the Son of God, needed so much to have His seasons of prayer. But the holiest need prayer the most. Some people manage to get along without much praying, but it is at the expense of their spiritual life. Not feeding their souls, they grow very lean. Luther used to say he had so much to do that He could not get along with less than three hours a day praying. Some of us would put it the other way, and say that we have so much to do that we have almost no time for praying. But Luther was wise. A great deal of praying needs always to go to a very little working. Then the habit of praying is important. Some people tell us that prayer should be spontaneous and that regular periods make it formal and take the life out of it; but if there are no regular seasons and places of prayer there will soon be no prayer at all. Jesus had habits of prayer.

Jesus, as He was nearing His cross, sought strength in two ways. He craved human sympathy. He wanted His disciples to be near Him, and to wait and watch with Him. In this they failed Him. Then He craved His Father's help. In this longing He was not disappointed. God never fails those who call upon Him in their distress. The cup did not pass from Him, but as He pleaded His agony became less and less intense, until His cries were quieted into submissive peace.

As Jesus came from the Garden He saw the torches flashing in the near distance. Every new line in the story of the betrayal shows new blackness in the heart of Judas. Going out from the supper table, he hastened to the priests, and quickly got under way with his band of soldiers and police. He knew very well where Jesus had gone. Then, when he had found Him, the manner in which he let the officers know which one of the company they were to arrest shows the deepest blackness of all—he went up to Him as to a dear friend, eager and ardent, and kissed Him; and the words mean that he kissed Him repeatedly, over and over, and with feigned warmth and affection. Let us remember how the treason grew in the heart of Judas, beginning in greed for money, growing into theft and falseness of life, ending at last in the blackest crime the world ever saw. We should watch the beginnings of evil in our hearts.

A picture in the royal gallery of Brussels represents Judas wandering about on the night after the betrayal. He comes by chance upon the workmen who have been making the cross on which Christ shall be crucified on the morrow. A fire nearby throws its light full on the faces of the men who are sleeping peacefully, while resting from their labor. Judas' face is somewhat in the shade, but it is wonderfully expressive of awful remorse and agony as he catches sight of the cross and the tools used in making it—the cross which his treachery had made possible. But still, though in the very torments of hell, as it appears, he clutches his moneybag and seems to hurry on into the night. That picture tells the story of the fruit of Judas' victory—the moneybag with thirty pieces of silver in it (and even that he could not keep long), carried off into the night of fiendish despair—that was all. The same terrible story of sin is repeated yet, whenever men sell their souls for money or for any price this world pays.

Jesus was not taken by surprise. He knew what it all meant when He saw the soldiers and officers with lanterns and torches and weapons, coming toward Him. He knew the meaning of the kiss from Judas. But He was not startled. He met the betrayal calmly. He stepped forth, saying, "Whom seek ye?" When they told Him, "Jesus of Nazareth," He said, "I am He." They were panic-stricken and fell to the ground. Here we have a glimpse of the power of Jesus. Though He seemed to be ensnared and unable to escape, yet really He never was more free than at that moment. He could have had legions of angels for a word, though even that would have been unnecessary, for He had almighty power in Himself, before which, had He put it forth, all His enemies would have been as nothing, We must remember that Christ's death was voluntary. He gave Himself as a sacrifice. He laid down His life for the sheep. Here we see the love of Jesus in freely offering Himself as our Redeemer. In this scene we have also a hint of the appalling effect Christ's look will have upon His enemies on the judgment day. One glance of His holy eye will send terror into all impenitent hearts and drive the ungodly forever away before the wind. They will call upon the hills and rocks to fall upon them, to hide them from the wrath of the Lamb, but in vain.

In the time of His own great danger Jesus did not forget His disciples, but sought and secured their safety. "If therefore ye seek me, let these go their way," He said. Illustrating the picture He had drawn of the Good Shepherd, He did not flee when He saw the wolf coming, leaving the sheep to be scattered; but gave His own life for the sheep. The incident illustrates also the great work of redemption. Jesus procures the deliverance of His people by surrendering Himself to shame and death, while they go their way in joy and safety. So watchful was He over His own in their time of panic and fear that as He had said, "Of those whom thou hast given me have I not lost one." And that is just as true now, after nineteen centuries, as it was that day. He never has lost a soul who trusted in Him. No one ever has perished who took refuge in the love of Christ. His infinite power protects all who submit themselves to Him as Redeemer and Savior. At the day of judgment Christ will be able to say these same words. We need not be afraid to trust ourselves to the saving of Christ. No matter what our peril may be in any condition or circumstances, we need never be afraid, if we are doing our part faithfully and trusting Him. No power can snatch us out of the hands of Christ.

We are not surprised to find the disciples interfering in behalf of their Master. It broke their hearts to see Him handled so roughly. Peter was always brave. He could not restrain himself, and, after drawing his sword, which he carried, he struck at one of the guards and cut off his ear. But Jesus checked his assault and said, "Put up thy sword . . . the cup which my Father hath given me, shall I not drink it?" We ought to take this word of Jesus for our own. He meant that no resistance such as Peter had attempted should be offered to His arrest; and the reason was that His betrayal, capture, and coming death belonged to "the cup" which the Father had given into His hands; and therefore must not be rejected. There are evils against which we should not lift a finger.

Just how far we ought to resist wrongs inflicted upon us by others is often a difficult question to settle. We remember the words of Christ elsewhere: "Resist not evil: but whosoever shall smite thee on thy right cheek, turn to him the other also. And if any man will sue thee at the law, and take away thy coat, let him have thy cloke also" [Matt. 5:39, 40].

Possibly this doctrine of nonresistance may sometimes be carried too far; but there is no doubt that far more frequently the erring is on the other side. At least we are very sure that if the wrongs threatened belong to "the cup" which the Father hath given us, we ought not to resist them.

32

Jesus Before Pilate

Scripture Reading: John 18:28–40

It was early in the morning. There was special hurry that day, for the
rulers wanted to get their business out of the way because of the approaching feast. The trials before the high priest and council pre-
ceded that before the governor. The rulers, when they could find absolutely nothing against Jesus, had sought to make out their case by bringing in hired witnesses. But even this testimony fell to the ground, no
two of the witnesses agreeing. The only hope was to compel Jesus to
convict Himself by some word He might speak. He stood silent, however, before them, until the high priest adjured Him to answer whether
He were the Christ or not. Then He could be silent no longer. On this
admission the sentence of condemnation was passed by the Sanhedrin.
This was as far as the council could go. They must wait now for the
approval of their sentence by the Roman governor.

Pilate was the one man in all the world who could give the final
word with regard to the sentence of Jesus. This put upon him a fearful
responsibility. While Jesus was standing before Pilate, apparently to be
tried by him, Pilate himself was really on trial before Jesus, and in the
light of that holy face the character of the Roman governor was plainly
revealed. Pilate was deeply impressed by the personality of His prisoner.
He was convinced of His innocence. He wanted to set Him free. But he
had not the courage to oppose the rulers, and so he let them have their

way and sent Jesus to His cross, even against his own conscience, and in spite of the pathetic pleadings of his wife.

The rulers carried their religious scruples even to the palace of Pilate. "They themselves went not into the judgment hall, lest they should be defiled; but that they might eat the Passover." They had no scruples about their treatment of an innocent man, but they were scrupulously conscientious about matters of mere ceremonial requirement. They would not set their feet on the Gentile's floor, for that would have defiled them and made them unworthy to sit down at the passover feast. Yet meanwhile their hearts were full of murderous thoughts and resolves. There always are people to be found who are most punctilious in their acts of devotion, but who in practical life are little better than heathen. We should learn well that the worst heresy is unlovingness, that God is grieved more for our bitter feeling, our lack of love, our spirit of hate and envy, than He is with little omissions in ceremonies and formalities.

When the rulers had presented Jesus to Pilate, he wanted to know what the charges against their prisoner were. He asked them, "What accusation bring ye against this man?" Jesus could not be put to death without Pilate's sentence. It was only fair, therefore, that he should ask His accusers what their charge against Him was. No man ever should be condemned without a trial. We have a right to ask the same question now of those who reject Christ. What wrong has He done? What faults have you found in His character? Whom has He injured? The rulers attempted no answer to Pilate's question—indeed, no answer was possible, for no accusation could be brought against Him. It would have been easy to bring a thousand witnesses to testify to the good things Jesus had done, the works of mercy, the deeds of kindness, the miracles of compassion; but in all the country not one person could have been found to testify to the smallest wrong thing that He had ever done to any being. His life had been a perpetual blessing wherever He had gone. His lips had ever been speaking words of comfort and love. He was hurried to death by men's hate, without reason or charge of any kind.

The rulers assumed an air of dignity in answer to Pilate's demand to know what charge they brought against Jesus, saying that if He were not an evildoer, they would not have brought Him before Pilate. Their bearing was haughty, and Pilate was offended by it. "Take ye him, and judge him according to your law." Pagan as Pilate was, and heartless, the presence of Jesus before him as prisoner filled his heart with dread. There was something about this prisoner which awed him. Ordinarily he cared nothing for justice, but now he sought to evade the responsibility of sentencing this Man. Instead of refusing to have anything to do with the sentencing of an innocent Man, Pilate sought all that morning by evasion simply to get clear of the case. Each time, however, Jesus came back and stood before him, waiting for His decision. So the scene closed, and Jesus was sent to His cross. In a little while Pilate fell into disgrace and committed suicide in his exile. When he went into the other world and found himself before the throne of the Judge, into whose eyes did the guilty Roman look? What a reversal there was! Once Pilate was judge, and Jesus stood at his bar; now Jesus is Judge, and Pilate is before Him. In like manner Jesus waits before every sinner, meek and lowly, with love and mercy, asking to be received, The scene will soon change, however, and those who reject Him here will stand before Him as their Judge.

If Jesus had been put to death under the Jewish law, it would have been by stoning. But again and again He had foretold that He would be lifted up, implying that He would die on a cross. Thus, unconsciously, the rulers were fulfilling our Lord's own prophecy regarding Himself. God keeps His hand on all events. In all the surging waves of the sea, not one drop of water ever rushes beyond the leash of law. In all the turmoil of human events no one ever gets beyond God's control. The whole fearful chapter of wickedness enacted around Christ's cross, even the most minute particular, was the fulfillment of prophecies made long before. We need never fear that the affairs of this world shall get beyond God's control. We never can drift beyond His love and care. A little bird built its nest under the iron track of a railroad. Day and night the heavy trains thundered along, with their terrific noise, but the little bird was not disturbed, and sat there in quiet peace, rearing her little ones in safety. So, amid this world's danger and rushing noise, a believer in God may rest in quiet confidence, undisturbed, undismayed.

There certainly seemed nothing kingly about Jesus at that time—at least in an earthly sense. He stood there, bound and suffering, with no followers, no friends, with neither throne nor scepter nor crown, with not even a place to lay His head. Little wonder is there that Pilate's question was put in tones of such surprise—"Art thou a king?" Yet Jesus was [and still is] King—King of angels and of men. Kingliness does not consist in purple robes, crowns of gold, and the pageantry of earthly honor. We have but to follow the account of this trial through to the end to see in this lowly, despised Man the highest type of kingliness. Study His bearing—His calm dignity, His gentle patience, His quiet self-control, His majestic silence under wrong and insult. While we look with love at Jesus so kingly amid all the scenes of His humiliation, let us take a lesson for ourselves. Let us learn to be patient under wrong and injury, to be gentle and uncomplaining in the rudest treatment.

Pilate sought again to be rid of the responsibility of sentencing Jesus to the cross by getting the people to choose Him as the one man among all the people to be set free at that feast. But in this, too, Pilate failed. "Then cried they all again, saying, Not this man, but Barabbas." They had their choice between Jesus the holy, the pure, the sinless Son of God, and Barabbas, the bandit, robber, murderer; and they chose Barabbas for liberty and life, and sent Jesus to death on the cross. We all agree in our condemnation of the rulers. But let us not forget that to every one of us a like choice comes. There are but two masters in the world—Christ and Satan. Both ask our allegiance, our obedience. We must make a choice—we cannot be neutral, for no man can serve two masters. In choosing Barabbas the Jews sent Jesus to a cross. He who rejects Christ now crucifies Him afresh and counts His blood an unholy thing.

33

Pilate Sentencing Jesus

Scripture Reading: 19:1–16

Pilate's portrait is hung up in the gallery of the world's great criminals. His is one of the names which never will be forgotten. The incident of the scourging is one of the darkest blots in the story of that terrible Friday. Pilate claimed that he could find no fault in Jesus, and that He should be released, yet, hoping that it would satisfy the Jews, he ordered Him to be scourged. The scourging must be considered as a part of Christ's sufferings as the world's Redeemer. The shame and indignity of being tied like a slave to a whipping post and then beaten until He seemed dead, we never can realize, for, thanks to the softening influence of the religion of Christ, such treatment even of the worst criminals is now unknown in civilized lands. There is, however, a word in Isaiah which gives a fresh meaning to this part of Christ's suffering. "With His stripes we are healed" [Is. 53:5], says the prophet. The peace we enjoy is ours, because the rod of chastisement fell upon Him, because He was smitten. Our soul's diseases are healed, their wounds made whole, because the body of Jesus was gashed and lacerated by the horrible scourge.

After the cruel scourging came the crowning with thorns and the mockery of Jesus as a King. "The soldiers plaited a crown of thorns, and put it on His head." We ought to look with great love and reverence at this picture—Jesus the Son of God, our Savior, standing there in the

556

midst of heathen soldiers, mocked and insulted by them. We know how truly He is a King, and what a glorious King He is. When the crusaders had captured the Holy City, Palestine became an independent kingdom. Godfrey, of Bouillon, was made king of Jerusalem, and it was proposed that he be crowned with a golden crown. But Godfrey's noble answer was, "I will not wear a crown of gold in the city where my Savior wore a crown of thorns." It is a sweet thought, too, that because Jesus wore a crown of thorns in the day of His shame, His redeemed ones shall wear crowns of glory in the life to come. In one sense this mock coronation of Jesus was very significant. Was He really ever more a King than when He was enduring His cross? All through John's gospel we have seen that Jesus spoke of His going to His cross as His being glorified. His cross really was His throne. It was on the cross that He fought the great battle and won the great victory of redemption. The cross was the ladder that led up to His throne. His crown of thorns, too, was fitter for Him than a crown of gold would have been, for He was the King of sorrow; He reached His glory by His sufferings; He saved His people by dying for them. He is adored and worshiped now as the King who has lifted men up by His own sorrows and blood to eternal life and blessedness.

Pilate showed pitiful weakness at every step in his dealing with Jesus. He knew there was no sin in Him, and yet he brought Him out to the people and surrendered Him to them. Behold the Man! Our eyes should be fixed upon Jesus as He stands there in the presence of the multitude. On His head is the crown of thorns, and around His torn and bleeding body is a purple robe, mock emblems of royalty. Behold the Man! Behold the Man enduring shame and contempt, set forth as a spectacle of mockery, that He might be presented at last in glory, and honored before angels and the Father. Behold the Man, reviled, yet reviling not again; hated, but still loving on; cruelly wronged, but speaking no resentful word. Behold the Man, the God-Man, wearing humanity, the Son of God humbling Himself and becoming obedient unto shame and death, that He might save our souls. Behold the Man, holy, sinless, undefiled, separate from sinners, yet bearing upon His own head as the Lamb of God the sin of the world.

The only righteous thing for a just judge to do when he finds His prisoner innocent is to set him free. Pilate brought Jesus out to the people, but said plainly, "I find no fault in him." Nobody could. Nobody ever did. The rulers tried zealously enough to find something that they use as a pretext, but they found nothing. They tried false witnesses, but even these could not agree in their witnessing. Now the keen Roman judge inquires into His character, into His life, into His motives, but finds nothing against Him. No other man has lived in whom no fault could be found. The holiest men have sinned. But Jesus was absolutely sinless. Why then did He suffer as a sinner? We know well the answer. They were our sins that they laid upon Him. "Christ hath redeemed us from the curse of the law, being made a curse for us" [Gal. 3:13]. Christ also hath once suffered for sins, "the Just for the unjust, that he might bring us to God." "Who His own self bare our sins in His own body on the tree." We never should forget this. In these days perhaps there is a tendency to forget the sacrifice of Christ in thinking of His salvation. Between us in our curse and our blessing stands the cross of our Savior. He was wounded for our transgressions and bruised for our iniquities. Let us praise the grace that took our sins, that we may stand whiter than snow before the throne of judgment.

The silences of Jesus are always as significant as His words. He was silent to Pilate. He understood Pilate's weak insincerity. Pilate had had opportunity enough to do the right thing for Jesus, but he had thrown away His chance. Now Jesus would answer no more of His questions. One lesson we must get from this silence is that if we reject Christ's offer of mercy and grace over and over, the time may come, will come, when Christ will be silent to us. And of all calamities that can possibly ever come to any soul none could be so great as that Christ should be silent to its prayers. "Then shall they call upon me, but I will not answer; they shall seek me early, but they shall not find me" [Prov. 1:28]. Another lesson we may learn from Christ's example is that there come times in all our lives when silence is better than speech. Often to words of reviling or to insult, silence is the only true Christian answer. To many of the assaults of skeptics on our religion and on our Lord it is better that we remain silent than that we speak. There is a time to speak boldly and without fear in the presence of Christ's enemies—Christ did speak several times in reply to Pilate—but there are also times when we should keep silence, attempting no answer.

Pilate tried to compel Jesus to answer him. "Knowest thou not that I have power to crucify thee?" The answer of Jesus is very clear. "Thou couldest have no power at all against me, except it were given thee from above." No man's power belongs to himself, to do with as he pleases; it is given him from God, the Source of all power. This is true of the authority of parents and teachers, and of the power possessed by civil magistrates. Men are eager to obtain positions of power, and they do not always realize the responsibility which is attached to such positions. Power belongs to God, and must be used for God, or its misuse will bring its sore penalty. It is a talent which is given to us to be accounted for, and no treason is worse than malfeasance in the employing of power. This is true all the way from the power of the child on the playground or in the home up to the power of the president of the nation or of the king on His throne. "Thou couldest have no power . . . except it were given thee from above."

There is another sweet thought suggested by the words "against me" in this sentence. Christ in this world was under the protection of His Father, and no one on earth could lift a finger against Him but by the Father's divine permission. What was true of Him, the Son of God, is true of each one of the sons of God in all their earthly life. Each believer, the humblest, the weakest, is kept in this world as the apple of God's eye. No one can lift a finger to touch one of God's little ones, save by divine permission. This shows how secure we are, amid all the world's dangers and enmities, while we trust ourselves, like little children, in our Father's keeping.

When Pilate ceased His weak efforts to have Jesus released, saying to the rulers, "Behold your King!" they cried out, "Away with him, crucify him." Thus they finally rejected their Messiah. We read at the beginning of John's gospel that "He came unto His own, and His own received him not" [1:11]. The whole story of His life was an illustration of this rejection of Him. Wherever He went they received Him not. Here and there a home opened its doors to Him, and now and then there was a devout heart that made hospitality for Him, but these receptions were so few that they could easily be counted. Crowds of the common people thronged after Him, and many heard Him gladly, but very few became His true disciples. Even on Palm Sunday, five days before He died, there was a vast multitude to cry, "Hosanna!" and wave palm branches; but soon the palms lay withered in the streets, and on Friday only cries of "Crucify him," were heard in the air. "He came unto His own, and His own received Him not." It is the saddest event in all history, this coming of the Son of God to this earth, bearing in His hands all divine and heavenly blessings, but finding only shut doors and shut hearts, being compelled to take away His gifts because men would not receive them. We read this old story and wonder how His own people could have treated Him so; yet how is it with us? Do we treat Him any better? We do not cry, "Crucify him," but we shut the doors of our hearts in His face and keep Him out. We reject and refuse His gifts which He comes all the way from heaven to bring to us. We may not with angry voice exclaim, "Away with him," but in our hearts many of us do keep Him away.

The struggle had ceased, and "Pilate delivered him therefore unto them to be crucified." He first tried every way to avoid the issue; then he temporized, hoping in some way to evade the responsibility. At least he yielded, and his name goes down through history pilloried forever as the man who delivered Jesus to be crucified, knowing and confessing that He was free from any crime. He was known in the world by no other act. Surely it is an unenviable notoriety. It had been a thousand times better for him if he had never been born, or if he had remained forever in quiet obscurity, instead of going to that high place of power in the land, in which he had to meet and deal with this most momentous question of history. We read in one of the Gospels that Pilate took water in the presence of the people and washed his hands, thus by symbol declaring that he was not responsible for the sentencing of Jesus to die. But the water did not wash away one particle of the stain of the guilt of that terrible sin. Pilate had the misfortune to be the only man in all the province who could send Jesus to the cross. Upon him, therefore, the final responsibility rested, no matter the pressure that was brought to bear upon him by the enemies of Jesus. The fact that others urge us to sin does not take away our guilt for that sin. No being in the universe can compel us to do wrong; if, then, we do wrong, the sin is our own. True, Jesus said there was one other whose guilt was even greater than Pilate's—that was the high priest. His sin was not only that he himself was determined to do wrong, but that he dragged others with him. We remember that the rulers replied to Pilate's act of washing his hands—"His blood be on us and on our children" [Matt. 27:25]. No one who has read the story of the next forty years can doubt that this self-imprecation was fulfilled. Forty years later thousands of the people were scourged and crucified. The crime of the rulers was successful, but what came of the success in the end? Let us learn that sin brings always terrible woe, and that the worst of all sin is sin against the Lord Jesus Christ.

34

The Crucifixion of Christ

Scripture Reading: John 19:17–30

An old legend said that Calvary was at the center of the earth. So it was, really, for the cross was the meeting place of two eternities—a past eternity of grace and hope, and a future eternity of faith, gratitude, love and devotion. It is the center of the earth, too, because toward it the eyes of all believers turn for pardon, comfort, light, joy, hope. As from all sections of the ancient camp the bitten people looked toward the brazen serpent on the pole at the center of the camp, so from all lands sin-stricken ones look in their penitence, and sorrow-stricken ones in their grief, toward the cross.

The first picture we see is Jesus leaving Pilate's judgment hall bearing His cross. The custom was that a criminal should carry to the place of execution the cross on which he should be fastened. The cross was heavy. Yet, heavy as it was, the wooden cross was not all the load Jesus carried that day. We know there was another still heavier, for He bore the burden of the world's sin. The old prophet said, "All we like sheep have gone astray . . . and the Lord hath laid on him the iniquity of us all" [Is. 53:6]. It would seem that none of the disciples were with Jesus as He went out to Calvary. John was caring for Mary, whom Jesus had committed to His care. She, with John and other friends, were presently watching by the cross. Certain other women were in the crowd, lamenting with Jesus. These He comforted even in His own great-sorrow.

562

When He staggered under His cross a passer-by was seized and compelled to carry His load. It would have indeed been a strange irony had the man who carried the cross missed the salvation whereof it is the instrument and the symbol.

The next picture shows us Jesus being nailed upon the cross. He was not alone, for two others were crucified with Him, although this was contrary to Jewish law. These were criminals, men suffering justly for their sin. Thus He was "numbered with the transgressors" [Mark 15:28, cf. Is. 53:12]. They put Jesus on the middle cross, as if He had been the greatest of the criminals. This was the place of the deepest dishonor. As He hung there He was at the lowest point of shame in the world, in the place of the worst sinner. This tells us that there is no known stage of sin or guilt possible on earth down to which Jesus cannot, will not, go as Savior. One of the criminals beside Him was saved that day, lifted up by Him out of his guilt and sin, and borne in His arms to Paradise. This shows us that no sinner is so low in degradation or condemnation that Jesus cannot lift him up to glory. But while we are looking at this one sinner who was saved that Good Friday, we must not fail to glance in sadness at his companion. He had the same opportunity for salvation that the other had, for he was equally close to Jesus, could hear His gracious words, see the blood dropping from His wounds, and behold His patience and compassion. Yet this man was not saved. He remained impenitent, though so close to the dying Redeemer. When people say they will take the chance of the dying thief on the cross, repenting at the last hour, they must remember that there were two dying thieves, equally close to Christ's cross, and that one of them was lost.

The next picture we see shows us Jesus Christ on His cross, and over His head the legend—JESUS OF NAZARETH THE KING OF THE JEWS. Jesus was indeed the King of the Jews, their own Messiah. He was also the King of the world. After He arose He said that all authority was given unto Him in heaven and on earth. In the visions of the Apocalypse we see Him in glory as King of kings. He did not seem kingly that hour on the cross. It was a strange throne for a king to occupy. Yet it was His throne, and the crucifixion was the point of His highest earthly honor. There His glory streamed out as at no other time in all His life. The love of God shone from the cross. It is the power of the cross that is changing the world today and drawing lives to the Savior.

The rulers asked Pilate to change the title he had put over the cross. They wanted him to write only that Jesus said He was King of the Jews. They did not themselves wish to have it suggested that He was indeed in any sense their king. But Pilate refused to make any change in the superscription. "What I have written I have written," he declared. He spoke a deeper truth than he knew. He was making a record which would stand forever, and which in spite of all the injustice and dishonor of the day was true. We are all writing, all the while, ineffaceably. What we have written we have written. Every act we perform, every word we speak, every thought we think and every influence we give out, goes down to stay on the page. This is well when the things we do are good, right and beautiful things; but it is just as true when they are sinful and unholy things. We should lay this truth to heart and should live so that we shall write down in the inexpungeable record of our lives only things we shall be glad to meet a thousand years hence. We never have the opportunity to go over our records to correct the mistakes we have made. As we write the words, so will they stand.

The next picture we see shows us the soldiers dividing the garments of Jesus among themselves. We can think of these men going about at their duty after that day, wearing the garments which Jesus had worn during His beautiful and holy life. We may carry the illustration farther, and think of ourselves and all redeemed ones as wearing the garments which Jesus prepared for us that day on the cross. The scene of the soldiers gambling for the scant possessions of Jesus, while the most stupendous event of all time was being enacted above their heads, suggests to us how indifferent the world is to the glory of God and the glorious things that God does. Elizabeth Barrett Browning speaks of those who sit down and pluck blackberries before the bushes in which God's presence is manifested. The glory of God is everywhere, but men are irreverent and are unmoved by even the holiest things.

The next picture shows us a little group of the dearest friends of Jesus, standing near the cross, while He was enduring His sorrows known and unknown. His mother was there, and John, the beloved disciple. When Jesus saw His mother His heart was touched with compassion for her, and He commended her to the beloved disciple, who from that time became as a son to her, taking her to his own home. In this scene we have a beautiful commentary on the Fifth Commandment.

Even on His cross, in the midst of the anguish of this terrible hour, He did not forget her who had borne Him, who had blessed His tender infancy and defenseless childhood with her rich, self-forgetful love. Every young person, or older one with parents living, who reads this fragment of the story of the cross, should remember the lesson and pay love's highest honor to the father or the mother to whom he owes so much.

The next picture shows us Jesus in His anguish of thirst. In response to His cry, "I thirst" one of the soldiers dipped a sponge in the sour wine that was provided for the watchers and held it up on a reed, that it might moisten His lips. This is the only one of the seven words on the cross in which Jesus referred to His own suffering. It is pleasant to think that one of the soldiers gave a kindly response to His cry. This is the only gleam of humanity in all the dark story of cruelty and hardness enacted around the cross. It is a comfort to us to know that even so small a kindness was wrought for Him who has filled the world with the fragrance of His love, blessing so many millions of suffering ones. For us the lesson is that we should train ourselves to deeds of thoughtful gentleness to all who are in distress. We remember that beautiful word of our Lord, that the giving of even a cup of cold water to a disciple in His name will not go unrewarded [see Matt. 10:42]. There are thirsty ones coming to us continually, and countless are the opportunities of doing good to them in Christ's name. We should not fail to put the cup to lips that are burning with life's fever. Since Jesus thirsted on the cross and was refreshed, if only by so much as the moisture of a sponge filled with sour wine, He is quick to recognize and reward any kindness to one of His that thirsts.

The last picture shows us Jesus dying. He said, "It is finished." Then He bowed His head and gave up His spirit. It was a cry of victory which fell from His lips. His work was finished. He had done each day the work given Him to do that day, and when the last hour of the day came there was nothing that He had left undone. We should learn the lesson and live as He lived, so as to have every part of our work finished when our end comes. But what was it that was finished when Jesus bowed His head on the cross? A famous picture represents Christ lifted up, and beneath Him an innumerable procession of the saints, advancing out of the darkness and coming into the light of His cross. There can be no doubt that He had such a vision of redemption while He hung there, for we are told that He endured the cross, despising the shame, because of the joy set before Him. "It is finished" was therefore a shout of victory as He completed the work of suffering and sacrificing that the world might be saved.

35

It Is Finished!

Scripture Reading: John 19:30

The three hours of darkness was ending. The light was breaking. The Scripture tells us that Jesus then cried in a loud, strong voice. It was not the cry of exhaustion and faintness; it was the shout of a victor. The cross seemed like defeat. Those who understood nothing of the meaning of the life and death of Christ would think of Him as a man who had failed, all of whose dreams and hopes had perished. But we who understand something at least of the meaning of His mission and of the great purpose of His life know that nothing failed, "It is finished," was the shout of a victor in the hour of His glorious success. It told of the completion of His work. All had been accomplished that He set out to do. His work was done. He had nothing more to do. There was no reason why He should live an hour longer, for the last task had now been done. A little while before, He said in His prayer in the upper room, "I have glorified thee on the earth: I have finished the work which thou gavest me to do." When He said in dying, "It is finished," He meant that there was nothing whatever left now for Him to do.

His friends did not think so. They thought His work was only beginning. He was but thirty-three years old, and at thirty-three we regard life as no more than well begun. He had been only three years in His public ministry. Think, too, what years these had been, how full of blessing to those whom He had touched with His life. We can

567

imagine Joseph and Nicodemus as they reverently took His body down from the cross and prepared it for burial, lamenting His early death, talking of what He might have done if only He had been spared longer. His disciples, too, in their anguish and their loss would speak together of the terrible bereavement they had suffered. He had just begun to live. He had gone about through the towns and villages, doing good for three years, healing, comforting, helping, blessing. What would fifty years of such ministry have meant to the world?

We talk the same way of our human friends who are taken away in early years. Their lives were full of promise. They had just begun to do beautiful things. They had shown a little of the power that was in them, to be a strength to others, to be a comfort to those who were in sorrow, to be inspirers of noble things. Our dreams for them were beginning to be realized. Then, suddenly, they slipped away and all was ended. We say that they could not be spared, that the world needed them longer. Over their graves we set up the broken shaft, symbol of incompleteness. It is a great comfort, then, to remember that life is not counted by the number of its years, but by what it puts into the years, few or many, that are lived.

> We live in deeds, not years; in thoughts, not breaths;
> In feelings, not in figures on a dial.
> We should count time by heart-throbs. He most lives
> Who thinks most, feels the noblest, acts the best.

A millionaire recently, when dying, sent for a clergyman and said to him, "Doctor, I have failed, for I have groveled." He had not lived dishonestly; he had not made his money by unjust treatment of others, by the oppression of the poor, or in any way that men called wrong. Men said he had lived well. He had failed, according to his own thought, because he had groveled, lived as if he were a worm. Eighty years of such life, with God and heaven and love left out, however stupendous the earthly success, will not count so much in eternity as one day of self-denying life of love, such as Jesus lived. Jesus, dying at thirty-three, had lived longer than any man who had reached fourscore years of selfishness, of groveling, of fame-seeking. When a friend dies early, with only a few years of life, but with those years filled with usefulness, helpfulness, unselfishness, and faithful doing of duty, do not say he had not done His work.

Another comforting truth started by the dying words of Jesus is that God allots to us our work, little or much, and the time in which it must be done. Jesus spoke often of His hour. Again and again we read that His hour had not yet come, meaning the hour when His work would be finished, His earthly life ended. "His hour was not yet come." Then, at last, He said His hour had come. The time of His death was not accidental. Then He spoke also of His work as what His Father had given Him to do. It was not a haphazard matter how much work He should do, or what particular work it should be. It was all given Him by His Father. When He said in His last moments, "It is finished," He meant that everything He had come into the world to do, all that the Father had given Him to do, He had done, and that now He had only to yield up His life into the hands of Him who gave it.

What was true of Him is true also of us. There is an appointed time to man on earth, and each one has his mission, his work to do. Whether it is a brief time or many years, it matters not; our only care should be to do what has been given us to do, and to fill our appointed days, short or long, with duty well done. We need not fret, then, if our time is short, if we have only a few years given us to work. Faithfulness while the day lasts is all that we need to care for. The things we wanted to do and longed to do, but could not do, were not part of our work at all—they belonged to some other one coming after us.

"It is finished." He meant fully accomplished, done perfectly. Not a word was unspoken which it was His to speak. Nothing, however small, was left undone which the Father had given Him to do. This never can be true of us. We do nothing perfectly. Our best work is marred and flawed by imperfections. We get the white pages from God day by day, and return them blotted and stained. Our lives are full of blanks, neglects—duties not performed, things left undone which we ought to have done. But all Christ's work was complete. He never omitted a kindness that was His to do, never passed by on the other side, to escape doing a service of love. We are never quite sure of the purity of our motives even for the most sacred and worthy deeds we do. "Which of you convinceth Me of sin?" [8:46]. Jesus could say as He looked into men's faces. But can we always say it? Why do we do our good things, our holy things? Is it really from love to God, and so for love to men, or is it sometimes from desire for praise? Everything in our lives is flecked and imperfect. We have to ask divine forgiveness on our best acts and words and thoughts.

But when Jesus said, "It is finished," He looked back upon a life work without a flaw, without an omission, without the slightest failure in thought or motive or deed. His life was brought under most searching light by the rulers in their eagerness to find something to accuse Him of when they sought justification for crucifying Him. But with all efforts to find a flaw, in the blaze of the most dazzling light, they found nothing. Herod sent Him back to Pilate with the testimony that he had found no fault in Him. Pilate declared the same of Him when he had examined Him. Then we have the witness of the Father, as He looked down upon Him and said out of the clouds of glory, "This is my beloved Son, in whom I am well pleased." Christ's work was not merely ended when He bowed His head on the cross and said, "It is finished"; it was completed. His life was perfect.

"It is finished." In a sense nothing He had done was finished; all His work was only begun, Luther spoke of the treatise He had made as narrating only "all that Jesus began both to do and to teach." All would go on forever. This is true of everything we ourselves do. They tell us that every word spoken into the air goes quivering on through space forever; that if you throw a pebble into the sea it starts wavelets which will ripple on and on till they break on every shore. Thus it is with every word we speak, with everything we do, with every influence that goes forth from our lives. We are starting things each day which will continue into eternity. Nothing we do is ever finished. We cannot know the end of any act, of any word. The same was true of the life and work of Christ. He only began the world's redemption. He ever lives at God's right hand, interceding for His church, blessing and saving man. His life seemed a failure the day He said this word. He had made but a slight impression upon the great world. He had gathered only a few friends, and they were men of no distinction, of no power or rank among men. He had been teaching for three years, speaking words of divine wisdom, but they had not been written down, and seemed now to be utterly lost. There were thousands of beginnings of blessing, but they were only merest beginnings, like seeds dropped into the soil.

We know what Christianity is today. The words Jesus spoke, which seemed altogether lost the day He died, have been filling the world with their benedictions. The influence of His life, which then had touched only a few lowly lives, has since touched nations and generations, and has changed all the world, has transformed millions of lives, and is bringing the nations up out of heathenism into holiness and happiness. The beginnings of the first Good Friday have developed into a glorious kingdom of light and love.

"It is finished." When Jesus said this He had reached the end of His sufferings. All His life He had been a sufferer. He came into the world to redeem the world by pain. He was the Man of sorrows. Perhaps we are in danger these days of losing sight of the place of the wounding of Christ in the redemption of the world. In Dr. G. Campbell Morgan's book, *The Crises of the Christ,* there is a chapter called "Man's Wounded God." The title is startling. Dr. Morgan reminds us that it is impossible to omit from the ascended and reigning One the wounds He bears. They are part of His personality. In glory He appears as a lamb that has been slain. He was our suffering Savior. You remember how vividly this is pictured even in the Old Testament. He was wounded for our transgressions, He was bruised for our iniquities. When He said, "It is finished," He had just passed through the three awful hours of darkness. What took place in His experience during those hours no mortal can ever know. We know only this, that in the mysterious depths of those hours, human redemption was accomplished. It was then that He redeemed us from the curse of the law by being made a curse for us. It was then that He who knew no sin was made sin for us, that we might be made the righteousness of God in Him.

As we hear His word of relief, "It is finished," we know that the work of redeeming love had been accomplished. The infinite meaning of the sufferings He endured in those hours we cannot fathom; earth has no line long enough to sound those holy depths; but we know that out of what was done on Calvary those hours come all the hopes of our lives. Every one of us had a share in those pains. In some mysterious way our sins were there, part of the awful blackness that obscured the sun, and also for a time hid the Father's face from the holy Sufferer. In some way, what took place there set us free from the curse of sin.

"It is finished," was the first announcement of the completion of redemption. It was the first proclamation of the gospel after the price had been paid. The Redeemer Himself made the announcement. Let us hear it today. Redemption is finished. We can be sure of eternal life if we accept this Savior as our Savior. There was nothing left undone in those hours that needed to be done to open the way for us to God, to put away sin, to provide eternal salvation for everyone who will accept it.

"It is finished." Think of the words a moment as words that we ourselves must speak, each of us. We are always finishing something. One by one duties come to us, and we must finish them quickly and leave them. How are we finishing them? Are we doing them as well as we can, or negligently? One by one the days come to us, white and beautiful, from God. What are we doing with them? What are we writing on the fair pages? One by one, in quick succession, opportunities come to us, opportunities to be kind, to be patient, to be forgiving, to help others, to honor Christ, to witness for Him, to plant a seed of truth in a heart, and we must meet them promptly, for a moment later they will be gone. What are we doing with our opportunities?

We are finishing a hundred things every day. What are we finishing? How are we finishing the things we do? Soon we shall come to the end of all our living, doing our last task, saying our last word. Friends will then lay us to rest in the grave, saying,

> Sleep.
>   Now that the charge is won,
>   Sleep in the narrow clod;
>   Now it is set of sun,
>   Sleep till the trump of God.
> Sleep.

When we come to the end of all our living and doing, what will be finished? What will we leave behind? Will it be something that will make the world forever better, purer, holier? When you and I say, "It is finished," what will be finished?

36

The Resurrection

Scripture Reading: John 20:11–23

John tells us that the new tomb in which Jesus was laid to rest was in a garden. This is more than a picture—it is a little parable of the meaning of the grave of Christ. It was in a garden. Wherever the gospel goes it makes gardens, turning deserts into places of blossoming beauty. Since Jesus died and rose again, every Christian's grave is in a garden. All about it bloom the flowers of hope and joy. Our dead shall rise again. Like His Master, the Christian cannot be held by death. Sad as bereavement is, the Christian has comforts which bloom like spring flowers and pour their fragrance on the air.

The first appearance of Jesus after He arose was to Mary Magdalene. She and other women had taken a tender part in the burial of Jesus, and then had come very early in the morning of the first day to the garden where the grave was. They were startled to find the grave open. They hasten to find Peter and John, and, having told them what they had discovered, Peter and John came quickly to the grave. John, being the younger and fleeter, first reached the tomb, but Peter, being the bolder, hurried in while John lingered. When Peter had pressed in, John followed him. In the grave they saw the linen cloths lying, but the body was gone. The two disciples, amazed by what they had seen, went to their home. Mary, however, could not tear herself away from the spot. She wept inconsolably because the body was no longer in the grave.

She did not realize that if the body had been there that morning she would have had real cause for weeping. Then the world's hopes would have been quenched, lost in the darkness of eternal night. What to her was a great grief was really the secret of a great joy. The things which we regard as causes of sorrow, if we could see them as God sees them, would appear to be secrets of joy. The empty grave, if only Mary had understood it, was the attestation of the Messiahship of Jesus.

Mary saw a vision of angels. She "seeth two angels in white sitting, the one at the head, and the other at the feet, where the body of Jesus had lain." We find angels all along the story of the life of Jesus. They sang at His birth. They ministered to Him after His temptation, and again in the Garden, after His agony. He said He could have called twelve legions of angels to His defense during His trial. Now we find angels watching in His tomb, and at the ascension we see them waiting to comfort His disciples as their Master parted from them. The presence of the angels in the empty grave suggests to us the change which Christ's resurrection made in the graves of all believing ones. We dread the tomb. It is a place of impenetrable darkness. But since Christ lay there, the sleeping places of His followers are all brightened. They are little beds in which the bodies of the saints rest until He who has the key to their graves shall come to call them again. If we had eyes to see, no doubt, as we lay our loved ones away, we should see angels sitting at the head and at the feet of each waiting one, keeping their sacred watch.

The angels tried to comfort Mary, asking her why she wept. She told them why very frankly, "Because they have taken away my Lord, and I know not where they have laid him." Just then she heard a movement behind her, and, turning back, saw Jesus Himself standing there. She did not know, however, who it was, and supposed He was the gardener. She was thinking of Him as dead, and did not recognize Him in the living man she saw. Then her eyes were dim with weeping, and she could not see. Many a time it is the same with us. Christ is close by us in our need or in our sorrow, but we cannot see Him, and so we miss the comfort of His presence. If only we would believe in the constant presence of Christ with us, and would make that presence real by our faith, our darkest hours would be lightened, our loneliest moments would be filled with companionship, and in our weakness we should have all the divine strength about us. It was said of Moses that "he endured, as seeing him who is invisible." Moses did not see God, but His faith made the presence of God as real to him as if he had seen Him with His human eyes. Such faith as this would change all life for those who believe in Christ.

The first recorded word from our Lord's lips after He arose is that which He spoke to Mary here, "Woman, why weepest thou?" The words were spoken to comfort one who was in sorrow. Jesus had always been a comforter—He comes to everyone who is in grief with the same question, "Why weepest thou?" He had come that morning from the grave, achieving His great victory over the last enemy. He was therefore the first who could have spoken such words, for before that, no one was able to wipe away the tears of sorrow. His question implied that there was no need for weeping. Mary was grieving for a dead Christ, and the living Christ was standing beside her. In our grief it is the same—He who comes to us is the risen One. The hand of Jesus has been wiping away tears ever since that morning. We may not get back our dead alive, but we have the blessed assurance that they have passed into the keeping of Christ, where they will be safe forever. Then some day we shall greet them and be greeted by them, alive.

Jesus revealed Himself to Mary by speaking her name. "Jesus saith unto her, Mary." The ancients believed that death washed away completely every memory of the earthly life, its friendships even passing from recollection. But we see Jesus here on the other side of death, and we find the old affections unchanged in Him. He took up the threads of the story with His friends just where they had been broken off three days before, and went on as if only a night's sleep had intervened. Death made no break in His life. Nothing was blotted out, nothing beautiful or good, nothing worthwhile. When our friends pass through death, whatever changes may be made in them, we know that there will be no change in their love for us.

> Death doth hide,
> But not divide.

When Mary heard her name spoken in the old familiar tones, she recognized Jesus. "She turned herself, and saith unto him, Rabboni." We do not recognize Jesus until He calls us by name. We love Him because He first loved us. Mary's answer showed the loyalty of her heart. She was ready now to devote her life to Him. Many people get only a fragment of the true thought of Christ. They believe in Him as their Savior, but do not think of Him as their Lord and Master. Their faith leads them to trust in Him for salvation, but it does not bring to them the comfort of a Savior living, present with them, helping them. They think of themselves as having been saved by Christ's death upon the cross, but do not realize that, important as the cross may be, their actual salvation comes through their attachment to and companionship with a living Master and Friend. Mary had a true conception—she took Christ as her Master. She surrendered herself to Him.

It was a strange word that Jesus spoke to Mary after she had recognized Him. "Touch me not . . . but go to my brethren, and say unto them." He probably meant to say to her that the old relationship was not to be reestablished. He was risen now, and the relationship must be spiritual. Further, He meant that there was no time now for the satisfying of love, however tender and true it was. Mary would have stayed at the Master's feet in the rapture of her joy and homage. But there was something else more important. Others must know of the joy. A message must be carried immediately to the other friends of Jesus. We are too apt, when we find a great joy, to wish to cherish it alone. But duty to others calls us away. When at the communion table, for example, we find a great gladness in fellowship with Christ, we must never forget that there are others outside the sacred walls, who are in sorrow, or in danger, and we should hasten to them with the message of Christ's love.

The scene in the upper room that night was a wonderful one. The disciples had assembled in fear and trembling, hiding away, lest harm might come to them. Suddenly Jesus Himself appeared. "Jesus came and stood in the midst, and saith unto them, Peace be unto you." This was the first appearance of Jesus to the disciples as a body. His first salutation to them was, "Peace be unto you." The words were familiar as a common greeting, but they had a new meaning to those men that night. They fell from the lips of the risen Christ. Wonderful among the gifts of Jesus to His disciples was the giving of His peace. It quiets the troubled heart. It changes sorrow into joy.

The disciples were awed by the presence of their Master, and to quiet their trembling fear He held up His hands. "He showed unto them His hands and His side. Then were the disciples glad, when they saw the

Lord." They were pierced hands which He held up. They bore the prints of the nails. Thus they assured these men that they were the same hands which had been nailed to the cross. The wounds told them first that He had indeed died for love of them. They told them, further, that He had risen also, His hands still bearing the marks of the nails. Christ is known everywhere by the print of the nails in His hands. A gospel without these marks is not a gospel. The preaching that does not tell men of the cross will not point men to salvation.

37

"Peace Be unto You"

Scripture Reading: John 20:19, 21, 26

No other benediction that could fall upon the ears of men could mean more than this: "Peace be unto you." This is a restless, striving, struggling world. Nation wars with nation. Business interests are in antagonism with other business interests. There are race wars which sometimes seem utterly unappeasable until one or the other race has been exterminated. Then there are family feuds which sometimes go on for generations, in deadly enmity. And there are personal quarrels, alienations, strifes, which separate friends. Besides all this, there is a restlessness in human hearts. Men are unhappy and not at peace in themselves. There is strife within the breast of nearly everyone.

No word Christ ever spoke caught more ears than when He said, "Come unto me . . . and I will give you rest" [Matt. 11:28], or "Peace be unto you." His words answered a universal need and a universal yearning.

"Peace be unto you." This was the first word the risen Christ spoke to His disciples as a body after He returned from the grave. This gives special significance to what He said. Three different times He spoke the same words—"Peace be unto you"; twice the evening of the day on which He rose, and once the following first-day evening. Yet, while He used precisely the same words, they had a different meaning each time, and were not merely a repetition. Look at the setting of the bene-

578

diction as He first uttered it. It was evening. The disciples had sought the quiet and safety of the upper room for a meeting together. The doors were carefully shut, for fear of the Jews. The little company was in sore dread of those who had crucified their Master. "Jesus . . . stood in the midst, and saith unto them, Peace be unto you. And when he had so said, he showed unto them His hands and His side." Why did He show them His hands and His side? Because of the wounds. He reminded them of His sufferings, through which alone peace could come to them.

The second use of the words was a few minutes later. "Then said Jesus to them again, Peace be unto you." Then He added, "As my Father hath sent me, even so send I you. And when he had said this, he breathed on them, and saith unto them, Receive ye the Holy Ghost." Here the benediction of peace is accompanied by the gift of the Spirit. There can be no true, deep peace in us save when the Holy Spirit holds sway in our hearts.

The third time the benediction was given was a week later. After eight days, again His disciples were within, and Thomas with them. "Then came Jesus, the doors being shut, and stood in the midst, and said, Peace be unto you. Then saith he to Thomas, Reach hither thy finger, and behold my hands; and reach hither thy hand, and thrust it into my side; and be not faithless, but believing." Here the purpose of the benediction was to help Thomas' slow faith.

"Peace be unto you." The spirit of Christianity is all in the direction of peace among nations. There is a picture called "Peace" which is suggestive. It shows a cannon lying in a meadow, in the grass, with a lamb feeding beside it, nibbling at its very mouth. But while the picture is beautiful, it is incomplete. The cannon, which once was used in war, dealing death, is still a cannon, useless, but ready to be used again in the old way. The prophet suggests a more fitting and complete picture when he says in His vision of the redeemed nation, "They shall beat their swords into plowshares, and their spears into pruninghooks; nation shall not lift up sword against nation, neither shall they learn war any more" [Is. 2:4; Mic. 4:3]. That is the kind of peace Christ would make. The sword shall not any longer be a sword, though rusty and unused, but shall be made into a plowshare, doing its work for humanity. In the artist's picture, it were truer to the spirit of Christianity if the cannon were not merely lying in the meadow, with the lamb feeding quietly beside it, but instead were cast into church bells to call the people to the house of God. The peace which our Master would make is not merely the laying down of arms, but a peace which shall bring good to both nations and restore them to fellowship. Christian peace is not merely a drawn battle, with the old bitterness remaining. The bitterness must be swallowed up in love. If two have been estranged through misunderstanding, or by whatever cause, Christ's peace leads them together in a new friendship which forgets the past and wipes out all traces of difference in a relationship of love.

"Peace I leave with you." This was the Master's bequest to His friends. He did not leave them gold and silver. He did not entail great estates upon them. He had none of these to leave. In His life the birds were better off than He, for in the world His hands had made He had not where to lay His head. When He died He had no grave in which His body might rest, and would have been buried in the potter's field, amid criminals and outcasts, had not a noble friend rescued Him from that ignominy and lent Him a new rock-hewn tomb for the three days and nights He slept. He was poor, and had no earthly inheritance to bequeath. But He left peace as a heritage. "Peace I leave with you."

"My peace I give unto you" [14:27] It was not merely peace, but His own peace, that He bequeathed to His friends. "My peace"! Think what Christ's peace was. It was the peace that He had had in His heart and life all His days. You know how serenely He met all experiences. He never lost His quietness and composure in any circumstances. Life had no terrors for Him. His was not an easy life. Soon after His public ministry began—opposition began, developing into bitter enmity, with plottings and schemings for His death. But nothing disturbed Him. He was never betrayed into fear or alarm. He knew what was before Him. The cross threw its dark shadows on His path long before He reached it. But with unruffled peace He moved on toward it. "My peace I give unto you." It is possible for Christ's followers to have the same peace the Master had. He bequeaths it to them—let them claim their inheritance. He gives it to them—let them accept the gift.

But why is it that so many Christians do not have this peace? What restless lives many of us live! Some of us scarcely ever have an hour of real peace. We fret at every trifle. We allow ourselves to be annoyed by the smallest things that do not go as we want them to go. We are full of discontents and complainings. We are envious at the prosperity of others. We vex ourselves over the things that are disagreeable in even the least way. We are continually dismayed by life's experiences. We are afraid to live and afraid to die. Is that the best that Christ can do for us? Is that the full meaning of His words here—"Peace be unto you; Peace I leave with you; My peace I give unto you"? Is that all that our religion can do for us? No; Jesus meant just what He said. He means for us to have His peace. We may have it too. He shows us His hands and says, "Peace be unto you. I have purchased peace for you." He breathes on us His divine Spirit, and says, "Peace be unto you." Let the peace of God into your heart today. You have had enough of restlessness, fret, anxiety and struggle. Let peace rule.

"Peace be unto you." "My peace I give unto you." When men have fought for their country, loyal patriots, and when the war is over, and the victory won, those who survive come home with wounds and scars, maimed and broken, and those who look upon them see the price of the peace which the country is enjoying, let us not forget that the peace which Christ gives cost Him suffering and shame and death. We have peace because He went to His cross.

In a gallery in Europe two pictures hang side by side. One is of a sea swept by storms—great waves, black clouds, lightning bolts, and on the wild water wrecks of vessels, with human forms struggling or dead. The artists calls His picture "Life." Hanging beside this picture is another, almost the same—a rough sea, billows, clouds, lightnings, wrecks, men struggling in the waters. In the center of this picture, however, a great rock rises up out of the wild sea, reaching above the highest waves, standing serene and firm in the midst of the storm. Then in the rock, far up, is a cleft of herbage and flowers growing, and as you look closely you see in the midst of the herbage a dove sitting quietly on her nest. The artist calls His picture "Peace." It represents the Christian's life. In the world there is tribulation. Peace does not come through the quieting of earth's storms. Christ does not make a little spot of calm for us, shutting off the storms. No; that rock rising above the waves tells the story. It is peace in the midst of the storm, in Christ. We have it in the hymn,

> Rock of Ages, cleft for me,
> Let me hide myself in Thee.

The Christian has no promise of less sorrow than His worldly neighbor, of an easier life, a life without struggle, pain, or buffeting. You remember how Christ got His peace—not by living in a little paradise, but in the enduring of all manner of suffering calmly and quietly. His peace was within. We must get our peace on fields of struggle. It must come through Christ's victory over the world. It must be Christ's gift. It must be in our heart.

President Eliot, of Harvard University, said at the dedication of an art gallery this: "The main object in every school should be, not to provide the children with means of earning a livelihood, but to show them how to live a happy and worthy life, inspired by ideals which will exalt and dignify both labor and leisure. To see beauty and to live it is to possess large securities for such a life."

To live only to get bread and clothes is a low aim. To live only to make money, to get on in the world, is an unworthy aim for an immortal being. We live worthily only when we live to grow into beautiful character and to do beautiful things of love. Peace is the highest mark of spiritual beauty.

There is a German legend of the origin of the moss rose. One day the angel of the flowers, weary in His ministry in the heat of the sun, sought a place to rest, but found none. Turned from every door, he lay down under the shelter of a rose and slept and was refreshed. He thanked the rose for the pleasure and comfort he had enjoyed in its shade, and then said that, to reward it, he would adorn it with a new charm. So soft, green moss grew around the stem, and those who looked at the flower saw the beautiful moss rose, loveliest of all the roses. So to those who are faithful to Christ He gives a new charm, life's highest and most heavenly adornment—peace.

We should be at peace with all men. If there is bitterness toward any human being, our peace is not Christ's peace. No matter what wrongs Jesus suffered, how unjustly or cruelly He was treated, He kept love in His heart. It is easy to cherish resentments. We like to say we have a right to be angry. Yes, but that is not the divine way. God forgives and forgets and loves on. Suppose God never forgave! Suppose He cherished resentments and refused to love us and to bless us! Let love heal all heart-hurts. If we think we have been treated wrongfully, let us forgive, and new beauty will come instead of a scar. The storm made a great gash on the mountainside, but grass, moss and flowers came, and the mountain was never so beautiful before as now it became.

> There was a wound once in a gentle heart
>> Whence all life's sweetness seemed to ebb and die;
> And love's confiding changed to bitter smart,
>> While slow, sad years went by.

> Yet as they passed, unseen an angel stole
>> And laid a balm of healing on the pain,
> Till love grew purer in the heart made whole,
>> And peace came back again.

We should have peace also in our own hearts. Why should we go on in the old restlessness and strife a day longer? Why should we worry so and fret when Christ offers us His own serene peace? No matter what may come to us in any possible future, nothing will come, if only we are obedient and true to God, which should break our peace. There will be mysteries, contradictions, perplexities, disappointments, but in all these a Hand divine will move, and nothing can make wrong out of life for us if we are truly Christ's. "The peace of God . . . shall keep your hearts and your minds through Christ Jesus" [Phil. 4:7].

> Peace, perfect peace, in this dark world of sin?
>> The blood of Jesus whispers peace within.

> Peace, perfect peace our future all unknown?
>> Jesus we know, and He is on the throne.

38

The Beloved Disciple

Scripture Reading: John 21:20

The name of John is not once mentioned in all his gospel. Again and again the writer refers to himself as "the disciple whom Jesus loved." He has been criticized for this, as if he had been vain and self-conceited in thus speaking of his own distinction among the disciples. But no grace is more marked in John than humility. He does not speak of himself as the disciple who loved Jesus. This would have been to claim preeminence among the disciples and would have shown a boastful and self-confident spirit. He said he was the disciple whom Jesus loved. He glorified the grace of Christ. He was what he was only because Christ loved him.

Right here we have one of the deepest truths of Christian life, one of the great secrets of Christian peace, an essential quality of faith—that our hope does not rest in our love for Christ, but in His love for us. People are often discouraged when they find in themselves so little that is good and beautiful. They cannot see that they love Christ any more this year than they did last. They do not find in themselves the beautiful fruits of the Spirit which they wish they could find. But there is another way to look at our lives which gives us more hope. It is John's way—not our love for Christ, but Christ's love for us.

At the best our love is variable in its moods and experiences. Today it glows with warmth and gladness, and we say we could die for our

Master. We know we love Him. Tomorrow, in some depression, we question whether we really love Him at all, our feelings respond so feebly to His name. A peace which depends on our loving Christ is as variable as our own consciousness. But when it is Christ's love for us that is our dependence, our peace is undisturbed by any earthly changes.

The usual conception of John is that he was gentle and affectionate, but not strong. Yet this is a mistaken conception. He was a man of magnificent strength. The ancient symbol of John was that of the eagle, soaring high, with broad wing, keen eye, fearless, rising into the depths of the heavens. When we see John at first, he had his faults. He was not always the disciple of gentleness and love. He was impetuous, fiery, intemperate in his zeal. We have an illustration of this quality in him in his impatience with the people of the Samaritan village to which his Master was not hospitably welcomed. His anger flamed hotly against them. He wished to call down fire from heaven upon the town and the people. He had not then learned the mind that was in Jesus Christ.

Another blemish in John at first was his desire for greatness. He supposed that Christ was to be an earthly king, ruling over the world. In this great kingdom John and his brother were ambitious to fill the highest offices. "Grant unto us to sit at thy right hand and at thy left." This, too, was contrary to the spirit of Christ. The places nearest to Him are reached by the paths of humility and service. He who becomes as a little child is greatest in the kingdom of heaven.

In our disappointment with ourselves it comforts us to be reminded that even the disciple whom Jesus loved was once a hot-headed zealot, ready to burn anyone who would not become a Christian, and a man with a worldly ambition clamoring for high office in Christ's kingdom. We want a religion that will take us as we are, with all our faults and imperfections, and make of us such a man as John's religion made of him. We have Robert Browning's longing:

> O for a man to arise in me,
> That the man I am might cease to be!

It is not every kind of religion that produces such men as John, "the disciple whom Jesus loved." Some people are Christians a long while, and yet never grow into sweetness of spirit, never become gentle, kind, longsuffering, thoughtful, unselfish. Not always does the resentful spirit become the spirit of mercy, forgiveness and charity, even after years. Not always does the eagerness for first places, for prominence, for distinction, grow into the lowly humility which we see in John in his later life. Instead of holding a prominent place among the apostles, he appears as a quiet, modest man, keeping close to Peter, walking in his shadow, sweetly accepting the second place. Instead of wishing to call down fire on those who would not honor his Master, he preached love as the great duty, as the one thing of Christian life. You know how this "disciple whom Jesus loved" came to stand at last as the ideal of love, not only in his teaching, but also in his life. We all want a religion that will do for a man what John's religion did for him. We desire that our life, with its resentments, its insincerities, its selfishness, its irritability, its vanity, its pride, its worldly ambition, can be made into the life of love which John attained. We are not satisfied with our faulty character, our poor living. We are not the kind of Christians we know we ought to be. Our religion does not seem to make us grow ever better. We attend church, we sing the hymns and join in the prayers, we enjoy the worship, we give to the cause of Christ, we go through the rounds of services and ordinances—but somehow we do not become sweeter, gentler, truer, braver, stronger, more Christlike.

What was John's religion? We may put it into one phrase—Christ and John were friends. It was a great, all-absorbing, overmastering friendship began that day when the Baptist said to two young men, as Jesus passed near, "Behold the Lamb of God" [1:29]. The two young men followed Him and were invited to His lodgings, spending the afternoon with Him. What took place during those hours we do not know, but we do know that a friendship began between one of the two—scarcely more than a boy then—and Jesus, whose bonds have never slackened since. For three and more years this friendship grew in sweetness and tenderness, and during those years it was that the wonderful transformation took place in the disciple.

We know a little about the power of a strong, rich, noble, human friendship in shaping, inspiring, uplifting lives.

There are many lives that are being saved, refined, sweetened, enriched by a human friendship. One of the best of the younger Christian men I have known I have seen lifted up from a life of ordinary ability and education into refinement, power and large usefulness by a gentle friendship. The girl whom he loved was rich-hearted, inspiring, showing in her own life the best ideals, and her love for him and his love for her lifted him up to love's nobility. She stayed with him only a few years, and then went home, but he walks among men today with a strength, an energy, and a force of character born of the holy friendship which meant so much to him.

George Eliot's *Silas Marner* is about a miser who hoarded his money. Someone took away his hoard, and his heart grew bitter over the wrong to him. Then a little child was left at his door. His poor, starved heart took in the little one, and love for her redeemed him from sordidness, bitterness and anguish of spirit. God saves many a life by sending to it a sweet human friendship. A church visitor climbed the rickety stairs to the miserable room where a woman lay in rags on a pile of straw. She bent over the poor woman, all vile with sin, said a loving word, and kissed her. That kiss saved her. Christ comes to sinners and saves them with love. That is the way He saved the prodigals of His time. He came to them and became their friend.

It is to a personal friendship with Himself that Christ is always inviting men. He does not come merely to make reforms, to start beneficent movements, to make the conditions of life better. He does not try to save the world by giving it better laws, by founding schools, by securing wholesome literature. Christ saves men by becoming their friend. John surrendered his heart and life to this friendship with Jesus. He opened every window and door to his new Master.

Another thing which helped on John's friendship with Christ was his trust. He never doubted. Thomas doubted and was slow to believe. This hindered the growth of his friendship with Jesus. Peter was one of our Savior's closest friends, but he was always saying rash words and doing rash things, which interrupted his fellowship with Christ. But John loved on in silence and trusted. At the Last Supper he leaned on the Master's breast. That is the place of confidence—the bosom is only for those who have a right to closest intimacy. It is the place of love, near the heart. It is the place of safety—in the secret place of the Most High. The bosom is the place of comfort. It was the darkest night the world ever saw that John lay on the bosom of Jesus. But he found comfort there. Men, trust in the secret of peace. "Thou wilt keep him in perfect peace whose mind is stayed on thee" [Is. 26:3]. That is what leaning on Christ's breast means. Do not think that that place of innermost love was for John only and has never been filled since that night. It is like heaven's gates—it is never closed, and whosoever will may come and lie there. It is a place for those who sorrow—oh, that all who have grief knew that they may creep in where John lay, and nestle there!

John's transformation is the model for all of us. No matter how many imperfections mar the beauty of our lives, we should not be discouraged. But we should never consent to let the faults remain. That is the way too many of us do. We condone our weaknesses and imperfections, pity them, and keep them. We should give ourselves no rest till they are cured. But how can we get these evil things out of our lives? How did John get rid of his faults? By letting the love of Christ possess him. Lying upon Christ's bosom, Christ's sweet, pure, wholesome life permeated John's life and made it sweet, pure and wholesome.

So it is the friendship of Christ alone that can transform us. You are a Christian not because you belong to a church, not because you have a good creed, not because you are living a fair moral life—you are a Christian because you and Christ are friends. What can a friend be to a friend? Let us think of the best that earth's richest-hearted friend can be to us and do for us. Then lift up this conception, multiplying it a thousand times. If it were possible to gather out of all history and from all the world the best and holiest things of pure, true friendship, and combine them all in one of great friendship, Christ's friendship would surpass the sum of them all.

Even our human friendships we prize as the dearest things on earth. They are more precious than rarest gems. We would lose everything else we have rather than give them up. Life without friendships would be empty and lonely. Yet the best earthly friendships are but little fragments of the friendship of Christ. It is perfect. Its touch is always gentle and full of healing. Its help is always wise. Its tenderness is like the warmth of a heavenly summer. If we have the friendship of Christ, we cannot be utterly bereft, though all human friends be taken away. To be Christ's friend is to be God's child, with all a child's privileges. This is one essential in being a Christian.

We could not say Paul is our friend, or John, but Jesus is living, away past death, and is with us evermore. He is our Friend as really as He was Mary's or John's.

Christ is our Friend. That means everything we need. No want can be unsupplied. No sorrow can be uncomforted. No evil can overmaster us. For time and for eternity we are safe. It will not be the streets of gold, and the gates of pearl, and the river and the trees that will make heaven for us—it will be the companionship, the friendship of Christ.

But we must not forget the other part of this friendship. We are to be Christ's friends, too. It is not much we can give to Him or do for Him. But He would have us loyal and true.

If a sacred human friendship exerts such influence over a true life, surely the consciousness that Christ is our Friend and we are His should check every evil thought, quell every bitter feeling, sweeten every emotion, and make all our life holy, true and heavenly.